DEADPOOL CLASSIC

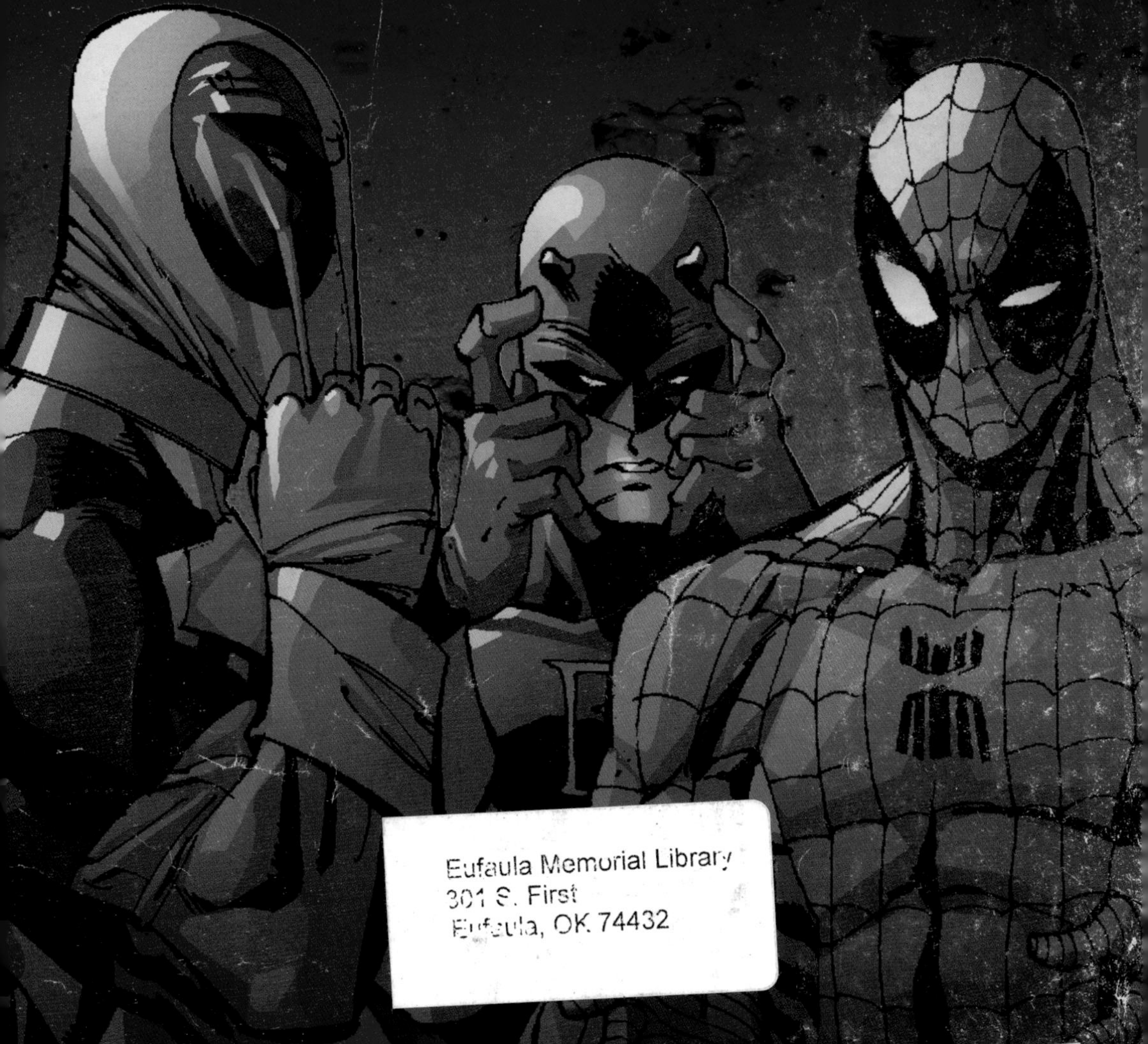

SUICIDE KINGS

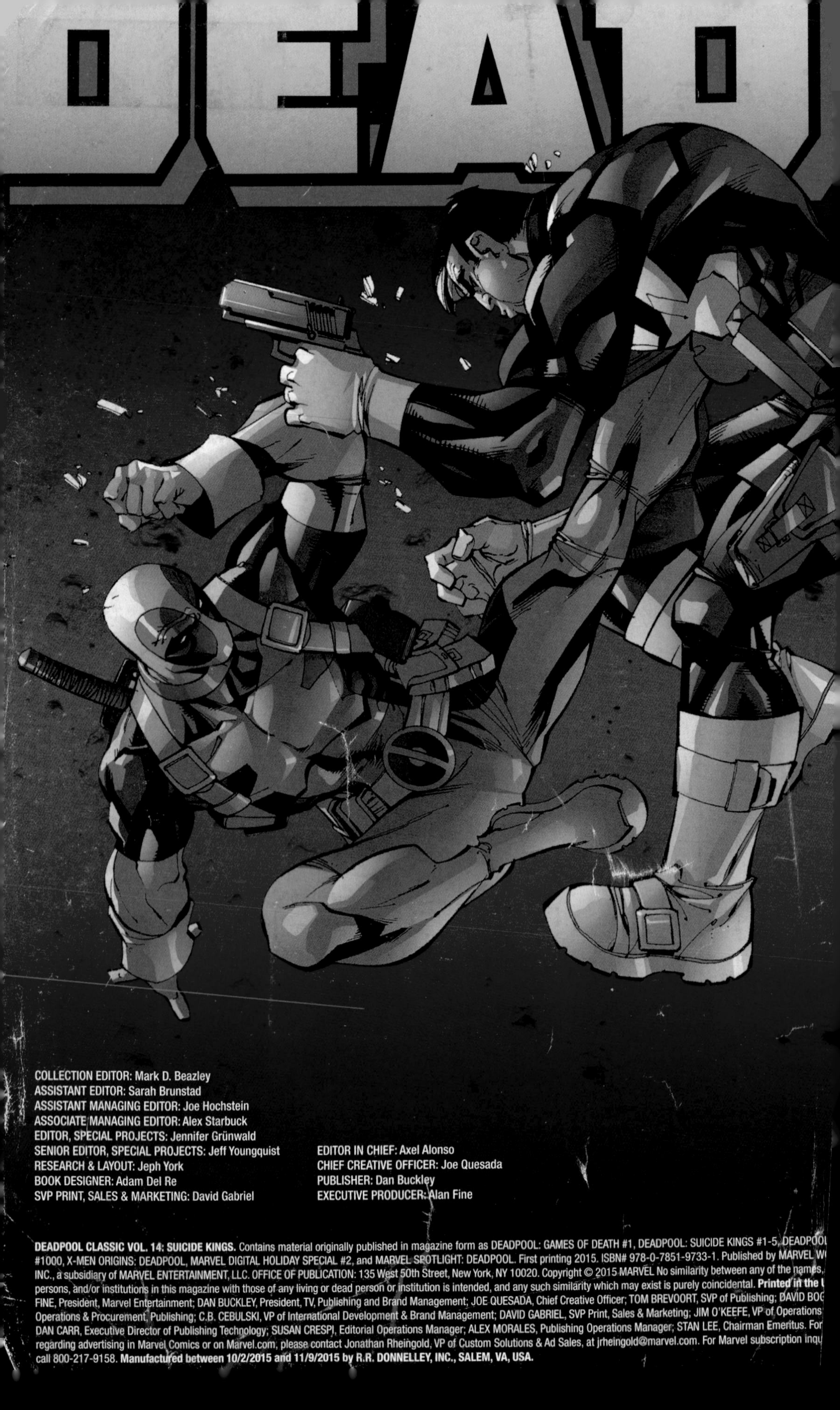

COLLECTION EDITOR: Mark D. Beazley
ASSISTANT EDITOR: Sarah Brunstad
ASSISTANT MANAGING EDITOR: Joe Hochstein
ASSOCIATE MANAGING EDITOR: Alex Starbuck
EDITOR, SPECIAL PROJECTS: Jennifer Grünwald
SENIOR EDITOR, SPECIAL PROJECTS: Jeff Youngquist
RESEARCH & LAYOUT: Jeph York
BOOK DESIGNER: Adam Del Re
SVP PRINT, SALES & MARKETING: David Gabriel

EDITOR IN CHIEF: Axel Alonso
CHIEF CREATIVE OFFICER: Joe Quesada
PUBLISHER: Dan Buckley
EXECUTIVE PRODUCER: Alan Fine

DEADPOOL CLASSIC VOL. 14: SUICIDE KINGS. Contains material originally published in magazine form as DEADPOOL: GAMES OF DEATH #1, DEADPOOL: SUICIDE KINGS #1-5, DEADPOOL #1000, X-MEN ORIGINS: DEADPOOL, MARVEL DIGITAL HOLIDAY SPECIAL #2, and MARVEL SPOTLIGHT: DEADPOOL. First printing 2015. ISBN# 978-0-7851-9733-1. Published by MARVEL W INC., a subsidiary of MARVEL ENTERTAINMENT, LLC. OFFICE OF PUBLICATION: 135 West 50th Street, New York, NY 10020. FINE, President, Marvel Entertainment; DAN BUCKLEY, President, TV, Publishing and Brand Management; JOE QUESADA, Chief Creative Officer; TOM BREVOORT, SVP of Publishing; DAVID BOG Operations & Procurement, Publishing; C.B. CEBULSKI, VP of International Development & Brand Management; DAVID GABRIEL, SVP Print, Sales & Marketing; JIM O'KEEFE, VP of Operations DAN CARR, Executive Director of Publishing Technology; SUSAN CRESPI, Editorial Operations Manager; ALEX MORALES, Publishing Operations Manager; STAN LEE, Chairman Emeritus. For regarding advertising in Marvel Comics or on Marvel.com, please contact Jonathan Rheingold, VP of Custom Solutions & Ad Sales, at jrheingold@marvel.com. For Marvel subscription inqu call 800-217-9158. **Manufactured between 10/2/2015 and 11/9/2015 by R.R. DONNELLEY, INC., SALEM, VA, USA.**

POOL CLASSIC

SUICIDE KINGS

DEADPOOL: GAMES OF DEATH
WRITER: Mike Benson
ARTIST: Shawn Crystal
COLORIST: Lee Loughridge
LETTERER: VC's Cory Petit
COVER ART: Greg Land
with Justin Ponsor

DEADPOOL: SUICIDE KINGS #1-5
WRITERS: Mike Benson
with Adam Glass (#3-5)
PENCILER: Carlo Barberi
INKER: Sandu Florea
COLORIST: Marte Gracia
LETTERER: VC's Cory Petit
COVER ART: Mike McKone
with Andres Mossa (#2 & #4)
& Morry Hollowell (#3 & #5)

MARVEL DIGITAL HOLIDAY SPECIAL #2
"MERRY FREAKIN' CHRISTMAS!!"
WRITER: Fred Van Lente
PENCILER: Sanford Greene
INKER: Nathan Massengill
COLORIST: John Rauch
LETTERER: Jeff Eckleberry
COVER ART: Ryan Stegman,
Andrew Pepoy
& Thomas Mason

DEADPOOL #900

"CLOSE ENCOUNTERS OF THE @#$ED-UP KIND"*
WRITER: Jason Aaron
PENCILER: Chris Staggs
INKER: Juan Vlasco
COLORIST: Marte Gracia

"SILENT BUT DEADLY"
WRITER: Fred Van Lente
ARTIST & COLORIST:
Dalibor Talajić

"SHRUNKEN MASTER"
WRITER: Mike Benson
ARTIST: Damion Scott
COLORIST: Lee Loughridge

"PINKY SWEAR"
WRITER: Joe Kelly
ARTIST: Rob Liefeld
COLORIST: Matt Yackey

"WHAT HAPPENS IN VEGAS…"
WRITER: Duane Swierczynski
ARTIST: Shawn Crystal
COLORIST: Lee Loughridge

"GREAT BALLS OF THUNDER ON THE DEEP BLUE SEA"
WRITER: Victor Gischler
PENCILER: Sanford Greene
INKER: Nathan Massengill
COLORIST: Dave McCaig

"ONE DOWN"
WRITER: Charlie Huston
ARTIST & COLORIST: Kyle Baker

LETTERER: VC'S Joe Sabino
COVER ART: Dave Johnson
Dedicated to the memory
of Bea Arthur

DEADPOOL #1000

"LUCK BE A LADY"
WRITER: Adam Glass
PENCILER: Paco Medina
INKER: Juan Vlasco
COLORIST: Edgar Delgado

"THE MALTESE BUNNY"
WRITER & ARTIST: David Lapham
COLORIST: Lee Loughridge

"APPETITE FOR DESTRUCTION"
WRITER: Rick Remender
ARTIST: Jerome Opeña
COLORIST: Edgar Delgado

"SILENTEST NIGHT"
WRITER: Fred Van Lente
PENCILER: Denys Cowan
INKER: Sandu Florea
COLORIST: Dan Brown

"A WEEK IN THE LIFE"
WRITER, ARTIST & COLORIST:
Peter Bagge

"TODAY I AM DA MAN!"
WRITER & ARTIST:
Howard Chaykin
COLORIST: Edgar Delgado

"NO LONGER IN A RELATIONSHIP"
WRITER, ARTIST & COLORIST:
Tim Hamilton

"CANADA, MAN!"
WRITER: Rob Williams
ARTIST: Phil Bond
COLORIST: Tomislav Tikulin

"MOUTH OF THE BORDER"
WRITER: Cullen Bunn
ARTIST: Matteo Scalera
COLORIST: Matthew Wilson

"TOO MANY DEADPOOLS"
WRITER, ARTIST & COLORIST:
Michael Kupperman

"A NIGHTMARE ON ELM TREE"
WRITER & ARTIST: Dean Haspiel
COLORIST: Joe Infurnari
Special Thanks to Reilly Brown

LETTERER: Jeff Eckleberry
COVER ART: Dave Johnson

X-MEN ORIGINS: DEADPOOL
"THE MAJOR MOTION PICTURE"
WRITER: Duane Swierczynski
ARTIST: Leandro Fernandez
COLORIST: Steve Buccellato
LETTERER: Jeff Eckleberry
COVER ART: Mark Brooks

MARVEL SPOTLIGHT: DEADPOOL
HEAD WRITER & EDITOR: John Rhett Thomas
SPOTLIGHT BULLPEN WRITERS: Jess Harrold & Chris Arrant
BOOK DESIGN: BLAMMO! Content & Design, Rommel Alama,
Michael Kronenberg & Lisa Baltozer
*The views and opinions expressed in this issue are solely those
of the writers, commentators or creative talent and do not express
or imply the views or opinions of Marvel Entertainment, Inc.*

ASSISTANT EDITORS: Jody LeHeup & Sebastian Girner
EDITORS: Axel Alonso with Sebastian Girner

VP, DIGITAL CONTENT: John Cerilli
DIGITAL COORDINATOR: Harry Go
DIGITAL PRODUCTION MANAGER: Tim Smith 3

Deadpool created by Rob Liefeld & Fabian Nicieza

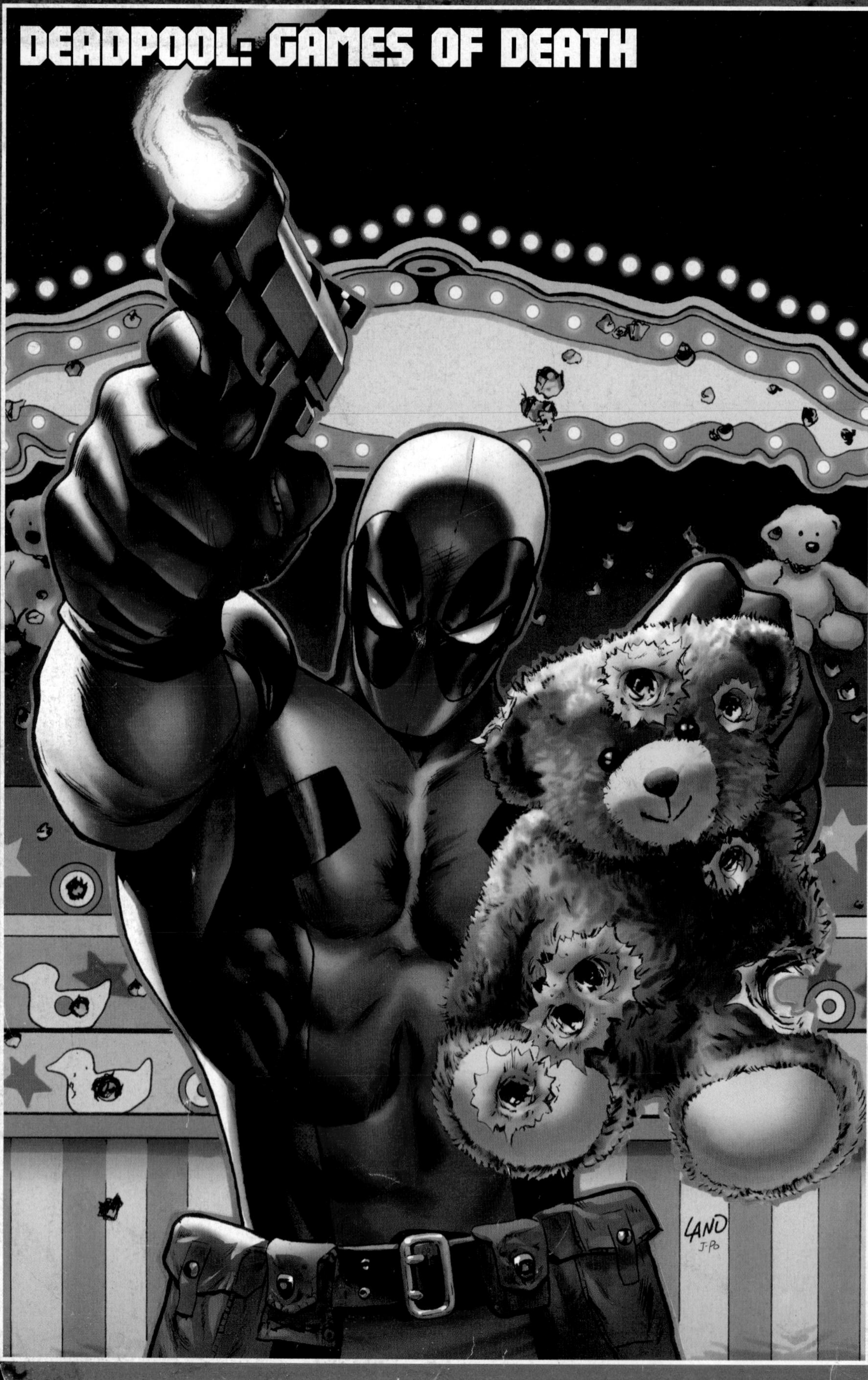
DEADPOOL: GAMES OF DEATH
LAND
J-Po

Some jobs are just too tough for your average fast talkin' hightech gun for hire. Sometimes…to get the job done right…you need someone crazier than a sack'a ferrets. You need Wade Wilson. The Crimson Comedian. The Regeneratin' Degenerate. The Merc with a Mouth…

DEADPOOL

Deadpool is a graduate *(VICTIM)* of the secret super-soldier program, Weapon X. There he was trained to be a living weapon *(EXPERIMENTED ON)* and hailed as the greatest of the program's warriors *(REJECTED AS A FAILURE)*. Now, he's not only one of the world's most dangerous men *(THAT'S TRUE)*, but he's also one of the world's most attractive bachelors *(ACTUALLY HE'S HIDEOUS)*. So ladies--*(IF YOU SAW HIS FACE YOU WOULD PROBABLY--)* Hey--*(--PUKE ALL OVER YOUR--)* Dude. *(WHAT?)* What are you doing? *(WHADDAYA YOU MEAN?)* Tryin' to give a bio here. *(WELL THEN GET YOUR FACTS STRAIGHT.)* It's *OUR* bio, bro! *(…OH…)*

Anyway. I'm a a hero *(MERCENARY)* and I'm out to make *(MONEY)* the world safe. Story. Go.

Dude! *(WHAT?!)* Nothing. Just shut up. *(YOU SHUT UP.)*

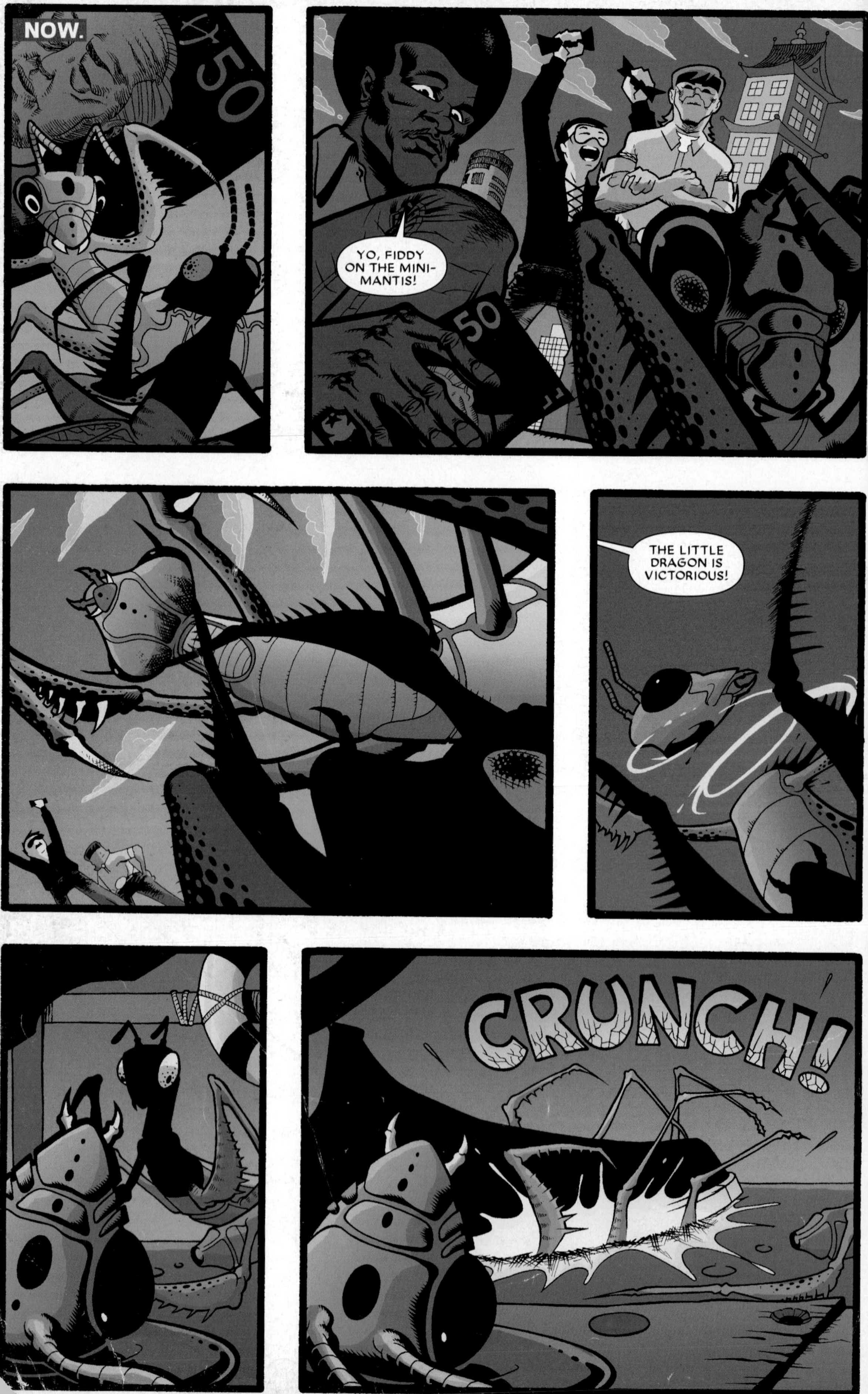
NOW.
YO, FIDDY ON THE MINI-MANTIS!
THE LITTLE DRAGON IS VICTORIOUS!
CRUNCH!

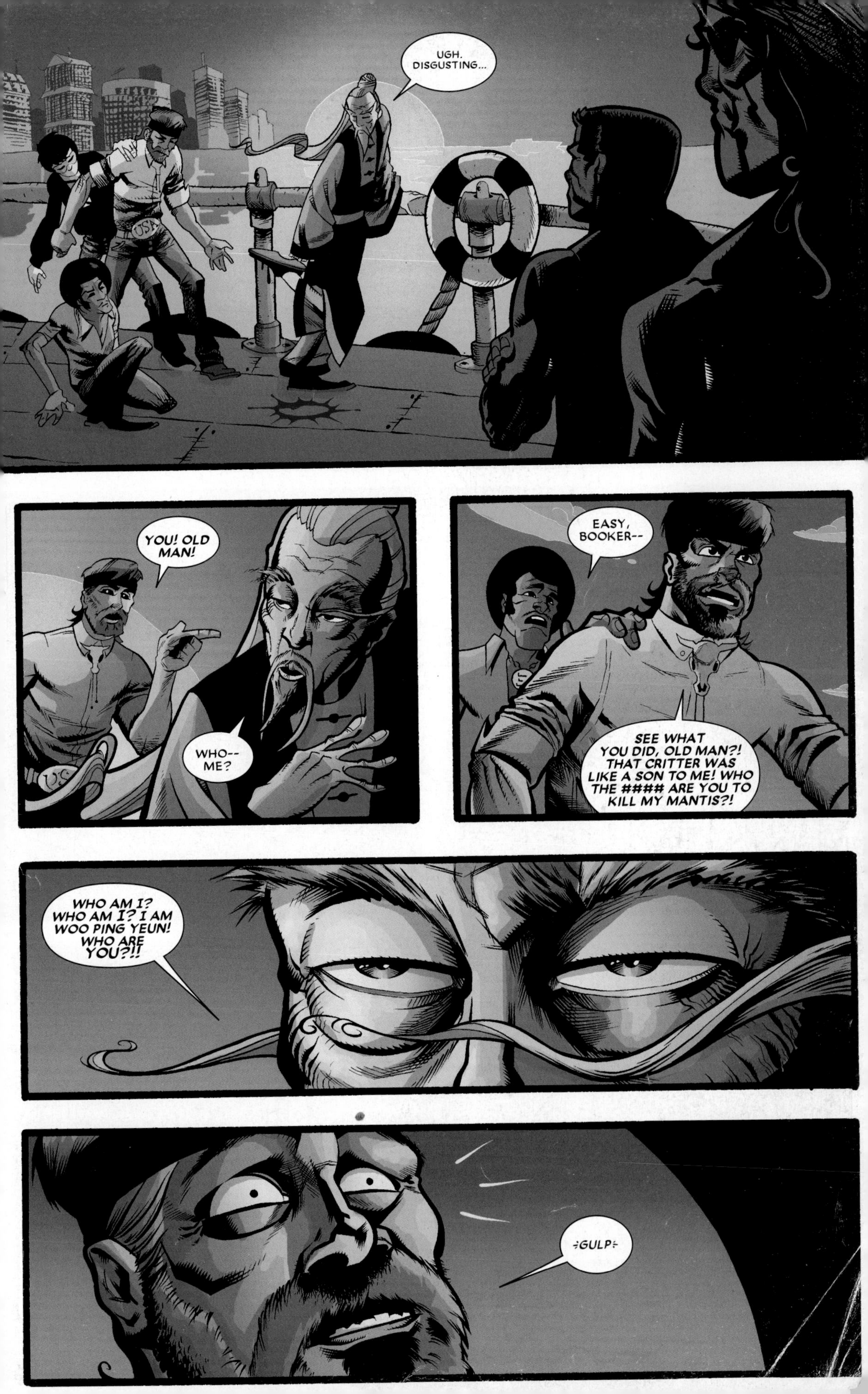
UGH. DISGUSTING...
YOU! OLD MAN!
WHO-- ME?
EASY, BOOKER--
SEE WHAT YOU DID, OLD MAN?! THAT CRITTER WAS LIKE A SON TO ME! WHO THE #### ARE YOU TO KILL MY MANTIS?!
WHO AM I? WHO AM I? I AM WOO PING YEUN! WHO ARE YOU?!!
GULP

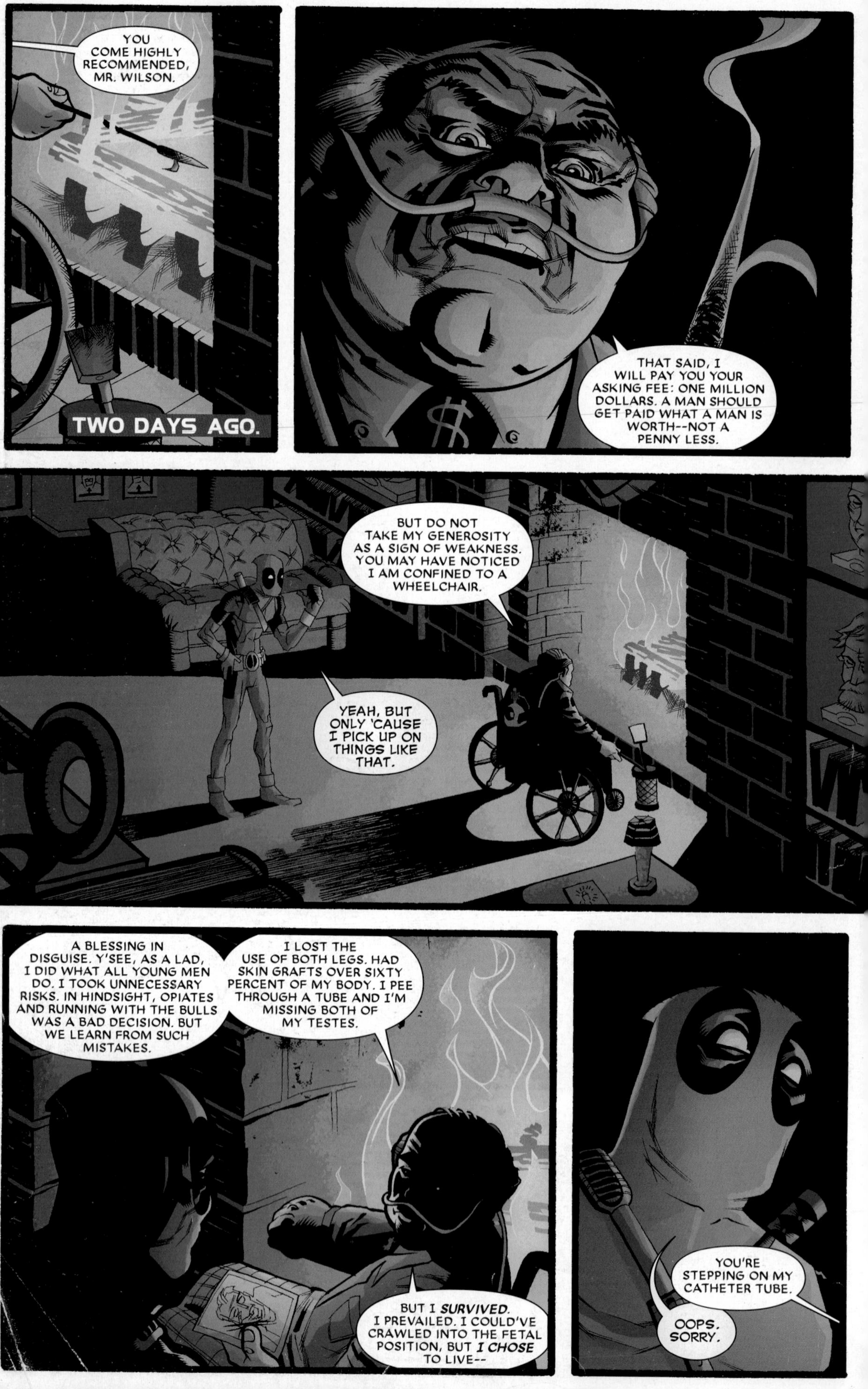
YOU COME HIGHLY RECOMMENDED, MR. WILSON.
TWO DAYS AGO.
THAT SAID, I WILL PAY YOU YOUR ASKING FEE: ONE MILLION DOLLARS. A MAN SHOULD GET PAID WHAT A MAN IS WORTH--NOT A PENNY LESS.
BUT DO NOT TAKE MY GENEROSITY AS A SIGN OF WEAKNESS. YOU MAY HAVE NOTICED I AM CONFINED TO A WHEELCHAIR.
YEAH, BUT ONLY 'CAUSE I PICK UP ON THINGS LIKE THAT.
A BLESSING IN DISGUISE. Y'SEE, AS A LAD, I DID WHAT ALL YOUNG MEN DO. I TOOK UNNECESSARY RISKS. IN HINDSIGHT, OPIATES AND RUNNING WITH THE BULLS WAS A BAD DECISION. BUT WE LEARN FROM SUCH MISTAKES.
I LOST THE USE OF BOTH LEGS. HAD SKIN GRAFTS OVER SIXTY PERCENT OF MY BODY. I PEE THROUGH A TUBE AND I'M MISSING BOTH OF MY TESTES.
BUT I *SURVIVED.* I PREVAILED. I COULD'VE CRAWLED INTO THE FETAL POSITION, BUT *I CHOSE* TO LIVE--
YOU'RE STEPPING ON MY CATHETER TUBE.
OOPS. SORRY.

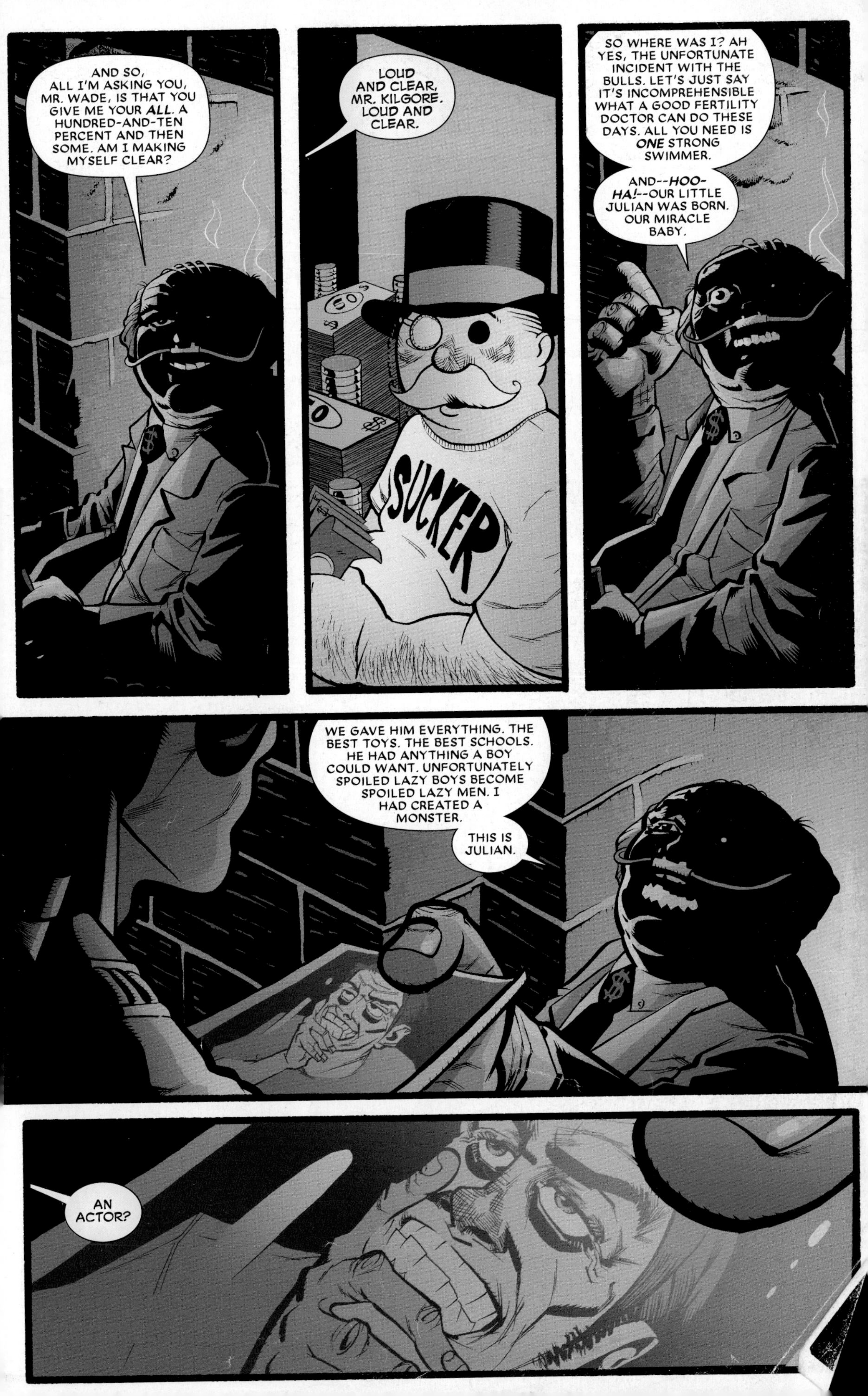
AND SO, ALL I'M ASKING YOU, MR. WADE, IS THAT YOU GIVE ME YOUR ALL. A HUNDRED-AND-TEN PERCENT AND THEN SOME. AM I MAKING MYSELF CLEAR?
LOUD AND CLEAR, MR. KILGORE. LOUD AND CLEAR.
SUCKER
SO WHERE WAS I? AH YES, THE UNFORTUNATE INCIDENT WITH THE BULLS. LET'S JUST SAY IT'S INCOMPREHENSIBLE WHAT A GOOD FERTILITY DOCTOR CAN DO THESE DAYS. ALL YOU NEED IS ONE STRONG SWIMMER.
AND--HOO-HA!--OUR LITTLE JULIAN WAS BORN. OUR MIRACLE BABY.
WE GAVE HIM EVERYTHING. THE BEST TOYS. THE BEST SCHOOLS. HE HAD ANYTHING A BOY COULD WANT. UNFORTUNATELY SPOILED LAZY BOYS BECOME SPOILED LAZY MEN. I HAD CREATED A MONSTER.
THIS IS JULIAN.
AN ACTOR?

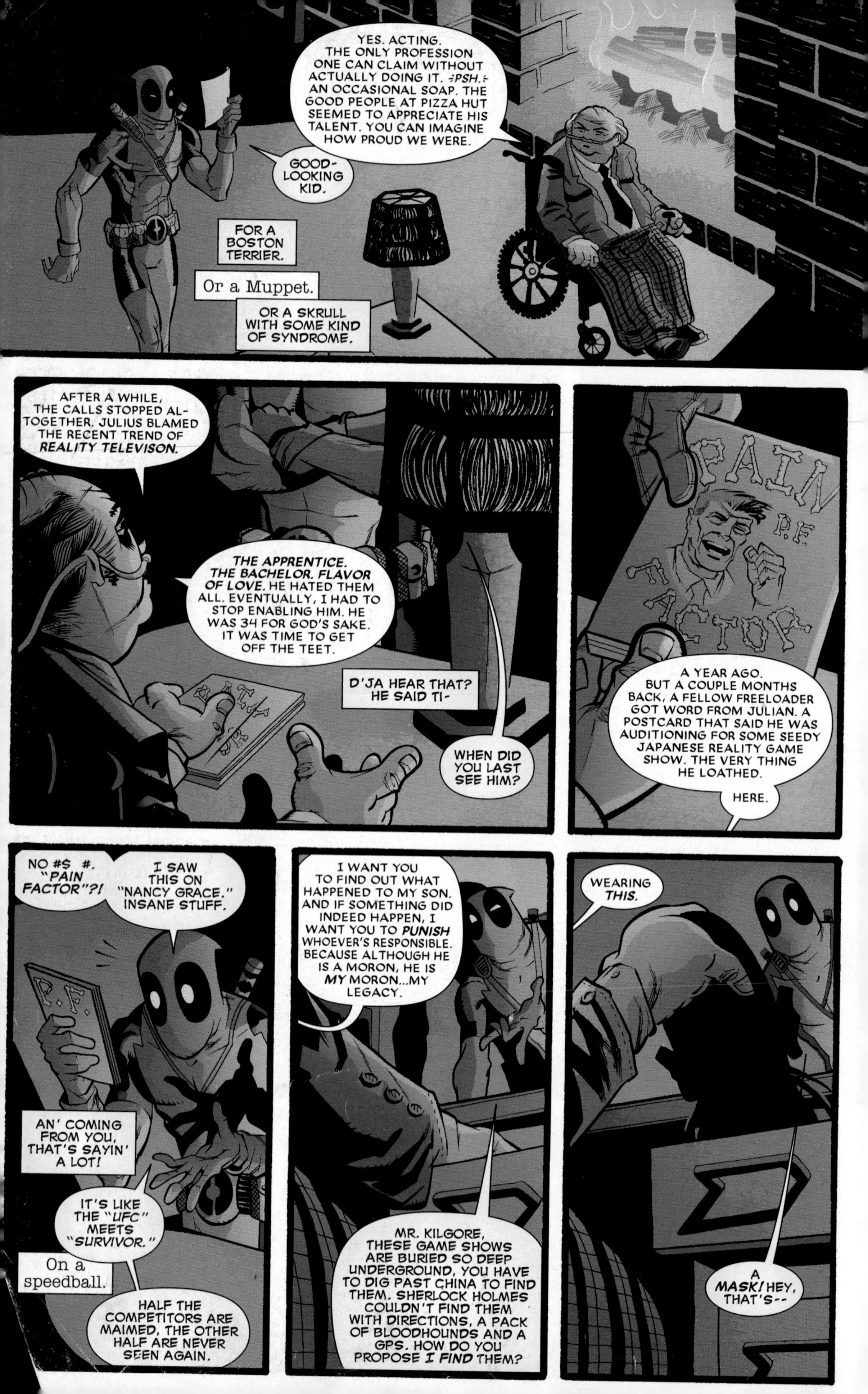
YES. ACTING. THE ONLY PROFESSION ONE CAN CLAIM WITHOUT ACTUALLY DOING IT. ÷PSH.÷ AN OCCASIONAL SOAP. THE GOOD PEOPLE AT PIZZA HUT SEEMED TO APPRECIATE HIS TALENT. YOU CAN IMAGINE HOW PROUD WE WERE.
GOOD-LOOKING KID.
FOR A BOSTON TERRIER.
Or a Muppet.
OR A SKRULL WITH SOME KIND OF SYNDROME.
AFTER A WHILE, THE CALLS STOPPED AL-TOGETHER. JULIUS BLAMED THE RECENT TREND OF REALITY TELEVISON.
THE APPRENTICE. THE BACHELOR. FLAVOR OF LOVE. HE HATED THEM ALL. EVENTUALLY, I HAD TO STOP ENABLING HIM. HE WAS 34 FOR GOD'S SAKE. IT WAS TIME TO GET OFF THE TEET.
D'JA HEAR THAT? HE SAID TI-
WHEN DID YOU LAST SEE HIM?
PAIN FACTOR
P.F.
A YEAR AGO. BUT A COUPLE MONTHS BACK, A FELLOW FREELOADER GOT WORD FROM JULIAN. A POSTCARD THAT SAID HE WAS AUDITIONING FOR SOME SEEDY JAPANESE REALITY GAME SHOW. THE VERY THING HE LOATHED.
HERE.
NO #$ #. "PAIN FACTOR"?!
I SAW THIS ON "NANCY GRACE." INSANE STUFF.
P.F.
AN' COMING FROM YOU, THAT'S SAYIN' A LOT!
IT'S LIKE THE "UFC" MEETS "SURVIVOR."
On a speedball.
HALF THE COMPETITORS ARE MAIMED, THE OTHER HALF ARE NEVER SEEN AGAIN.
I WANT YOU TO FIND OUT WHAT HAPPENED TO MY SON. AND IF SOMETHING DID INDEED HAPPEN, I WANT YOU TO PUNISH WHOEVER'S RESPONSIBLE. BECAUSE ALTHOUGH HE IS A MORON, HE IS MY MORON...MY LEGACY.
MR. KILGORE, THESE GAME SHOWS ARE BURIED SO DEEP UNDERGROUND, YOU HAVE TO DIG PAST CHINA TO FIND THEM. SHERLOCK HOLMES COULDN'T FIND THEM WITH DIRECTIONS, A PACK OF BLOODHOUNDS AND A GPS. HOW DO YOU PROPOSE I FIND THEM?
WEARING THIS.
A MASK! HEY, THAT'S--

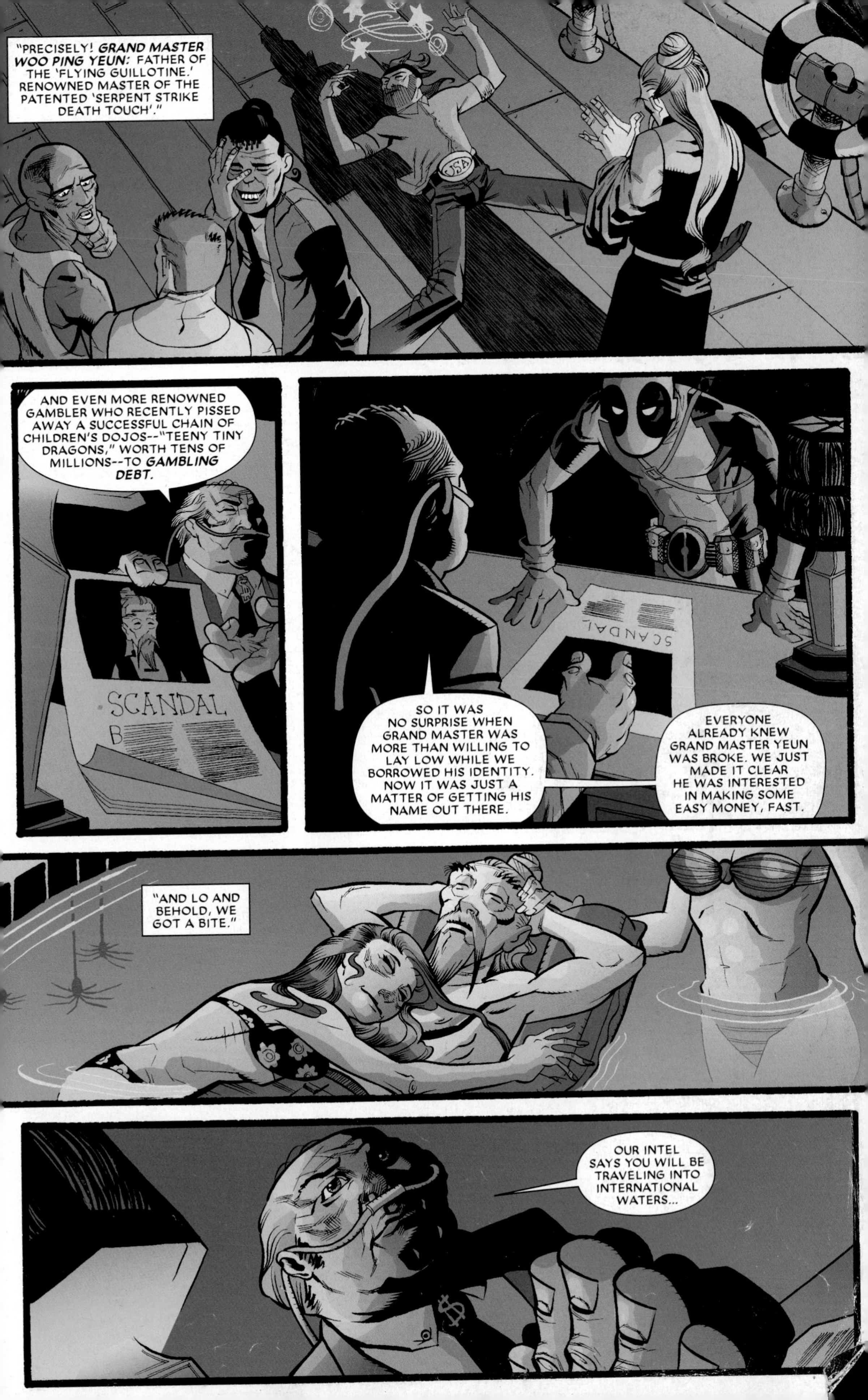
"PRECISELY! GRAND MASTER WOO PING YEUN: FATHER OF THE 'FLYING GUILLOTINE.' RENOWNED MASTER OF THE PATENTED 'SERPENT STRIKE DEATH TOUCH'."
USA
AND EVEN MORE RENOWNED GAMBLER WHO RECENTLY PISSED AWAY A SUCCESSFUL CHAIN OF CHILDREN'S DOJOS--"TEENY TINY DRAGONS," WORTH TENS OF MILLIONS--TO GAMBLING DEBT.
SCANDAL
SCANDAL
SO IT WAS NO SURPRISE WHEN GRAND MASTER WAS MORE THAN WILLING TO LAY LOW WHILE WE BORROWED HIS IDENTITY. NOW IT WAS JUST A MATTER OF GETTING HIS NAME OUT THERE.
EVERYONE ALREADY KNEW GRAND MASTER YEUN WAS BROKE. WE JUST MADE IT CLEAR HE WAS INTERESTED IN MAKING SOME EASY MONEY, FAST.
"AND LO AND BEHOLD, WE GOT A BITE."
OUR INTEL SAYS YOU WILL BE TRAVELING INTO INTERNATIONAL WATERS...

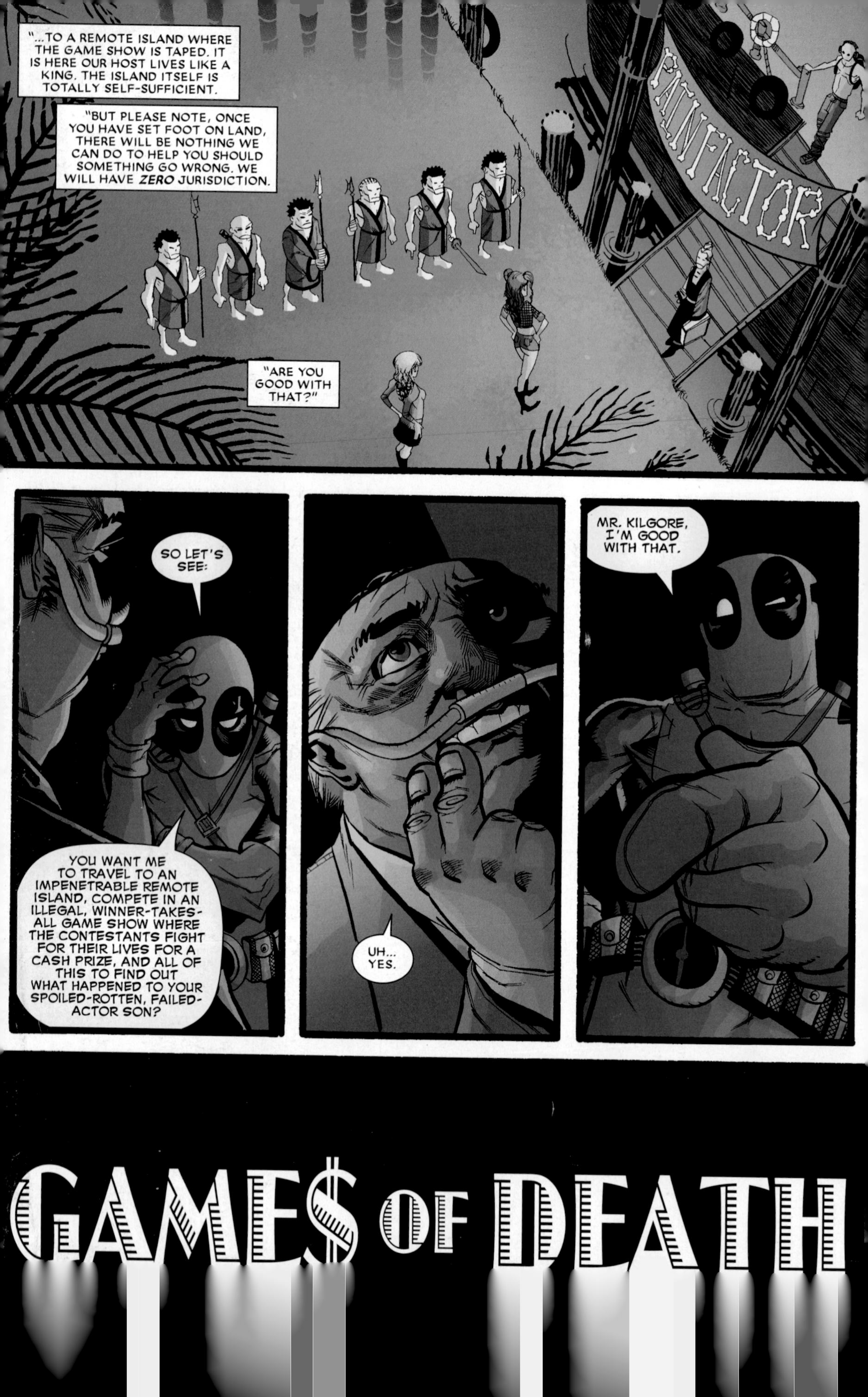
"...TO A REMOTE ISLAND WHERE THE GAME SHOW IS TAPED. IT IS HERE OUR HOST LIVES LIKE A KING. THE ISLAND ITSELF IS TOTALLY SELF-SUFFICIENT.
"BUT PLEASE NOTE, ONCE YOU HAVE SET FOOT ON LAND, THERE WILL BE NOTHING WE CAN DO TO HELP YOU SHOULD SOMETHING GO WRONG. WE WILL HAVE *ZERO* JURISDICTION.
PAIN FACTOR
"ARE YOU GOOD WITH THAT?"
SO LET'S SEE:
YOU WANT ME TO TRAVEL TO AN IMPENETRABLE REMOTE ISLAND, COMPETE IN AN ILLEGAL, WINNER-TAKES-ALL GAME SHOW WHERE THE CONTESTANTS FIGHT FOR THEIR LIVES FOR A CASH PRIZE, AND ALL OF THIS TO FIND OUT WHAT HAPPENED TO YOUR SPOILED-ROTTEN, FAILED-ACTOR SON?
UH... YES.
MR. KILGORE, I'M GOOD WITH THAT.
GAME$ OF DEATH

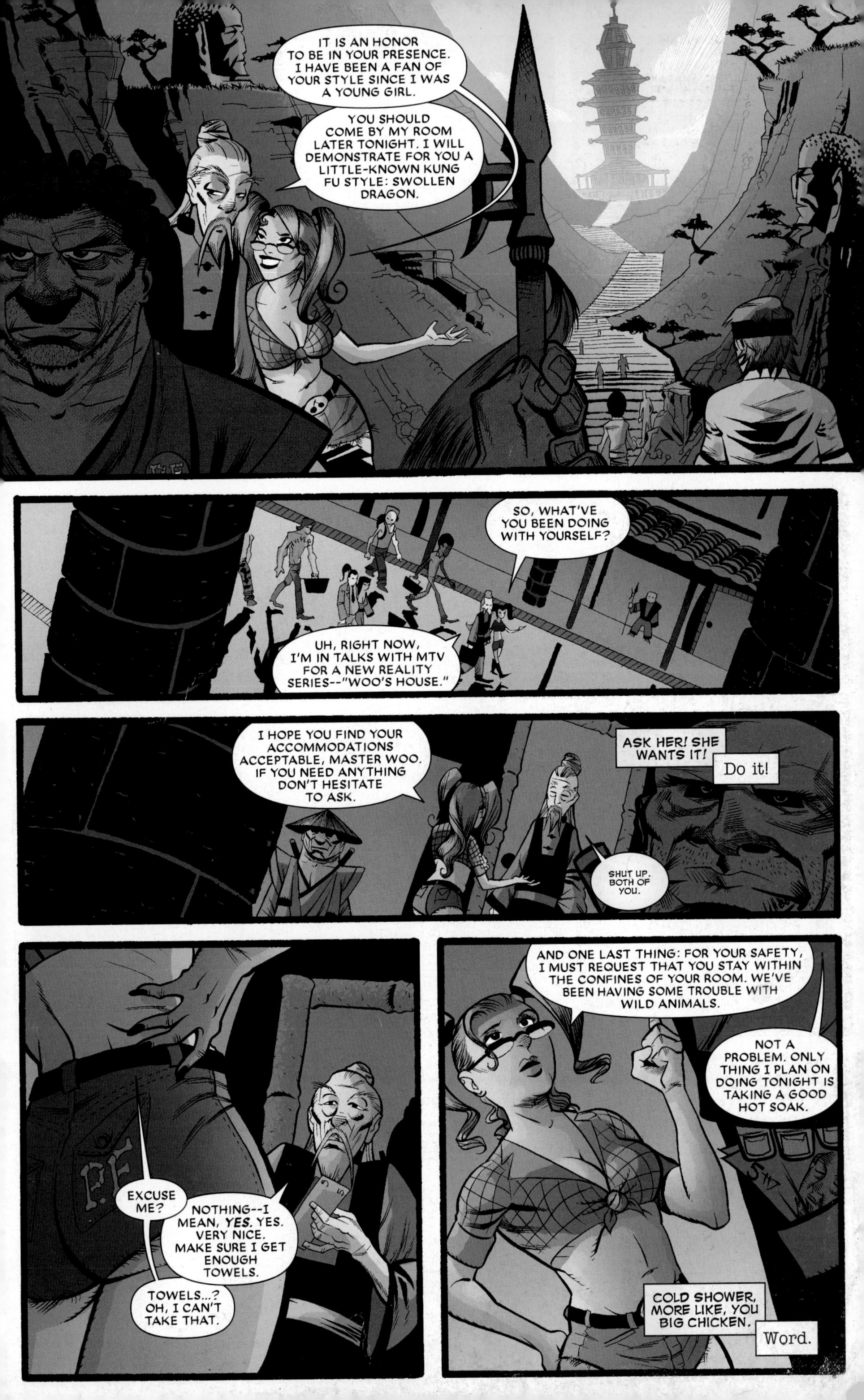
IT IS AN HONOR TO BE IN YOUR PRESENCE. I HAVE BEEN A FAN OF YOUR STYLE SINCE I WAS A YOUNG GIRL.
YOU SHOULD COME BY MY ROOM LATER TONIGHT. I WILL DEMONSTRATE FOR YOU A LITTLE-KNOWN KUNG FU STYLE: SWOLLEN DRAGON.
SO, WHAT'VE YOU BEEN DOING WITH YOURSELF?
UH, RIGHT NOW, I'M IN TALKS WITH MTV FOR A NEW REALITY SERIES--"WOO'S HOUSE."
I HOPE YOU FIND YOUR ACCOMMODATIONS ACCEPTABLE, MASTER WOO. IF YOU NEED ANYTHING DON'T HESITATE TO ASK.
ASK HER! SHE WANTS IT!
Do it!
SHUT UP. BOTH OF YOU.
EXCUSE ME?
NOTHING--I MEAN, YES. YES. VERY NICE. MAKE SURE I GET ENOUGH TOWELS.
TOWELS...? OH, I CAN'T TAKE THAT.
AND ONE LAST THING: FOR YOUR SAFETY, I MUST REQUEST THAT YOU STAY WITHIN THE CONFINES OF YOUR ROOM. WE'VE BEEN HAVING SOME TROUBLE WITH WILD ANIMALS.
NOT A PROBLEM. ONLY THING I PLAN ON DOING TONIGHT IS TAKING A GOOD HOT SOAK.
COLD SHOWER, MORE LIKE, YOU BIG CHICKEN.
Word.

SO, WHEN WILL WE BE MEETING WITH OUR ILLUSTRIOUS HOST?

TOMORROW AT THE GAMES. AGAIN, IF THERE'S *ANYTHING* YOU NEED...

C'MON, DUDE. SHE SAID *ANYTHING!*

Do it!

THEN GOOD NIGHT, UM....

THEY CALL ME POO-EN.

THERE'S A JOKE IN THERE BUT I'M NOT GONNA TOUCH IT.

A LOVELY NAME.

If you're a Cambodian hooker.

AH, MARRONE A MI.

GUESS I'M GONNA HAVE TO BLOW OFF STEAM ANOTHER WAY TONIGHT.

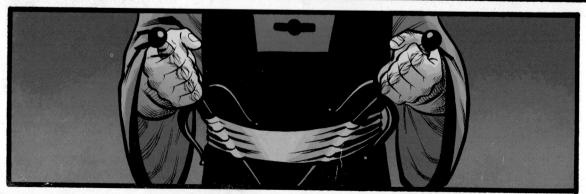

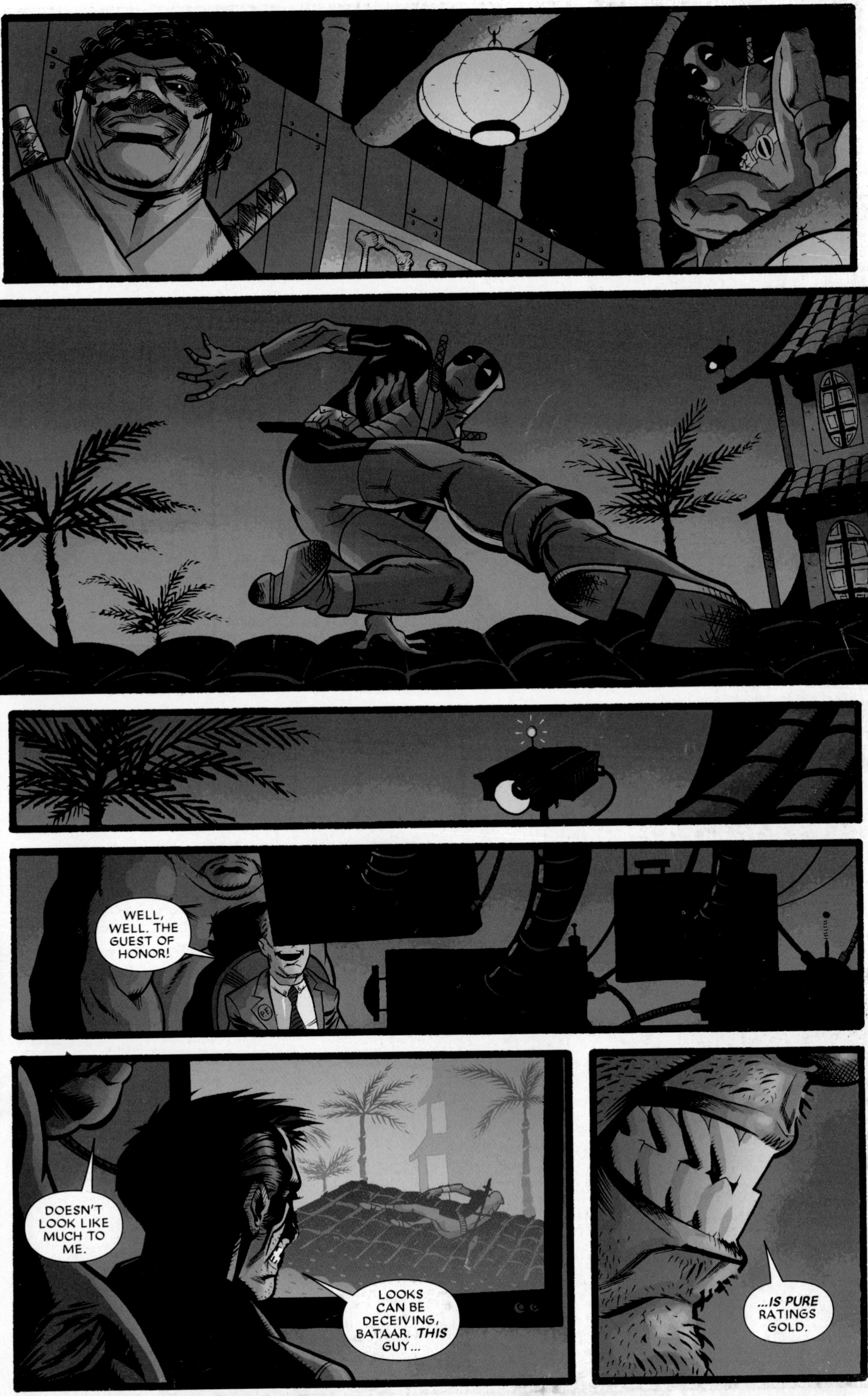
WELL, WELL. THE GUEST OF HONOR!
DOESN'T LOOK LIKE MUCH TO ME.
LOOKS CAN BE DECEIVING, BATAAR. THIS GUY...
...IS PURE RATINGS GOLD.

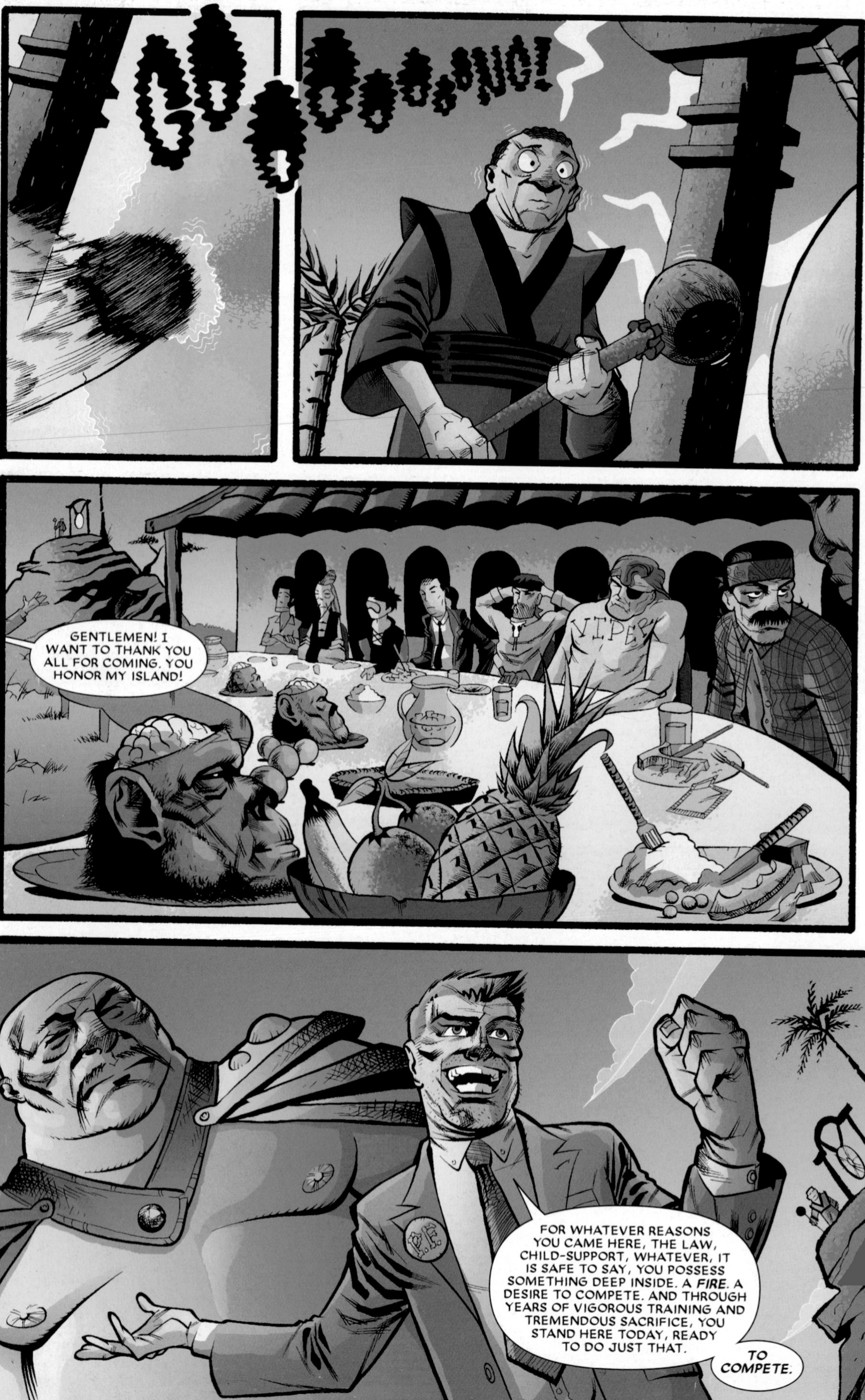
GOOOOOOOONG!
GENTLEMEN! I WANT TO THANK YOU ALL FOR COMING. YOU HONOR MY ISLAND!
VIPER
FOR WHATEVER REASONS YOU CAME HERE, THE LAW, CHILD-SUPPORT, WHATEVER, IT IS SAFE TO SAY, YOU POSSESS SOMETHING DEEP INSIDE. A FIRE. A DESIRE TO COMPETE. AND THROUGH YEARS OF VIGOROUS TRAINING AND TREMENDOUS SACRIFICE, YOU STAND HERE TODAY, READY TO DO JUST THAT.
TO COMPETE.

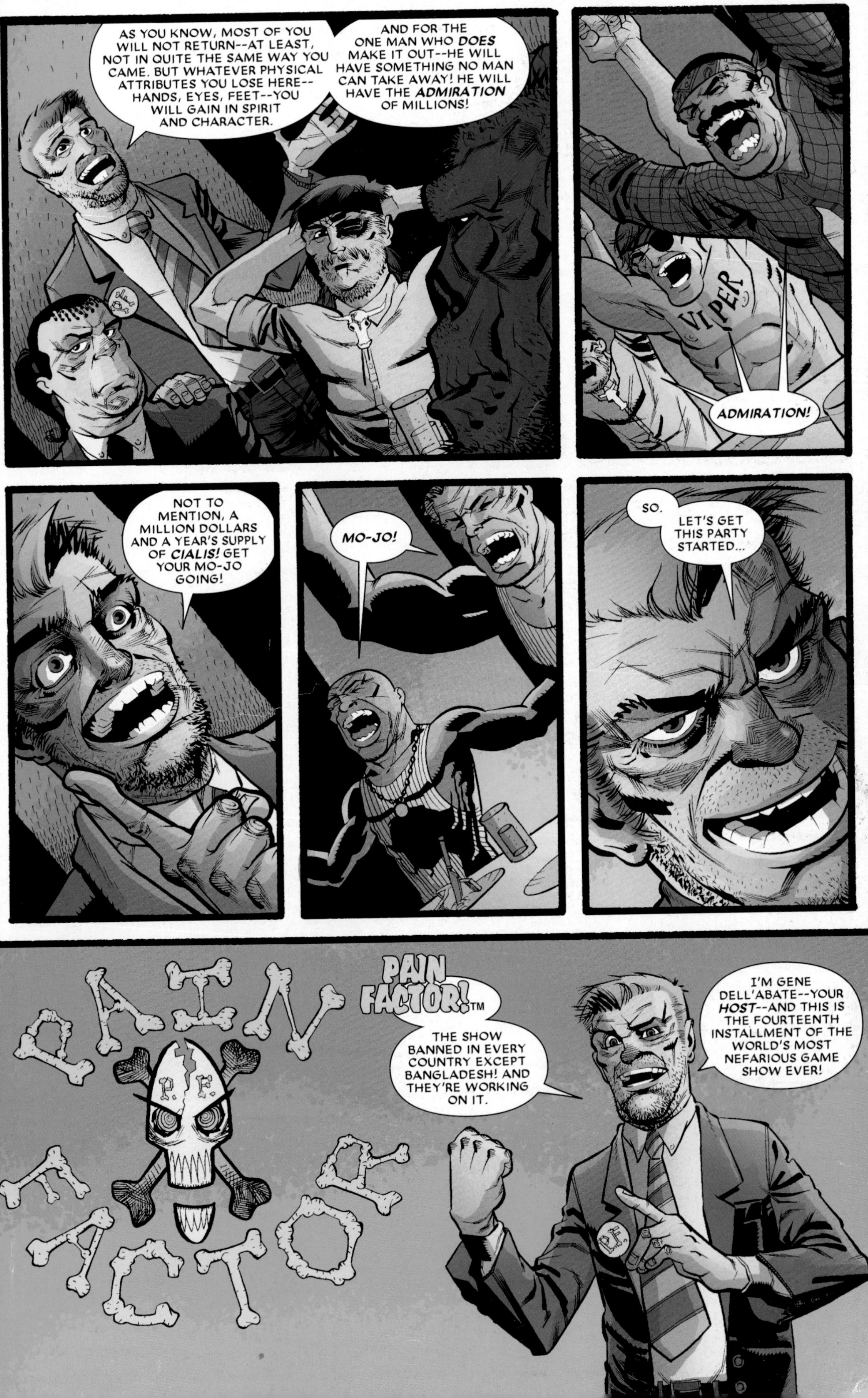
AS YOU KNOW, MOST OF YOU WILL NOT RETURN--AT LEAST, NOT IN QUITE THE SAME WAY YOU CAME. BUT WHATEVER PHYSICAL ATTRIBUTES YOU LOSE HERE--HANDS, EYES, FEET--YOU WILL GAIN IN SPIRIT AND CHARACTER.
AND FOR THE ONE MAN WHO DOES MAKE IT OUT--HE WILL HAVE SOMETHING NO MAN CAN TAKE AWAY! HE WILL HAVE THE ADMIRATION OF MILLIONS!
VIPER
ADMIRATION!
NOT TO MENTION, A MILLION DOLLARS AND A YEAR'S SUPPLY OF CIALIS! GET YOUR MO-JO GOING!
MO-JO!
SO.
LET'S GET THIS PARTY STARTED...
PAIN FACTOR
P.F.
PAIN FACTOR!™
THE SHOW BANNED IN EVERY COUNTRY EXCEPT BANGLADESH! AND THEY'RE WORKING ON IT.
I'M GENE DELL'ABATE--YOUR HOST--AND THIS IS THE FOURTEENTH INSTALLMENT OF THE WORLD'S MOST NEFARIOUS GAME SHOW EVER!
P.F.

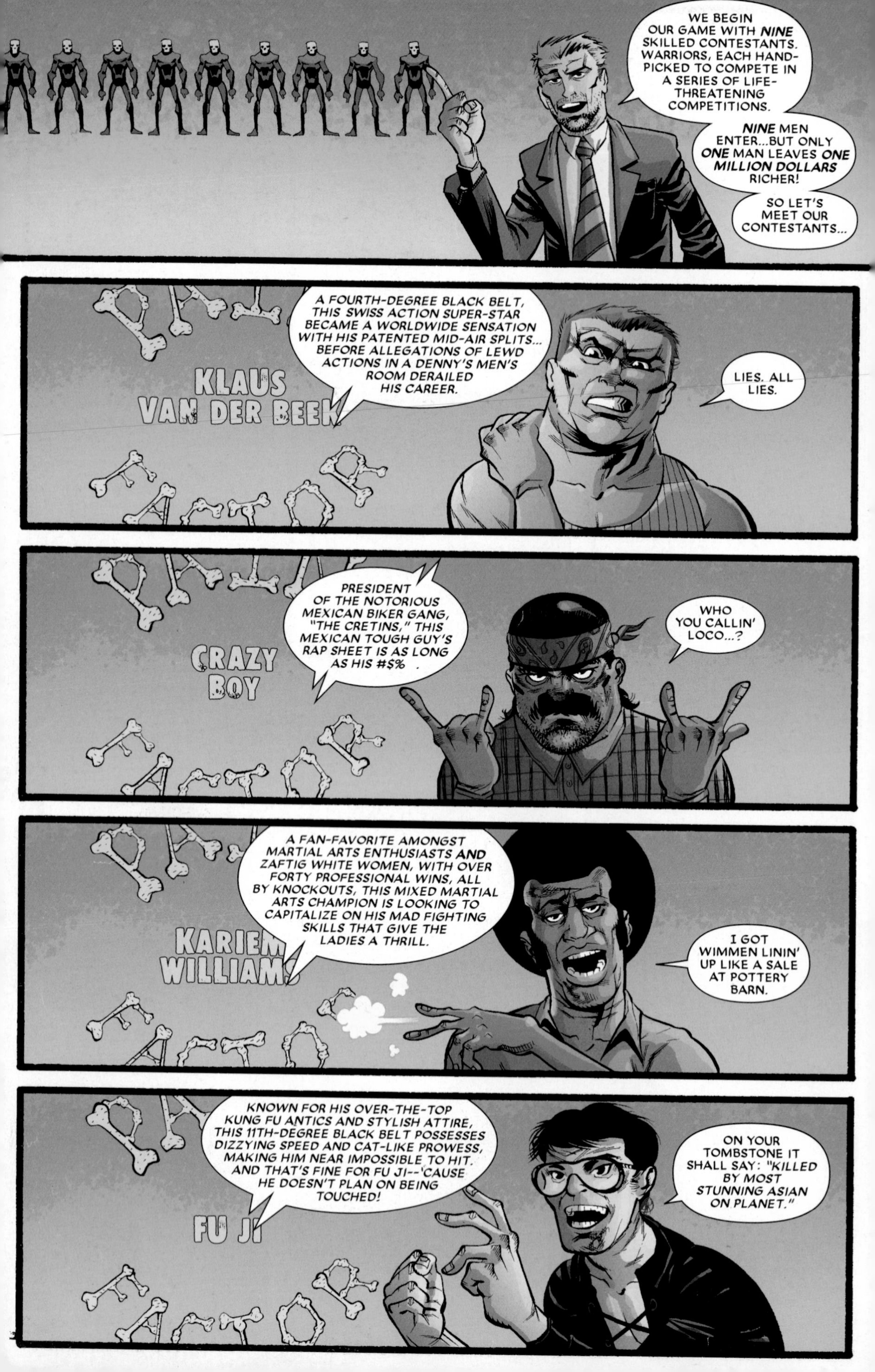
WE BEGIN OUR GAME WITH NINE SKILLED CONTESTANTS. WARRIORS, EACH HAND-PICKED TO COMPETE IN A SERIES OF LIFE-THREATENING COMPETITIONS.
NINE MEN ENTER...BUT ONLY ONE MAN LEAVES ONE MILLION DOLLARS RICHER!
SO LET'S MEET OUR CONTESTANTS...
KLAUS VAN DER BEEK
A FOURTH-DEGREE BLACK BELT, THIS SWISS ACTION SUPER-STAR BECAME A WORLDWIDE SENSATION WITH HIS PATENTED MID-AIR SPLITS... BEFORE ALLEGATIONS OF LEWD ACTIONS IN A DENNY'S MEN'S ROOM DERAILED HIS CAREER.
LIES. ALL LIES.
CRAZY BOY
PRESIDENT OF THE NOTORIOUS MEXICAN BIKER GANG, "THE CRETINS," THIS MEXICAN TOUGH GUY'S RAP SHEET IS AS LONG AS HIS #$%.
WHO YOU CALLIN' LOCO...?
KARIEM WILLIAMS
A FAN-FAVORITE AMONGST MARTIAL ARTS ENTHUSIASTS AND ZAFTIG WHITE WOMEN, WITH OVER FORTY PROFESSIONAL WINS, ALL BY KNOCKOUTS, THIS MIXED MARTIAL ARTS CHAMPION IS LOOKING TO CAPITALIZE ON HIS MAD FIGHTING SKILLS THAT GIVE THE LADIES A THRILL.
I GOT WIMMEN LININ' UP LIKE A SALE AT POTTERY BARN.
FU JI
KNOWN FOR HIS OVER-THE-TOP KUNG FU ANTICS AND STYLISH ATTIRE, THIS 11TH-DEGREE BLACK BELT POSSESSES DIZZYING SPEED AND CAT-LIKE PROWESS, MAKING HIM NEAR IMPOSSIBLE TO HIT. AND THAT'S FINE FOR FU JI--'CAUSE HE DOESN'T PLAN ON BEING TOUCHED!
ON YOUR TOMBSTONE IT SHALL SAY: "KILLED BY MOST STUNNING ASIAN ON PLANET."

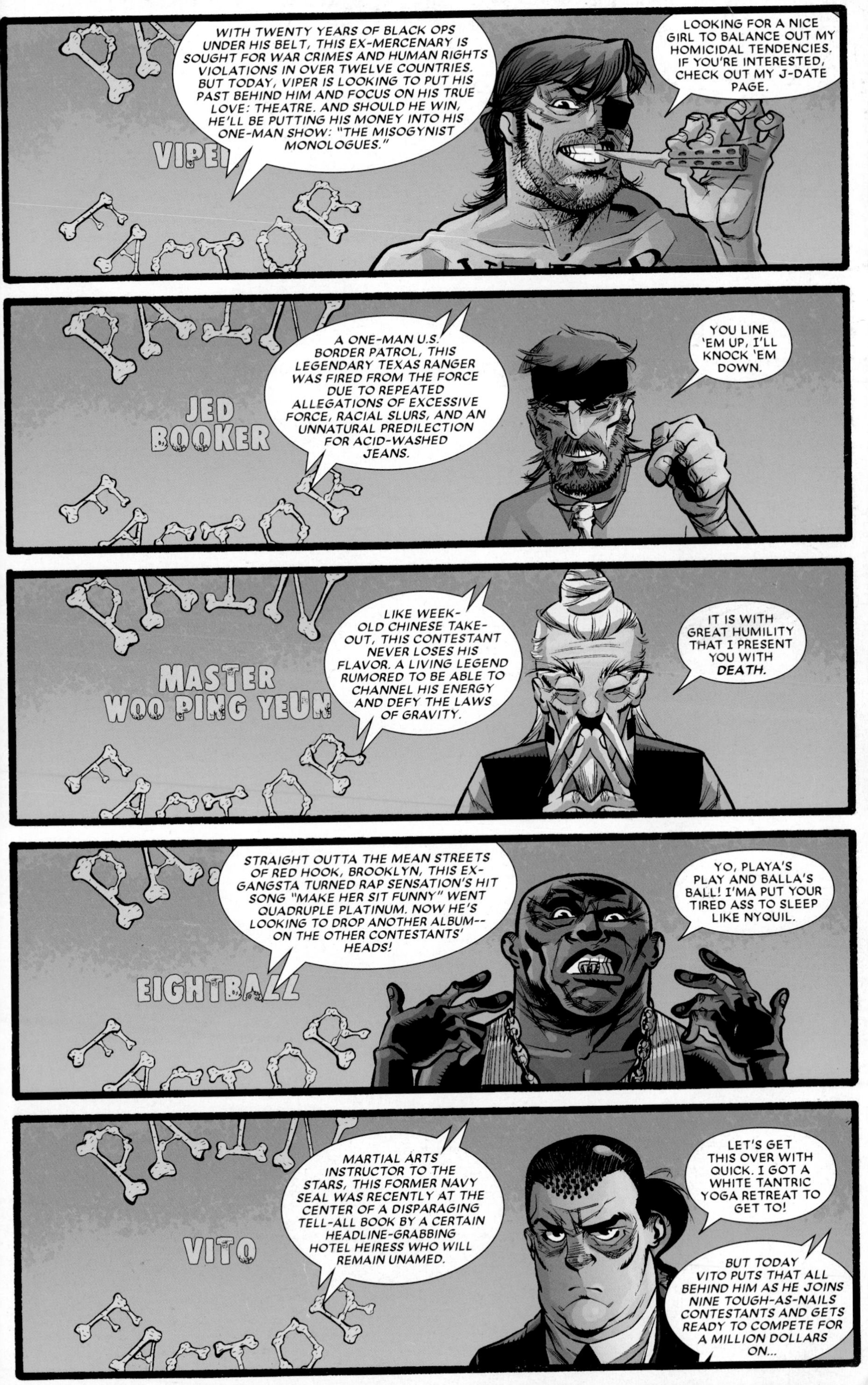

VIPE
WITH TWENTY YEARS OF BLACK OPS UNDER HIS BELT, THIS EX-MERCENARY IS SOUGHT FOR WAR CRIMES AND HUMAN RIGHTS VIOLATIONS IN OVER TWELVE COUNTRIES. BUT TODAY, VIPER IS LOOKING TO PUT HIS PAST BEHIND HIM AND FOCUS ON HIS TRUE LOVE: THEATRE. AND SHOULD HE WIN, HE'LL BE PUTTING HIS MONEY INTO HIS ONE-MAN SHOW: "THE MISOGYNIST MONOLOGUES."
LOOKING FOR A NICE GIRL TO BALANCE OUT MY HOMICIDAL TENDENCIES. IF YOU'RE INTERESTED, CHECK OUT MY J-DATE PAGE.
JED BOOKER
A ONE-MAN U.S. BORDER PATROL, THIS LEGENDARY TEXAS RANGER WAS FIRED FROM THE FORCE DUE TO REPEATED ALLEGATIONS OF EXCESSIVE FORCE, RACIAL SLURS, AND AN UNNATURAL PREDILECTION FOR ACID-WASHED JEANS.
YOU LINE 'EM UP, I'LL KNOCK 'EM DOWN.
MASTER WOO PING YEUN
LIKE WEEK-OLD CHINESE TAKE-OUT, THIS CONTESTANT NEVER LOSES HIS FLAVOR. A LIVING LEGEND RUMORED TO BE ABLE TO CHANNEL HIS ENERGY AND DEFY THE LAWS OF GRAVITY.
IT IS WITH GREAT HUMILITY THAT I PRESENT YOU WITH *DEATH.*
EIGHTBALL
STRAIGHT OUTTA THE MEAN STREETS OF RED HOOK, BROOKLYN, THIS EX-GANGSTA TURNED RAP SENSATION'S HIT SONG "MAKE HER SIT FUNNY" WENT QUADRUPLE PLATINUM. NOW HE'S LOOKING TO DROP ANOTHER ALBUM--ON THE OTHER CONTESTANTS' HEADS!
YO, PLAYA'S PLAY AND BALLA'S BALL! I'MA PUT YOUR TIRED ASS TO SLEEP LIKE NYQUIL.
VITO
MARTIAL ARTS INSTRUCTOR TO THE STARS, THIS FORMER NAVY SEAL WAS RECENTLY AT THE CENTER OF A DISPARAGING TELL-ALL BOOK BY A CERTAIN HEADLINE-GRABBING HOTEL HEIRESS WHO WILL REMAIN UNAMED.
LET'S GET THIS OVER WITH QUICK. I GOT A WHITE TANTRIC YOGA RETREAT TO GET TO!
BUT TODAY VITO PUTS THAT ALL BEHIND HIM AS HE JOINS NINE TOUGH-AS-NAILS CONTESTANTS AND GETS READY TO COMPETE FOR A MILLION DOLLARS ON...

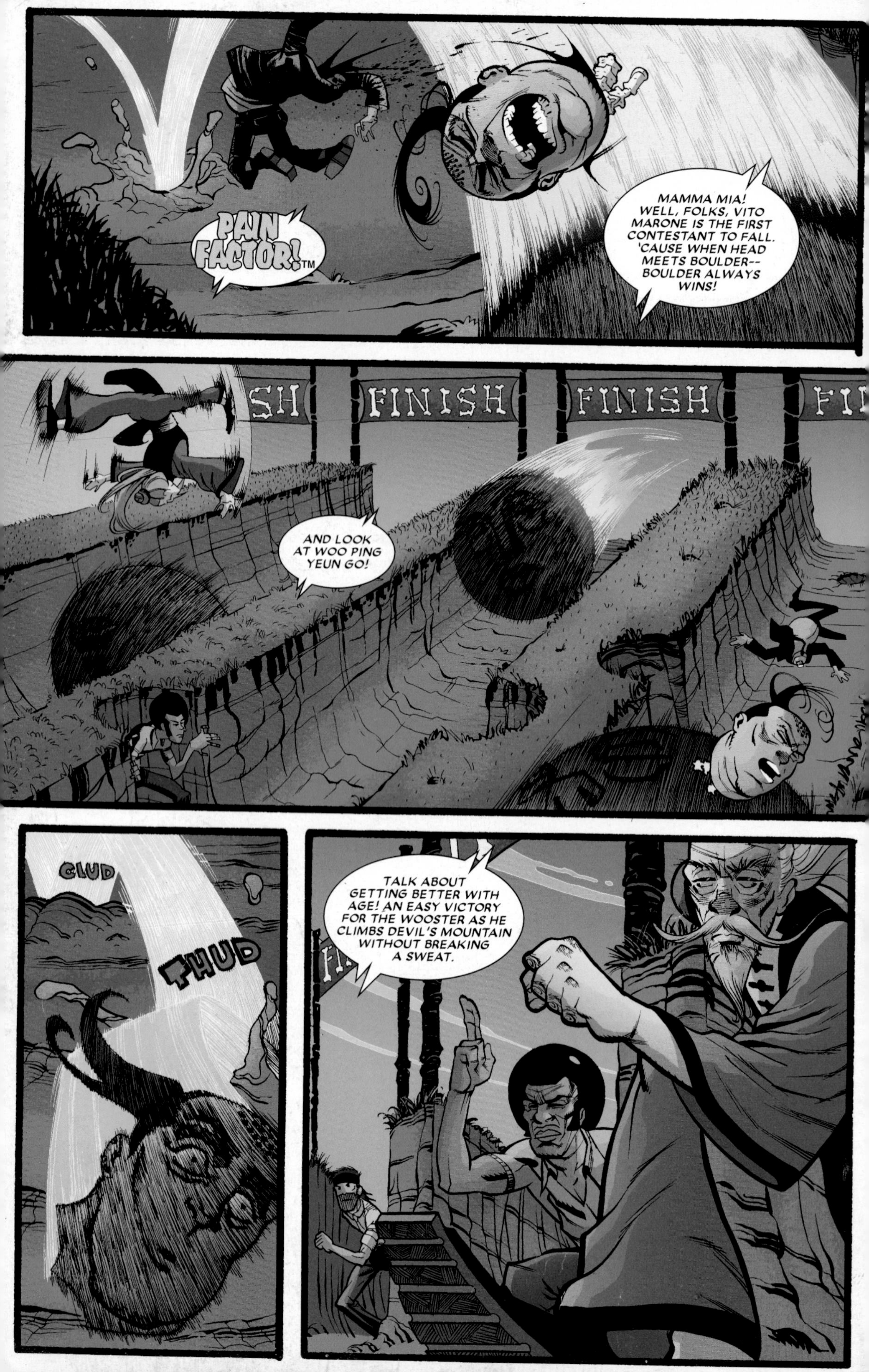
PAIN FACTOR!™
MAMMA MIA! WELL, FOLKS, VITO MARONE IS THE FIRST CONTESTANT TO FALL. 'CAUSE WHEN HEAD MEETS BOULDER-- BOULDER ALWAYS WINS!
FINISH
FINISH
AND LOOK AT WOO PING YEUN GO!
GLUD
THUD
TALK ABOUT GETTING BETTER WITH AGE! AN EASY VICTORY FOR THE WOOSTER AS HE CLIMBS DEVIL'S MOUNTAIN WITHOUT BREAKING A SWEAT.

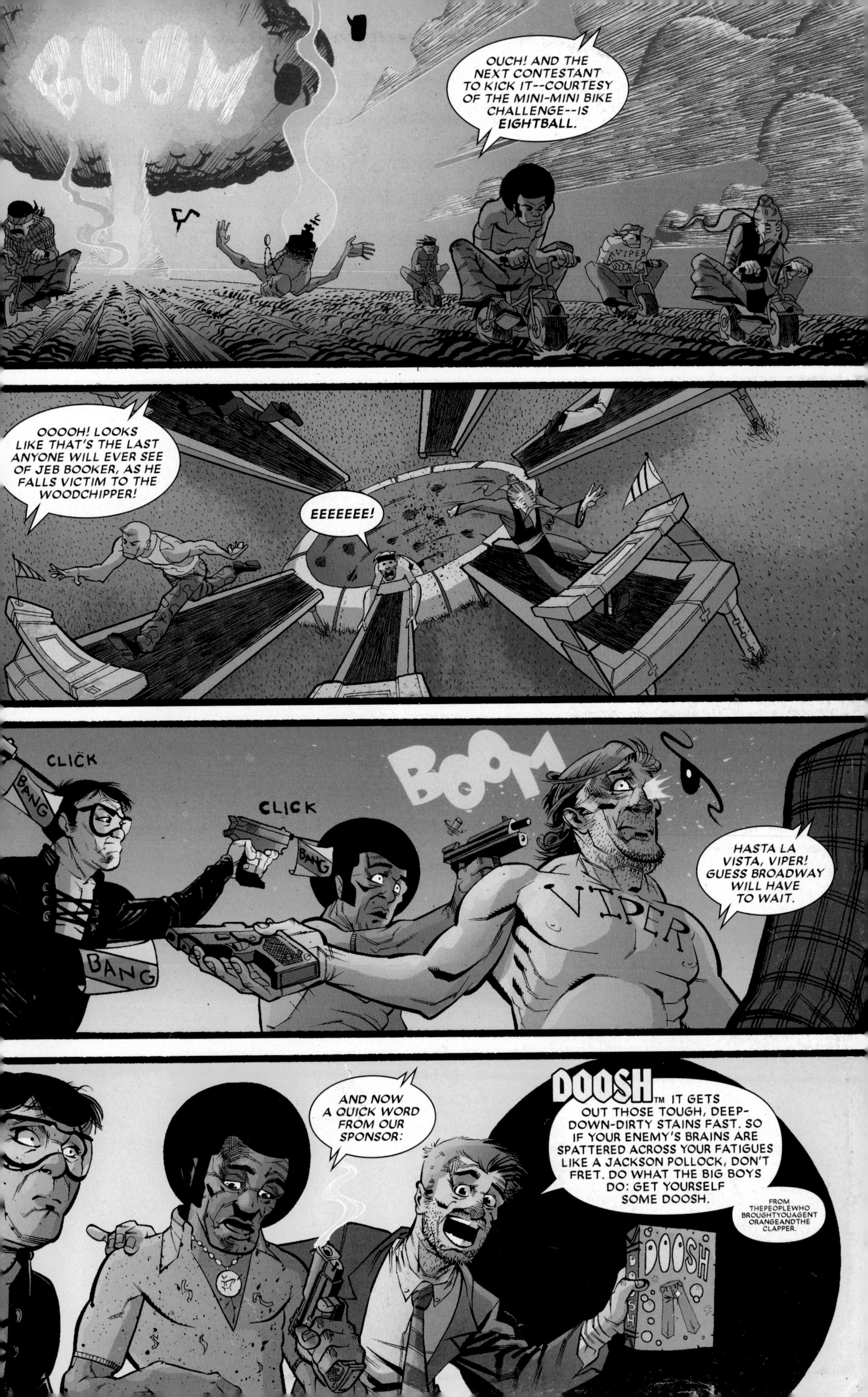
BOOM
OUCH! AND THE NEXT CONTESTANT TO KICK IT--COURTESY OF THE MINI-MINI BIKE CHALLENGE--IS EIGHTBALL.
VIPER
OOOOH! LOOKS LIKE THAT'S THE LAST ANYONE WILL EVER SEE OF JEB BOOKER, AS HE FALLS VICTIM TO THE WOODCHIPPER!
EEEEEEE!
CLICK
BANG
CLICK
BANG
BOOM
BANG
VIPER
HASTA LA VISTA, VIPER! GUESS BROADWAY WILL HAVE TO WAIT.
AND NOW A QUICK WORD FROM OUR SPONSOR:
DOOSH™ IT GETS OUT THOSE TOUGH, DEEP-DOWN-DIRTY STAINS FAST. SO IF YOUR ENEMY'S BRAINS ARE SPATTERED ACROSS YOUR FATIGUES LIKE A JACKSON POLLOCK, DON'T FRET. DO WHAT THE BIG BOYS DO: GET YOURSELF SOME DOOSH.
FROM THEPEOPLEWHO BROUGHTYOUAGENT ORANGEANDTHE CLAPPER.
DOOSH

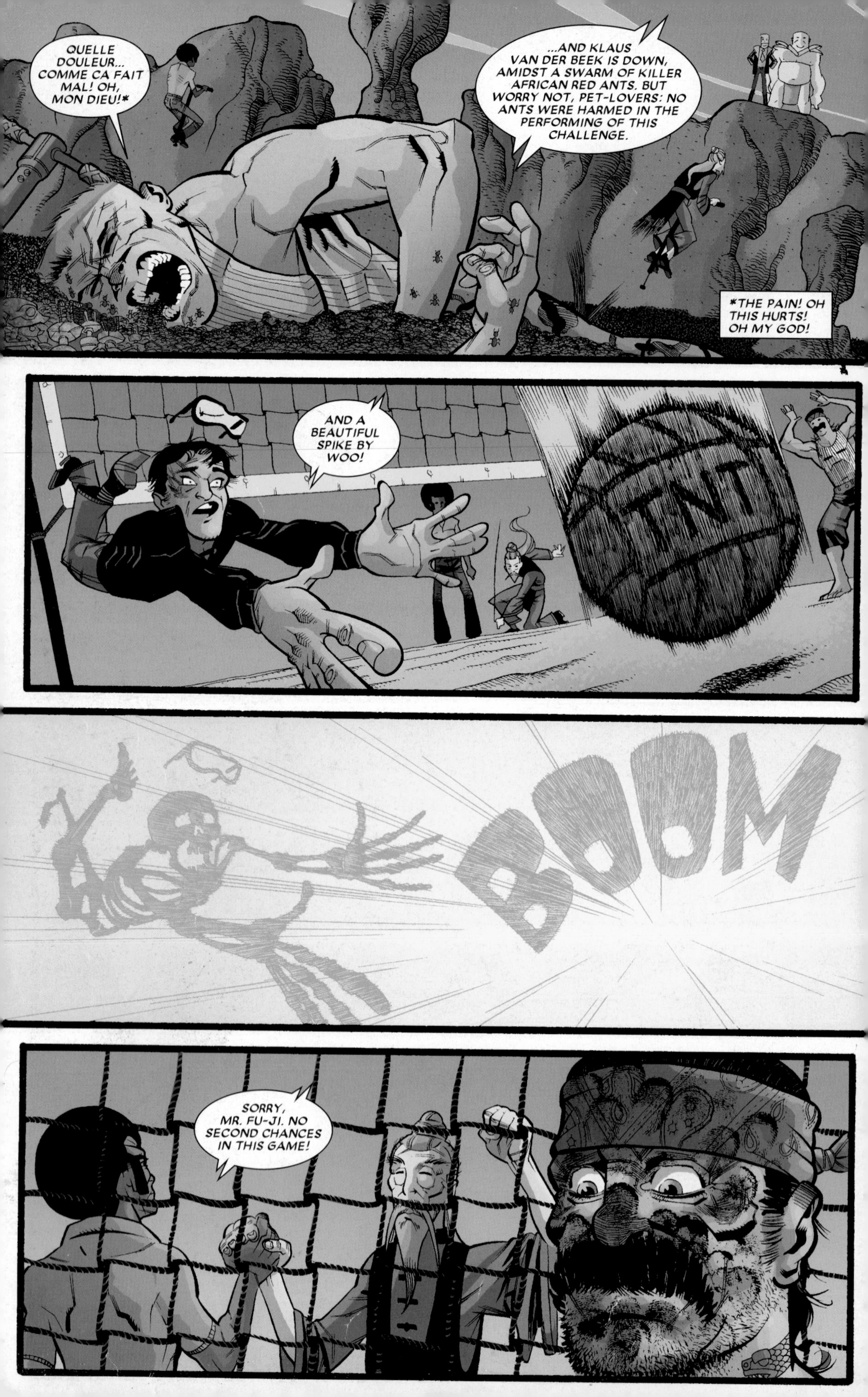
QUELLE DOULEUR... COMME CA FAIT MAL! OH, MON DIEU!*
...AND KLAUS VAN DER BEEK IS DOWN, AMIDST A SWARM OF KILLER AFRICAN RED ANTS. BUT WORRY NOT, PET-LOVERS: NO ANTS WERE HARMED IN THE PERFORMING OF THIS CHALLENGE.
*THE PAIN! OH THIS HURTS! OH MY GOD!
AND A BEAUTIFUL SPIKE BY WOO!
TNT
BOOOM
SORRY, MR. FU-JI. NO SECOND CHANCES IN THIS GAME!

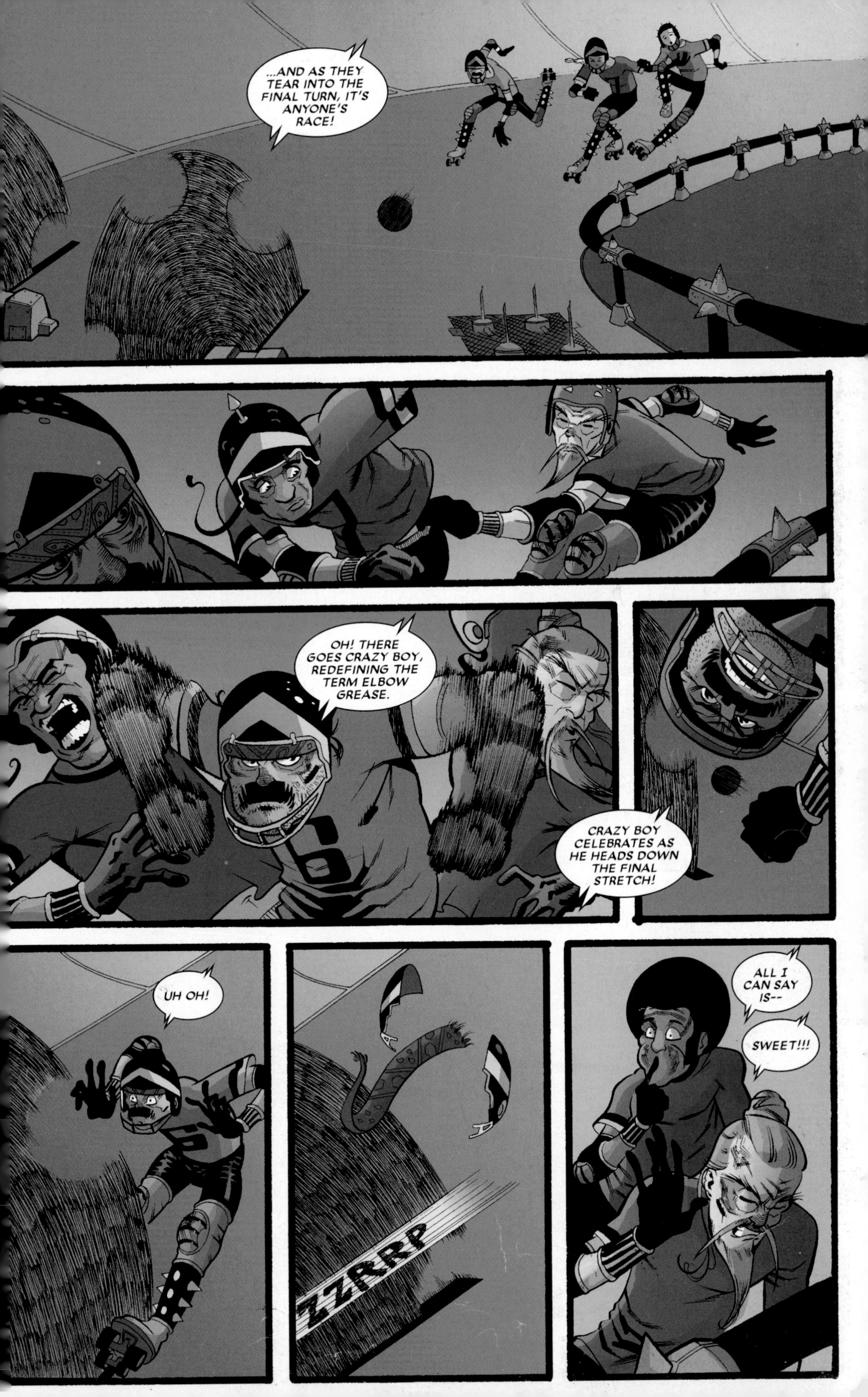
...AND AS THEY TEAR INTO THE FINAL TURN, IT'S ANYONE'S RACE!
OH! THERE GOES CRAZY BOY, REDEFINING THE TERM ELBOW GREASE.
CRAZY BOY CELEBRATES AS HE HEADS DOWN THE FINAL STRETCH!
UH OH!
ZZRRRP
ALL I CAN SAY IS--
SWEET!!!

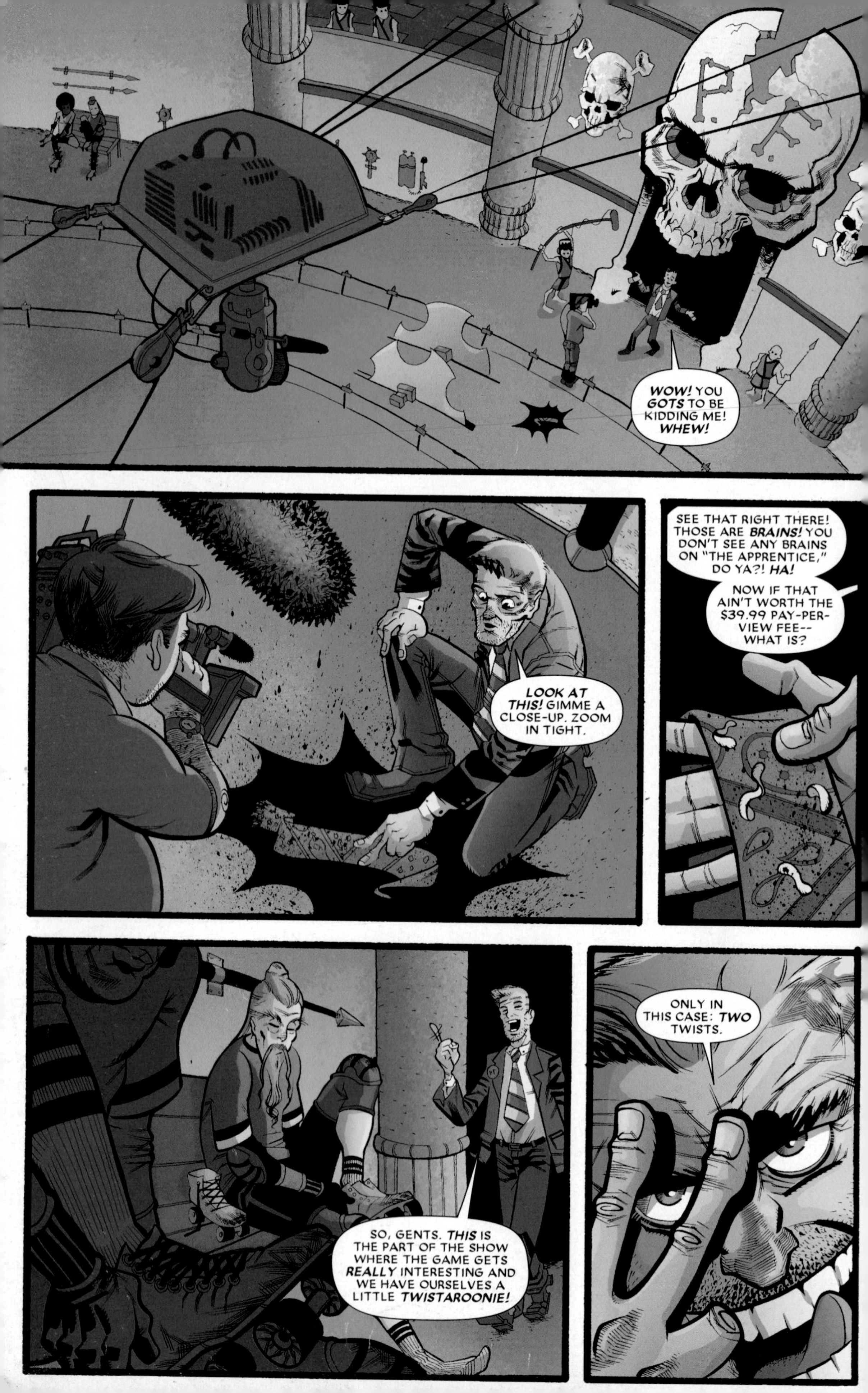
WOW! YOU GOTS TO BE KIDDING ME! WHEW!
LOOK AT THIS! GIMME A CLOSE-UP. ZOOM IN TIGHT.
SEE THAT RIGHT THERE! THOSE ARE BRAINS! YOU DON'T SEE ANY BRAINS ON "THE APPRENTICE," DO YA?! HA!
NOW IF THAT AIN'T WORTH THE $39.99 PAY-PER-VIEW FEE-- WHAT IS?
SO, GENTS. THIS IS THE PART OF THE SHOW WHERE THE GAME GETS REALLY INTERESTING AND WE HAVE OURSELVES A LITTLE TWISTAROONIE!
ONLY IN THIS CASE: TWO TWISTS.

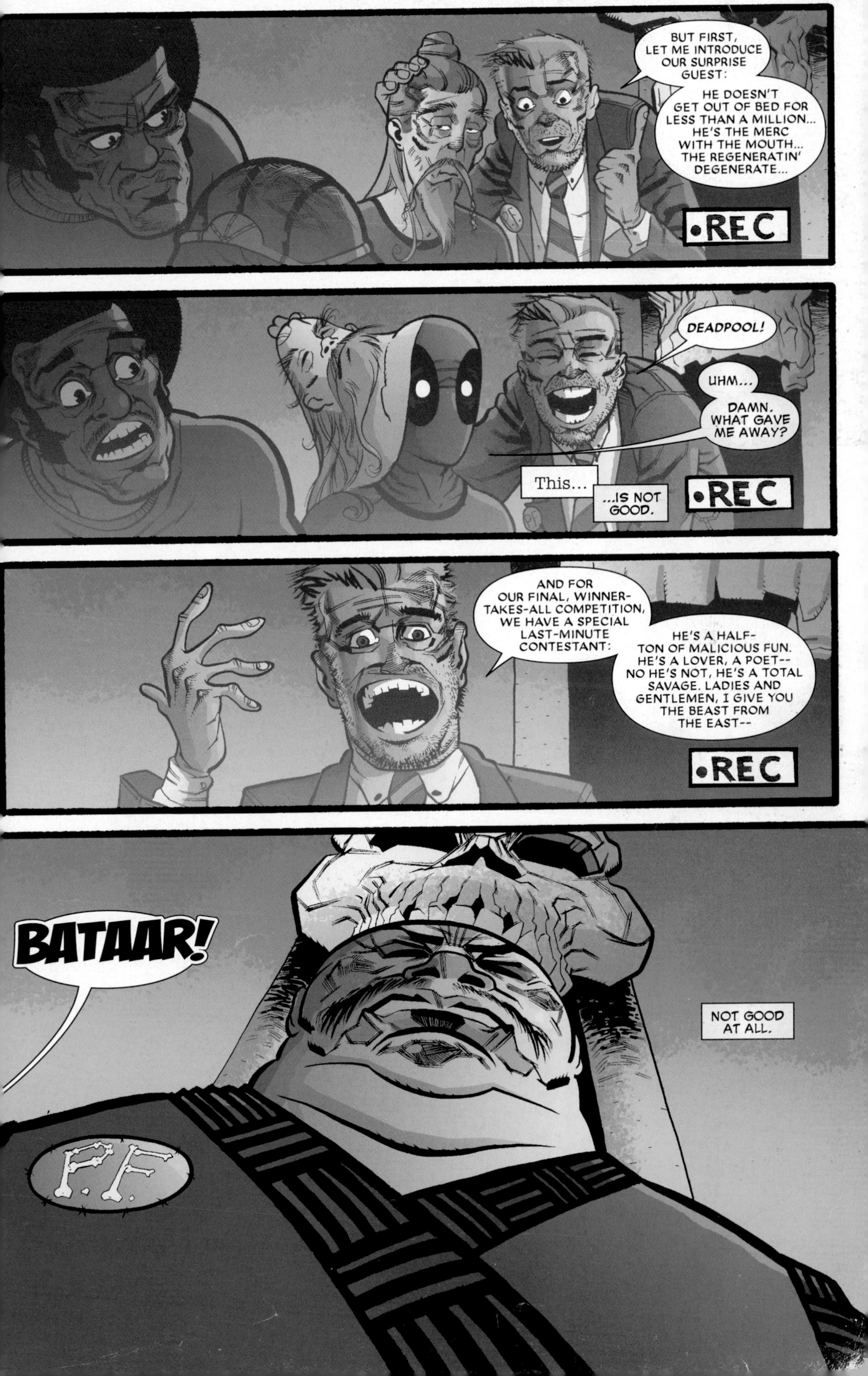
BUT FIRST, LET ME INTRODUCE OUR SURPRISE GUEST:
HE DOESN'T GET OUT OF BED FOR LESS THAN A MILLION... HE'S THE MERC WITH THE MOUTH... THE REGENERATIN' DEGENERATE...
•REC
DEADPOOL!
UHM...
DAMN. WHAT GAVE ME AWAY?
This...
...IS NOT GOOD.
•REC
AND FOR OUR FINAL, WINNER-TAKES-ALL COMPETITION, WE HAVE A SPECIAL LAST-MINUTE CONTESTANT:
HE'S A HALF-TON OF MALICIOUS FUN. HE'S A LOVER, A POET-- NO HE'S NOT, HE'S A TOTAL SAVAGE. LADIES AND GENTLEMEN, I GIVE YOU THE BEAST FROM THE EAST--
•REC
BATAAR!
NOT GOOD AT ALL.
P.F.

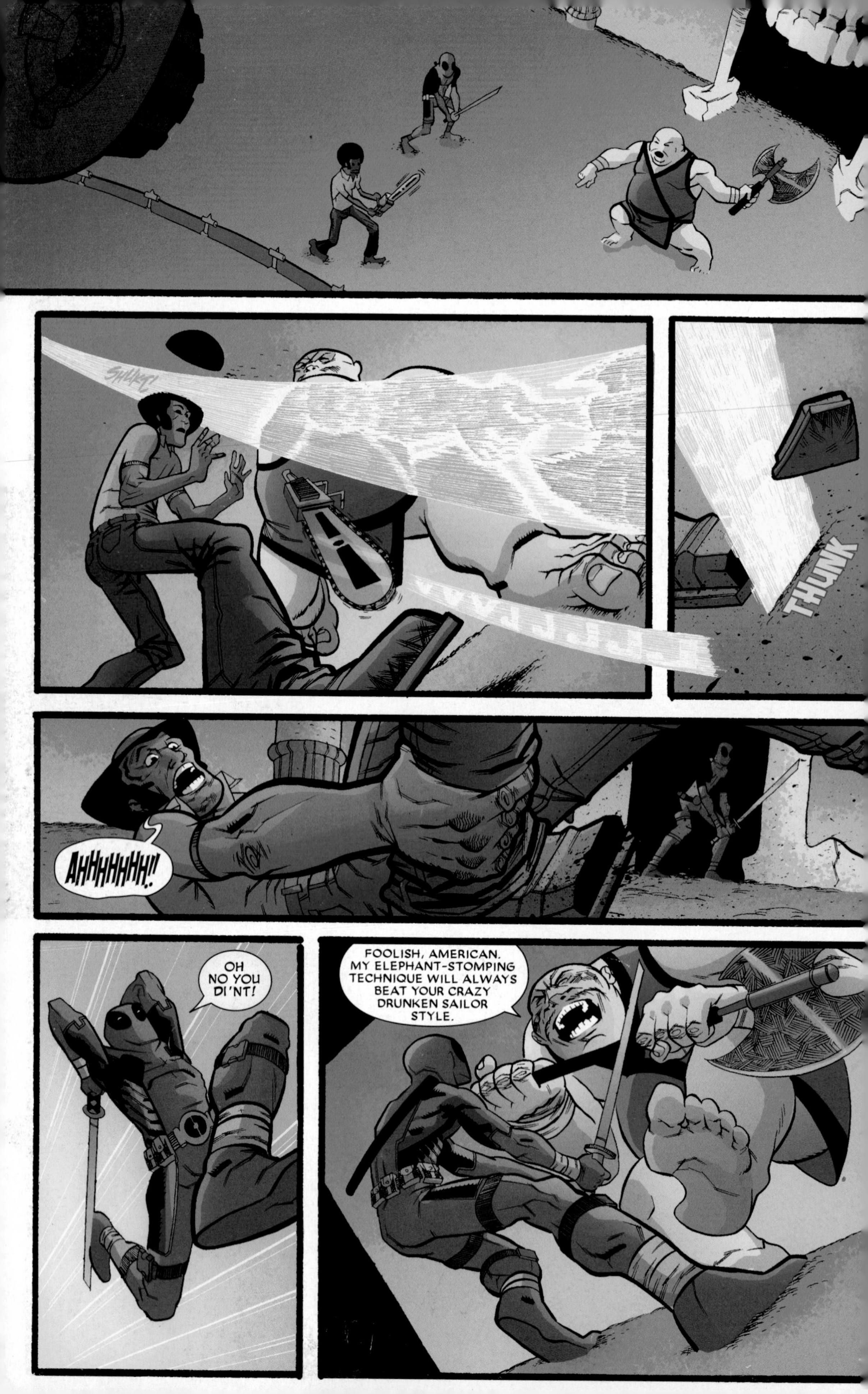
THUNK
AHHHHHHH!!
OH NO YOU DI'NT!
FOOLISH, AMERICAN. MY ELEPHANT-STOMPING TECHNIQUE WILL ALWAYS BEAT YOUR CRAZY DRUNKEN SAILOR STYLE.

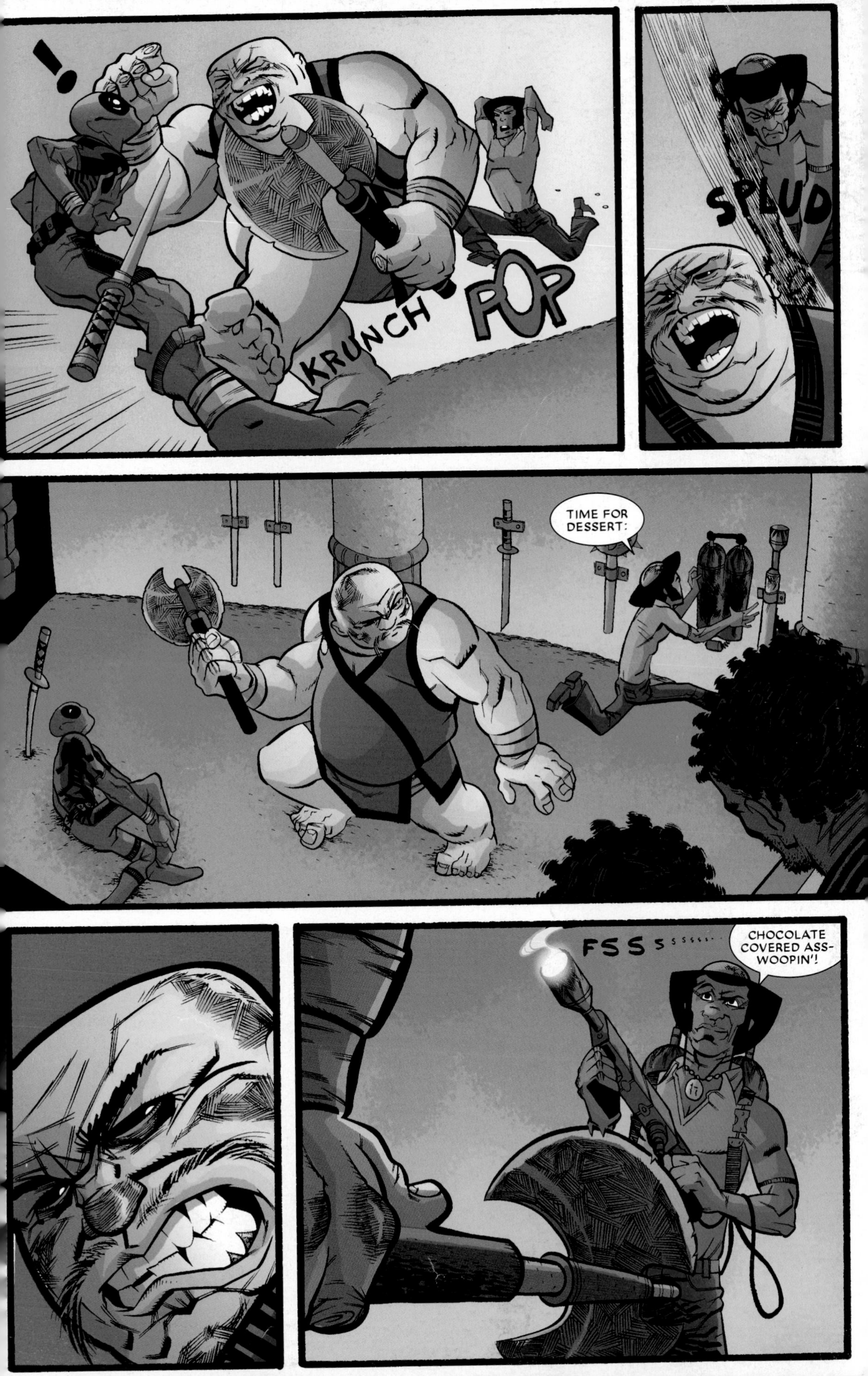
!
KRUNCH
POP
SPLUD
TIME FOR DESSERT:
FSSsssssss...
CHOCOLATE COVERED ASS-WOOPIN'!

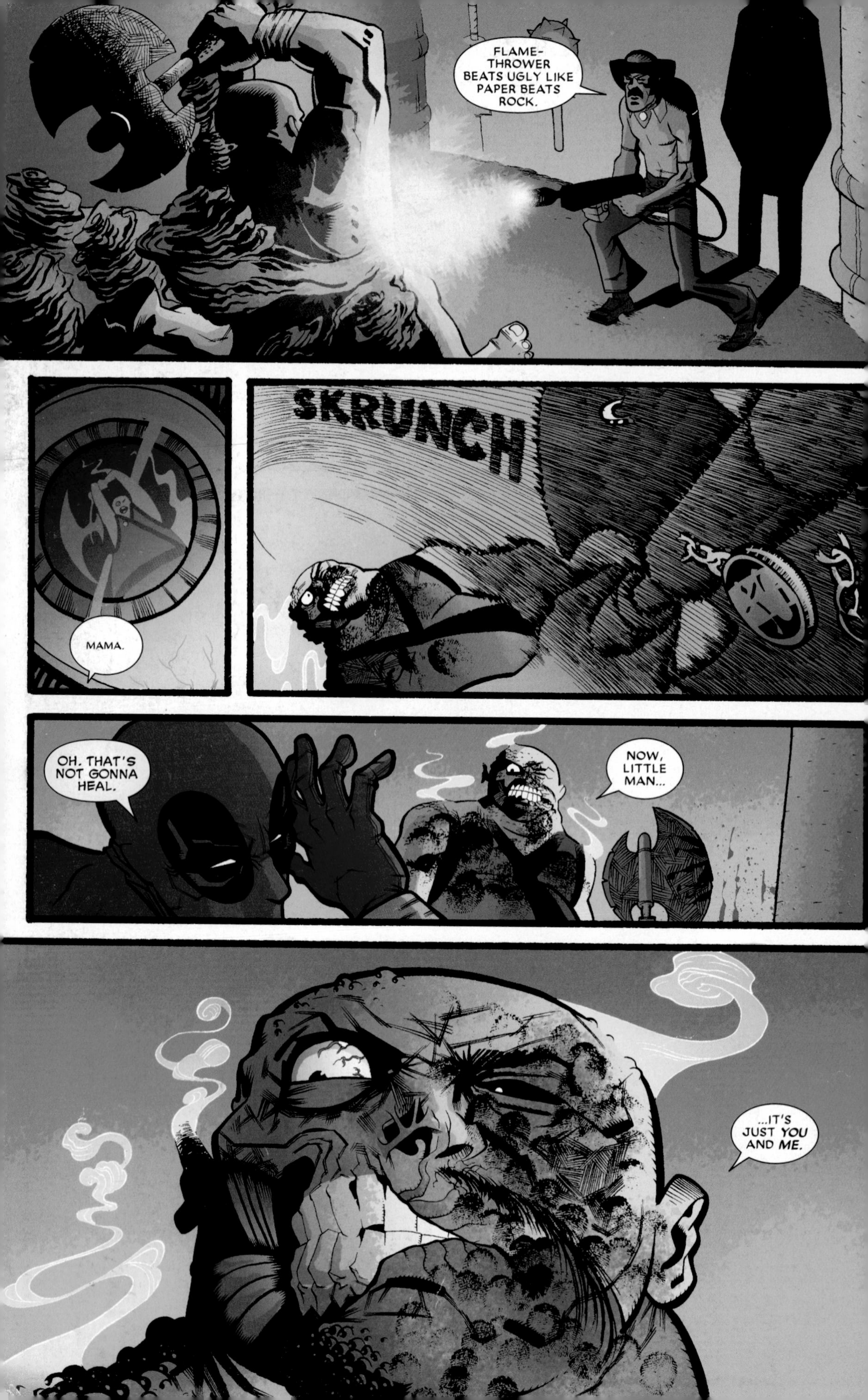
FLAME-THROWER BEATS UGLY LIKE PAPER BEATS ROCK.
MAMA.
SKRUNCH
OH. THAT'S NOT GONNA HEAL.
NOW, LITTLE MAN...
...IT'S JUST YOU AND ME.

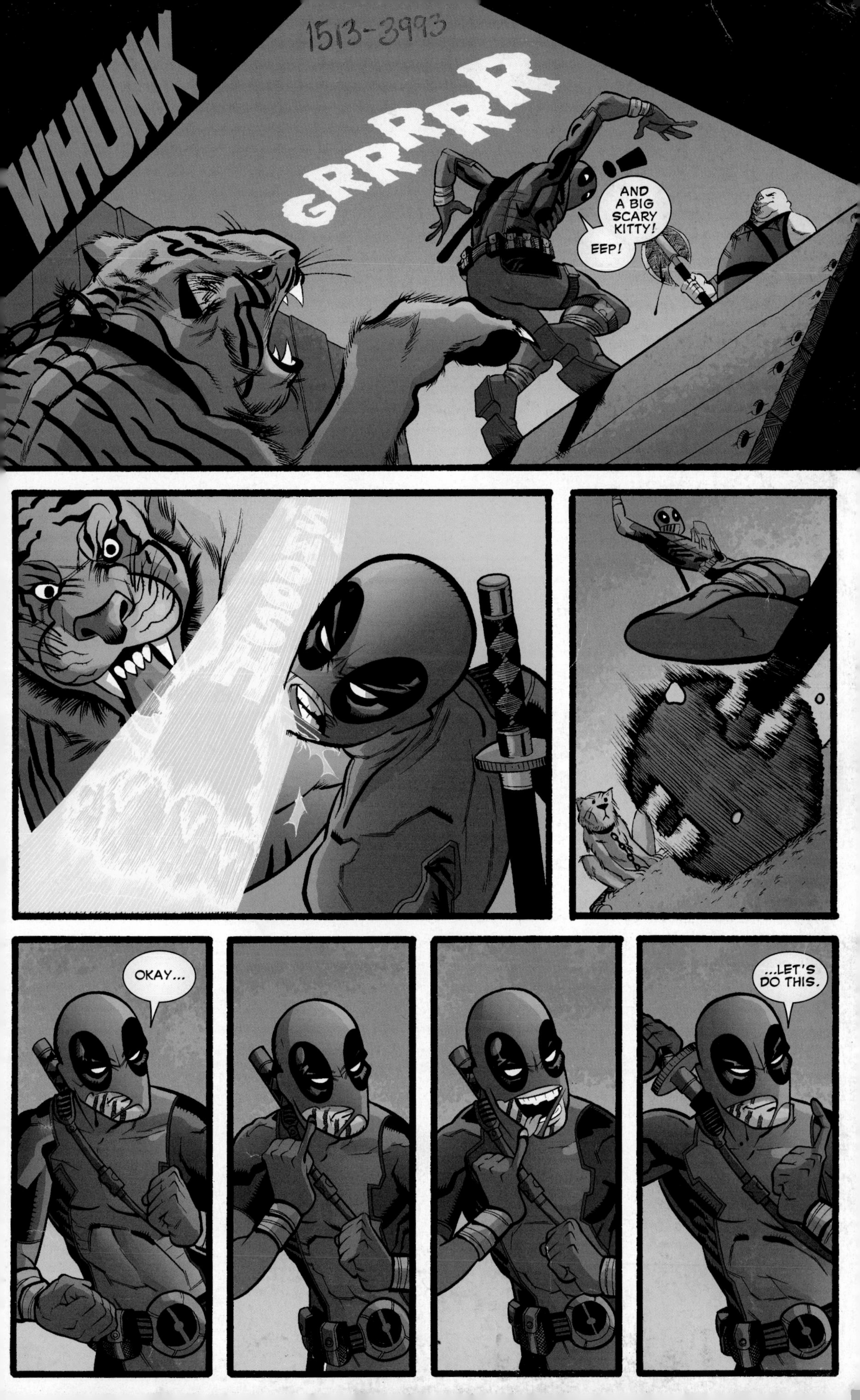
1513-3993
WHUNK
GRRRR
!
AND A BIG SCARY KITTY!
EEP!
OKAY...
...LET'S DO THIS.

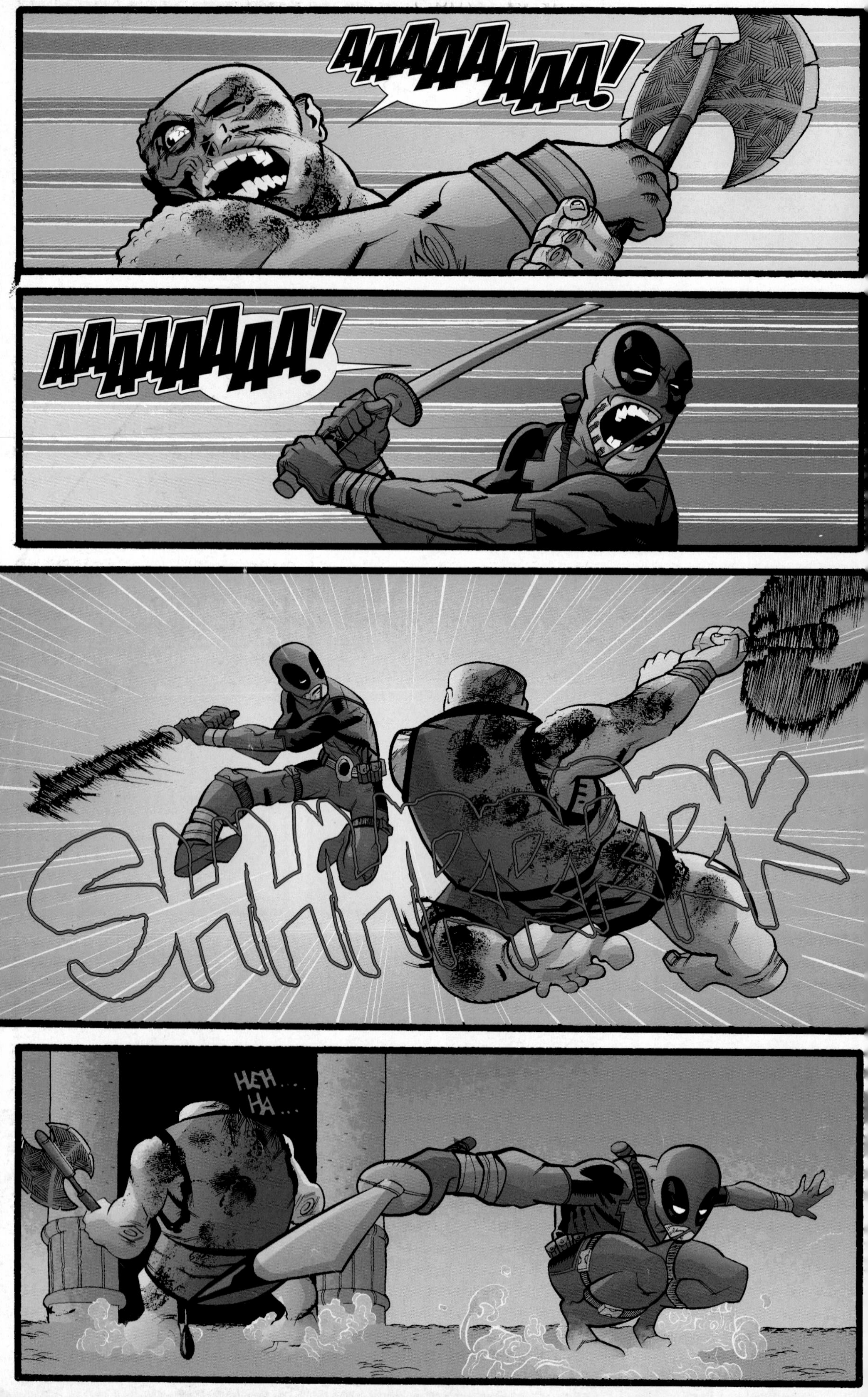
AAAAAAAAA!
AAAAAAAAA!
SHHHHRAK
HEH... HA...

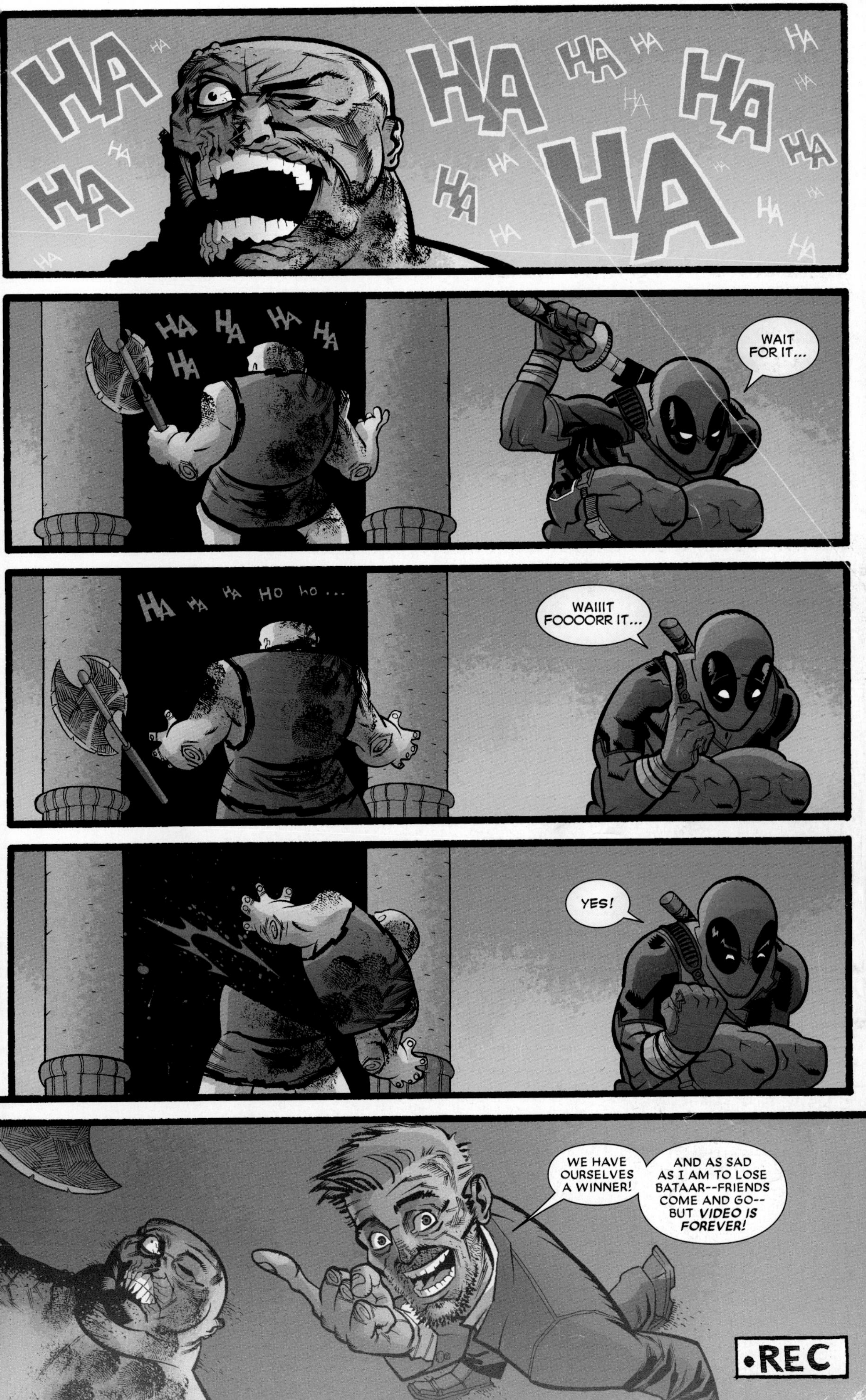
HA HA HA HA HA HA HA HA HA HA HA HA HA HA HA HA HA HA HA HA HA HA
HA HA HA HA HA HA
WAIT FOR IT...
HA HA HA HO ho...
WAIIIT FOOOORR IT...
YES!
WE HAVE OURSELVES A WINNER!
AND AS SAD AS I AM TO LOSE BATAAR--FRIENDS COME AND GO--BUT *VIDEO IS FOREVER!*
•REC

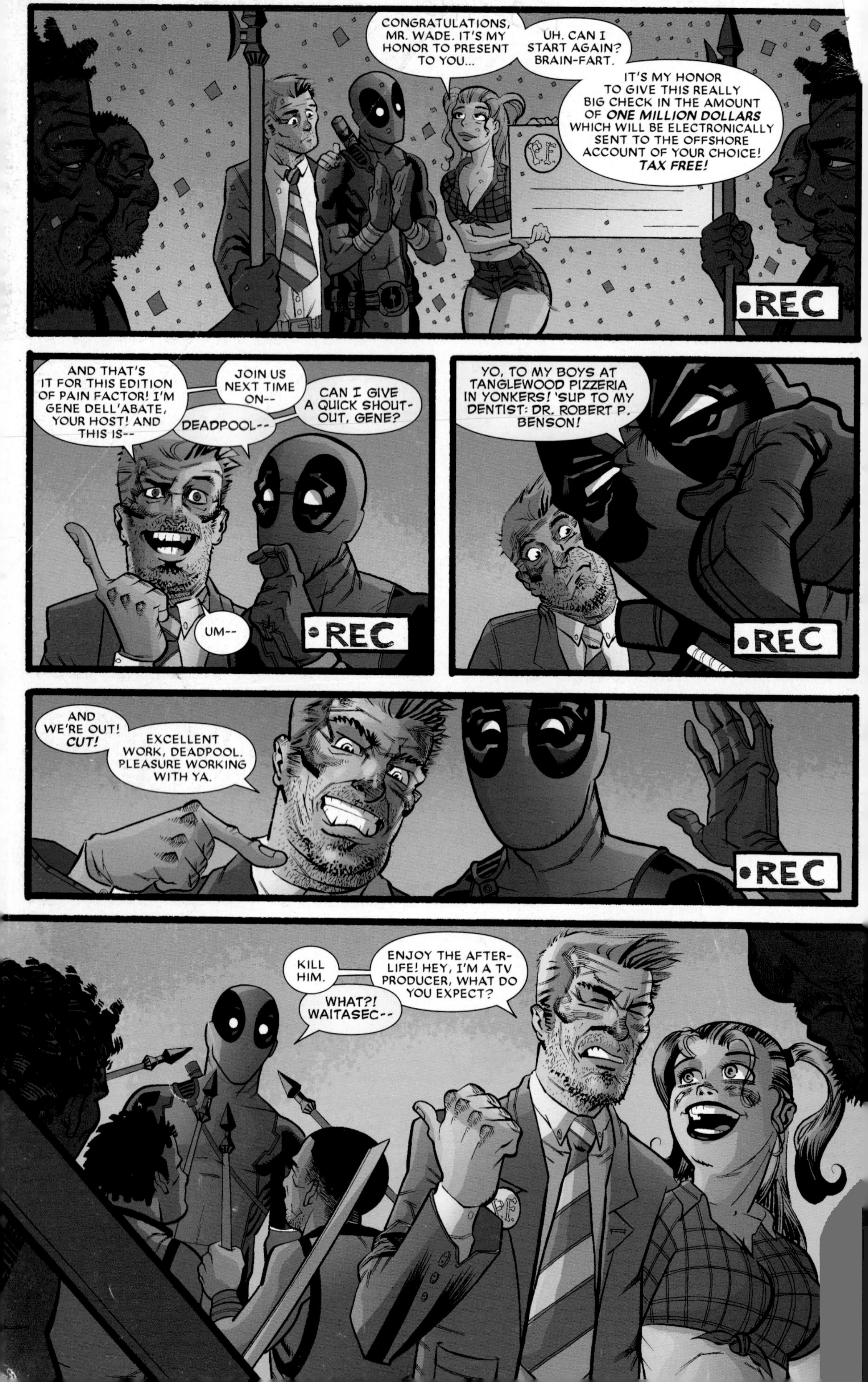

CONGRATULATIONS, MR. WADE. IT'S MY HONOR TO PRESENT TO YOU...
UH. CAN I START AGAIN? BRAIN-FART.
IT'S MY HONOR TO GIVE THIS REALLY BIG CHECK IN THE AMOUNT OF ONE MILLION DOLLARS WHICH WILL BE ELECTRONICALLY SENT TO THE OFFSHORE ACCOUNT OF YOUR CHOICE! TAX FREE!
P.F.
•REC
AND THAT'S IT FOR THIS EDITION OF PAIN FACTOR! I'M GENE DELL'ABATE, YOUR HOST! AND THIS IS--
JOIN US NEXT TIME ON--
DEADPOOL--
CAN I GIVE A QUICK SHOUT-OUT, GENE?
UM--
•REC
YO, TO MY BOYS AT TANGLEWOOD PIZZERIA IN YONKERS! 'SUP TO MY DENTIST: DR. ROBERT P. BENSON!
•REC
AND WE'RE OUT! CUT!
EXCELLENT WORK, DEADPOOL. PLEASURE WORKING WITH YA.
•REC
KILL HIM.
ENJOY THE AFTER-LIFE! HEY, I'M A TV PRODUCER, WHAT DO YOU EXPECT?
WHAT?! WAITASEC--
P.F

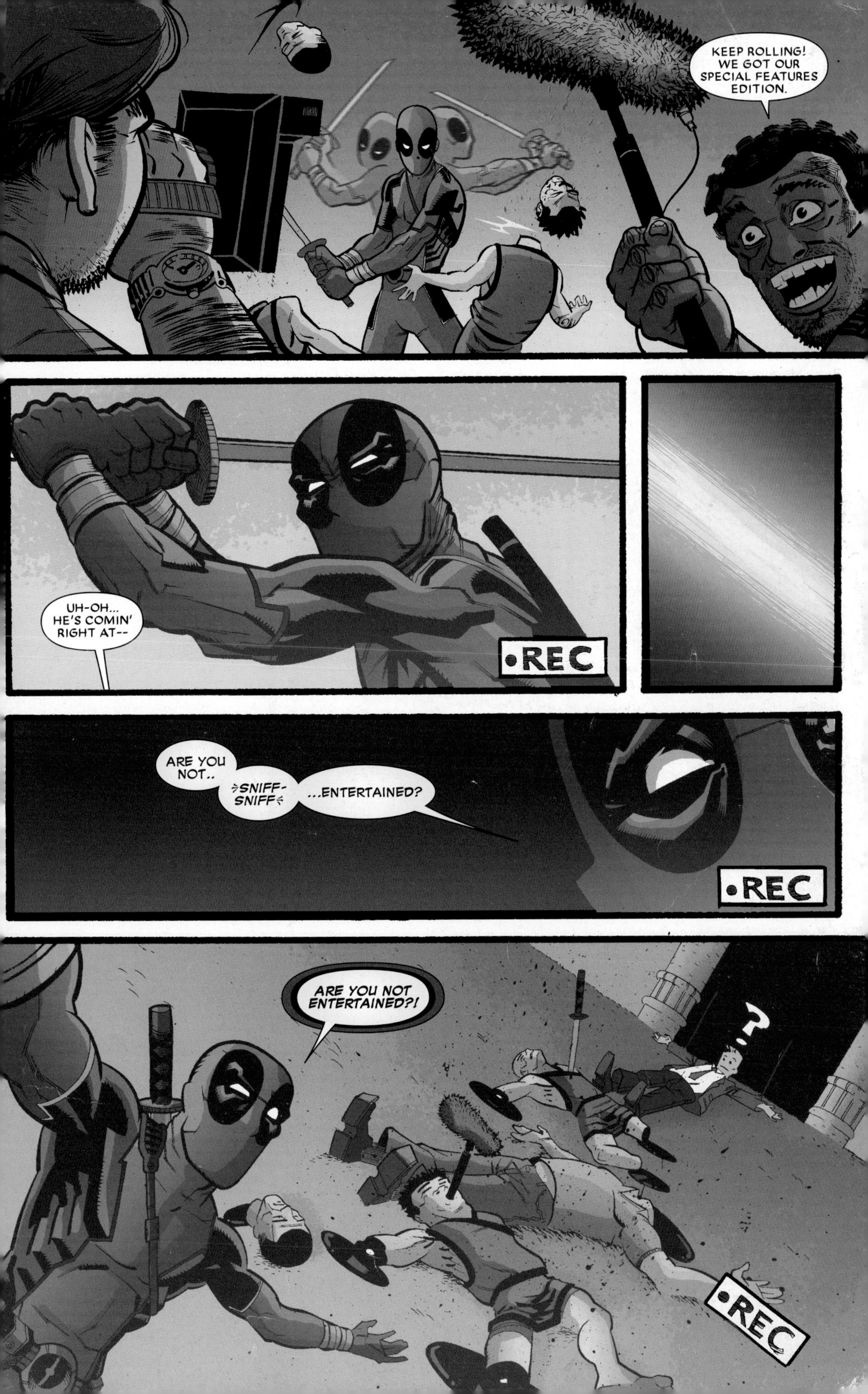
KEEP ROLLING! WE GOT OUR SPECIAL FEATURES EDITION.
UH-OH... HE'S COMIN' RIGHT AT--
•REC
ARE YOU NOT..
SNIFF-SNIFF
...ENTERTAINED?
•REC
ARE YOU NOT ENTERTAINED?!
?
•REC

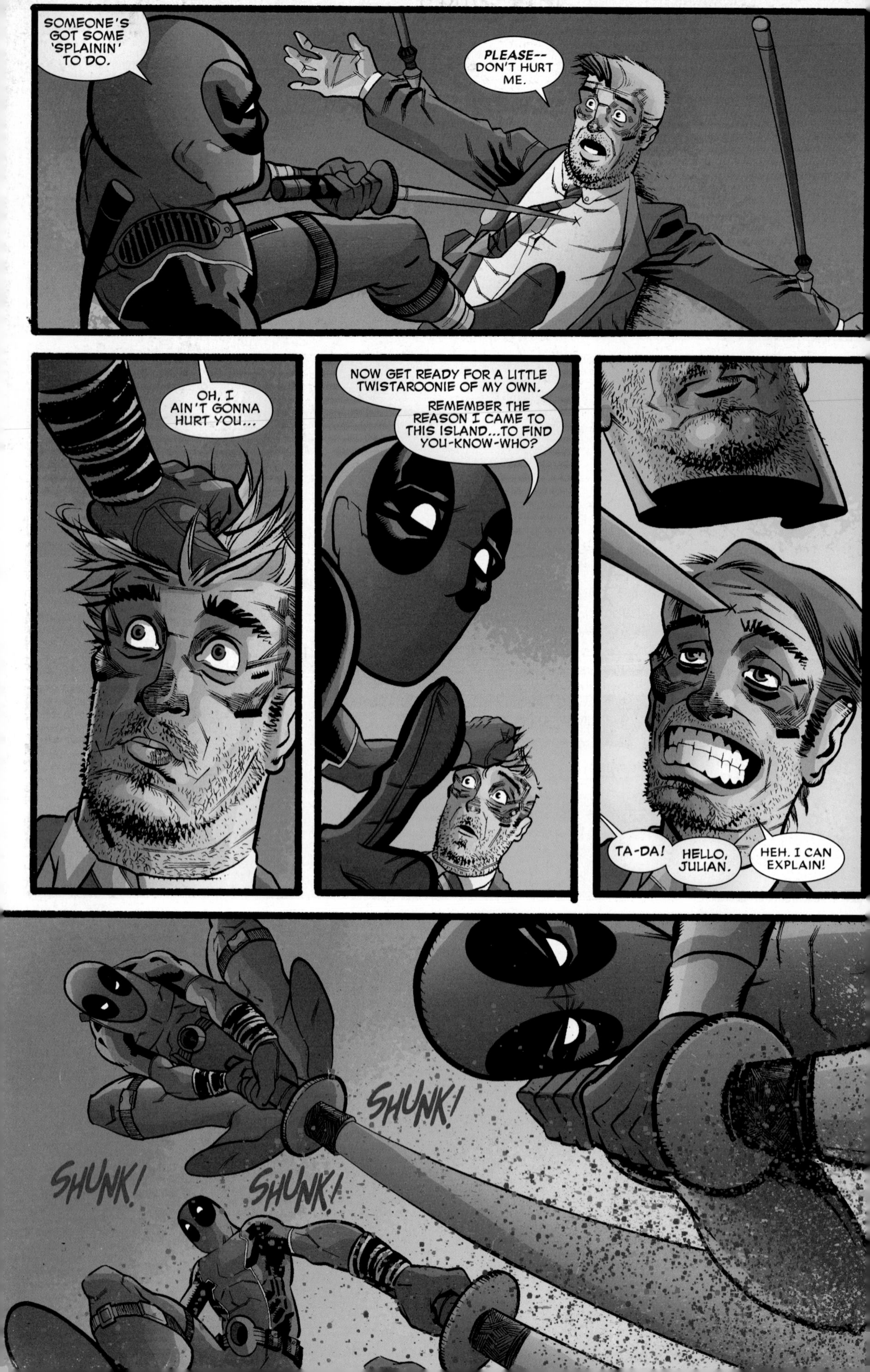
SOMEONE'S GOT SOME 'SPLAININ' TO DO.
PLEASE-- DON'T HURT ME.
OH, I AIN'T GONNA HURT YOU...
NOW GET READY FOR A LITTLE TWISTAROONIE OF MY OWN.
REMEMBER THE REASON I CAME TO THIS ISLAND...TO FIND YOU-KNOW-WHO?
TA-DA!
HELLO, JULIAN.
HEH. I CAN EXPLAIN!
SHUNK!
SHUNK!
SHUNK!

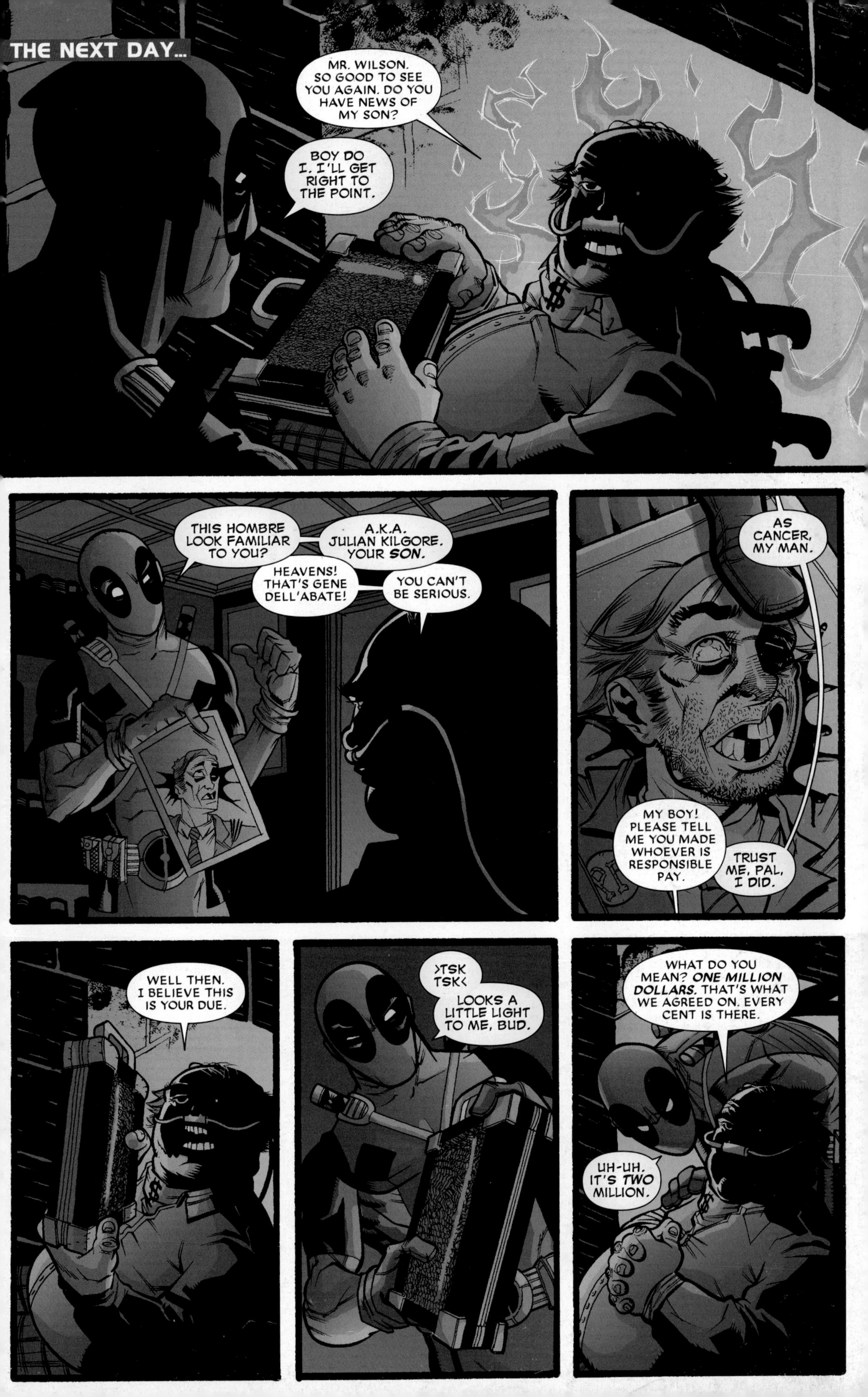
THE NEXT DAY...
MR. WILSON. SO GOOD TO SEE YOU AGAIN. DO YOU HAVE NEWS OF MY SON?
BOY DO I. I'LL GET RIGHT TO THE POINT.
THIS HOMBRE LOOK FAMILIAR TO YOU?
A.K.A. JULIAN KILGORE. YOUR SON.
HEAVENS! THAT'S GENE DELL'ABATE!
YOU CAN'T BE SERIOUS.
AS CANCER, MY MAN.
MY BOY! PLEASE TELL ME YOU MADE WHOEVER IS RESPONSIBLE PAY.
TRUST ME, PAL, I DID.
WELL THEN. I BELIEVE THIS IS YOUR DUE.
>TSK TSK<
LOOKS A LITTLE LIGHT TO ME, BUD.
WHAT DO YOU MEAN? ONE MILLION DOLLARS. THAT'S WHAT WE AGREED ON. EVERY CENT IS THERE.
UH-UH. IT'S TWO MILLION.

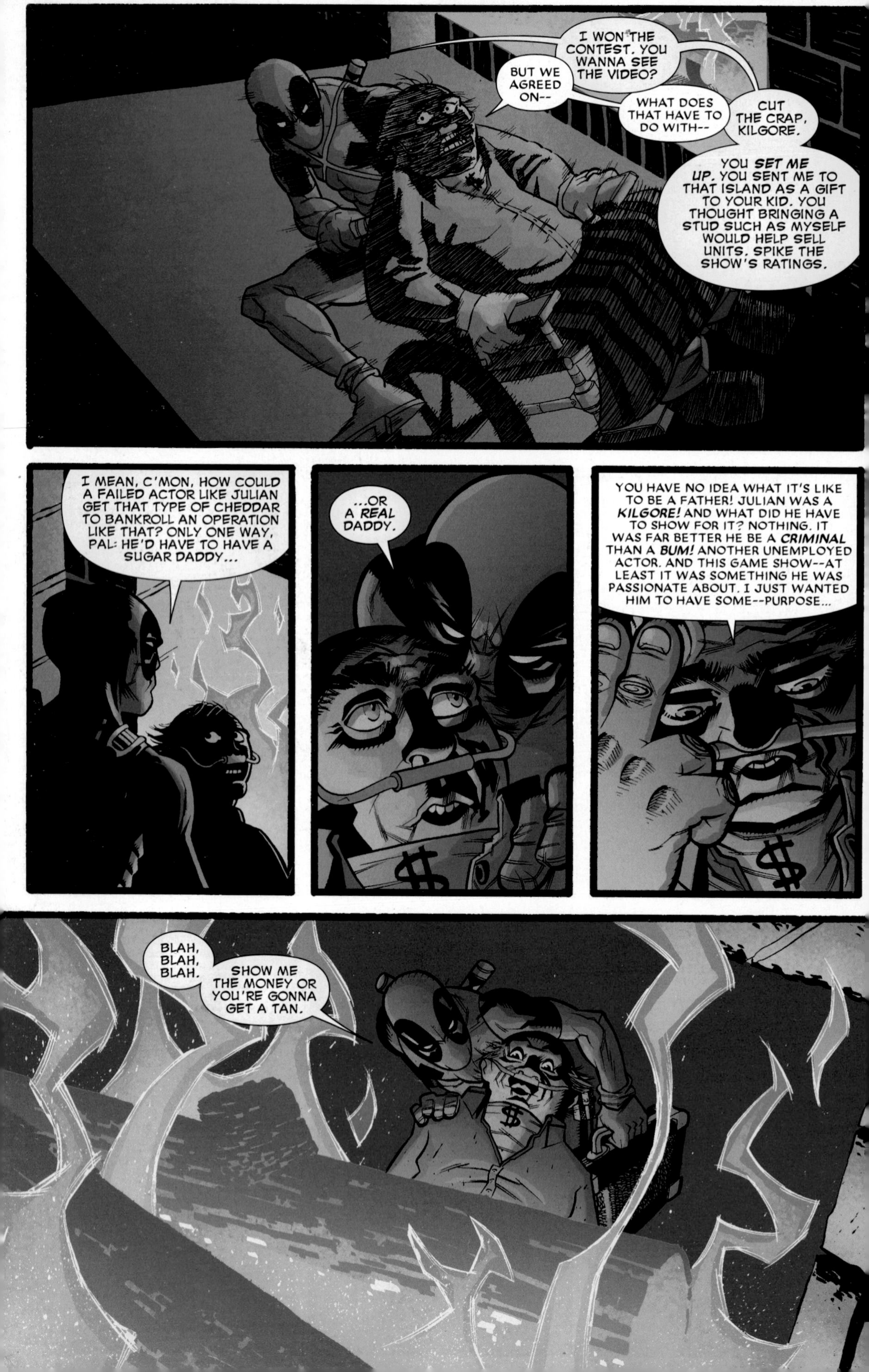
I WON THE CONTEST. YOU WANNA SEE THE VIDEO?
BUT WE AGREED ON--
WHAT DOES THAT HAVE TO DO WITH--
CUT THE CRAP, KILGORE.
YOU SET ME UP. YOU SENT ME TO THAT ISLAND AS A GIFT TO YOUR KID. YOU THOUGHT BRINGING A STUD SUCH AS MYSELF WOULD HELP SELL UNITS. SPIKE THE SHOW'S RATINGS.
I MEAN, C'MON, HOW COULD A FAILED ACTOR LIKE JULIAN GET THAT TYPE OF CHEDDAR TO BANKROLL AN OPERATION LIKE THAT? ONLY ONE WAY, PAL: HE'D HAVE TO HAVE A SUGAR DADDY...
...OR A REAL DADDY.
YOU HAVE NO IDEA WHAT IT'S LIKE TO BE A FATHER! JULIAN WAS A KILGORE! AND WHAT DID HE HAVE TO SHOW FOR IT? NOTHING. IT WAS FAR BETTER HE BE A CRIMINAL THAN A BUM! ANOTHER UNEMPLOYED ACTOR. AND THIS GAME SHOW--AT LEAST IT WAS SOMETHING HE WAS PASSIONATE ABOUT. I JUST WANTED HIM TO HAVE SOME--PURPOSE...
BLAH, BLAH, BLAH.
SHOW ME THE MONEY OR YOU'RE GONNA GET A TAN.

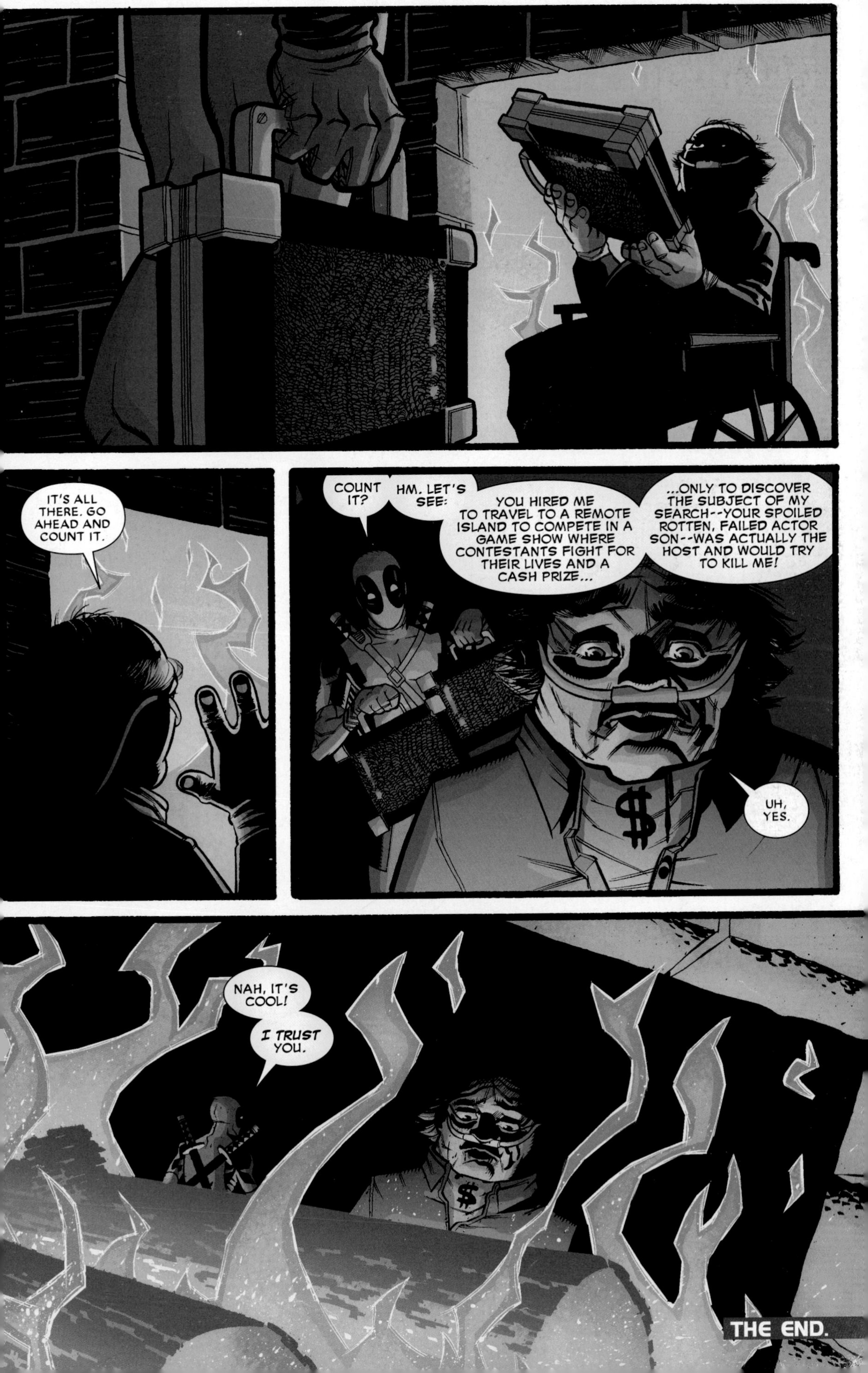
IT'S ALL THERE. GO AHEAD AND COUNT IT.
COUNT IT?
HM. LET'S SEE:
YOU HIRED ME TO TRAVEL TO A REMOTE ISLAND TO COMPETE IN A GAME SHOW WHERE CONTESTANTS FIGHT FOR THEIR LIVES AND A CASH PRIZE...
...ONLY TO DISCOVER THE SUBJECT OF MY SEARCH--YOUR SPOILED ROTTEN, FAILED ACTOR SON--WAS ACTUALLY THE HOST AND WOULD TRY TO KILL ME!
UH, YES.
NAH, IT'S COOL!
I TRUST YOU.
THE END.

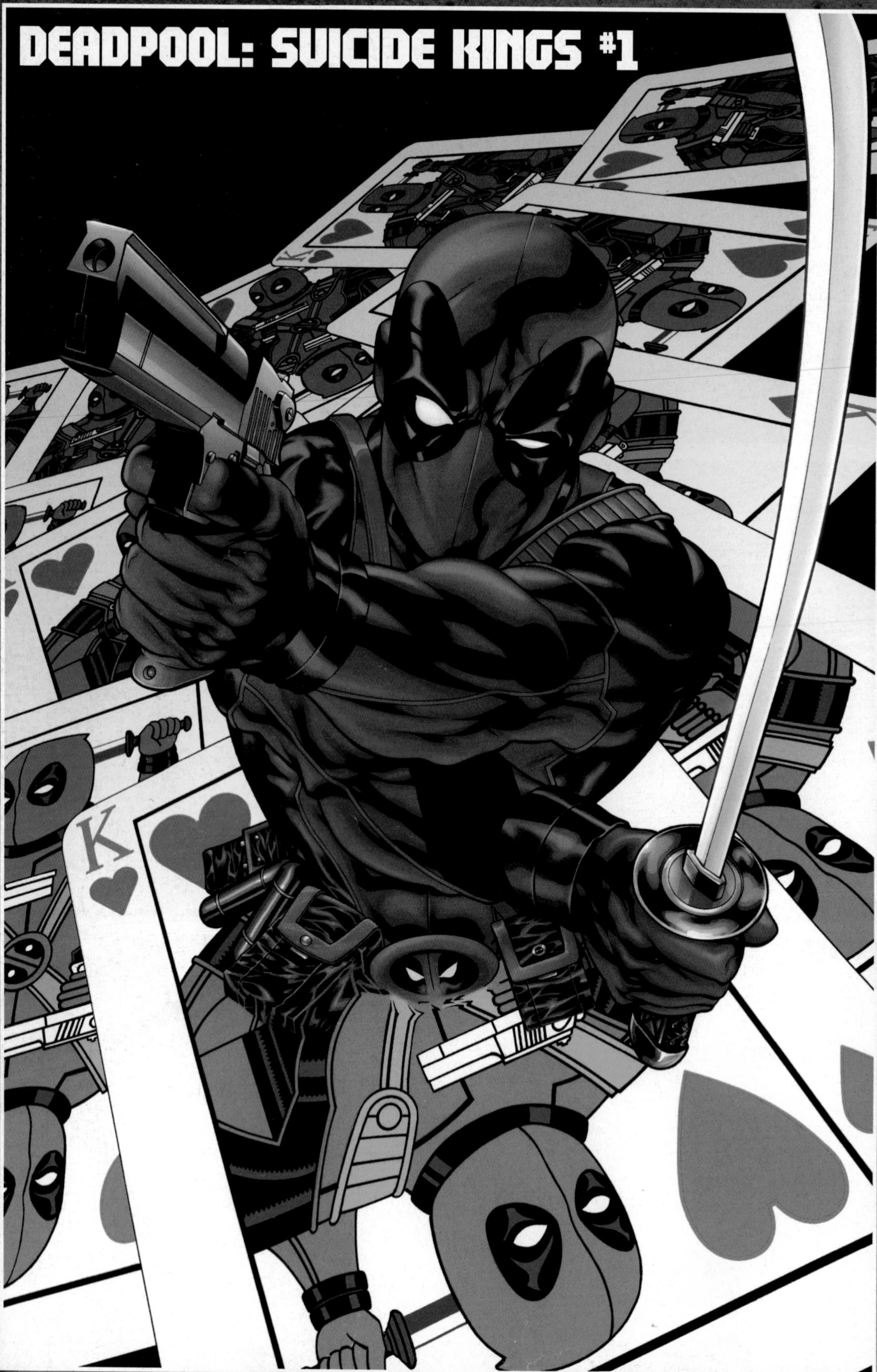
DEADPOOL: SUICIDE KINGS #1

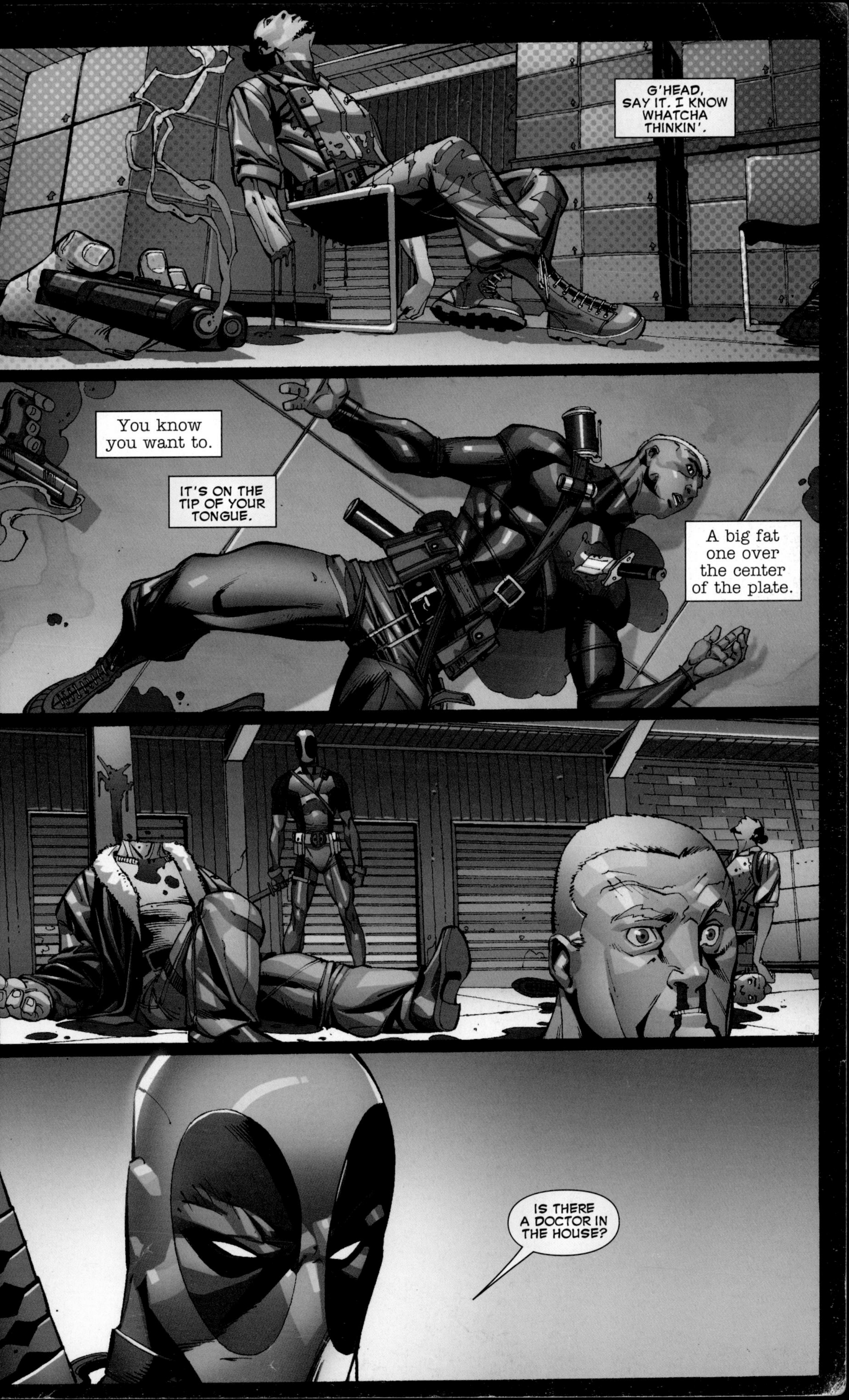
G'HEAD, SAY IT. I KNOW WHATCHA THINKIN'.
You know you want to.
IT'S ON THE TIP OF YOUR TONGUE.
A big fat one over the center of the plate.
IS THERE A DOCTOR IN THE HOUSE?

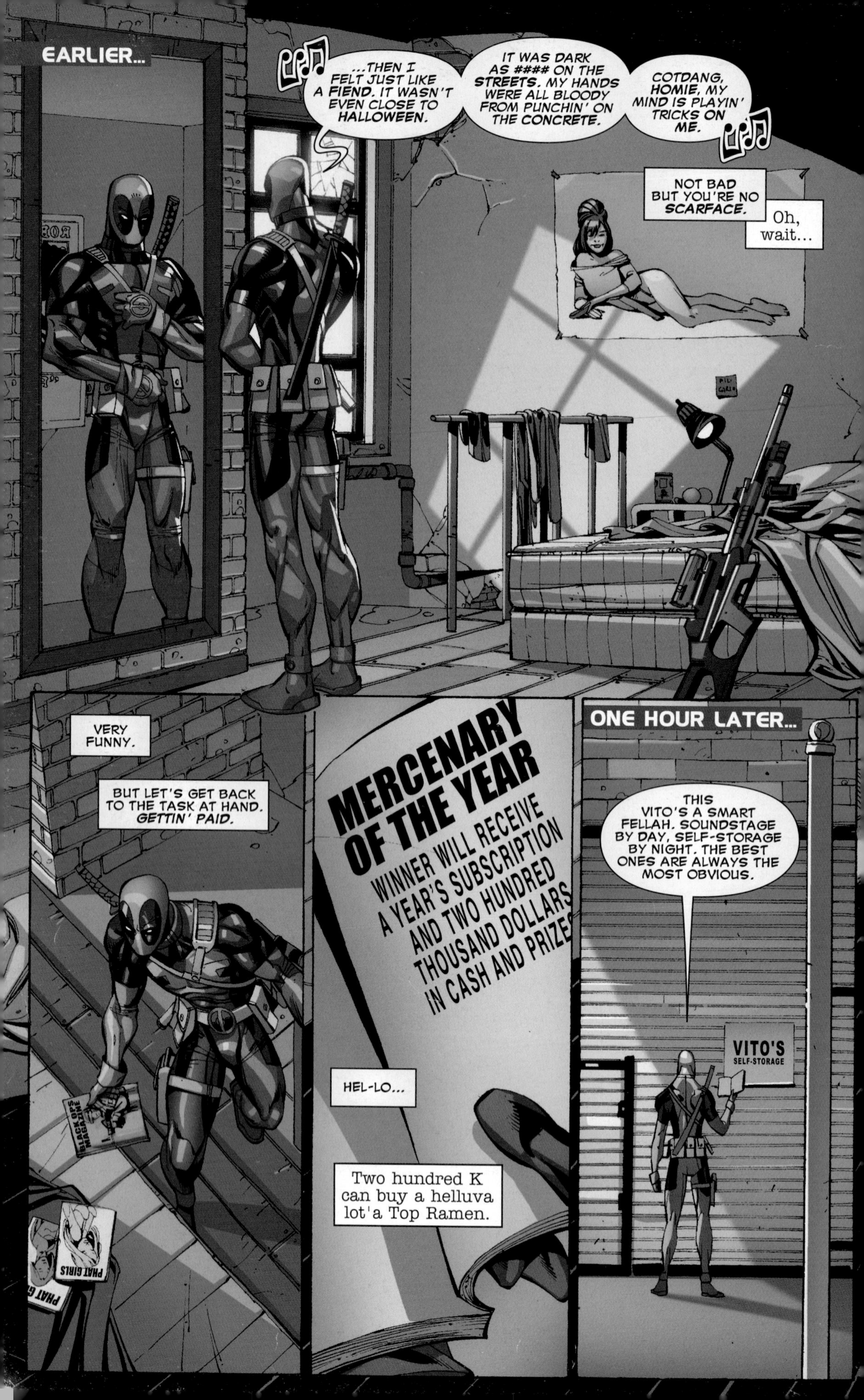
EARLIER...
...THEN I FELT JUST LIKE A FIEND. IT WASN'T EVEN CLOSE TO HALLOWEEN.
IT WAS DARK AS #### ON THE STREETS. MY HANDS WERE ALL BLOODY FROM PUNCHIN' ON THE CONCRETE.
COTDANG, HOMIE, MY MIND IS PLAYIN' TRICKS ON ME.
NOT BAD BUT YOU'RE NO SCARFACE.
Oh, wait...
VERY FUNNY.
BUT LET'S GET BACK TO THE TASK AT HAND. GETTIN' PAID.
BLACK OPS MAGAZINE
PHAT GIRLS
MERCENARY OF THE YEAR
WINNER WILL RECEIVE A YEAR'S SUBSCRIPTION AND TWO HUNDRED THOUSAND DOLLARS IN CASH AND PRIZES
HEL-LO...
Two hundred K can buy a helluva lot'a Top Ramen.
ONE HOUR LATER...
THIS VITO'S A SMART FELLAH. SOUNDSTAGE BY DAY, SELF-STORAGE BY NIGHT. THE BEST ONES ARE ALWAYS THE MOST OBVIOUS.
VITO'S SELF-STORAGE

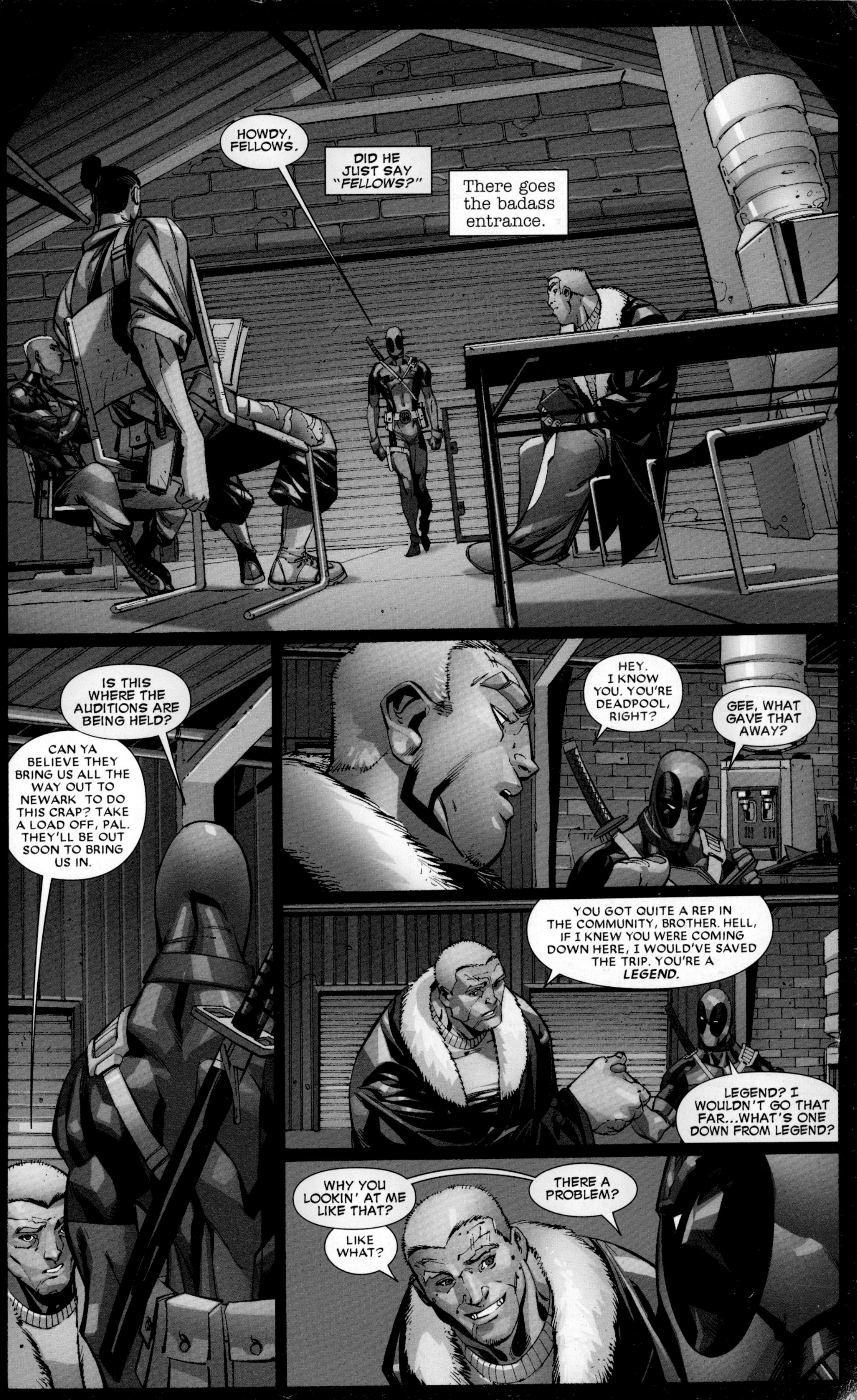
HOWDY, FELLOWS.
DID HE JUST SAY "FELLOWS?"
There goes the badass entrance.
IS THIS WHERE THE AUDITIONS ARE BEING HELD?
CAN YA BELIEVE THEY BRING US ALL THE WAY OUT TO NEWARK TO DO THIS CRAP? TAKE A LOAD OFF, PAL. THEY'LL BE OUT SOON TO BRING US IN.
HEY. I KNOW YOU. YOU'RE DEADPOOL, RIGHT?
GEE, WHAT GAVE THAT AWAY?
YOU GOT QUITE A REP IN THE COMMUNITY, BROTHER. HELL, IF I KNEW YOU WERE COMING DOWN HERE, I WOULD'VE SAVED THE TRIP. YOU'RE A LEGEND.
LEGEND? I WOULDN'T GO THAT FAR...WHAT'S ONE DOWN FROM LEGEND?
WHY YOU LOOKIN' AT ME LIKE THAT?
THERE A PROBLEM?
LIKE WHAT?

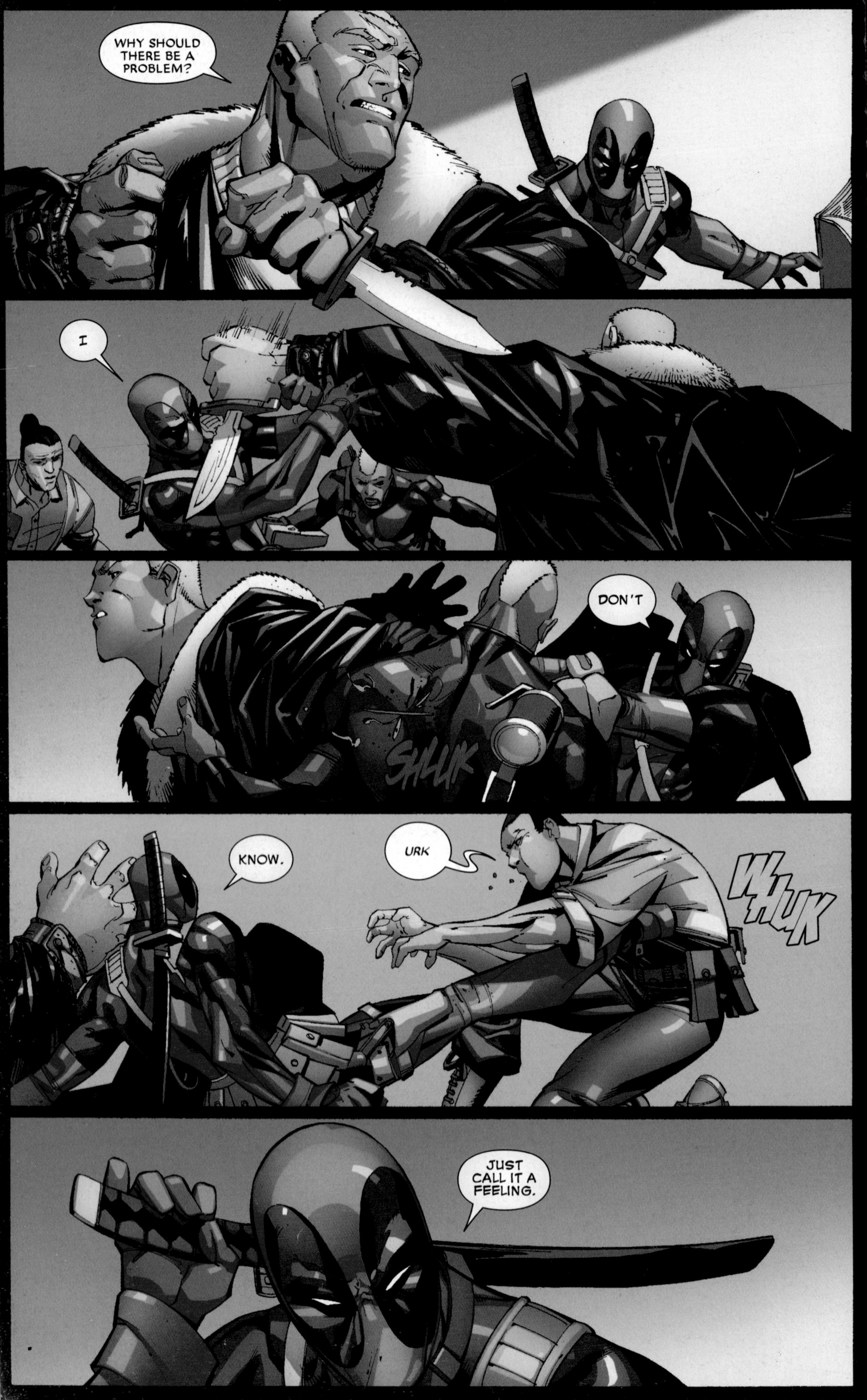
WHY SHOULD THERE BE A PROBLEM?
I
DON'T
SHLUK
KNOW.
URK
WHUK
JUST CALL IT A FEELING.

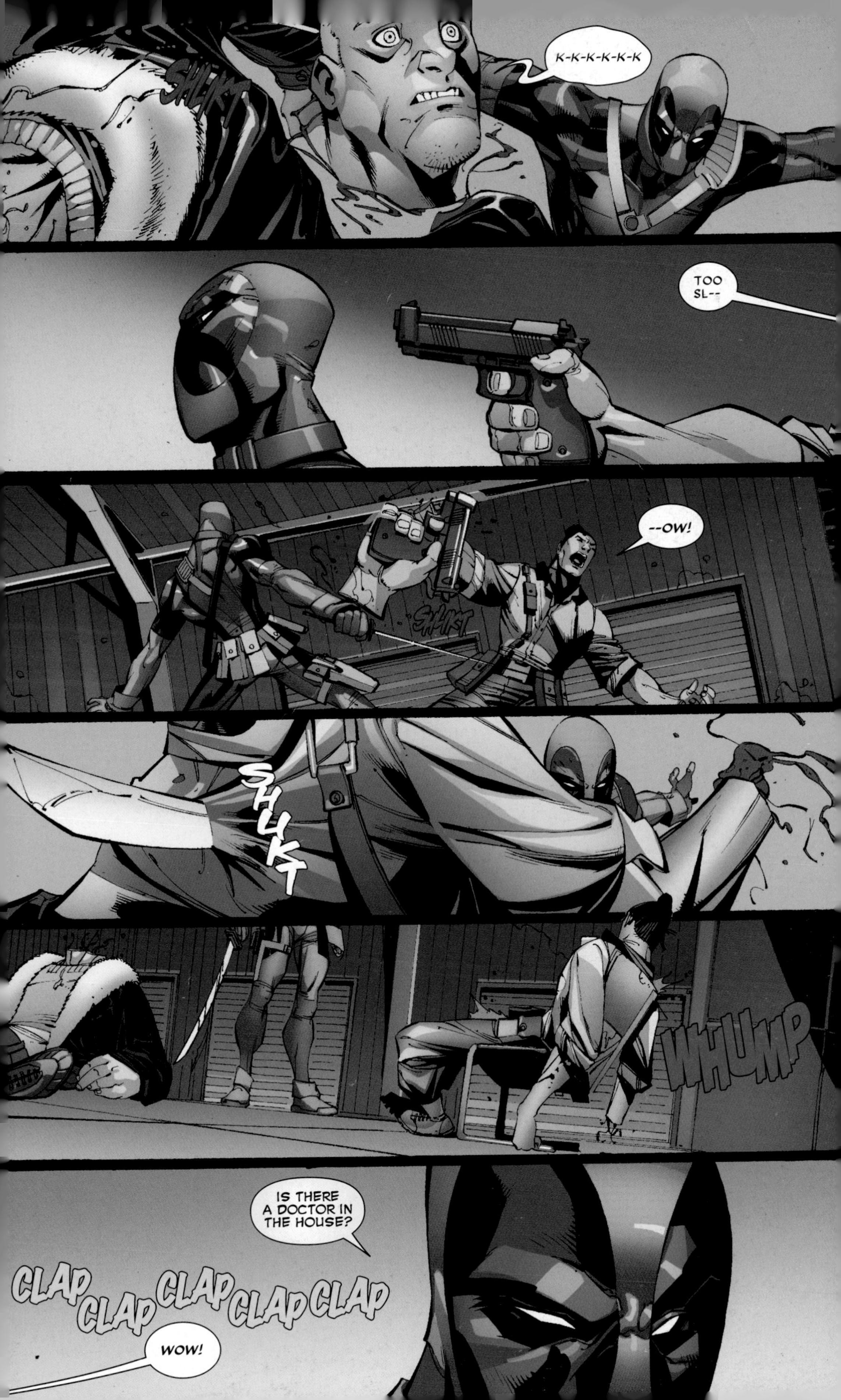
SHLIKT
K-K-K-K-K-K
TOO SL--
--OW!
SHLIKT
SHUKT
WHUMP
IS THERE A DOCTOR IN THE HOUSE?
CLAP CLAP CLAP CLAP CLAP
WOW!

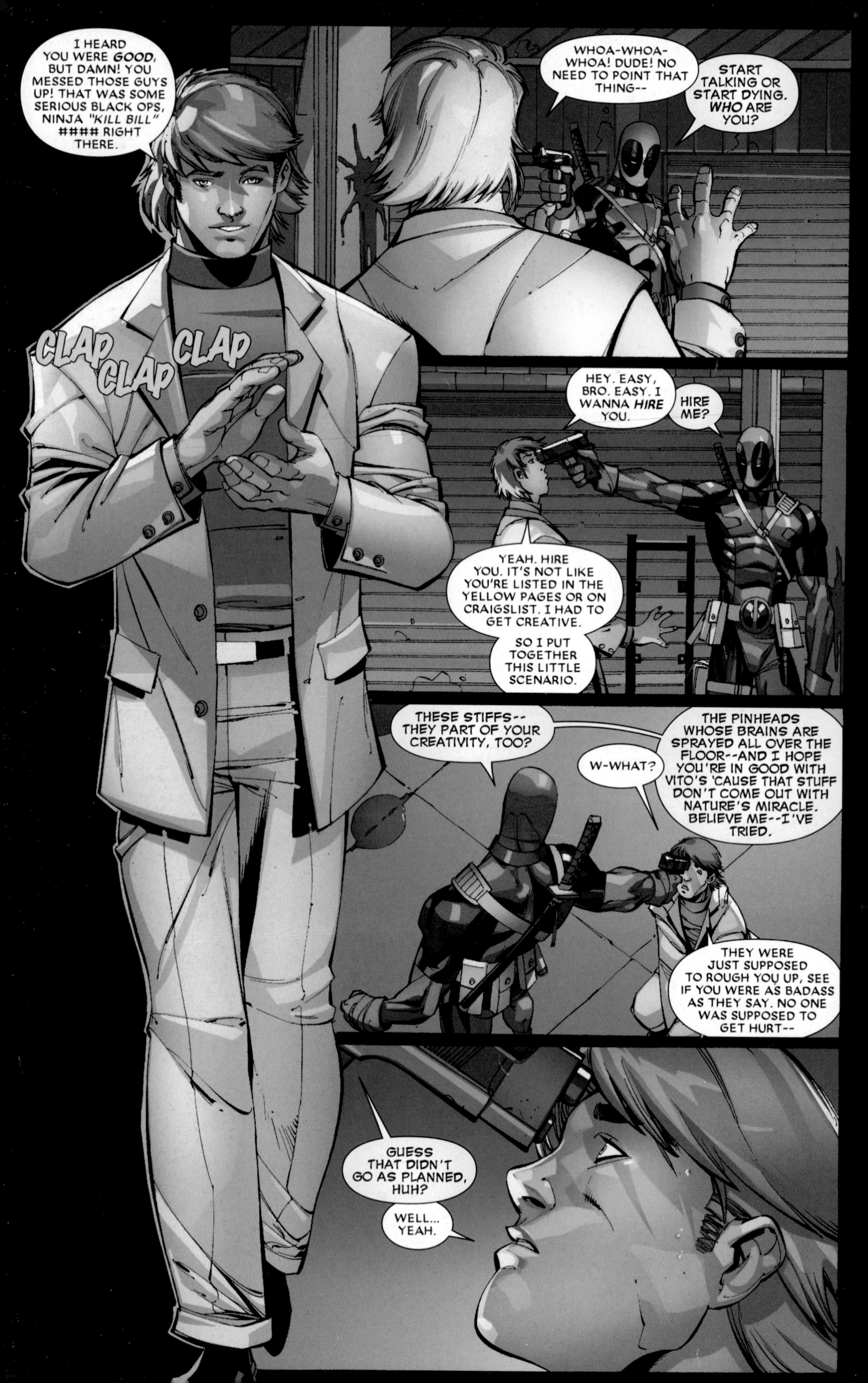
I HEARD YOU WERE GOOD, BUT DAMN! YOU MESSED THOSE GUYS UP! THAT WAS SOME SERIOUS BLACK OPS, NINJA "KILL BILL" #### RIGHT THERE.
CLAP CLAP CLAP
WHOA-WHOA-WHOA! DUDE! NO NEED TO POINT THAT THING--
START TALKING OR START DYING. WHO ARE YOU?
HEY. EASY, BRO. EASY. I WANNA HIRE YOU.
HIRE ME?
YEAH. HIRE YOU. IT'S NOT LIKE YOU'RE LISTED IN THE YELLOW PAGES OR ON CRAIGSLIST. I HAD TO GET CREATIVE.
SO I PUT TOGETHER THIS LITTLE SCENARIO.
THESE STIFFS-- THEY PART OF YOUR CREATIVITY, TOO?
W-WHAT?
THE PINHEADS WHOSE BRAINS ARE SPRAYED ALL OVER THE FLOOR--AND I HOPE YOU'RE IN GOOD WITH VITO'S 'CAUSE THAT STUFF DON'T COME OUT WITH NATURE'S MIRACLE. BELIEVE ME--I'VE TRIED.
THEY WERE JUST SUPPOSED TO ROUGH YOU UP, SEE IF YOU WERE AS BADASS AS THEY SAY. NO ONE WAS SUPPOSED TO GET HURT--
GUESS THAT DIDN'T GO AS PLANNED, HUH?
WELL... YEAH.

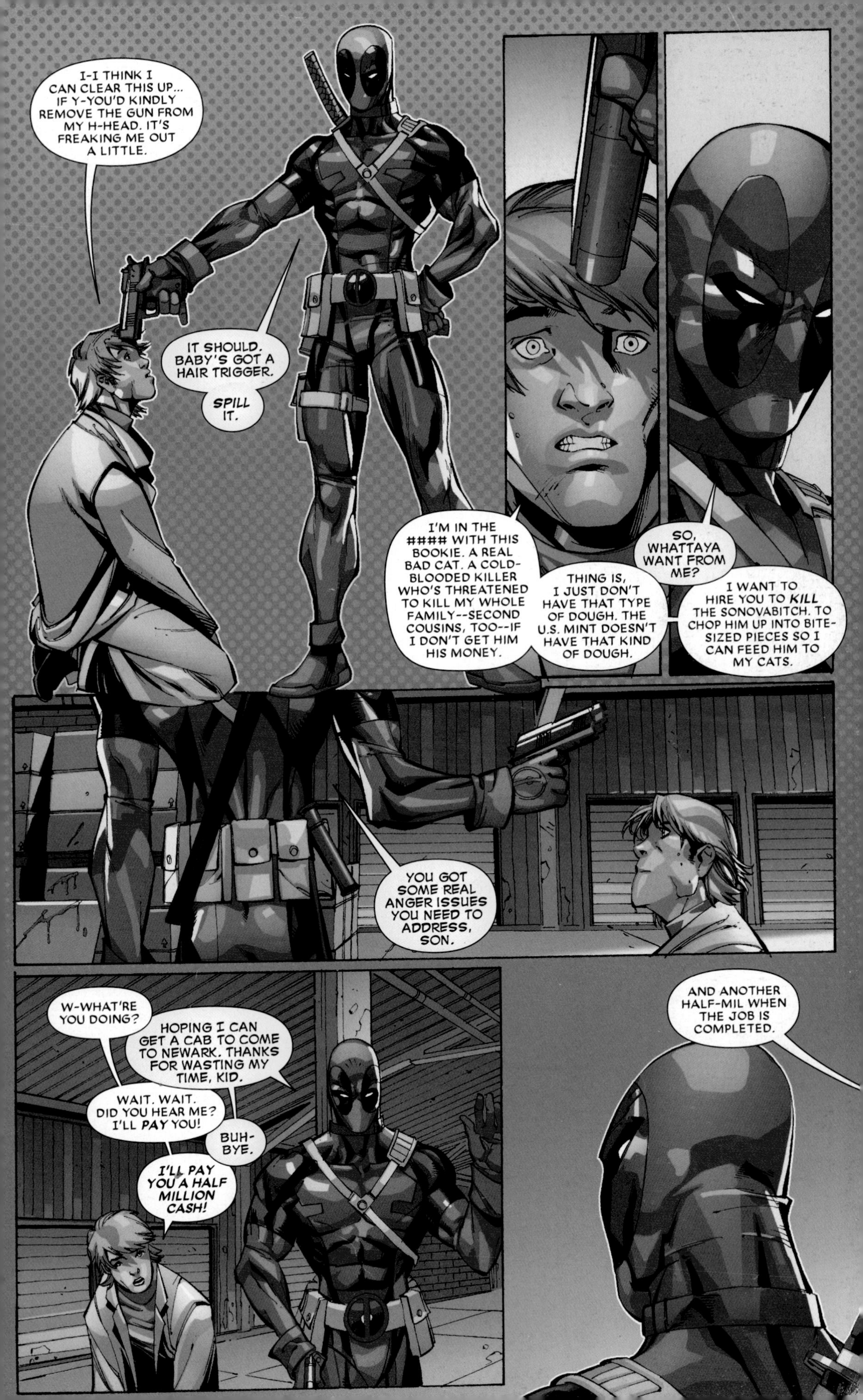
I-I THINK I CAN CLEAR THIS UP... IF Y-YOU'D KINDLY REMOVE THE GUN FROM MY H-HEAD. IT'S FREAKING ME OUT A LITTLE.
IT SHOULD. BABY'S GOT A HAIR TRIGGER.
SPILL IT.
I'M IN THE #### WITH THIS BOOKIE. A REAL BAD CAT. A COLD-BLOODED KILLER WHO'S THREATENED TO KILL MY WHOLE FAMILY--SECOND COUSINS, TOO--IF I DON'T GET HIM HIS MONEY.
THING IS, I JUST DON'T HAVE THAT TYPE OF DOUGH. THE U.S. MINT DOESN'T HAVE THAT KIND OF DOUGH.
SO, WHATTAYA WANT FROM ME?
I WANT TO HIRE YOU TO KILL THE SONOVABITCH. TO CHOP HIM UP INTO BITE-SIZED PIECES SO I CAN FEED HIM TO MY CATS.
YOU GOT SOME REAL ANGER ISSUES YOU NEED TO ADDRESS, SON.
W-WHAT'RE YOU DOING?
HOPING I CAN GET A CAB TO COME TO NEWARK. THANKS FOR WASTING MY TIME, KID.
WAIT. WAIT. DID YOU HEAR ME? I'LL PAY YOU!
BUH-BYE.
I'LL PAY YOU A HALF MILLION CASH!
AND ANOTHER HALF-MIL WHEN THE JOB IS COMPLETED.

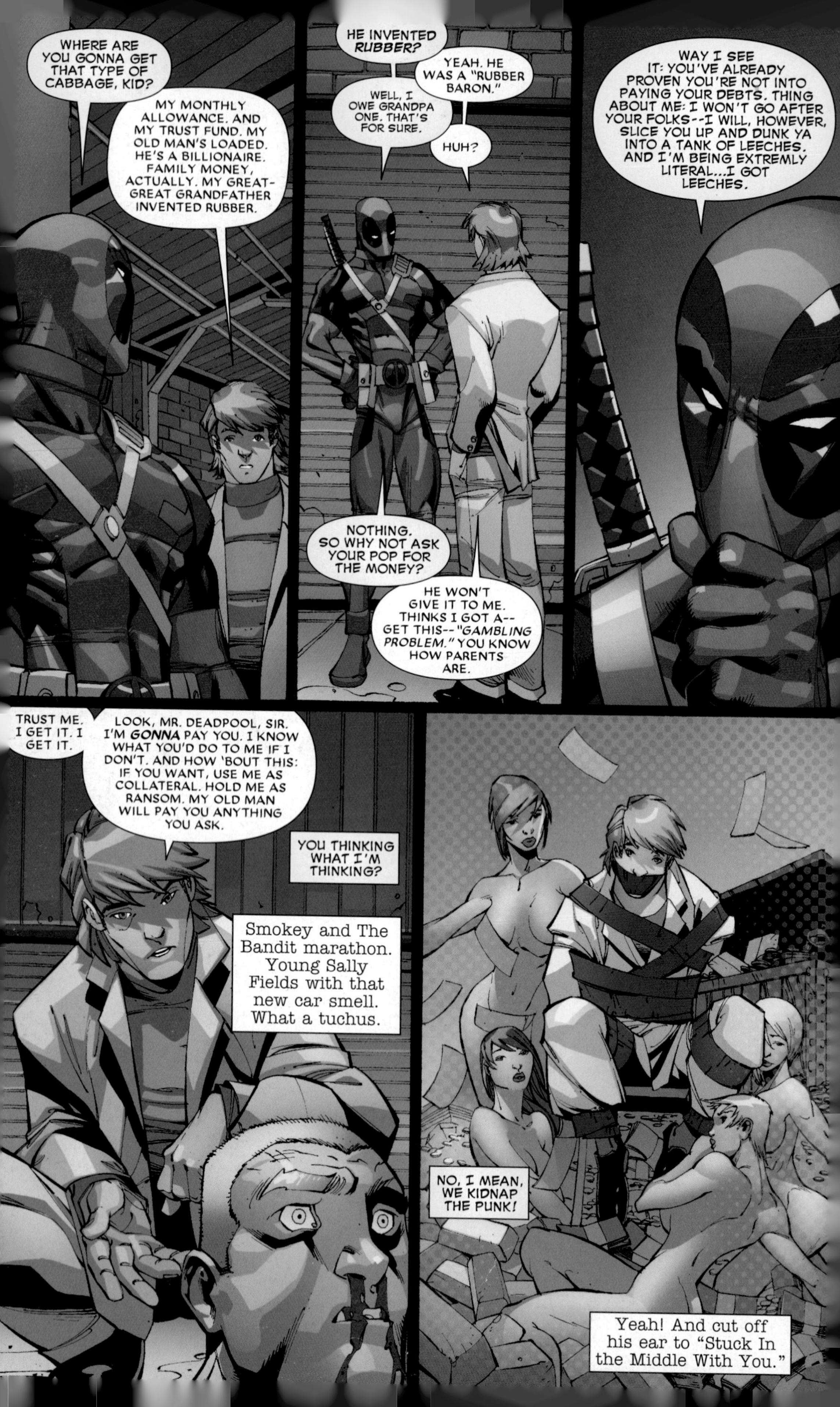

WHERE ARE YOU GONNA GET THAT TYPE OF CABBAGE, KID?
MY MONTHLY ALLOWANCE. AND MY TRUST FUND. MY OLD MAN'S LOADED. HE'S A BILLIONAIRE. FAMILY MONEY, ACTUALLY. MY GREAT-GREAT GRANDFATHER INVENTED RUBBER.
HE INVENTED RUBBER?
YEAH. HE WAS A "RUBBER BARON."
WELL, I OWE GRANDPA ONE. THAT'S FOR SURE.
HUH?
NOTHING. SO WHY NOT ASK YOUR POP FOR THE MONEY?
HE WON'T GIVE IT TO ME. THINKS I GOT A-- GET THIS-- "GAMBLING PROBLEM." YOU KNOW HOW PARENTS ARE.
WAY I SEE IT: YOU'VE ALREADY PROVEN YOU'RE NOT INTO PAYING YOUR DEBTS. THING ABOUT ME: I WON'T GO AFTER YOUR FOLKS--I WILL, HOWEVER, SLICE YOU UP AND DUNK YA INTO A TANK OF LEECHES. AND I'M BEING EXTREMLY LITERAL...I GOT LEECHES.
TRUST ME. I GET IT. I GET IT.
LOOK, MR. DEADPOOL, SIR. I'M GONNA PAY YOU. I KNOW WHAT YOU'D DO TO ME IF I DON'T. AND HOW 'BOUT THIS: IF YOU WANT, USE ME AS COLLATERAL. HOLD ME AS RANSOM. MY OLD MAN WILL PAY YOU ANYTHING YOU ASK.
YOU THINKING WHAT I'M THINKING?
Smokey and The Bandit marathon. Young Sally Fields with that new car smell. What a tuchus.
NO, I MEAN, WE KIDNAP THE PUNK!
Yeah! And cut off his ear to "Stuck In the Middle With You."

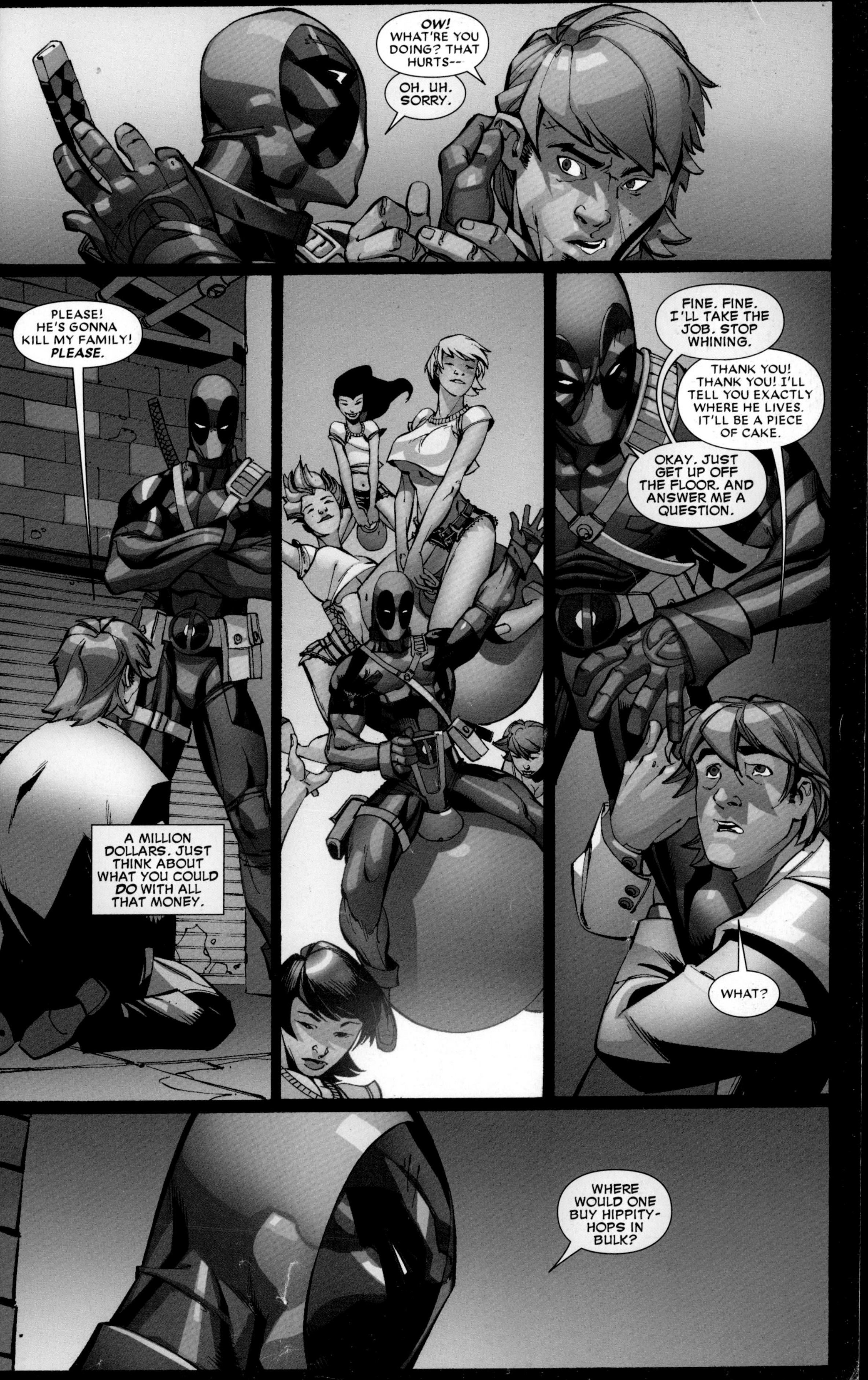
OW! WHAT'RE YOU DOING? THAT HURTS--
OH. UH. SORRY.
PLEASE! HE'S GONNA KILL MY FAMILY! PLEASE.
A MILLION DOLLARS. JUST THINK ABOUT WHAT YOU COULD DO WITH ALL THAT MONEY.
FINE. FINE. I'LL TAKE THE JOB. STOP WHINING.
THANK YOU! THANK YOU! I'LL TELL YOU EXACTLY WHERE HE LIVES. IT'LL BE A PIECE OF CAKE.
OKAY. JUST GET UP OFF THE FLOOR. AND ANSWER ME A QUESTION.
WHAT?
WHERE WOULD ONE BUY HIPPITY-HOPS IN BULK?

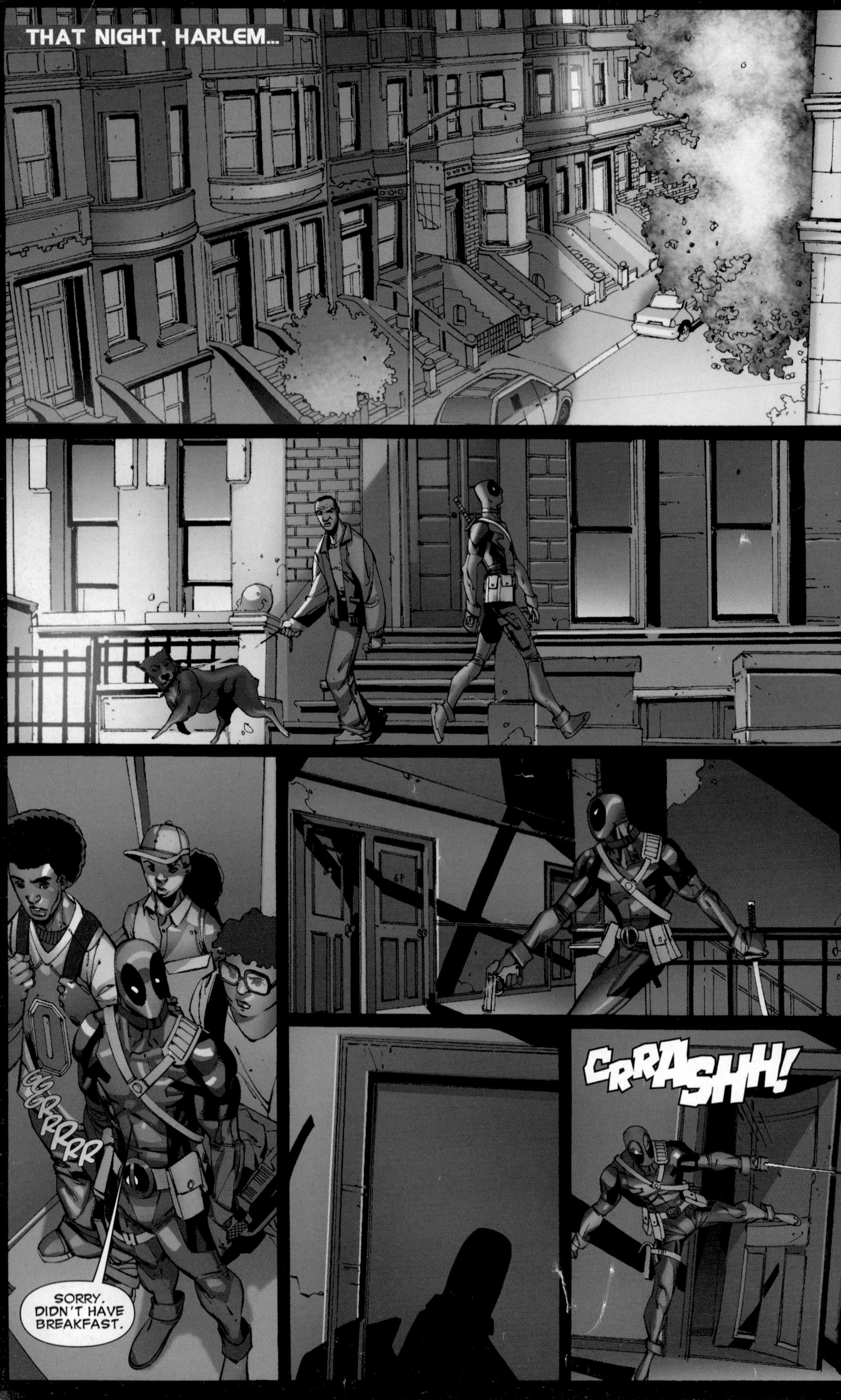
THAT NIGHT, HARLEM...
GGGRRRRR
SORRY. DIDN'T HAVE BREAKFAST.
CRRASHH!

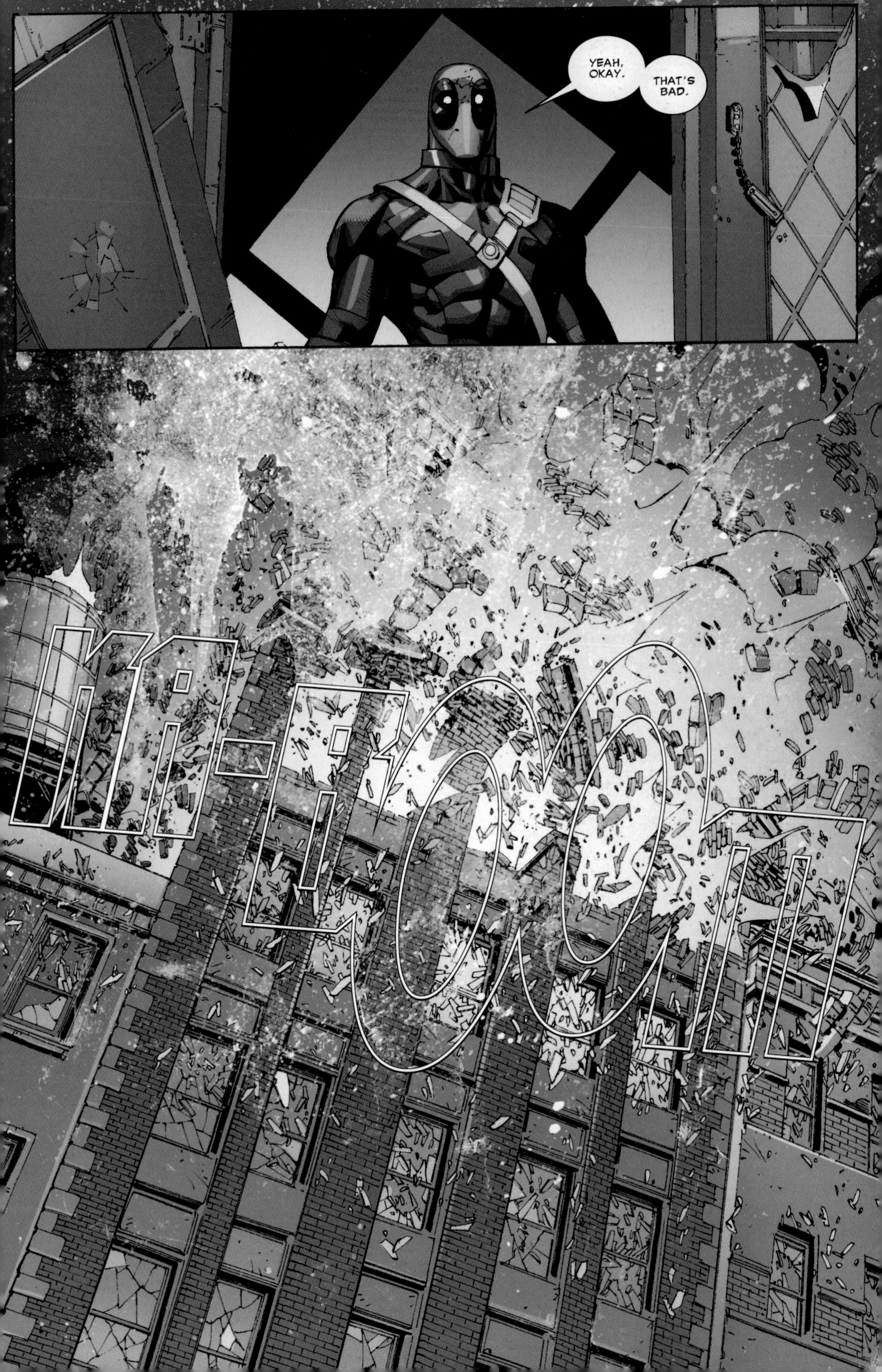
YEAH, OKAY.
THAT'S BAD.
KA-BOOM

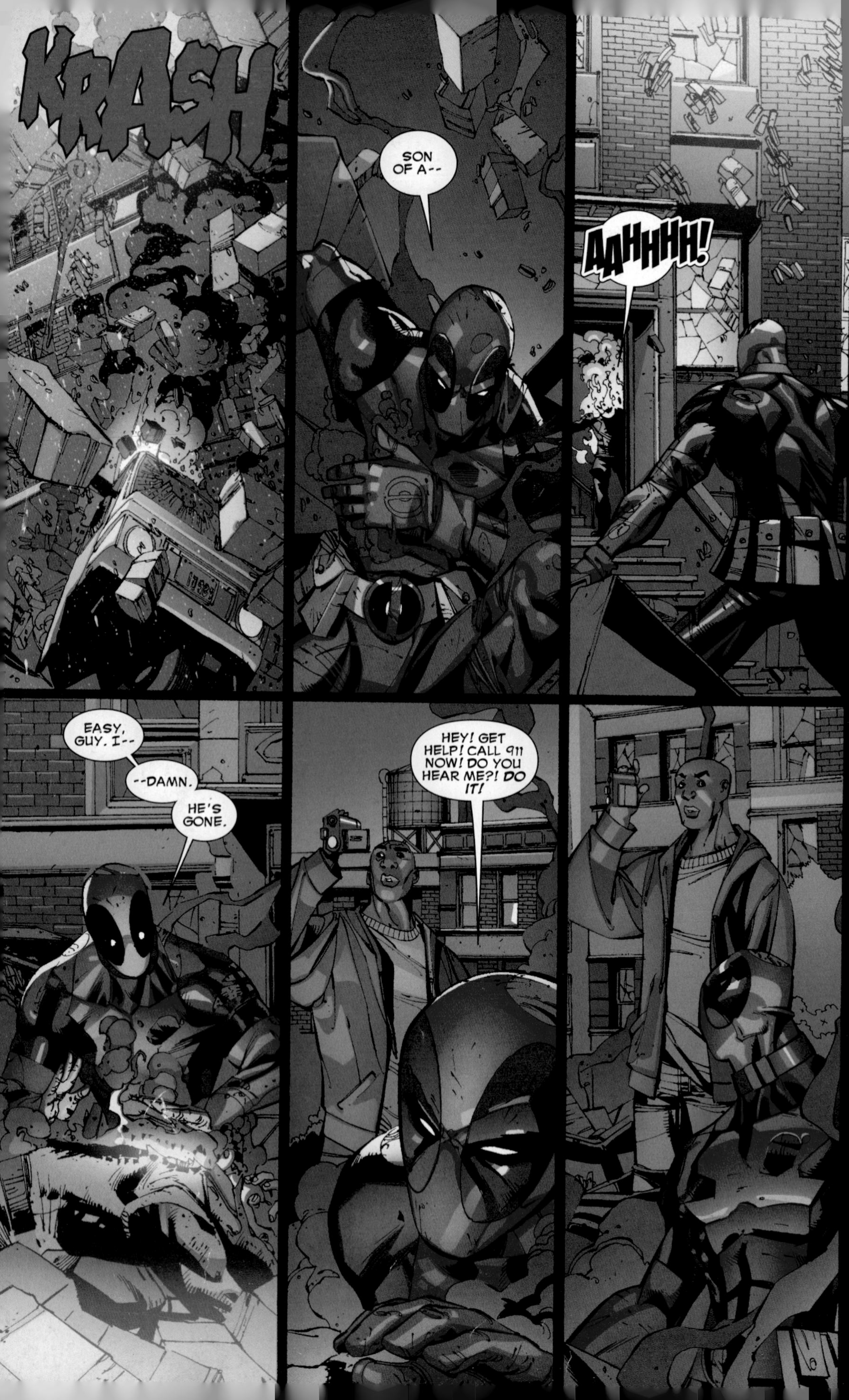
KRASH
SON OF A--
AAHHHH!
EASY, GUY. I--
--DAMN.
HE'S GONE.
HEY! GET HELP! CALL 911 NOW! DO YOU HEAR ME?! DO IT!

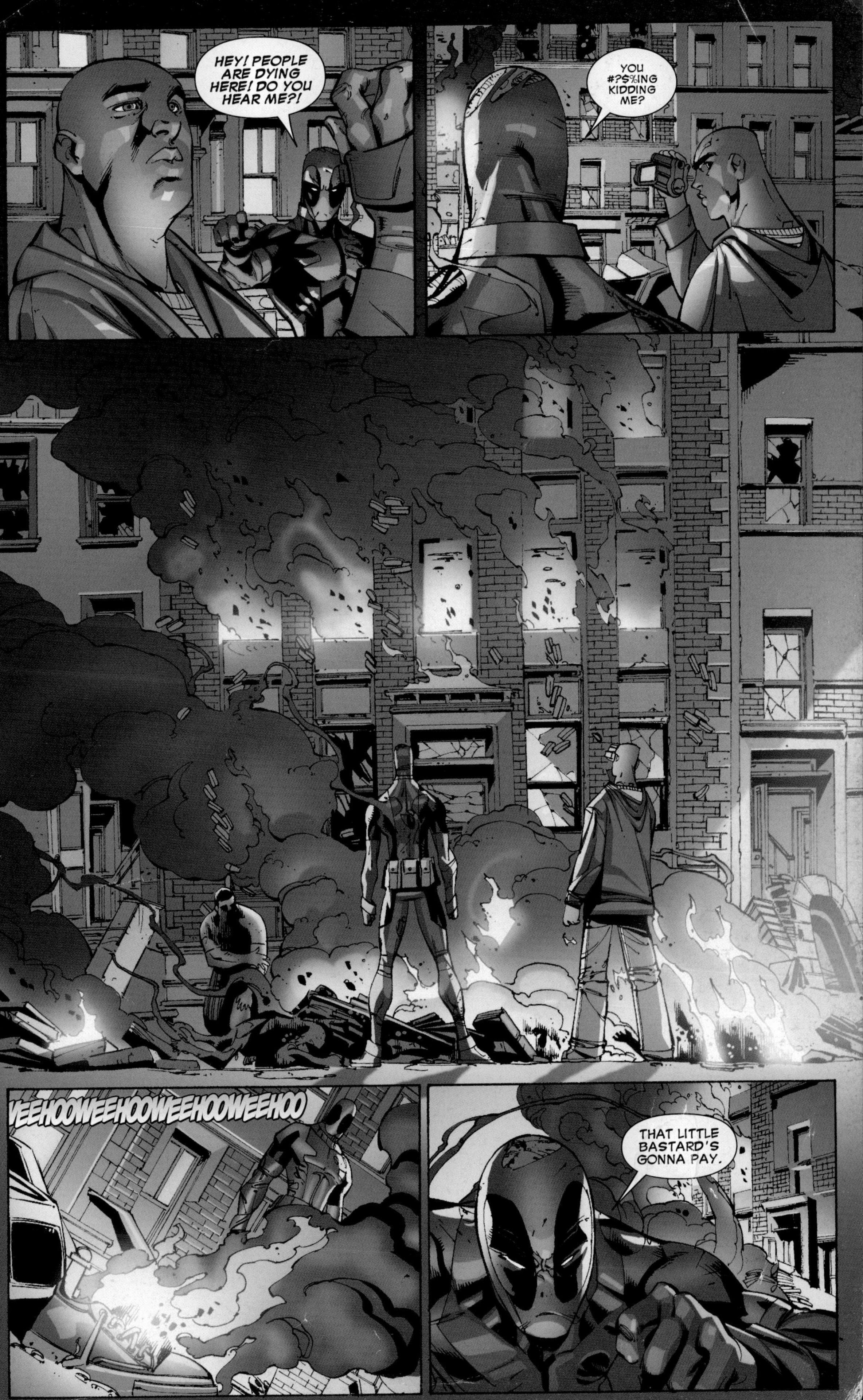
HEY! PEOPLE ARE DYING HERE! DO YOU HEAR ME?!
YOU #?$%ING KIDDING ME?
WEEHOOWEEHOOWEEHOOWEEHOO
THAT LITTLE BASTARD'S GONNA PAY.

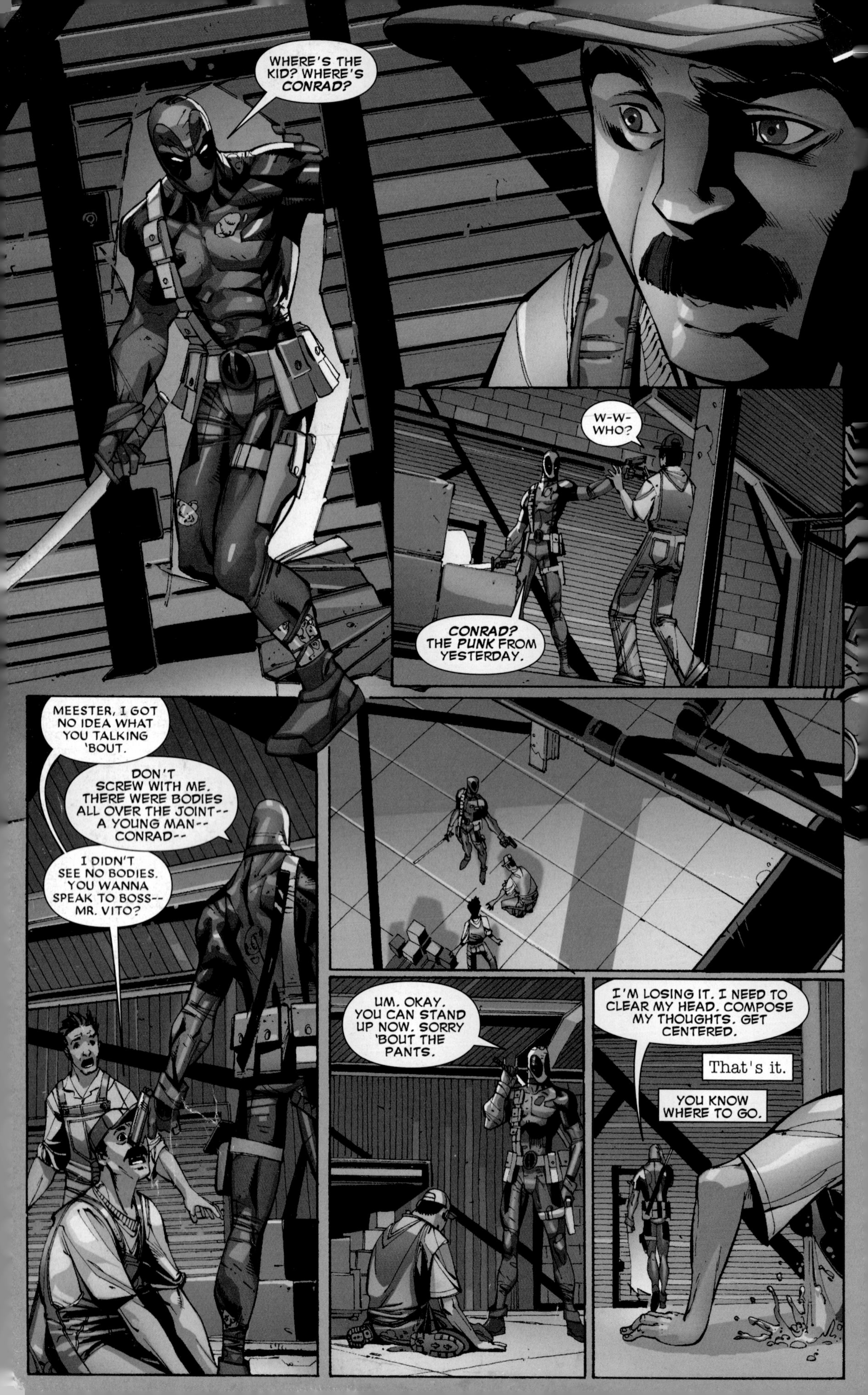

WHERE'S THE KID? WHERE'S CONRAD?
W-W-WHO?
CONRAD? THE PUNK FROM YESTERDAY.
MEESTER, I GOT NO IDEA WHAT YOU TALKING 'BOUT.
DON'T SCREW WITH ME. THERE WERE BODIES ALL OVER THE JOINT-- A YOUNG MAN-- CONRAD--
I DIDN'T SEE NO BODIES. YOU WANNA SPEAK TO BOSS-- MR. VITO?
UM. OKAY. YOU CAN STAND UP NOW. SORRY 'BOUT THE PANTS.
I'M LOSING IT. I NEED TO CLEAR MY HEAD. COMPOSE MY THOUGHTS. GET CENTERED.
That's it.
YOU KNOW WHERE TO GO.

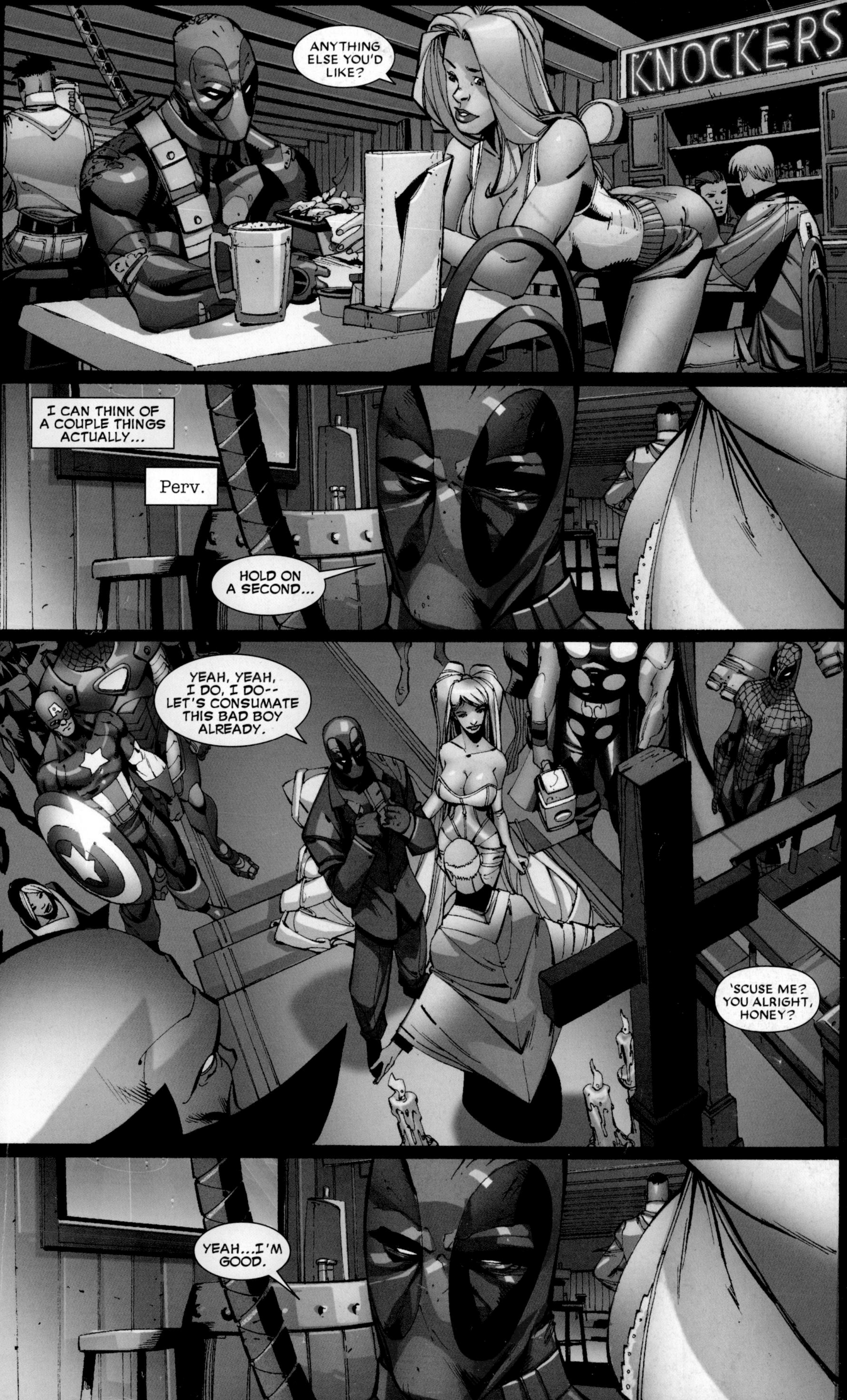

KNOCKERS
ANYTHING ELSE YOU'D LIKE?
I CAN THINK OF A COUPLE THINGS ACTUALLY...
Perv.
HOLD ON A SECOND...
YEAH, YEAH, I DO, I DO-- LET'S CONSUMATE THIS BAD BOY ALREADY.
'SCUSE ME? YOU ALRIGHT, HONEY?
YEAH...I'M GOOD.

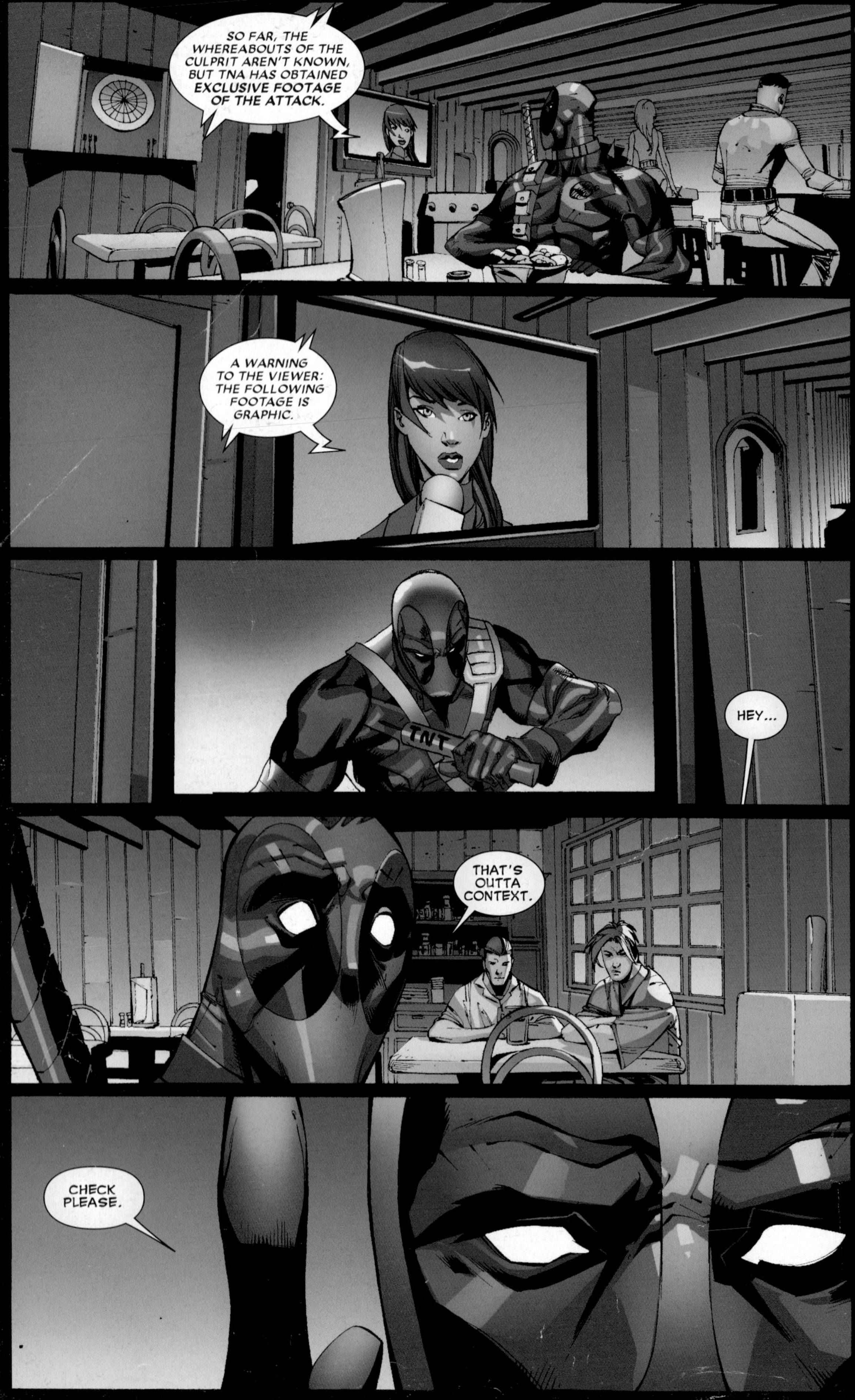
SO FAR, THE WHEREABOUTS OF THE CULPRIT AREN'T KNOWN, BUT TNA HAS OBTAINED EXCLUSIVE FOOTAGE OF THE ATTACK.
A WARNING TO THE VIEWER: THE FOLLOWING FOOTAGE IS GRAPHIC.
TNT
HEY...
THAT'S OUTTA CONTEXT.
CHECK PLEASE.

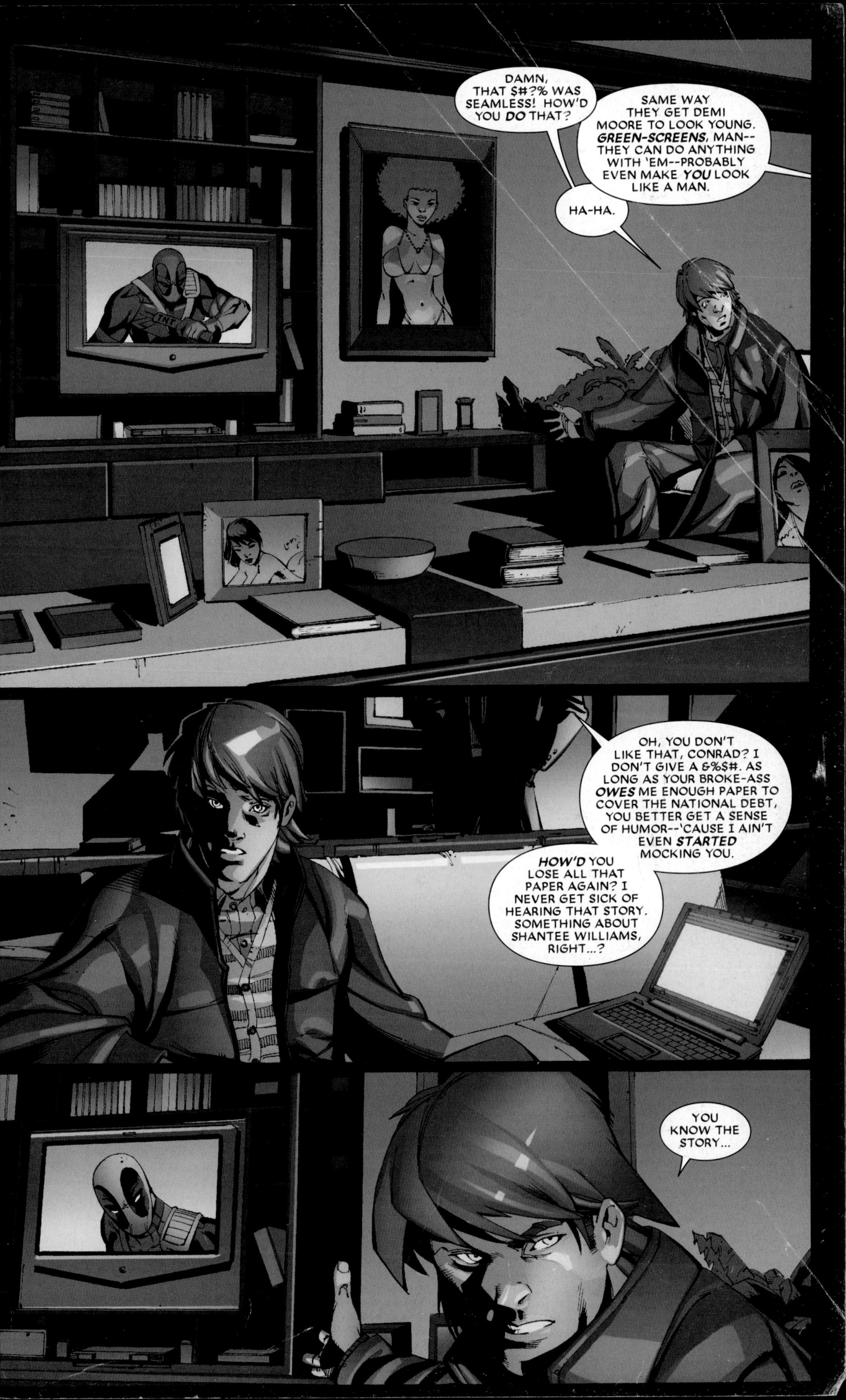
DAMN, THAT $#?% WAS SEAMLESS! HOW'D YOU *DO* THAT?
SAME WAY THEY GET DEMI MOORE TO LOOK YOUNG. *GREEN-SCREENS*, MAN--THEY CAN DO ANYTHING WITH 'EM--PROBABLY EVEN MAKE *YOU* LOOK LIKE A MAN.
HA-HA.
OH, YOU DON'T LIKE THAT, CONRAD? I DON'T GIVE A &%$#. AS LONG AS YOUR BROKE-ASS *OWES* ME ENOUGH PAPER TO COVER THE NATIONAL DEBT, YOU BETTER GET A SENSE OF HUMOR--'CAUSE I AIN'T EVEN *STARTED* MOCKING YOU.
HOW'D YOU LOSE ALL THAT PAPER AGAIN? I NEVER GET SICK OF HEARING THAT STORY. SOMETHING ABOUT SHANTEE WILLIAMS, RIGHT...?
YOU KNOW THE STORY...

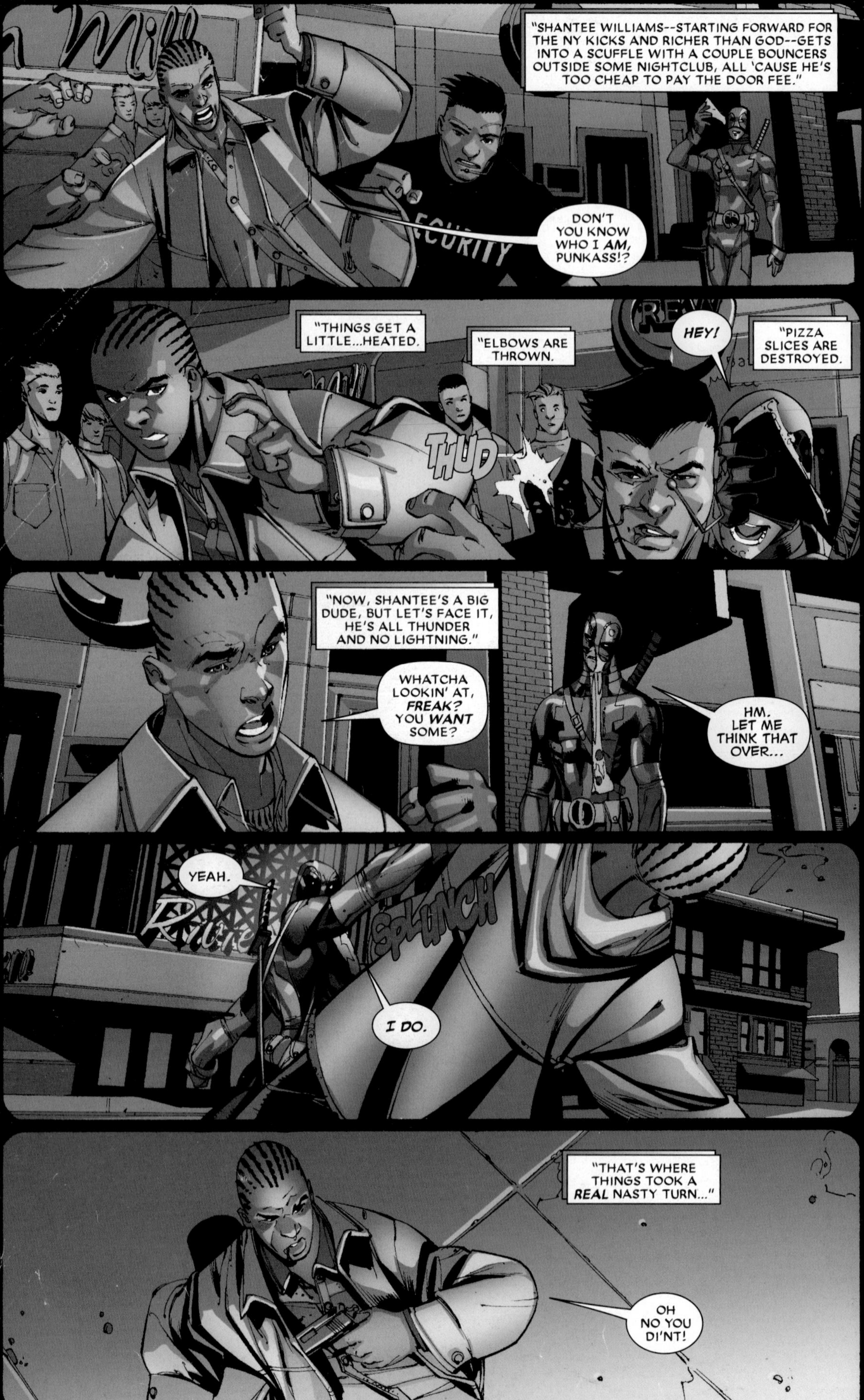
"SHANTEE WILLIAMS--STARTING FORWARD FOR THE NY KICKS AND RICHER THAN GOD--GETS INTO A SCUFFLE WITH A COUPLE BOUNCERS OUTSIDE SOME NIGHTCLUB, ALL 'CAUSE HE'S TOO CHEAP TO PAY THE DOOR FEE."
DON'T YOU KNOW WHO I AM, PUNKASS!?
SECURITY
"THINGS GET A LITTLE...HEATED.
"ELBOWS ARE THROWN.
HEY!
"PIZZA SLICES ARE DESTROYED.
THUD
"NOW, SHANTEE'S A BIG DUDE, BUT LET'S FACE IT, HE'S ALL THUNDER AND NO LIGHTNING."
WHATCHA LOOKIN' AT, FREAK? YOU WANT SOME?
HM. LET ME THINK THAT OVER...
YEAH.
SPLUNCH
I DO.
"THAT'S WHERE THINGS TOOK A REAL NASTY TURN..."
OH NO YOU DI'NT!

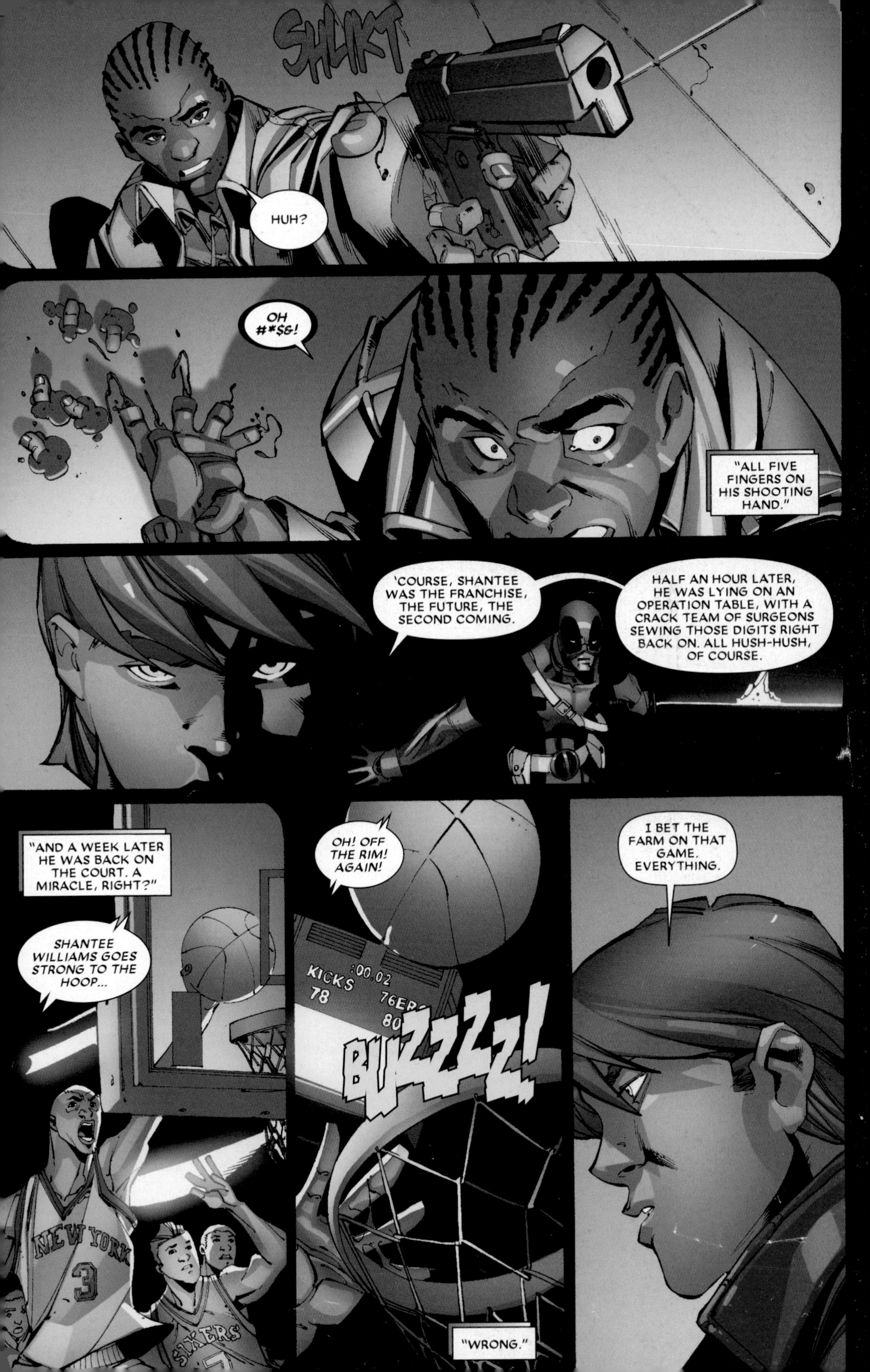
SHLIKT
HUH?
OH #*$&!
"ALL FIVE FINGERS ON HIS SHOOTING HAND."
'COURSE, SHANTEE WAS THE FRANCHISE, THE FUTURE, THE SECOND COMING.
HALF AN HOUR LATER, HE WAS LYING ON AN OPERATION TABLE, WITH A CRACK TEAM OF SURGEONS SEWING THOSE DIGITS RIGHT BACK ON. ALL HUSH-HUSH, OF COURSE.
"AND A WEEK LATER HE WAS BACK ON THE COURT. A MIRACLE, RIGHT?"
SHANTEE WILLIAMS GOES STRONG TO THE HOOP...
NEW YORK
3
SIXERS
OH! OFF THE RIM! AGAIN!
:00.02
KICKS
78
80
BUZZZZ!
"WRONG."
I BET THE FARM ON THAT GAME. EVERYTHING.

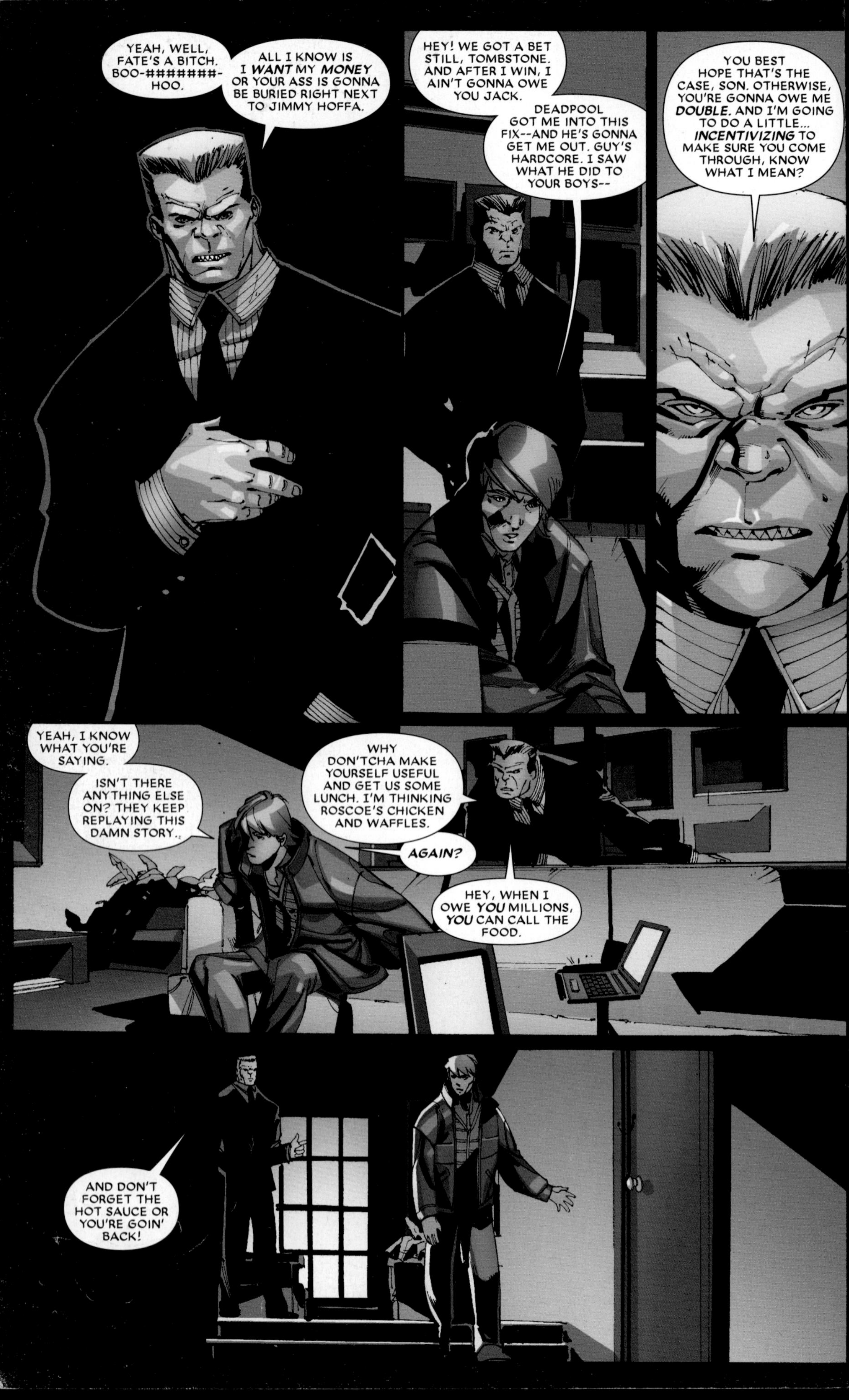
YEAH, WELL, FATE'S A BITCH. BOO-#######-HOO.
ALL I KNOW IS I WANT MY MONEY OR YOUR ASS IS GONNA BE BURIED RIGHT NEXT TO JIMMY HOFFA.
HEY! WE GOT A BET STILL, TOMBSTONE. AND AFTER I WIN, I AIN'T GONNA OWE YOU JACK.
DEADPOOL GOT ME INTO THIS FIX--AND HE'S GONNA GET ME OUT. GUY'S HARDCORE. I SAW WHAT HE DID TO YOUR BOYS--
YOU BEST HOPE THAT'S THE CASE, SON. OTHERWISE, YOU'RE GONNA OWE ME DOUBLE. AND I'M GOING TO DO A LITTLE... INCENTIVIZING TO MAKE SURE YOU COME THROUGH, KNOW WHAT I MEAN?
YEAH, I KNOW WHAT YOU'RE SAYING.
ISN'T THERE ANYTHING ELSE ON? THEY KEEP REPLAYING THIS DAMN STORY.
WHY DON'TCHA MAKE YOURSELF USEFUL AND GET US SOME LUNCH. I'M THINKING ROSCOE'S CHICKEN AND WAFFLES.
AGAIN?
HEY, WHEN I OWE YOU MILLIONS, YOU CAN CALL THE FOOD.
AND DON'T FORGET THE HOT SAUCE OR YOU'RE GOIN' BACK!

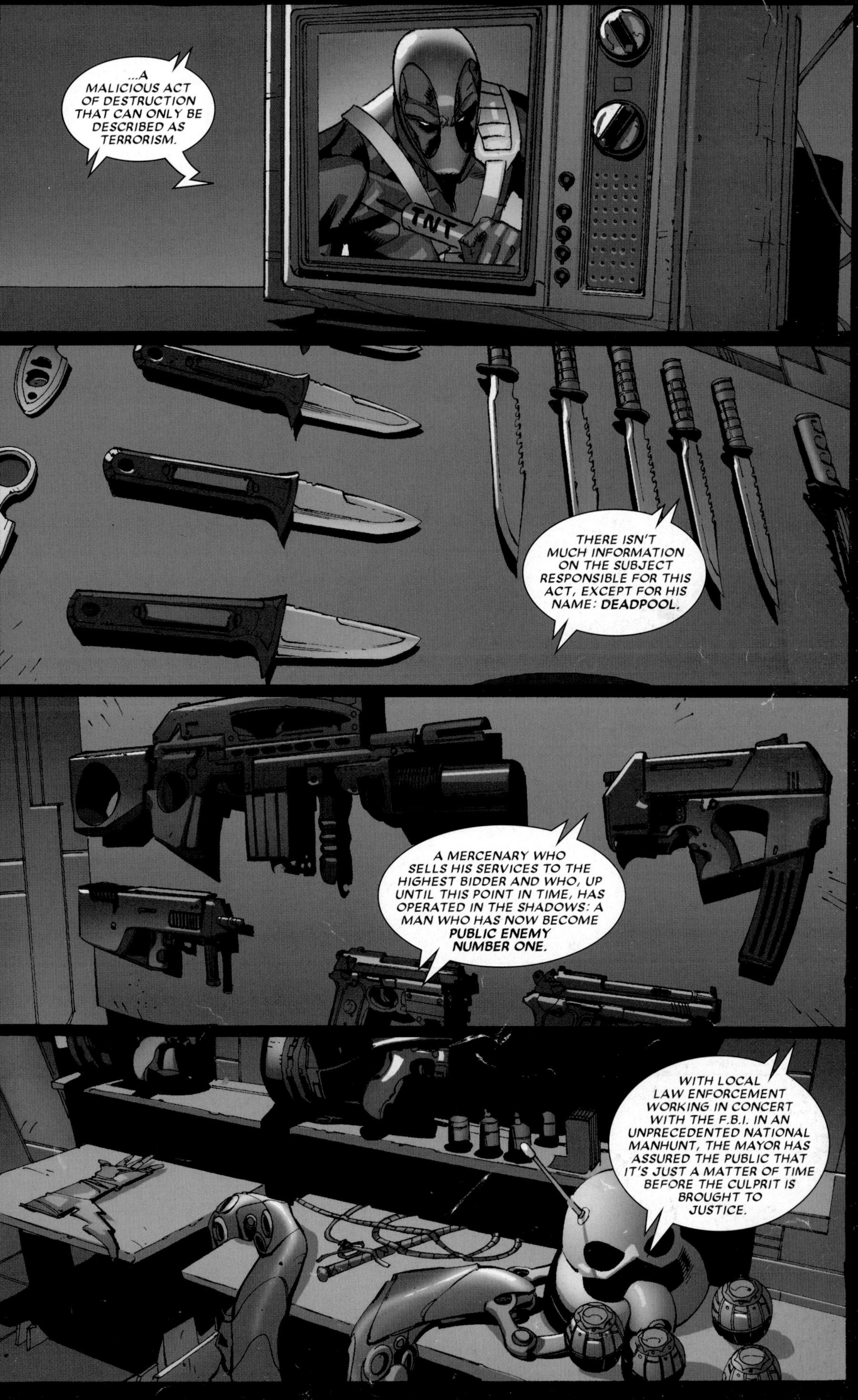
...A MALICIOUS ACT OF DESTRUCTION THAT CAN ONLY BE DESCRIBED AS TERRORISM.
TNT
THERE ISN'T MUCH INFORMATION ON THE SUBJECT RESPONSIBLE FOR THIS ACT, EXCEPT FOR HIS NAME: DEADPOOL.
A MERCENARY WHO SELLS HIS SERVICES TO THE HIGHEST BIDDER AND WHO, UP UNTIL THIS POINT IN TIME, HAS OPERATED IN THE SHADOWS: A MAN WHO HAS NOW BECOME PUBLIC ENEMY NUMBER ONE.
WITH LOCAL LAW ENFORCEMENT WORKING IN CONCERT WITH THE F.B.I. IN AN UNPRECEDENTED NATIONAL MANHUNT, THE MAYOR HAS ASSURED THE PUBLIC THAT IT'S JUST A MATTER OF TIME BEFORE THE CULPRIT IS BROUGHT TO JUSTICE.

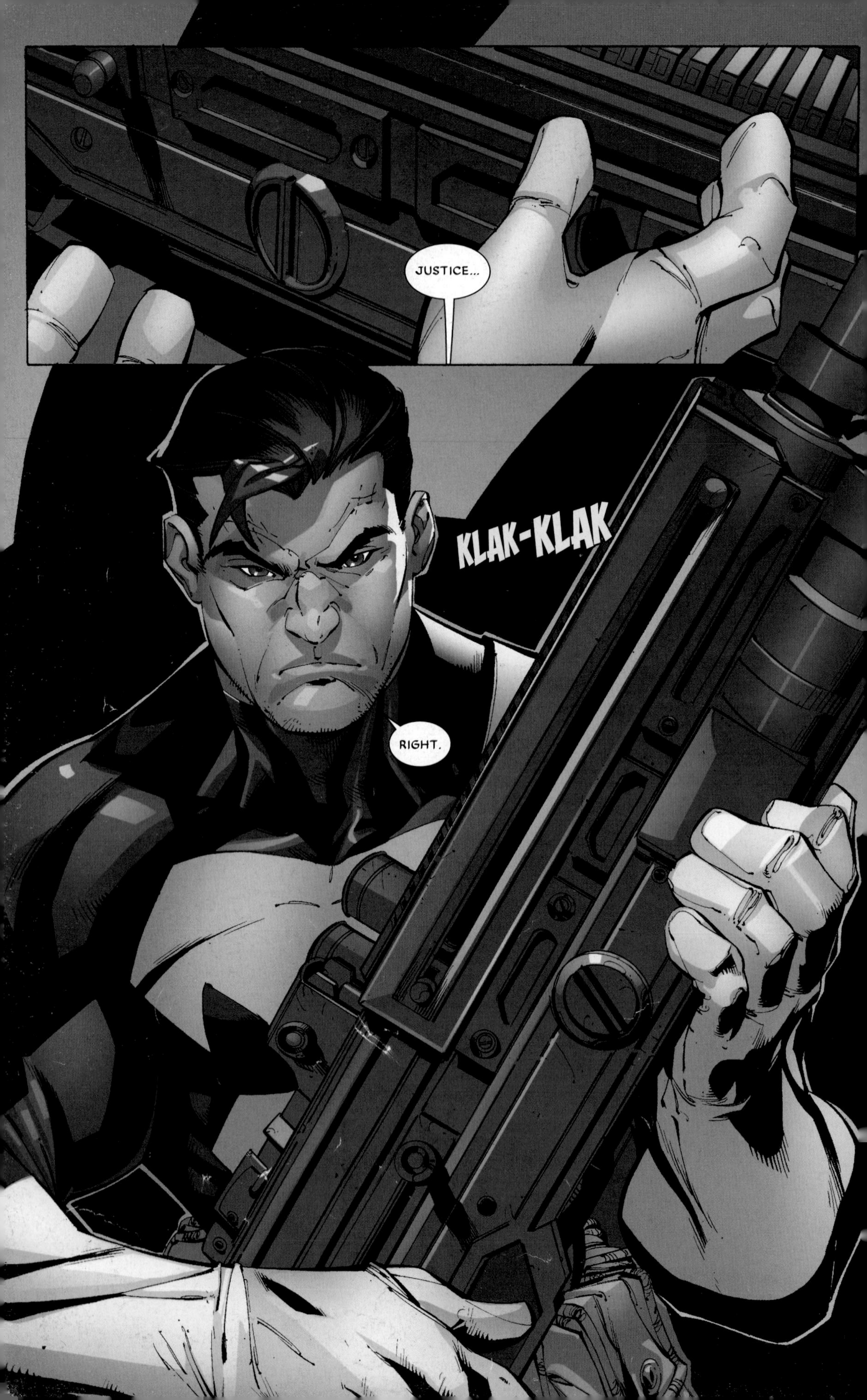
JUSTICE...
KLAK-KLAK
RIGHT.

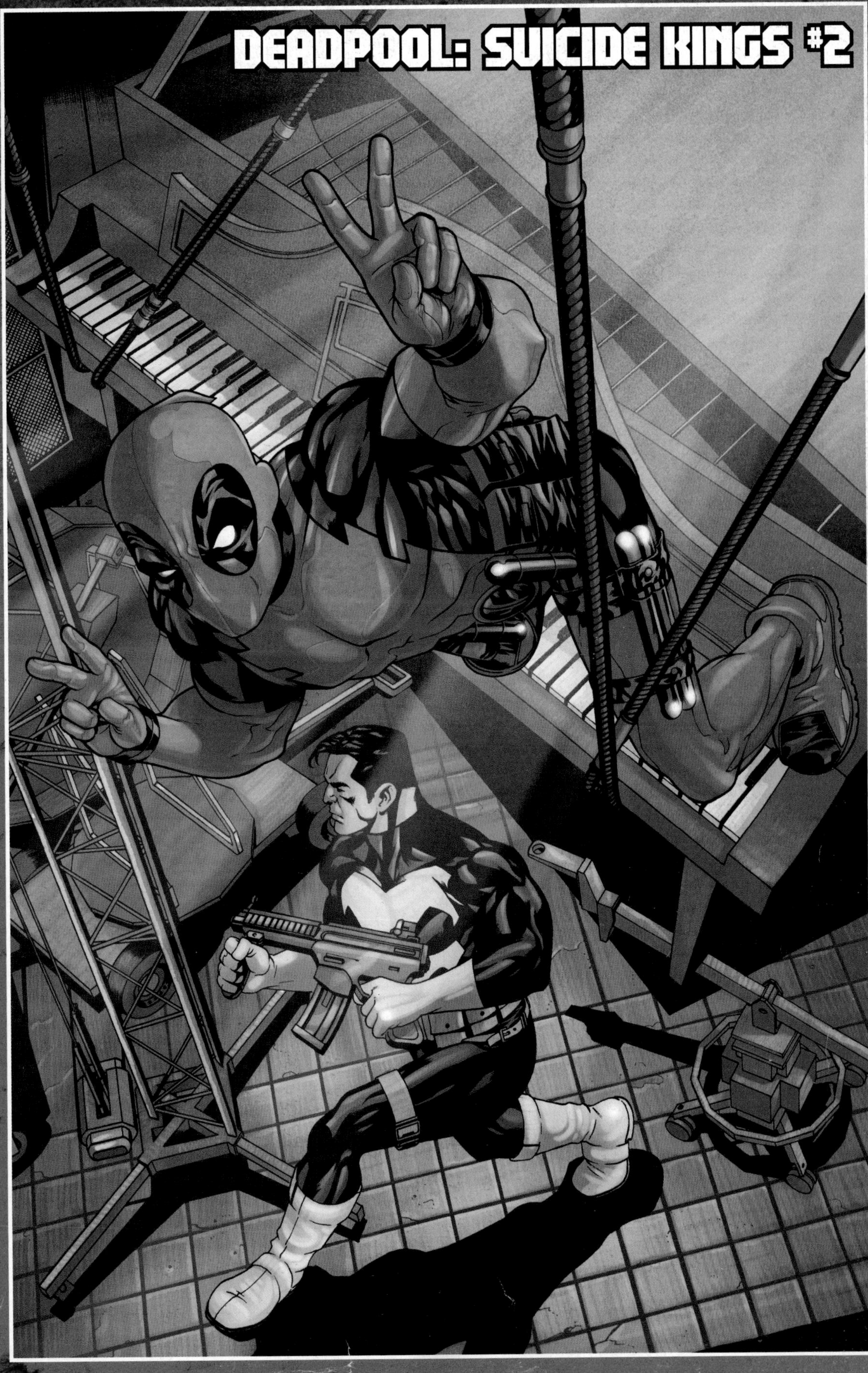
DEADPOOL: SUICIDE KINGS #2

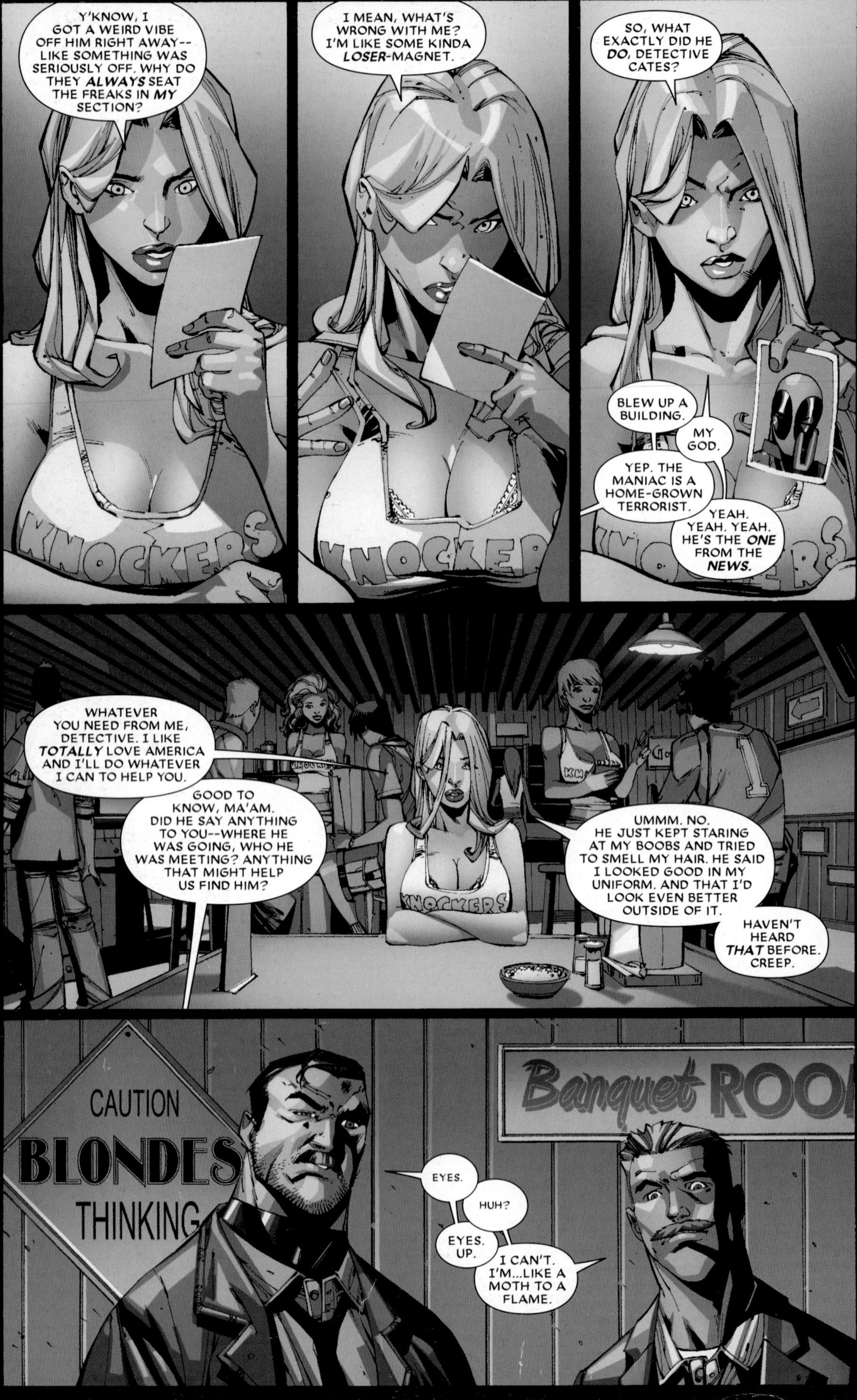
Y'KNOW, I GOT A WEIRD VIBE OFF HIM RIGHT AWAY--LIKE SOMETHING WAS SERIOUSLY OFF. WHY DO THEY *ALWAYS* SEAT THE FREAKS IN *MY* SECTION?
KNOCKERS
I MEAN, WHAT'S WRONG WITH ME? I'M LIKE SOME KINDA *LOSER*-MAGNET.
KNOCKERS
SO, WHAT EXACTLY DID HE *DO*, DETECTIVE CATES?
BLEW UP A BUILDING.
MY GOD.
YEP. THE MANIAC IS A HOME-GROWN TERRORIST.
YEAH. YEAH. YEAH. HE'S THE *ONE* FROM THE *NEWS.*
WHATEVER YOU NEED FROM ME, DETECTIVE. I LIKE *TOTALLY* LOVE AMERICA AND I'LL DO WHATEVER I CAN TO HELP YOU.
GOOD TO KNOW, MA'AM. DID HE SAY ANYTHING TO YOU--WHERE HE WAS GOING, WHO HE WAS MEETING? ANYTHING THAT MIGHT HELP US FIND HIM?
KNOCKERS
UMMM. NO. HE JUST KEPT STARING AT MY BOOBS AND TRIED TO SMELL MY HAIR. HE SAID I LOOKED GOOD IN MY UNIFORM. AND THAT I'D LOOK EVEN BETTER OUTSIDE OF IT.
HAVEN'T HEARD *THAT* BEFORE. CREEP.
CAUTION
BLONDES
THINKING
Banquet ROO
EYES.
HUH?
EYES. UP.
I CAN'T. I'M...LIKE A MOTH TO A FLAME.

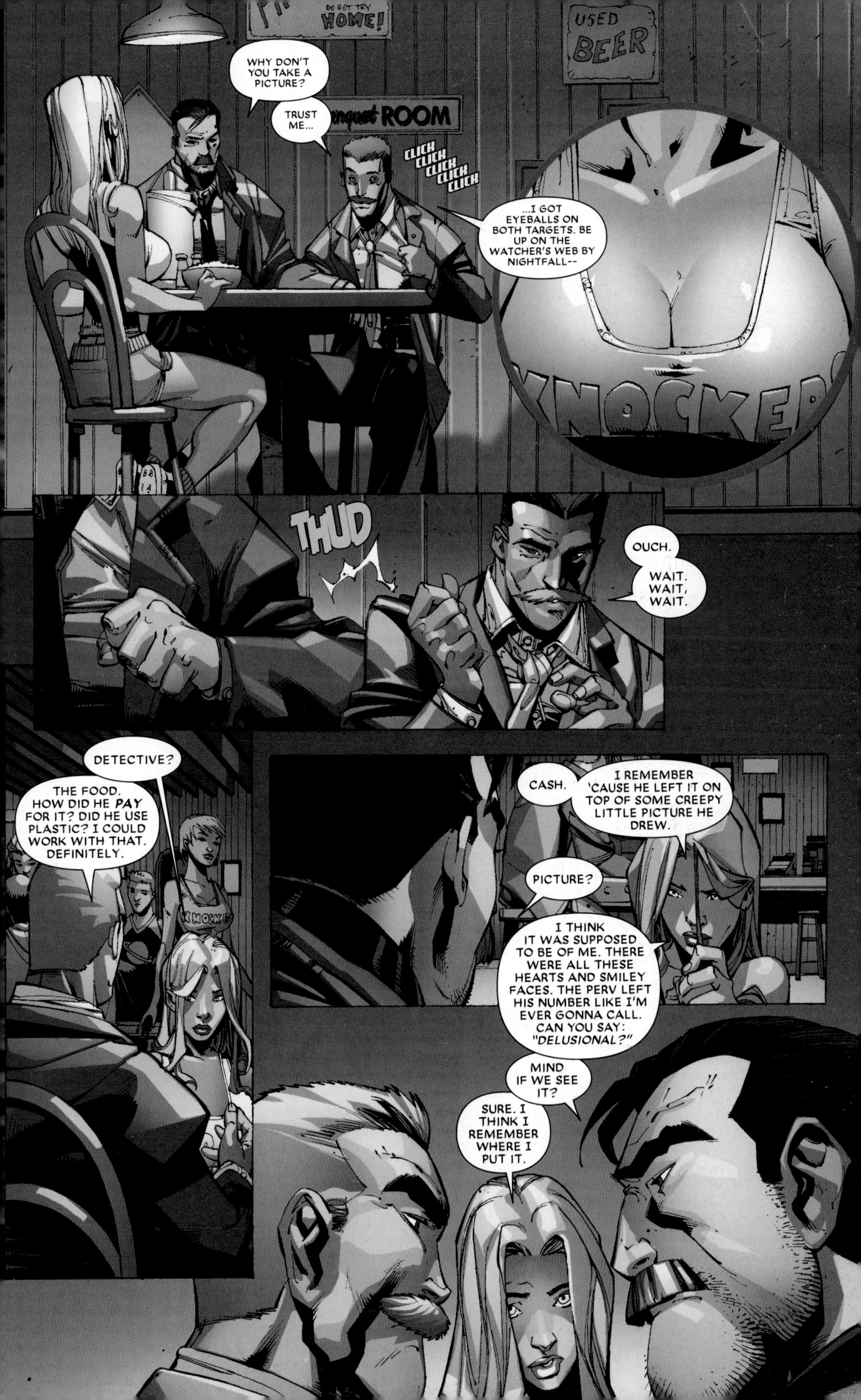
DO NOT TRY
HOME!
USED BEER
WHY DON'T YOU TAKE A PICTURE?
TRUST ME...
ROOM
CLICK CLICK CLICK CLICK CLICK
...I GOT EYEBALLS ON BOTH TARGETS. BE UP ON THE WATCHER'S WEB BY NIGHTFALL--
KNOCKER
THUD
OUCH.
WAIT. WAIT, WAIT.
DETECTIVE?
THE FOOD. HOW DID HE *PAY* FOR IT? DID HE USE PLASTIC? I COULD WORK WITH THAT. DEFINITELY.
CASH.
I REMEMBER 'CAUSE HE LEFT IT ON TOP OF SOME CREEPY LITTLE PICTURE HE DREW.
PICTURE?
I THINK IT WAS SUPPOSED TO BE OF ME. THERE WERE ALL THESE HEARTS AND SMILEY FACES. THE PERV LEFT HIS NUMBER LIKE I'M EVER GONNA CALL. CAN YOU SAY: *"DELUSIONAL?"*
MIND IF WE SEE IT?
SURE. I THINK I REMEMBER WHERE I PUT IT.

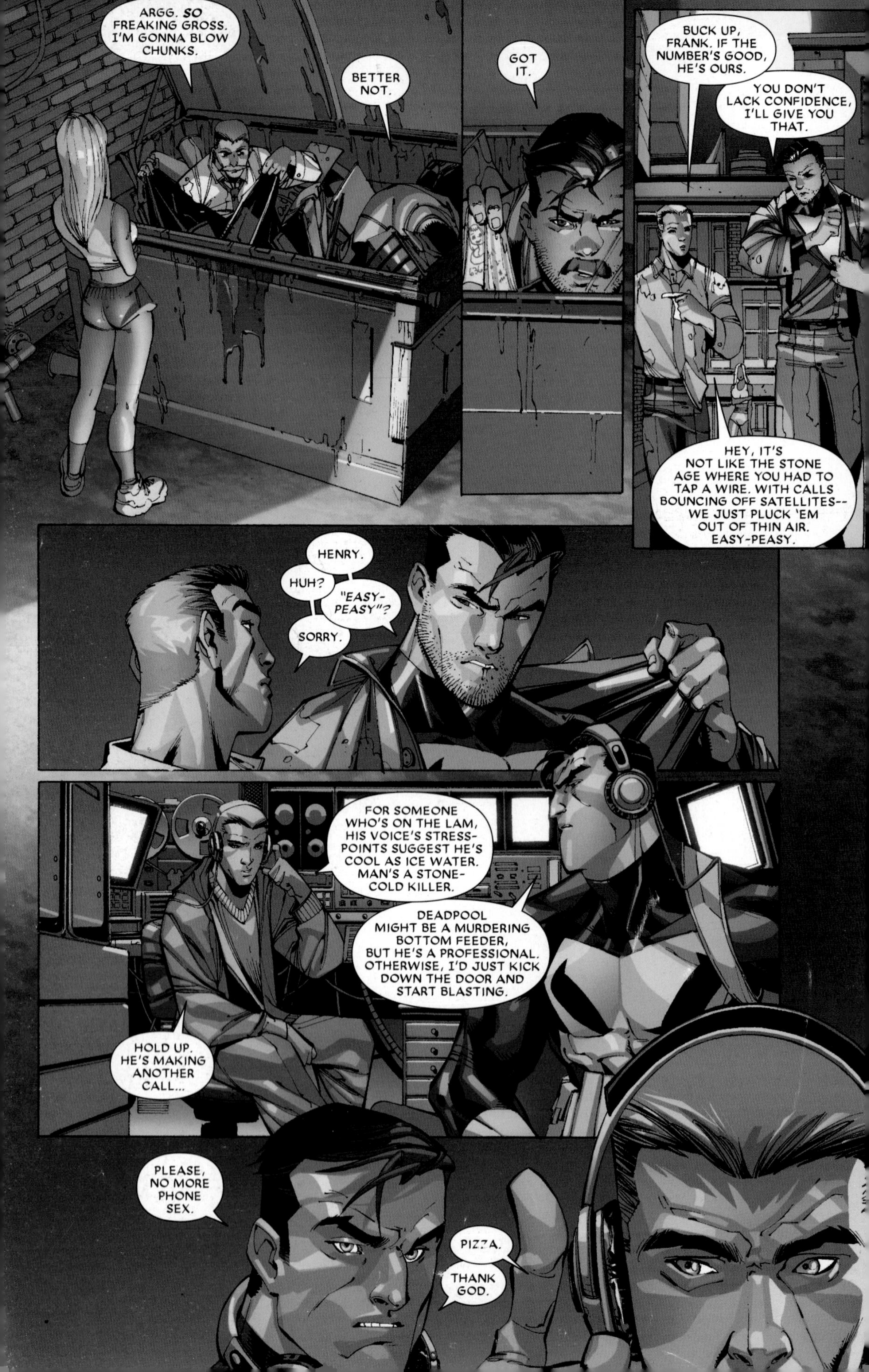

ARGG. SO FREAKING GROSS. I'M GONNA BLOW CHUNKS.
BETTER NOT.
GOT IT.
BUCK UP, FRANK. IF THE NUMBER'S GOOD, HE'S OURS.
YOU DON'T LACK CONFIDENCE, I'LL GIVE YOU THAT.
HEY, IT'S NOT LIKE THE STONE AGE WHERE YOU HAD TO TAP A WIRE. WITH CALLS BOUNCING OFF SATELLITES-- WE JUST PLUCK 'EM OUT OF THIN AIR. EASY-PEASY.
HENRY.
HUH?
"EASY-PEASY"?
SORRY.
FOR SOMEONE WHO'S ON THE LAM, HIS VOICE'S STRESS-POINTS SUGGEST HE'S COOL AS ICE WATER. MAN'S A STONE-COLD KILLER.
DEADPOOL MIGHT BE A MURDERING BOTTOM FEEDER, BUT HE'S A PROFESSIONAL. OTHERWISE, I'D JUST KICK DOWN THE DOOR AND START BLASTING.
HOLD UP. HE'S MAKING ANOTHER CALL...
PLEASE, NO MORE PHONE SEX.
PIZZA.
THANK GOD.

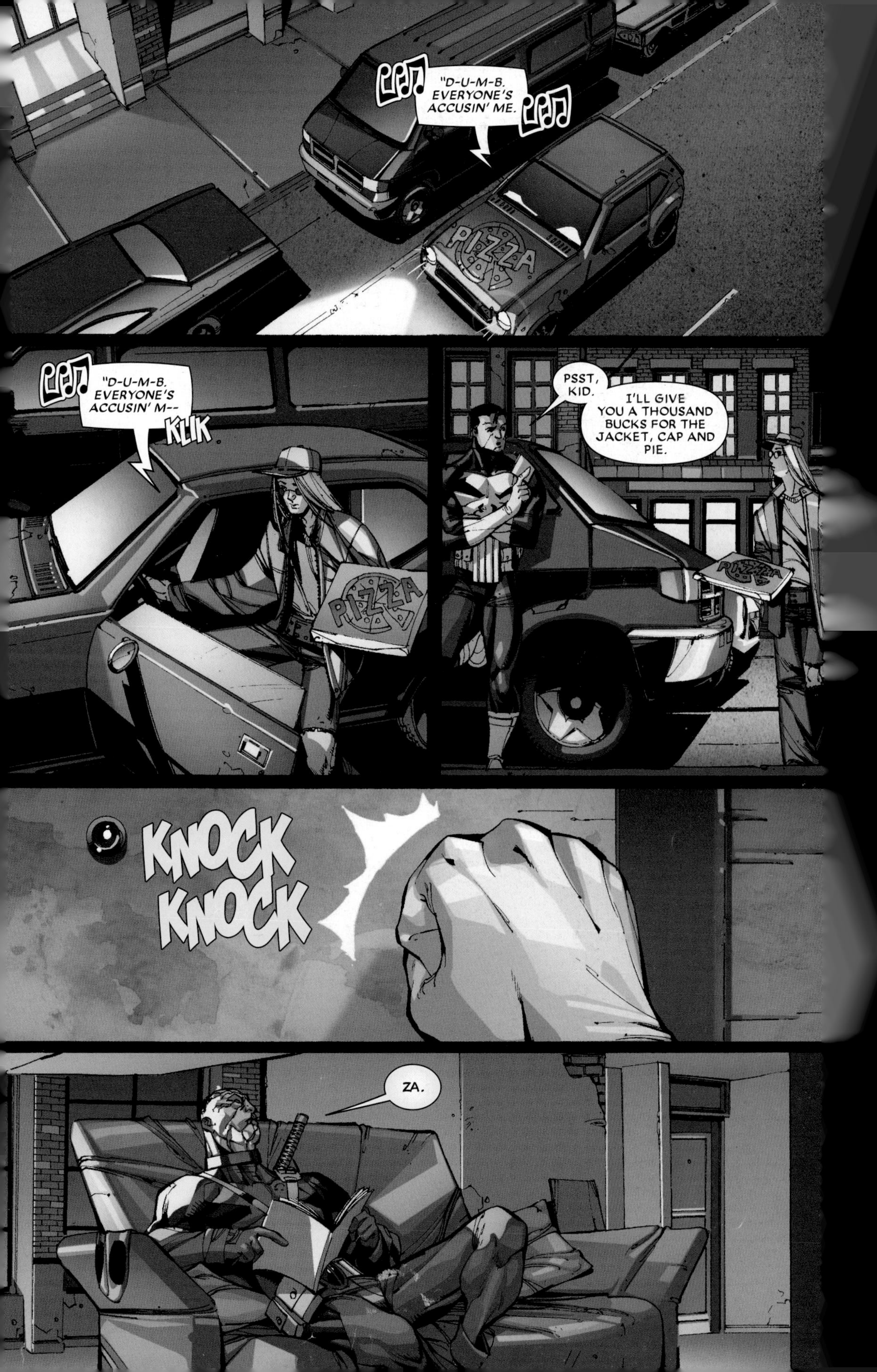
"D-U-M-B. EVERYONE'S ACCUSIN' ME.
"D-U-M-B. EVERYONE'S ACCUSIN' M--
KLIK
PSST, KID.
I'LL GIVE YOU A THOUSAND BUCKS FOR THE JACKET, CAP AND PIE.
KNOCK KNOCK
ZA.

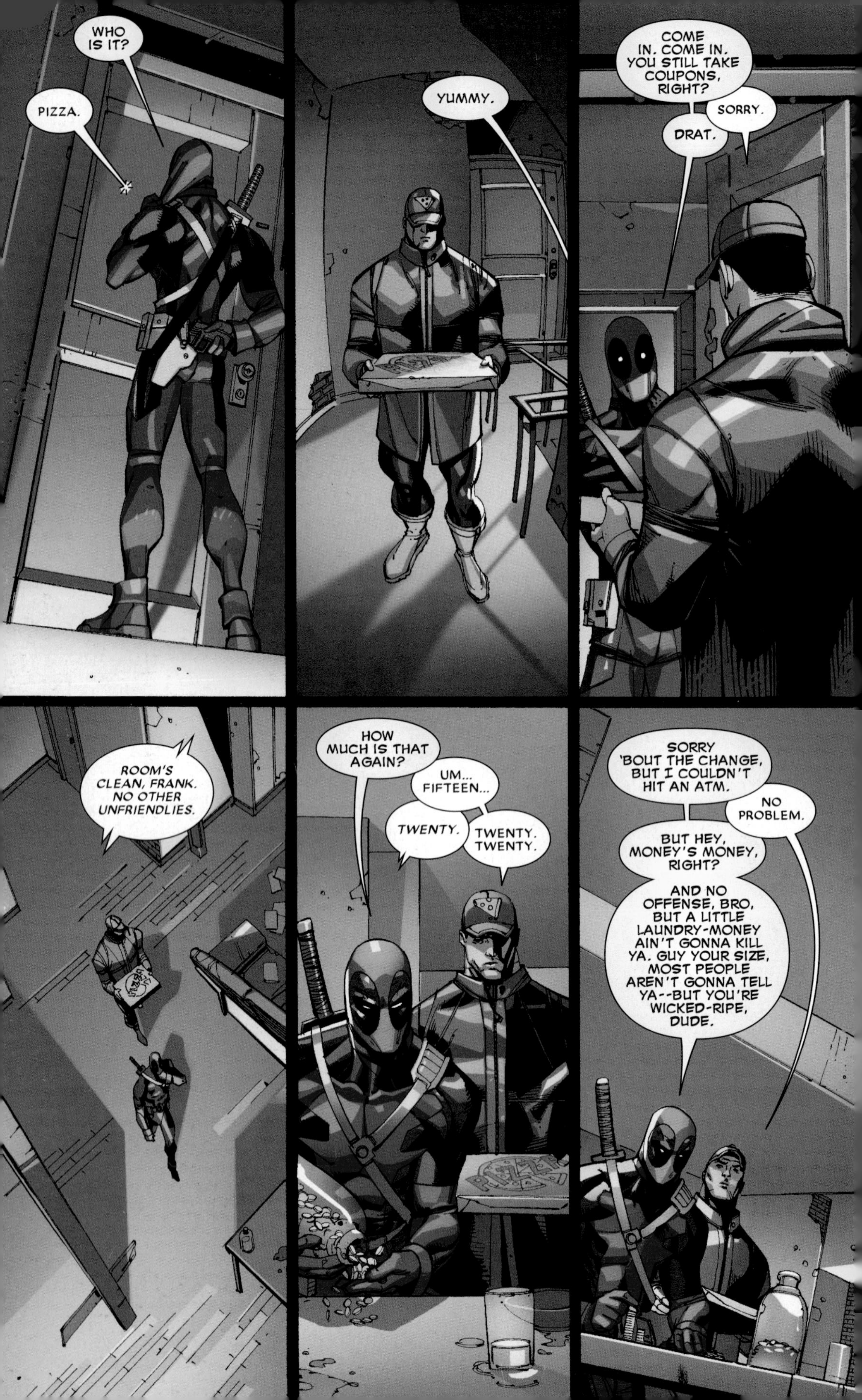
WHO IS IT?
PIZZA.
YUMMY.
COME IN. COME IN. YOU STILL TAKE COUPONS, RIGHT?
SORRY.
DRAT.
ROOM'S CLEAN, FRANK. NO OTHER UNFRIENDLIES.
HOW MUCH IS THAT AGAIN?
UM... FIFTEEN...
TWENTY.
TWENTY. TWENTY.
SORRY 'BOUT THE CHANGE, BUT I COULDN'T HIT AN ATM.
NO PROBLEM.
BUT HEY, MONEY'S MONEY, RIGHT?
AND NO OFFENSE, BRO, BUT A LITTLE LAUNDRY-MONEY AIN'T GONNA KILL YA. GUY YOUR SIZE, MOST PEOPLE AREN'T GONNA TELL YA--BUT YOU'RE WICKED-RIPE, DUDE.

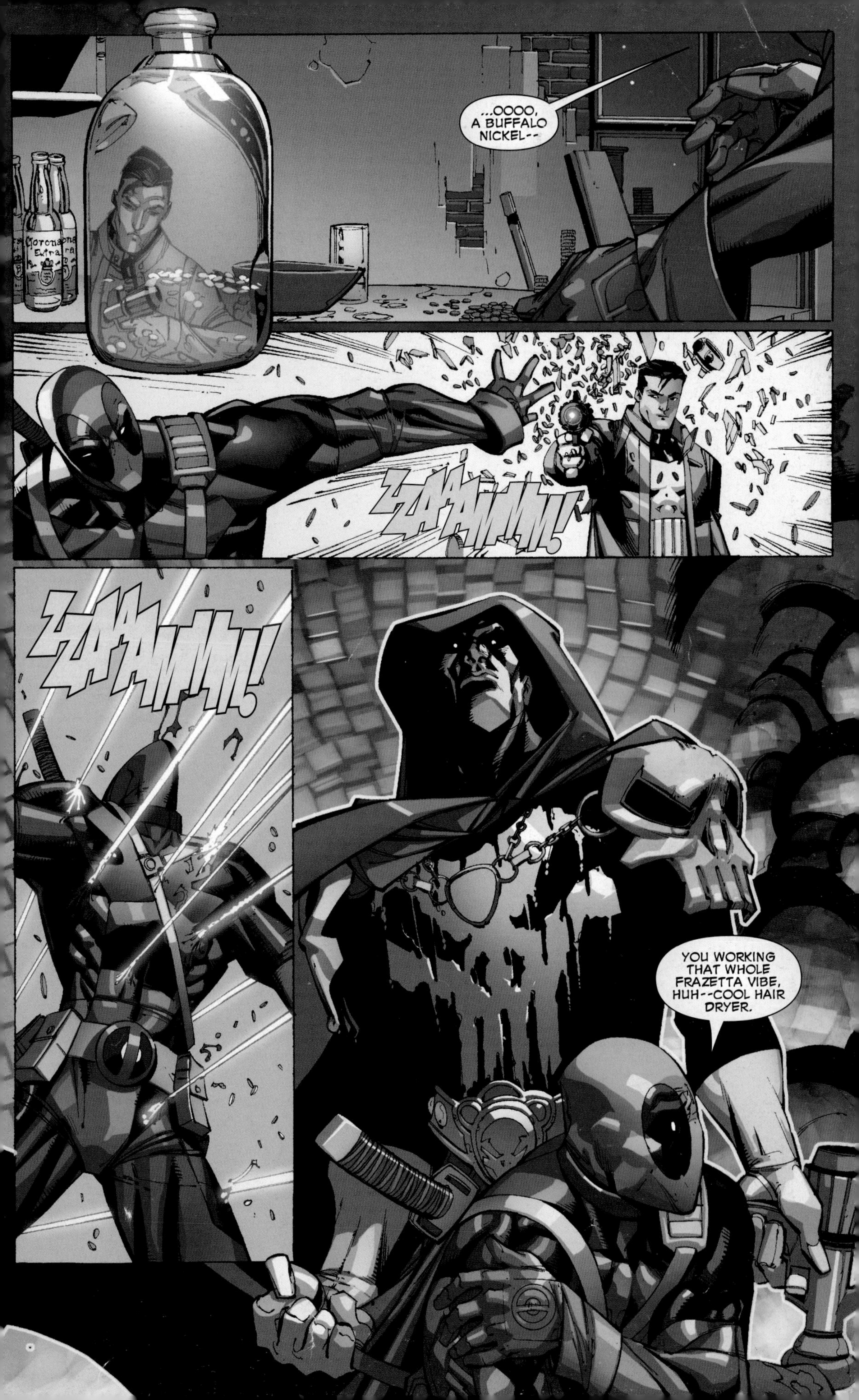
...OOOO, A BUFFALO NICKEL--
Corona Extra
ZZAAAMMM!
ZZAAAMMMM!
YOU WORKING THAT WHOLE FRAZETTA VIBE, HUH--COOL HAIR DRYER.

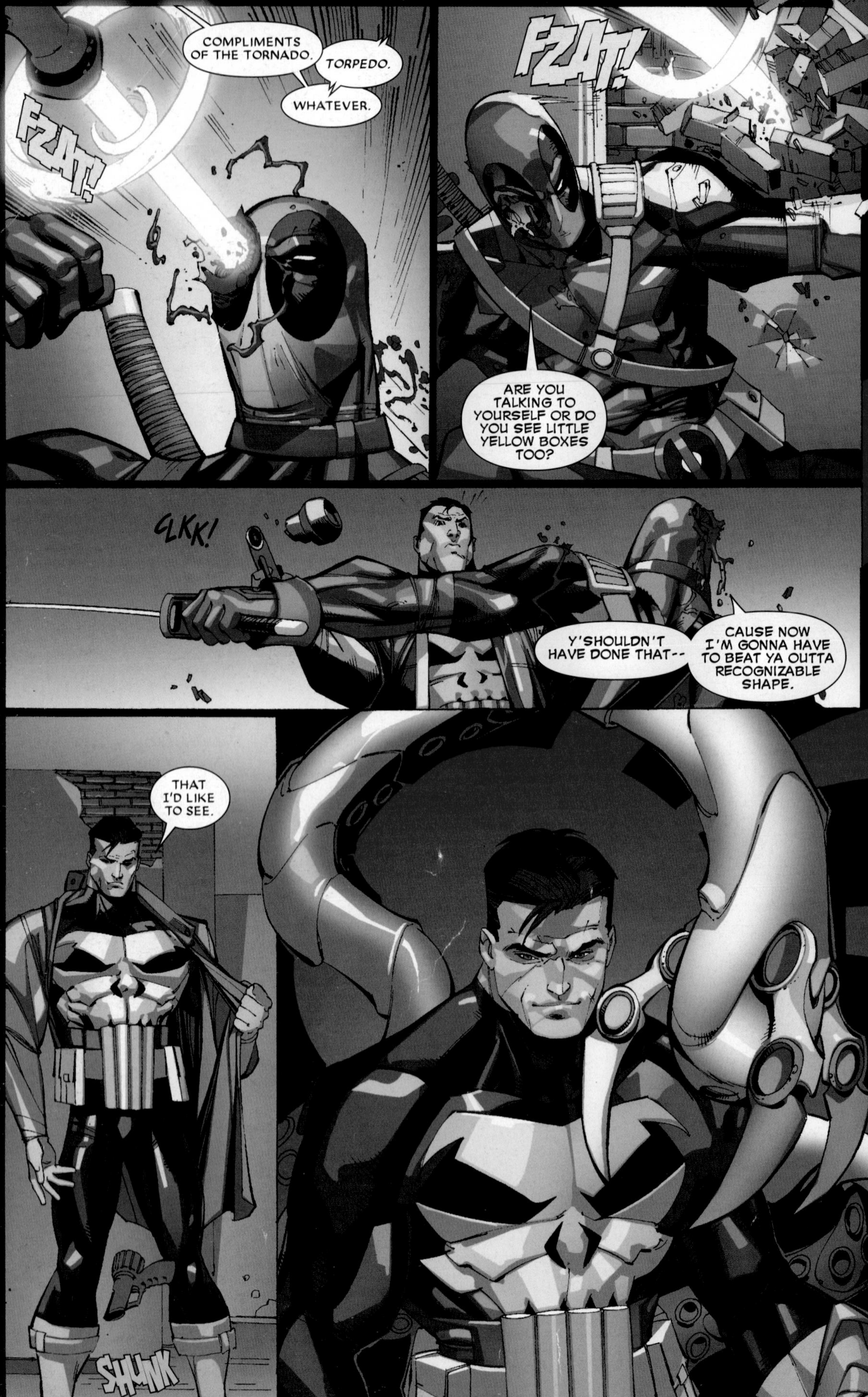
COMPLIMENTS OF THE TORNADO.
TORPEDO.
WHATEVER.
FZAT!
FZAT!
ARE YOU TALKING TO YOURSELF OR DO YOU SEE LITTLE YELLOW BOXES TOO?
CLKK!
Y'SHOULDN'T HAVE DONE THAT--
CAUSE NOW I'M GONNA HAVE TO BEAT YA OUTTA RECOGNIZABLE SHAPE.
THAT I'D LIKE TO SEE.
SHUNK

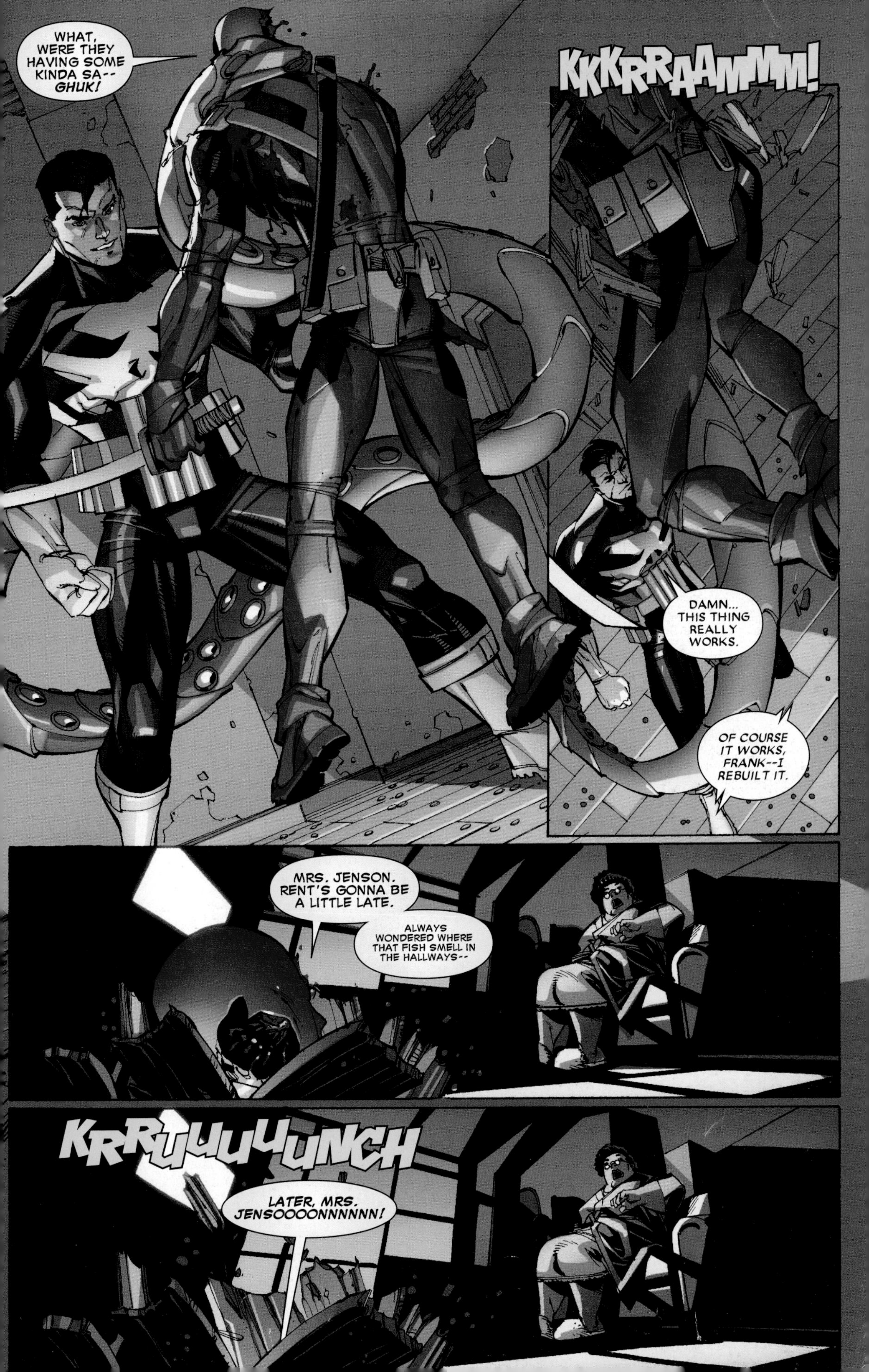

WHAT, WERE THEY HAVING SOME KINDA SA-- GHUK!
KKKRRAAMMM!
DAMN... THIS THING REALLY WORKS.
OF COURSE IT WORKS, FRANK--I REBUILT IT.
MRS. JENSON. RENT'S GONNA BE A LITTLE LATE.
ALWAYS WONDERED WHERE THAT FISH SMELL IN THE HALLWAYS--
KRRUUUUUNCH
LATER, MRS. JENSOOOONNNNNN!

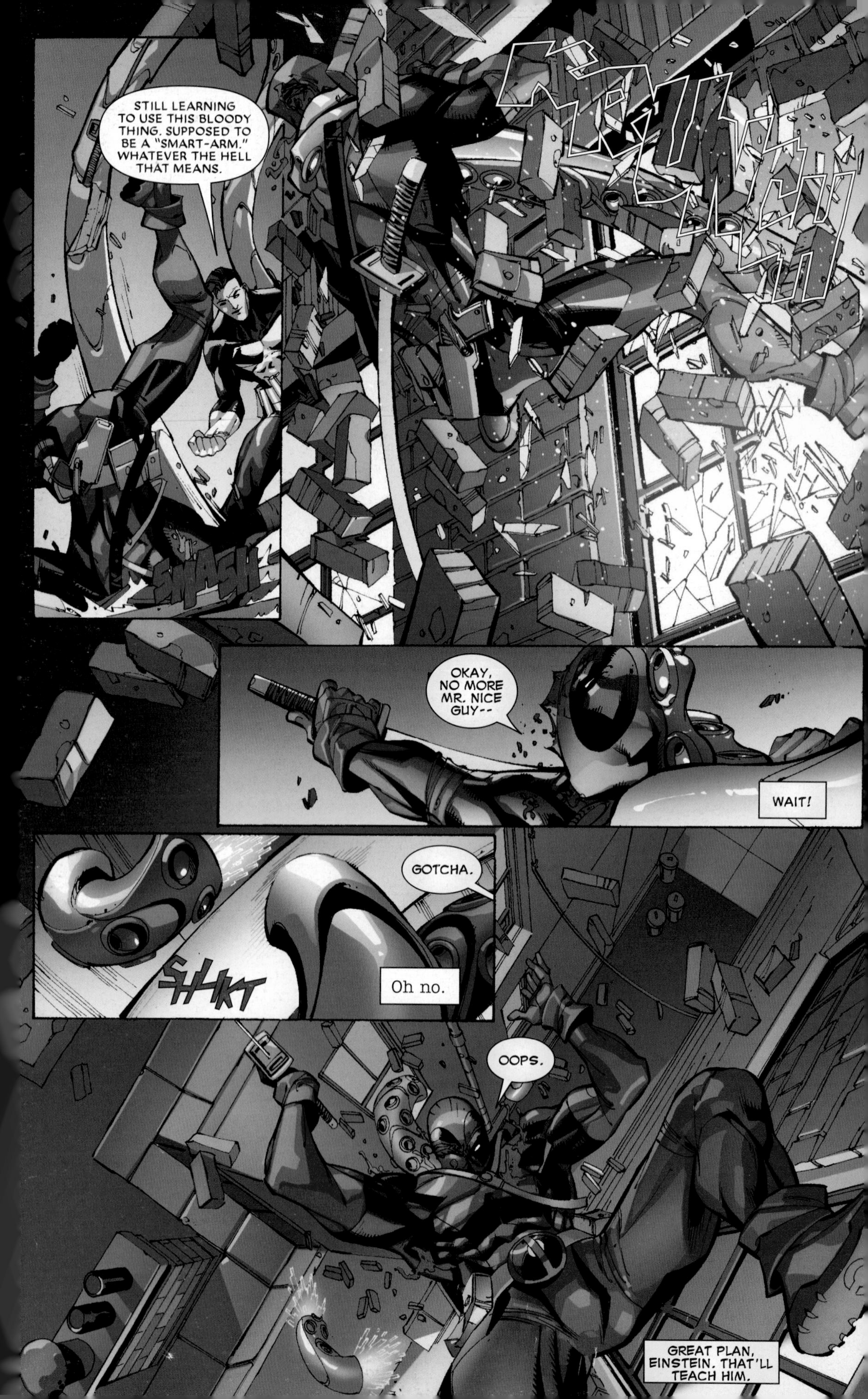
STILL LEARNING TO USE THIS BLOODY THING. SUPPOSED TO BE A "SMART-ARM." WHATEVER THE HELL THAT MEANS.
SMASH
OKAY, NO MORE MR. NICE GUY--
WAIT!
GOTCHA.
SHIKT
Oh no.
OOPS.
GREAT PLAN, EINSTEIN. THAT'LL TEACH HIM.

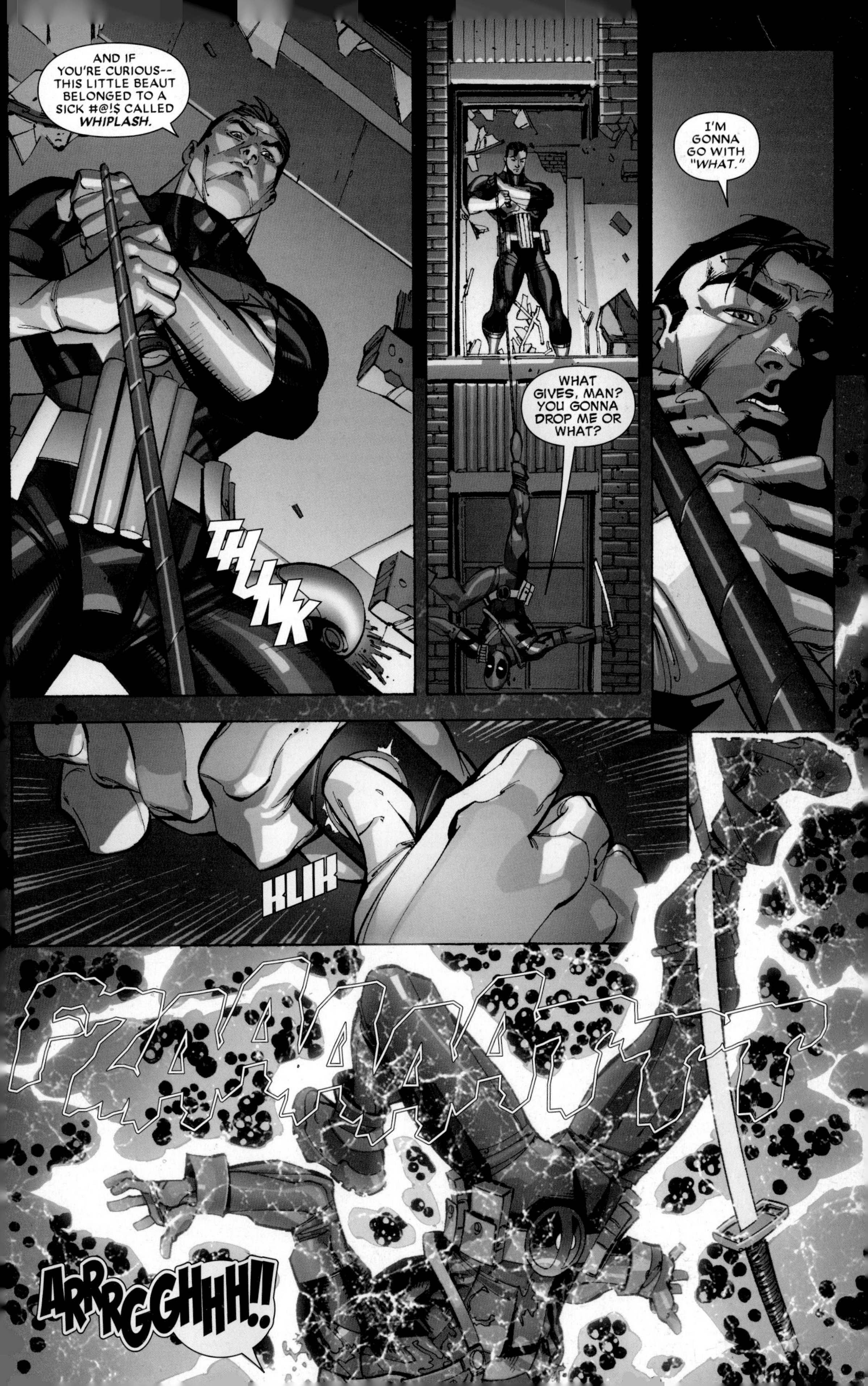
AND IF YOU'RE CURIOUS-- THIS LITTLE BEAUT BELONGED TO A SICK #@!$ CALLED *WHIPLASH.*
THUNK
WHAT GIVES, MAN? YOU GONNA DROP ME OR WHAT?
I'M GONNA GO WITH *"WHAT."*
KLIK
ARRRGGHHH!!

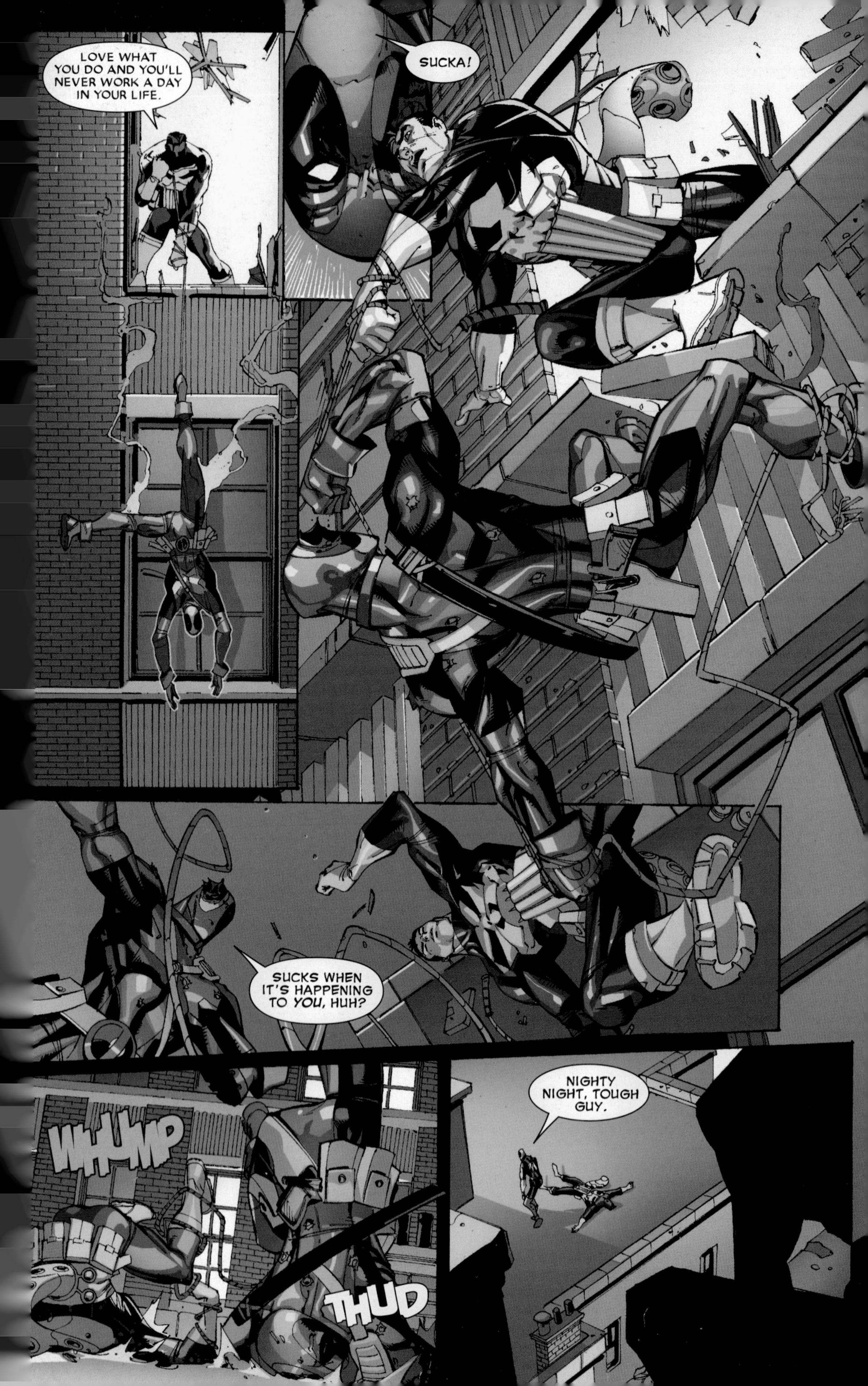
LOVE WHAT YOU DO AND YOU'LL NEVER WORK A DAY IN YOUR LIFE.
SUCKA!
SUCKS WHEN IT'S HAPPENING TO *YOU*, HUH?
WHUMP
THUD
NIGHTY NIGHT, TOUGH GUY.

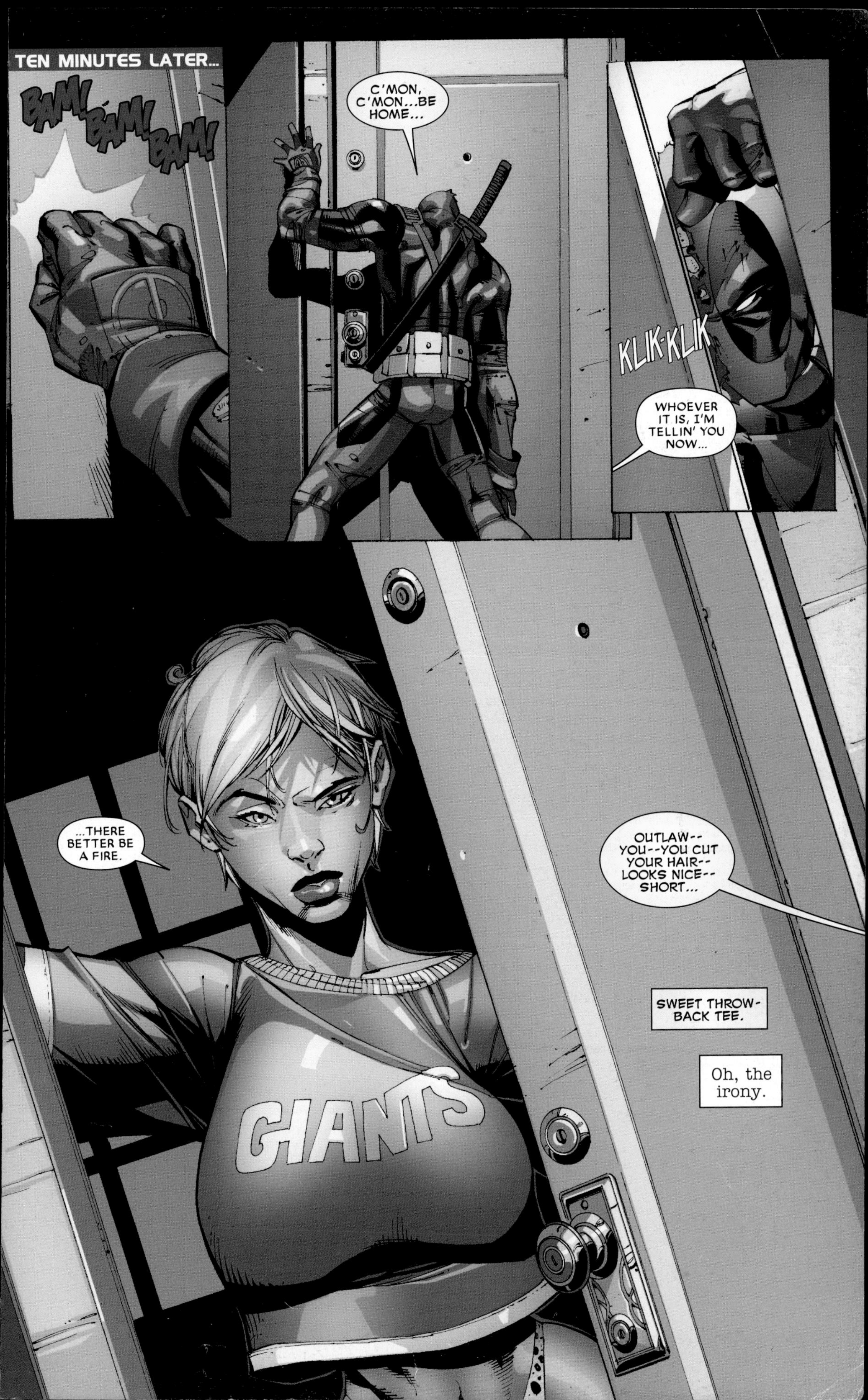
TEN MINUTES LATER...
BAM! BAM! BAM!
C'MON, C'MON...BE HOME...
KLIK-KLIK
WHOEVER IT IS, I'M TELLIN' YOU NOW...
...THERE BETTER BE A FIRE.
OUTLAW-- YOU--YOU CUT YOUR HAIR-- LOOKS NICE-- SHORT...
SWEET THROW-BACK TEE.
Oh, the irony.
GIANTS

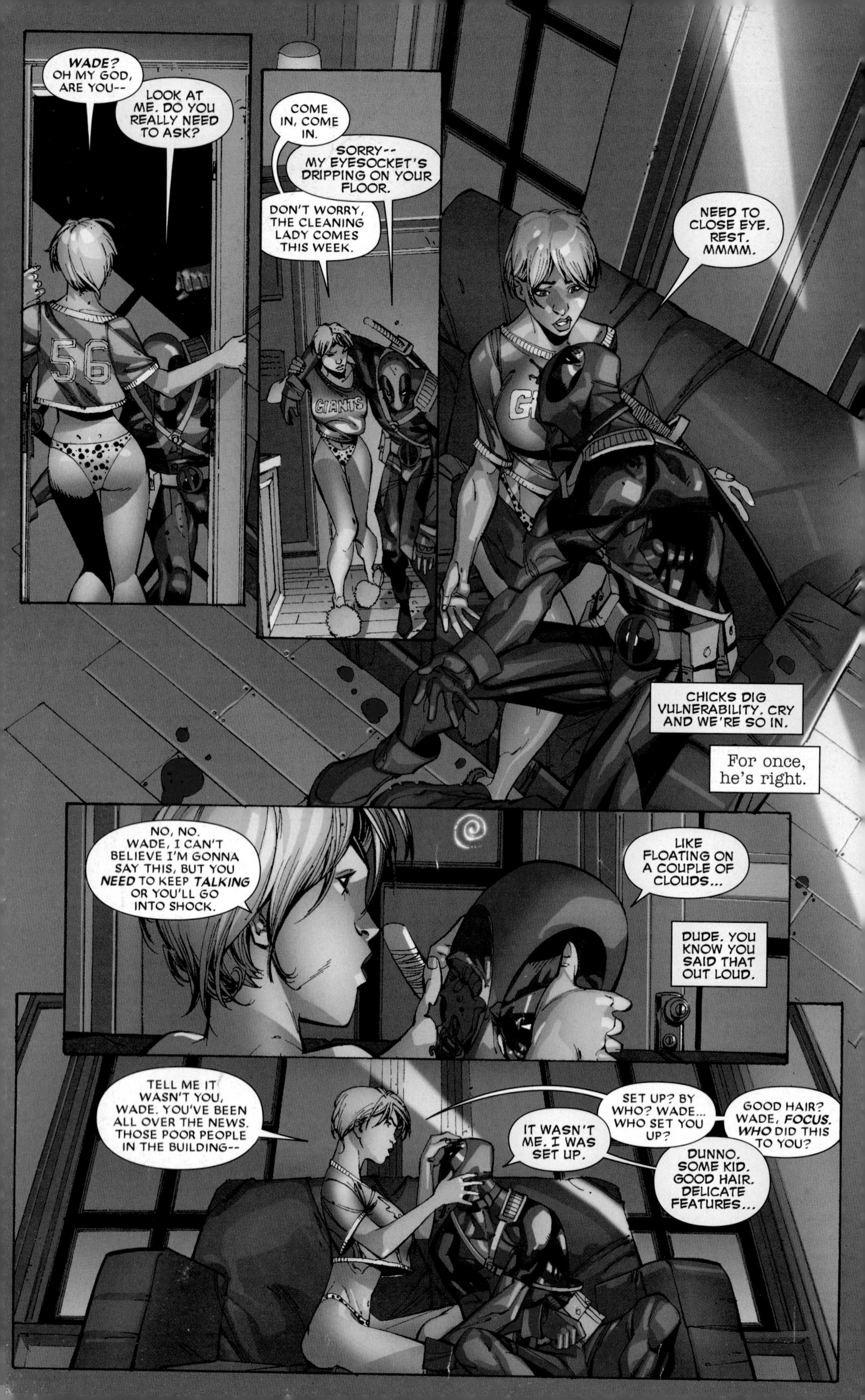
WADE? OH MY GOD, ARE YOU--
LOOK AT ME. DO YOU REALLY NEED TO ASK?
COME IN, COME IN.
SORRY-- MY EYESOCKET'S DRIPPING ON YOUR FLOOR.
DON'T WORRY, THE CLEANING LADY COMES THIS WEEK.
NEED TO CLOSE EYE. REST. MMMM.
CHICKS DIG VULNERABILITY. CRY AND WE'RE SO IN.
For once, he's right.
NO, NO. WADE, I CAN'T BELIEVE I'M GONNA SAY THIS, BUT YOU NEED TO KEEP TALKING OR YOU'LL GO INTO SHOCK.
LIKE FLOATING ON A COUPLE OF CLOUDS...
DUDE. YOU KNOW YOU SAID THAT OUT LOUD.
TELL ME IT WASN'T YOU, WADE. YOU'VE BEEN ALL OVER THE NEWS. THOSE POOR PEOPLE IN THE BUILDING--
IT WASN'T ME. I WAS SET UP.
SET UP? BY WHO? WADE... WHO SET YOU UP?
DUNNO. SOME KID. GOOD HAIR. DELICATE FEATURES...
GOOD HAIR? WADE, FOCUS. WHO DID THIS TO YOU?

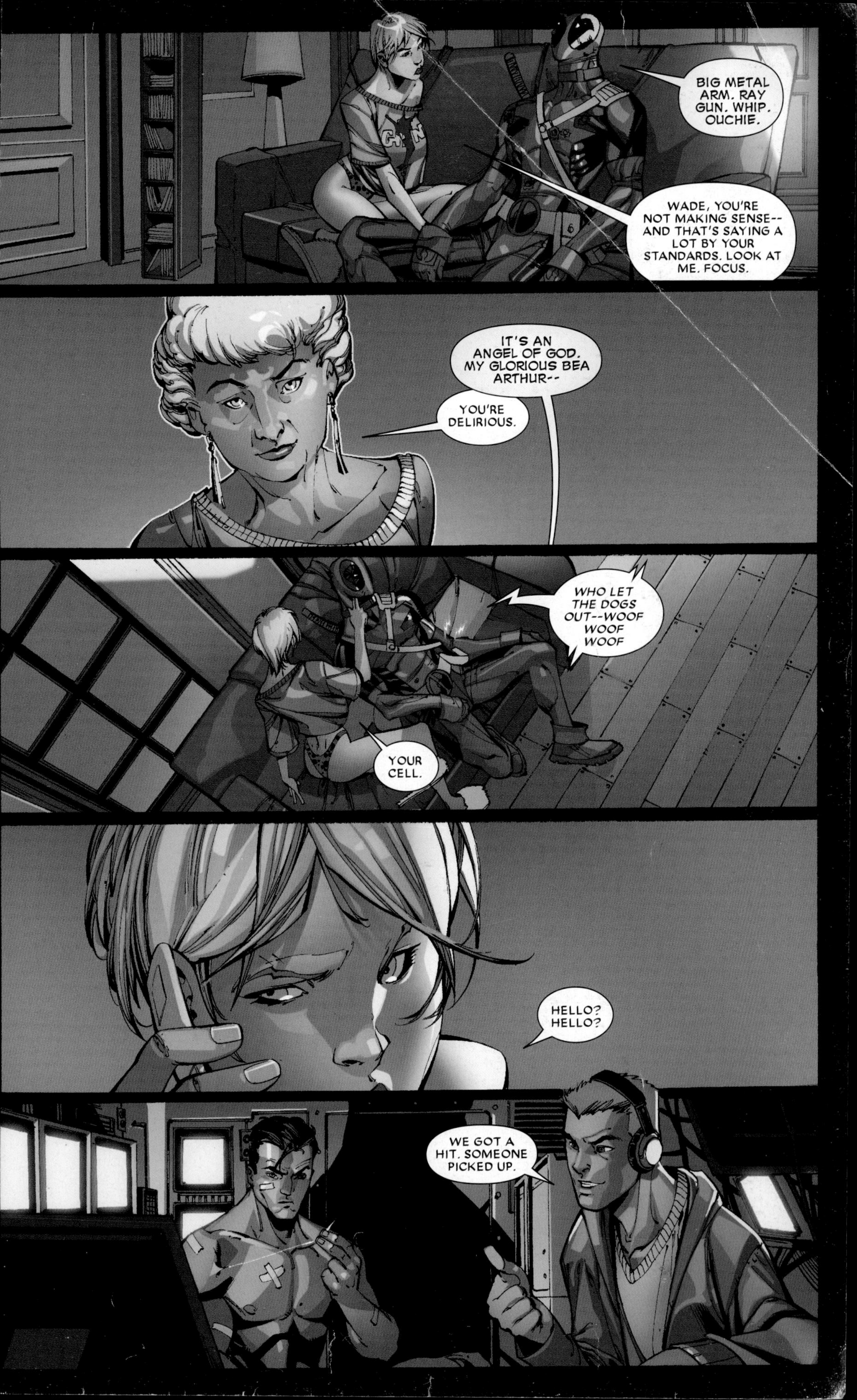
BIG METAL ARM. RAY GUN. WHIP. OUCHIE.
WADE, YOU'RE NOT MAKING SENSE--AND THAT'S SAYING A LOT BY YOUR STANDARDS. LOOK AT ME. FOCUS.
IT'S AN ANGEL OF GOD. MY GLORIOUS BEA ARTHUR--
YOU'RE DELIRIOUS.
WHO LET THE DOGS OUT--WOOF WOOF WOOF
YOUR CELL.
HELLO? HELLO?
WE GOT A HIT. SOMEONE PICKED UP.

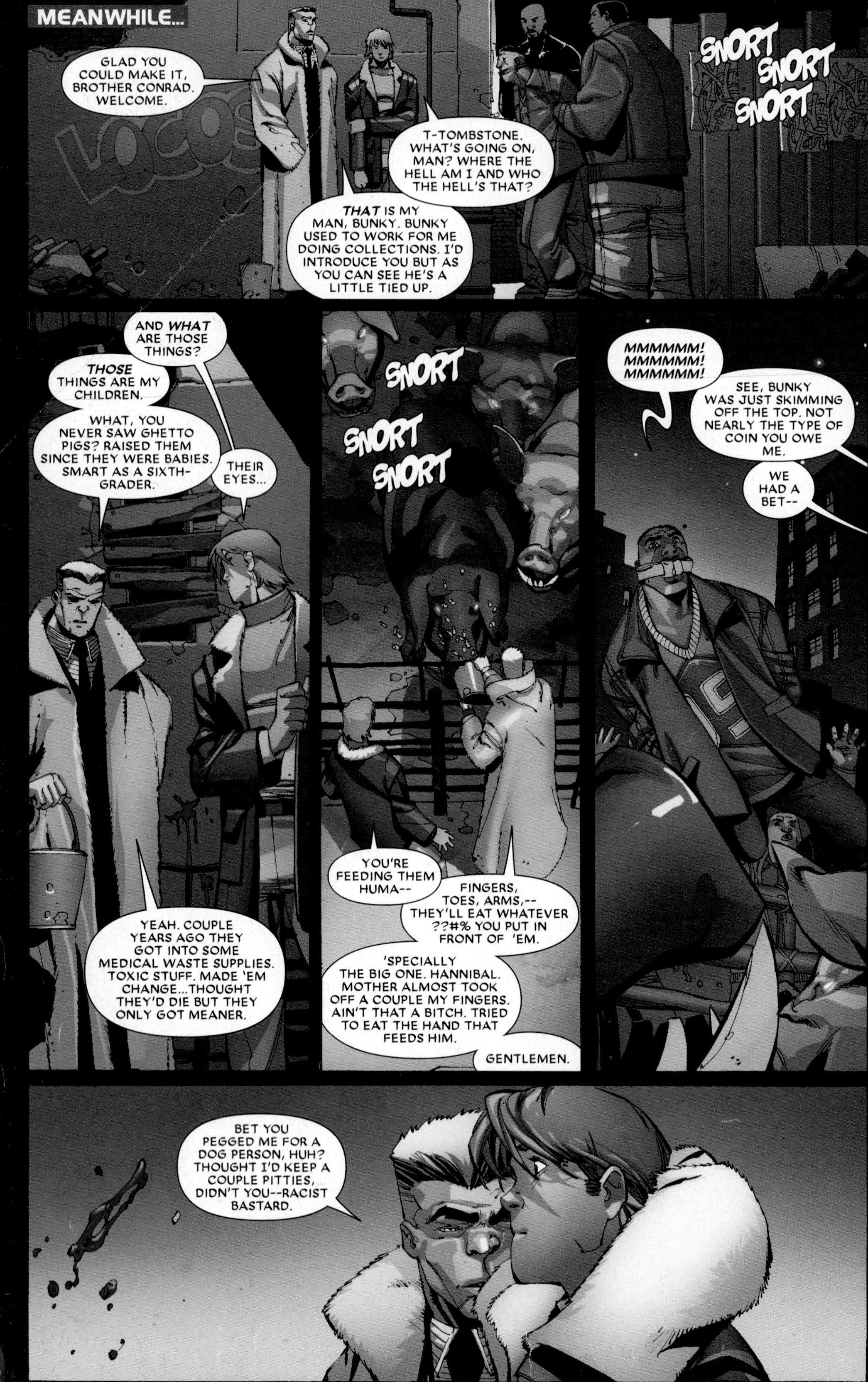
MEANWHILE...
GLAD YOU COULD MAKE IT, BROTHER CONRAD. WELCOME.
T-TOMBSTONE. WHAT'S GOING ON, MAN? WHERE THE HELL AM I AND WHO THE HELL'S THAT?
THAT IS MY MAN, BUNKY. BUNKY USED TO WORK FOR ME DOING COLLECTIONS. I'D INTRODUCE YOU BUT AS YOU CAN SEE HE'S A LITTLE TIED UP.
SNORT SNORT SNORT
AND *WHAT* ARE THOSE THINGS?
THOSE THINGS ARE MY CHILDREN.
WHAT, YOU NEVER SAW GHETTO PIGS? RAISED THEM SINCE THEY WERE BABIES. SMART AS A SIXTH-GRADER.
THEIR EYES...
YEAH. COUPLE YEARS AGO THEY GOT INTO SOME MEDICAL WASTE SUPPLIES. TOXIC STUFF. MADE 'EM CHANGE...THOUGHT THEY'D DIE BUT THEY ONLY GOT MEANER.
SNORT
SNORT
SNORT
YOU'RE FEEDING THEM HUMA--
FINGERS, TOES, ARMS,-- THEY'LL EAT WHATEVER ??#% YOU PUT IN FRONT OF 'EM.
'SPECIALLY THE BIG ONE. HANNIBAL. MOTHER ALMOST TOOK OFF A COUPLE MY FINGERS. AIN'T THAT A BITCH. TRIED TO EAT THE HAND THAT FEEDS HIM.
GENTLEMEN.
MMMMMM! MMMMMM! MMMMMM!
SEE, BUNKY WAS JUST SKIMMING OFF THE TOP. NOT NEARLY THE TYPE OF COIN YOU OWE ME.
WE HAD A BET--
BET YOU PEGGED ME FOR A DOG PERSON, HUH? THOUGHT I'D KEEP A COUPLE PITTIES, DIDN'T YOU--RACIST BASTARD.

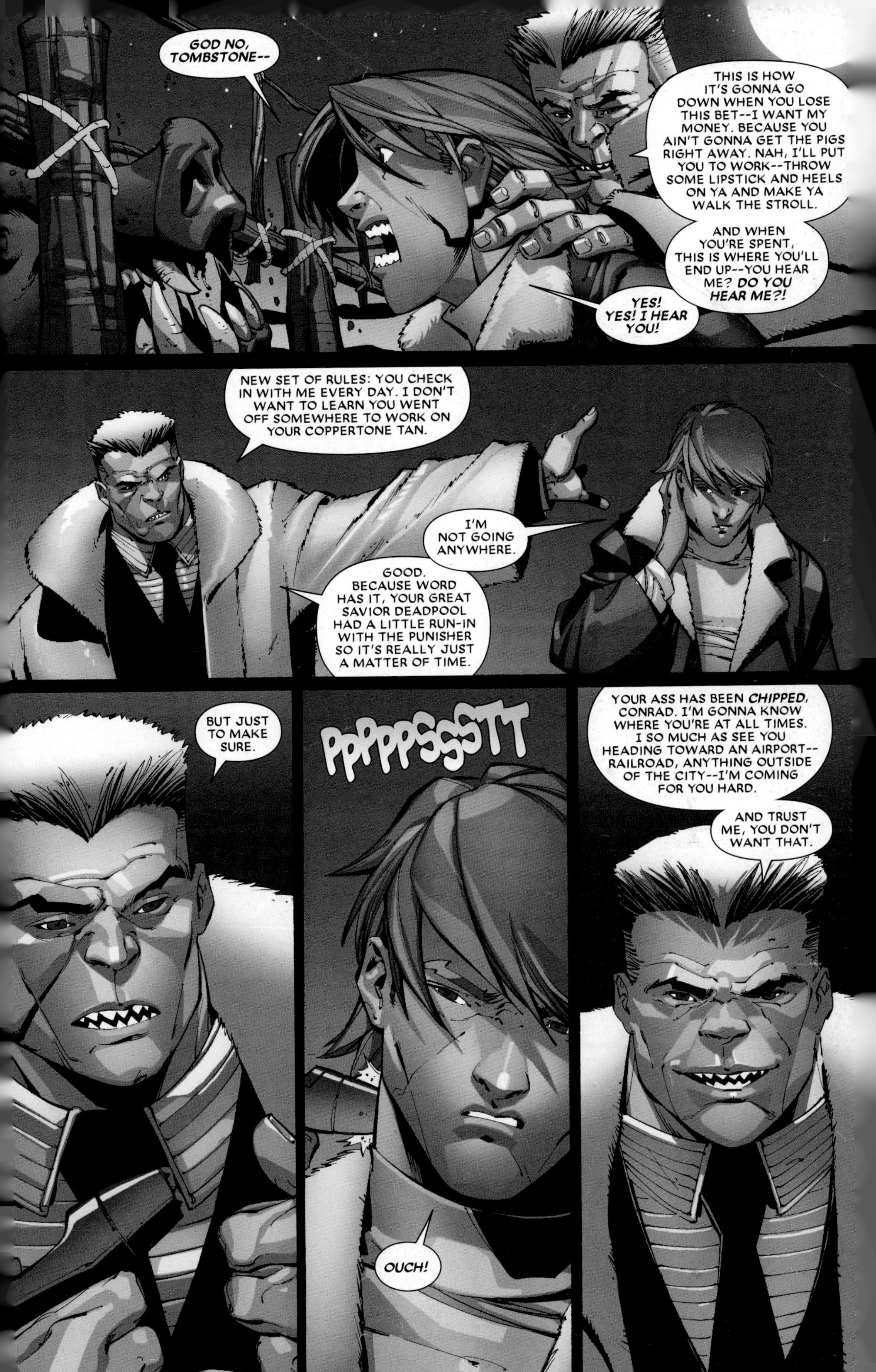
GOD NO, TOMBSTONE--
THIS IS HOW IT'S GONNA GO DOWN WHEN YOU LOSE THIS BET--I WANT MY MONEY. BECAUSE YOU AIN'T GONNA GET THE PIGS RIGHT AWAY. NAH, I'LL PUT YOU TO WORK--THROW SOME LIPSTICK AND HEELS ON YA AND MAKE YA WALK THE STROLL.
AND WHEN YOU'RE SPENT, THIS IS WHERE YOU'LL END UP--YOU HEAR ME? DO YOU HEAR ME?!
YES! YES! I HEAR YOU!
NEW SET OF RULES: YOU CHECK IN WITH ME EVERY DAY. I DON'T WANT TO LEARN YOU WENT OFF SOMEWHERE TO WORK ON YOUR COPPERTONE TAN.
I'M NOT GOING ANYWHERE.
GOOD. BECAUSE WORD HAS IT, YOUR GREAT SAVIOR DEADPOOL HAD A LITTLE RUN-IN WITH THE PUNISHER SO IT'S REALLY JUST A MATTER OF TIME.
BUT JUST TO MAKE SURE.
PPPPPSSSSTT
OUCH!
YOUR ASS HAS BEEN CHIPPED, CONRAD. I'M GONNA KNOW WHERE YOU'RE AT ALL TIMES. I SO MUCH AS SEE YOU HEADING TOWARD AN AIRPORT--RAILROAD, ANYTHING OUTSIDE OF THE CITY--I'M COMING FOR YOU HARD.
AND TRUST ME, YOU DON'T WANT THAT.

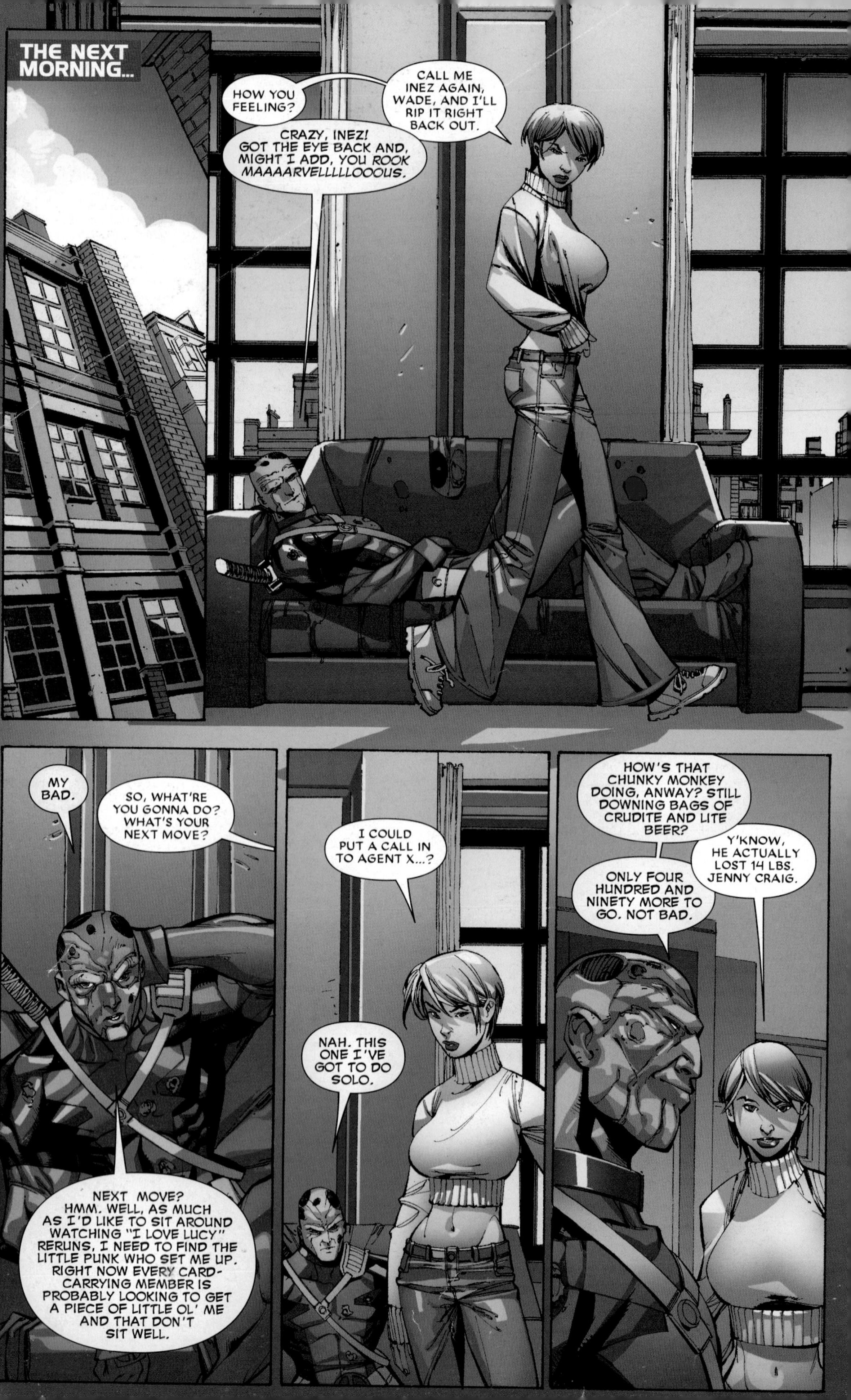
THE NEXT MORNING...
HOW YOU FEELING?
CRAZY, INEZ! GOT THE EYE BACK AND, MIGHT I ADD, YOU ROOK MAAAARVELLLLLOOOUS.
CALL ME INEZ AGAIN, WADE, AND I'LL RIP IT RIGHT BACK OUT.
MY BAD.
SO, WHAT'RE YOU GONNA DO? WHAT'S YOUR NEXT MOVE?
NEXT MOVE? HMM. WELL, AS MUCH AS I'D LIKE TO SIT AROUND WATCHING "I LOVE LUCY" RERUNS, I NEED TO FIND THE LITTLE PUNK WHO SET ME UP. RIGHT NOW EVERY CARD-CARRYING MEMBER IS PROBABLY LOOKING TO GET A PIECE OF LITTLE OL' ME AND THAT DON'T SIT WELL.
I COULD PUT A CALL IN TO AGENT X...?
NAH. THIS ONE I'VE GOT TO DO SOLO.
HOW'S THAT CHUNKY MONKEY DOING, ANWAY? STILL DOWNING BAGS OF CRUDITE AND LITE BEER?
Y'KNOW, HE ACTUALLY LOST 14 LBS. JENNY CRAIG.
ONLY FOUR HUNDRED AND NINETY MORE TO GO. NOT BAD.

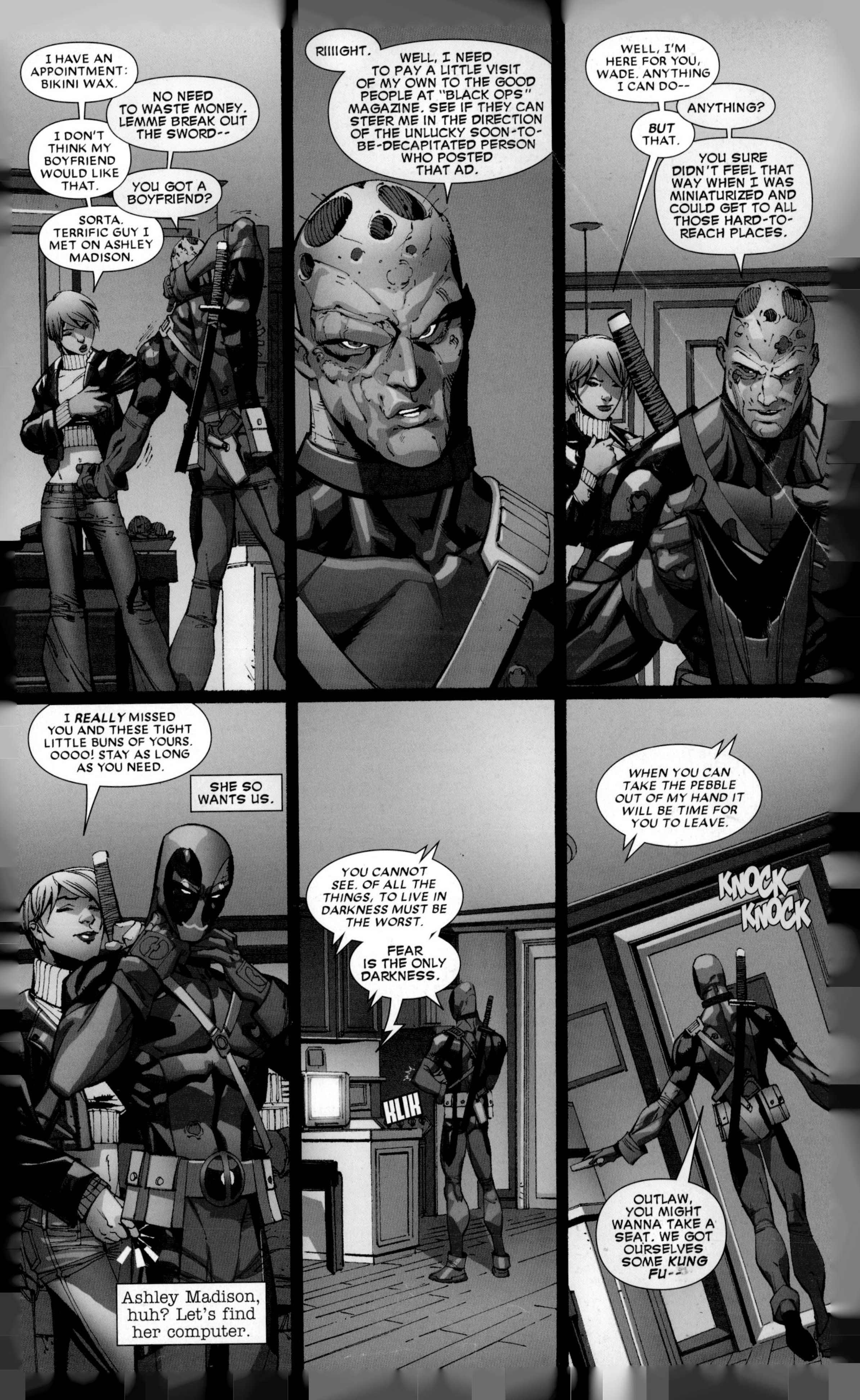
I HAVE AN APPOINTMENT: BIKINI WAX.
NO NEED TO WASTE MONEY. LEMME BREAK OUT THE SWORD--
I DON'T THINK MY BOYFRIEND WOULD LIKE THAT.
YOU GOT A BOYFRIEND?
SORTA. TERRIFIC GUY I MET ON ASHLEY MADISON.
RIIIIGHT.
WELL, I NEED TO PAY A LITTLE VISIT OF MY OWN TO THE GOOD PEOPLE AT "BLACK OPS" MAGAZINE. SEE IF THEY CAN STEER ME IN THE DIRECTION OF THE UNLUCKY SOON-TO-BE-DECAPITATED PERSON WHO POSTED THAT AD.
WELL, I'M HERE FOR YOU, WADE. ANYTHING I CAN DO--
ANYTHING?
BUT THAT.
YOU SURE DIDN'T FEEL THAT WAY WHEN I WAS MINIATURIZED AND COULD GET TO ALL THOSE HARD-TO-REACH PLACES.
I REALLY MISSED YOU AND THESE TIGHT LITTLE BUNS OF YOURS. OOOO! STAY AS LONG AS YOU NEED.
SHE SO WANTS US.
Ashley Madison, huh? Let's find her computer.
YOU CANNOT SEE. OF ALL THE THINGS, TO LIVE IN DARKNESS MUST BE THE WORST.
FEAR IS THE ONLY DARKNESS.
KLIK
WHEN YOU CAN TAKE THE PEBBLE OUT OF MY HAND IT WILL BE TIME FOR YOU TO LEAVE.
KNOCK KNOCK
OUTLAW, YOU MIGHT WANNA TAKE A SEAT. WE GOT OURSELVES SOME KUNG FU--

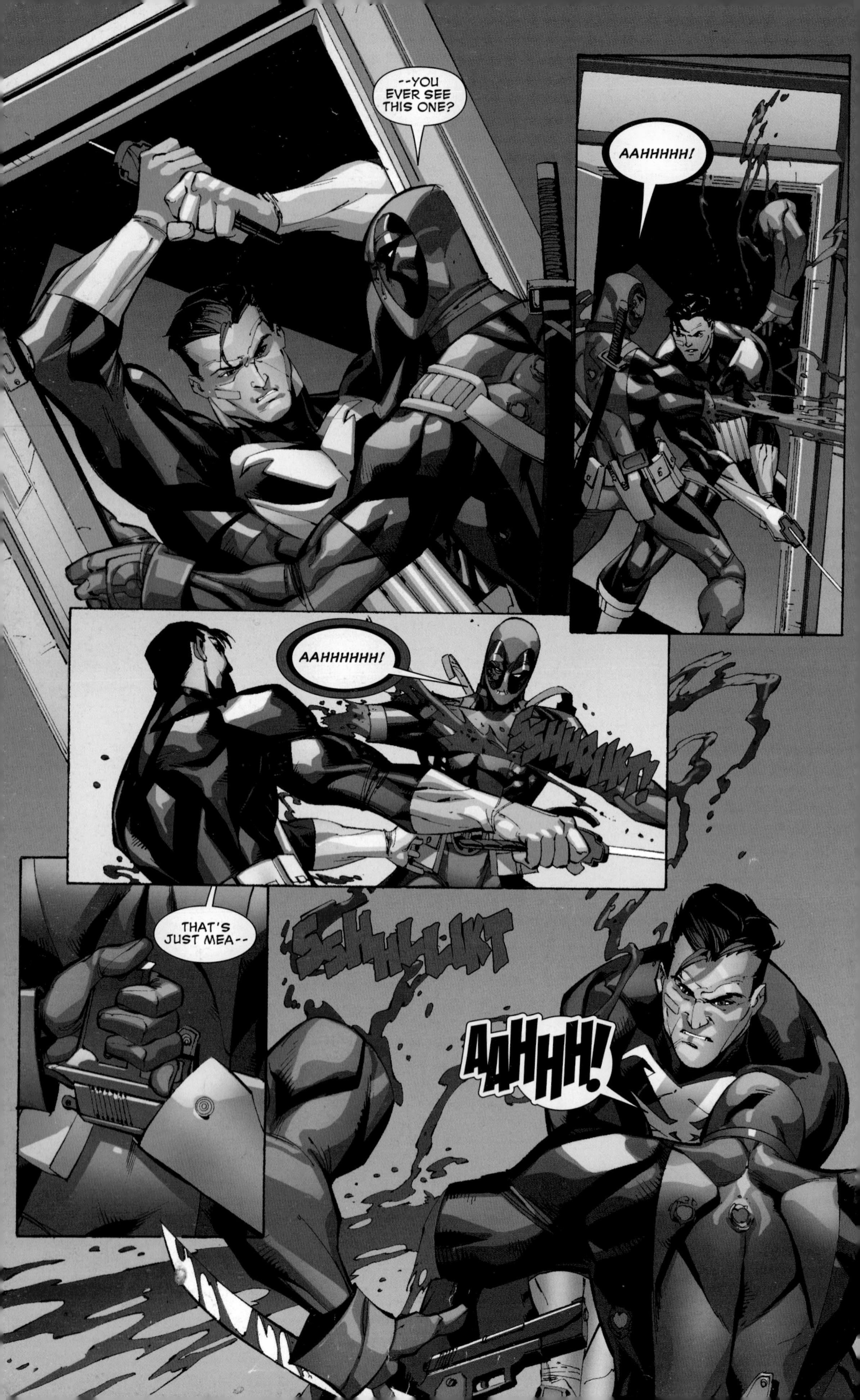
--YOU EVER SEE THIS ONE?
AAHHHHH!
AAHHHHHH!
SSHHRAKT!
THAT'S JUST MEA--
SSHHLLKT
AAHHH!

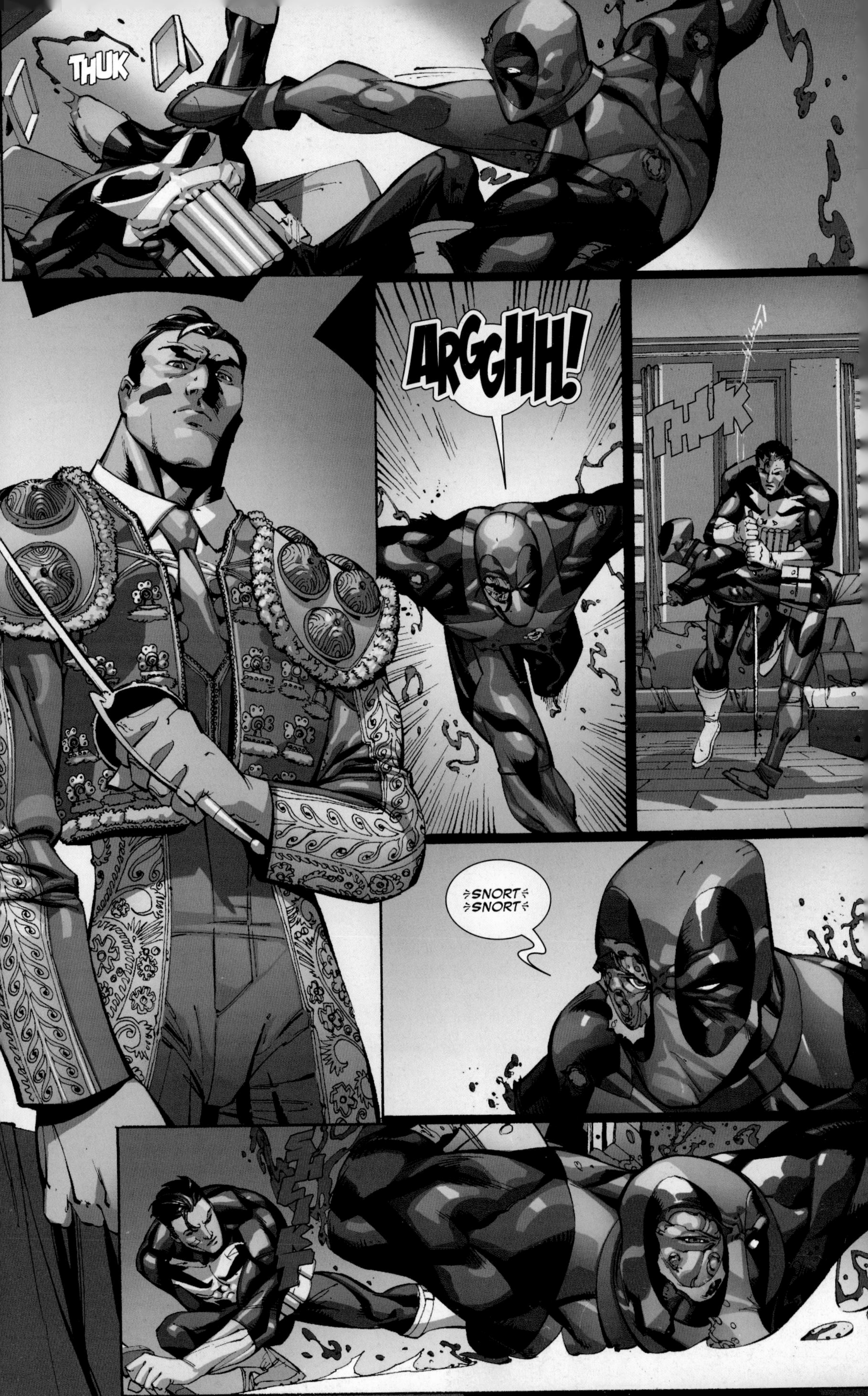
THUK
ARGGHH!
THUK
SNORT SNORT

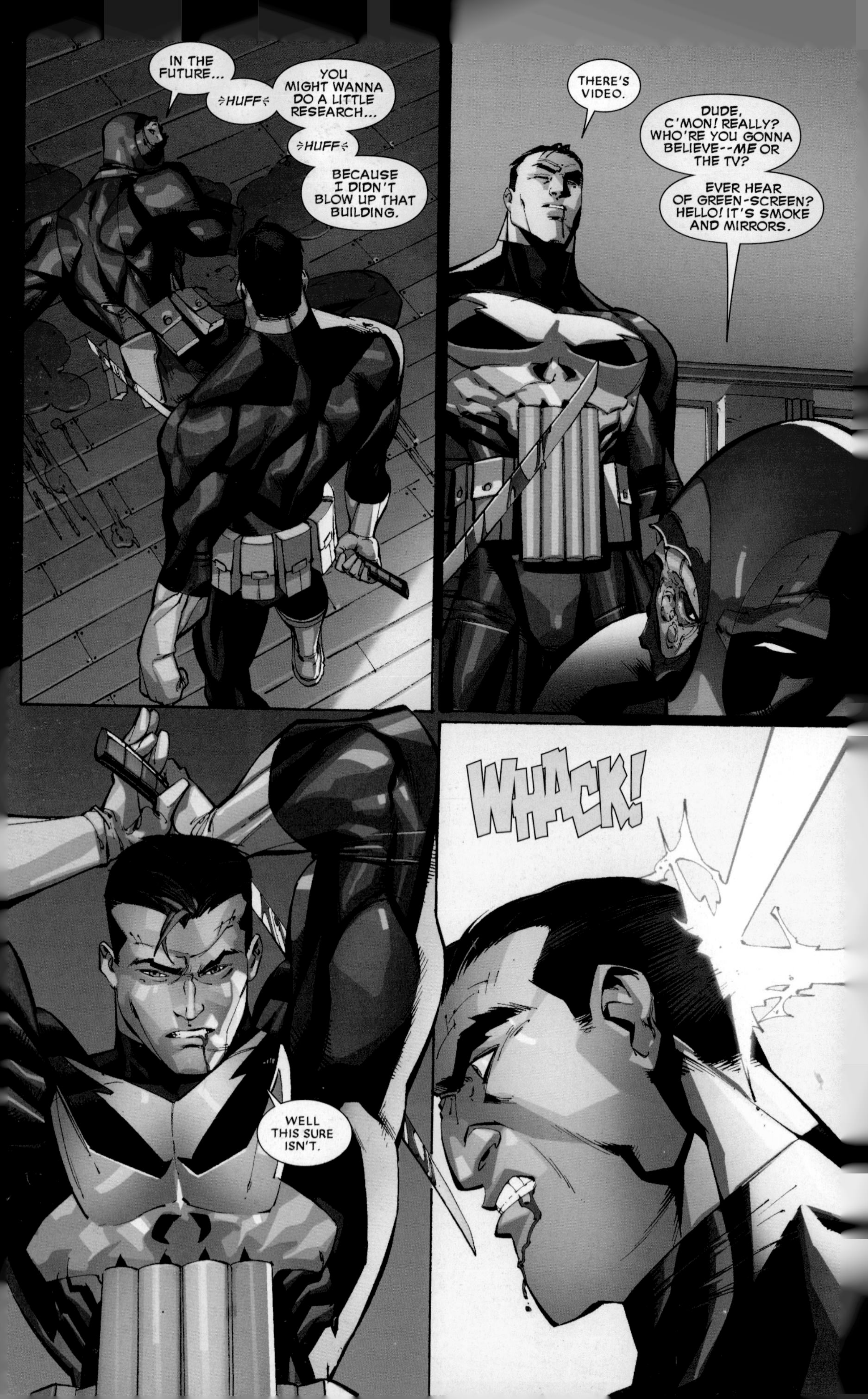
IN THE FUTURE...
HUFF
YOU MIGHT WANNA DO A LITTLE RESEARCH...
HUFF
BECAUSE I DIDN'T BLOW UP THAT BUILDING.
THERE'S VIDEO.
DUDE, C'MON! REALLY? WHO'RE YOU GONNA BELIEVE--ME OR THE TV?
EVER HEAR OF GREEN-SCREEN? HELLO! IT'S SMOKE AND MIRRORS.
WELL THIS SURE ISN'T.
WHACK!

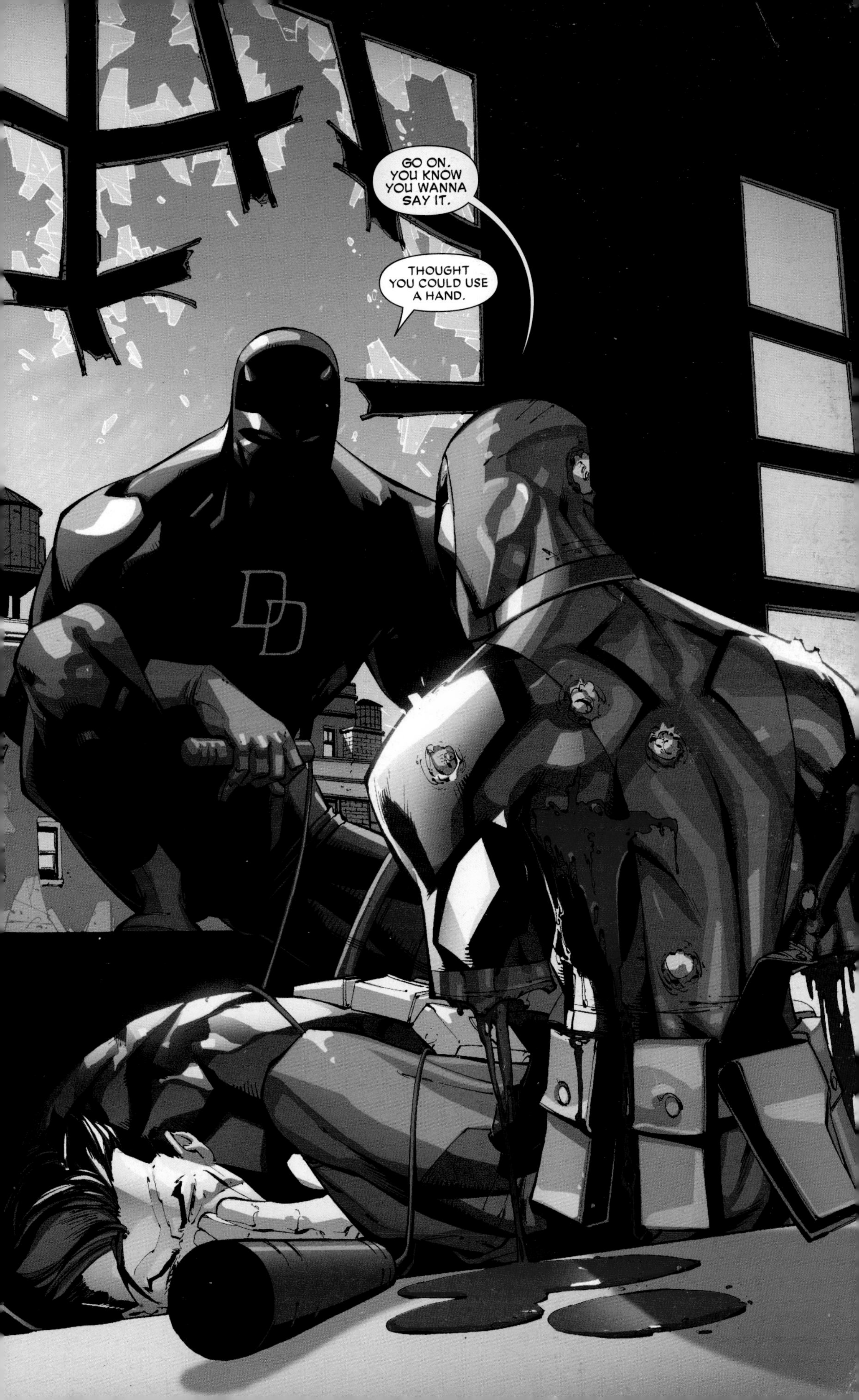
GO ON. YOU KNOW YOU WANNA SAY IT.
THOUGHT YOU COULD USE A HAND.

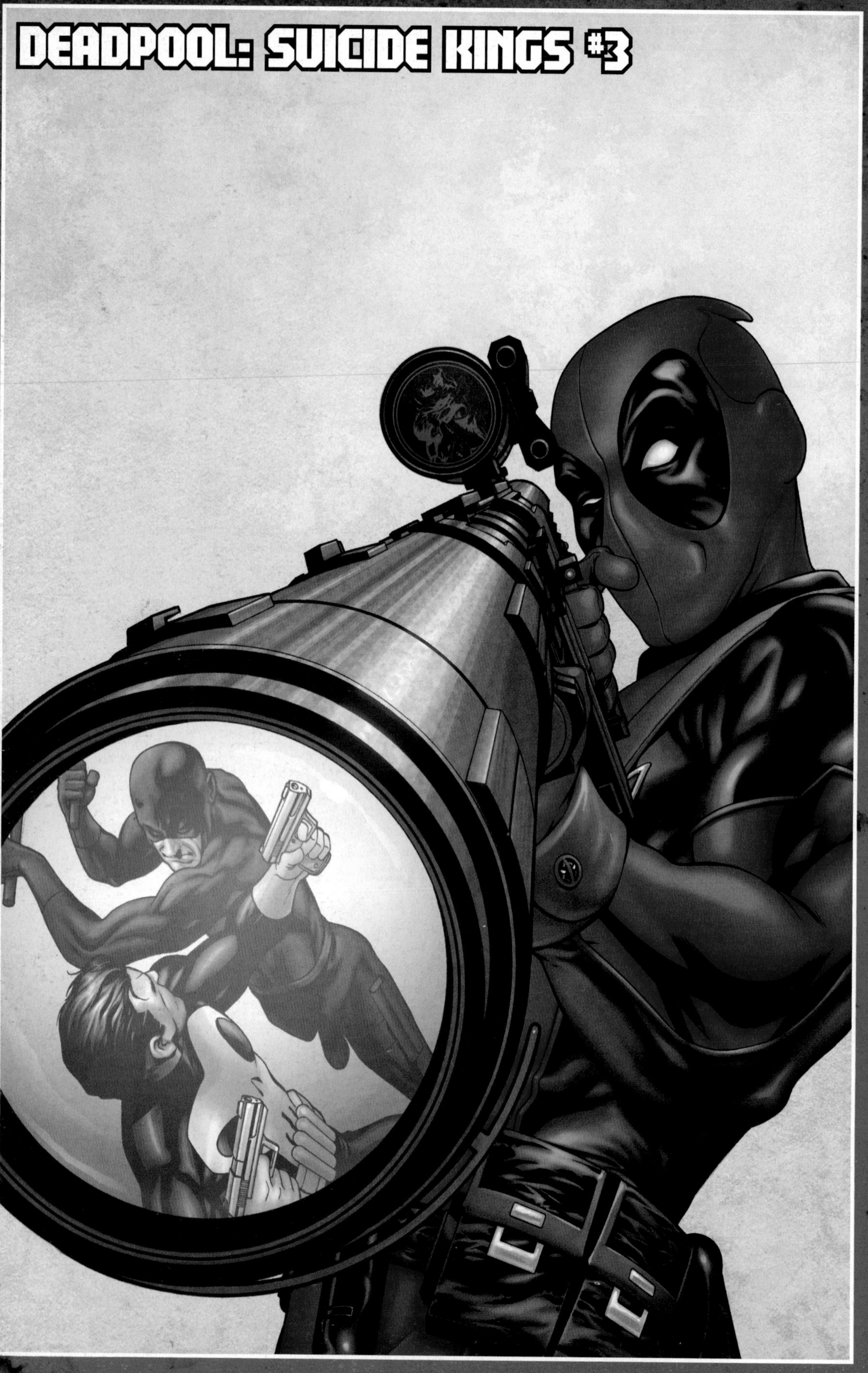
DEADPOOL: SUICIDE KINGS #3

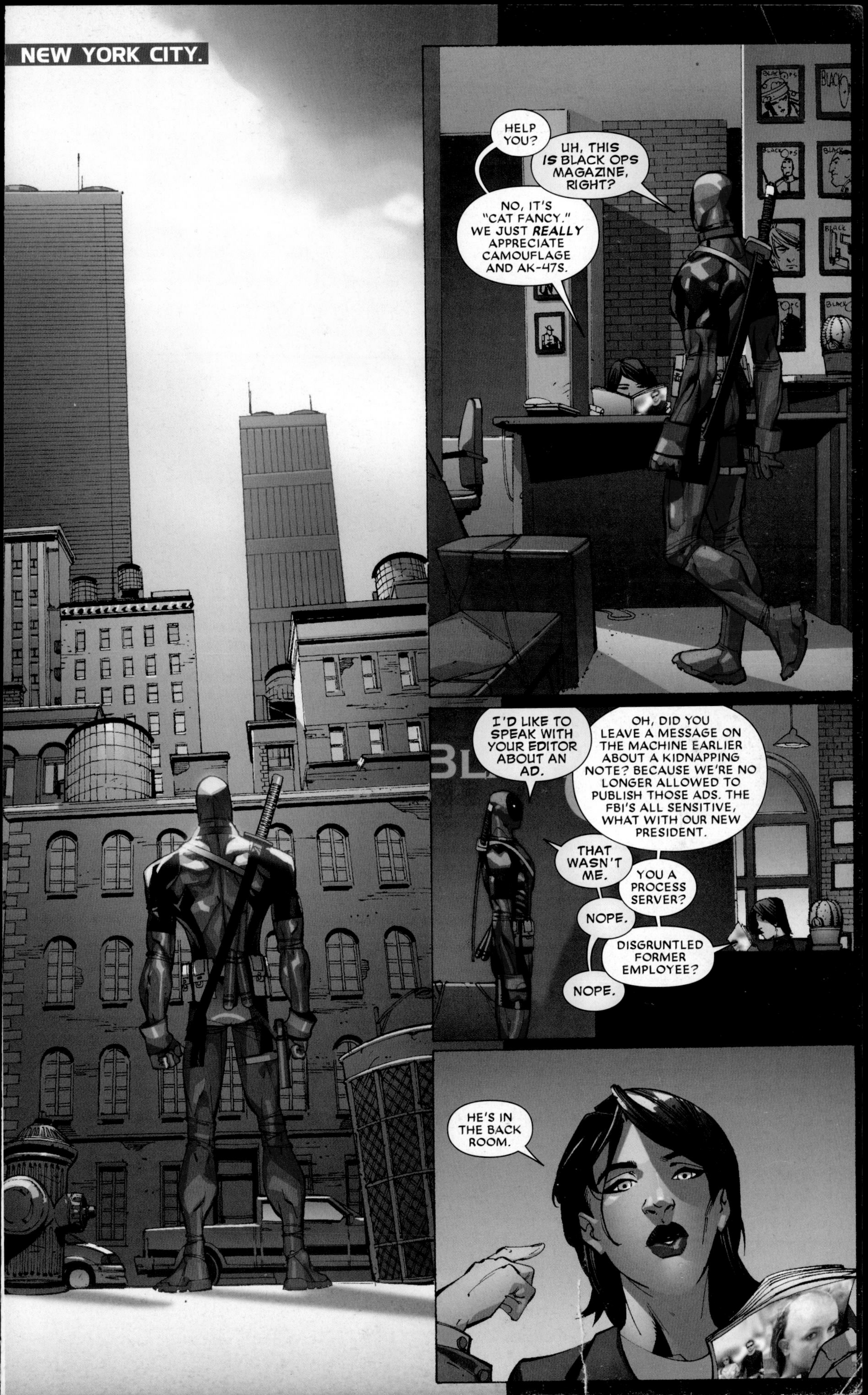
NEW YORK CITY.
HELP YOU?
UH, THIS IS BLACK OPS MAGAZINE, RIGHT?
NO, IT'S "CAT FANCY." WE JUST REALLY APPRECIATE CAMOUFLAGE AND AK-47S.
I'D LIKE TO SPEAK WITH YOUR EDITOR ABOUT AN AD.
OH, DID YOU LEAVE A MESSAGE ON THE MACHINE EARLIER ABOUT A KIDNAPPING NOTE? BECAUSE WE'RE NO LONGER ALLOWED TO PUBLISH THOSE ADS. THE FBI'S ALL SENSITIVE, WHAT WITH OUR NEW PRESIDENT.
THAT WASN'T ME.
YOU A PROCESS SERVER?
NOPE.
DISGRUNTLED FORMER EMPLOYEE?
NOPE.
HE'S IN THE BACK ROOM.

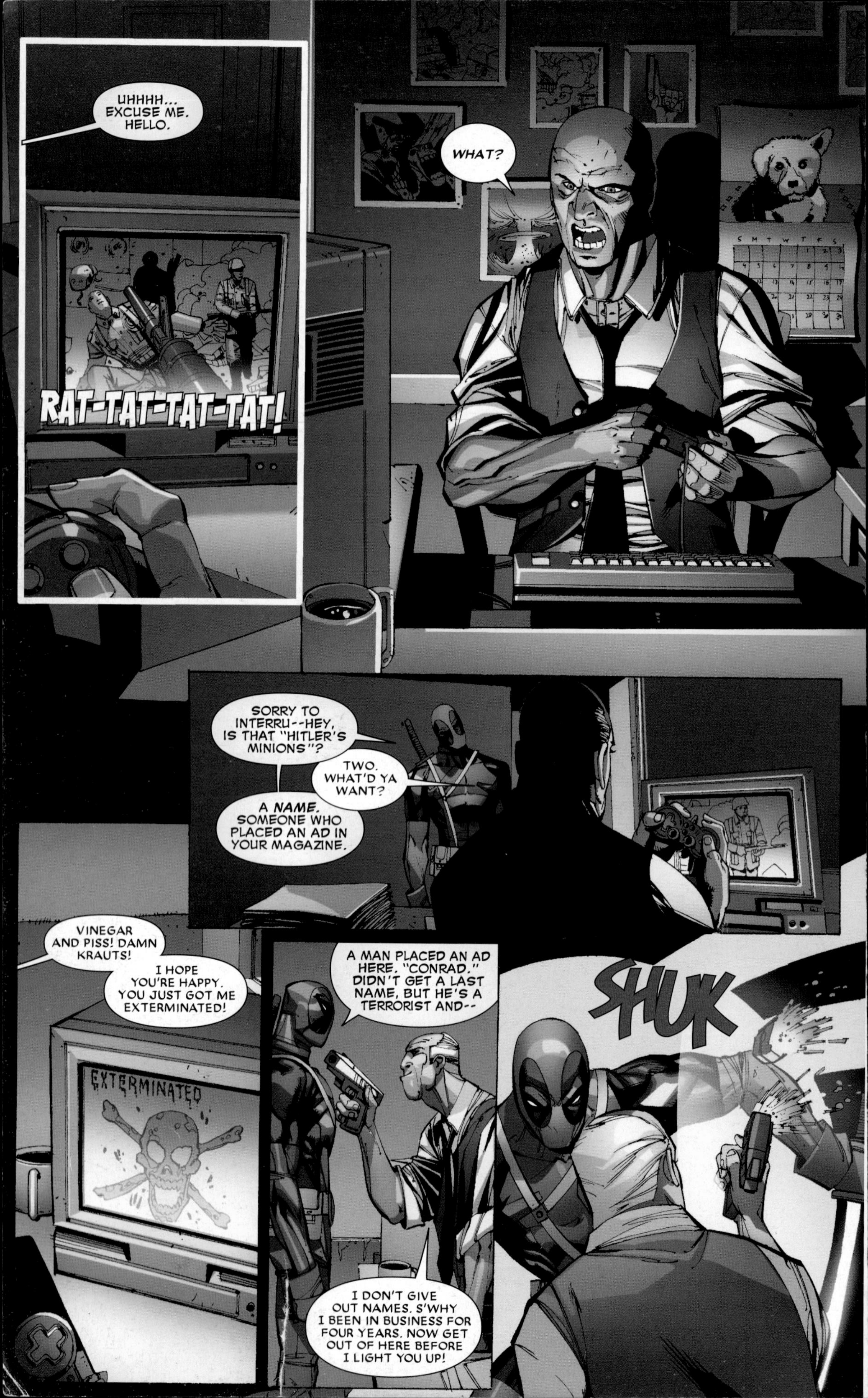
UHHHH... EXCUSE ME. HELLO.
RAT-TAT-TAT-TAT!
WHAT?
SORRY TO INTERRU--HEY, IS THAT "HITLER'S MINIONS"?
TWO. WHAT'D YA WANT?
A NAME. SOMEONE WHO PLACED AN AD IN YOUR MAGAZINE.
VINEGAR AND PISS! DAMN KRAUTS!
I HOPE YOU'RE HAPPY. YOU JUST GOT ME EXTERMINATED!
EXTERMINATED
A MAN PLACED AN AD HERE. "CONRAD." DIDN'T GET A LAST NAME, BUT HE'S A TERRORIST AND--
I DON'T GIVE OUT NAMES. S'WHY I BEEN IN BUSINESS FOR FOUR YEARS. NOW GET OUT OF HERE BEFORE I LIGHT YOU UP!
SHUK

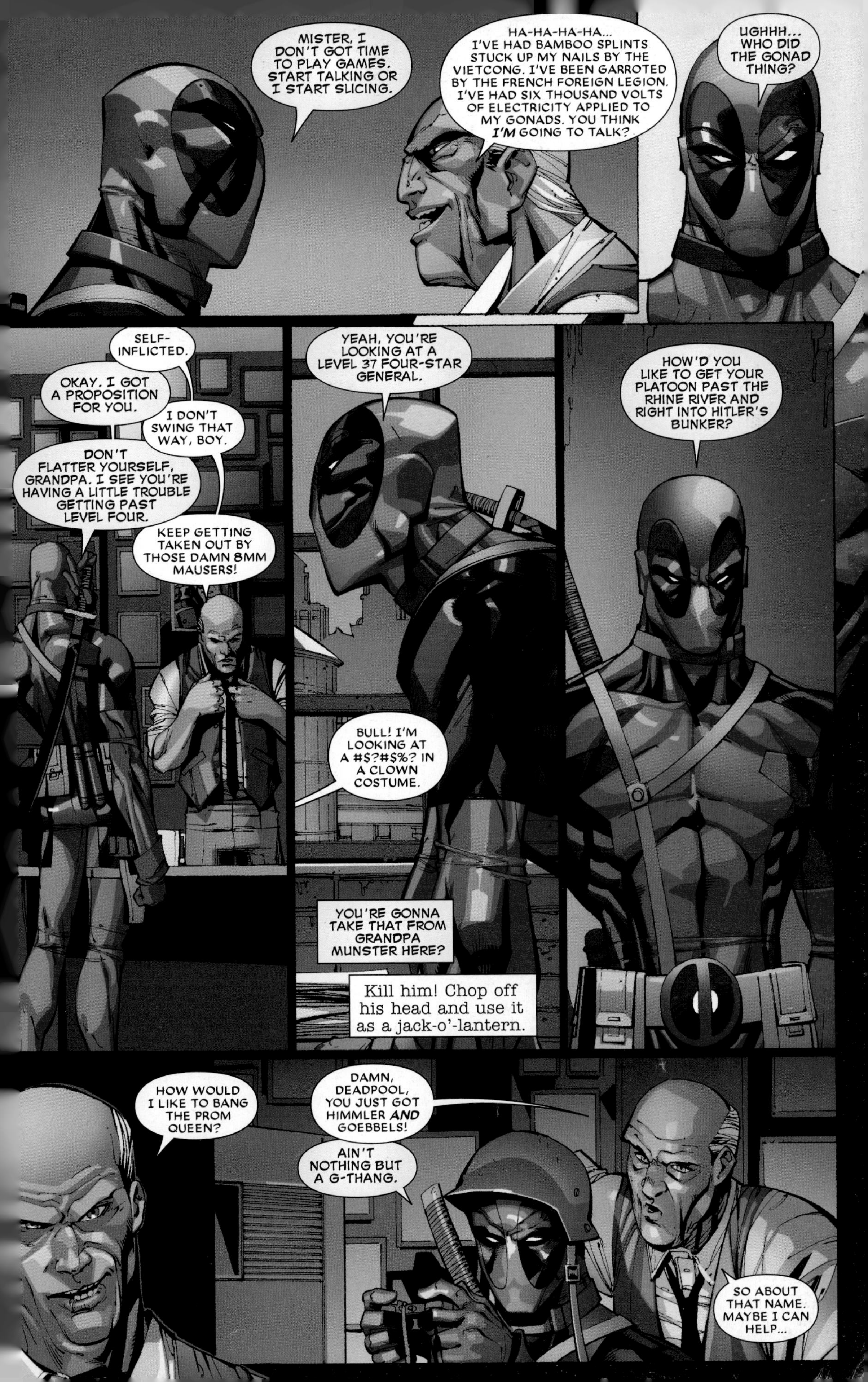

MISTER, I DON'T GOT TIME TO PLAY GAMES. START TALKING OR I START SLICING.
HA-HA-HA-HA... I'VE HAD BAMBOO SPLINTS STUCK UP MY NAILS BY THE VIETCONG. I'VE BEEN GARROTED BY THE FRENCH FOREIGN LEGION. I'VE HAD SIX THOUSAND VOLTS OF ELECTRICITY APPLIED TO MY GONADS. YOU THINK *I'M* GOING TO TALK?
UGHHH... WHO *DID* THE GONAD THING?
SELF-INFLICTED.
OKAY. I GOT A PROPOSITION FOR YOU.
I DON'T SWING THAT WAY, BOY.
DON'T FLATTER YOURSELF, GRANDPA. I SEE YOU'RE HAVING A LITTLE TROUBLE GETTING PAST LEVEL FOUR.
KEEP GETTING TAKEN OUT BY THOSE DAMN 8MM MAUSERS!
YEAH, YOU'RE LOOKING AT A LEVEL 37 FOUR-STAR GENERAL.
BULL! I'M LOOKING AT A #$?#$%? IN A CLOWN COSTUME.
YOU'RE GONNA TAKE THAT FROM GRANDPA MUNSTER HERE?
Kill him! Chop off his head and use it as a jack-o'-lantern.
HOW'D YOU LIKE TO GET YOUR PLATOON PAST THE RHINE RIVER AND RIGHT INTO HITLER'S BUNKER?
HOW WOULD I LIKE TO BANG THE PROM QUEEN?
DAMN, DEADPOOL, YOU JUST GOT HIMMLER *AND* GOEBBELS!
AIN'T NOTHING BUT A G-THANG.
SO ABOUT THAT NAME. MAYBE I CAN HELP...

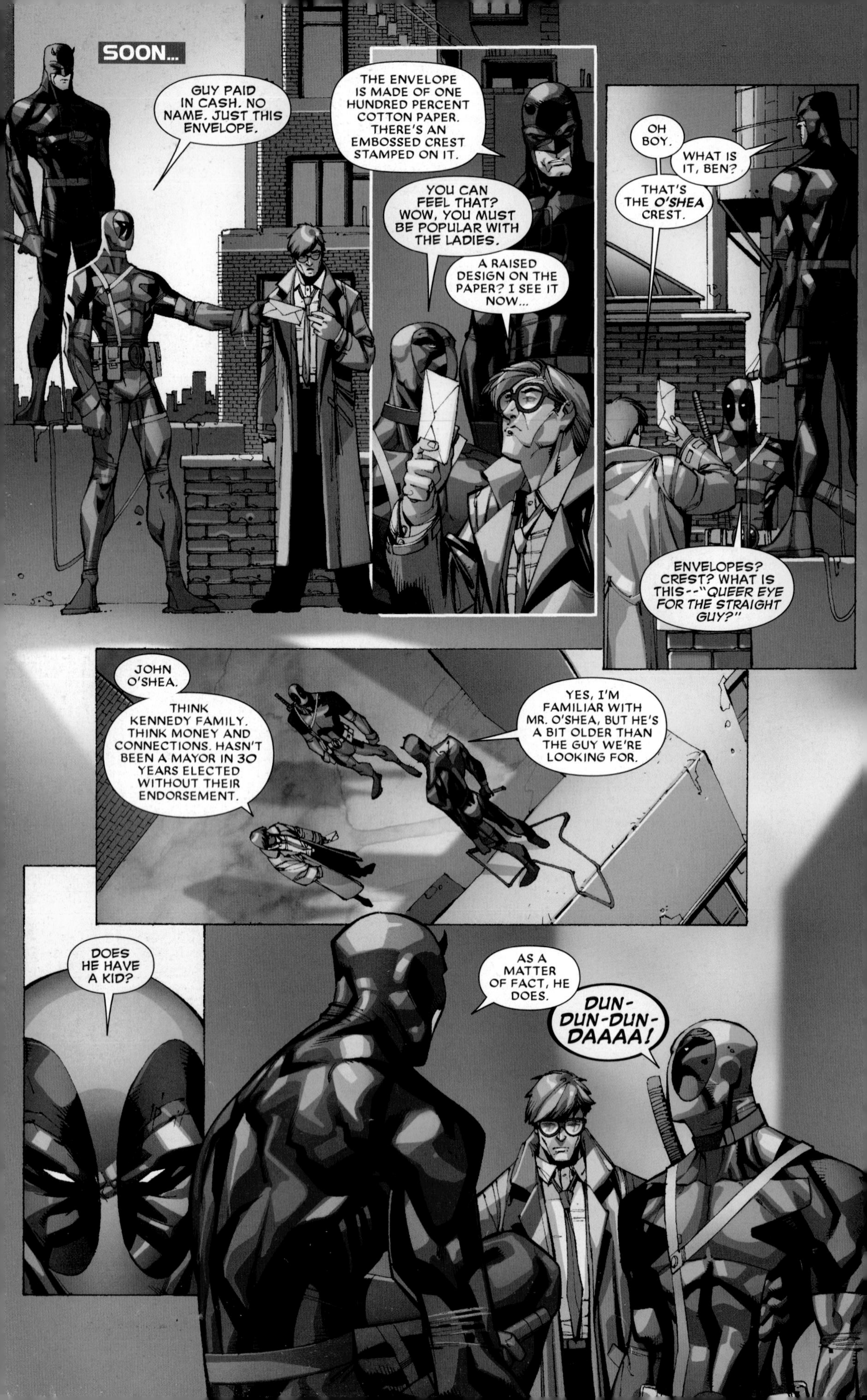
SOON...
GUY PAID IN CASH. NO NAME. JUST THIS ENVELOPE.
THE ENVELOPE IS MADE OF ONE HUNDRED PERCENT COTTON PAPER. THERE'S AN EMBOSSED CREST STAMPED ON IT.
YOU CAN FEEL THAT? WOW, YOU MUST BE POPULAR WITH THE LADIES.
A RAISED DESIGN ON THE PAPER? I SEE IT NOW...
OH BOY.
WHAT IS IT, BEN?
THAT'S THE O'SHEA CREST.
ENVELOPES? CREST? WHAT IS THIS--"QUEER EYE FOR THE STRAIGHT GUY?"
JOHN O'SHEA.
THINK KENNEDY FAMILY. THINK MONEY AND CONNECTIONS. HASN'T BEEN A MAYOR IN 30 YEARS ELECTED WITHOUT THEIR ENDORSEMENT.
YES, I'M FAMILIAR WITH MR. O'SHEA, BUT HE'S A BIT OLDER THAN THE GUY WE'RE LOOKING FOR.
DOES HE HAVE A KID?
AS A MATTER OF FACT, HE DOES.
DUN-DUN-DUN-DAAAA!

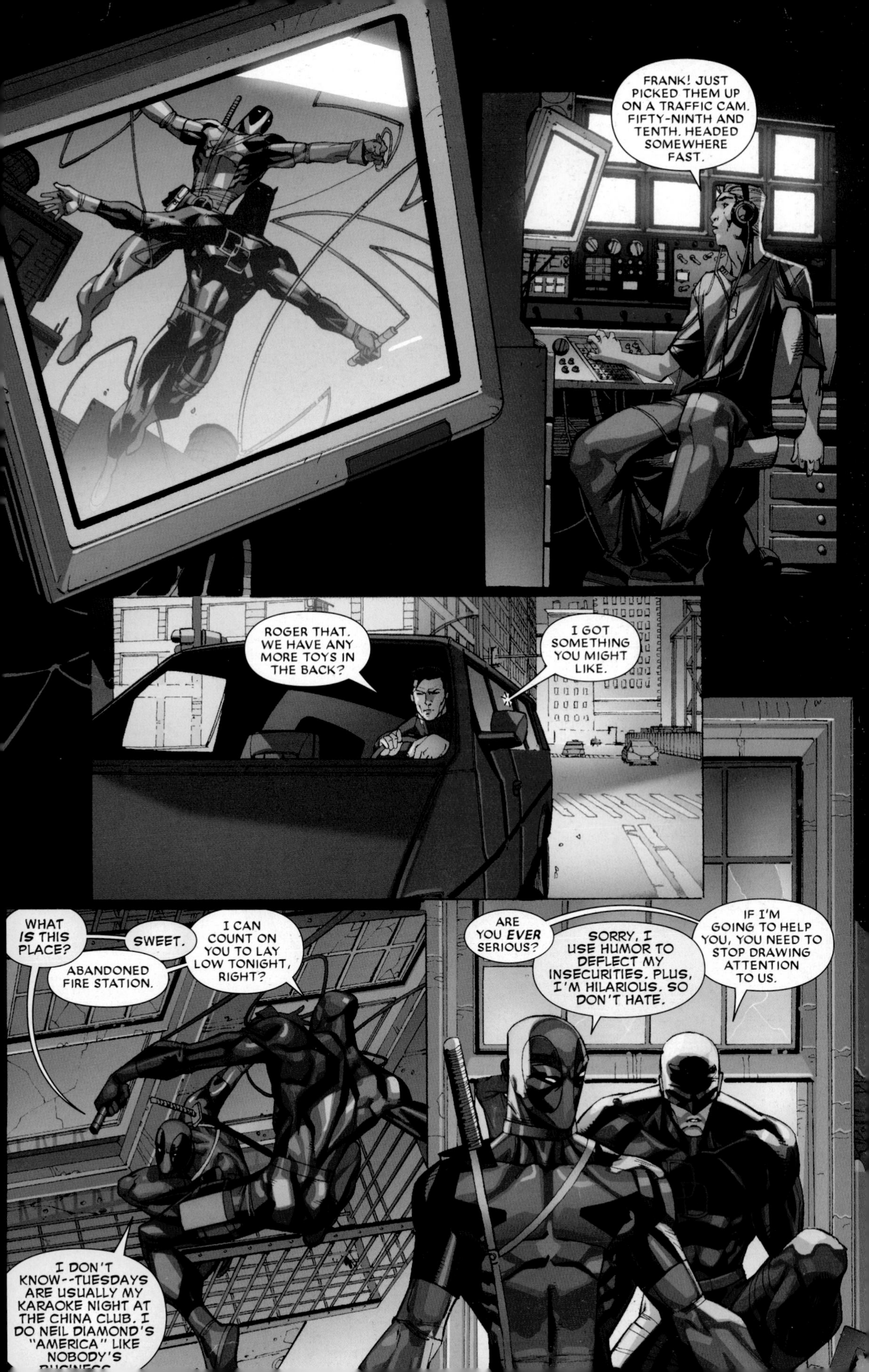
FRANK! JUST PICKED THEM UP ON A TRAFFIC CAM. FIFTY-NINTH AND TENTH. HEADED SOMEWHERE FAST.
ROGER THAT. WE HAVE ANY MORE TOYS IN THE BACK?
I GOT SOMETHING YOU MIGHT LIKE.
WHAT IS THIS PLACE?
ABANDONED FIRE STATION.
SWEET.
I CAN COUNT ON YOU TO LAY LOW TONIGHT, RIGHT?
I DON'T KNOW--TUESDAYS ARE USUALLY MY KARAOKE NIGHT AT THE CHINA CLUB. I DO NEIL DIAMOND'S "AMERICA" LIKE NOBODY'S
ARE YOU EVER SERIOUS?
SORRY, I USE HUMOR TO DEFLECT MY INSECURITIES. PLUS, I'M HILARIOUS. SO DON'T HATE.
IF I'M GOING TO HELP YOU, YOU NEED TO STOP DRAWING ATTENTION TO US.

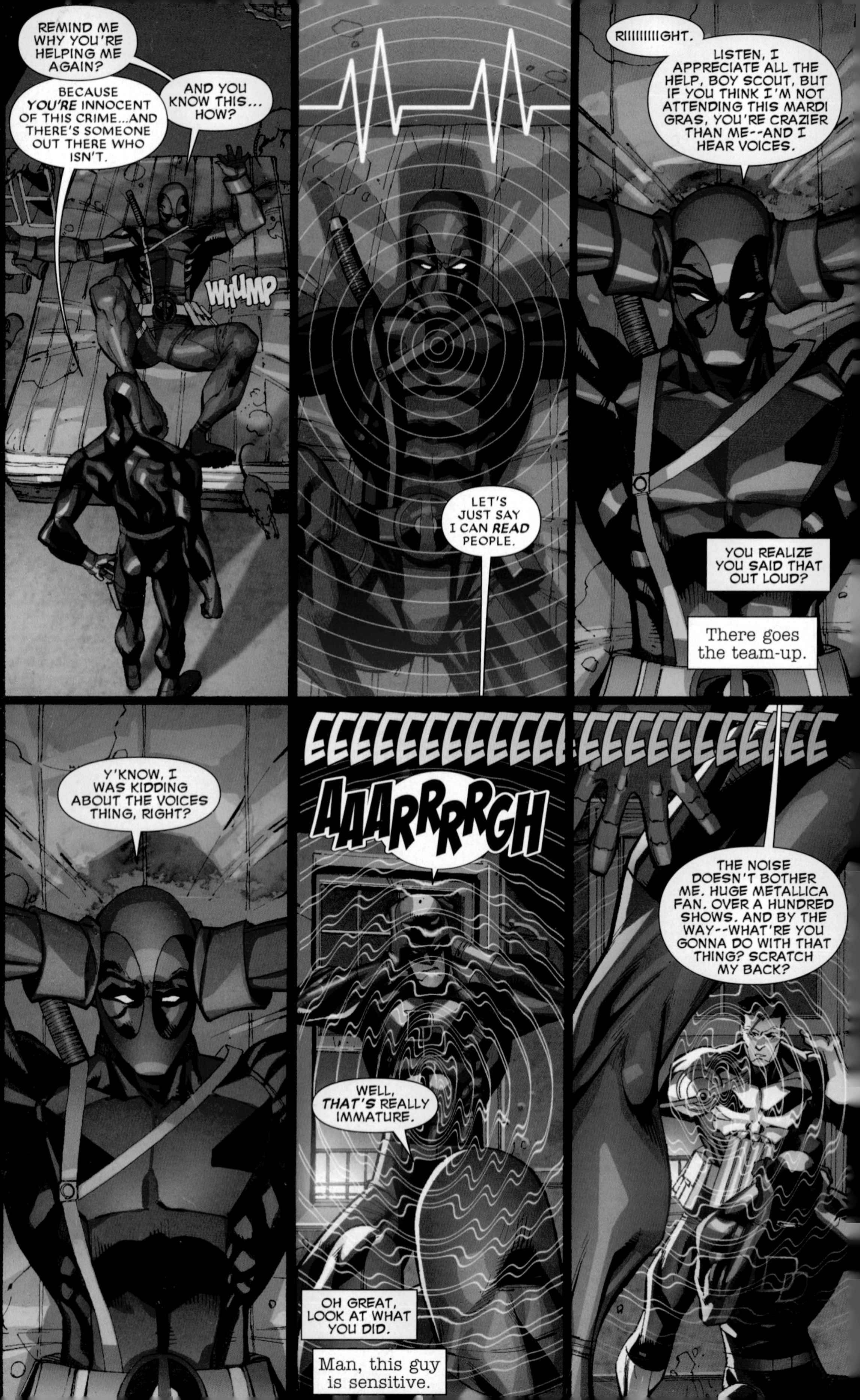

REMIND ME WHY YOU'RE HELPING ME AGAIN?
BECAUSE YOU'RE INNOCENT OF THIS CRIME...AND THERE'S SOMEONE OUT THERE WHO ISN'T.
AND YOU KNOW THIS... HOW?
WHUMP
LET'S JUST SAY I CAN READ PEOPLE.
RIIIIIIIIIGHT.
LISTEN, I APPRECIATE ALL THE HELP, BOY SCOUT, BUT IF YOU THINK I'M NOT ATTENDING THIS MARDI GRAS, YOU'RE CRAZIER THAN ME--AND I HEAR VOICES.
YOU REALIZE YOU SAID THAT OUT LOUD?
There goes the team-up.
Y'KNOW, I WAS KIDDING ABOUT THE VOICES THING, RIGHT?
EEEEEEEEEEEEEEEEEEEEEEEEEEEE
AAARRRRGH
WELL, THAT'S REALLY IMMATURE.
OH GREAT, LOOK AT WHAT YOU DID.
Man, this guy is sensitive.
THE NOISE DOESN'T BOTHER ME. HUGE METALLICA FAN. OVER A HUNDRED SHOWS. AND BY THE WAY--WHAT'RE YOU GONNA DO WITH THAT THING? SCRATCH MY BACK?

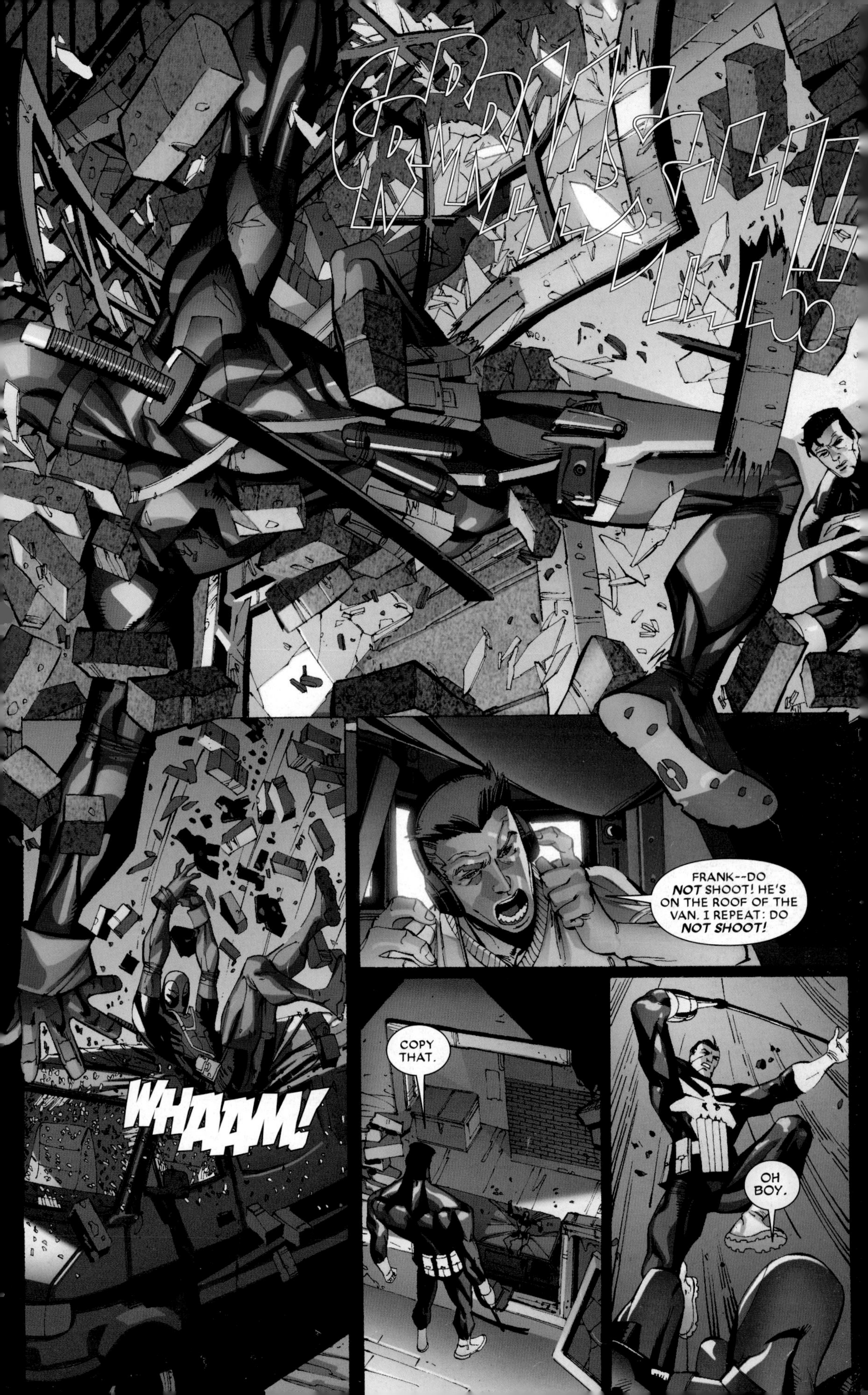
WHAAM!
FRANK--DO NOT SHOOT! HE'S ON THE ROOF OF THE VAN. I REPEAT: DO NOT SHOOT!
COPY THAT.
OH BOY.

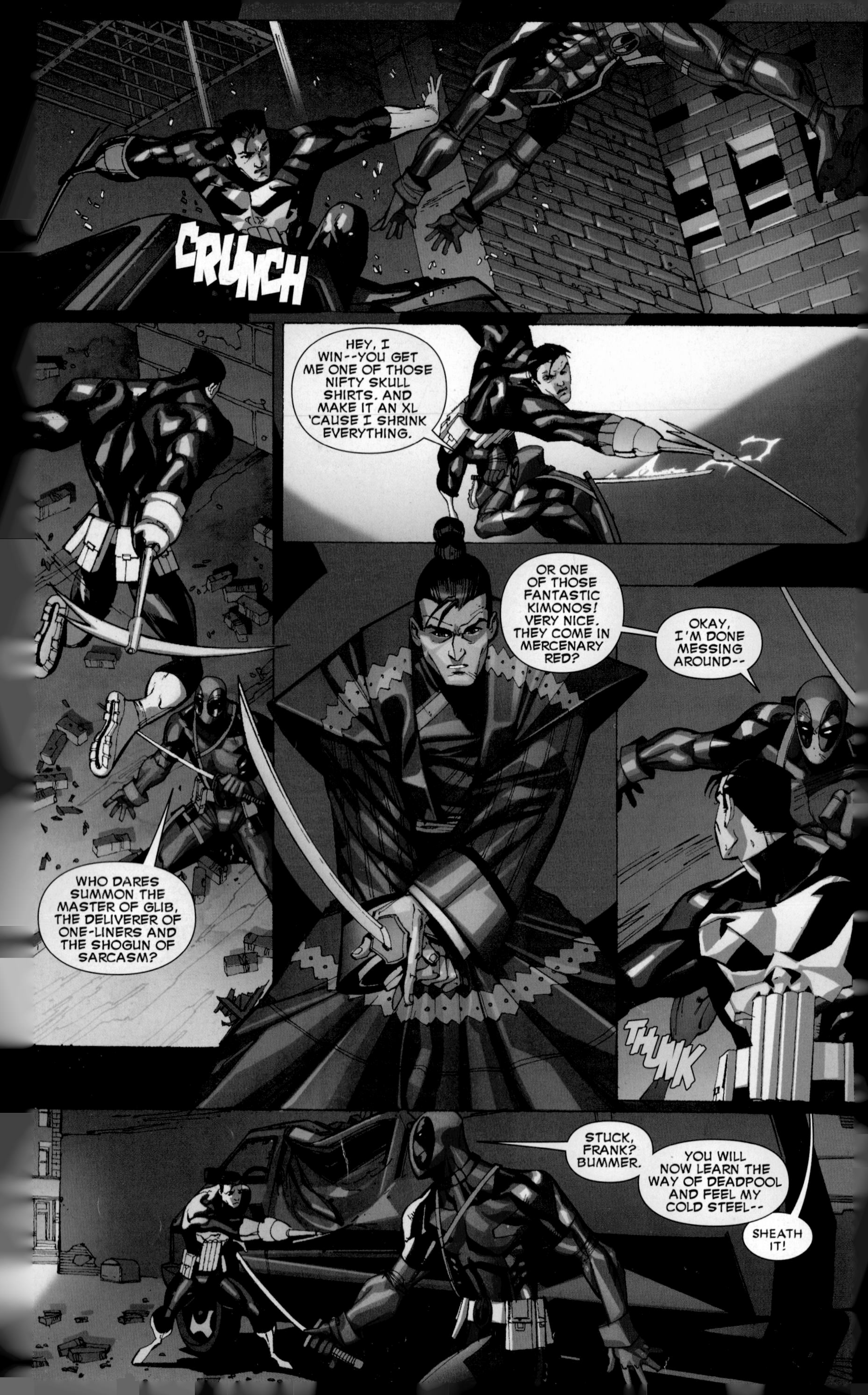
CRUNCH
HEY, I WIN--YOU GET ME ONE OF THOSE NIFTY SKULL SHIRTS. AND MAKE IT AN XL 'CAUSE I SHRINK EVERYTHING.
WHO DARES SUMMON THE MASTER OF GLIB, THE DELIVERER OF ONE-LINERS AND THE SHOGUN OF SARCASM?
OR ONE OF THOSE FANTASTIC KIMONOS! VERY NICE. THEY COME IN MERCENARY RED?
OKAY, I'M DONE MESSING AROUND--
THUNK
STUCK, FRANK? BUMMER.
YOU WILL NOW LEARN THE WAY OF DEADPOOL AND FEEL MY COLD STEEL--
SHEATH IT!

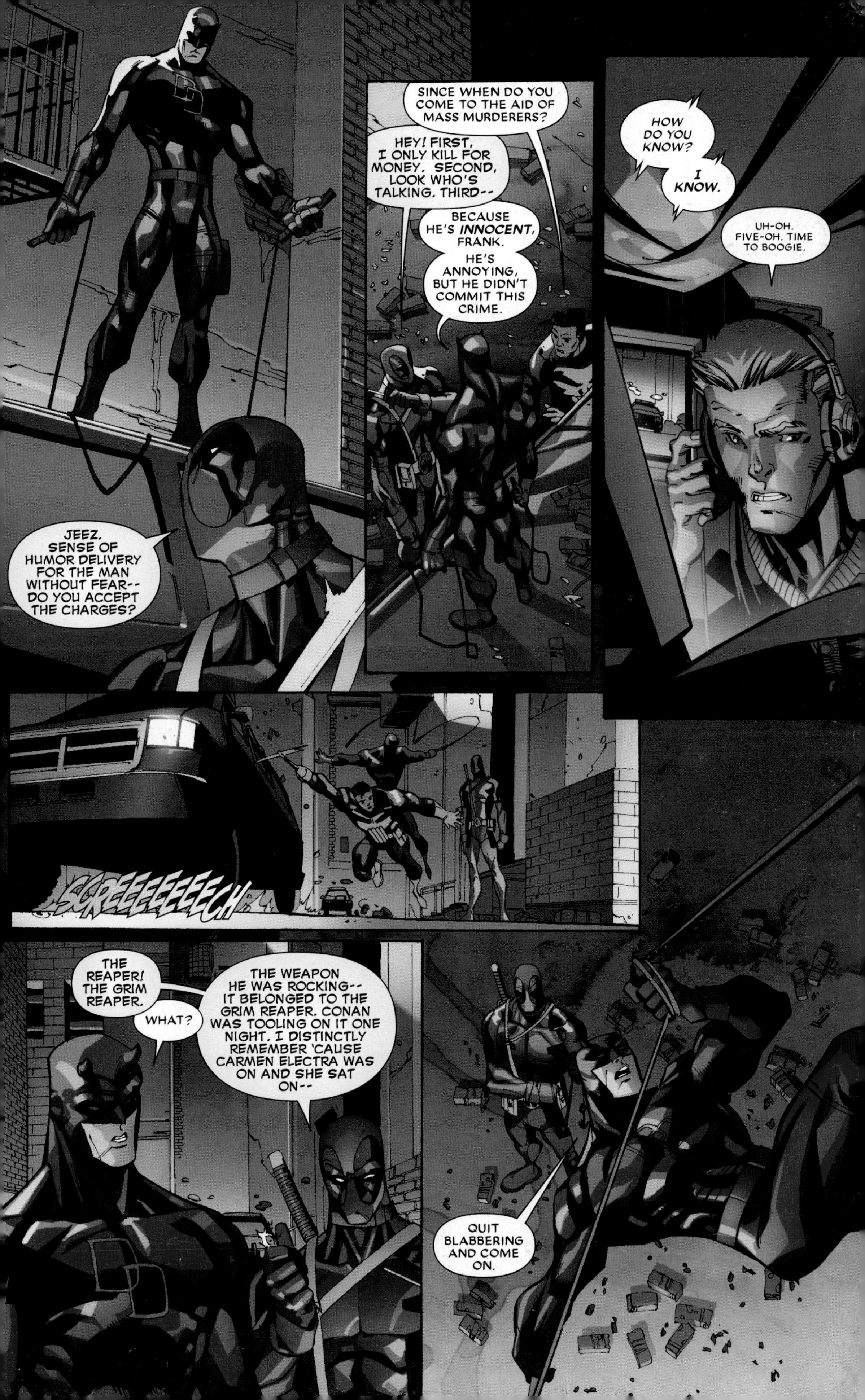
JEEZ. SENSE OF HUMOR DELIVERY FOR THE MAN WITHOUT FEAR-- DO YOU ACCEPT THE CHARGES?
SINCE WHEN DO YOU COME TO THE AID OF MASS MURDERERS?
HEY! FIRST, I ONLY KILL FOR MONEY. SECOND, LOOK WHO'S TALKING. THIRD--
BECAUSE HE'S INNOCENT, FRANK.
HE'S ANNOYING, BUT HE DIDN'T COMMIT THIS CRIME.
HOW DO YOU KNOW?
I KNOW.
UH-OH. FIVE-OH. TIME TO BOOGIE.
SCREEEEEEEECH
THE REAPER! THE GRIM REAPER.
WHAT?
THE WEAPON HE WAS ROCKING-- IT BELONGED TO THE GRIM REAPER. CONAN WAS TOOLING ON IT ONE NIGHT. I DISTINCTLY REMEMBER 'CAUSE CARMEN ELECTRA WAS ON AND SHE SAT ON--
QUIT BLABBERING AND COME ON.

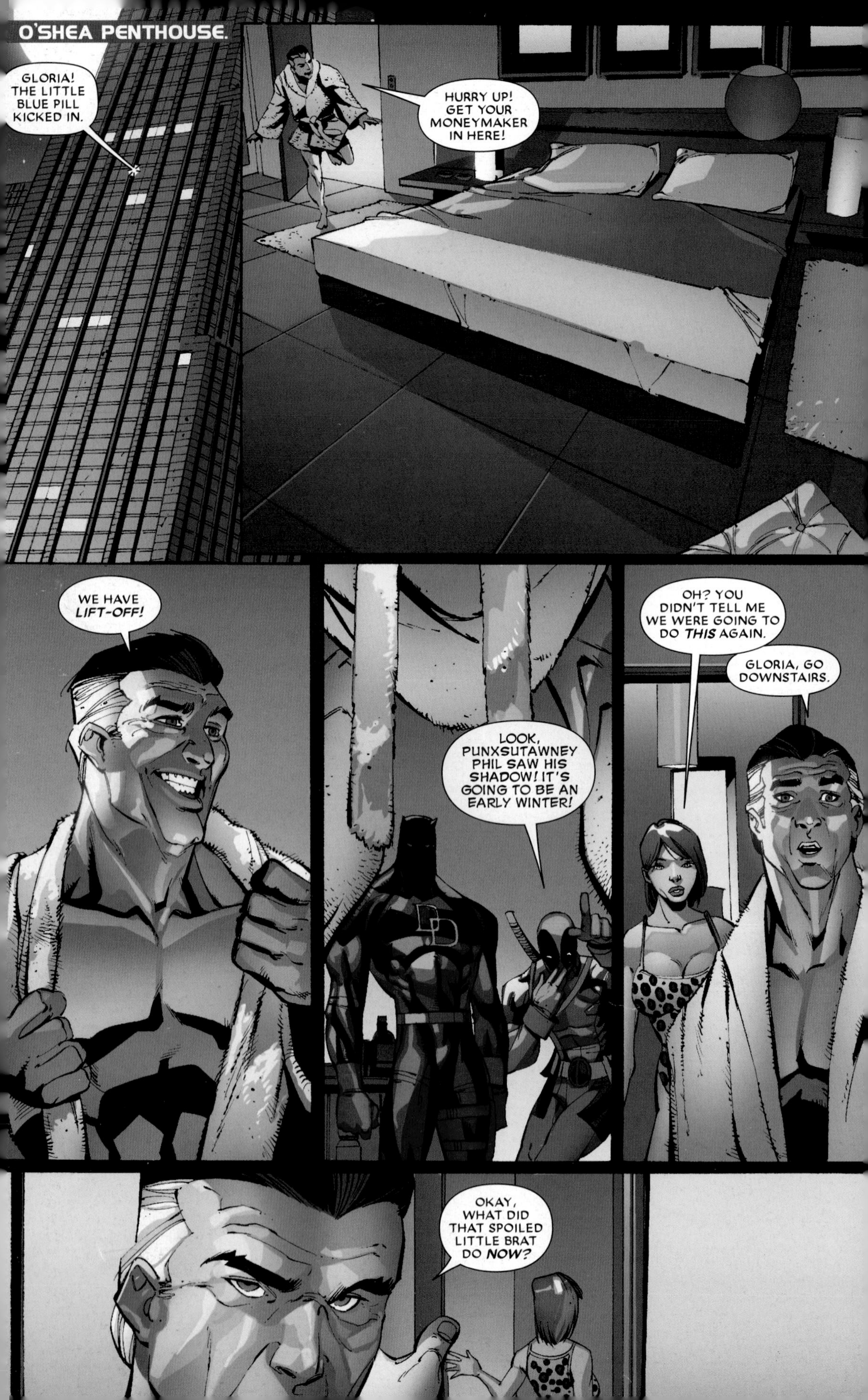
O'SHEA PENTHOUSE.
GLORIA! THE LITTLE BLUE PILL KICKED IN.
HURRY UP! GET YOUR MONEYMAKER IN HERE!
WE HAVE *LIFT-OFF!*
LOOK, PUNXSUTAWNEY PHIL SAW HIS *SHADOW!* IT'S GOING TO BE AN EARLY WINTER!
OH? YOU DIDN'T TELL ME WE WERE GOING TO DO *THIS* AGAIN.
GLORIA, GO DOWNSTAIRS.
OKAY, WHAT DID THAT SPOILED LITTLE BRAT DO *NOW?*

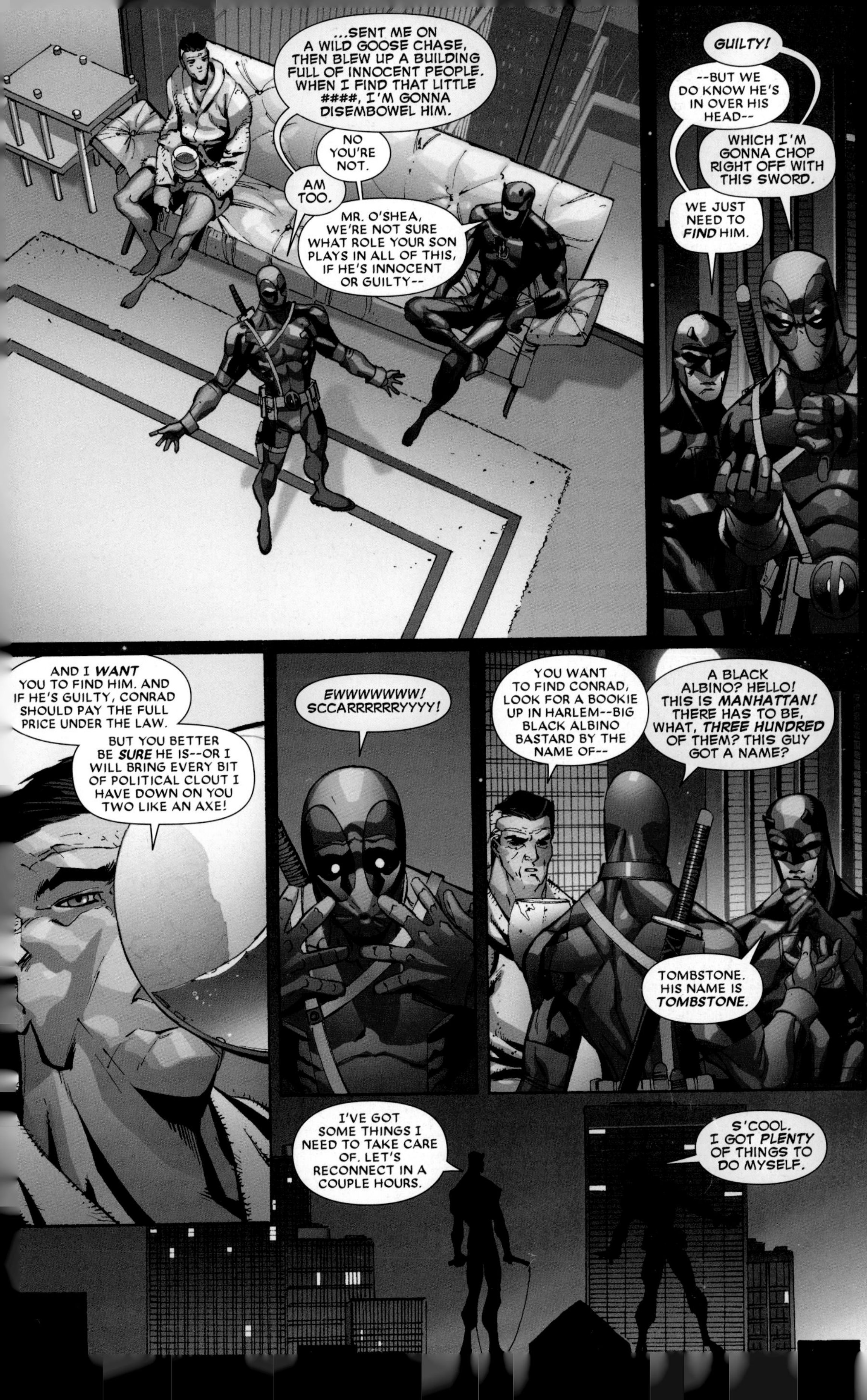
...SENT ME ON A WILD GOOSE CHASE, THEN BLEW UP A BUILDING FULL OF INNOCENT PEOPLE. WHEN I FIND THAT LITTLE ####, I'M GONNA DISEMBOWEL HIM.
NO YOU'RE NOT.
AM TOO.
MR. O'SHEA, WE'RE NOT SURE WHAT ROLE YOUR SON PLAYS IN ALL OF THIS, IF HE'S INNOCENT OR GUILTY--
GUILTY!
--BUT WE DO KNOW HE'S IN OVER HIS HEAD--
WHICH I'M GONNA CHOP RIGHT OFF WITH THIS SWORD.
WE JUST NEED TO FIND HIM.
AND I WANT YOU TO FIND HIM. AND IF HE'S GUILTY, CONRAD SHOULD PAY THE FULL PRICE UNDER THE LAW.
BUT YOU BETTER BE SURE HE IS--OR I WILL BRING EVERY BIT OF POLITICAL CLOUT I HAVE DOWN ON YOU TWO LIKE AN AXE!
EWWWWWWW! SCCARRRRRRYYYY!
YOU WANT TO FIND CONRAD, LOOK FOR A BOOKIE UP IN HARLEM--BIG BLACK ALBINO BASTARD BY THE NAME OF--
A BLACK ALBINO? HELLO! THIS IS MANHATTAN! THERE HAS TO BE, WHAT, THREE HUNDRED OF THEM? THIS GUY GOT A NAME?
TOMBSTONE. HIS NAME IS TOMBSTONE.
I'VE GOT SOME THINGS I NEED TO TAKE CARE OF. LET'S RECONNECT IN A COUPLE HOURS.
S'COOL. I GOT PLENTY OF THINGS TO DO MYSELF.

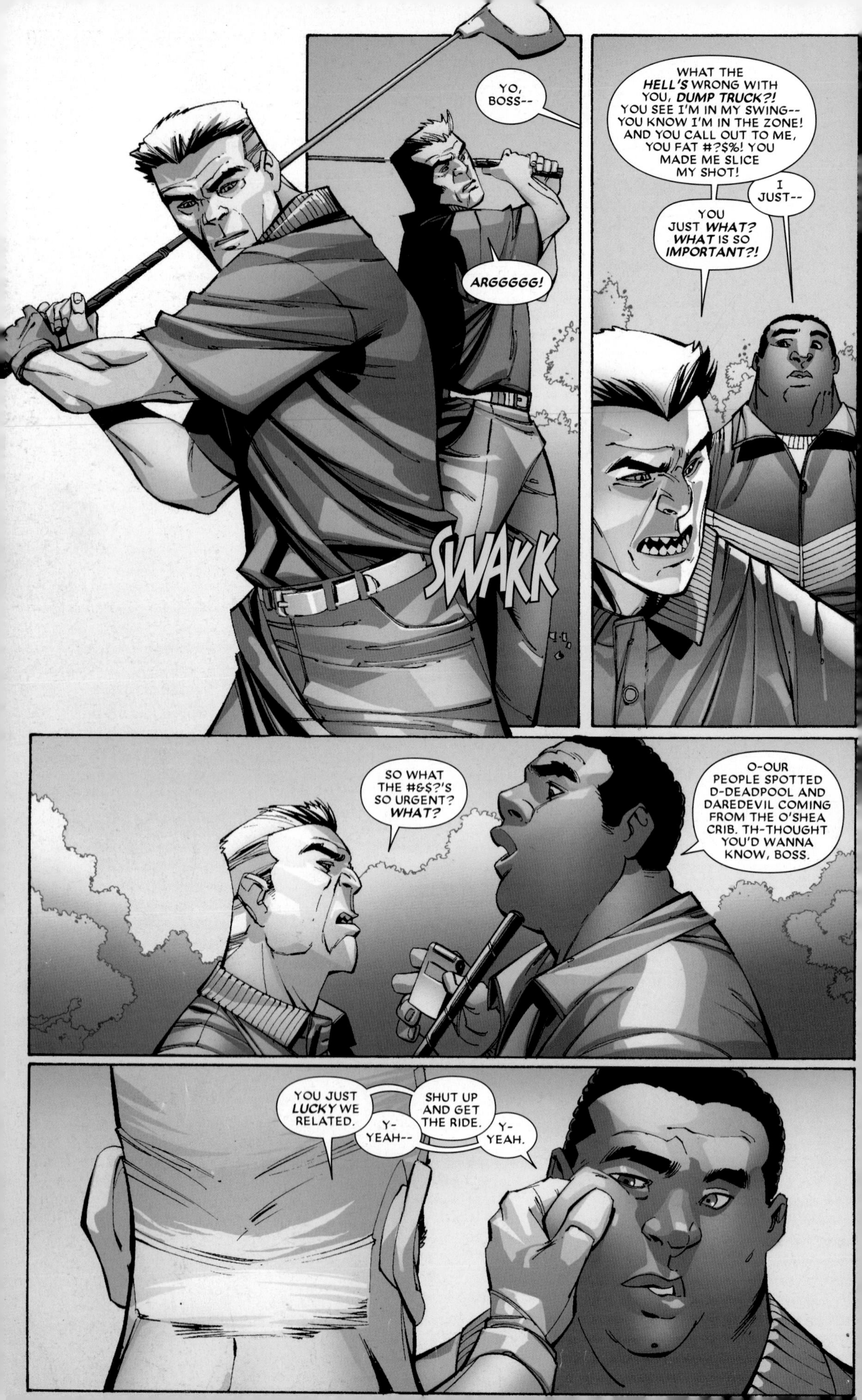
YO, BOSS--
ARGGGGG!
SWAKK
WHAT THE HELL'S WRONG WITH YOU, DUMP TRUCK?! YOU SEE I'M IN MY SWING-- YOU KNOW I'M IN THE ZONE! AND YOU CALL OUT TO ME, YOU FAT #?$%! YOU MADE ME SLICE MY SHOT!
I JUST--
YOU JUST WHAT? WHAT IS SO IMPORTANT?!
SO WHAT THE #&$?'S SO URGENT? WHAT?
O-OUR PEOPLE SPOTTED D-DEADPOOL AND DAREDEVIL COMING FROM THE O'SHEA CRIB. TH-THOUGHT YOU'D WANNA KNOW, BOSS.
YOU JUST LUCKY WE RELATED.
Y-YEAH--
SHUT UP AND GET THE RIDE.
Y-YEAH.

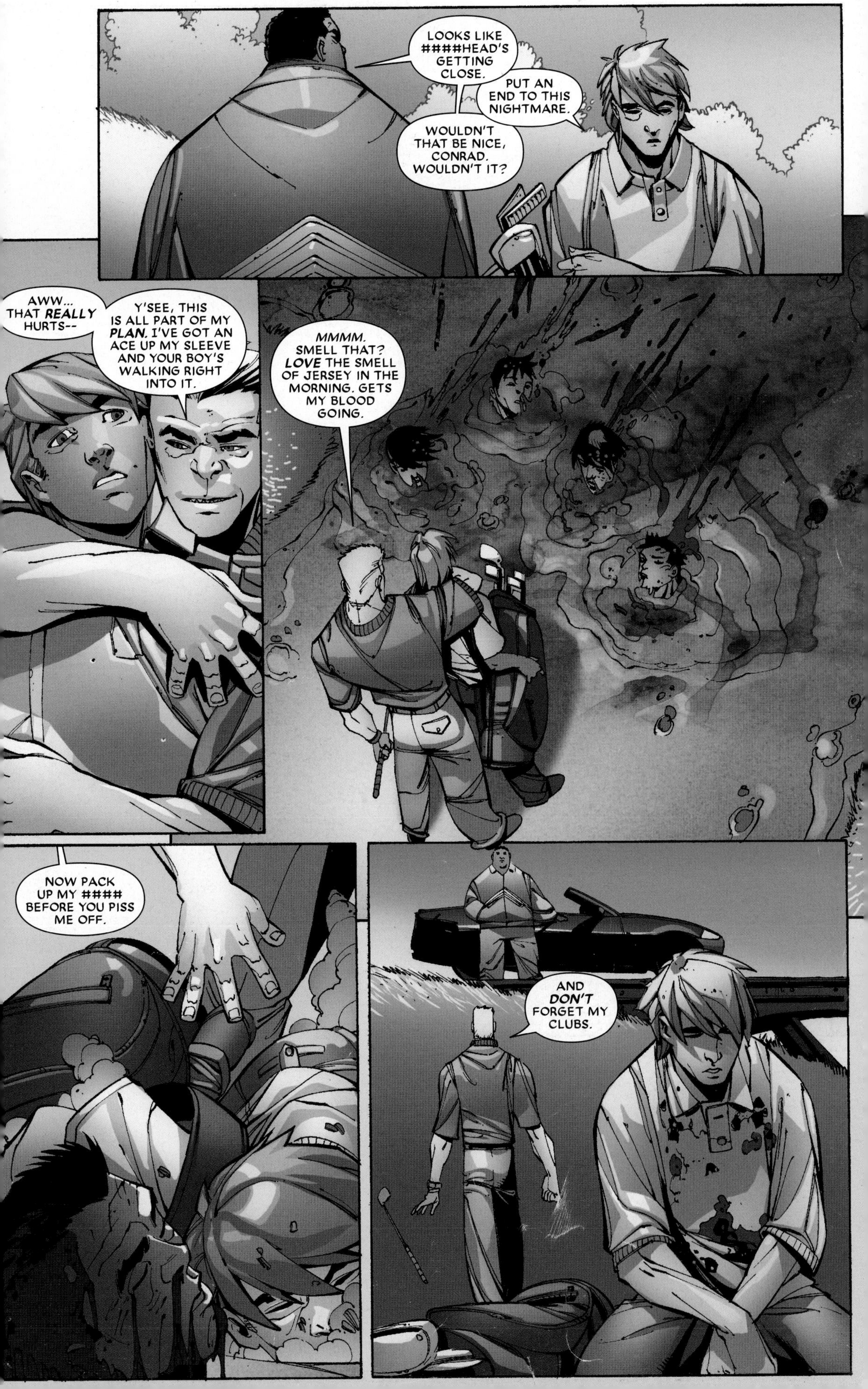
LOOKS LIKE ####HEAD'S GETTING CLOSE.
PUT AN END TO THIS NIGHTMARE.
WOULDN'T THAT BE NICE, CONRAD. WOULDN'T IT?
AWW... THAT REALLY HURTS--
Y'SEE, THIS IS ALL PART OF MY PLAN. I'VE GOT AN ACE UP MY SLEEVE AND YOUR BOY'S WALKING RIGHT INTO IT.
MMMM. SMELL THAT? LOVE THE SMELL OF JERSEY IN THE MORNING. GETS MY BLOOD GOING.
NOW PACK UP MY #### BEFORE YOU PISS ME OFF.
AND DON'T FORGET MY CLUBS.

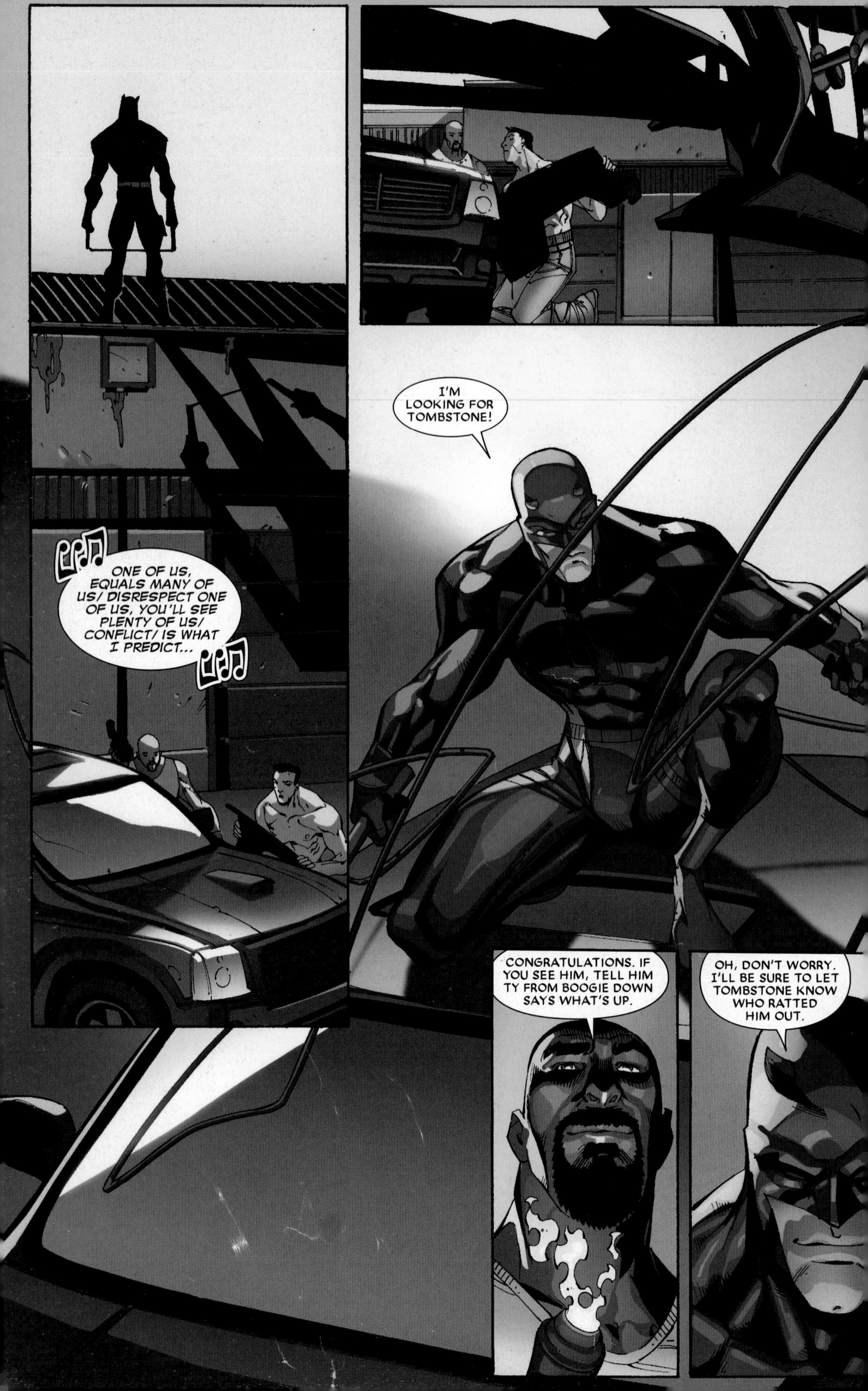

ONE OF US, EQUALS MANY OF US/ DISRESPECT ONE OF US, YOU'LL SEE PLENTY OF US/ CONFLICT/ IS WHAT I PREDICT...
I'M LOOKING FOR TOMBSTONE!
CONGRATULATIONS. IF YOU SEE HIM, TELL HIM TY FROM BOOGIE DOWN SAYS WHAT'S UP.
OH, DON'T WORRY. I'LL BE SURE TO LET TOMBSTONE KNOW WHO RATTED HIM OUT.

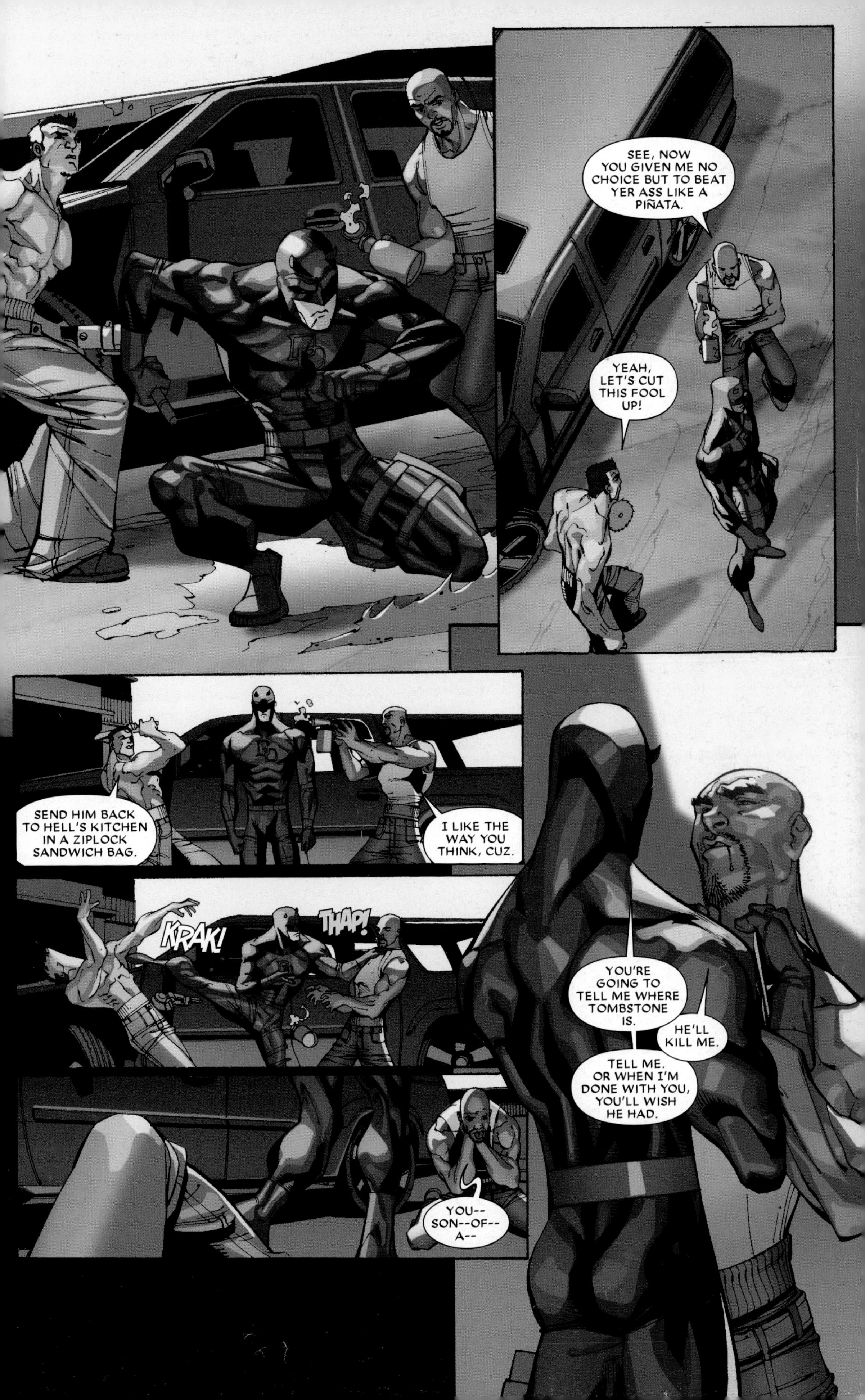
SEE, NOW YOU GIVEN ME NO CHOICE BUT TO BEAT YER ASS LIKE A PIÑATA.
YEAH, LET'S CUT THIS FOOL UP!
SEND HIM BACK TO HELL'S KITCHEN IN A ZIPLOCK SANDWICH BAG.
I LIKE THE WAY YOU THINK, CUZ.
KRAK!
THAP!
YOU-- SON--OF-- A--
YOU'RE GOING TO TELL ME WHERE TOMBSTONE IS.
HE'LL KILL ME.
TELL ME. OR WHEN I'M DONE WITH YOU, YOU'LL WISH HE HAD.

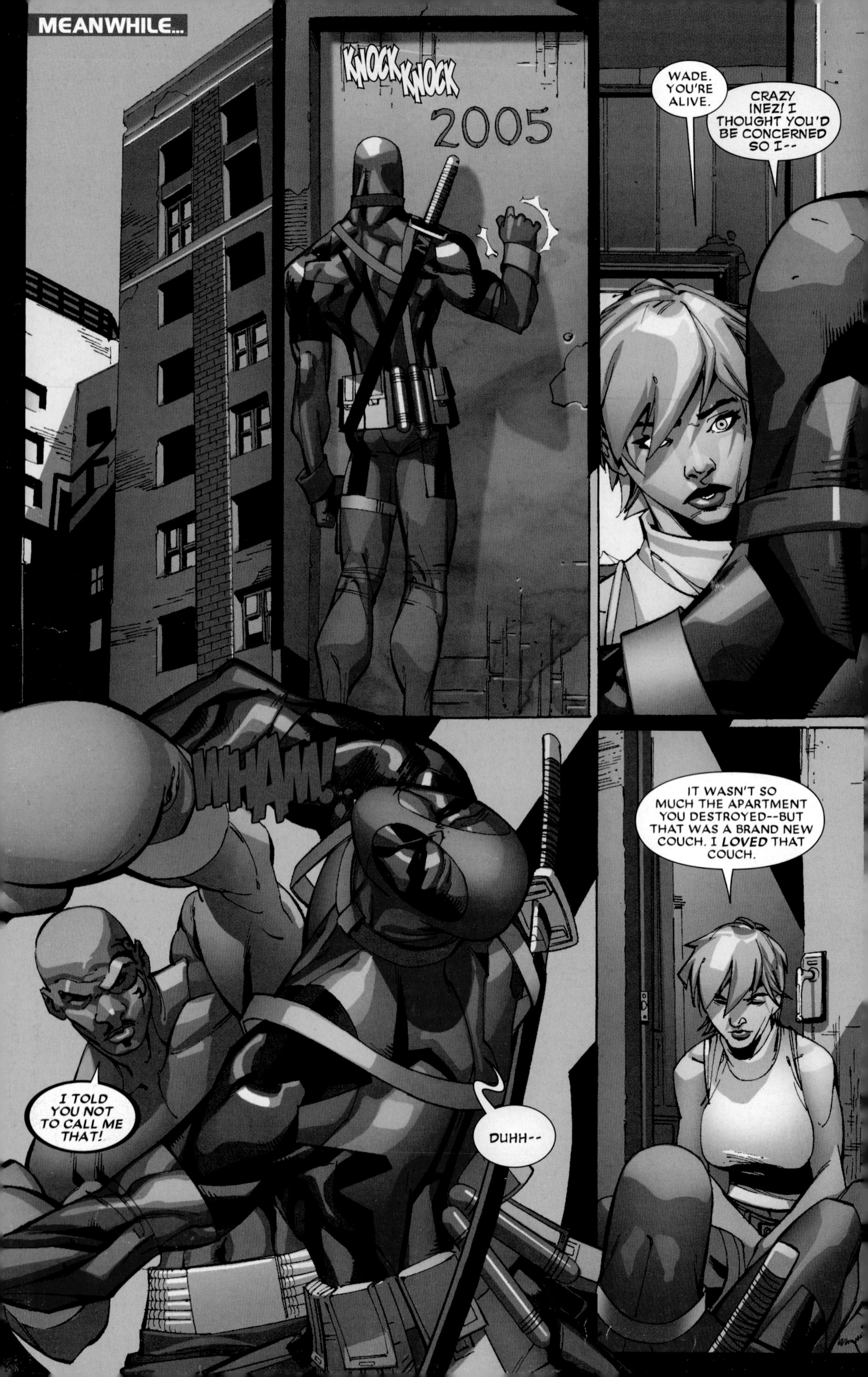
MEANWHILE...
KNOCK KNOCK
2005
WADE. YOU'RE ALIVE.
CRAZY INEZ! I THOUGHT YOU'D BE CONCERNED SO I--
WHAM!
I TOLD YOU NOT TO CALL ME THAT!
DUHH--
IT WASN'T SO MUCH THE APARTMENT YOU DESTROYED--BUT THAT WAS A BRAND NEW COUCH. I *LOVED* THAT COUCH.

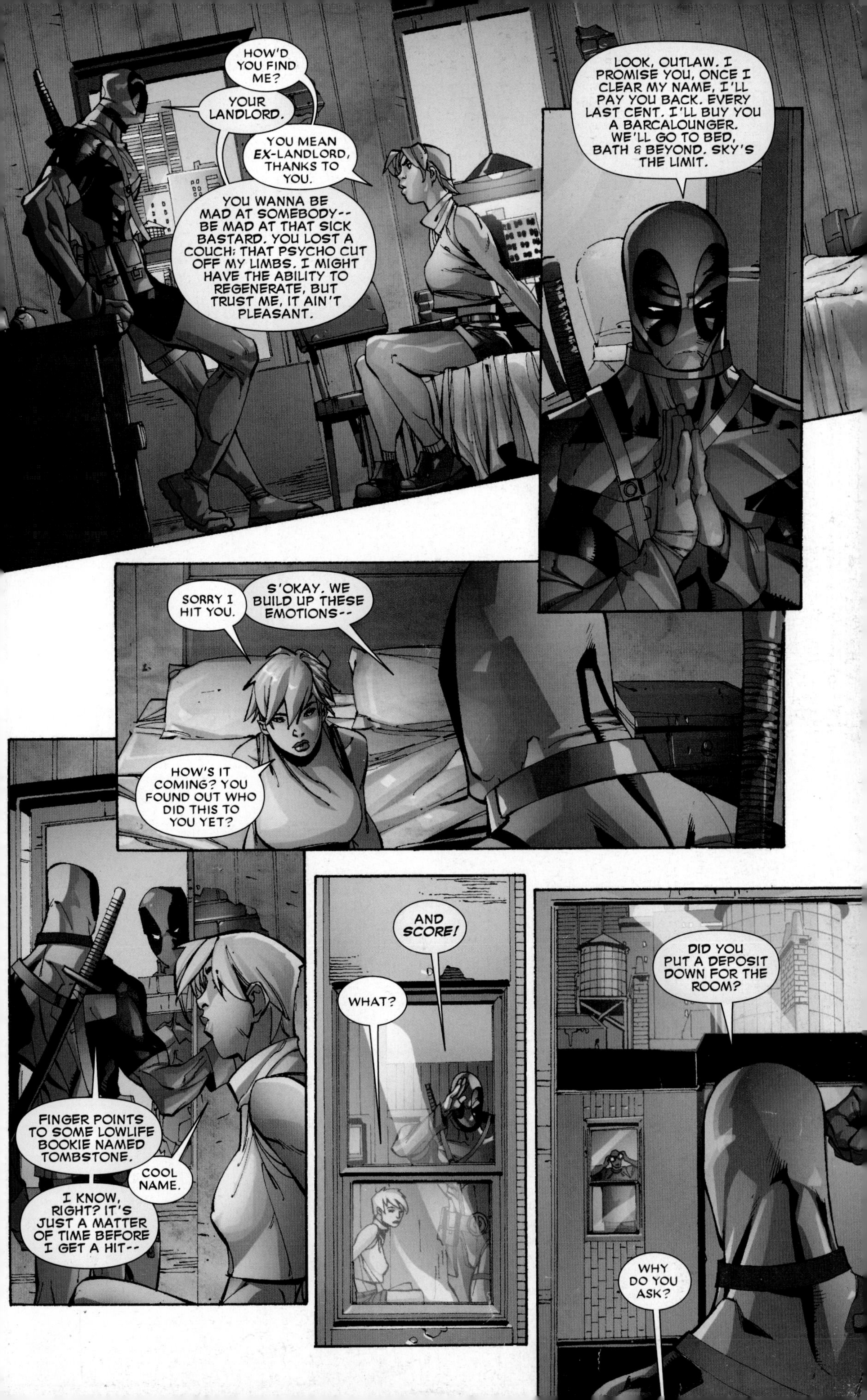
HOW'D YOU FIND ME?
YOUR LANDLORD.
YOU MEAN EX-LANDLORD, THANKS TO YOU.
YOU WANNA BE MAD AT SOMEBODY-- BE MAD AT THAT SICK BASTARD. YOU LOST A COUCH; THAT PSYCHO CUT OFF MY LIMBS. I MIGHT HAVE THE ABILITY TO REGENERATE, BUT TRUST ME, IT AIN'T PLEASANT.
LOOK, OUTLAW. I PROMISE YOU, ONCE I CLEAR MY NAME, I'LL PAY YOU BACK. EVERY LAST CENT. I'LL BUY YOU A BARCALOUNGER. WE'LL GO TO BED, BATH & BEYOND. SKY'S THE LIMIT.
SORRY I HIT YOU.
S'OKAY. WE BUILD UP THESE EMOTIONS--
HOW'S IT COMING? YOU FOUND OUT WHO DID THIS TO YOU YET?
FINGER POINTS TO SOME LOWLIFE BOOKIE NAMED TOMBSTONE.
COOL NAME.
I KNOW, RIGHT? IT'S JUST A MATTER OF TIME BEFORE I GET A HIT--
AND SCORE!
WHAT?
DID YOU PUT A DEPOSIT DOWN FOR THE ROOM?
WHY DO YOU ASK?

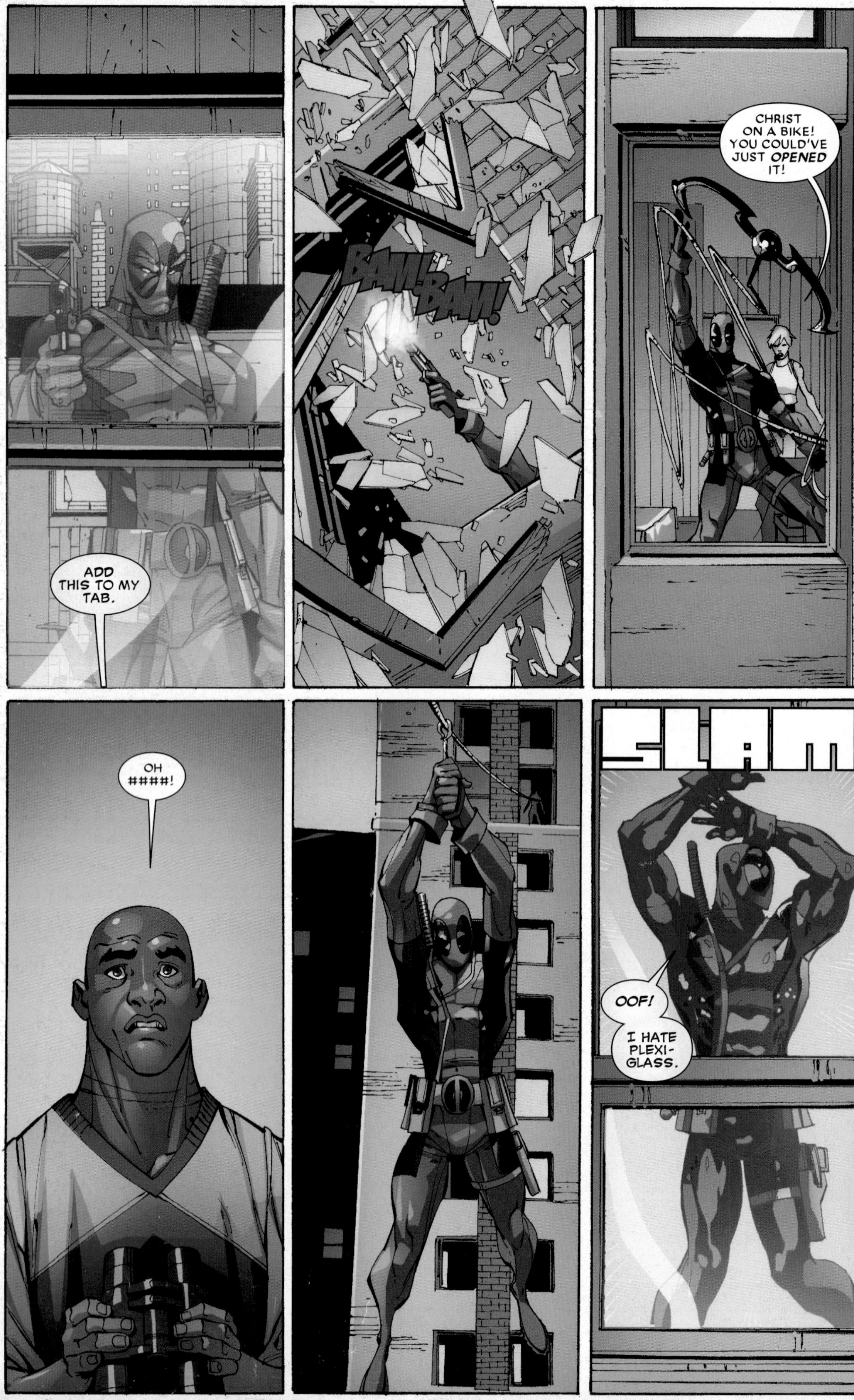
ADD THIS TO MY TAB.
BAM! BAM!
CHRIST ON A BIKE! YOU COULD'VE JUST *OPENED* IT!
OH ####!
SLAM
OOF!
I HATE PLEXI-GLASS.

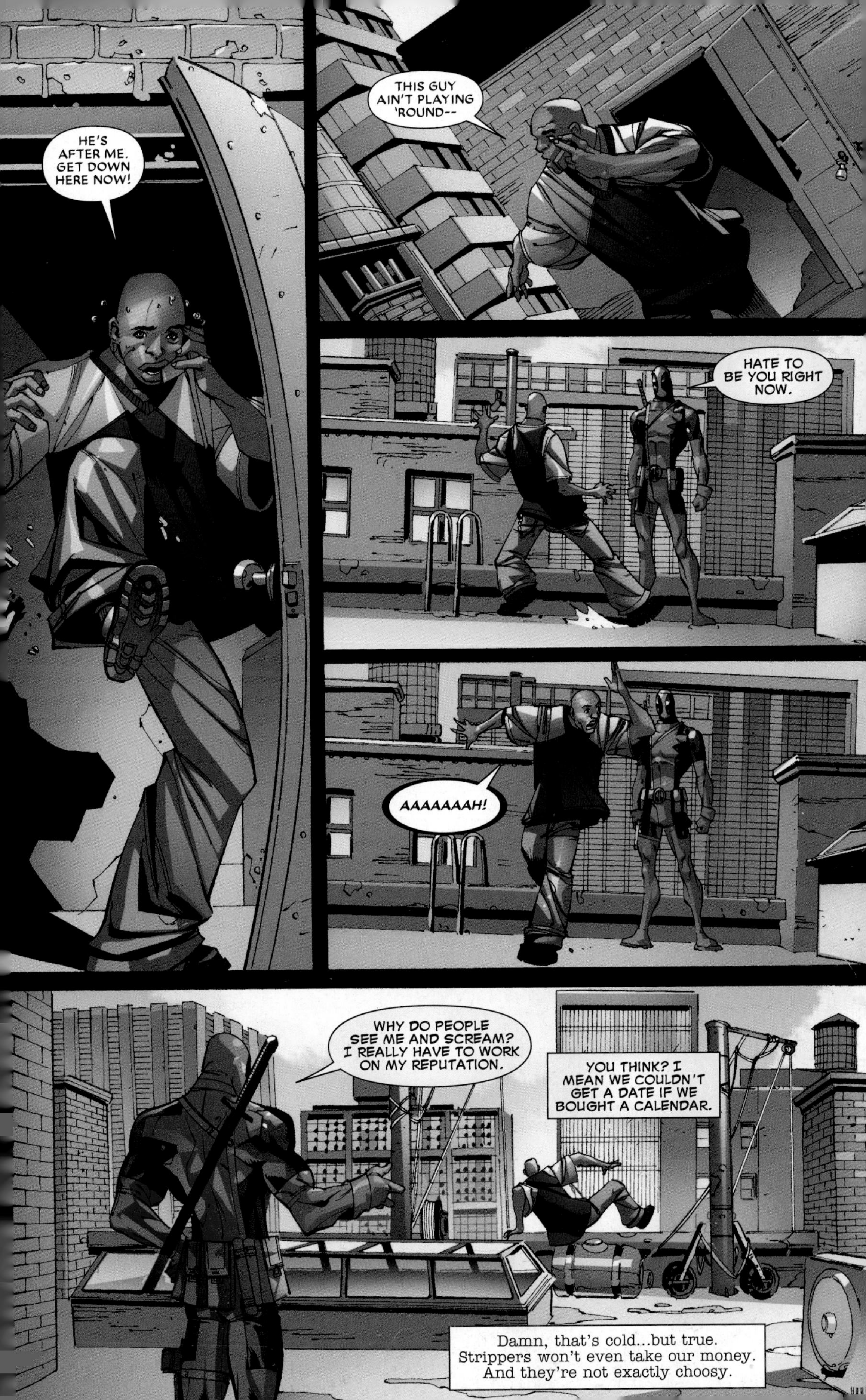
HE'S AFTER ME. GET DOWN HERE NOW!
THIS GUY AIN'T PLAYING 'ROUND--
HATE TO BE YOU RIGHT NOW.
AAAAAAAH!
WHY DO PEOPLE SEE ME AND SCREAM? I REALLY HAVE TO WORK ON MY REPUTATION.
YOU THINK? I MEAN WE COULDN'T GET A DATE IF WE BOUGHT A CALENDAR.
Damn, that's cold...but true. Strippers won't even take our money. And they're not exactly choosy.

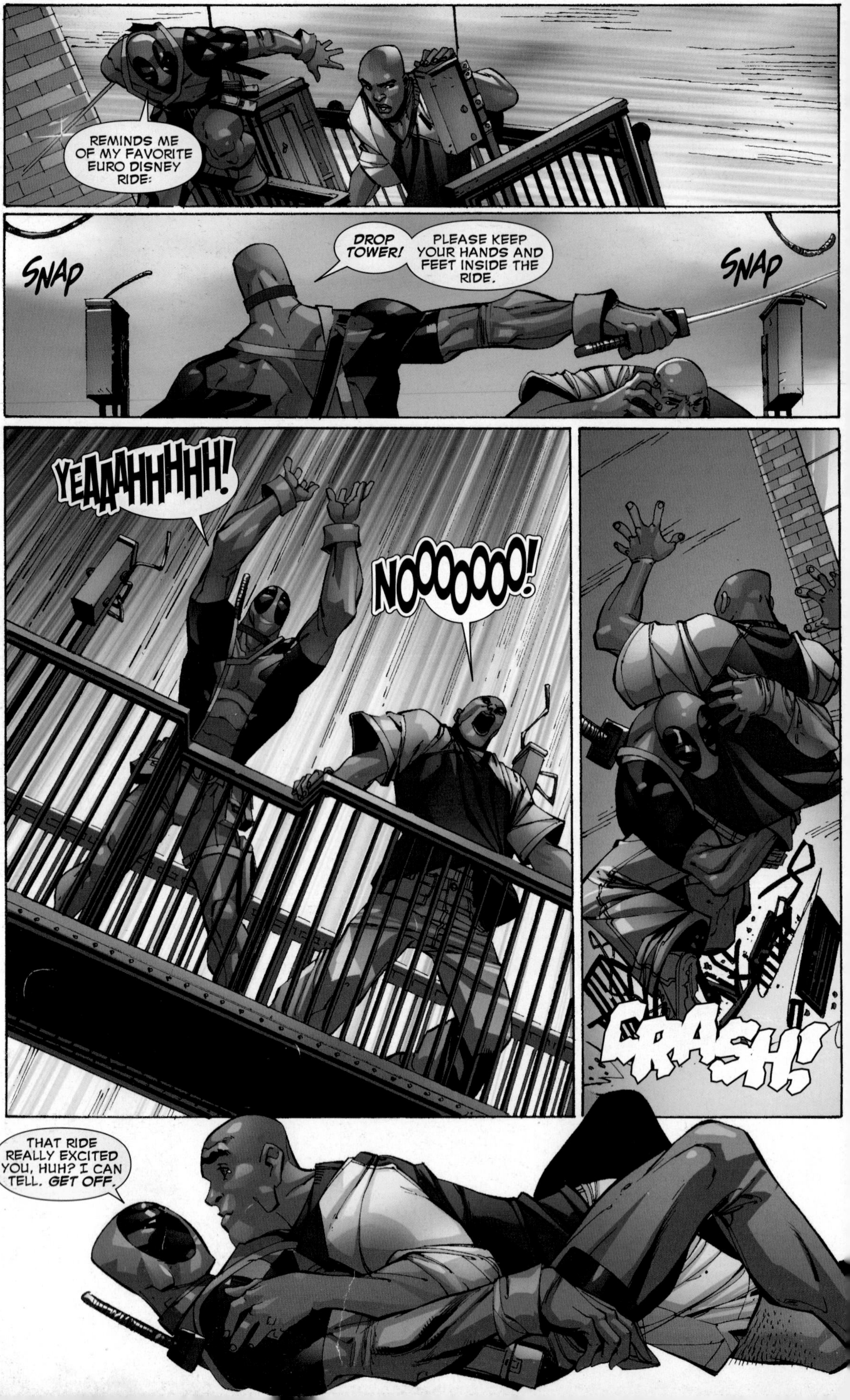
REMINDS ME OF MY FAVORITE EURO DISNEY RIDE:
SNAP
DROP TOWER!
PLEASE KEEP YOUR HANDS AND FEET INSIDE THE RIDE.
SNAP
YEAAAHHHHH!
NOOOOOOO!
CRASH!
THAT RIDE REALLY EXCITED YOU, HUH? I CAN TELL. *GET OFF*.

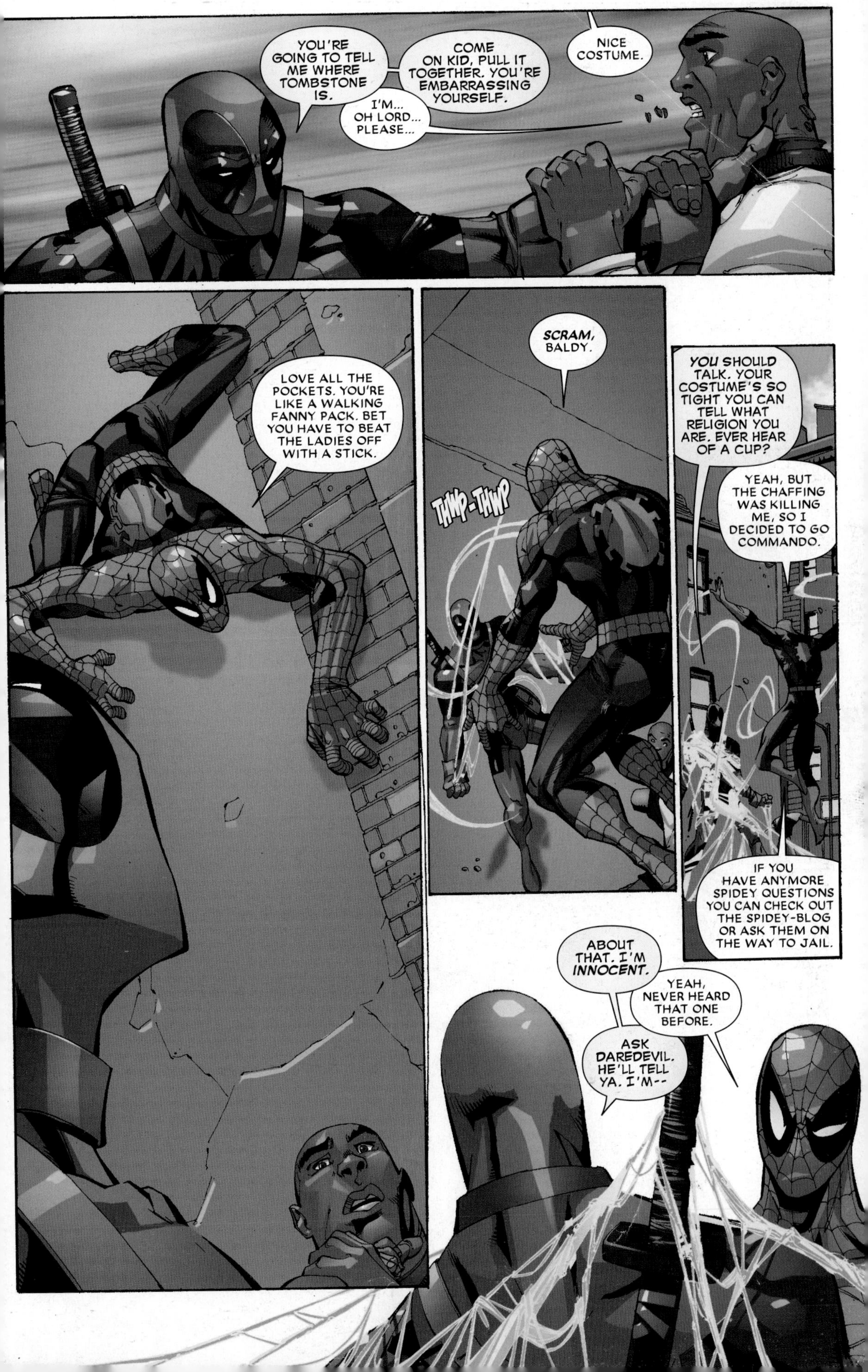

YOU'RE GOING TO TELL ME WHERE TOMBSTONE IS.
COME ON KID, PULL IT TOGETHER. YOU'RE EMBARRASSING YOURSELF.
I'M... OH LORD... PLEASE...
NICE COSTUME.
LOVE ALL THE POCKETS. YOU'RE LIKE A WALKING FANNY PACK. BET YOU HAVE TO BEAT THE LADIES OFF WITH A STICK.
SCRAM, BALDY.
THWP-THWP
YOU SHOULD TALK. YOUR COSTUME'S SO TIGHT YOU CAN TELL WHAT RELIGION YOU ARE. EVER HEAR OF A CUP?
YEAH, BUT THE CHAFFING WAS KILLING ME, SO I DECIDED TO GO COMMANDO.
IF YOU HAVE ANYMORE SPIDEY QUESTIONS YOU CAN CHECK OUT THE SPIDEY-BLOG OR ASK THEM ON THE WAY TO JAIL.
ABOUT THAT. I'M INNOCENT.
YEAH, NEVER HEARD THAT ONE BEFORE.
ASK DAREDEVIL. HE'LL TELL YA. I'M--

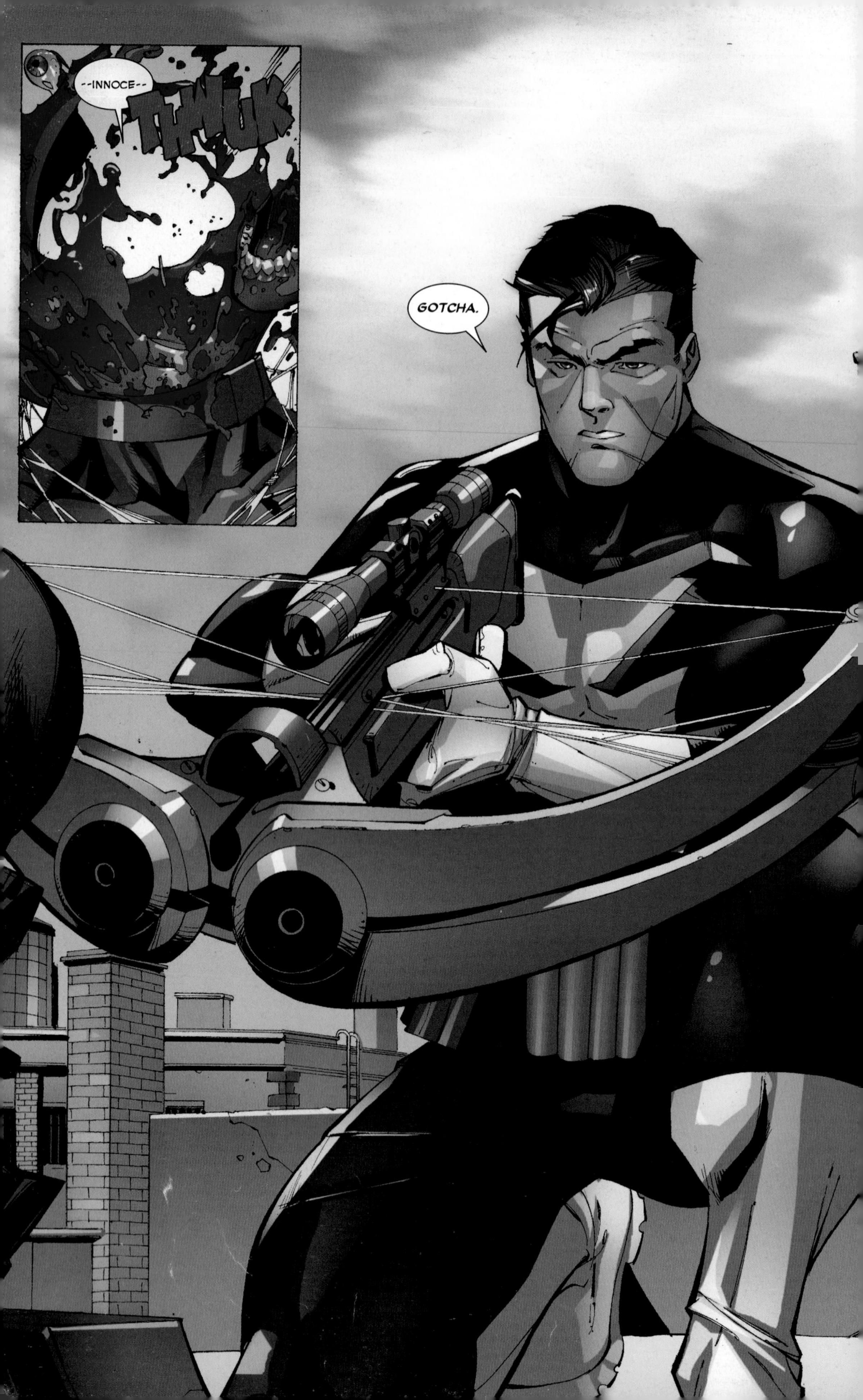
--INNOCE--
THWUK
GOTCHA.

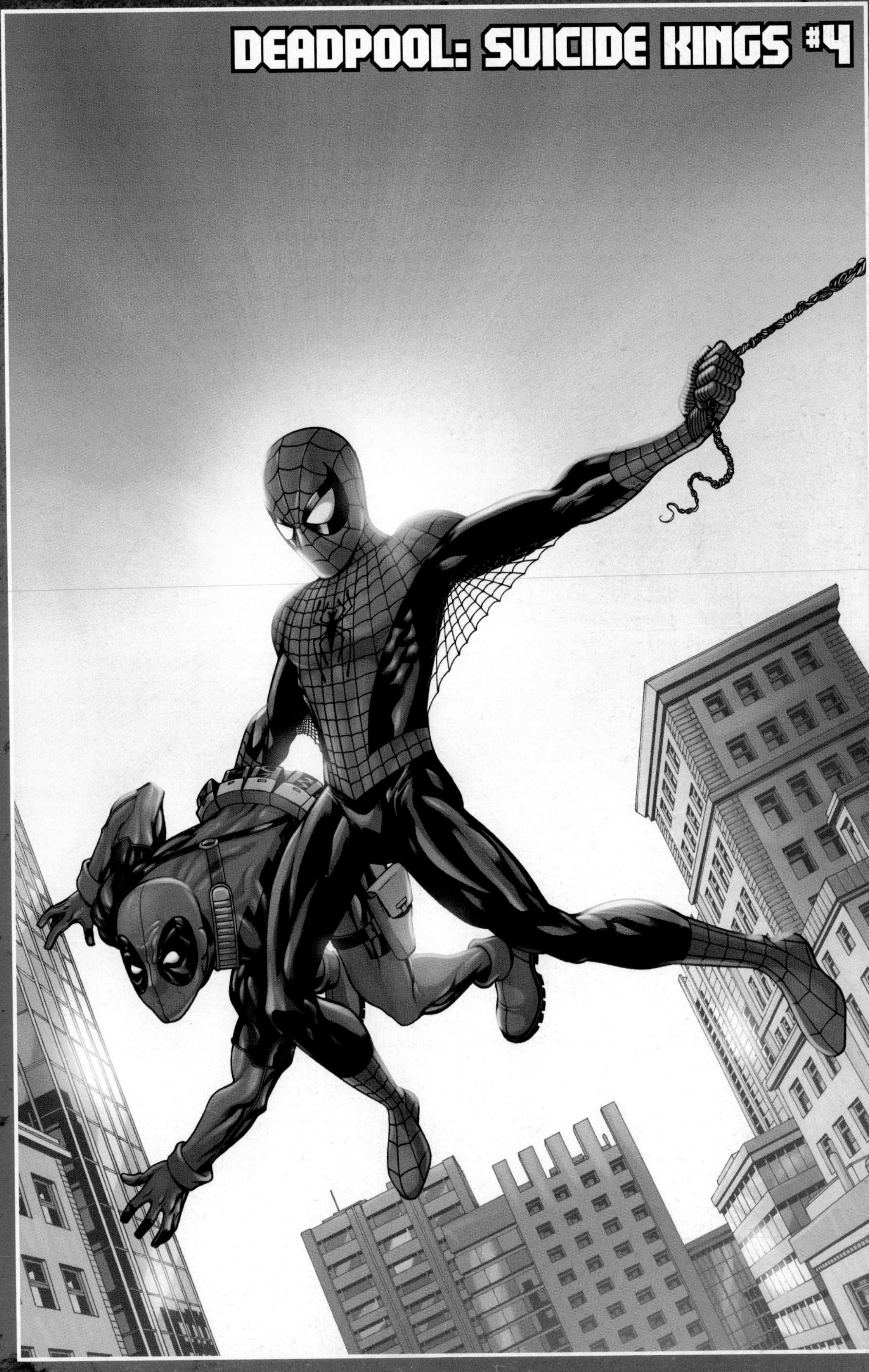
DEADPOOL: SUICIDE KINGS #4

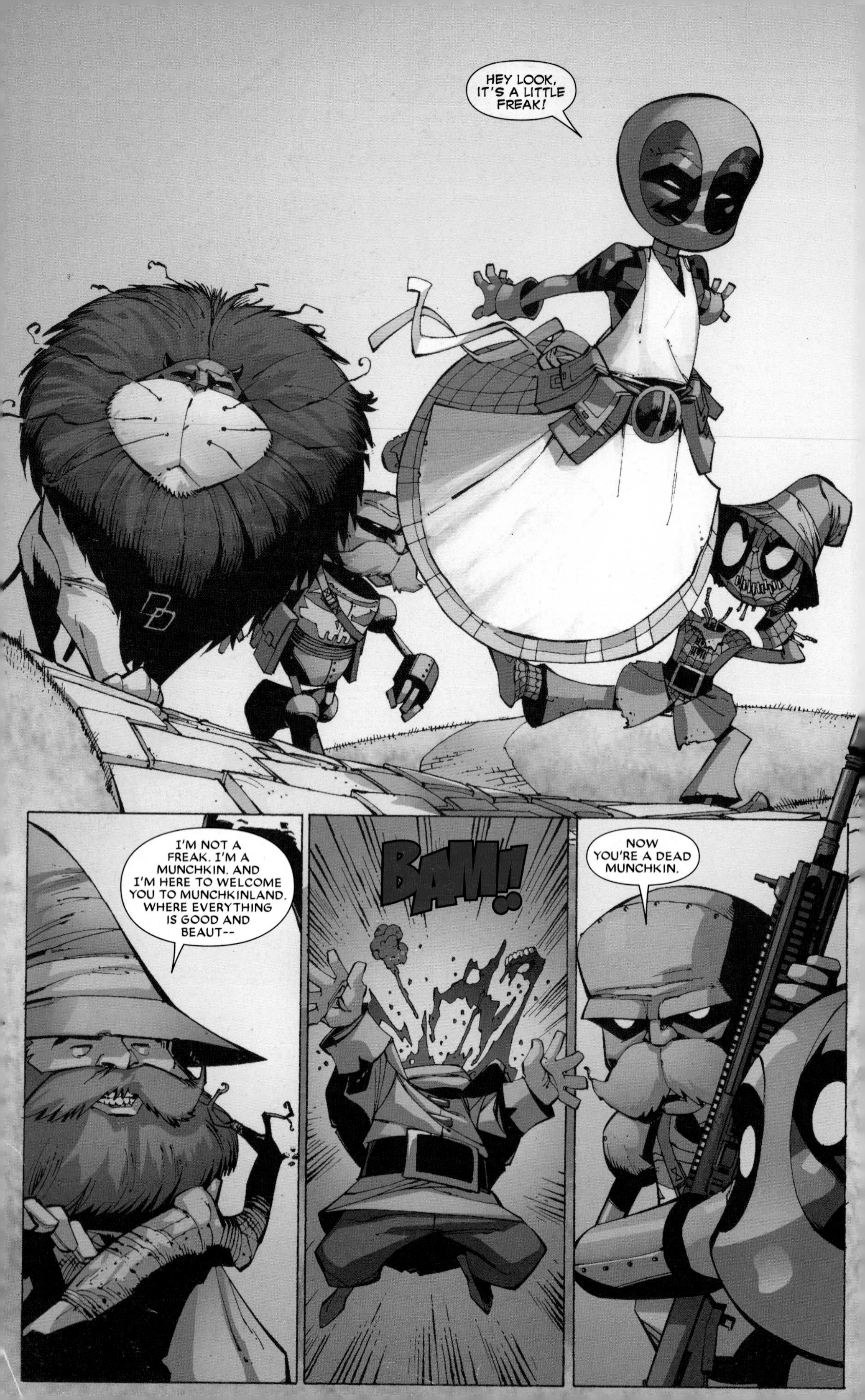
HEY LOOK, IT'S A LITTLE FREAK!
I'M NOT A FREAK. I'M A MUNCHKIN, AND I'M HERE TO WELCOME YOU TO MUNCHKINLAND, WHERE EVERYTHING IS GOOD AND BEAUT--
BAM!!
NOW YOU'RE A DEAD MUNCHKIN.

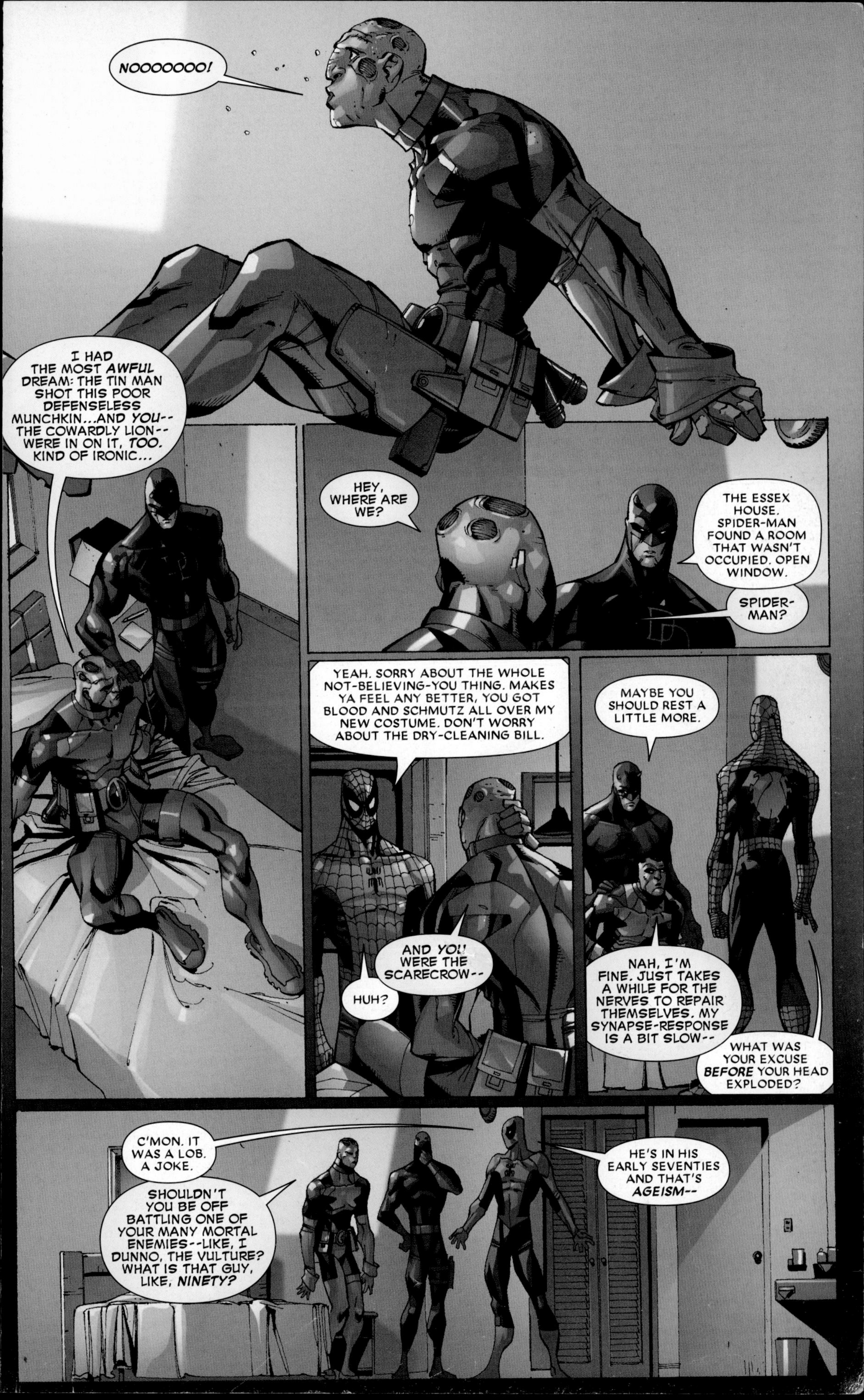
NOOOOOOO!
I HAD THE MOST AWFUL DREAM: THE TIN MAN SHOT THIS POOR DEFENSELESS MUNCHKIN...AND YOU--THE COWARDLY LION--WERE IN ON IT, TOO. KIND OF IRONIC...
HEY, WHERE ARE WE?
THE ESSEX HOUSE. SPIDER-MAN FOUND A ROOM THAT WASN'T OCCUPIED. OPEN WINDOW.
SPIDER-MAN?
YEAH. SORRY ABOUT THE WHOLE NOT-BELIEVING-YOU THING. MAKES YA FEEL ANY BETTER, YOU GOT BLOOD AND SCHMUTZ ALL OVER MY NEW COSTUME. DON'T WORRY ABOUT THE DRY-CLEANING BILL.
AND YOU WERE THE SCARECROW--
HUH?
MAYBE YOU SHOULD REST A LITTLE MORE.
NAH, I'M FINE. JUST TAKES A WHILE FOR THE NERVES TO REPAIR THEMSELVES. MY SYNAPSE-RESPONSE IS A BIT SLOW--
WHAT WAS YOUR EXCUSE BEFORE YOUR HEAD EXPLODED?
C'MON. IT WAS A LOB. A JOKE.
SHOULDN'T YOU BE OFF BATTLING ONE OF YOUR MANY MORTAL ENEMIES--LIKE, I DUNNO, THE VULTURE? WHAT IS THAT GUY, LIKE, NINETY?
HE'S IN HIS EARLY SEVENTIES AND THAT'S AGEISM--

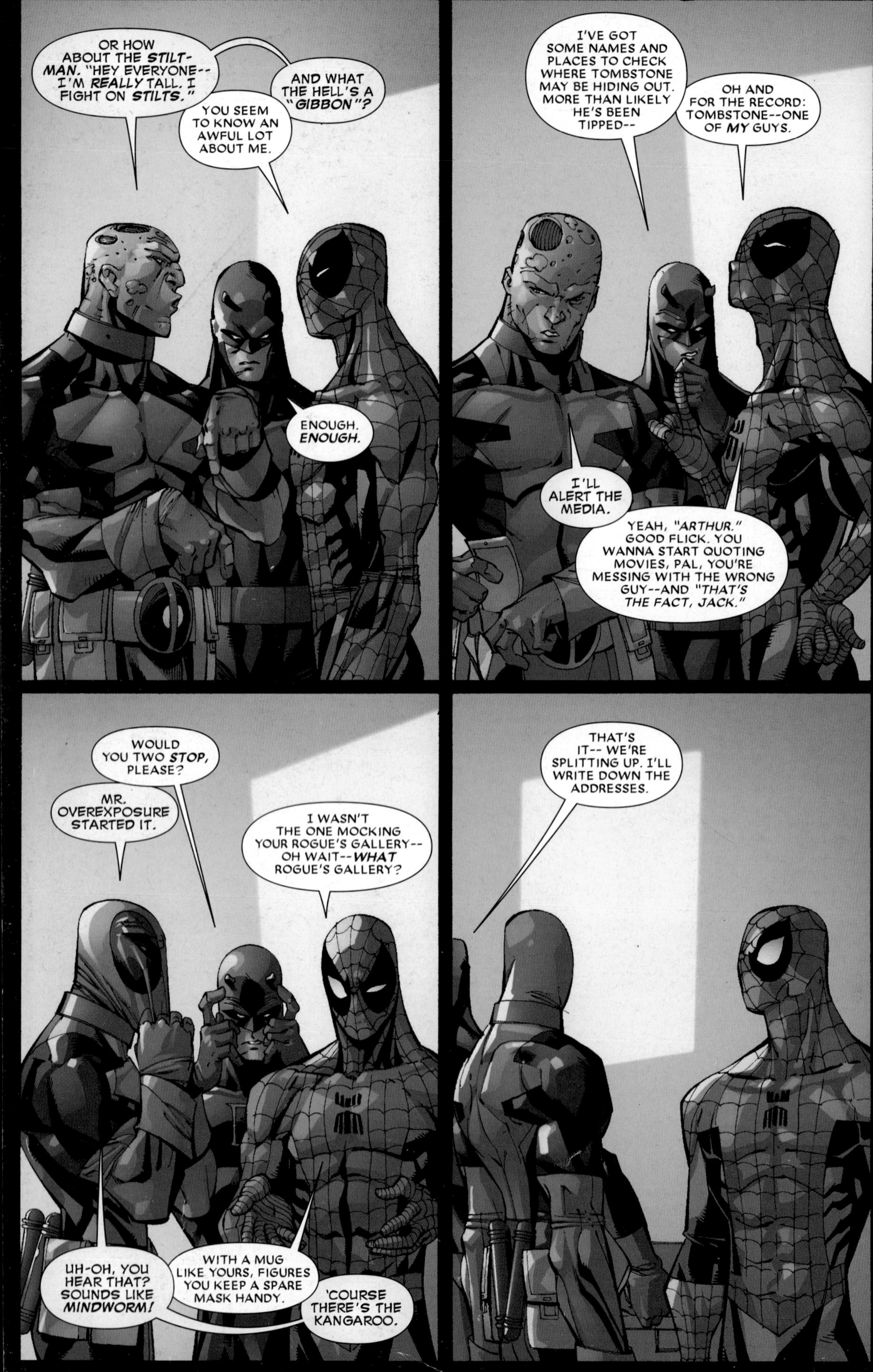
OR HOW ABOUT THE **STILT-MAN.** "HEY EVERYONE-- I'M **REALLY** TALL. I FIGHT ON **STILTS.**"
AND WHAT THE HELL'S A "**GIBBON**"?
YOU SEEM TO KNOW AN AWFUL LOT ABOUT ME.
ENOUGH. **ENOUGH.**
I'VE GOT SOME NAMES AND PLACES TO CHECK WHERE TOMBSTONE MAY BE HIDING OUT. MORE THAN LIKELY HE'S BEEN TIPPED--
OH AND FOR THE RECORD: TOMBSTONE--ONE OF **MY** GUYS.
I'LL ALERT THE MEDIA.
YEAH, "*ARTHUR.*" GOOD FLICK. YOU WANNA START QUOTING MOVIES, PAL, YOU'RE MESSING WITH THE WRONG GUY--AND "*THAT'S THE FACT, JACK.*"
WOULD YOU TWO **STOP,** PLEASE?
MR. OVEREXPOSURE STARTED IT.
I WASN'T THE ONE MOCKING YOUR ROGUE'S GALLERY-- OH WAIT--**WHAT** ROGUE'S GALLERY?
UH-OH, YOU HEAR THAT? SOUNDS LIKE **MINDWORM!**
WITH A MUG LIKE YOURS, FIGURES YOU KEEP A SPARE MASK HANDY.
'COURSE THERE'S THE KANGAROO.
THAT'S IT-- WE'RE SPLITTING UP. I'LL WRITE DOWN THE ADDRESSES.

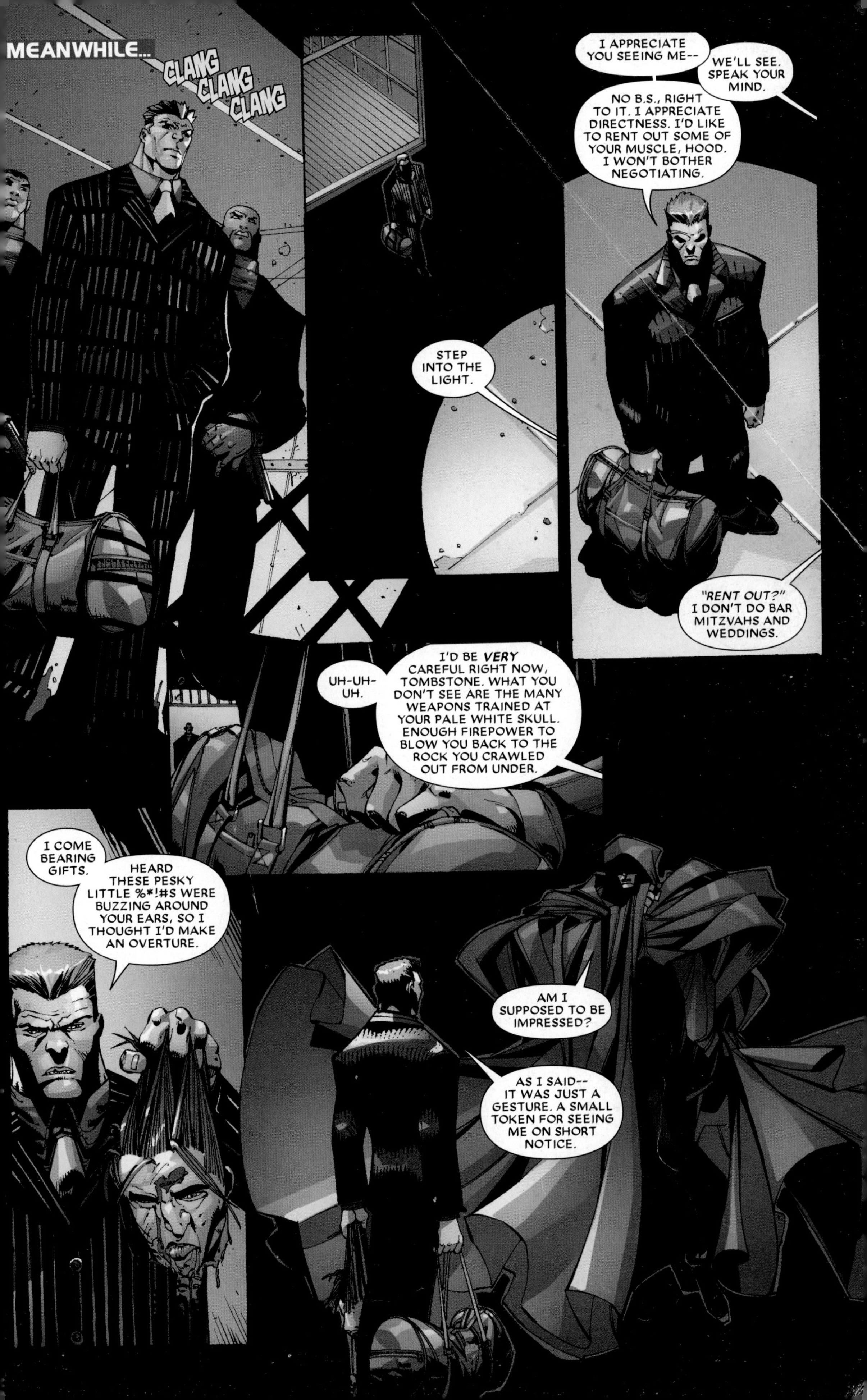
MEANWHILE...
CLANG CLANG CLANG
I APPRECIATE YOU SEEING ME--
WE'LL SEE. SPEAK YOUR MIND.
NO B.S., RIGHT TO IT. I APPRECIATE DIRECTNESS. I'D LIKE TO RENT OUT SOME OF YOUR MUSCLE, HOOD. I WON'T BOTHER NEGOTIATING.
STEP INTO THE LIGHT.
"RENT OUT?" I DON'T DO BAR MITZVAHS AND WEDDINGS.
UH-UH-UH.
I'D BE VERY CAREFUL RIGHT NOW, TOMBSTONE. WHAT YOU DON'T SEE ARE THE MANY WEAPONS TRAINED AT YOUR PALE WHITE SKULL. ENOUGH FIREPOWER TO BLOW YOU BACK TO THE ROCK YOU CRAWLED OUT FROM UNDER.
I COME BEARING GIFTS.
HEARD THESE PESKY LITTLE %*!#S WERE BUZZING AROUND YOUR EARS, SO I THOUGHT I'D MAKE AN OVERTURE.
AM I SUPPOSED TO BE IMPRESSED?
AS I SAID-- IT WAS JUST A GESTURE. A SMALL TOKEN FOR SEEING ME ON SHORT NOTICE.

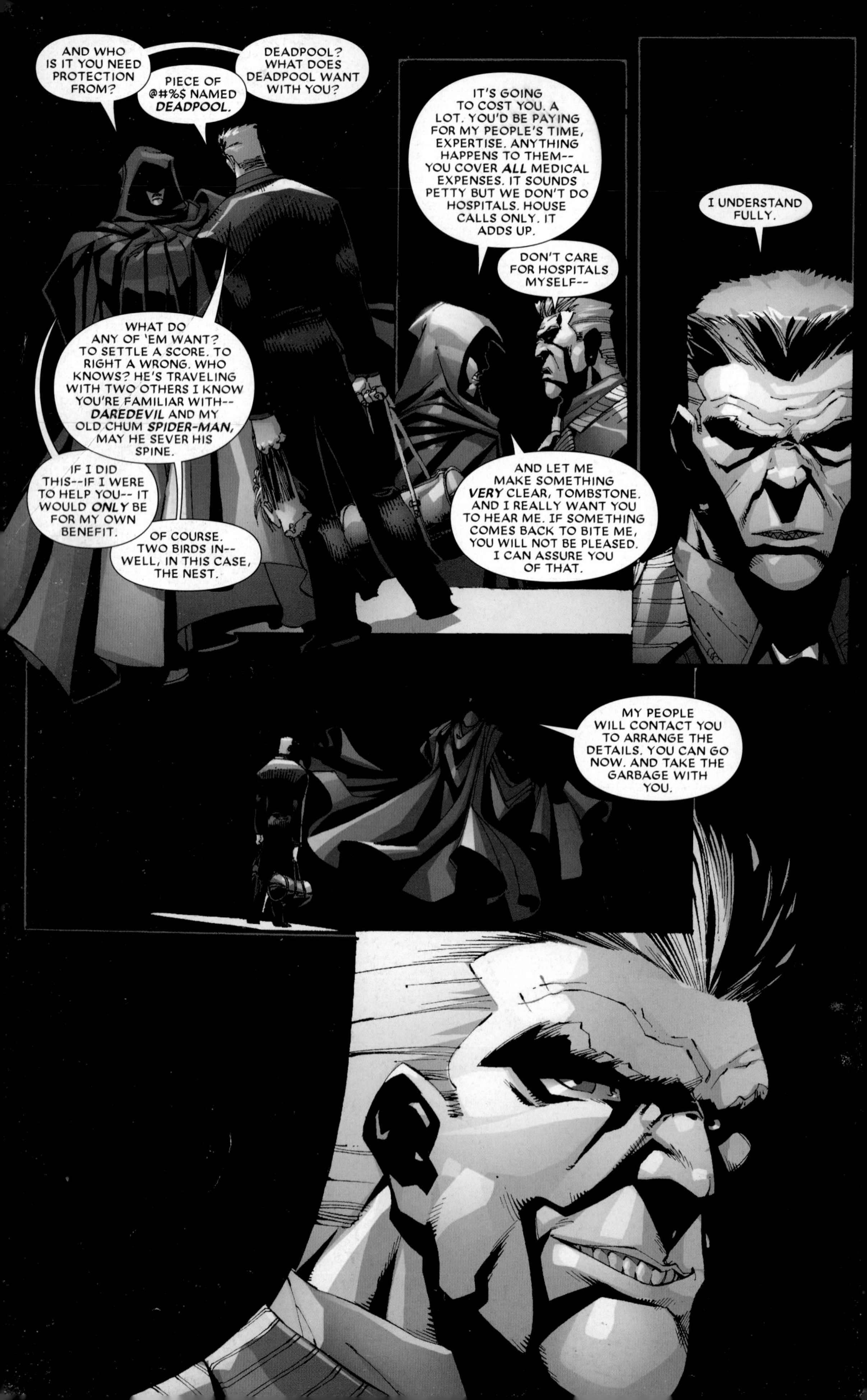
AND WHO IS IT YOU NEED PROTECTION FROM?
PIECE OF @#%$ NAMED DEADPOOL.
DEADPOOL? WHAT DOES DEADPOOL WANT WITH YOU?
WHAT DO ANY OF 'EM WANT? TO SETTLE A SCORE. TO RIGHT A WRONG. WHO KNOWS? HE'S TRAVELING WITH TWO OTHERS I KNOW YOU'RE FAMILIAR WITH-- DAREDEVIL AND MY OLD CHUM SPIDER-MAN, MAY HE SEVER HIS SPINE.
IF I DID THIS--IF I WERE TO HELP YOU-- IT WOULD ONLY BE FOR MY OWN BENEFIT.
OF COURSE. TWO BIRDS IN-- WELL, IN THIS CASE, THE NEST.
IT'S GOING TO COST YOU. A LOT. YOU'D BE PAYING FOR MY PEOPLE'S TIME, EXPERTISE. ANYTHING HAPPENS TO THEM-- YOU COVER ALL MEDICAL EXPENSES. IT SOUNDS PETTY BUT WE DON'T DO HOSPITALS. HOUSE CALLS ONLY. IT ADDS UP.
DON'T CARE FOR HOSPITALS MYSELF--
AND LET ME MAKE SOMETHING VERY CLEAR, TOMBSTONE. AND I REALLY WANT YOU TO HEAR ME. IF SOMETHING COMES BACK TO BITE ME, YOU WILL NOT BE PLEASED. I CAN ASSURE YOU OF THAT.
I UNDERSTAND FULLY.
MY PEOPLE WILL CONTACT YOU TO ARRANGE THE DETAILS. YOU CAN GO NOW. AND TAKE THE GARBAGE WITH YOU.

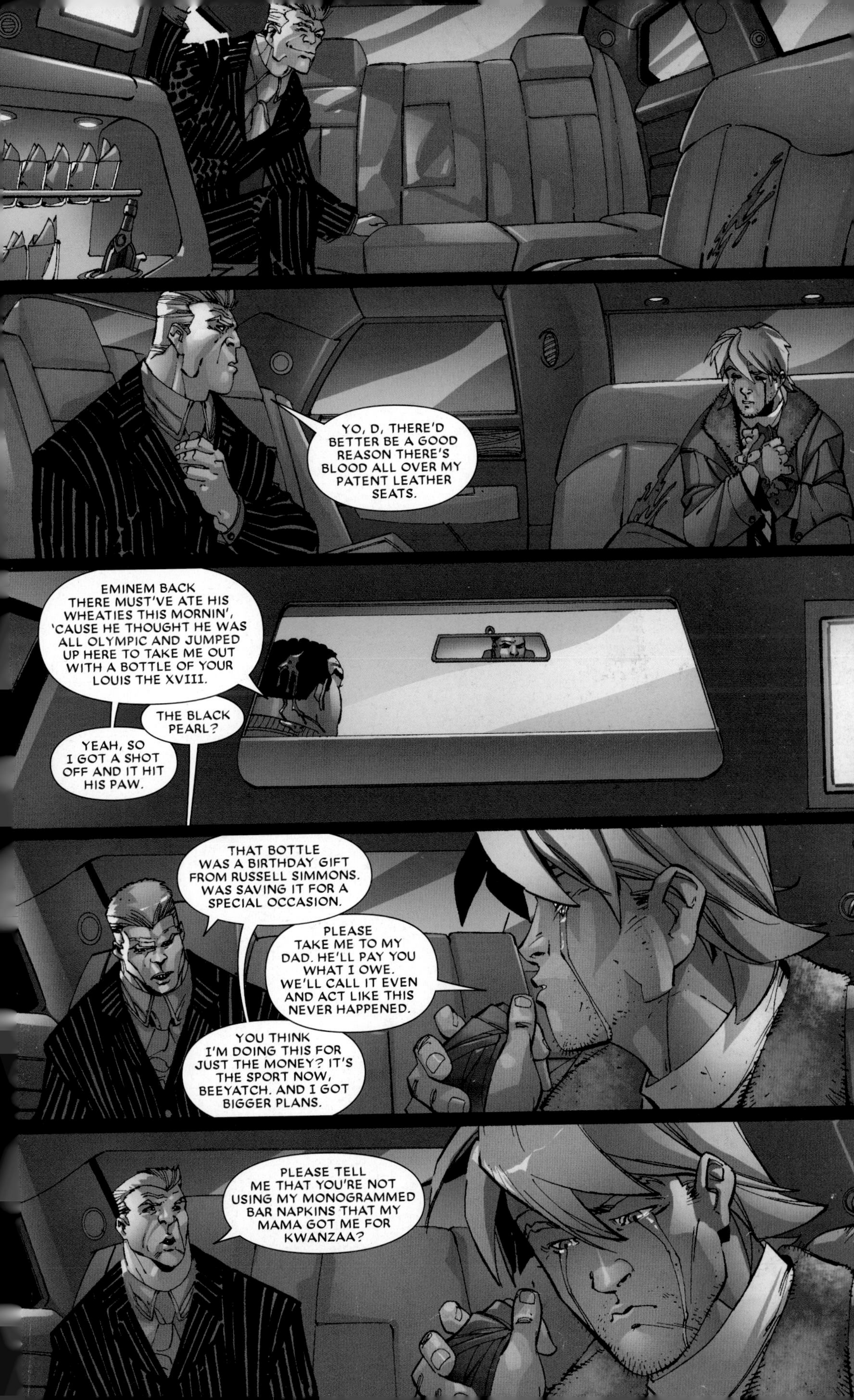

YO, D, THERE'D BETTER BE A GOOD REASON THERE'S BLOOD ALL OVER MY PATENT LEATHER SEATS.
EMINEM BACK THERE MUST'VE ATE HIS WHEATIES THIS MORNIN', 'CAUSE HE THOUGHT HE WAS ALL OLYMPIC AND JUMPED UP HERE TO TAKE ME OUT WITH A BOTTLE OF YOUR LOUIS THE XVIII.
THE BLACK PEARL?
YEAH, SO I GOT A SHOT OFF AND IT HIT HIS PAW.
THAT BOTTLE WAS A BIRTHDAY GIFT FROM RUSSELL SIMMONS. WAS SAVING IT FOR A SPECIAL OCCASION.
PLEASE TAKE ME TO MY DAD. HE'LL PAY YOU WHAT I OWE. WE'LL CALL IT EVEN AND ACT LIKE THIS NEVER HAPPENED.
YOU THINK I'M DOING THIS FOR JUST THE MONEY? IT'S THE SPORT NOW, BEEYATCH. AND I GOT BIGGER PLANS.
PLEASE TELL ME THAT YOU'RE NOT USING MY MONOGRAMMED BAR NAPKINS THAT MY MAMA GOT ME FOR KWANZAA?

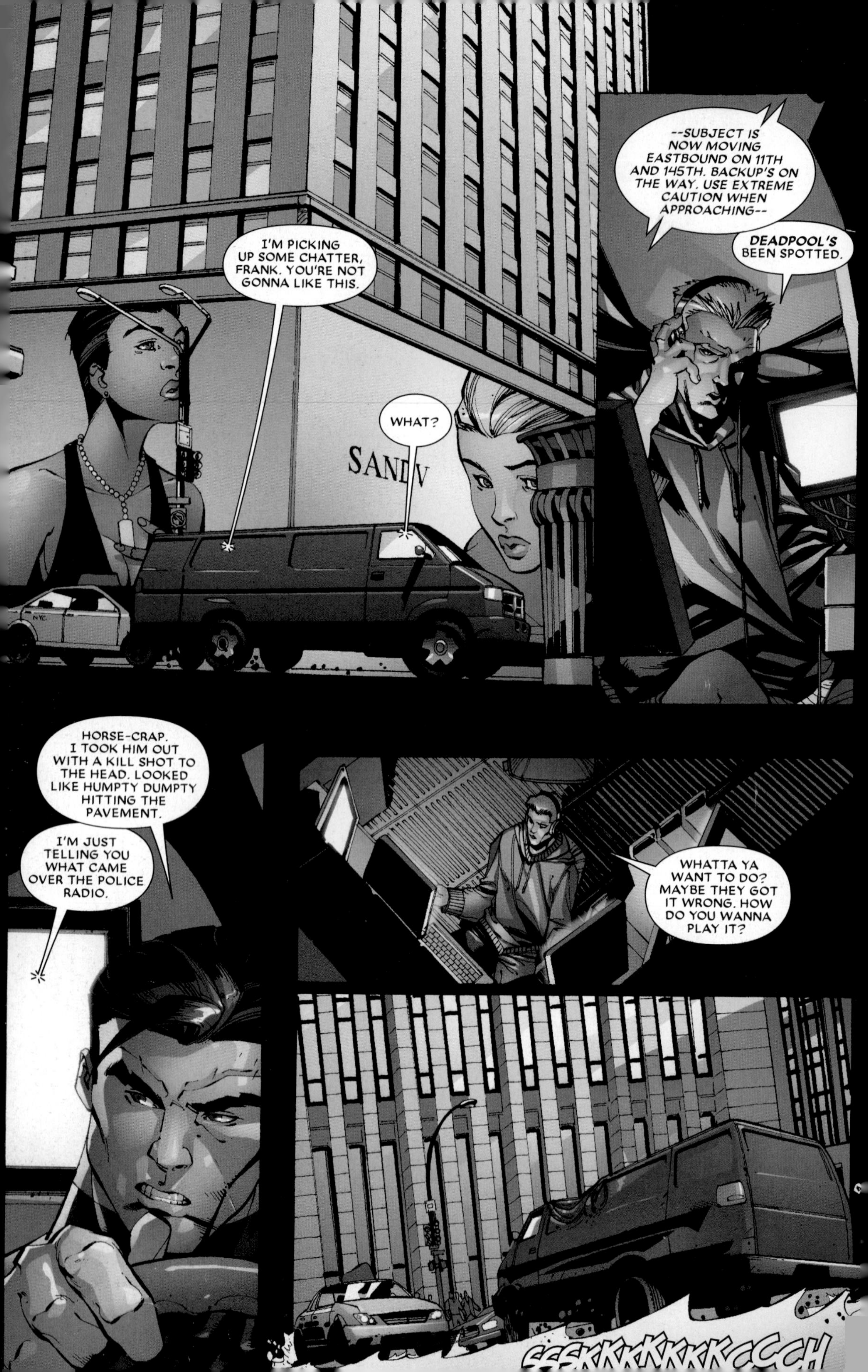
I'M PICKING UP SOME CHATTER, FRANK. YOU'RE NOT GONNA LIKE THIS.
WHAT?
SANDV
--SUBJECT IS NOW MOVING EASTBOUND ON 11TH AND 145TH. BACKUP'S ON THE WAY. USE EXTREME CAUTION WHEN APPROACHING--
DEADPOOL'S BEEN SPOTTED.
HORSE-CRAP. I TOOK HIM OUT WITH A KILL SHOT TO THE HEAD. LOOKED LIKE HUMPTY DUMPTY HITTING THE PAVEMENT.
I'M JUST TELLING YOU WHAT CAME OVER THE POLICE RADIO.
WHATTA YA WANT TO DO? MAYBE THEY GOT IT WRONG. HOW DO YOU WANNA PLAY IT?
SSSKKKKKKKCCCH

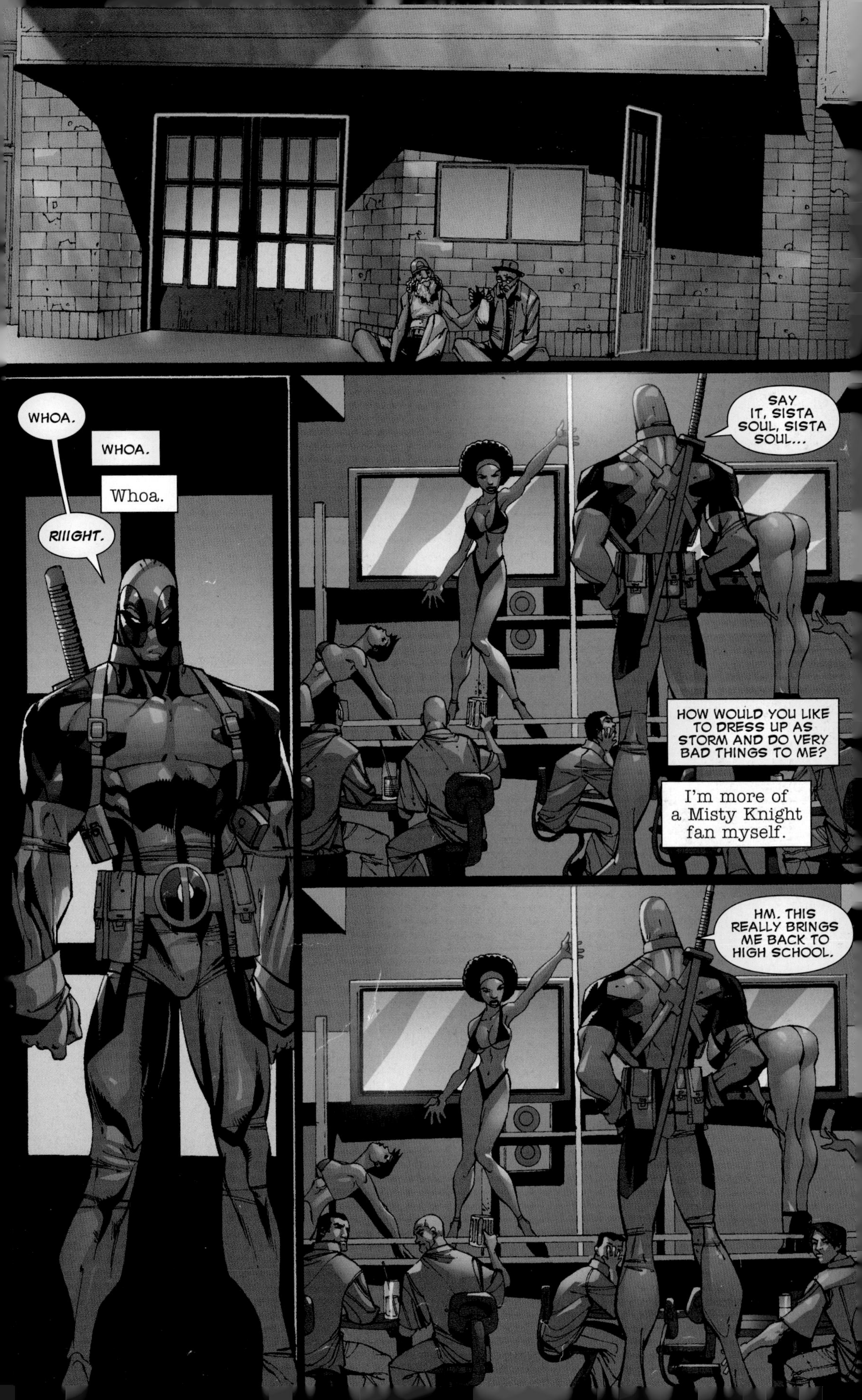
WHOA.
WHOA.
Whoa.
RIIIGHT.
SAY IT, SISTA SOUL, SISTA SOUL...
HOW WOULD YOU LIKE TO DRESS UP AS STORM AND DO VERY BAD THINGS TO ME?
I'm more of a Misty Knight fan myself.
HM. THIS REALLY BRINGS ME BACK TO HIGH SCHOOL.

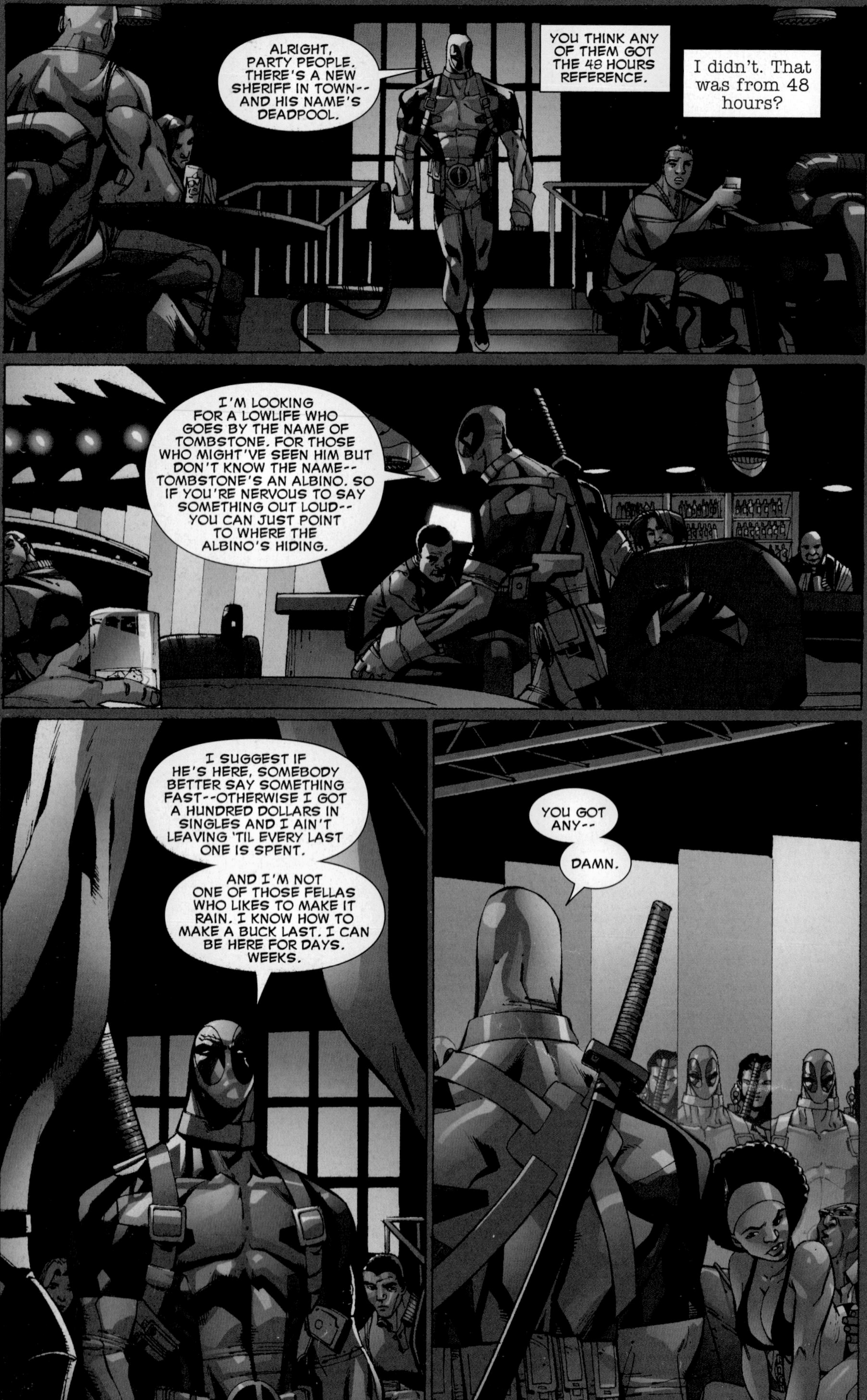
ALRIGHT, PARTY PEOPLE. THERE'S A NEW SHERIFF IN TOWN--AND HIS NAME'S DEADPOOL.
YOU THINK ANY OF THEM GOT THE 48 HOURS REFERENCE.
I didn't. That was from 48 hours?
I'M LOOKING FOR A LOWLIFE WHO GOES BY THE NAME OF TOMBSTONE. FOR THOSE WHO MIGHT'VE SEEN HIM BUT DON'T KNOW THE NAME--TOMBSTONE'S AN ALBINO. SO IF YOU'RE NERVOUS TO SAY SOMETHING OUT LOUD--YOU CAN JUST POINT TO WHERE THE ALBINO'S HIDING.
I SUGGEST IF HE'S HERE, SOMEBODY BETTER SAY SOMETHING FAST--OTHERWISE I GOT A HUNDRED DOLLARS IN SINGLES AND I AIN'T LEAVING 'TIL EVERY LAST ONE IS SPENT.
AND I'M NOT ONE OF THOSE FELLAS WHO LIKES TO MAKE IT RAIN. I KNOW HOW TO MAKE A BUCK LAST. I CAN BE HERE FOR DAYS. WEEKS.
YOU GOT ANY--
DAMN.

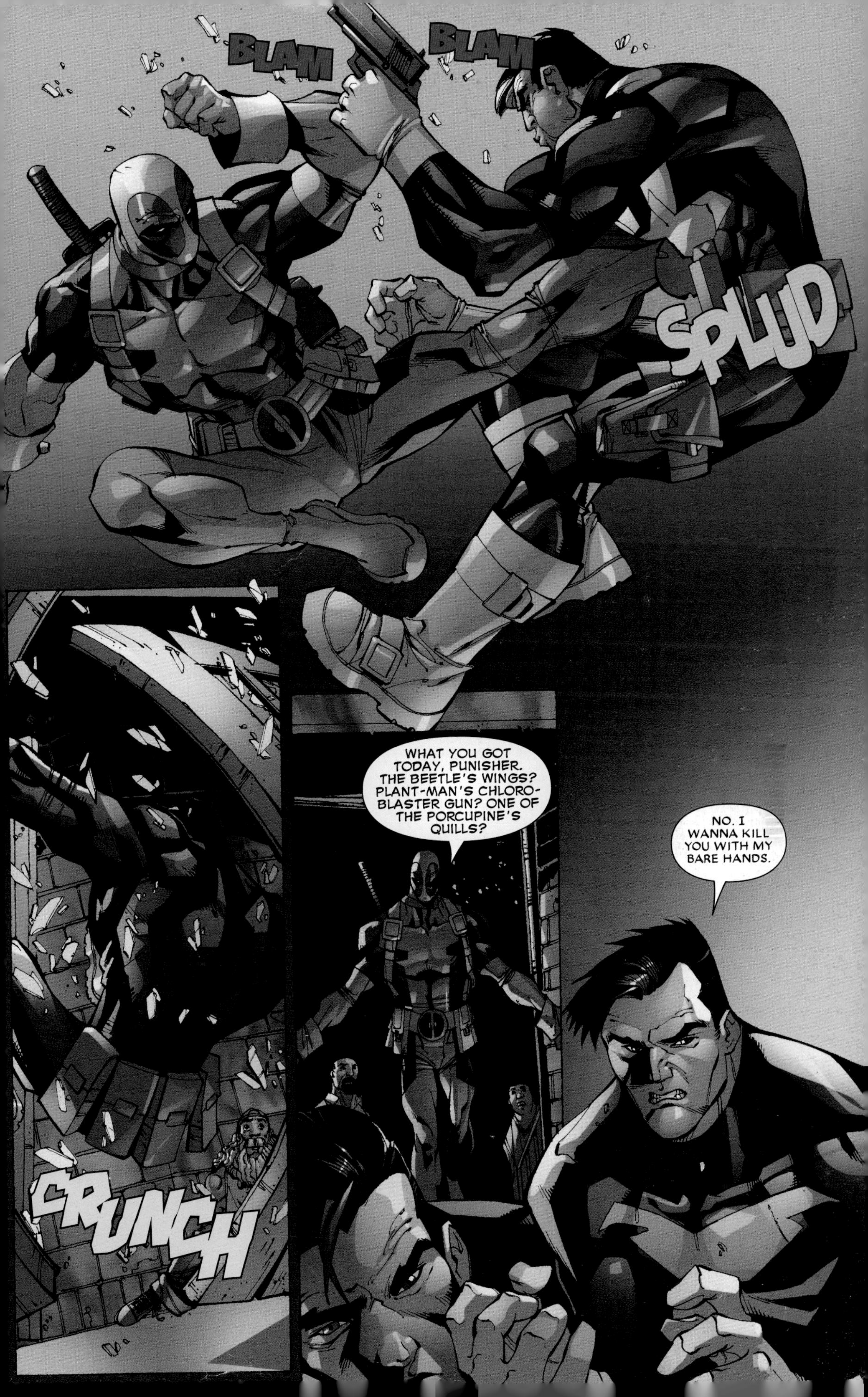
BLAM
BLAM
SPLUD
CRUNCH
WHAT YOU GOT TODAY, PUNISHER. THE BEETLE'S WINGS? PLANT-MAN'S CHLORO-BLASTER GUN? ONE OF THE PORCUPINE'S QUILLS?
NO. I WANNA KILL YOU WITH MY BARE HANDS.

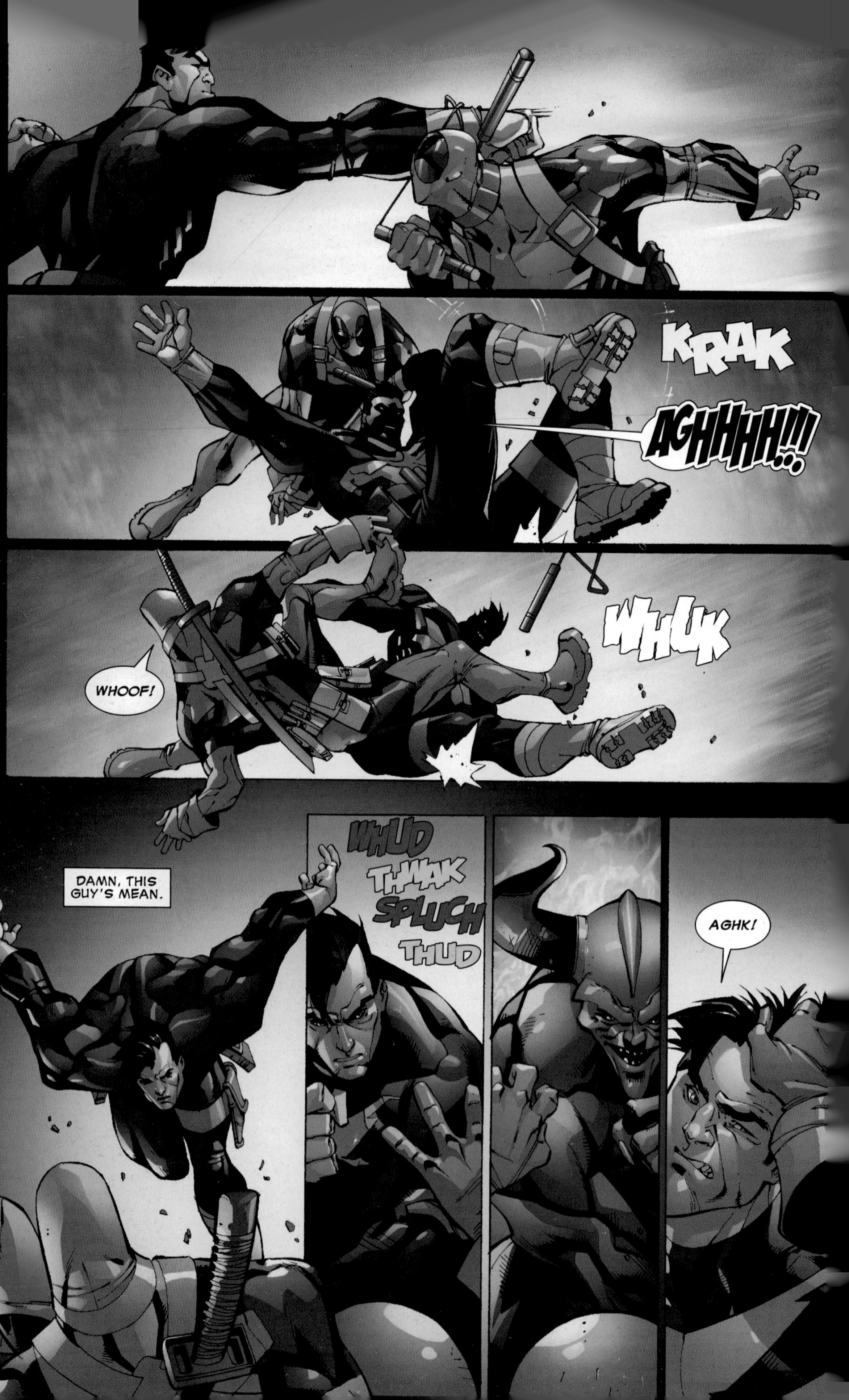
KRAK
AGHHHH!!!
WHOOF!
WHUK
DAMN, THIS GUY'S MEAN.
WHUD
THWAK
SPLUCH
THUD
AGHK!

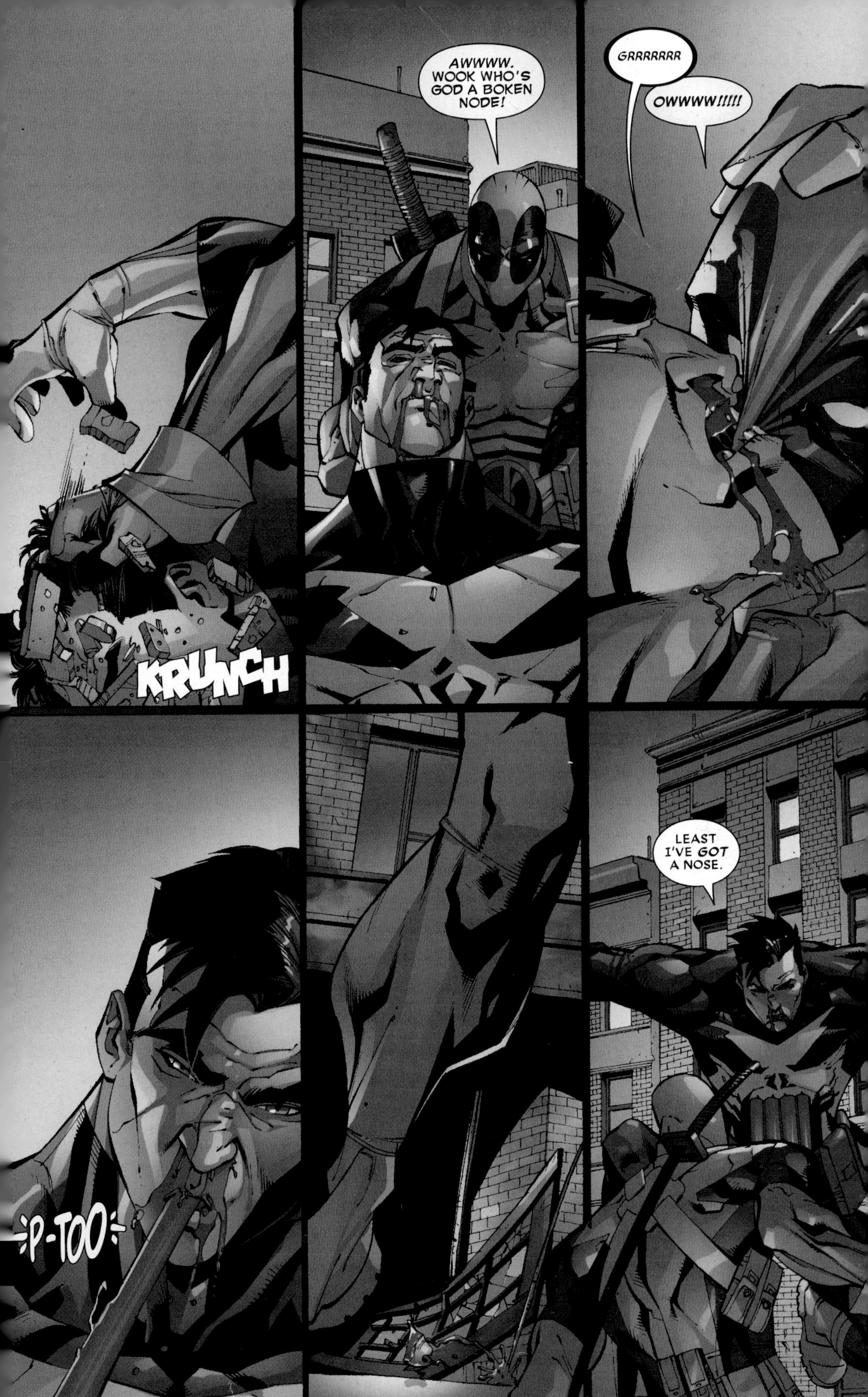
KRUNCH
AWWWW. WOOK WHO'S GOD A BOKEN NODE!
GRRRRRRR
OWWWW!!!!!
P-TOO
LEAST I'VE GOT A NOSE.

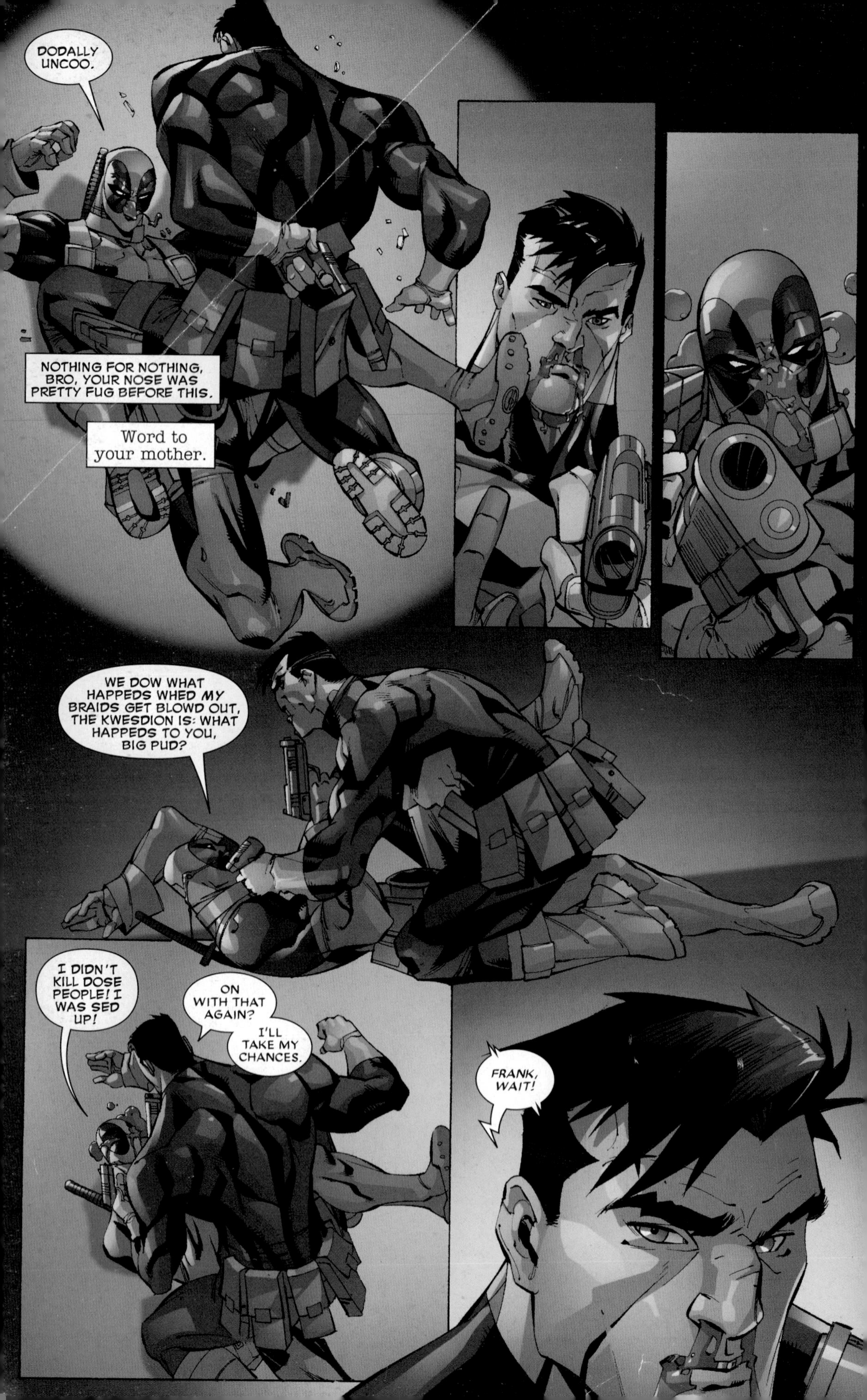
DODALLY UNCOO.
NOTHING FOR NOTHING, BRO, YOUR NOSE WAS PRETTY FUG BEFORE THIS.
Word to your mother.
WE DOW WHAT HAPPEDS WHED MY BRAIDS GET BLOWD OUT, THE KWESDION IS: WHAT HAPPEDS TO YOU, BIG PUD?
I DIDN'T KILL DOSE PEOPLE! I WAS SED UP!
ON WITH THAT AGAIN?
I'LL TAKE MY CHANCES.
FRANK, WAIT!

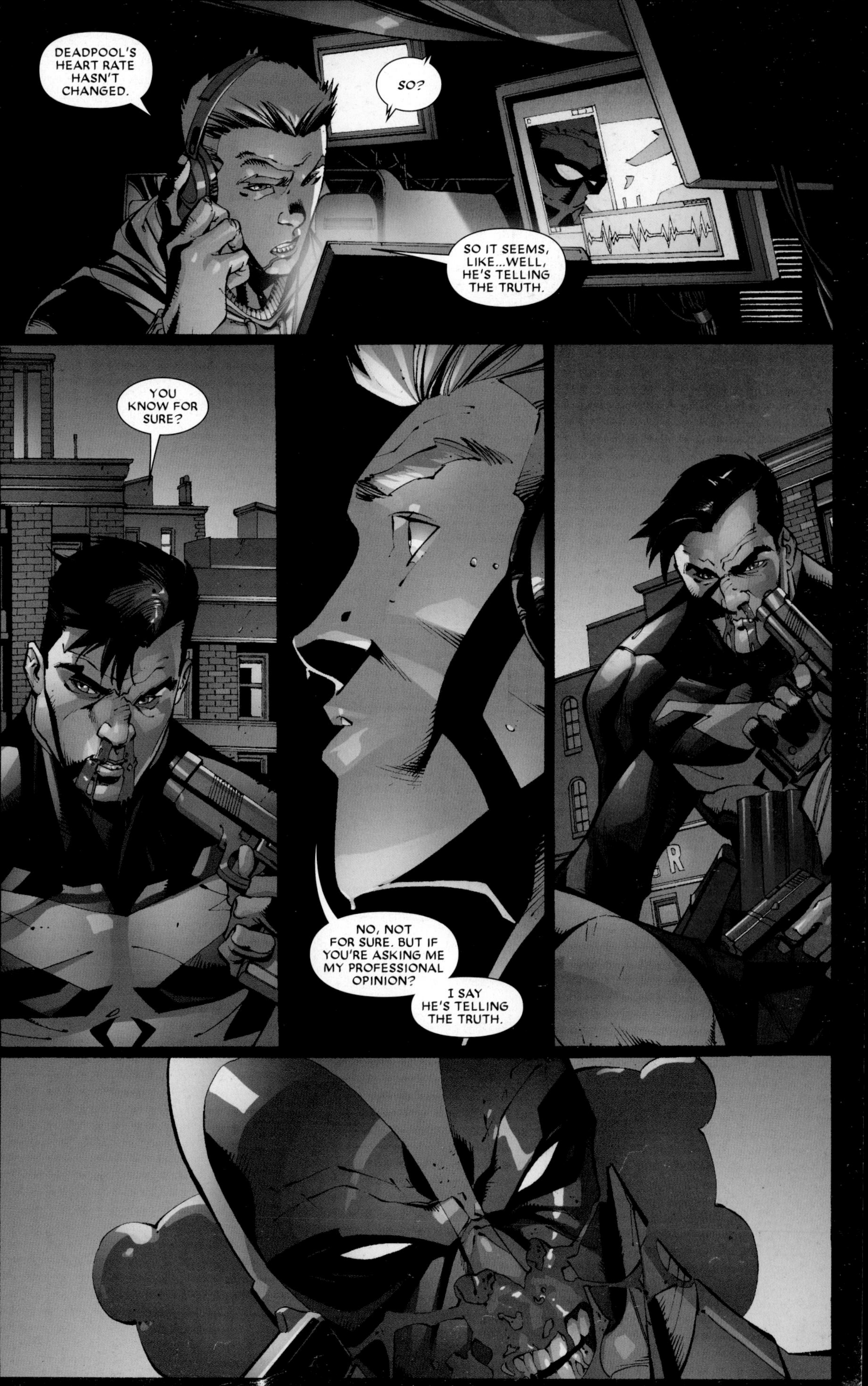
DEADPOOL'S HEART RATE HASN'T CHANGED.
SO?
SO IT SEEMS, LIKE...WELL, HE'S TELLING THE TRUTH.
YOU KNOW FOR SURE?
NO, NOT FOR SURE. BUT IF YOU'RE ASKING ME MY PROFESSIONAL OPINION?
I SAY HE'S TELLING THE TRUTH.

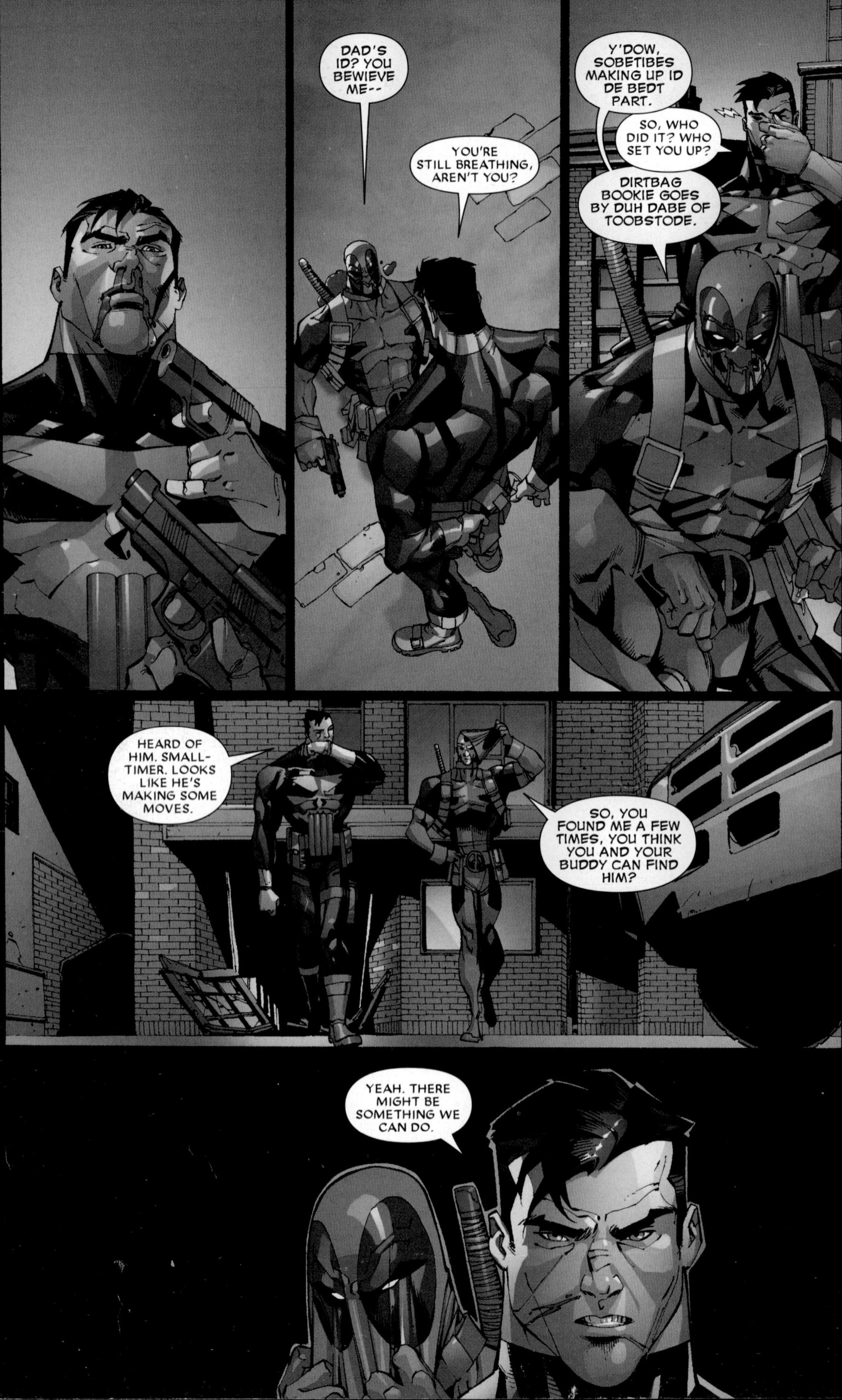
DAD'S ID? YOU BEWIEVE ME--
YOU'RE STILL BREATHING, AREN'T YOU?
Y'DOW, SOBETIBES MAKING UP ID DE BEDT PART.
SO, WHO DID IT? WHO SET YOU UP?
DIRTBAG BOOKIE GOES BY DUH DABE OF TOOBSTODE.
HEARD OF HIM. SMALL-TIMER. LOOKS LIKE HE'S MAKING SOME MOVES.
SO, YOU FOUND ME A FEW TIMES, YOU THINK YOU AND YOUR BUDDY CAN FIND HIM?
YEAH. THERE MIGHT BE SOMETHING WE CAN DO.

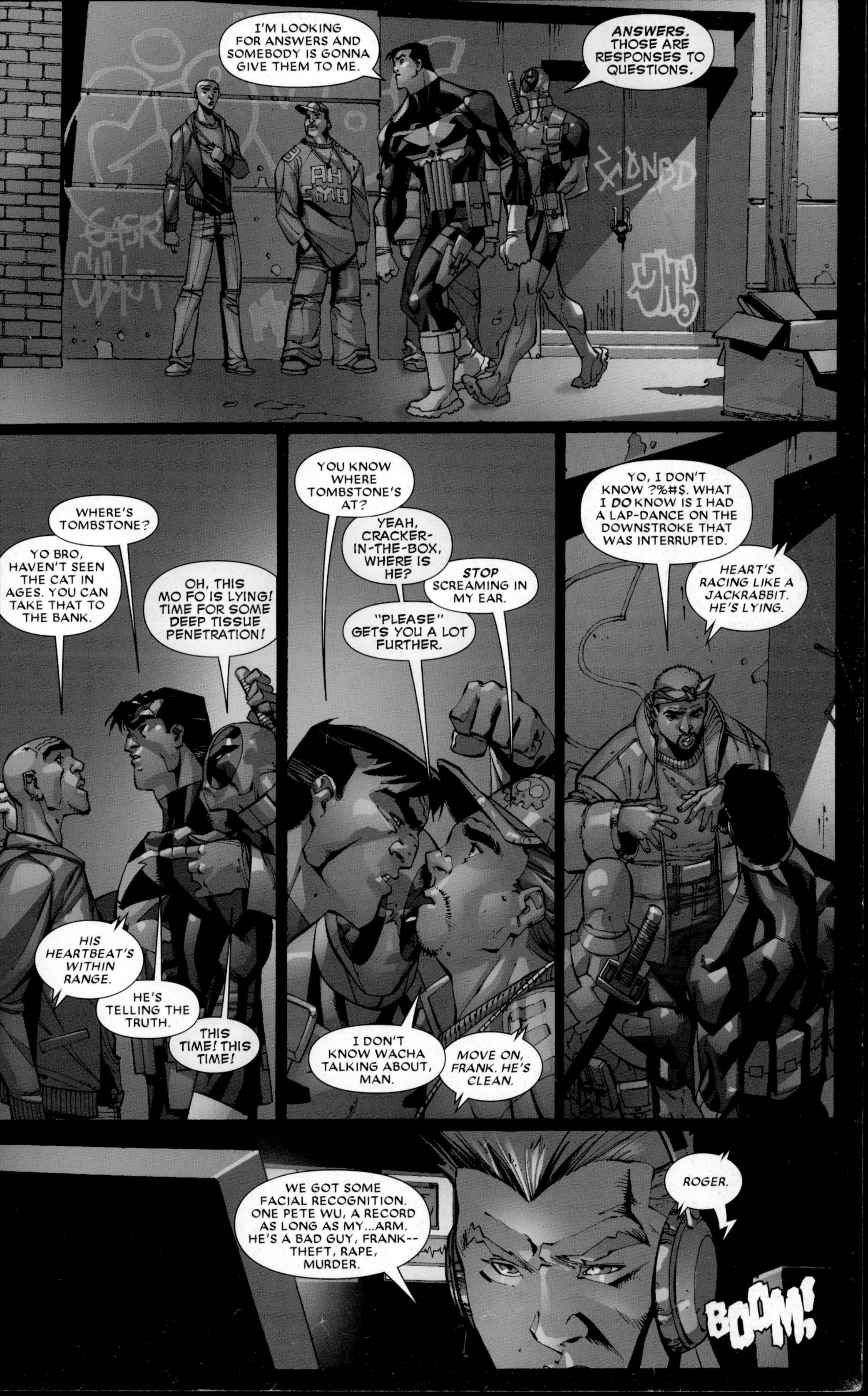
I'M LOOKING FOR ANSWERS AND SOMEBODY IS GONNA GIVE THEM TO ME.
ANSWERS. THOSE ARE RESPONSES TO QUESTIONS.
WHERE'S TOMBSTONE?
YO BRO, HAVEN'T SEEN THE CAT IN AGES. YOU CAN TAKE THAT TO THE BANK.
OH, THIS MO FO IS LYING! TIME FOR SOME DEEP TISSUE PENETRATION!
HIS HEARTBEAT'S WITHIN RANGE.
HE'S TELLING THE TRUTH.
THIS TIME! THIS TIME!
YOU KNOW WHERE TOMBSTONE'S AT?
YEAH, CRACKER-IN-THE-BOX, WHERE IS HE?
STOP SCREAMING IN MY EAR.
"PLEASE" GETS YOU A LOT FURTHER.
I DON'T KNOW WACHA TALKING ABOUT, MAN.
MOVE ON, FRANK. HE'S CLEAN.
YO, I DON'T KNOW ?%#$. WHAT I DO KNOW IS I HAD A LAP-DANCE ON THE DOWNSTROKE THAT WAS INTERRUPTED.
HEART'S RACING LIKE A JACKRABBIT. HE'S LYING.
WE GOT SOME FACIAL RECOGNITION. ONE PETE WU, A RECORD AS LONG AS MY...ARM. HE'S A BAD GUY, FRANK-- THEFT, RAPE, MURDER.
ROGER.
BOOM!

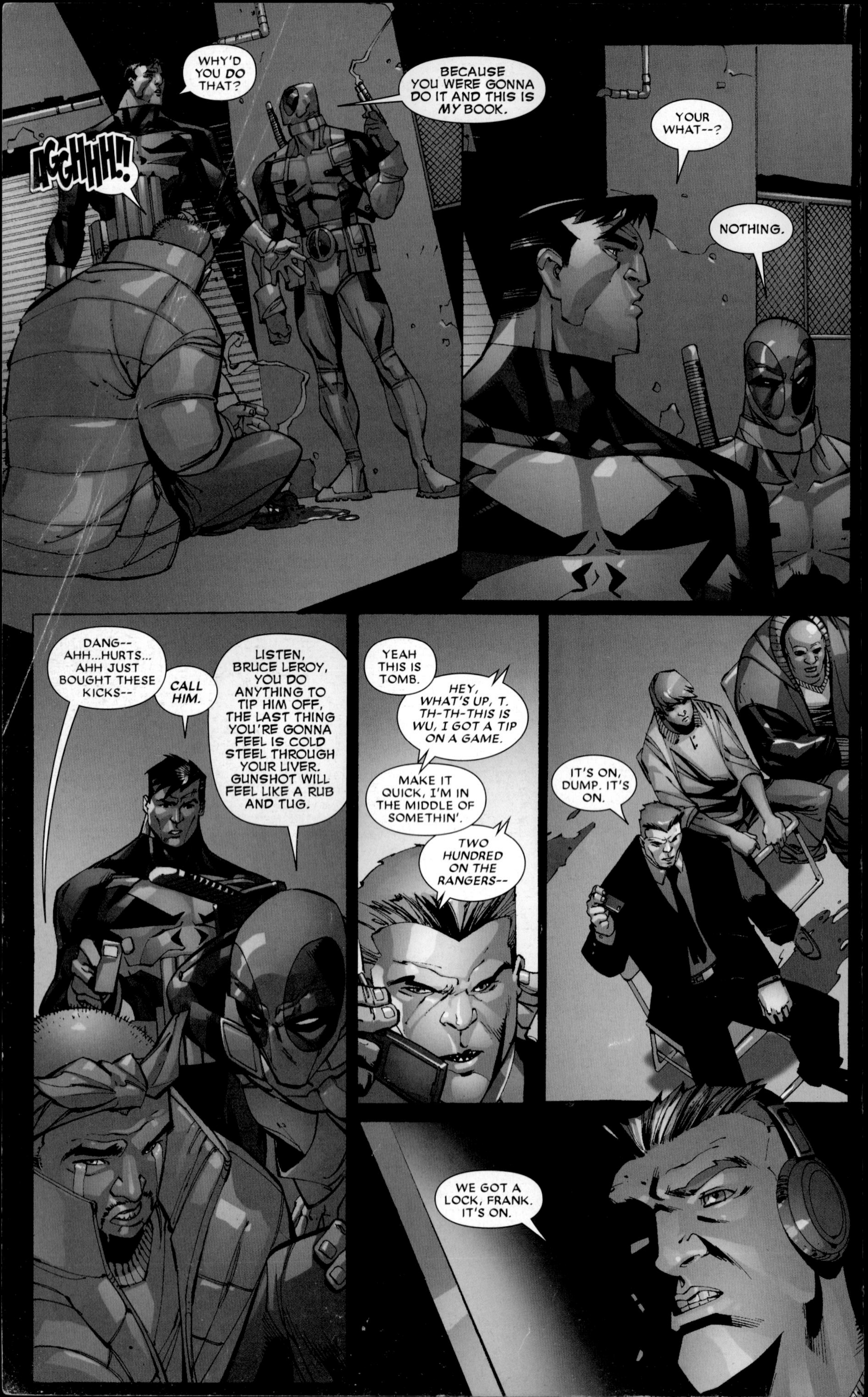
WHY'D YOU DO THAT?
BECAUSE YOU WERE GONNA DO IT AND THIS IS MY BOOK.
AGGHHH!!
YOUR WHAT--?
NOTHING.
DANG-- AHH...HURTS... AHH JUST BOUGHT THESE KICKS--
CALL HIM.
LISTEN, BRUCE LEROY, YOU DO ANYTHING TO TIP HIM OFF, THE LAST THING YOU'RE GONNA FEEL IS COLD STEEL THROUGH YOUR LIVER. GUNSHOT WILL FEEL LIKE A RUB AND TUG.
YEAH THIS IS TOMB.
HEY, WHAT'S UP, T. TH-TH-THIS IS WU, I GOT A TIP ON A GAME.
MAKE IT QUICK, I'M IN THE MIDDLE OF SOMETHIN'.
TWO HUNDRED ON THE RANGERS--
IT'S ON, DUMP. IT'S ON.
WE GOT A LOCK, FRANK. IT'S ON.

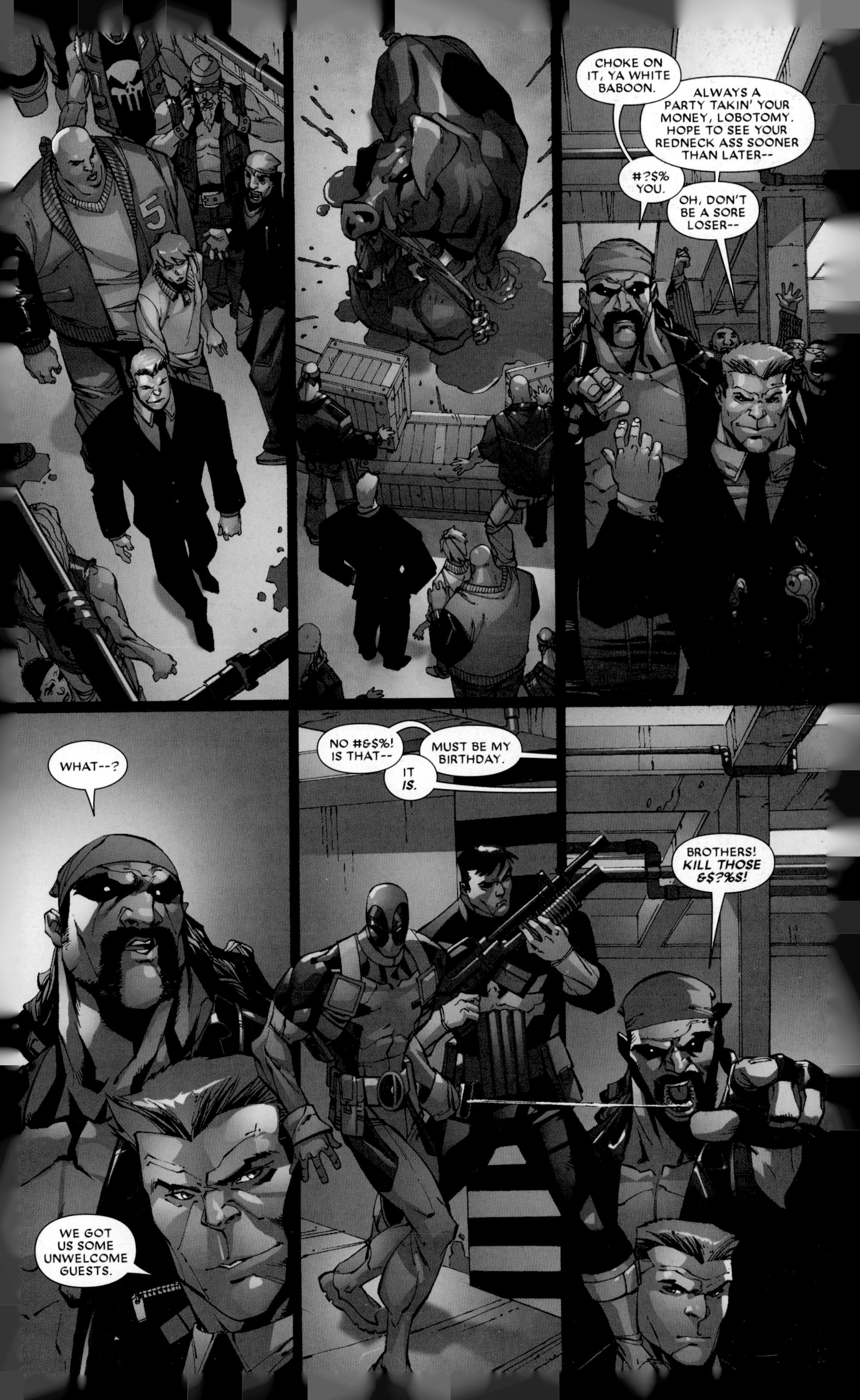
CHOKE ON IT, YA WHITE BABOON.
ALWAYS A PARTY TAKIN' YOUR MONEY, LOBOTOMY. HOPE TO SEE YOUR REDNECK ASS SOONER THAN LATER--
#?$% YOU.
OH, DON'T BE A SORE LOSER--
WHAT--?
WE GOT US SOME UNWELCOME GUESTS.
NO #&$%! IS THAT--
MUST BE MY BIRTHDAY.
IT *IS.*
BROTHERS! ***KILL THOSE &$?%S!***

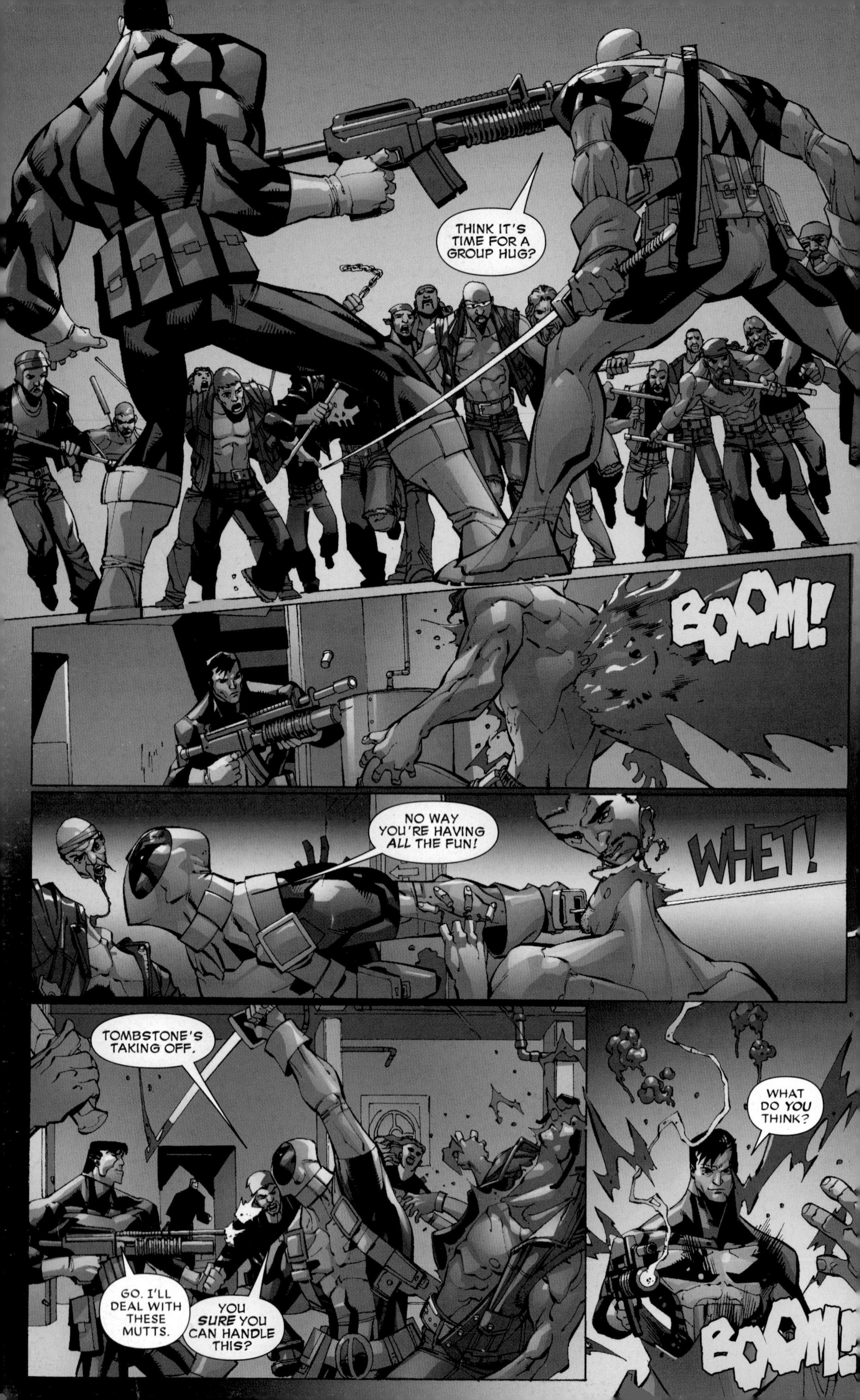
THINK IT'S TIME FOR A GROUP HUG?
BOOM!
NO WAY YOU'RE HAVING *ALL* THE FUN!
WHET!
TOMBSTONE'S TAKING OFF.
GO. I'LL DEAL WITH THESE MUTTS.
YOU *SURE* YOU CAN HANDLE THIS?
WHAT DO *YOU* THINK?
BOOM!

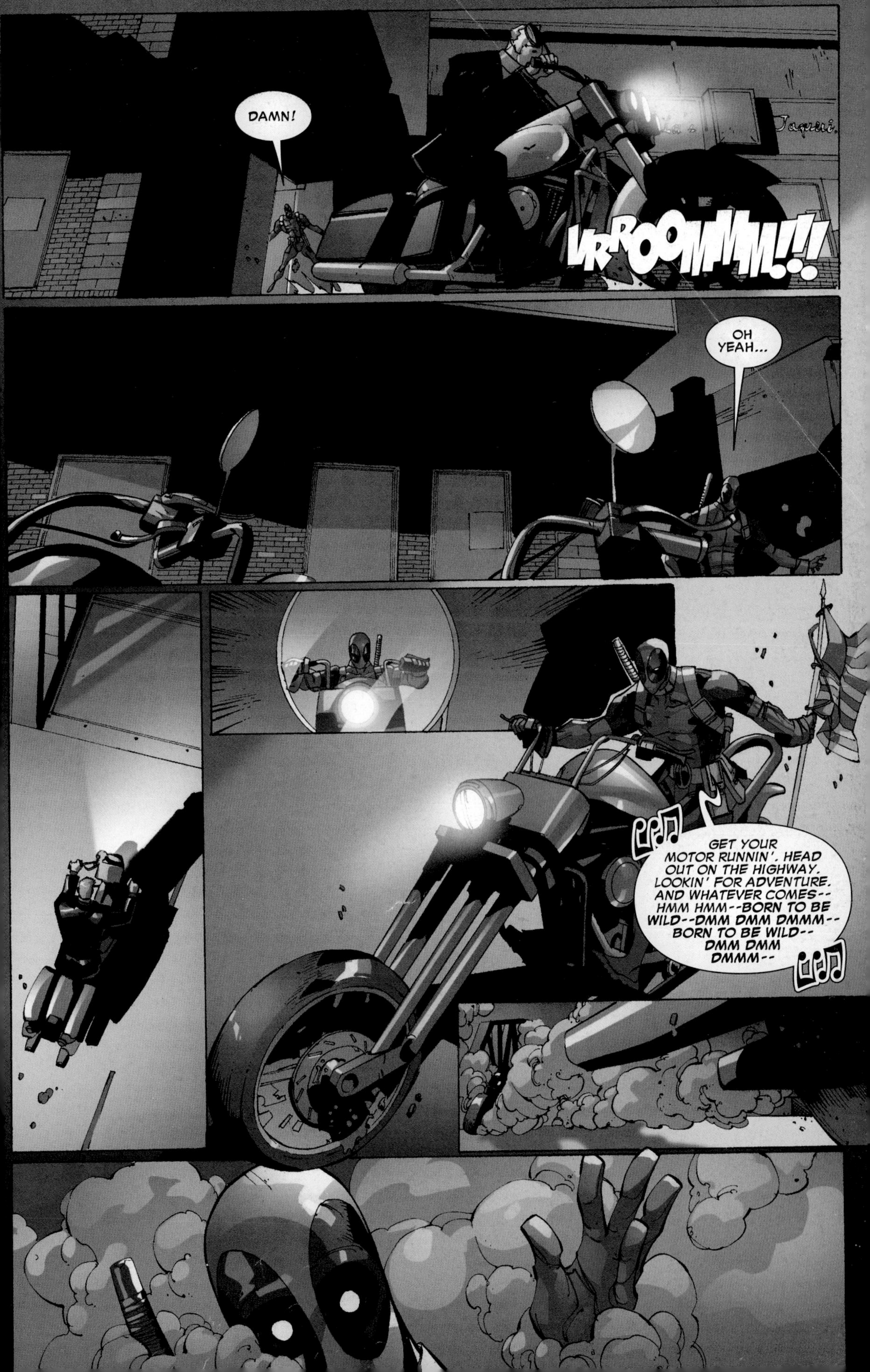
DAMN!
VRROOMMM!!!
OH YEAH...
GET YOUR MOTOR RUNNIN'. HEAD OUT ON THE HIGHWAY. LOOKIN' FOR ADVENTURE. AND WHATEVER COMES-- HMM HMM--BORN TO BE WILD--DMM DMM DMMM--BORN TO BE WILD--DMM DMM DMMM--

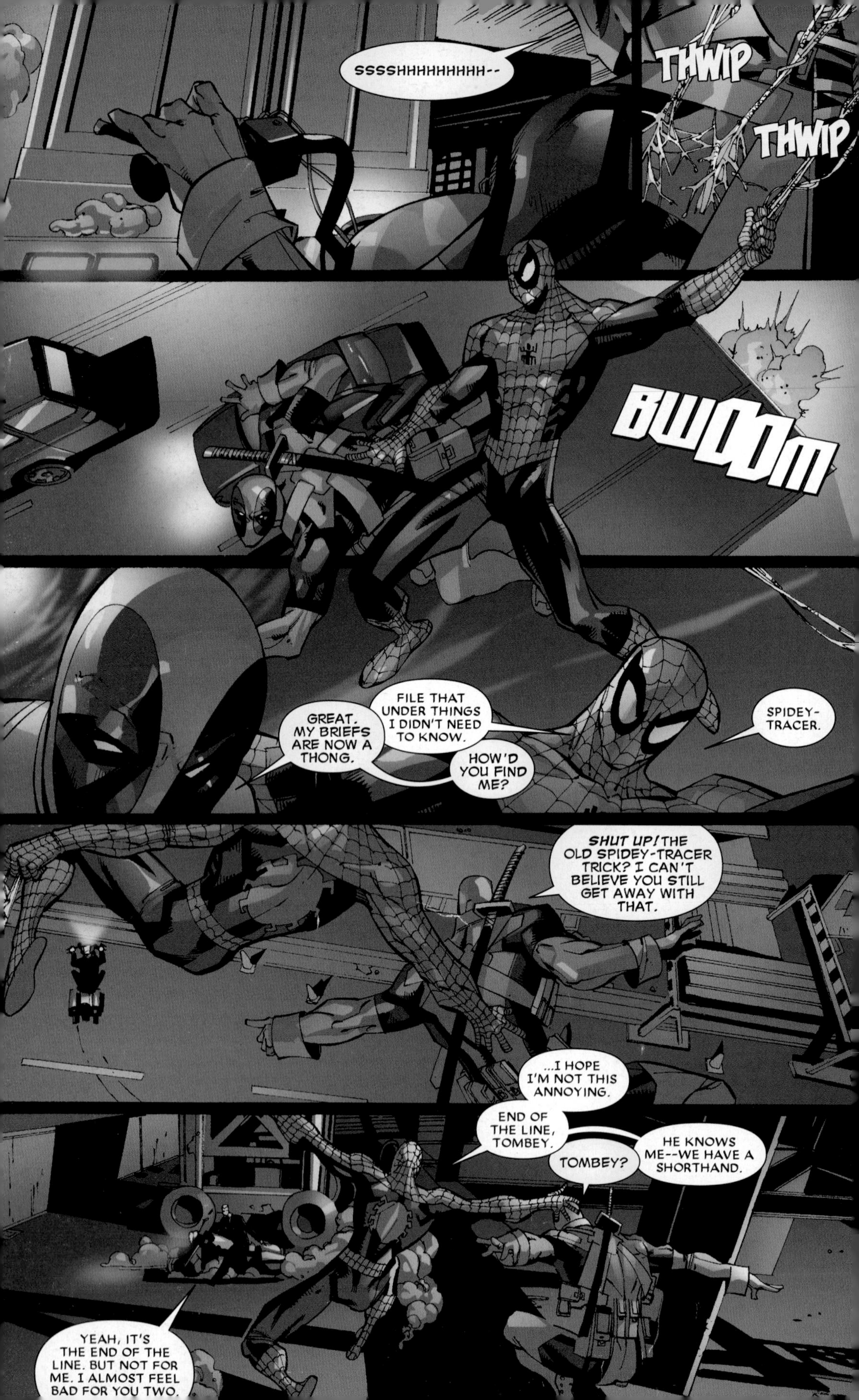
SSSSHHHHHHHHH--
THWIP
THWIP
BWOOM
GREAT. MY BRIEFS ARE NOW A THONG.
FILE THAT UNDER THINGS I DIDN'T NEED TO KNOW.
HOW'D YOU FIND ME?
SPIDEY-TRACER.
SHUT UP! THE OLD SPIDEY-TRACER TRICK? I CAN'T BELIEVE YOU STILL GET AWAY WITH THAT.
...I HOPE I'M NOT THIS ANNOYING.
END OF THE LINE, TOMBEY.
TOMBEY?
HE KNOWS ME--WE HAVE A SHORTHAND.
YEAH, IT'S THE END OF THE LINE. BUT NOT FOR ME. I ALMOST FEEL BAD FOR YOU TWO.

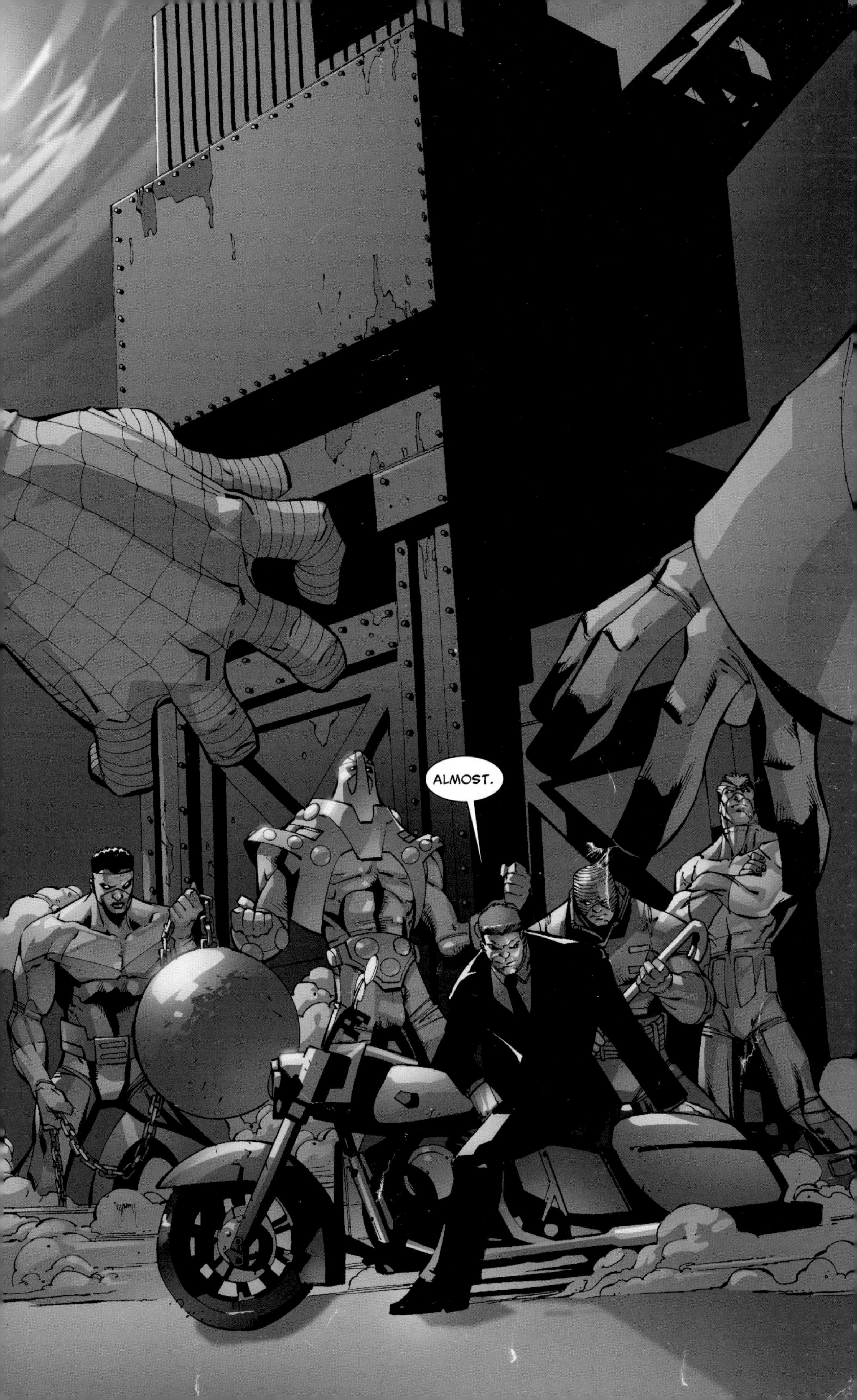
ALMOST.

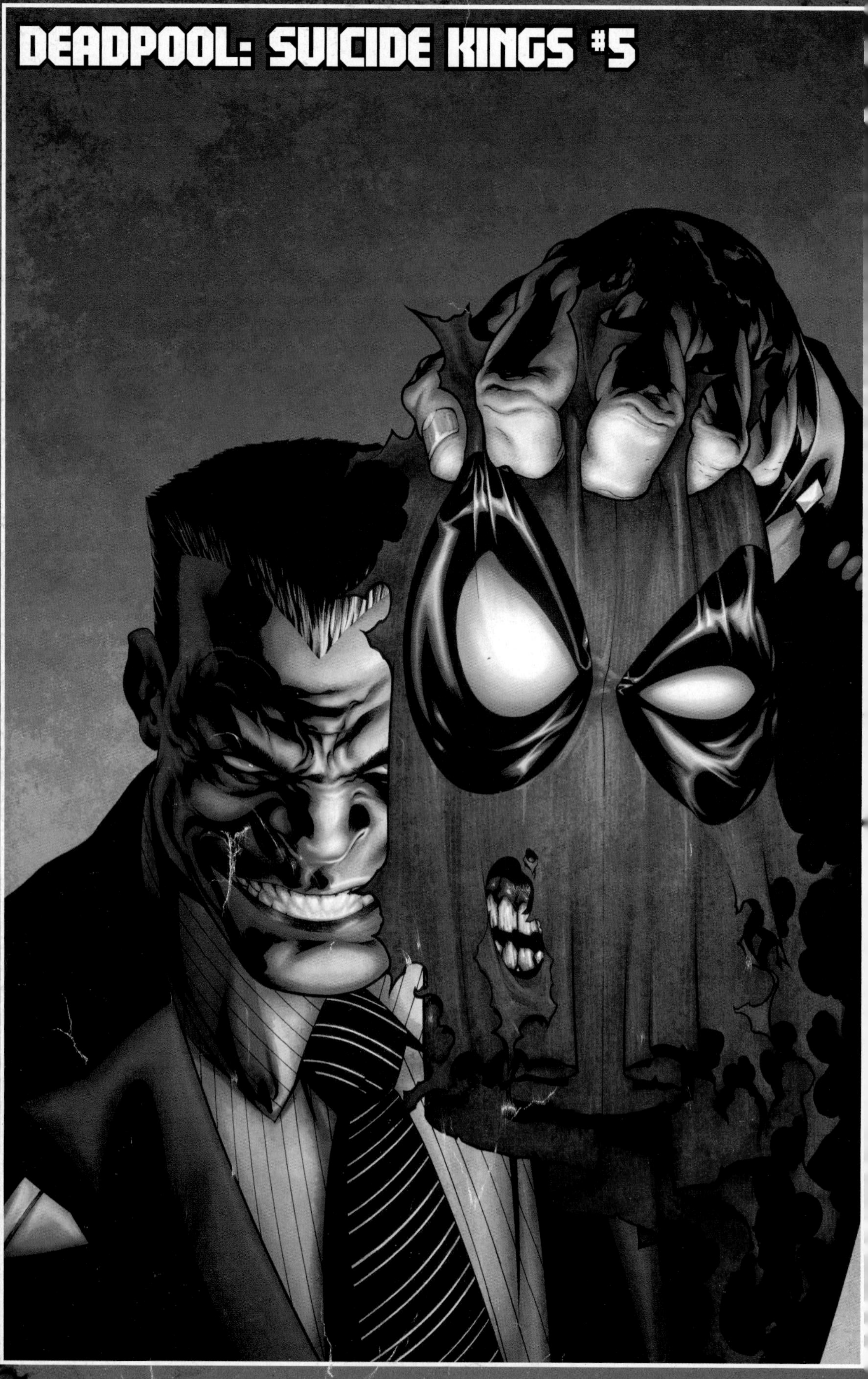
DEADPOOL: SUICIDE KINGS #5

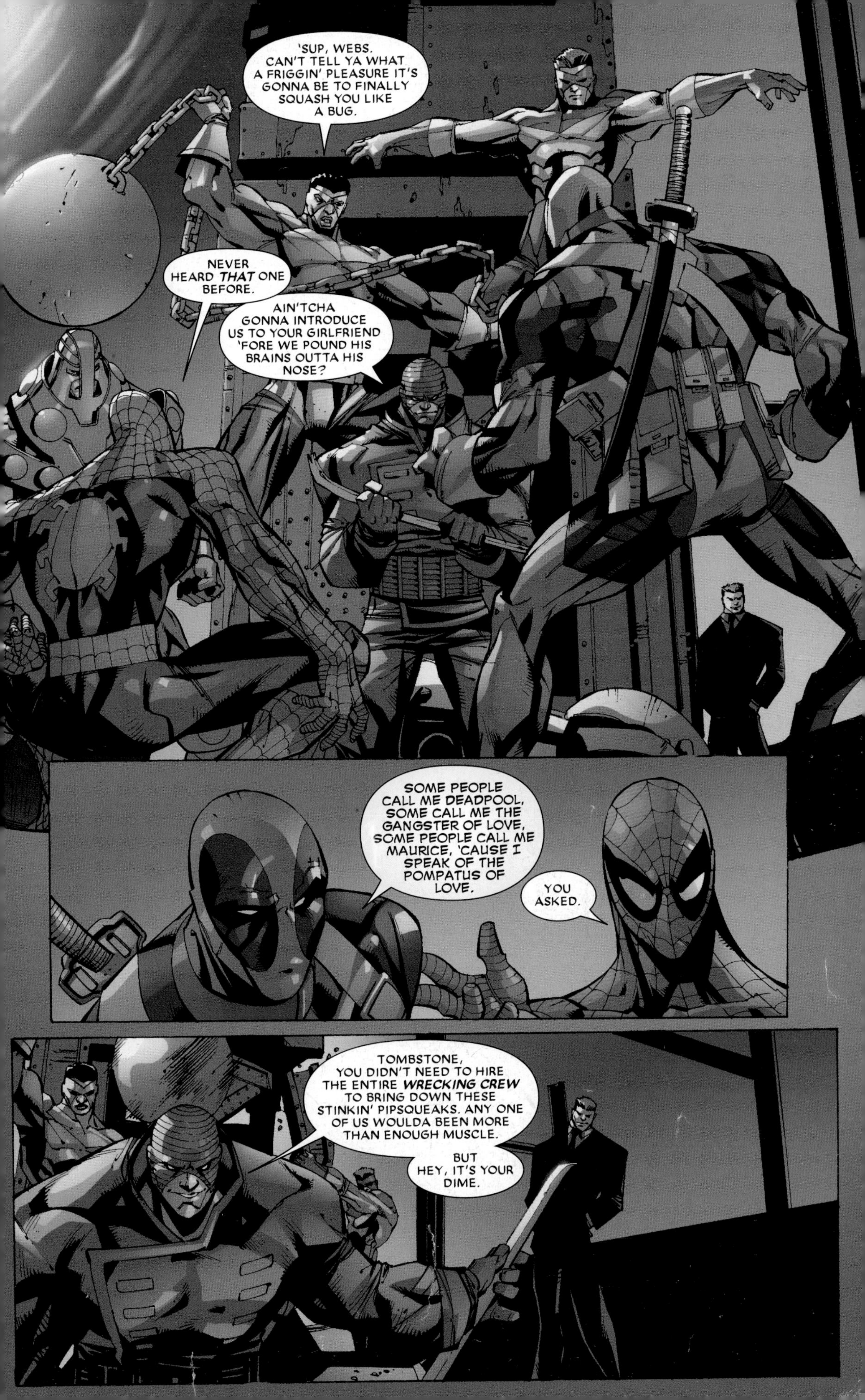

'SUP, WEBS. CAN'T TELL YA WHAT A FRIGGIN' PLEASURE IT'S GONNA BE TO FINALLY SQUASH YOU LIKE A BUG.
NEVER HEARD *THAT* ONE BEFORE.
AIN'TCHA GONNA INTRODUCE US TO YOUR GIRLFRIEND 'FORE WE POUND HIS BRAINS OUTTA HIS NOSE?
SOME PEOPLE CALL ME DEADPOOL, SOME CALL ME THE GANGSTER OF LOVE, SOME PEOPLE CALL ME MAURICE, 'CAUSE I SPEAK OF THE POMPATUS OF LOVE.
YOU ASKED.
TOMBSTONE, YOU DIDN'T NEED TO HIRE THE ENTIRE *WRECKING CREW* TO BRING DOWN THESE STINKIN' PIPSQUEAKS. ANY ONE OF US WOULDA BEEN MORE THAN ENOUGH MUSCLE.
BUT HEY, IT'S YOUR DIME.

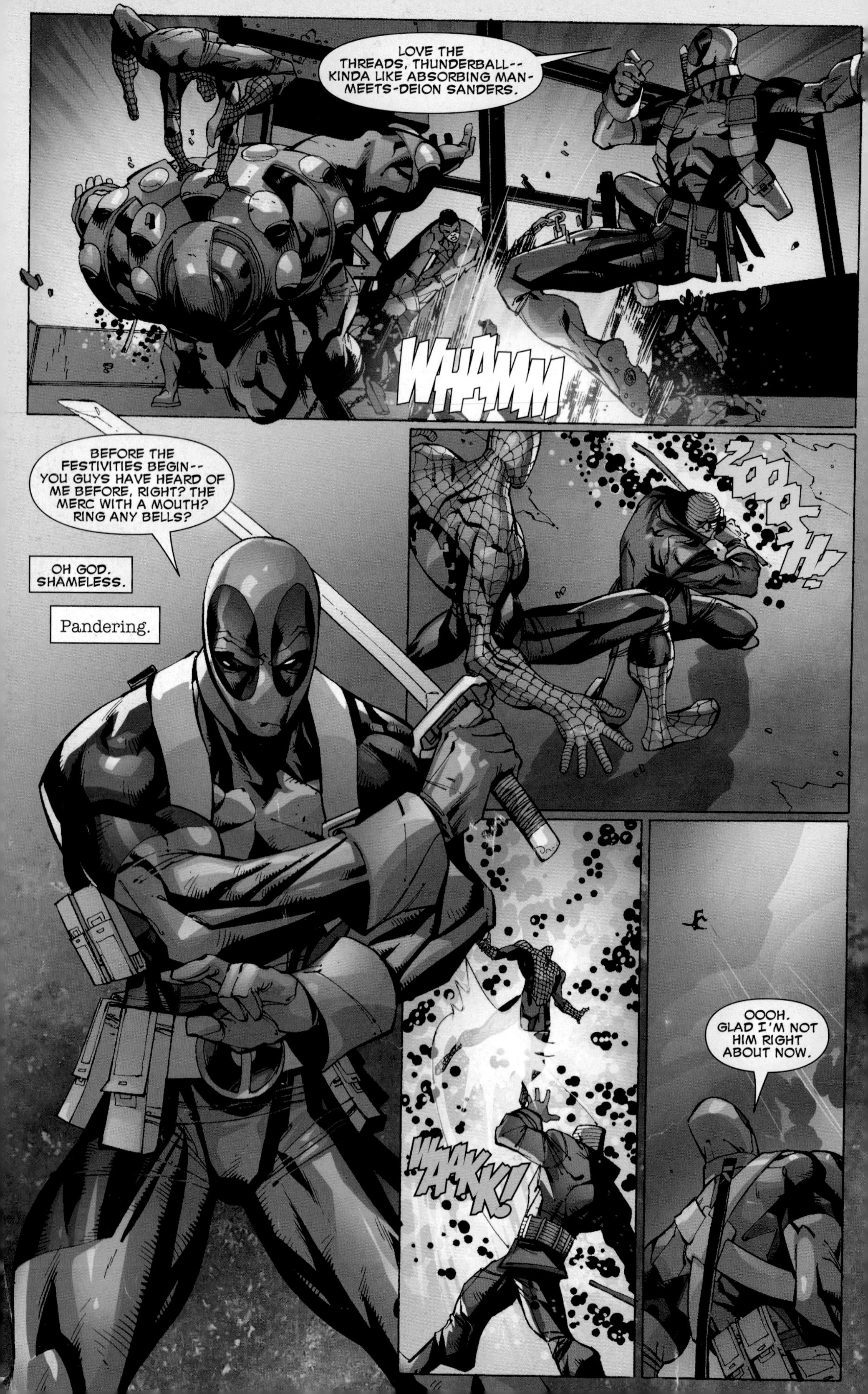
LOVE THE THREADS, THUNDERBALL-- KINDA LIKE ABSORBING MAN-MEETS-DEION SANDERS.
WHAMM
BEFORE THE FESTIVITIES BEGIN-- YOU GUYS HAVE HEARD OF ME BEFORE, RIGHT? THE MERC WITH A MOUTH? RING ANY BELLS?
OH GOD. SHAMELESS.
Pandering.
ZOOOCH!
WAKK!
OOOH. GLAD I'M NOT HIM RIGHT ABOUT NOW.

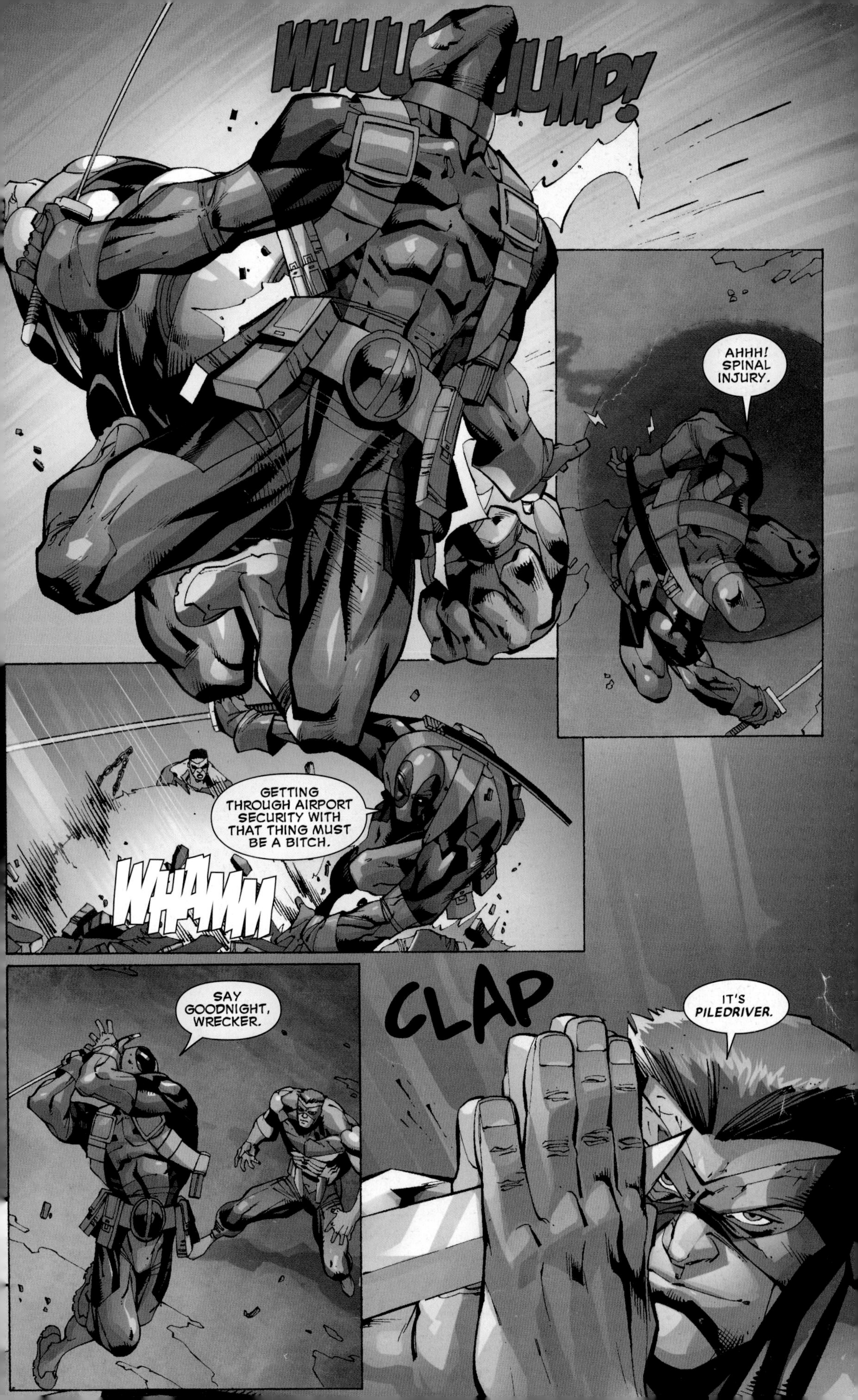
WHUUMP!
AHHH! SPINAL INJURY.
GETTING THROUGH AIRPORT SECURITY WITH THAT THING MUST BE A BITCH.
WHAMM
SAY GOODNIGHT, WRECKER.
CLAP
IT'S PILEDRIVER.

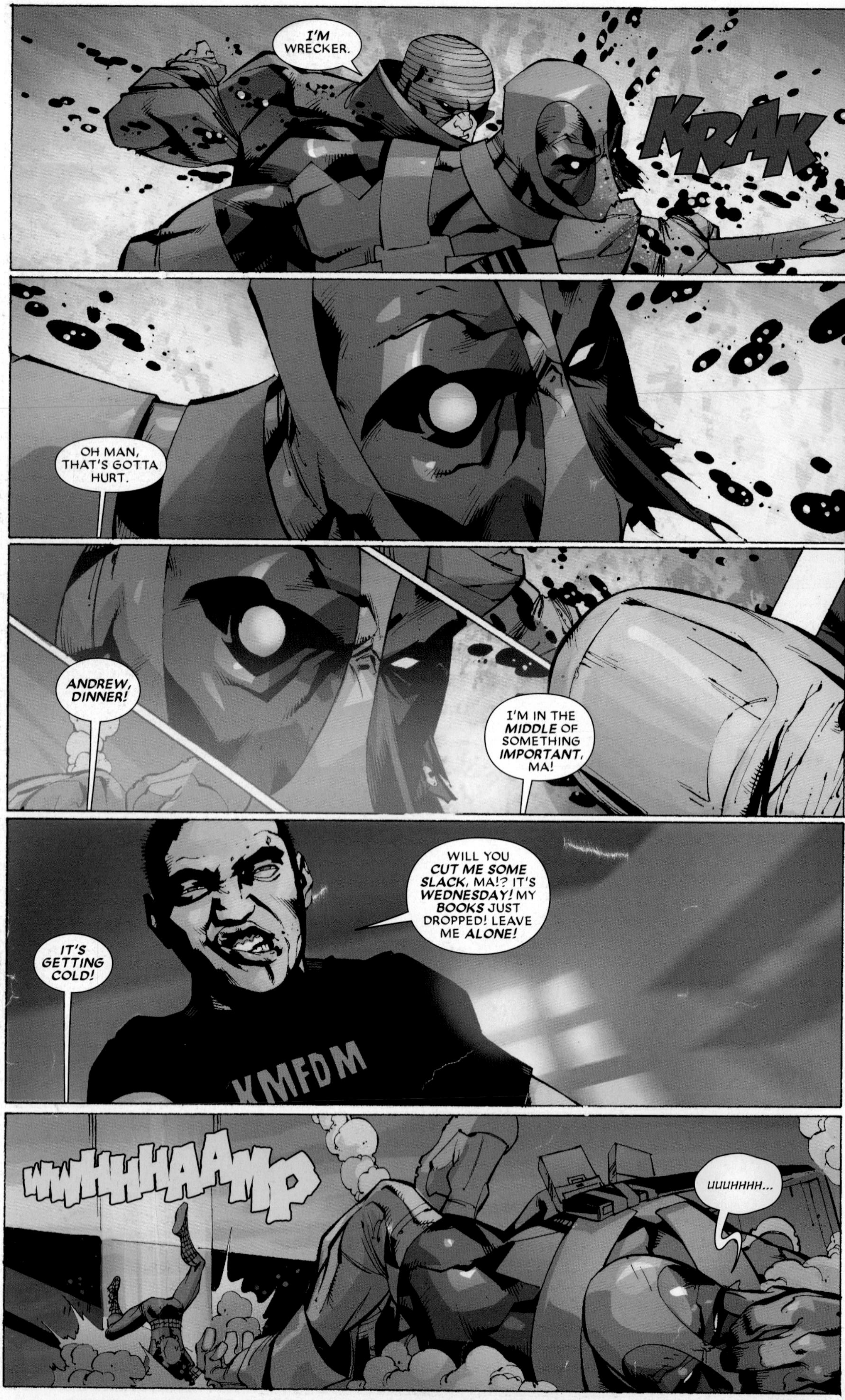
I'M WRECKER.
KRAK
OH MAN, THAT'S GOTTA HURT.
ANDREW, DINNER!
I'M IN THE MIDDLE OF SOMETHING IMPORTANT, MA!
WILL YOU CUT ME SOME SLACK, MA!? IT'S WEDNESDAY! MY BOOKS JUST DROPPED! LEAVE ME ALONE!
IT'S GETTING COLD!
KMFDM
WWHHHAAMP
UUUHHHH...

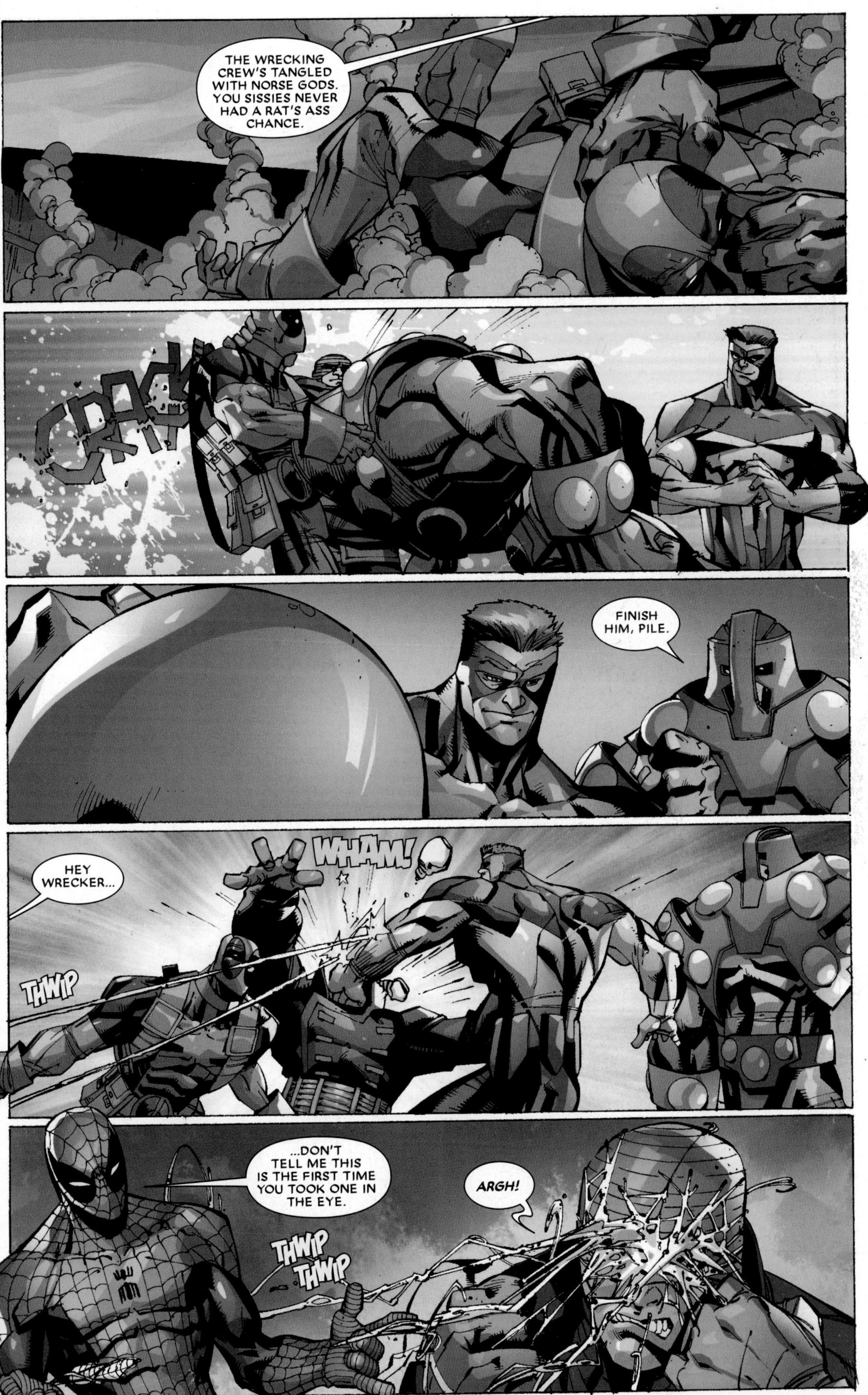
THE WRECKING CREW'S TANGLED WITH NORSE GODS. YOU SISSIES NEVER HAD A RAT'S ASS CHANCE.
CRACK
FINISH HIM, PILE.
HEY WRECKER...
WHAM!
THWIP
...DON'T TELL ME THIS IS THE FIRST TIME YOU TOOK ONE IN THE EYE.
ARGH!
THWIP THWIP

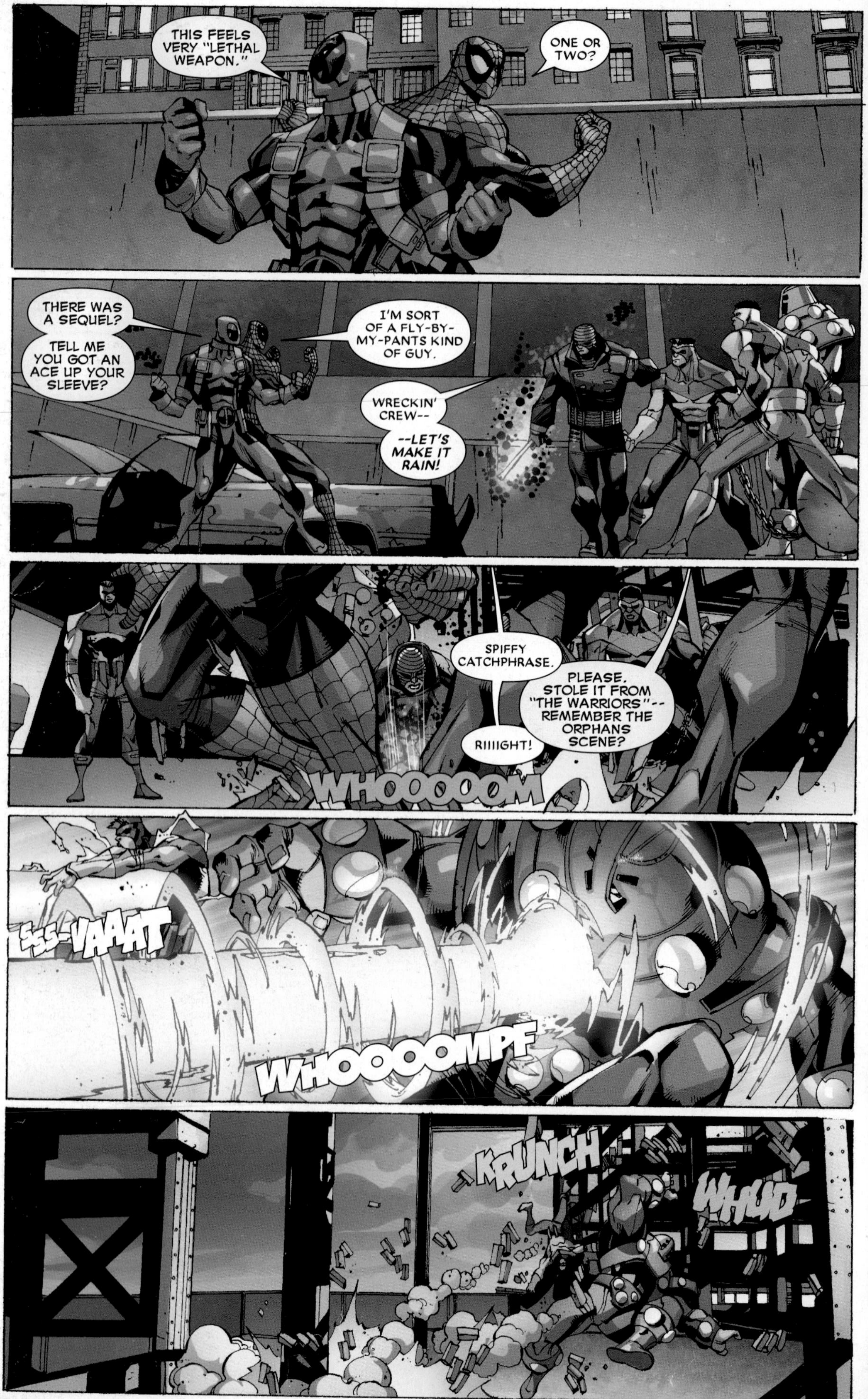
THIS FEELS VERY "LETHAL WEAPON."
ONE OR TWO?
THERE WAS A SEQUEL?
TELL ME YOU GOT AN ACE UP YOUR SLEEVE?
I'M SORT OF A FLY-BY-MY-PANTS KIND OF GUY.
WRECKIN' CREW--
--LET'S MAKE IT RAIN!
SPIFFY CATCHPHRASE.
PLEASE. STOLE IT FROM "THE WARRIORS"--REMEMBER THE ORPHANS SCENE?
RIIIIGHT!
WHOOOOOOM
SSS-VAAAT
WHOOOOOMPF
KRUNCH
WHUD

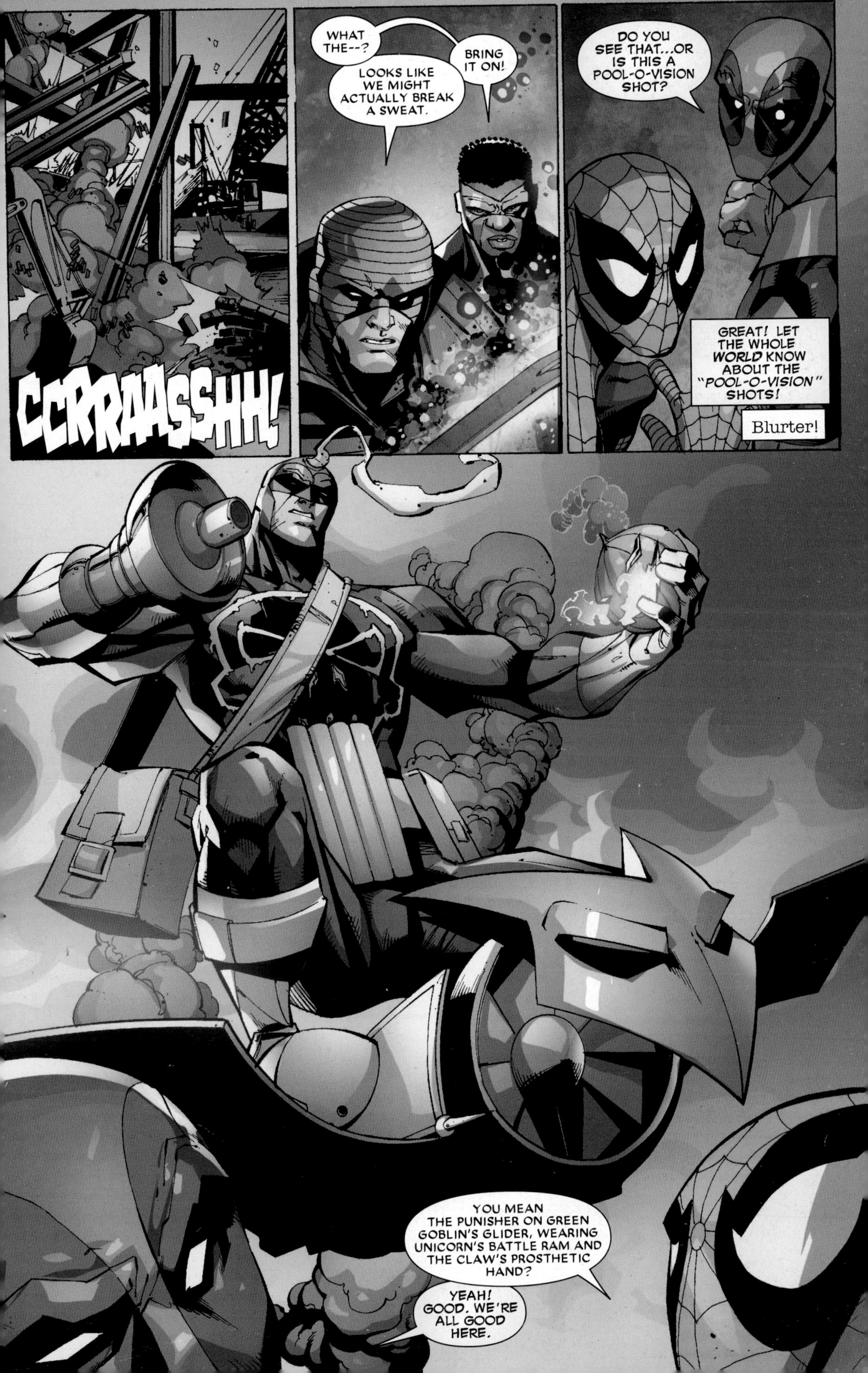
CCRRAASSHH!
WHAT THE--?
LOOKS LIKE WE MIGHT ACTUALLY BREAK A SWEAT.
BRING IT ON!
DO YOU SEE THAT...OR IS THIS A POOL-O-VISION SHOT?
GREAT! LET THE WHOLE WORLD KNOW ABOUT THE "POOL-O-VISION" SHOTS!
Blurter!
YOU MEAN THE PUNISHER ON GREEN GOBLIN'S GLIDER, WEARING UNICORN'S BATTLE RAM AND THE CLAW'S PROSTHETIC HAND?
YEAH! GOOD. WE'RE ALL GOOD HERE.

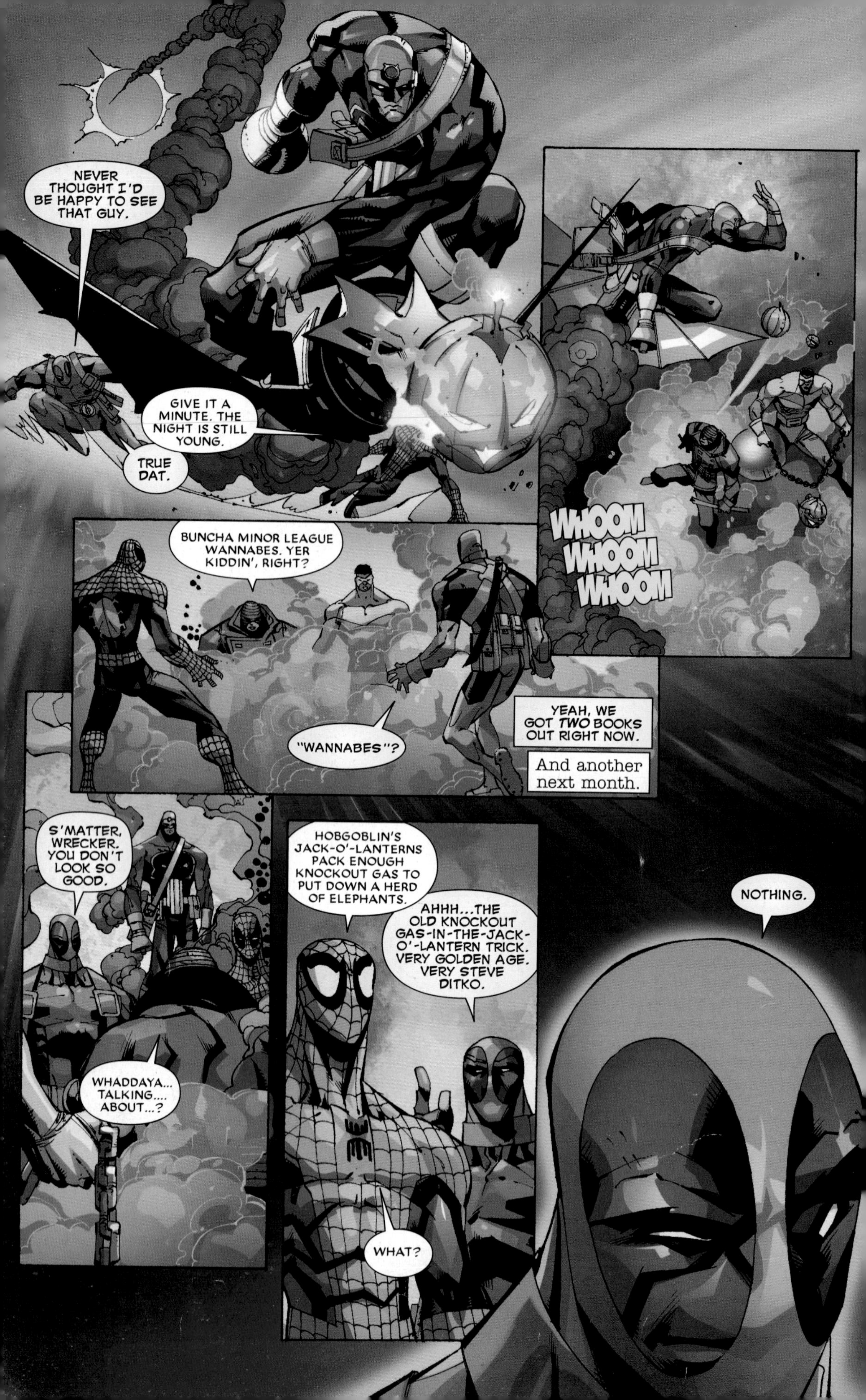
NEVER THOUGHT I'D BE HAPPY TO SEE THAT GUY.
GIVE IT A MINUTE. THE NIGHT IS STILL YOUNG.
TRUE DAT.
WHOOM WHOOM WHOOM
BUNCHA MINOR LEAGUE WANNABES. YER KIDDIN', RIGHT?
"WANNABES"?
YEAH, WE GOT TWO BOOKS OUT RIGHT NOW.
And another next month.
S'MATTER, WRECKER. YOU DON'T LOOK SO GOOD.
WHADDAYA... TALKING.... ABOUT...?
HOBGOBLIN'S JACK-O'-LANTERNS PACK ENOUGH KNOCKOUT GAS TO PUT DOWN A HERD OF ELEPHANTS.
AHHH...THE OLD KNOCKOUT GAS-IN-THE-JACK-O'-LANTERN TRICK. VERY GOLDEN AGE. VERY STEVE DITKO.
WHAT?
NOTHING.

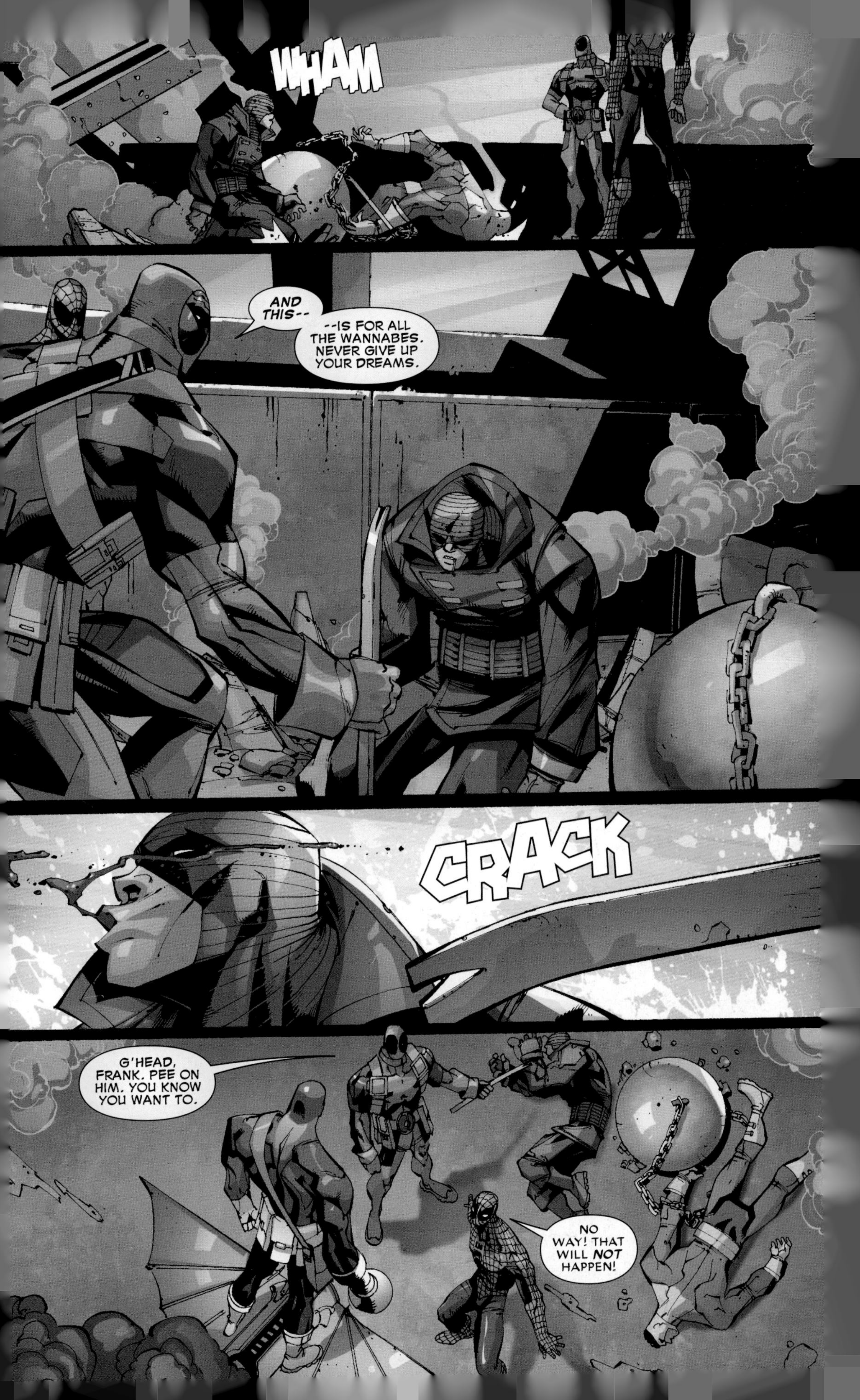
WHAM
AND THIS--
--IS FOR ALL THE WANNABES. NEVER GIVE UP YOUR DREAMS.
CRACK
G'HEAD, FRANK. PEE ON HIM. YOU KNOW YOU WANT TO.
NO WAY! THAT WILL NOT HAPPEN!

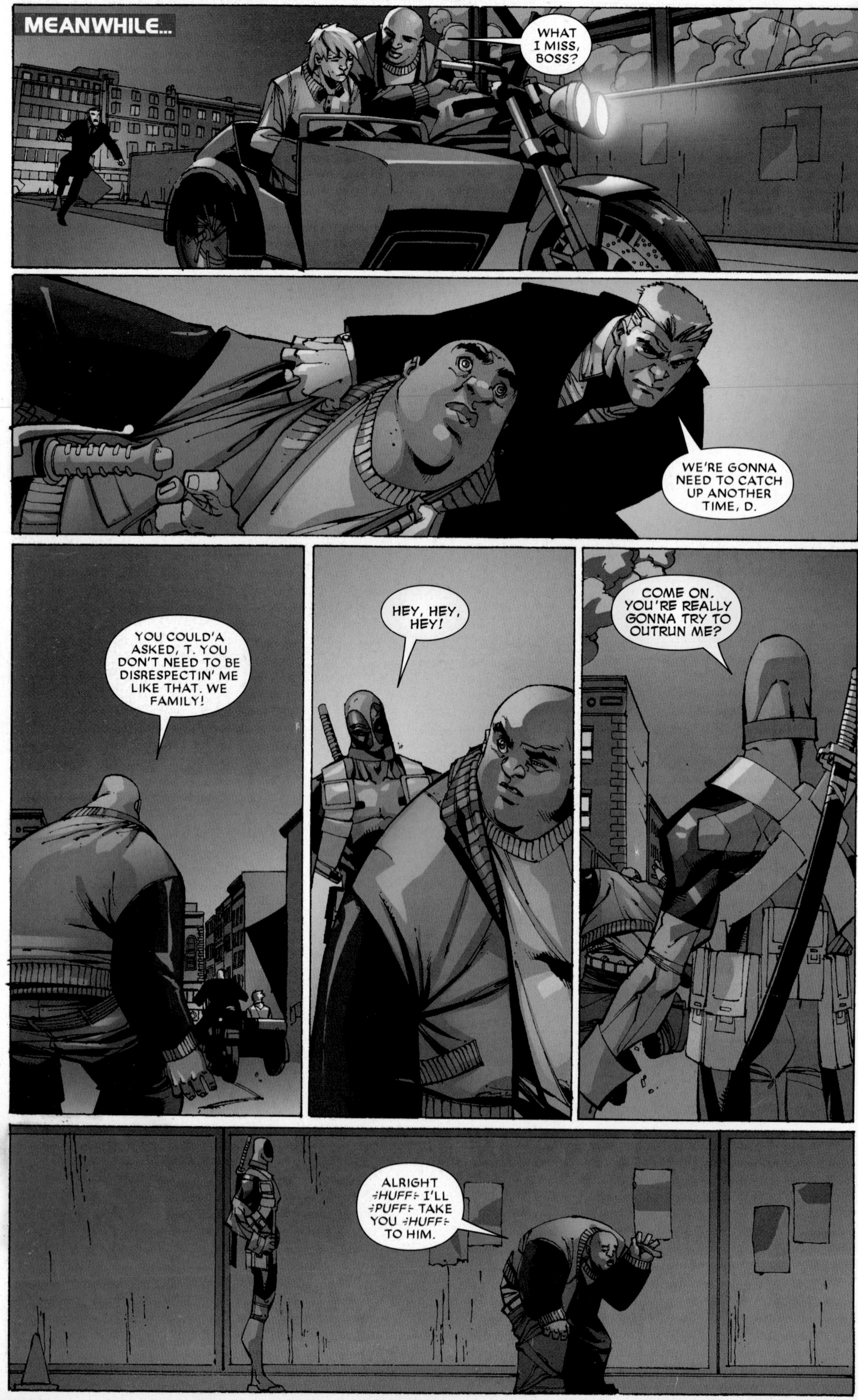
MEANWHILE...
WHAT I MISS, BOSS?
WE'RE GONNA NEED TO CATCH UP ANOTHER TIME, D.
YOU COULD'A ASKED, T. YOU DON'T NEED TO BE DISRESPECTIN' ME LIKE THAT. WE FAMILY!
HEY, HEY, HEY!
COME ON. YOU'RE REALLY GONNA TRY TO OUTRUN ME?
ALRIGHT ≠HUFF≠ I'LL ≠PUFF≠ TAKE YOU ≠HUFF≠ TO HIM.

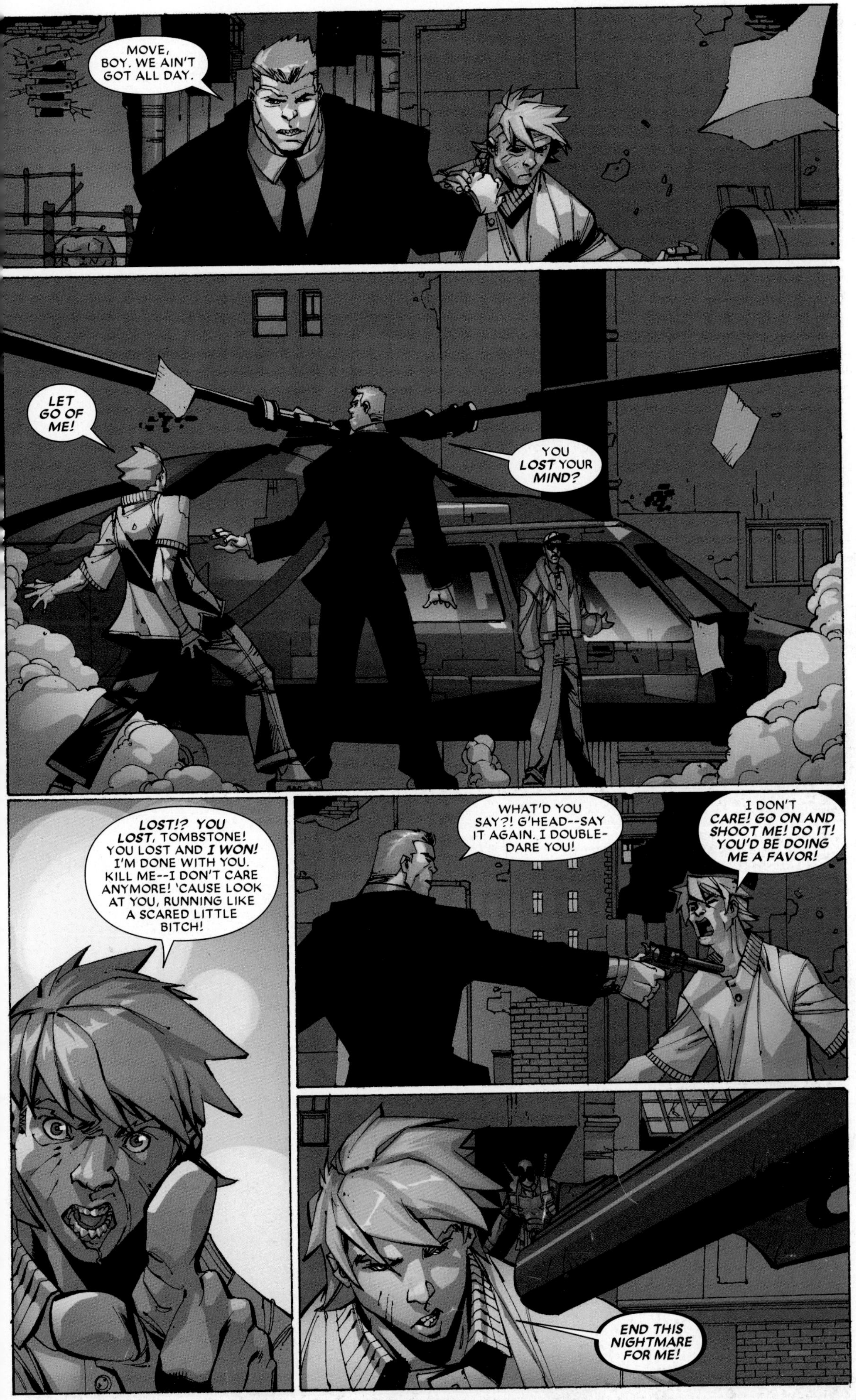
MOVE, BOY. WE AIN'T GOT ALL DAY.
LET GO OF ME!
YOU LOST YOUR MIND?
LOST!? YOU LOST, TOMBSTONE! YOU LOST AND I WON! I'M DONE WITH YOU. KILL ME--I DON'T CARE ANYMORE! 'CAUSE LOOK AT YOU, RUNNING LIKE A SCARED LITTLE BITCH!
WHAT'D YOU SAY?! G'HEAD--SAY IT AGAIN. I DOUBLE-DARE YOU!
I DON'T CARE! GO ON AND SHOOT ME! DO IT! YOU'D BE DOING ME A FAVOR!
END THIS NIGHTMARE FOR ME!

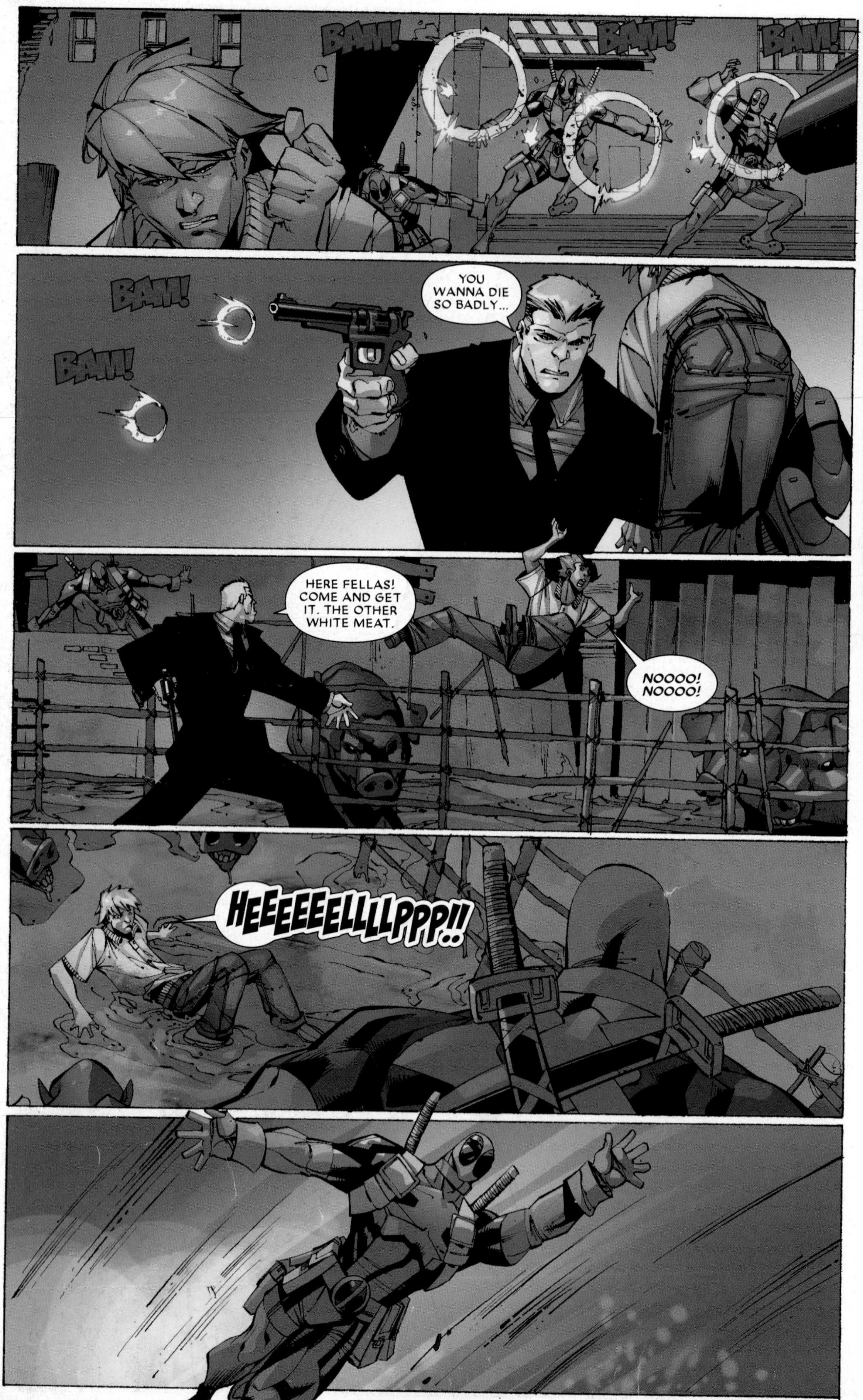
BAM!
BAM!
BAM!
BAM!
BAM!
YOU WANNA DIE SO BADLY...
HERE FELLAS! COME AND GET IT. THE OTHER WHITE MEAT.
NOOOO! NOOOO!
HEEEEEELLLLPPP!!

:SNORT:
:SNORT:
:SNORT:

OHMY GODNOOOO! NOOOO!

SHLKT

SSSQQUUUEELL!

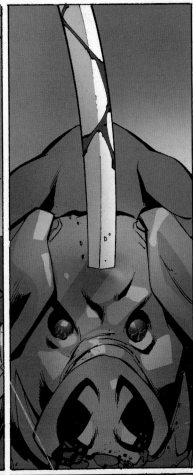

I'M HAVING A REAL "LORD OF THE FLIES" MOMENT.

SSSQQUUUEELL!

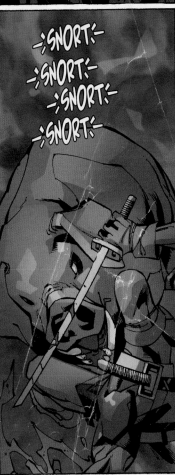

:SNORT:
:SNORT:
:SNORT:
:SNORT:

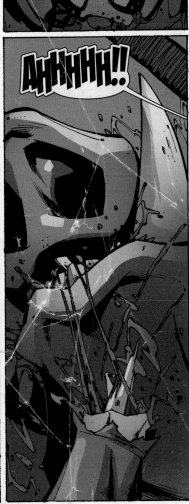

AHHHHH!!

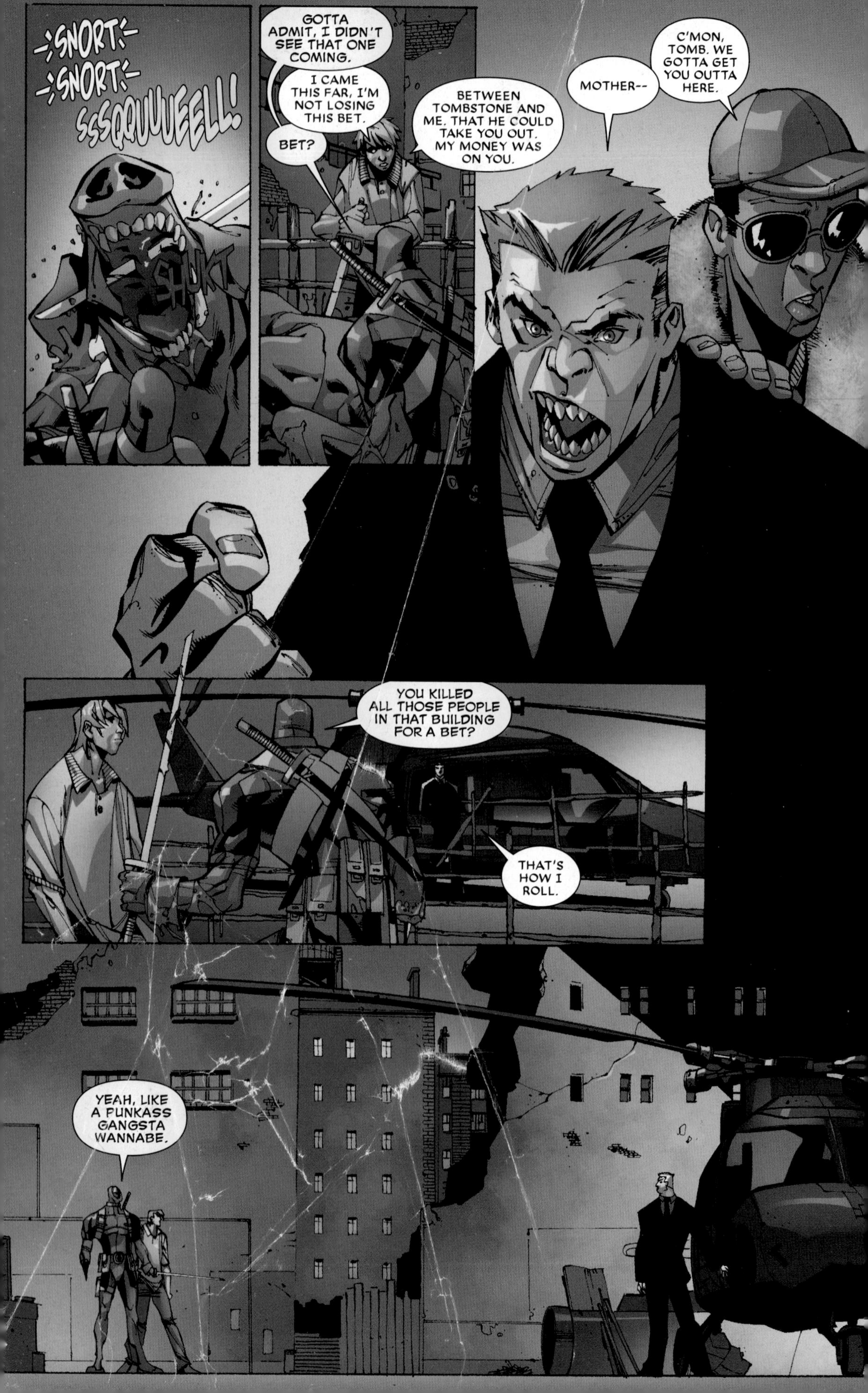
SNORT
SNORT
SSSQQUUUUEELL!
SHUKT
GOTTA ADMIT, I DIDN'T SEE THAT ONE COMING.
I CAME THIS FAR, I'M NOT LOSING THIS BET.
BET?
BETWEEN TOMBSTONE AND ME. THAT HE COULD TAKE YOU OUT. MY MONEY WAS ON YOU.
MOTHER--
C'MON, TOMB. WE GOTTA GET YOU OUTTA HERE.
YOU KILLED ALL THOSE PEOPLE IN THAT BUILDING FOR A BET?
THAT'S HOW I ROLL.
YEAH, LIKE A PUNKASS GANGSTA WANNABE.

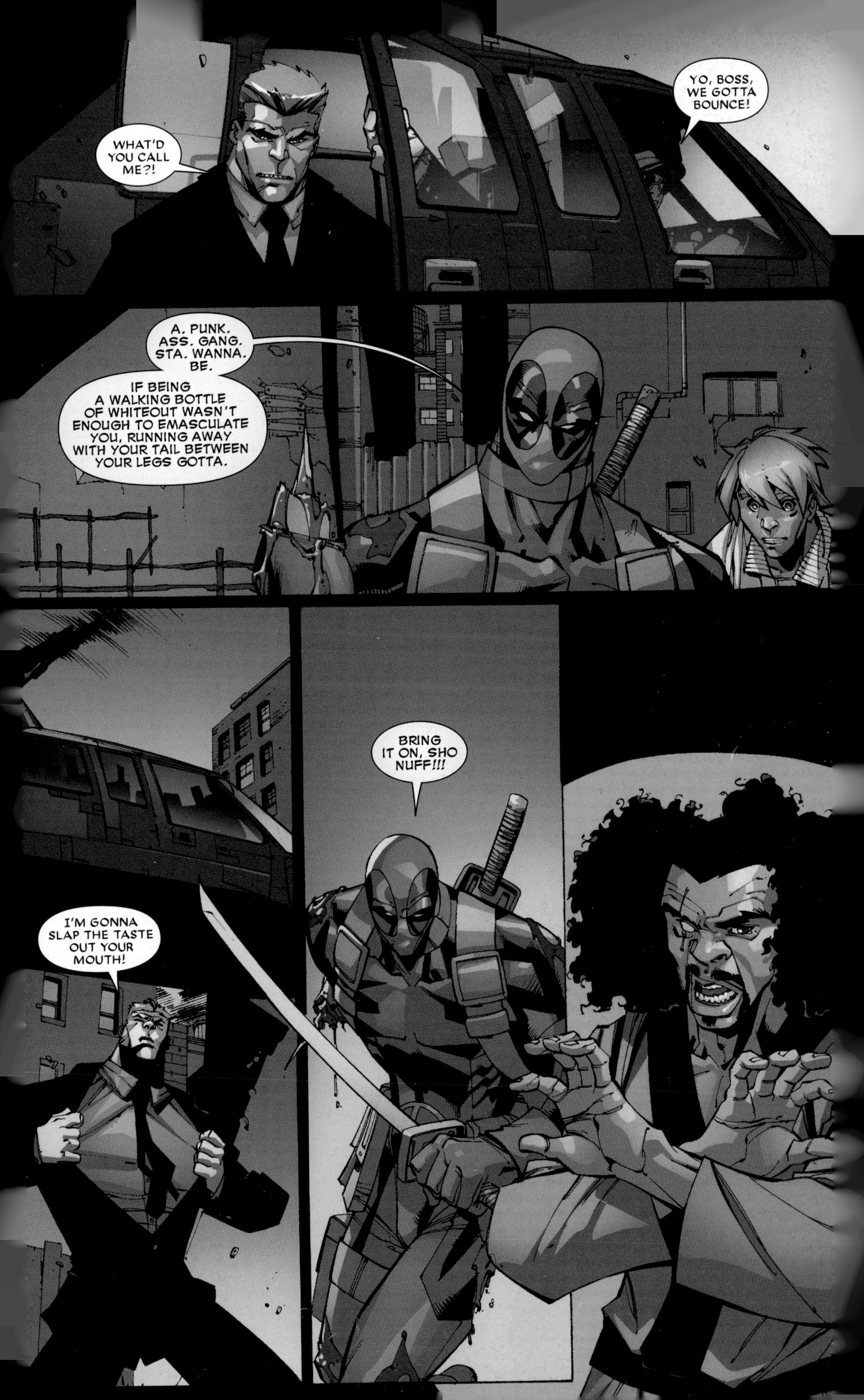
WHAT'D YOU CALL ME?!
YO, BOSS, WE GOTTA BOUNCE!
A. PUNK. ASS. GANG. STA. WANNA. BE.
IF BEING A WALKING BOTTLE OF WHITEOUT WASN'T ENOUGH TO EMASCULATE YOU, RUNNING AWAY WITH YOUR TAIL BETWEEN YOUR LEGS GOTTA.
I'M GONNA SLAP THE TASTE OUT YOUR MOUTH!
BRING IT ON, SHO NUFF!!!

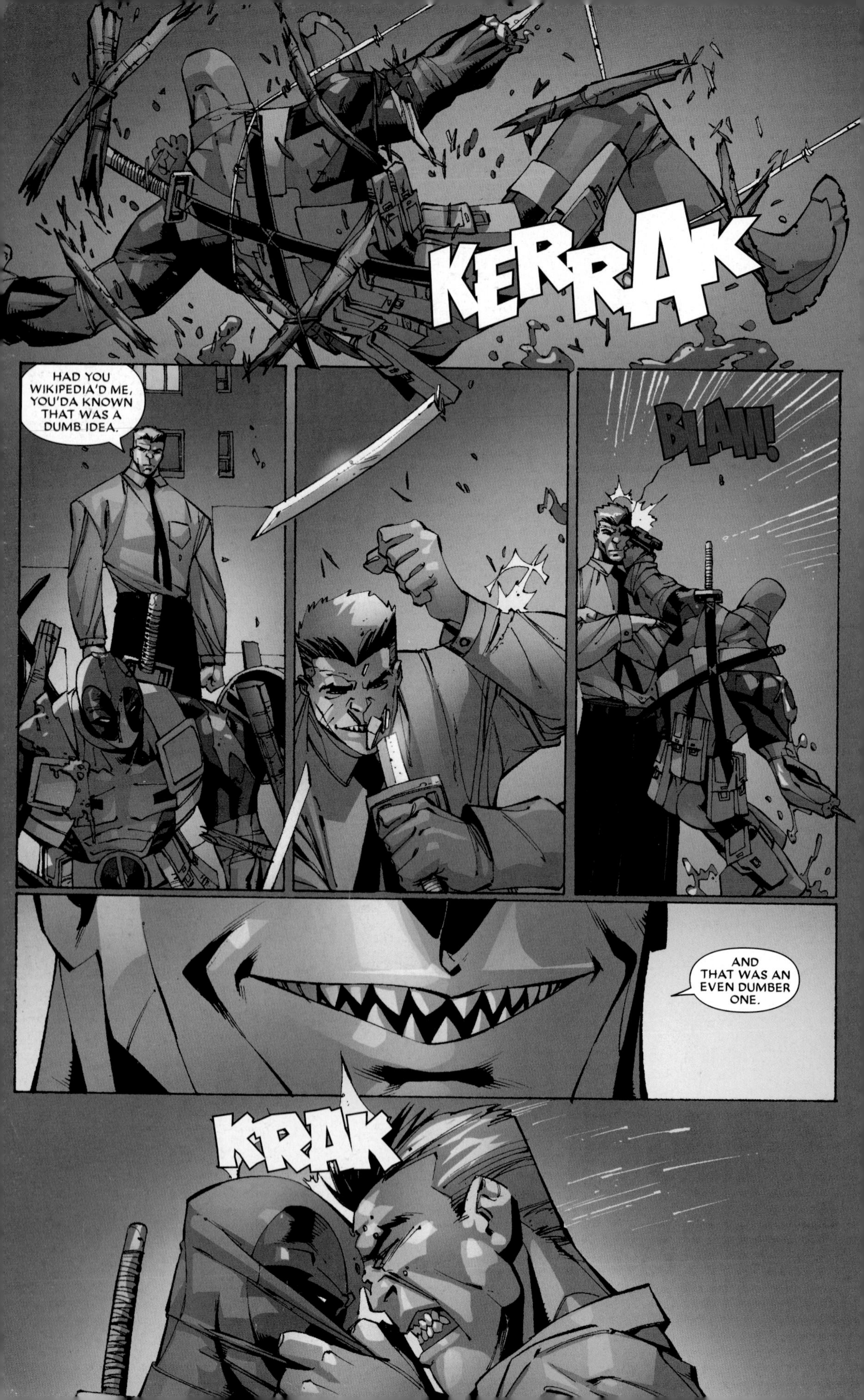
KERRAK
HAD YOU WIKIPEDIA'D ME, YOU'DA KNOWN THAT WAS A DUMB IDEA.
BLAM!
AND THAT WAS AN EVEN DUMBER ONE.
KRAK

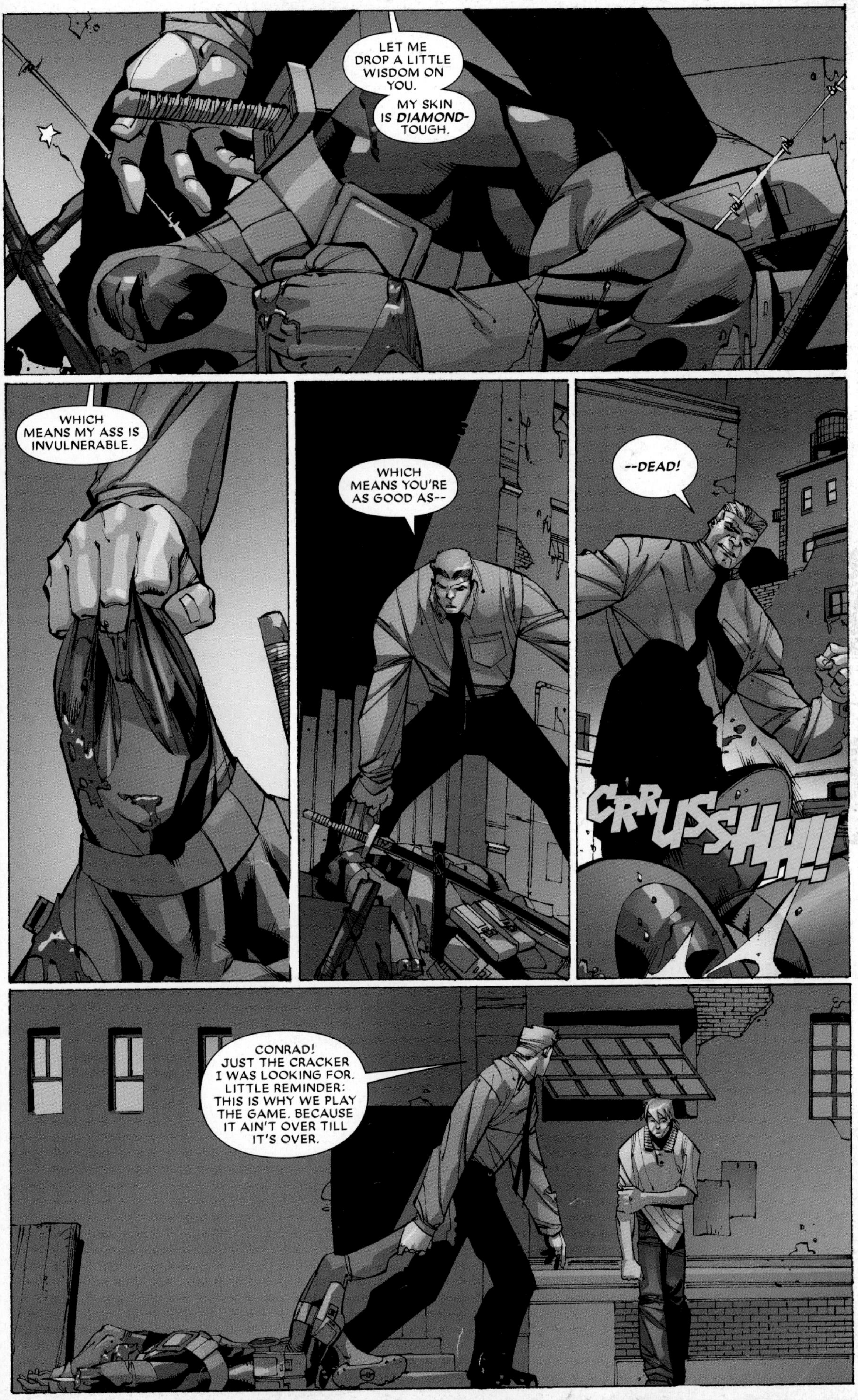
LET ME DROP A LITTLE WISDOM ON YOU.
MY SKIN IS DIAMOND-TOUGH.
WHICH MEANS MY ASS IS INVULNERABLE.
WHICH MEANS YOU'RE AS GOOD AS--
--DEAD!
CRRUSSHH!!
CONRAD! JUST THE CRACKER I WAS LOOKING FOR. LITTLE REMINDER: THIS IS WHY WE PLAY THE GAME. BECAUSE IT AIN'T OVER TILL IT'S OVER.

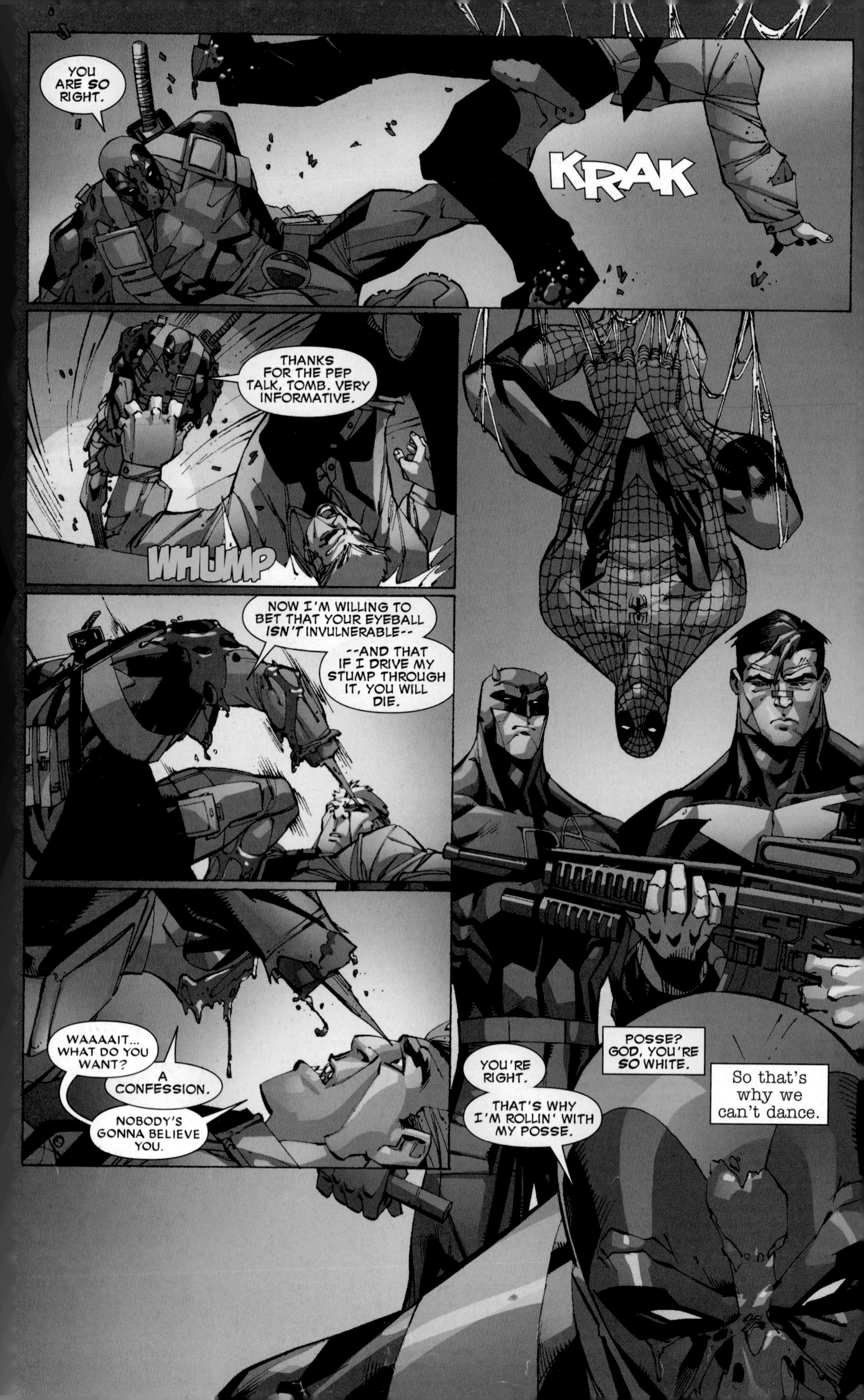
YOU ARE SO RIGHT.
KRAK
THANKS FOR THE PEP TALK, TOMB. VERY INFORMATIVE.
WHUMP
NOW I'M WILLING TO BET THAT YOUR EYEBALL ISN'T INVULNERABLE--
--AND THAT IF I DRIVE MY STUMP THROUGH IT, YOU WILL DIE.
WAAAAIT... WHAT DO YOU WANT?
A CONFESSION.
NOBODY'S GONNA BELIEVE YOU.
YOU'RE RIGHT.
THAT'S WHY I'M ROLLIN' WITH MY POSSE.
POSSE? GOD, YOU'RE SO WHITE.
So that's why we can't dance.

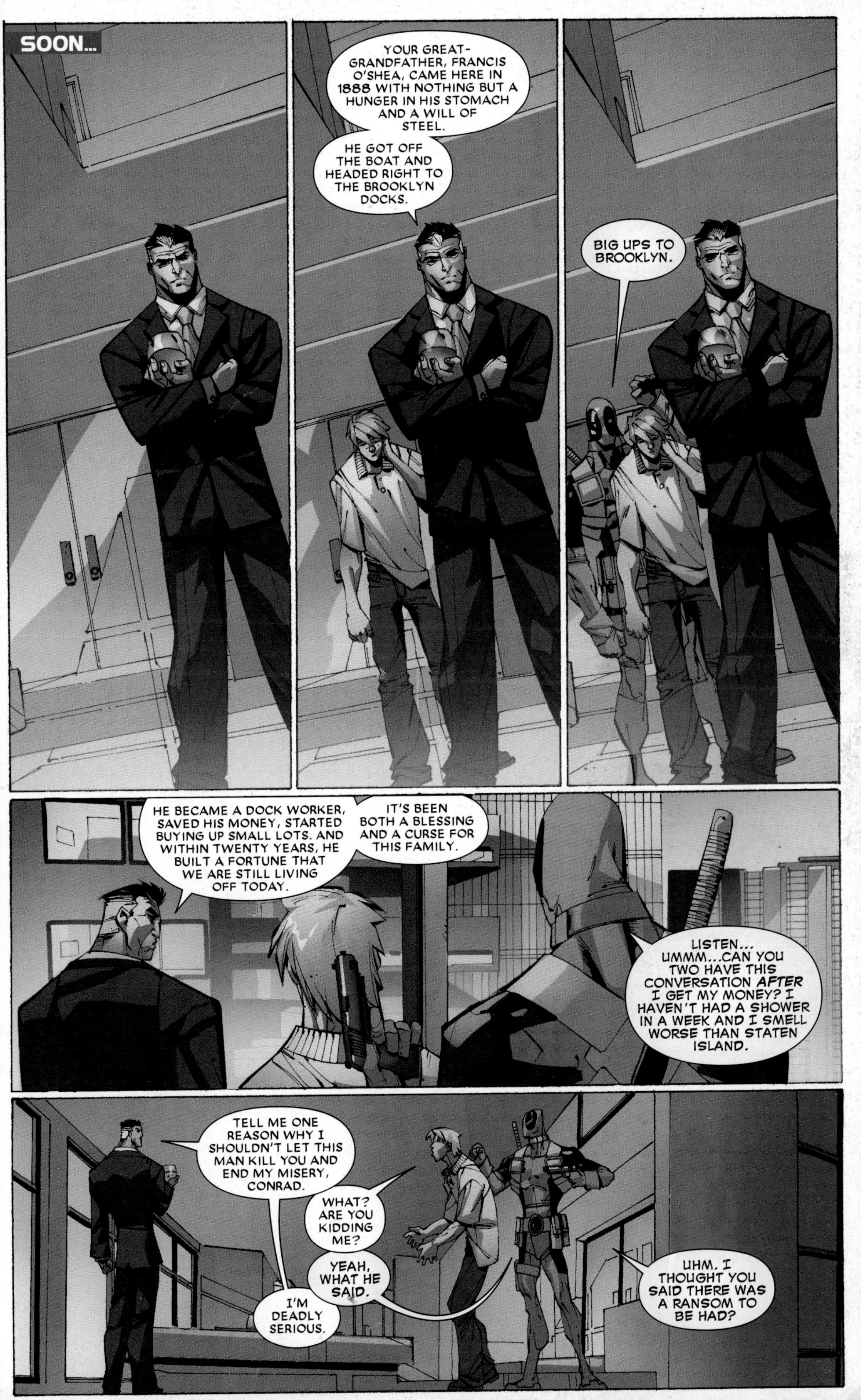
SOON...
YOUR GREAT-GRANDFATHER, FRANCIS O'SHEA, CAME HERE IN 1888 WITH NOTHING BUT A HUNGER IN HIS STOMACH AND A WILL OF STEEL.
HE GOT OFF THE BOAT AND HEADED RIGHT TO THE BROOKLYN DOCKS.
BIG UPS TO BROOKLYN.
HE BECAME A DOCK WORKER, SAVED HIS MONEY, STARTED BUYING UP SMALL LOTS. AND WITHIN TWENTY YEARS, HE BUILT A FORTUNE THAT WE ARE STILL LIVING OFF TODAY.
IT'S BEEN BOTH A BLESSING AND A CURSE FOR THIS FAMILY.
LISTEN... UMMM...CAN YOU TWO HAVE THIS CONVERSATION *AFTER* I GET MY MONEY? I HAVEN'T HAD A SHOWER IN A WEEK AND I SMELL WORSE THAN STATEN ISLAND.
TELL ME ONE REASON WHY I SHOULDN'T LET THIS MAN KILL YOU AND END MY MISERY, CONRAD.
WHAT? ARE YOU KIDDING ME?
YEAH, WHAT HE **SAID.**
I'M DEADLY SERIOUS.
UHM. I THOUGHT YOU SAID THERE WAS A RANSOM TO BE HAD?

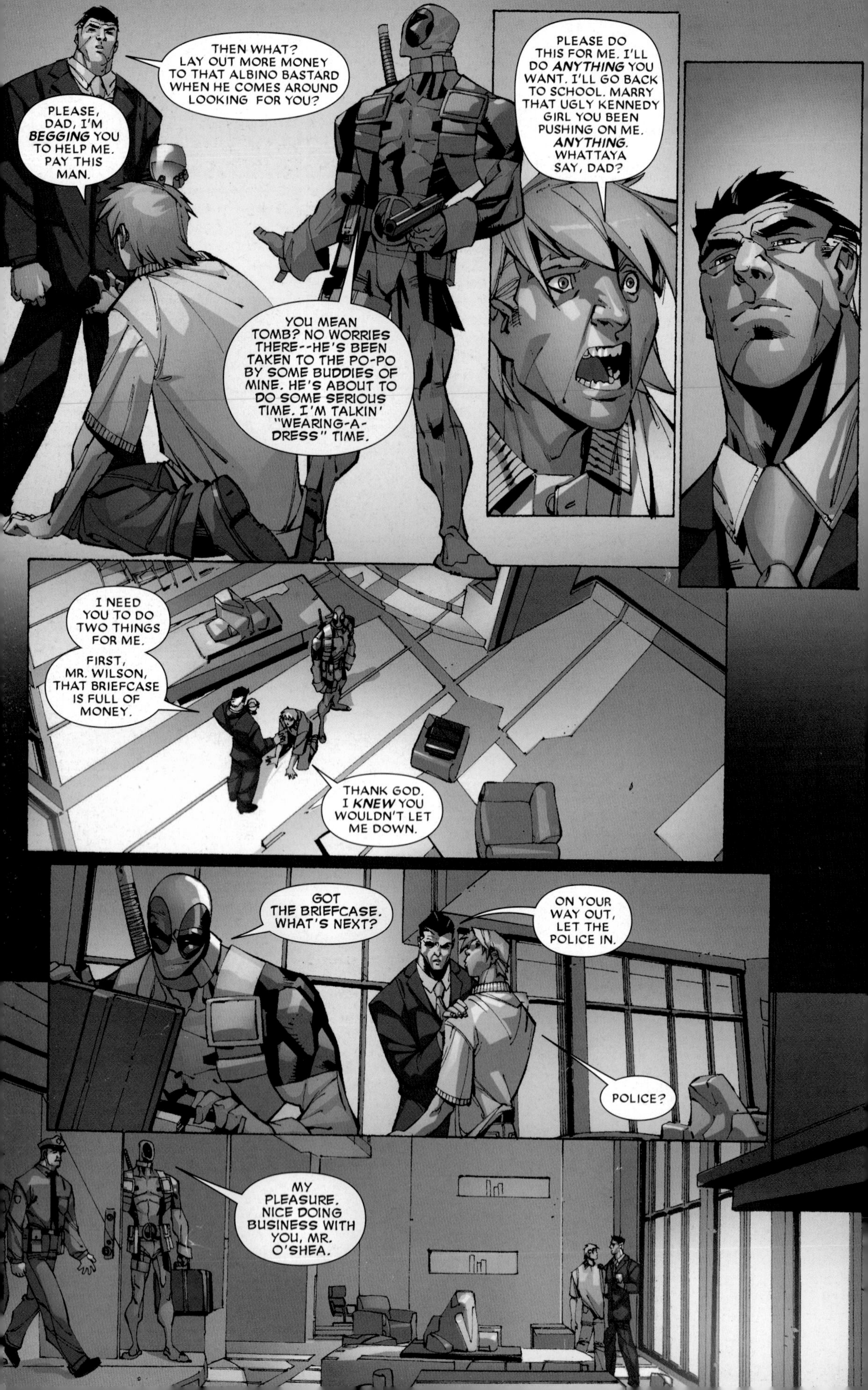
PLEASE, DAD, I'M BEGGING YOU TO HELP ME. PAY THIS MAN.
THEN WHAT? LAY OUT MORE MONEY TO THAT ALBINO BASTARD WHEN HE COMES AROUND LOOKING FOR YOU?
YOU MEAN TOMB? NO WORRIES THERE--HE'S BEEN TAKEN TO THE PO-PO BY SOME BUDDIES OF MINE. HE'S ABOUT TO DO SOME SERIOUS TIME. I'M TALKIN' "WEARING-A-DRESS" TIME.
PLEASE DO THIS FOR ME. I'LL DO ANYTHING YOU WANT. I'LL GO BACK TO SCHOOL. MARRY THAT UGLY KENNEDY GIRL YOU BEEN PUSHING ON ME. ANYTHING. WHATTAYA SAY, DAD?
I NEED YOU TO DO TWO THINGS FOR ME.
FIRST, MR. WILSON, THAT BRIEFCASE IS FULL OF MONEY.
THANK GOD. I KNEW YOU WOULDN'T LET ME DOWN.
GOT THE BRIEFCASE. WHAT'S NEXT?
ON YOUR WAY OUT, LET THE POLICE IN.
POLICE?
MY PLEASURE. NICE DOING BUSINESS WITH YOU, MR. O'SHEA.

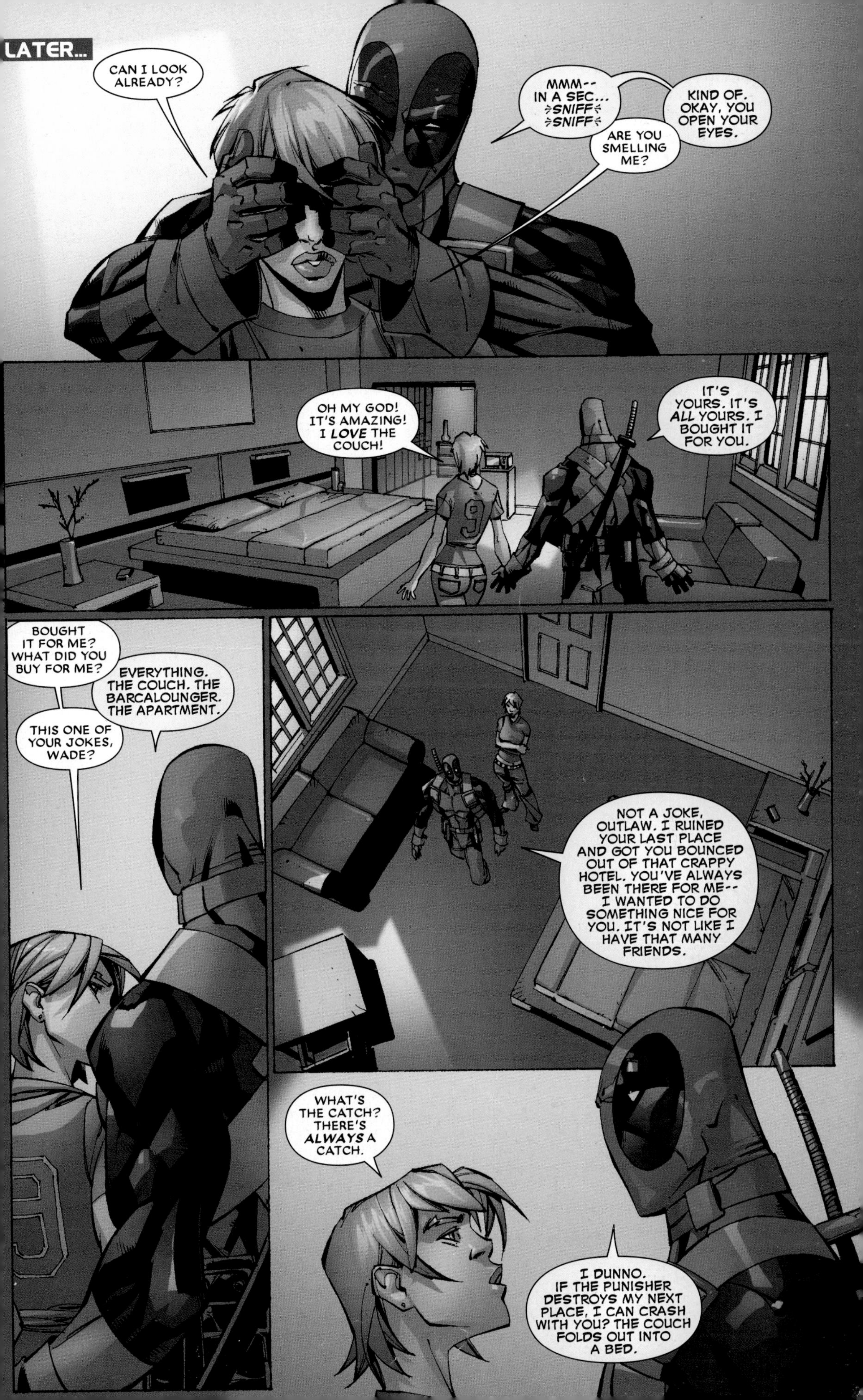
LATER...
CAN I LOOK ALREADY?
MMM-- IN A SEC... *SNIFF* *SNIFF*
ARE YOU SMELLING ME?
KIND OF. OKAY, YOU OPEN YOUR EYES.
OH MY GOD! IT'S AMAZING! I LOVE THE COUCH!
IT'S YOURS. IT'S ALL YOURS. I BOUGHT IT FOR YOU.
BOUGHT IT FOR ME? WHAT DID YOU BUY FOR ME?
EVERYTHING. THE COUCH. THE BARCALOUNGER. THE APARTMENT.
THIS ONE OF YOUR JOKES, WADE?
NOT A JOKE, OUTLAW. I RUINED YOUR LAST PLACE AND GOT YOU BOUNCED OUT OF THAT CRAPPY HOTEL. YOU'VE ALWAYS BEEN THERE FOR ME-- I WANTED TO DO SOMETHING NICE FOR YOU. IT'S NOT LIKE I HAVE THAT MANY FRIENDS.
WHAT'S THE CATCH? THERE'S ALWAYS A CATCH.
I DUNNO. IF THE PUNISHER DESTROYS MY NEXT PLACE, I CAN CRASH WITH YOU? THE COUCH FOLDS OUT INTO A BED.

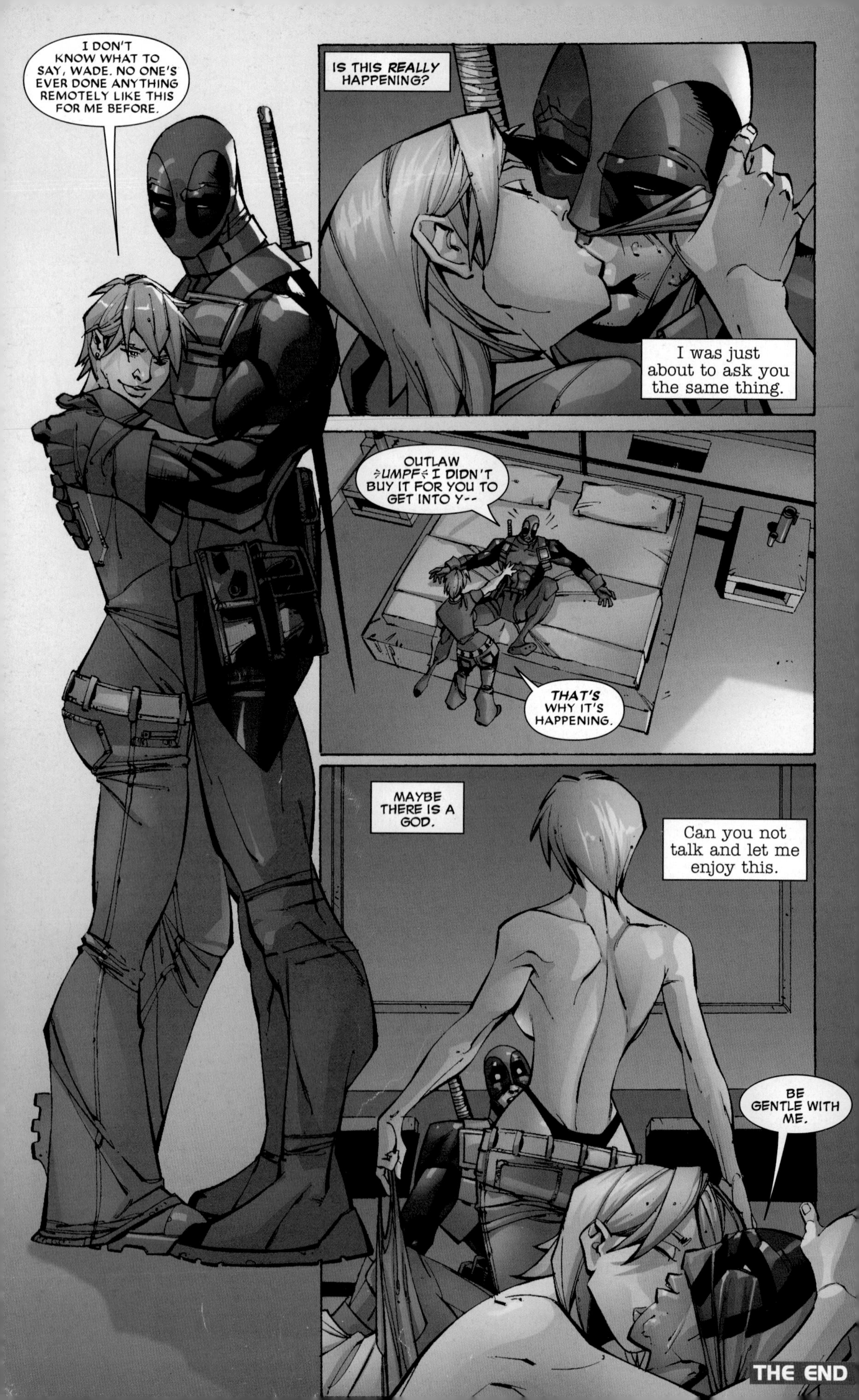
I DON'T KNOW WHAT TO SAY, WADE. NO ONE'S EVER DONE ANYTHING REMOTELY LIKE THIS FOR ME BEFORE.
IS THIS *REALLY* HAPPENING?
I was just about to ask you the same thing.
OUTLAW ⇒UMPF⇐ I DIDN'T BUY IT FOR YOU TO GET INTO Y--
THAT'S WHY IT'S HAPPENING.
MAYBE THERE IS A GOD.
Can you not talk and let me enjoy this.
BE GENTLE WITH ME.
THE END

DEADPOOL: SUICIDE KINGS #1-3 2ND PRINTING VARIANTS

THESE 2ND-PRINTING COVERS COMBINE TO FORM A SINGLE IMAGE.
ART BY CARLO BARBERI, SANDU FLOREA & MARTE GRACIA.

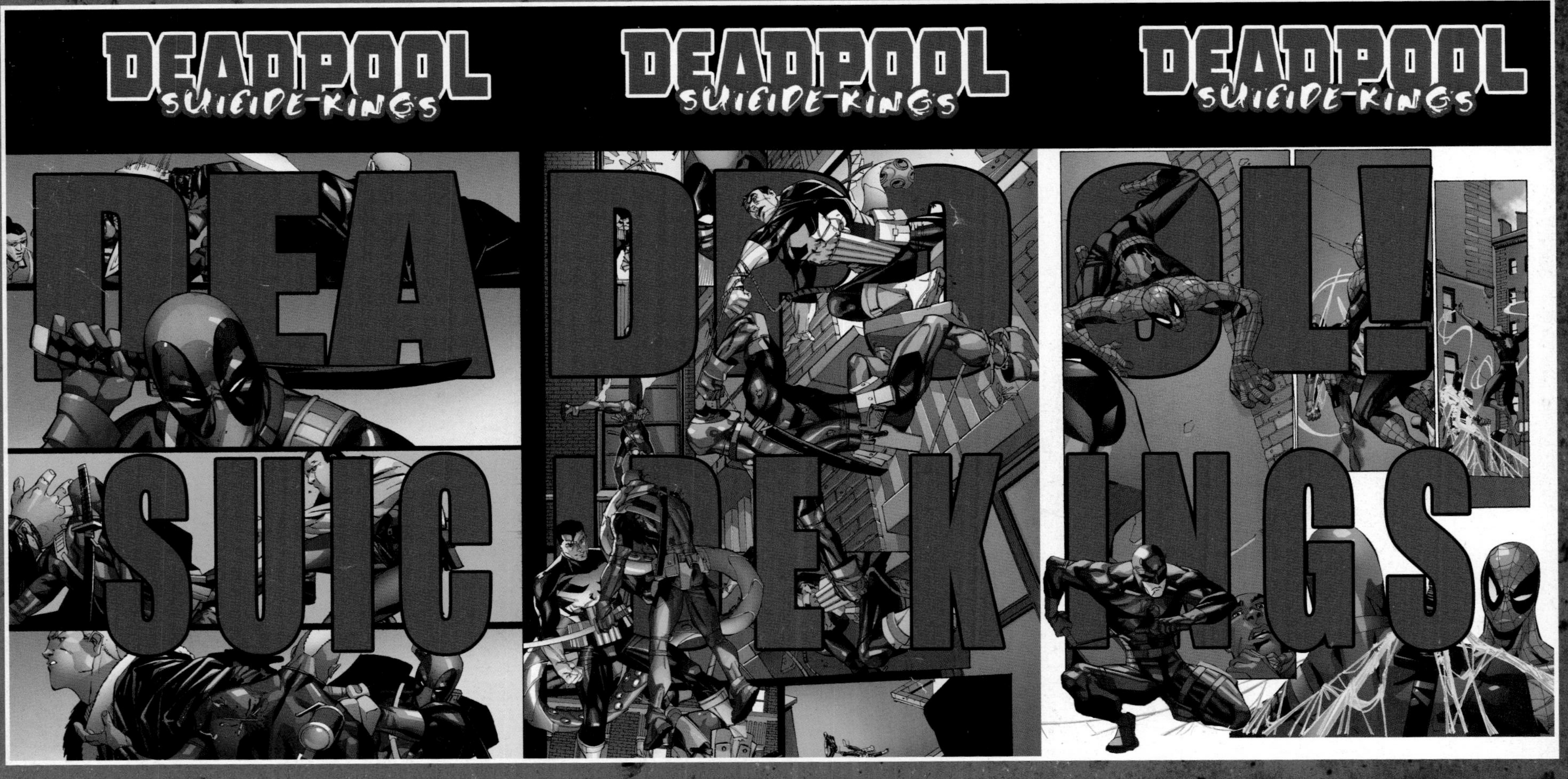
DEADPOOL
SUICIDE KINGS
DEADPOOL
SUICIDE KINGS
DEADPOOL
SUICIDE KINGS
DEADPOOL!
SUICIDE KINGS

MARVEL DIGITAL HOLIDAY SPECIAL#2

FIRST PRINTED IN *MARVEL HOLIDAY MAGAZINE 2010*; THAT MAGAZINE'S TWO COVERS COMBINE TO FORM A SINGLE IMAGE.

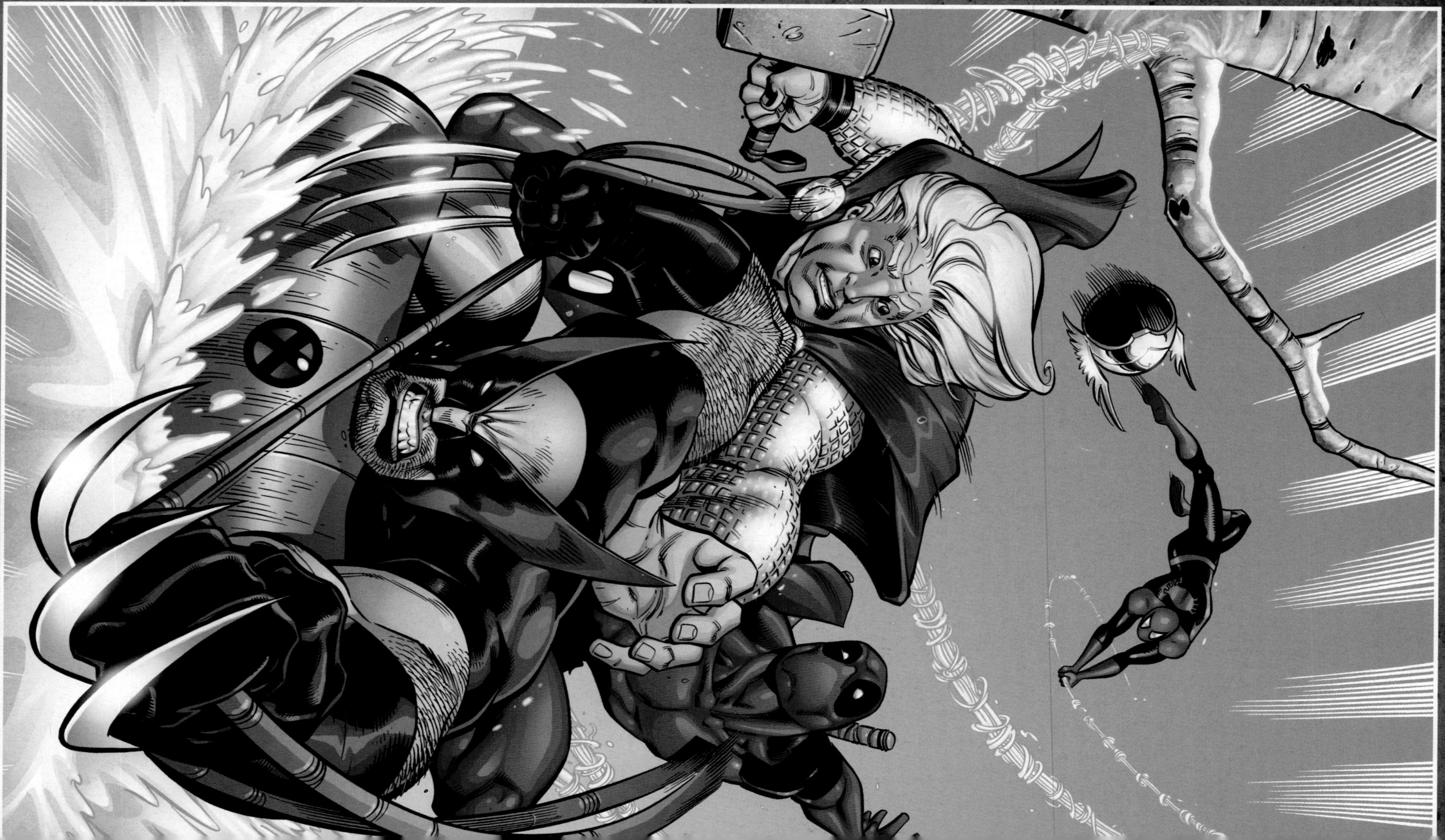

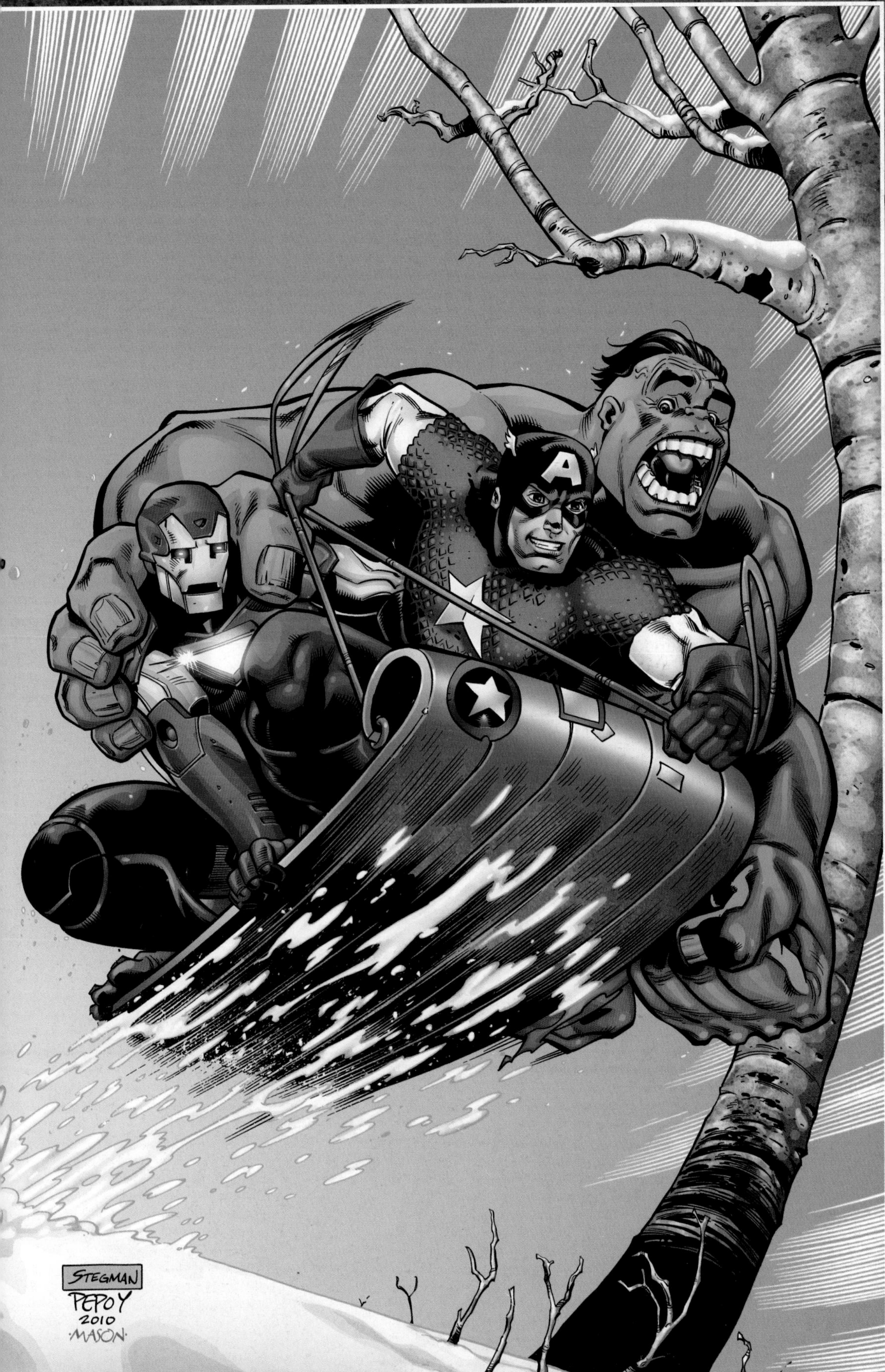
STEGMAN
PEPOY
2010
MASON

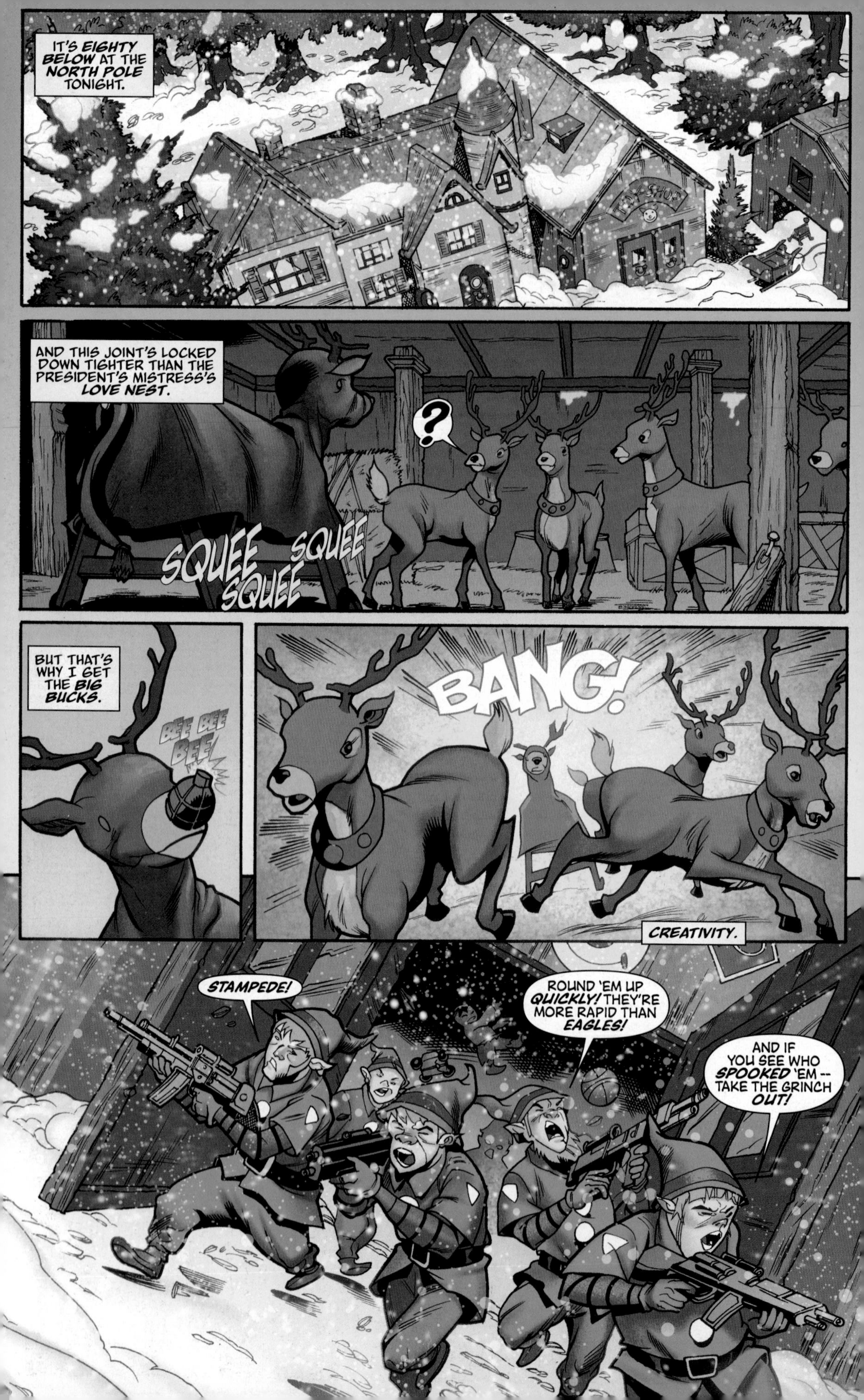
IT'S EIGHTY BELOW AT THE NORTH POLE TONIGHT.
AND THIS JOINT'S LOCKED DOWN TIGHTER THAN THE PRESIDENT'S MISTRESS'S LOVE NEST.
?
SQUEE SQUEE SQUEE
BUT THAT'S WHY I GET THE BIG BUCKS.
BEE BEE BEE
BANG!
CREATIVITY.
STAMPEDE!
ROUND 'EM UP QUICKLY! THEY'RE MORE RAPID THAN EAGLES!
AND IF YOU SEE WHO SPOOKED 'EM -- TAKE THE GRINCH OUT!

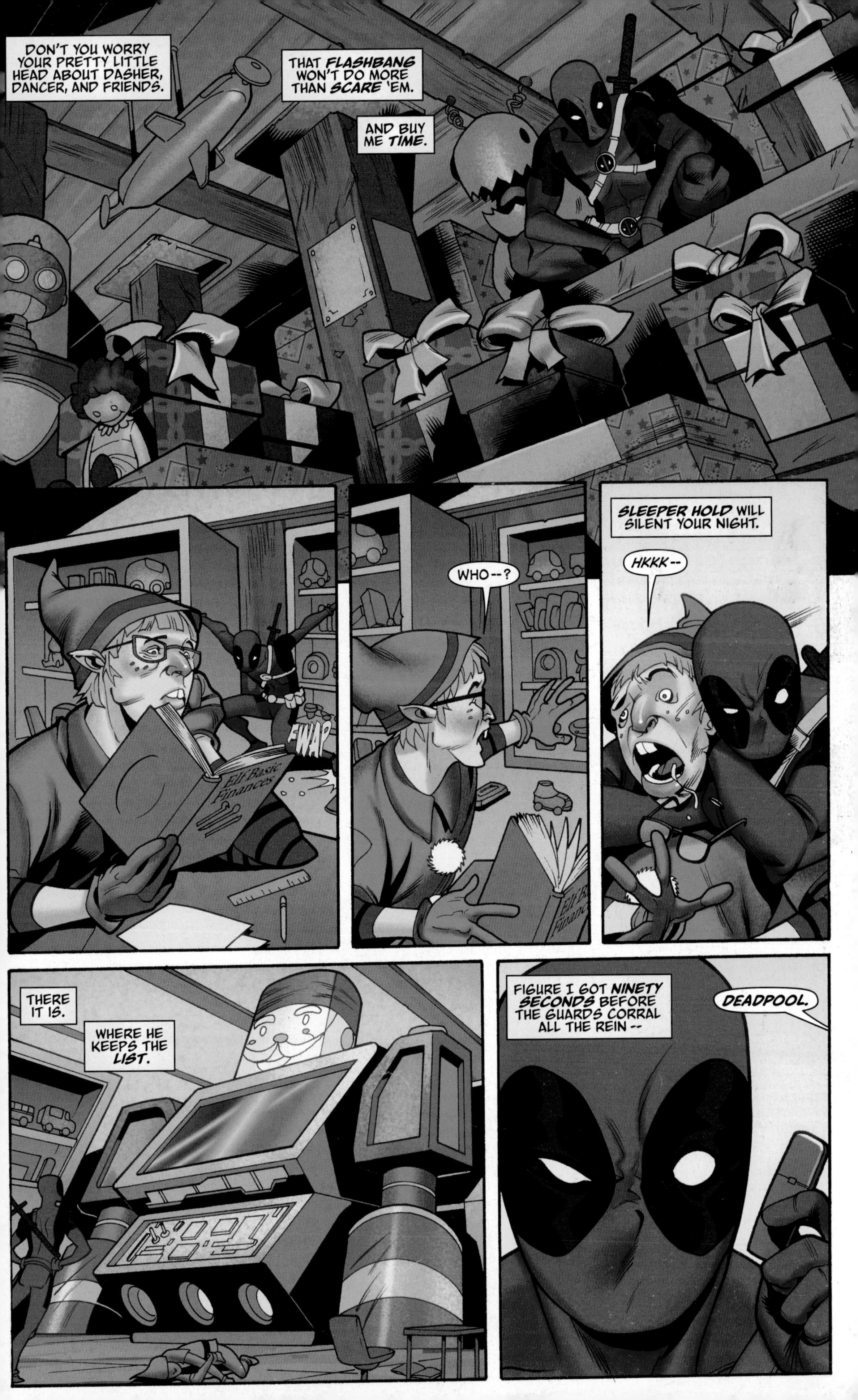
DON'T YOU WORRY YOUR PRETTY LITTLE HEAD ABOUT DASHER, DANCER, AND FRIENDS.
THAT FLASHBANG WON'T DO MORE THAN SCARE 'EM.
AND BUY ME TIME.
FWAP
Elf Basic Finances
WHO--?
SLEEPER HOLD WILL SILENT YOUR NIGHT.
HKKK--
THERE IT IS.
WHERE HE KEEPS THE LIST.
FIGURE I GOT NINETY SECONDS BEFORE THE GUARDS CORRAL ALL THE REIN--
DEADPOOL.

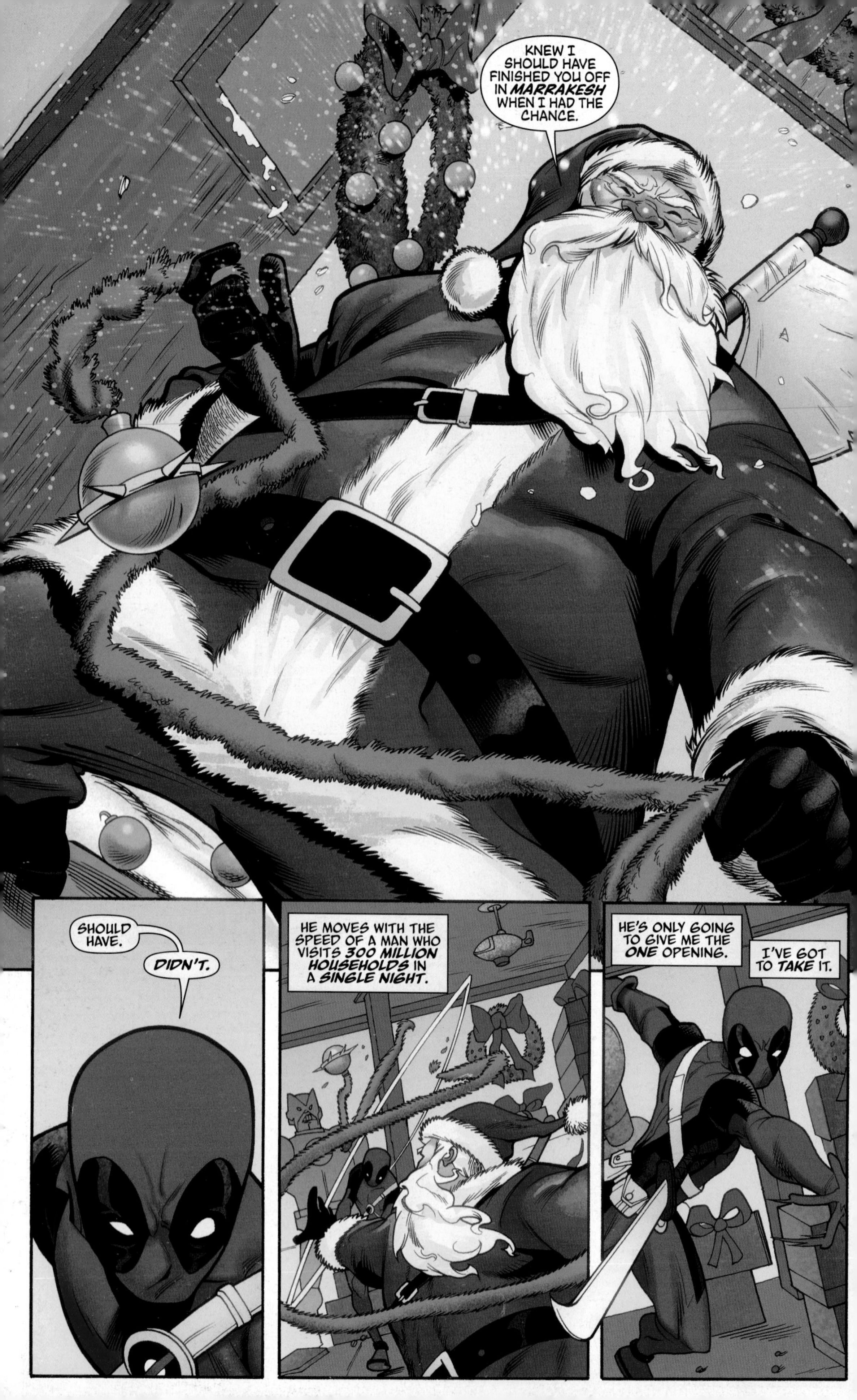
KNEW I SHOULD HAVE FINISHED YOU OFF IN MARRAKESH WHEN I HAD THE CHANCE.
SHOULD HAVE.
DIDN'T.
HE MOVES WITH THE SPEED OF A MAN WHO VISITS 300 MILLION HOUSEHOLDS IN A SINGLE NIGHT.
HE'S ONLY GOING TO GIVE ME THE ONE OPENING.
I'VE GOT TO TAKE IT.

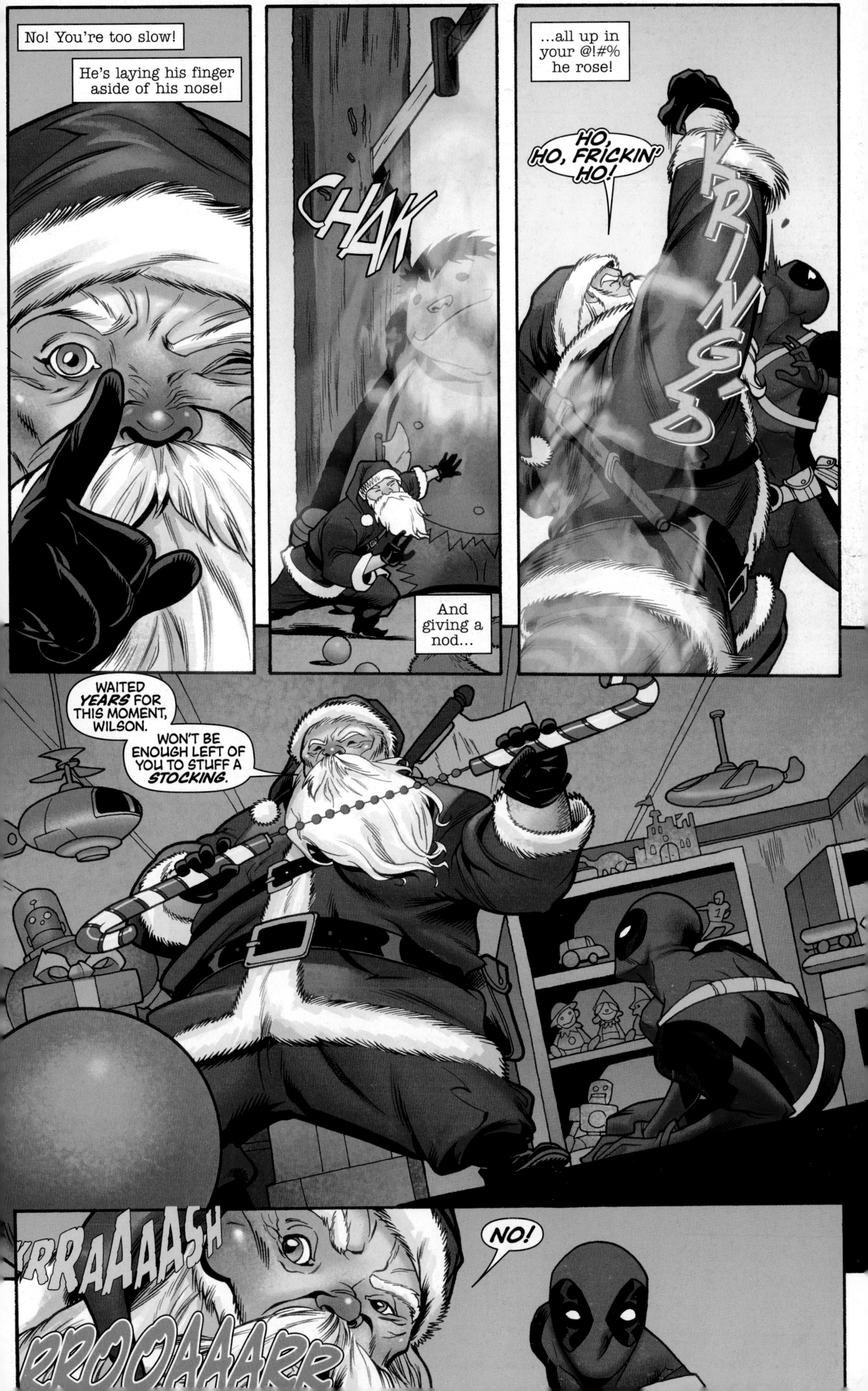
No! You're too slow!
He's laying his finger aside of his nose!
CHAK
And giving a nod...
...all up in your @!#% he rose!
HO, HO, FRICKIN' HO!
KRING!D
WAITED YEARS FOR THIS MOMENT, WILSON.
WON'T BE ENOUGH LEFT OF YOU TO STUFF A STOCKING.
KRRAAAASH
NO!
RROOAAARR

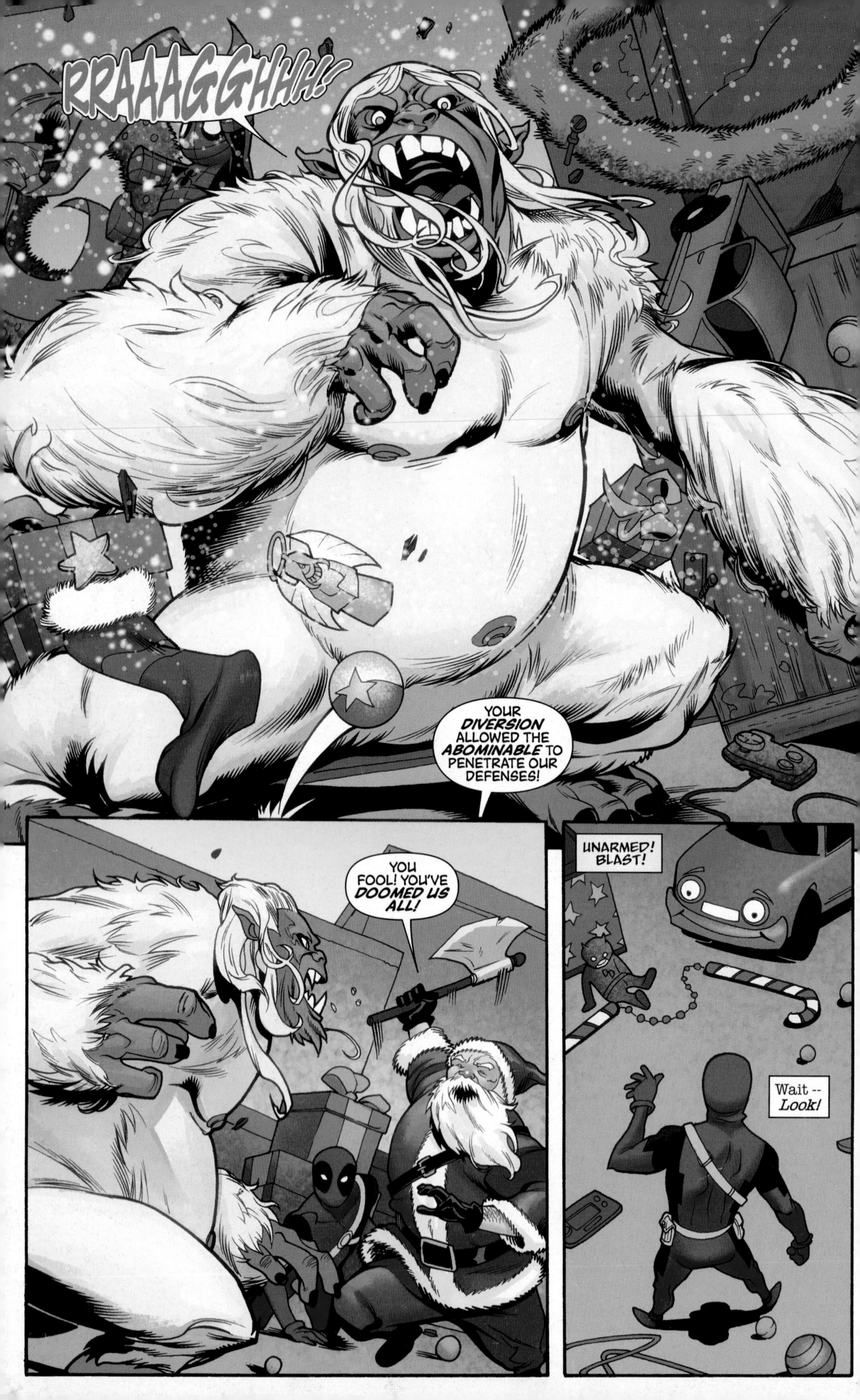
RRAAAGGHHH!
YOUR *DIVERSION* ALLOWED THE *ABOMINABLE* TO PENETRATE OUR DEFENSES!
YOU FOOL! YOU'VE *DOOMED US ALL!*
UNARMED! BLAST!
Wait -- *Look!*

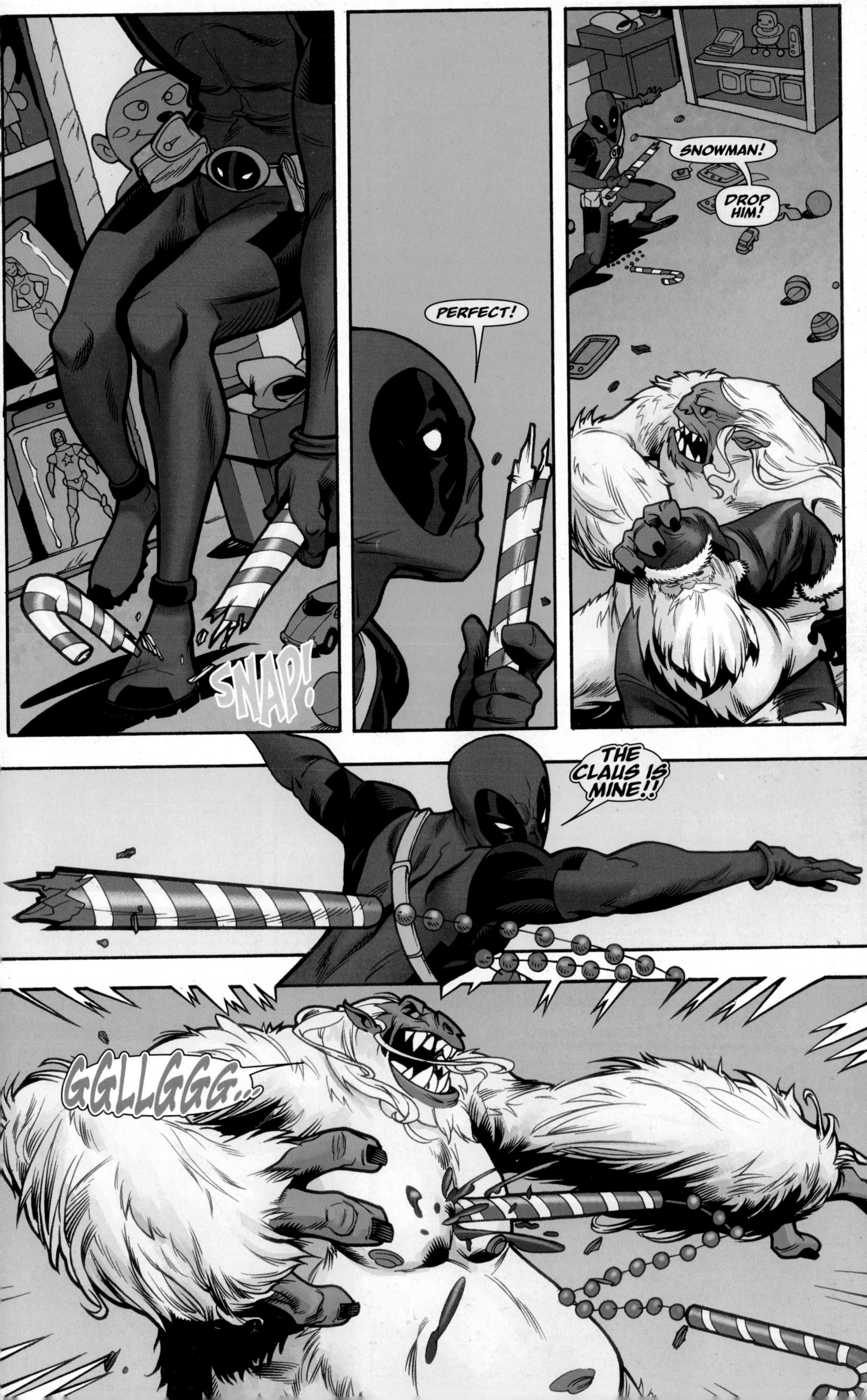
SNAP!
PERFECT!
SNOWMAN!
DROP HIM!
THE CLAUS IS MINE!!
GGLLGGG...

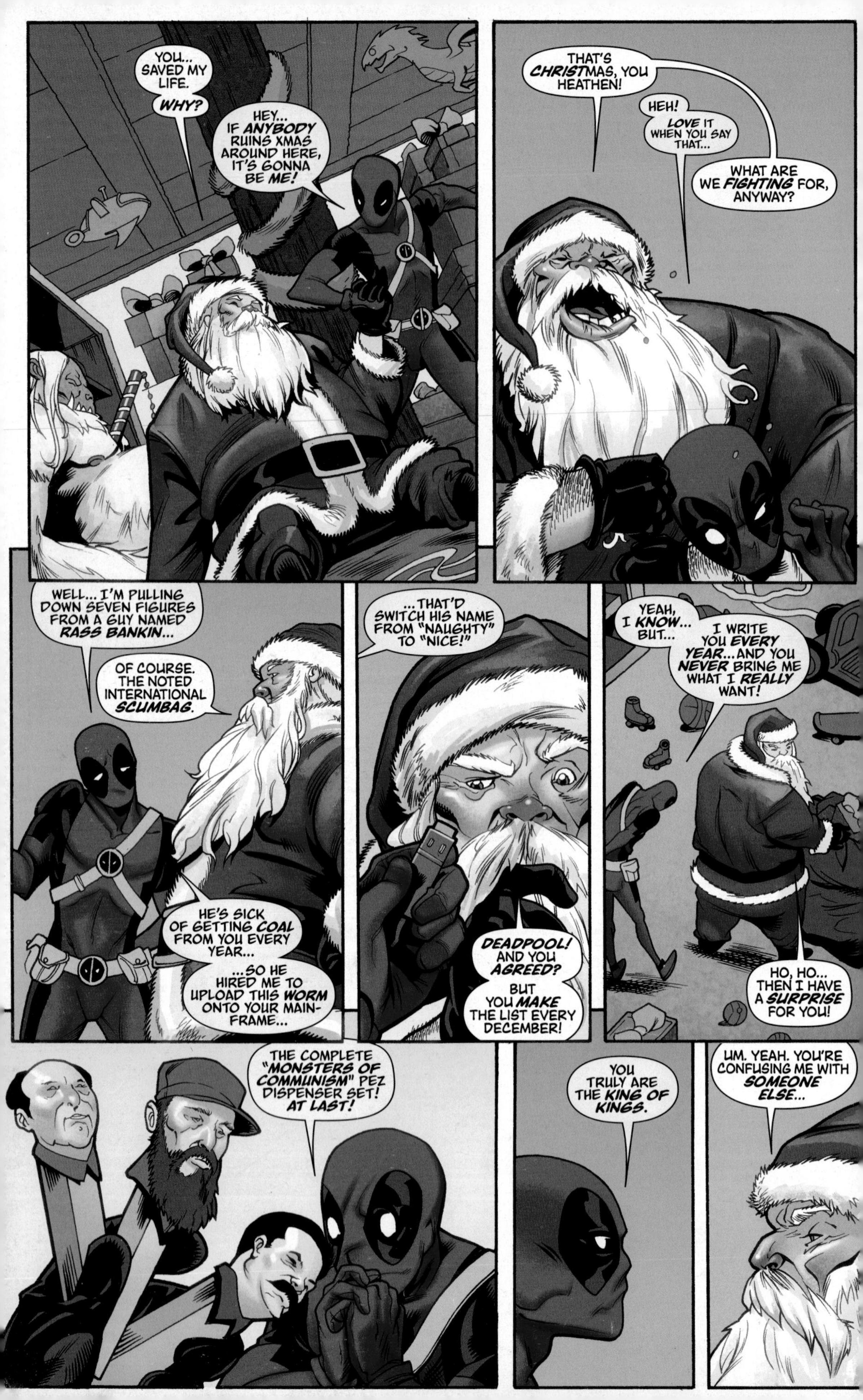

YOU... SAVED MY LIFE. WHY?
HEY... IF ANYBODY RUINS XMAS AROUND HERE, IT'S GONNA BE ME!
THAT'S CHRISTMAS, YOU HEATHEN!
HEH! LOVE IT WHEN YOU SAY THAT...
WHAT ARE WE FIGHTING FOR, ANYWAY?
WELL... I'M PULLING DOWN SEVEN FIGURES FROM A GUY NAMED RASS BANKIN...
OF COURSE. THE NOTED INTERNATIONAL SCUMBAG.
HE'S SICK OF GETTING COAL FROM YOU EVERY YEAR...
...SO HE HIRED ME TO UPLOAD THIS WORM ONTO YOUR MAIN-FRAME...
...THAT'D SWITCH HIS NAME FROM "NAUGHTY" TO "NICE!"
DEADPOOL! AND YOU AGREED?
BUT YOU MAKE THE LIST EVERY DECEMBER!
YEAH, I KNOW... BUT...
I WRITE YOU EVERY YEAR... AND YOU NEVER BRING ME WHAT I REALLY WANT!
HO, HO... THEN I HAVE A SURPRISE FOR YOU!
THE COMPLETE "MONSTERS OF COMMUNISM" PEZ DISPENSER SET! AT LAST!
YOU TRULY ARE THE KING OF KINGS.
UM. YEAH. YOU'RE CONFUSING ME WITH SOMEONE ELSE...

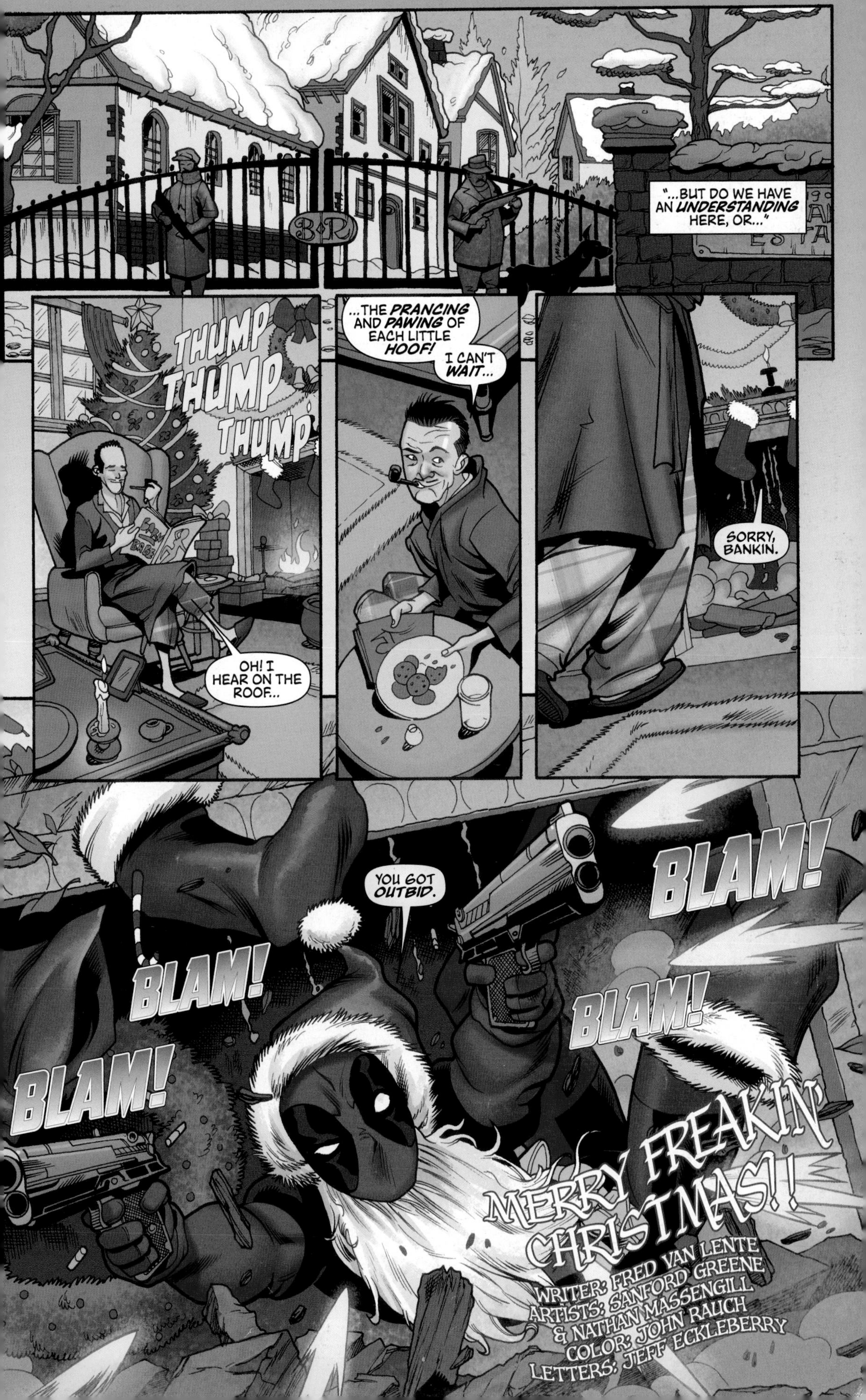
"...BUT DO WE HAVE AN UNDERSTANDING HERE, OR..."
THUMP THUMP THUMP
OH! I HEAR ON THE ROOF...
...THE PRANCING AND PAWING OF EACH LITTLE HOOF!
I CAN'T WAIT...
SORRY, BANKIN.
YOU GOT OUTBID.
BLAM!
BLAM!
BLAM!
BLAM!
MERRY FREAKIN' CHRISTMAS!!
WRITER: FRED VAN LENTE
ARTISTS: SANFORD GREENE & NATHAN MASSENGILL
COLOR: JOHN RAUCH
LETTERS: JEFF ECKLEBERRY

DEADPOOL #900

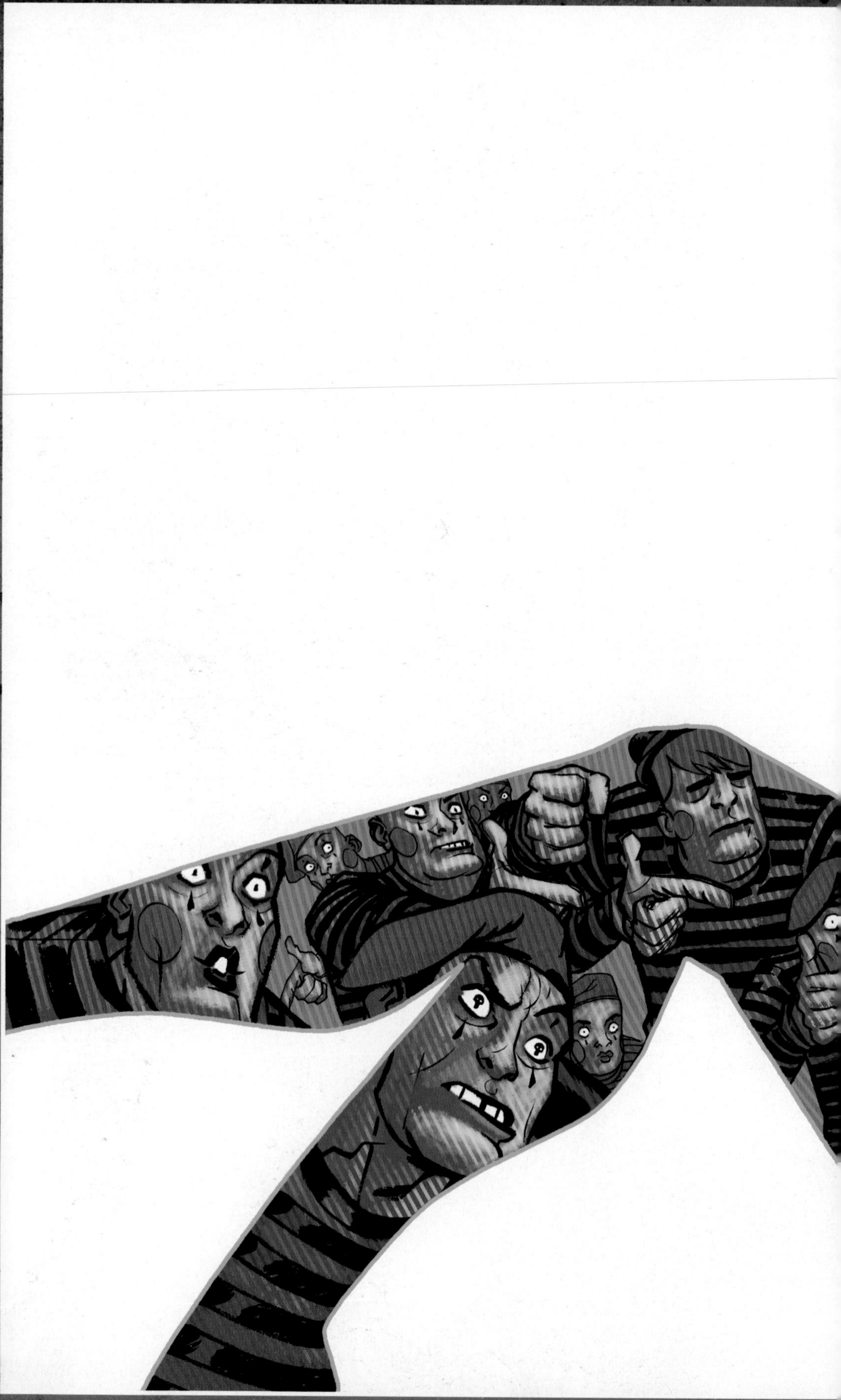

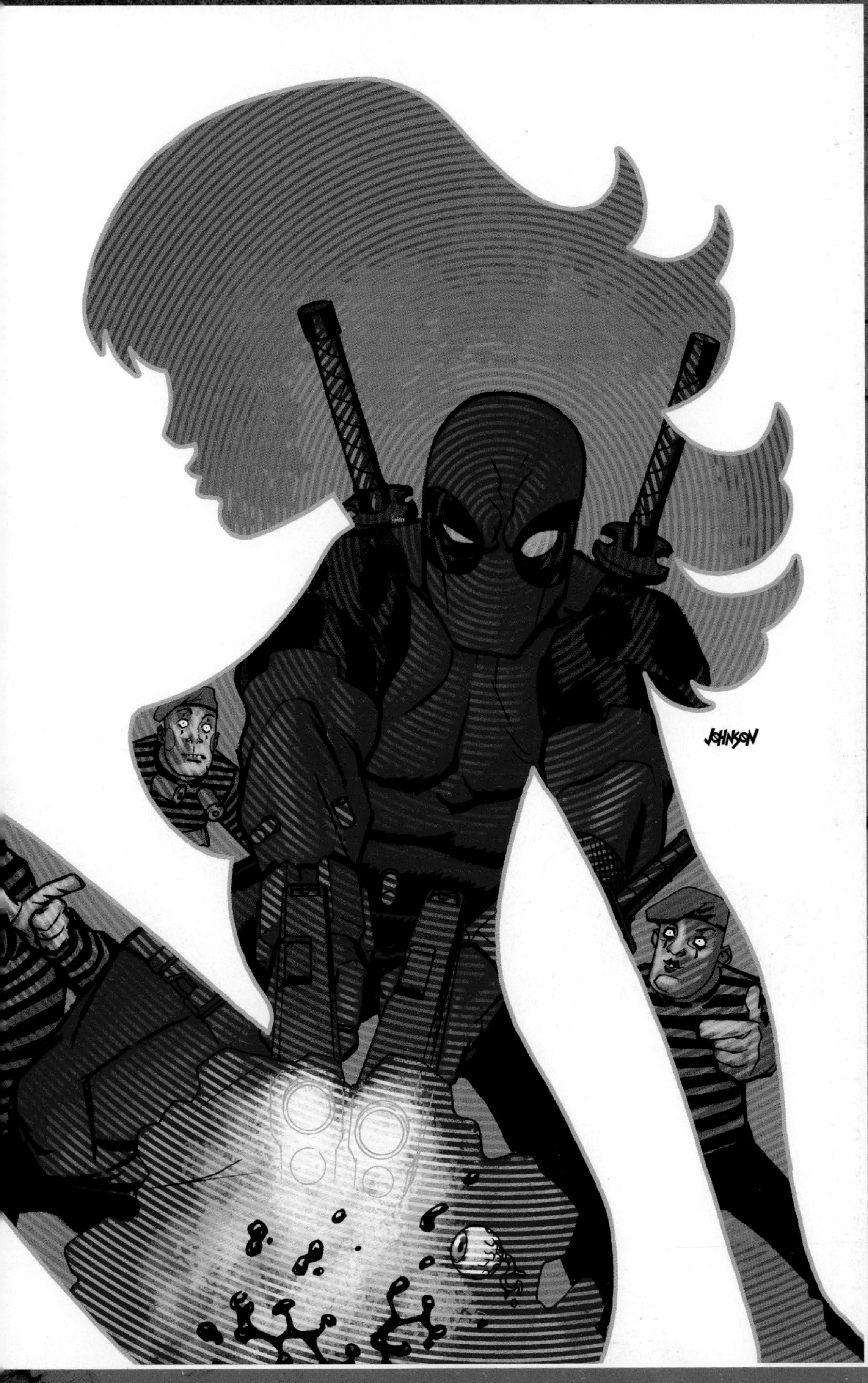
JOHNSON

DEADPOOL #900 VARIANT BY DAVE JOHNSON

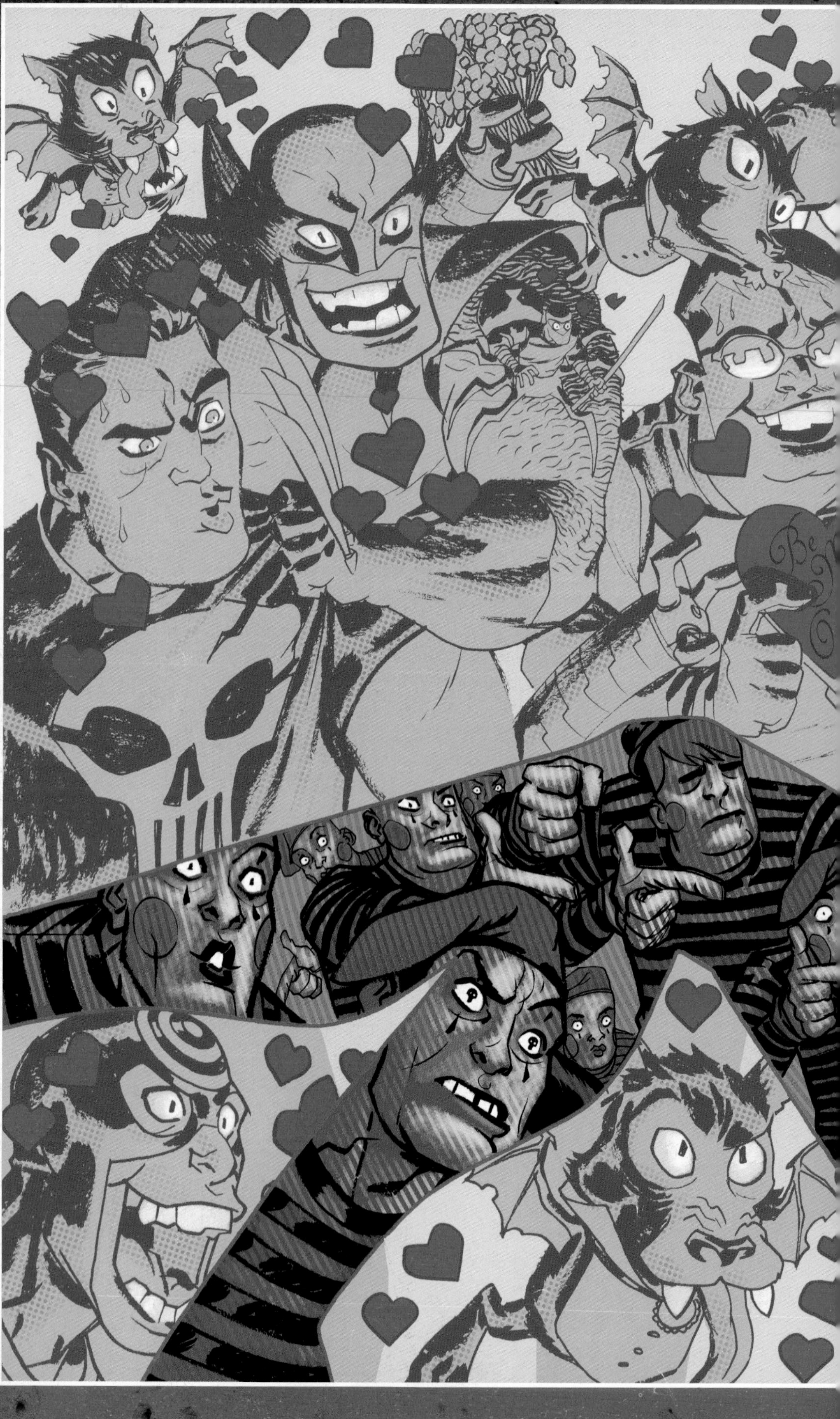

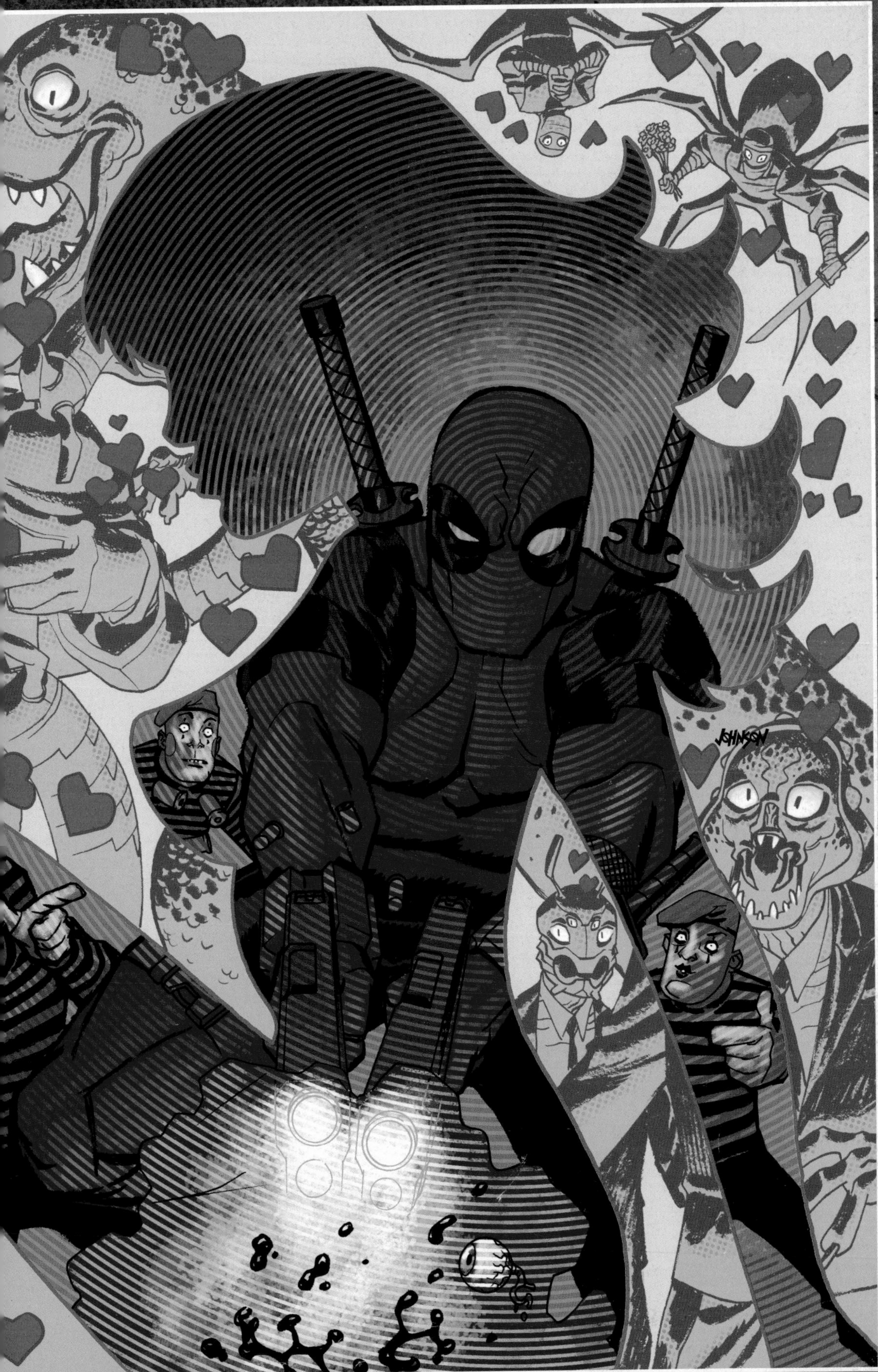
JOHNSON

Some jobs are just too tough for your average fast-talkin' high-tech gun-for-hire. Sometimes...to get the job done right...you need someone crazier than a sack'a ferrets. You need Wade Wilson. The Crimson Comedian. The Regeneratin' Degenerate. The Merc with a Mouth...

DEADPOOL

Well it's been a long time coming (I'M PRETTY SURE EVERY HERO/VILLAIN HAS KILLED US AT LEAST ONCE. Probably.) but we're finally here at the BIG issue #900 (HOW FITTING THAT MY SERIES IS THE FIRST COMIC EVER TO HIT THAT NUMBER, BABY! Must have been all the weekly shipping during my three picture movie career.)! But now that we've reached the BIG #900 and after all those years of carrying second-rate heroes on my shoulders, once again it's me (AND ME), good ol' Wade Wilson, starring in his own series (I DIDN'T LIKE YOU GUYS ANYWAY!).

But instead of getting on with this BIG issue I'll briefly recap my recent team-up issues, as if everyone wasn't buying them religiously (THAT'S RIGHT, I'M TALKING TO YOU!). For the past one hundred and sixty-eight issues I've been side by side with the likes of Wolverine (YES, HE SMELLS), Captain America ("I COME BACK FROM THE DEAD ALL THE TIME AND NO ONE CARES!"), Thor (DOES ANYONE STILL WEAR A CAPE?), and Spider-Man (RED LOOKS BETTER ON ME).

Then there was the woman who stole my heart (LITERALLY). I never thought I'd love again after Black Widow (DUDE, SHE CHOPPED US INTO PIECES...I'm easy), but then Lady Deadpool came along! I never found out who she was but I'll never forget that smokin' body (PRETTY SURE IT WAS JARVIS...Impossible, I'd recognize Jarvis' figure anywhere). And who could forget my brief stint as a teen in those Young Deadpool years pairing up with Power Pack, the New Warriors, and Franklin Richards...what a kid...(DID YOU KNOW HE HAS PSYCHOTIC POWERS? Psionic powers, psionic.)

Now that all of you lazy bums are caught up we can get on with the show! By the way, did I mention this issue is HUGE??? Enjoy it, folks (OR ELSE), this is the once in a lifetime, never before seen in comics history issue #900 of a comic! Wahooo! I can't wait...why are you waiting? Start turning those pages (IMMEDIATELY!).

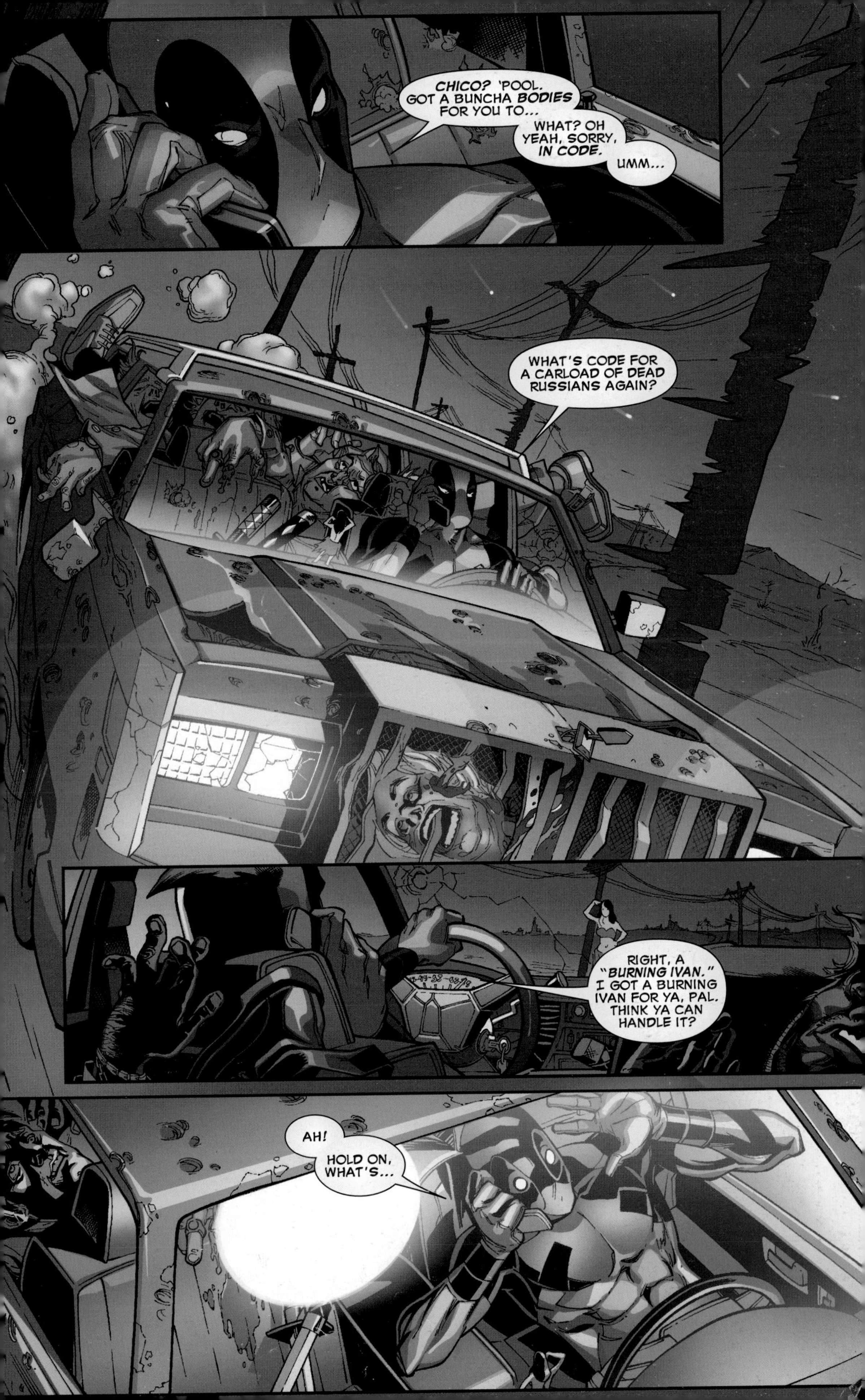
CHICO? 'POOL. GOT A BUNCHA BODIES FOR YOU TO...
WHAT? OH YEAH, SORRY, IN CODE.
UMM...
WHAT'S CODE FOR A CARLOAD OF DEAD RUSSIANS AGAIN?
RIGHT, A "BURNING IVAN." I GOT A BURNING IVAN FOR YA, PAL. THINK YA CAN HANDLE IT?
AH!
HOLD ON, WHAT'S...

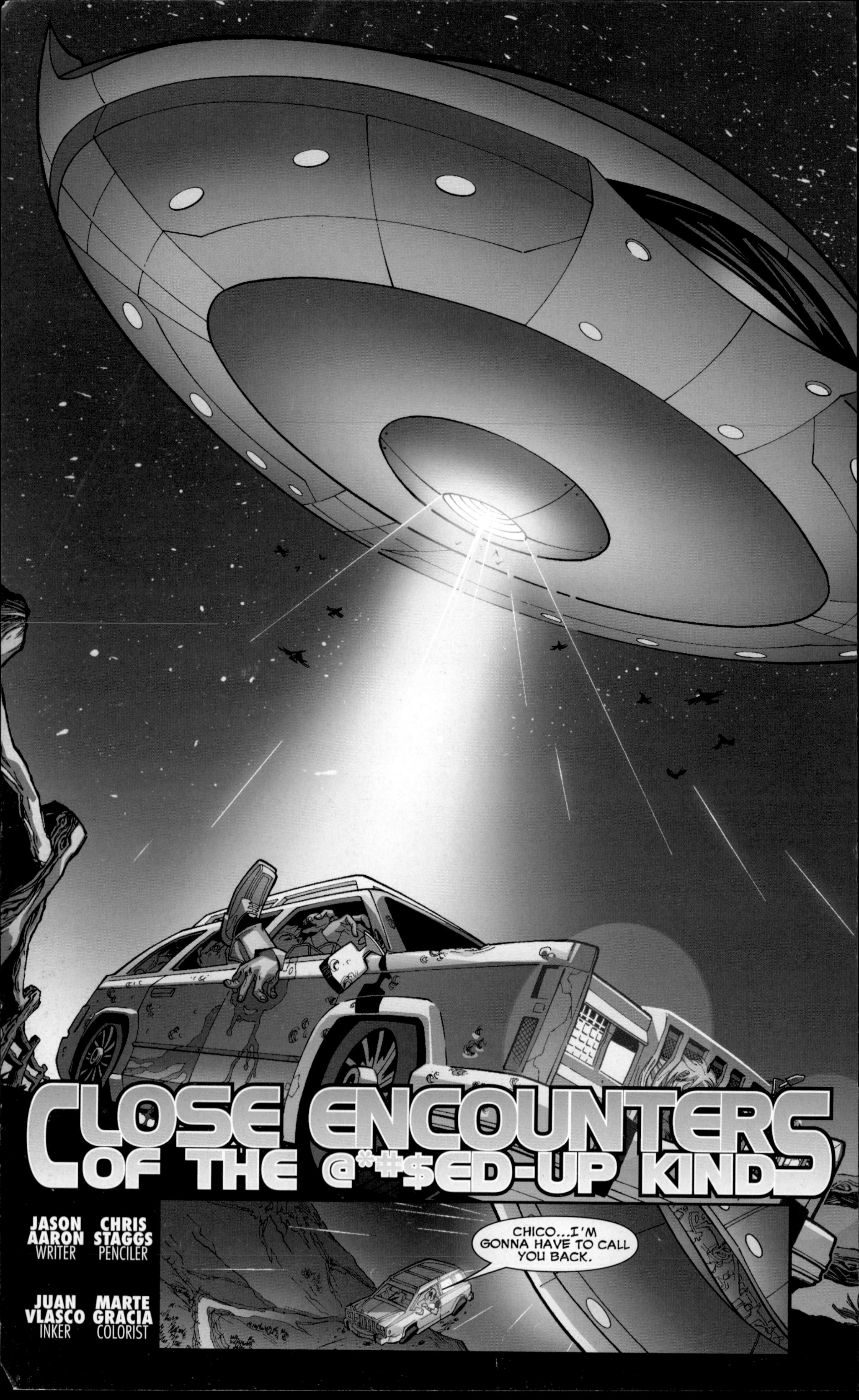
CLOSE ENCOUNTERS
OF THE @*#$ED-UP KIND
JASON AARON WRITER
CHRIS STAGGS PENCILER
JUAN VLASCO INKER
MARTE GRACIA COLORIST
CHICO...I'M GONNA HAVE TO CALL YOU BACK.

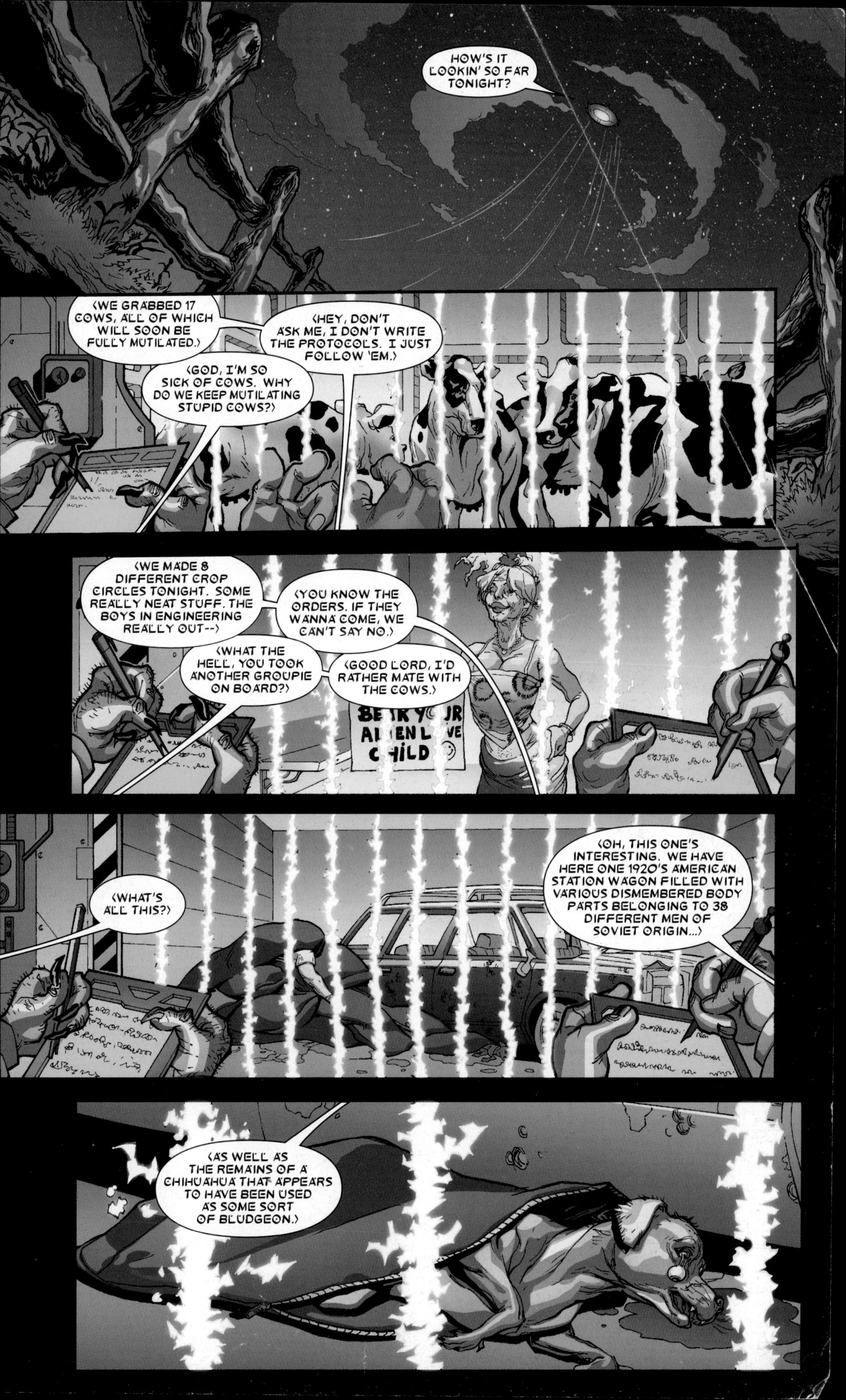
HOW'S IT LOOKIN' SO FAR TONIGHT?
<WE GRABBED 17 COWS, ALL OF WHICH WILL SOON BE FULLY MUTILATED.>
<HEY, DON'T ASK ME, I DON'T WRITE THE PROTOCOLS. I JUST FOLLOW 'EM.>
<GOD, I'M SO SICK OF COWS. WHY DO WE KEEP MUTILATING STUPID COWS?>
<WE MADE 8 DIFFERENT CROP CIRCLES TONIGHT. SOME REALLY NEAT STUFF. THE BOYS IN ENGINEERING REALLY OUT-->
<YOU KNOW THE ORDERS. IF THEY WANNA COME, WE CAN'T SAY NO.>
<WHAT THE HELL, YOU TOOK ANOTHER GROUPIE ON BOARD?>
<GOOD LORD, I'D RATHER MATE WITH THE COWS.>
<WHAT'S ALL THIS?>
<OH, THIS ONE'S INTERESTING. WE HAVE HERE ONE 1920'S AMERICAN STATION WAGON FILLED WITH VARIOUS DISMEMBERED BODY PARTS BELONGING TO 38 DIFFERENT MEN OF SOVIET ORIGIN...>
<AS WELL AS THE REMAINS OF A CHIHUAHUA THAT APPEARS TO HAVE BEEN USED AS SOME SORT OF BLUDGEON.>

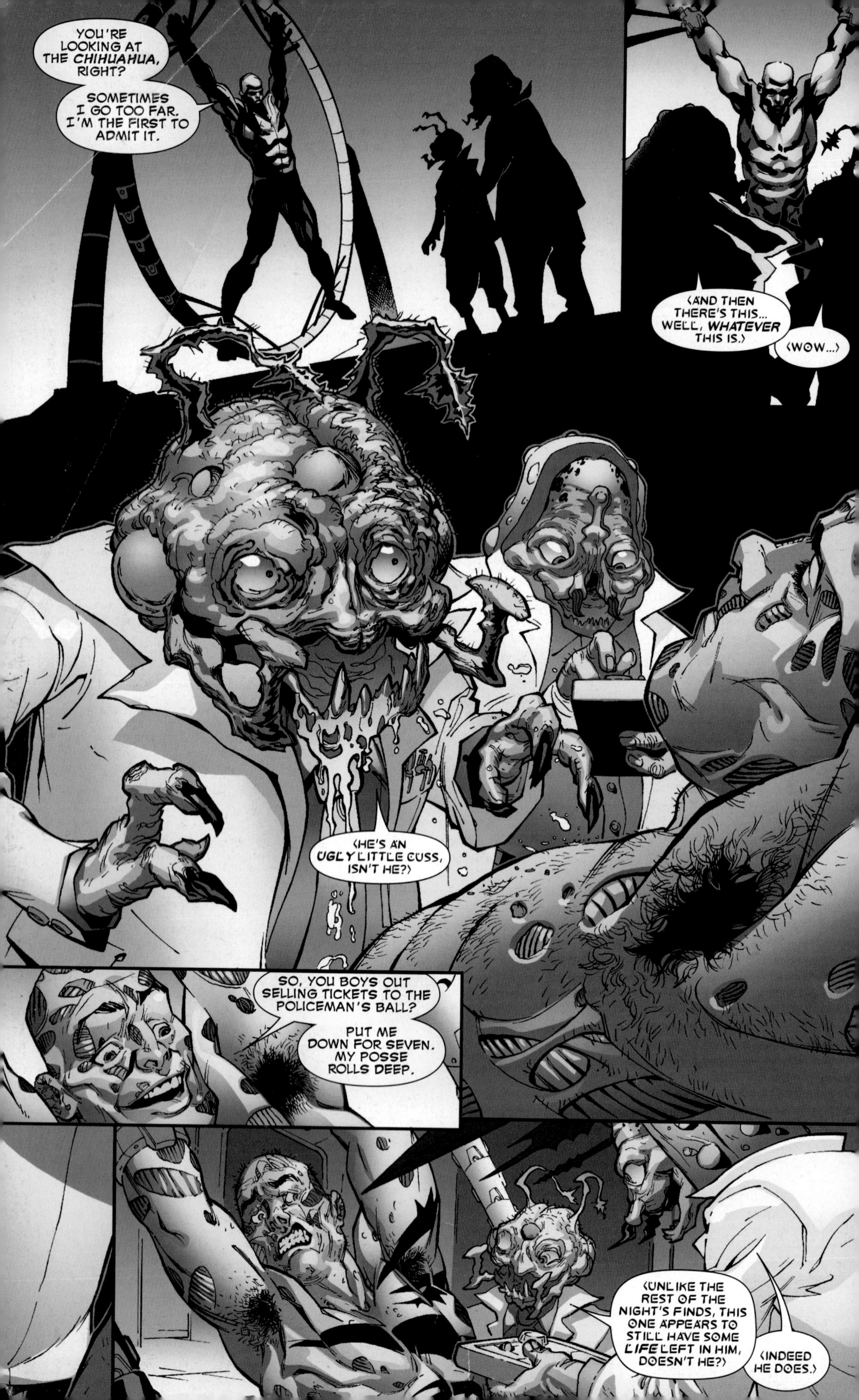
YOU'RE LOOKING AT THE *CHIHUAHUA*, RIGHT?
SOMETIMES I GO TOO FAR. I'M THE FIRST TO ADMIT IT.
‹AND THEN THERE'S THIS... WELL, *WHATEVER* THIS IS.›
‹WOW...›
‹HE'S AN *UGLY* LITTLE CUSS, ISN'T HE?›
SO, YOU BOYS OUT SELLING TICKETS TO THE POLICEMAN'S BALL?
PUT ME DOWN FOR SEVEN. MY POSSE ROLLS DEEP.
‹UNLIKE THE REST OF THE NIGHT'S FINDS, THIS ONE APPEARS TO STILL HAVE SOME *LIFE* LEFT IN HIM, DOESN'T HE?›
‹INDEED HE DOES.›

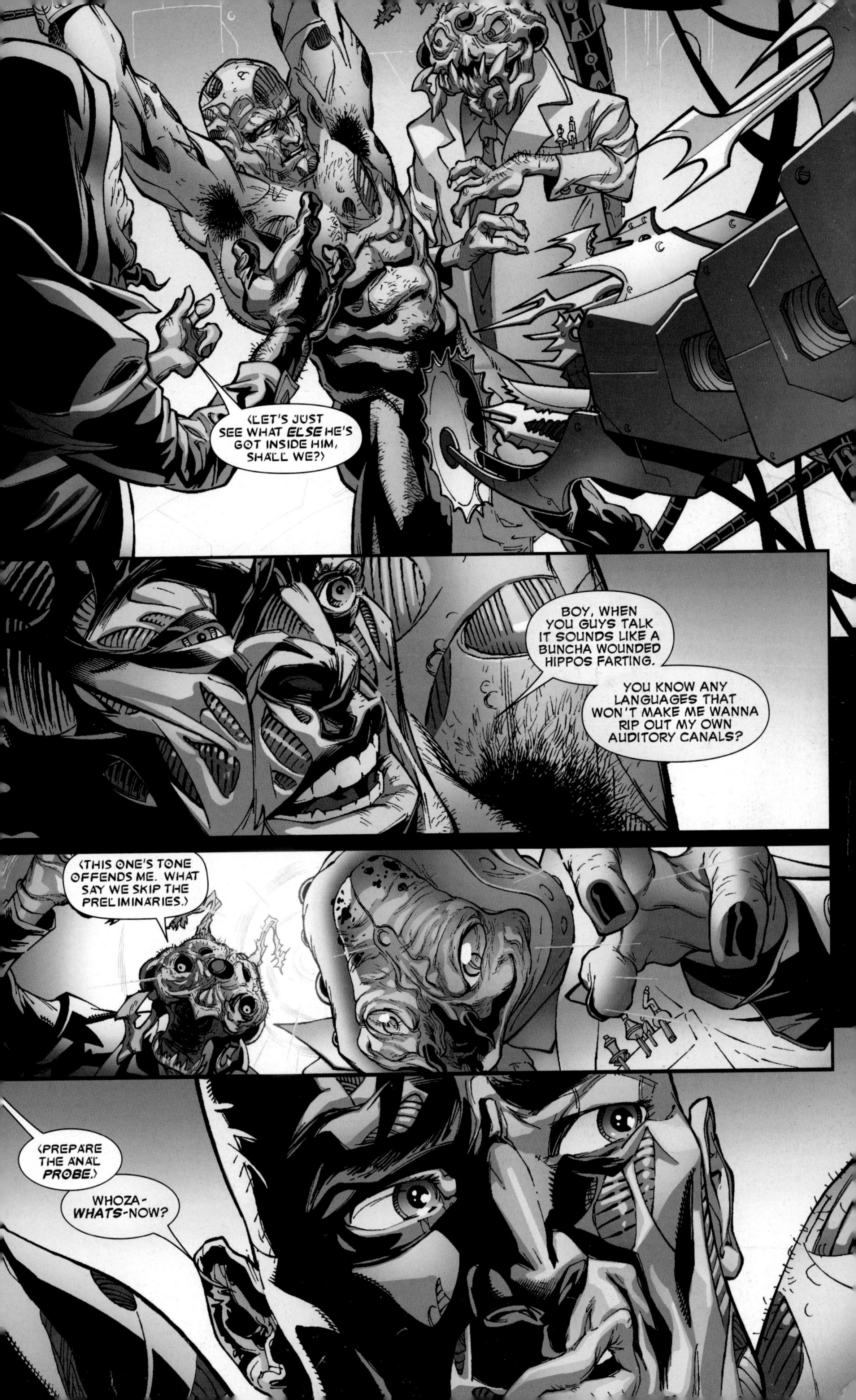
‹LET'S JUST SEE WHAT *ELSE* HE'S GOT INSIDE HIM, SHALL WE?›
BOY, WHEN YOU GUYS TALK IT SOUNDS LIKE A BUNCHA WOUNDED HIPPOS FARTING.
YOU KNOW ANY LANGUAGES THAT WON'T MAKE ME WANNA RIP OUT MY OWN AUDITORY CANALS?
‹THIS ONE'S TONE OFFENDS ME. WHAT SAY WE SKIP THE PRELIMINARIES.›
‹PREPARE THE ANAL *PROBE*.›
WHOZA-*WHATS*-NOW?

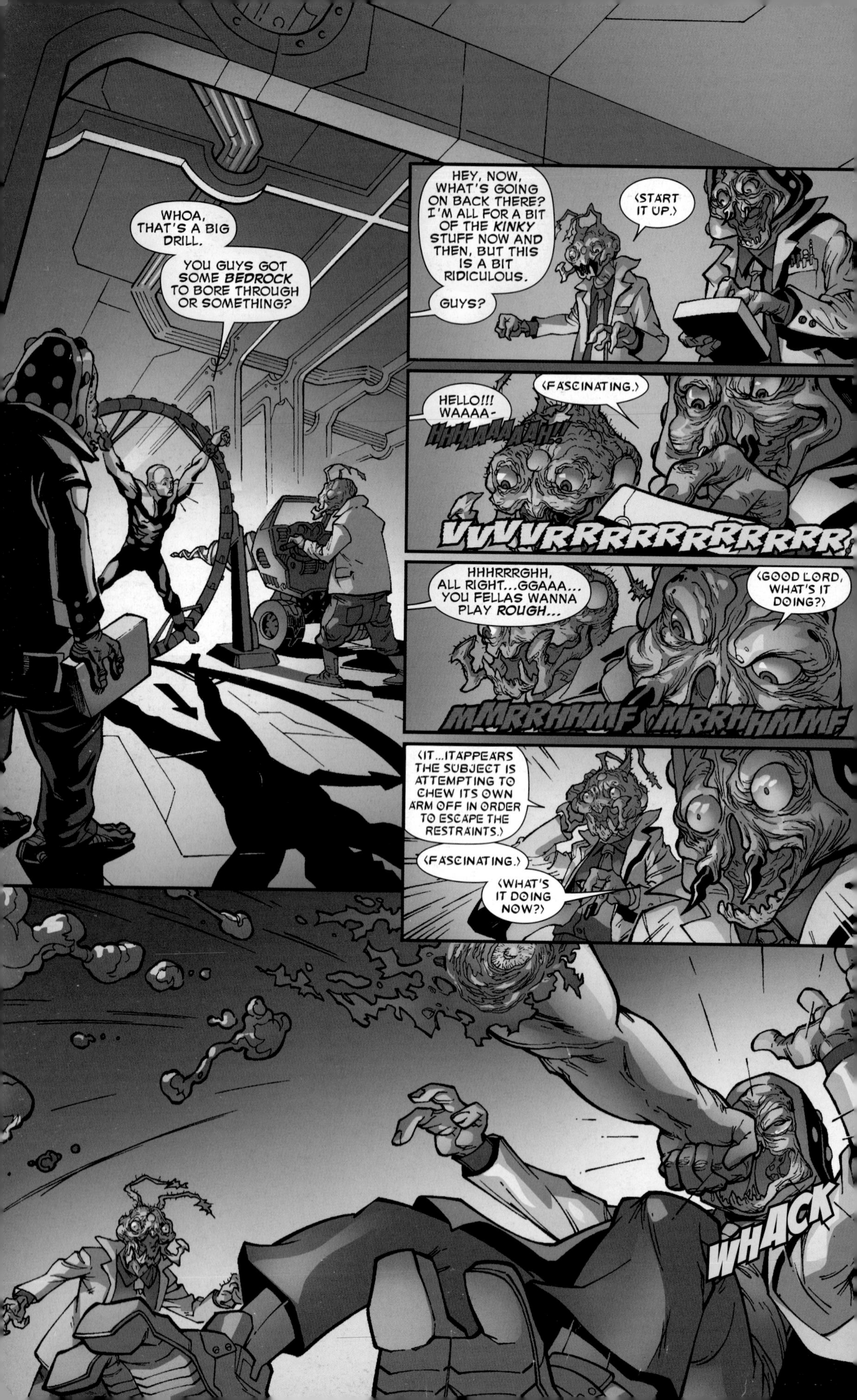
WHOA, THAT'S A BIG DRILL.
YOU GUYS GOT SOME BEDROCK TO BORE THROUGH OR SOMETHING?
HEY, NOW, WHAT'S GOING ON BACK THERE? I'M ALL FOR A BIT OF THE KINKY STUFF NOW AND THEN, BUT THIS IS A BIT RIDICULOUS.
GUYS?
‹START IT UP.›
HELLO!!! WAAAA-HHHAAAAAAH!!
‹FASCINATING.›
VVVVRRRRRRRRRRRR
HHHRRRGHH, ALL RIGHT...GGAAA... YOU FELLAS WANNA PLAY ROUGH...
‹GOOD LORD, WHAT'S IT DOING?›
MMRRHHMF MMRRHHMMF
‹IT...IT APPEARS THE SUBJECT IS ATTEMPTING TO CHEW ITS OWN ARM OFF IN ORDER TO ESCAPE THE RESTRAINTS.›
‹FASCINATING.›
‹WHAT'S IT DOING NOW?›
WHACK

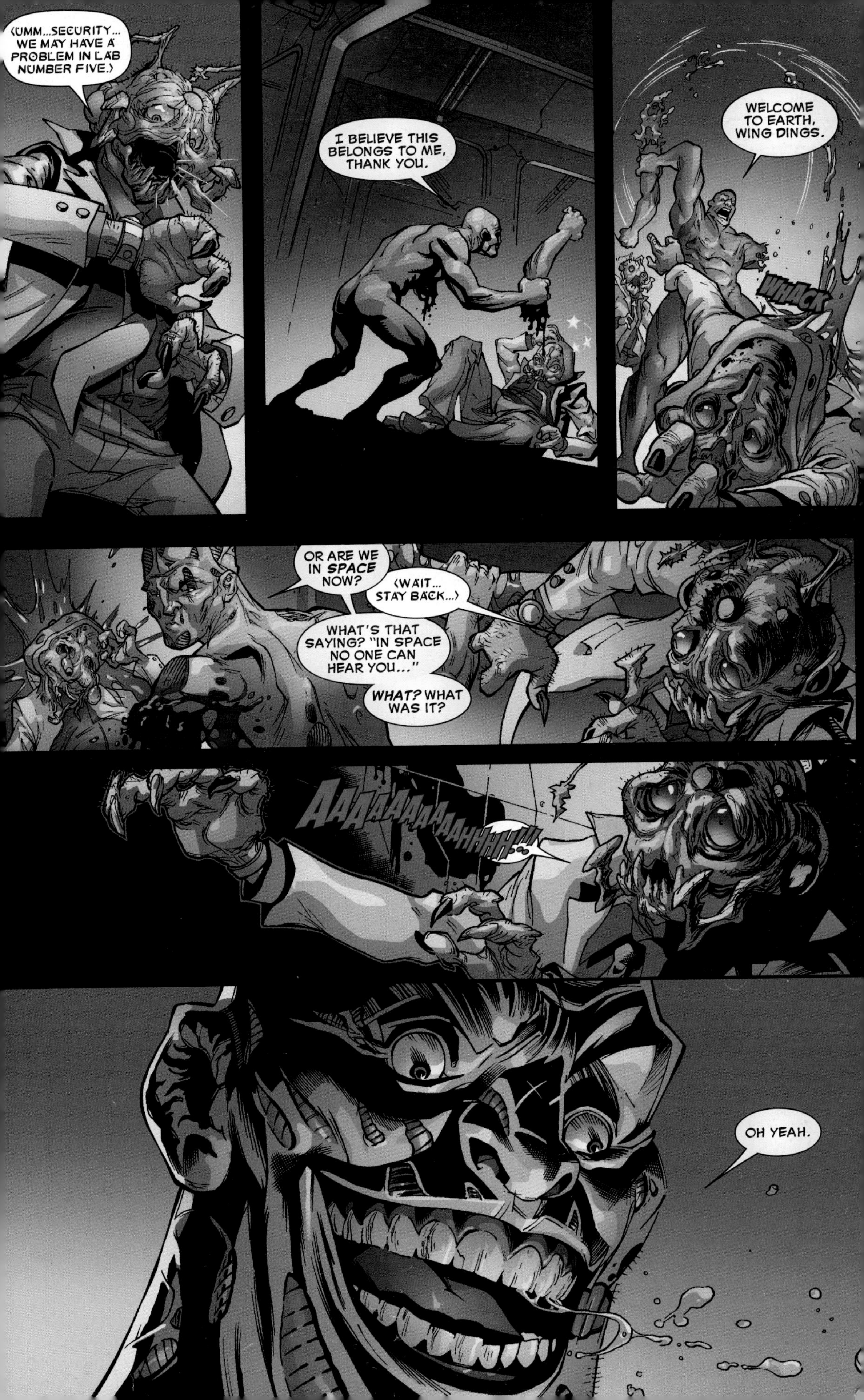
‹UMM...SECURITY... WE MAY HAVE A PROBLEM IN LAB NUMBER FIVE.›
I BELIEVE THIS BELONGS TO ME, THANK YOU.
WELCOME TO EARTH, WING DINGS.
WHACK
OR ARE WE IN SPACE NOW?
‹WAIT... STAY BACK...›
WHAT'S THAT SAYING? "IN SPACE NO ONE CAN HEAR YOU..."
WHAT? WHAT WAS IT?
AAAAAAAAAAAHHHH!!
OH YEAH.

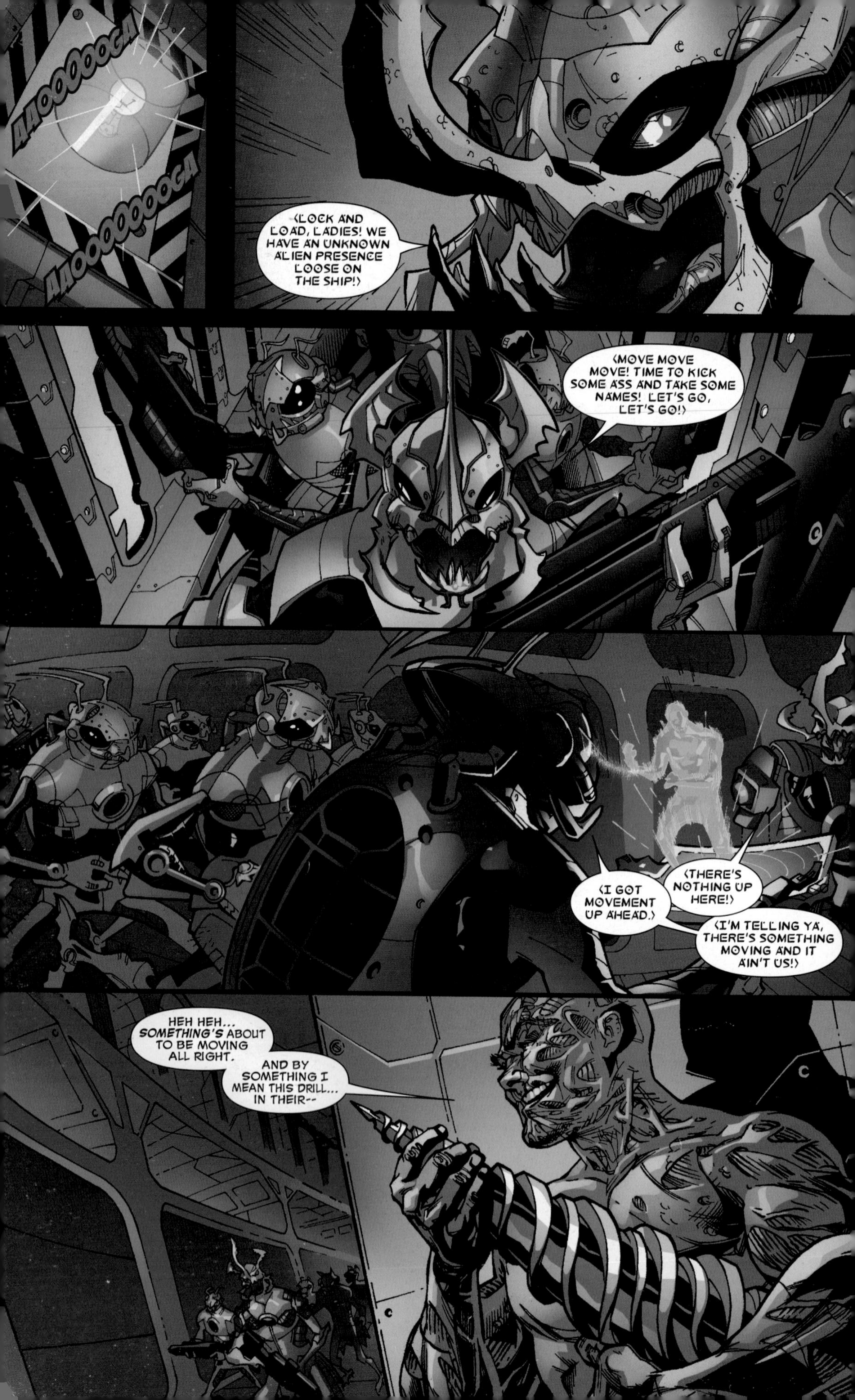
AAOOOOOOGA
AAOOOOOOOOGA
‹LOCK AND LOAD, LADIES! WE HAVE AN UNKNOWN ALIEN PRESENCE LOOSE ON THE SHIP!›
‹MOVE MOVE MOVE! TIME TO KICK SOME ASS AND TAKE SOME NAMES! LET'S GO, LET'S GO!›
‹THERE'S NOTHING UP HERE!›
‹I GOT MOVEMENT UP AHEAD.›
‹I'M TELLING YA, THERE'S SOMETHING MOVING AND IT AIN'T US!›
HEH HEH... SOMETHING'S ABOUT TO BE MOVING ALL RIGHT.
AND BY SOMETHING I MEAN THIS DRILL... IN THEIR--

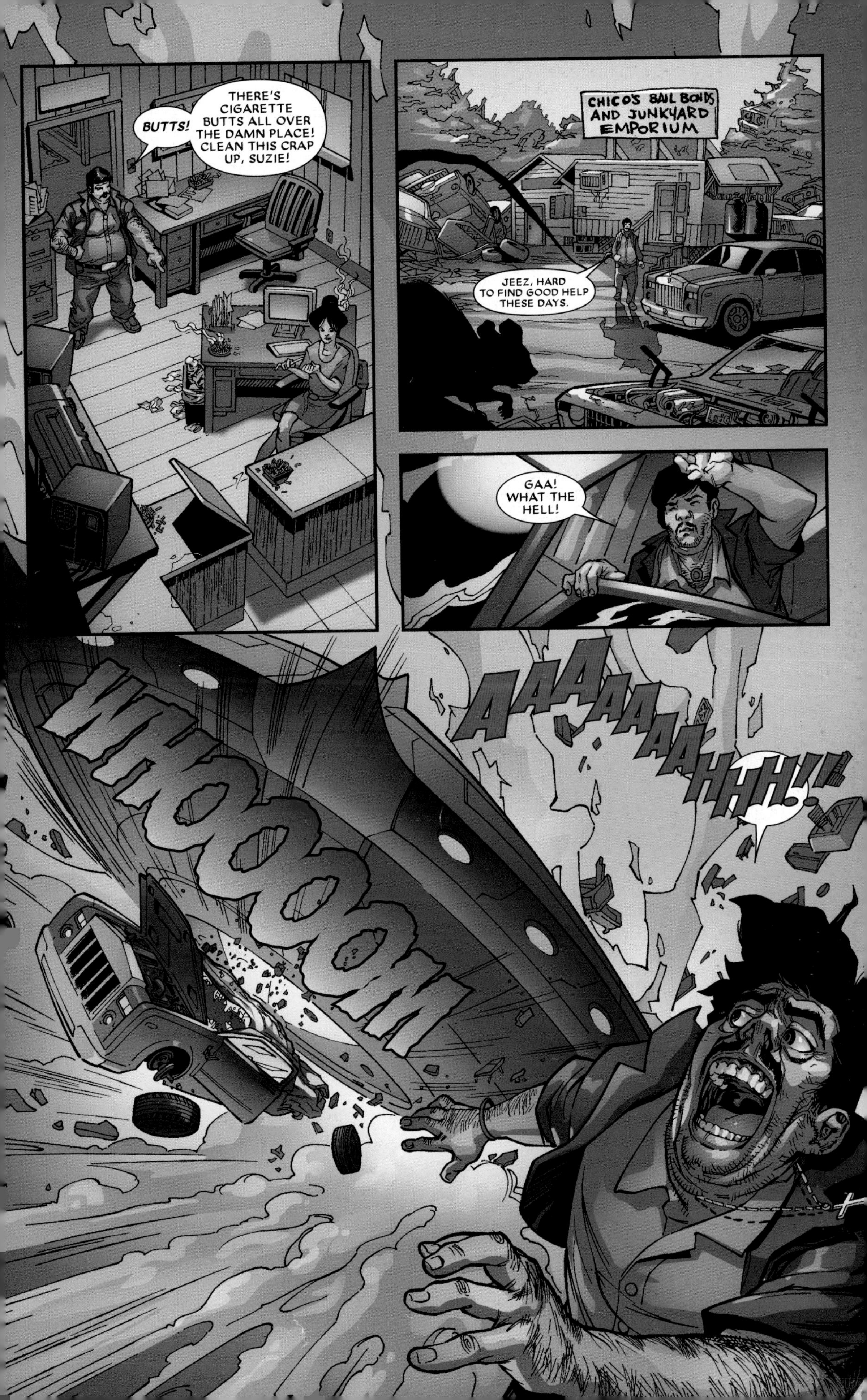
BUTTS!
THERE'S CIGARETTE BUTTS ALL OVER THE DAMN PLACE! CLEAN THIS CRAP UP, SUZIE!
CHICO'S BAIL BONDS AND JUNKYARD EMPORIUM
JEEZ, HARD TO FIND GOOD HELP THESE DAYS.
GAA! WHAT THE HELL!
WHOOOOOM
AAAAAAAHHH!!

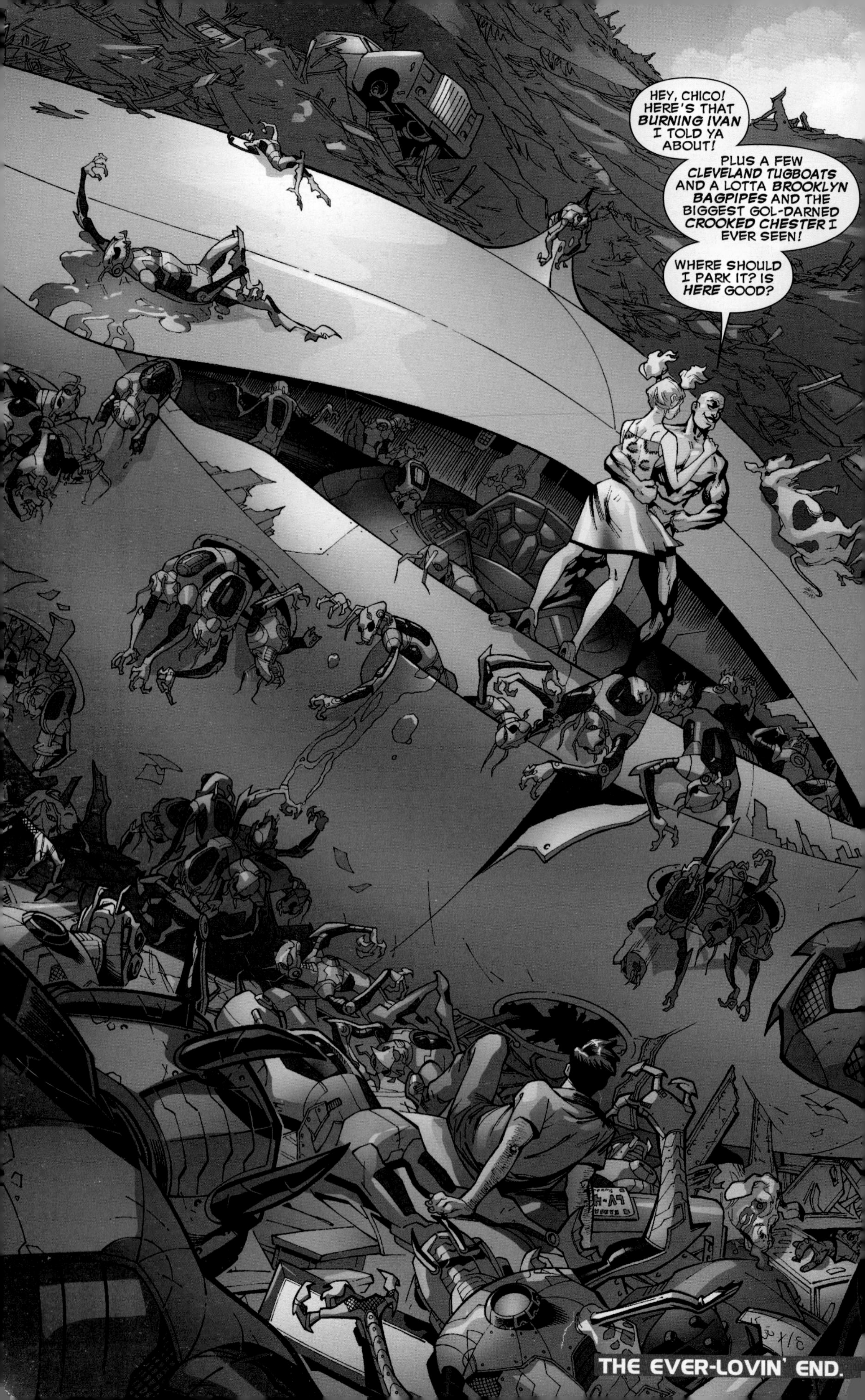
HEY, CHICO! HERE'S THAT *BURNING IVAN* I TOLD YA ABOUT!
PLUS A FEW *CLEVELAND TUGBOATS* AND A LOTTA *BROOKLYN BAGPIPES* AND THE BIGGEST GOL-DARNED *CROOKED CHESTER* I EVER SEEN!
WHERE SHOULD I PARK IT? IS *HERE* GOOD?
THE EVER-LOVIN' END.

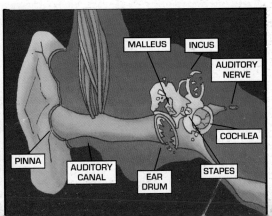

MALLEUS

INCUS

AUDITORY NERVE

PINNA

AUDITORY CANAL

EAR DRUM

COCHLEA

STAPES

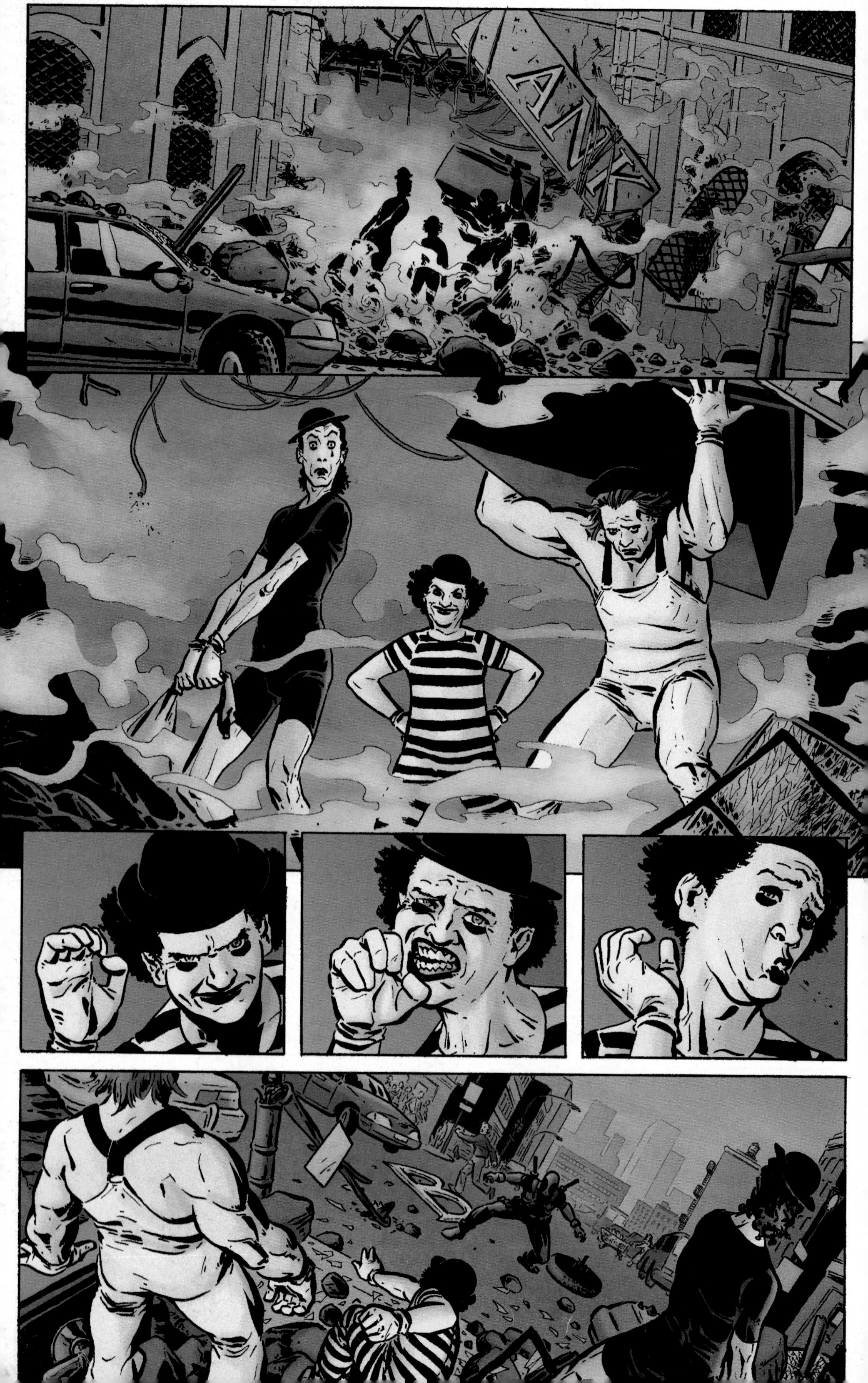

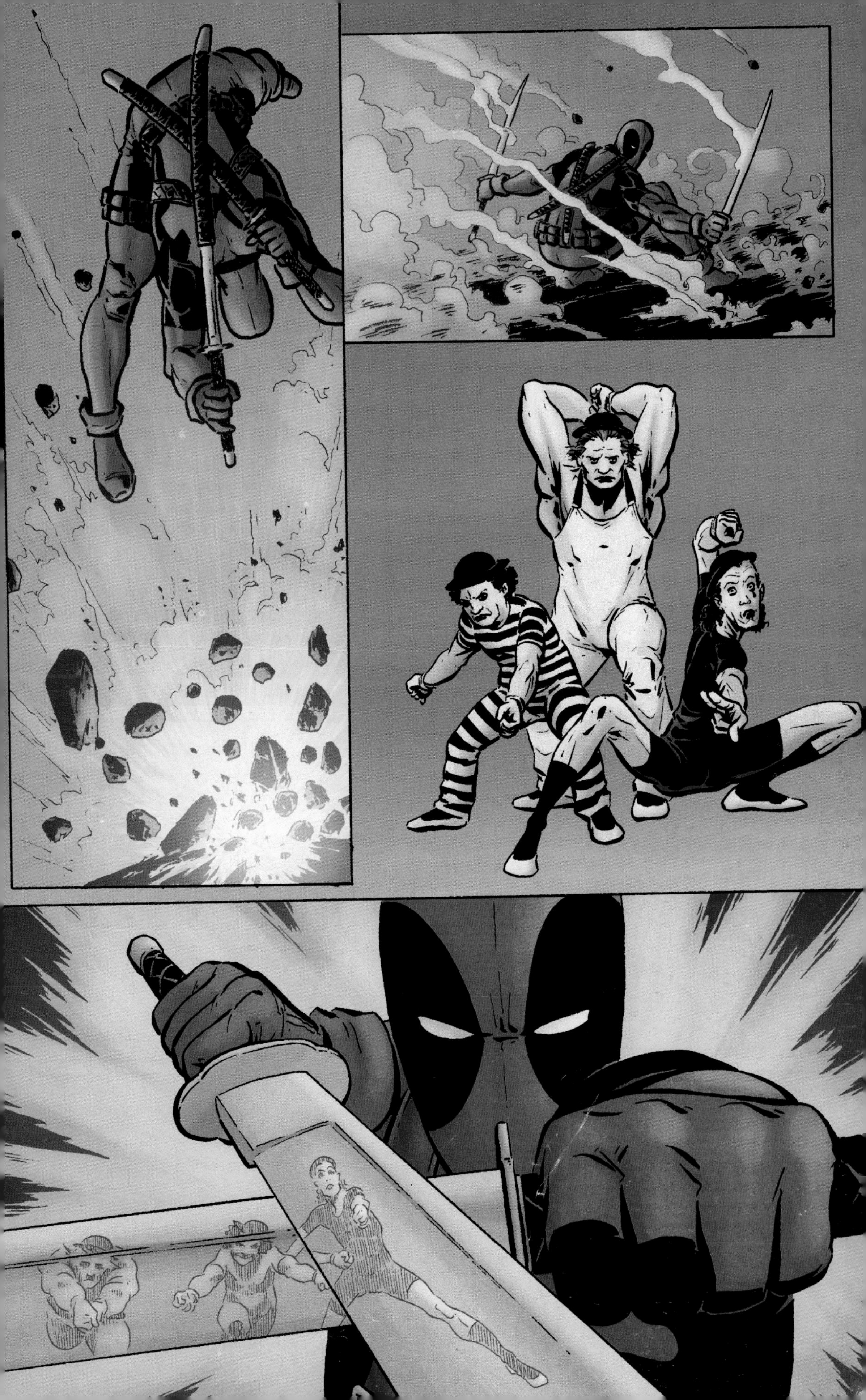

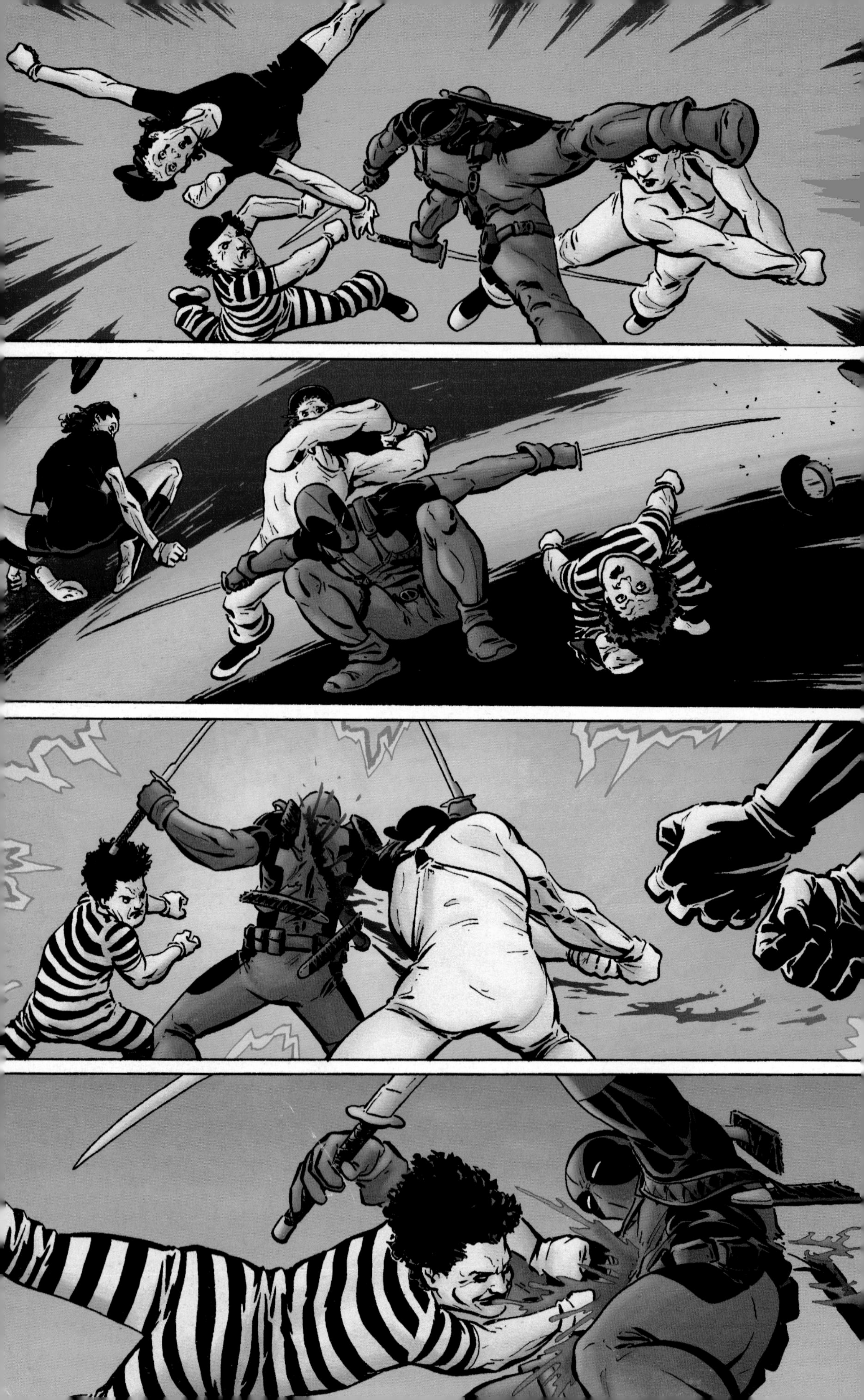

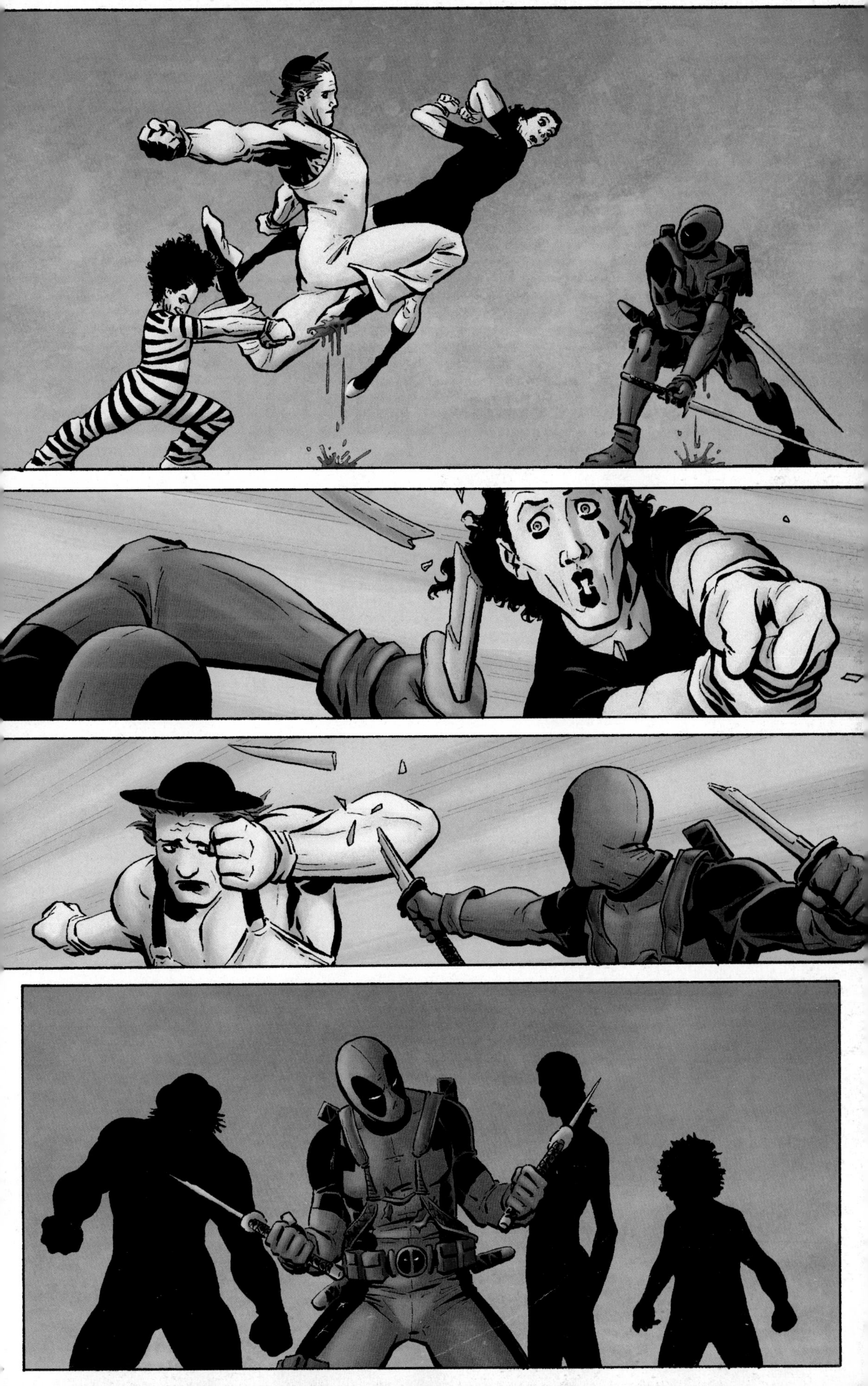

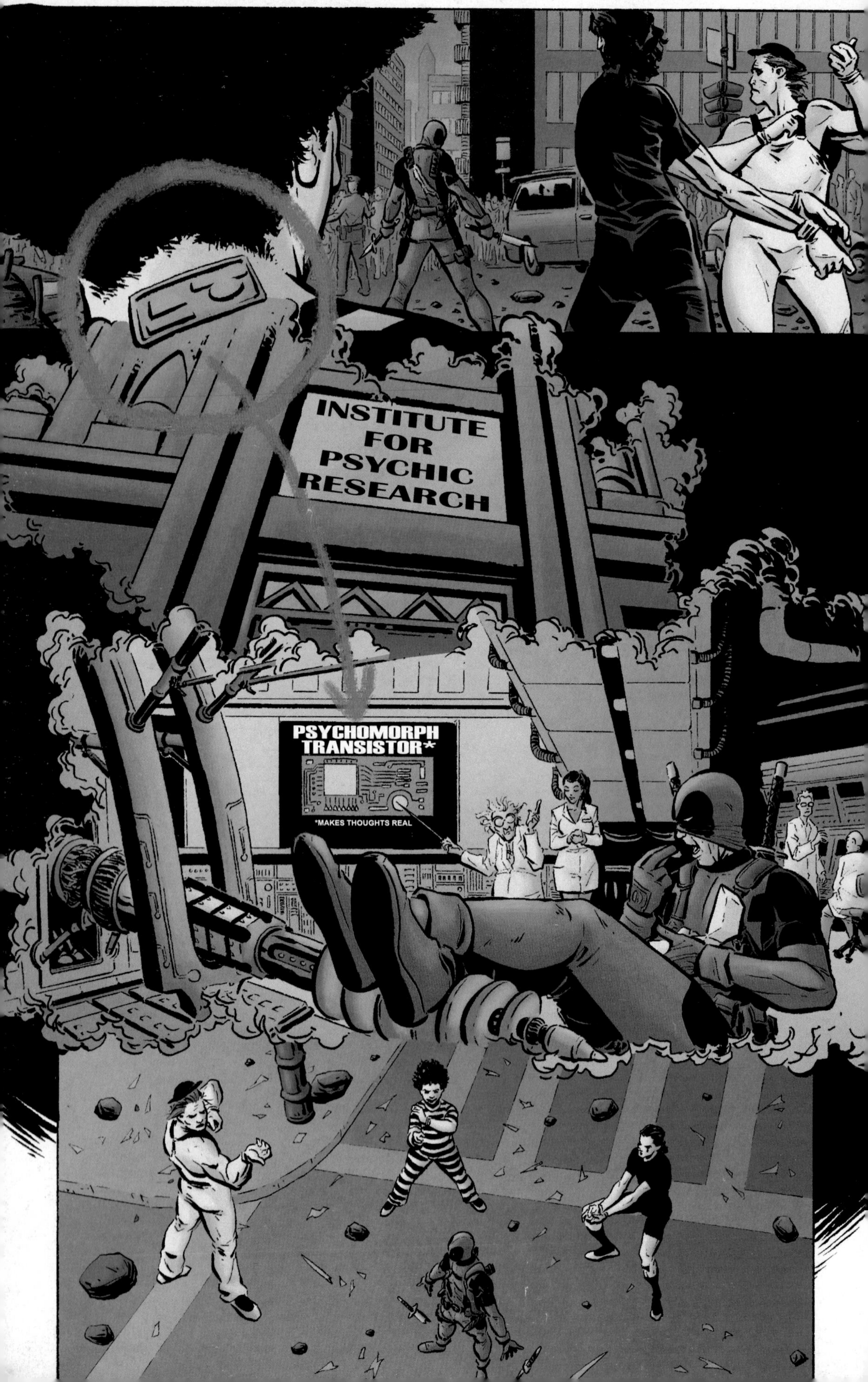
INSTITUTE FOR PSYCHIC RESEARCH
PSYCHOMORPH TRANSISTOR*
*MAKES THOUGHTS REAL

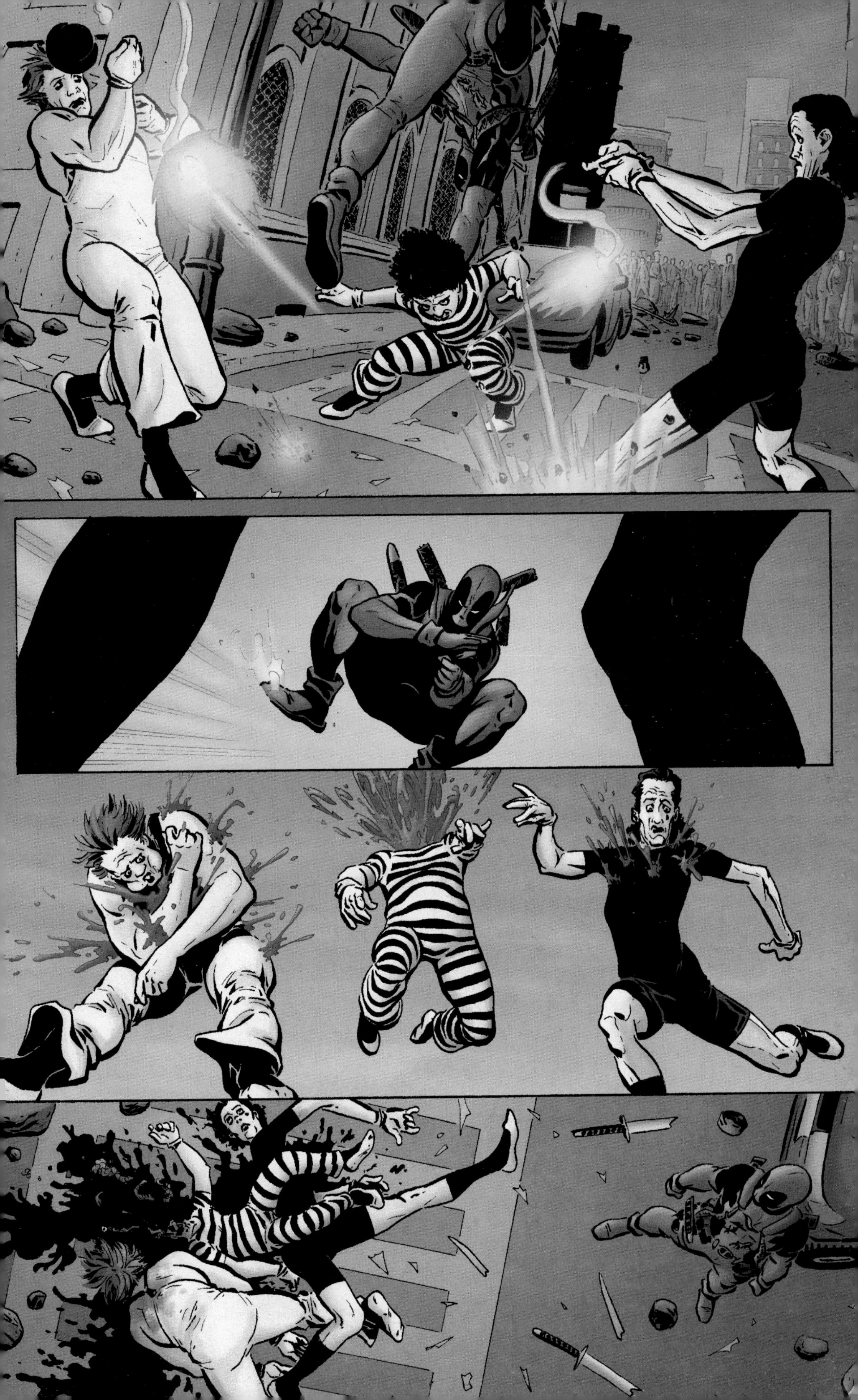

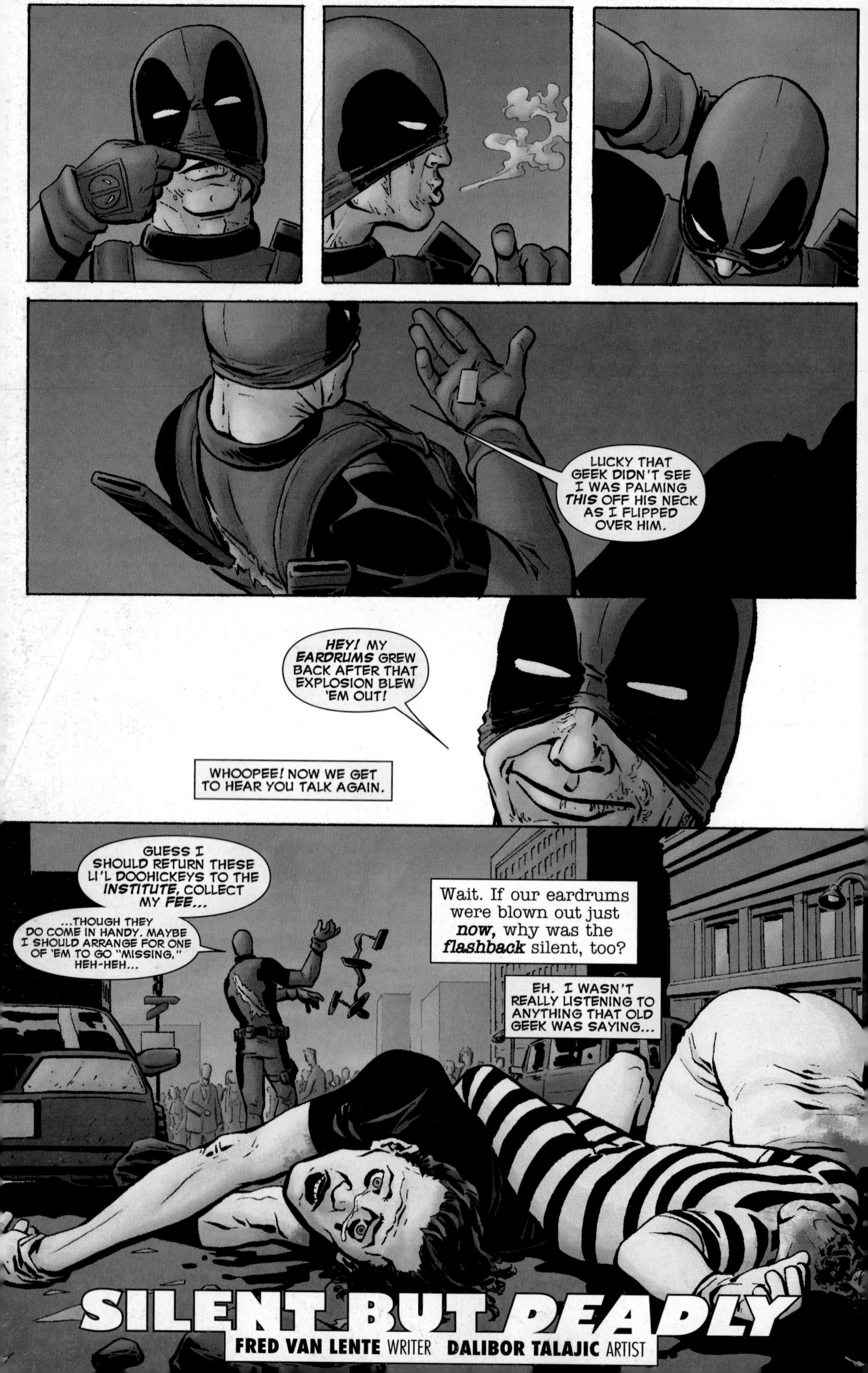

LUCKY THAT GEEK DIDN'T SEE I WAS PALMING THIS OFF HIS NECK AS I FLIPPED OVER HIM.
HEY! MY EARDRUMS GREW BACK AFTER THAT EXPLOSION BLEW 'EM OUT!
WHOOPEE! NOW WE GET TO HEAR YOU TALK AGAIN.
GUESS I SHOULD RETURN THESE LI'L DOOHICKEYS TO THE INSTITUTE, COLLECT MY FEE...
...THOUGH THEY DO COME IN HANDY. MAYBE I SHOULD ARRANGE FOR ONE OF 'EM TO GO "MISSING," HEH-HEH...
Wait. If our eardrums were blown out just now, why was the flashback silent, too?
EH. I WASN'T REALLY LISTENING TO ANYTHING THAT OLD GEEK WAS SAYING...
SILENT BUT DEADLY
FRED VAN LENTE WRITER DALIBOR TALAJIC ARTIST

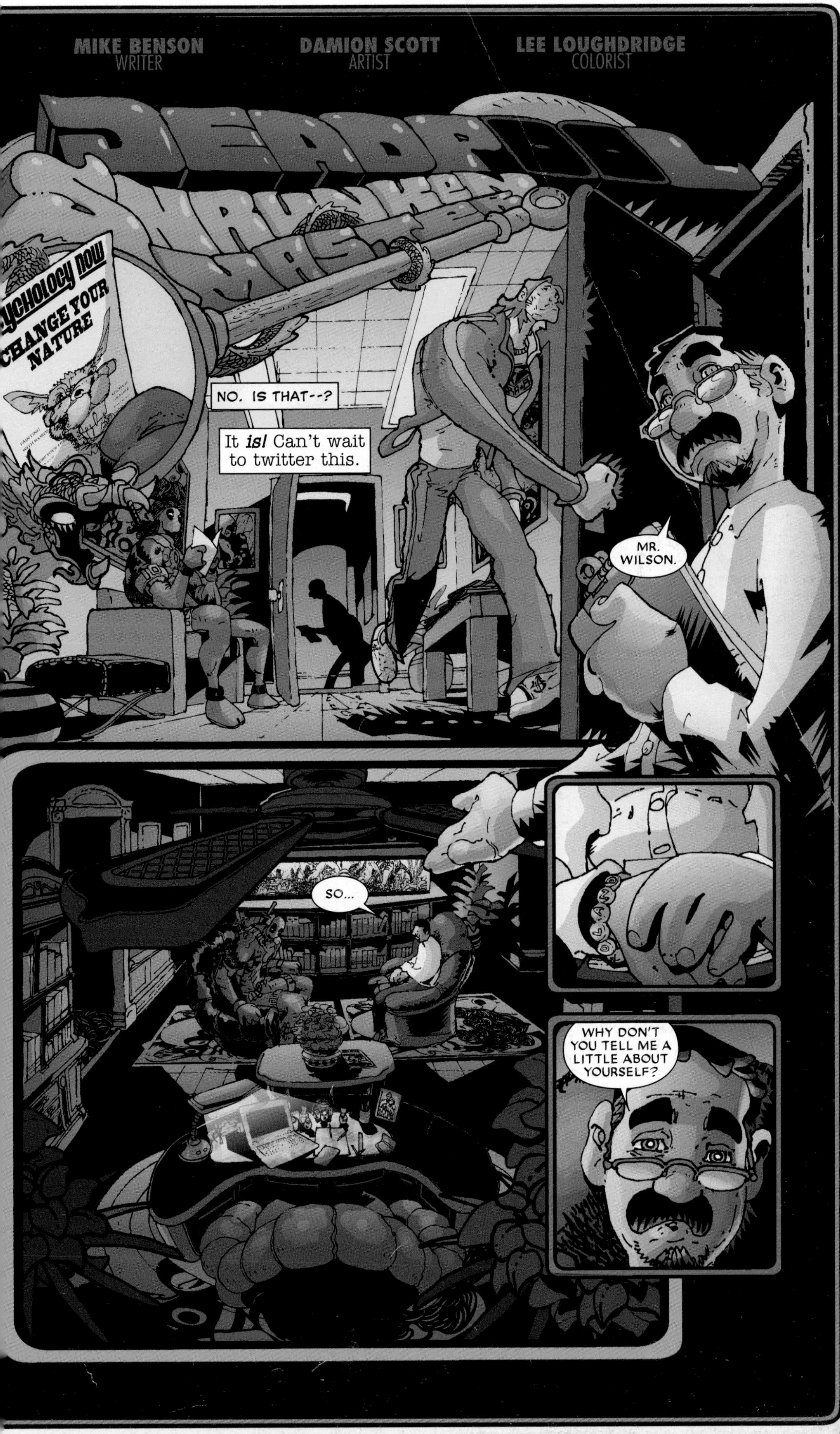

MIKE BENSON
WRITER
DAMION SCOTT
ARTIST
LEE LOUGHDRIDGE
COLORIST
ychology now
CHANGE YOUR NATURE
NO. IS THAT--?
It is! Can't wait to twitter this.
MR. WILSON.
SO...
WHY DON'T YOU TELL ME A LITTLE ABOUT YOURSELF?

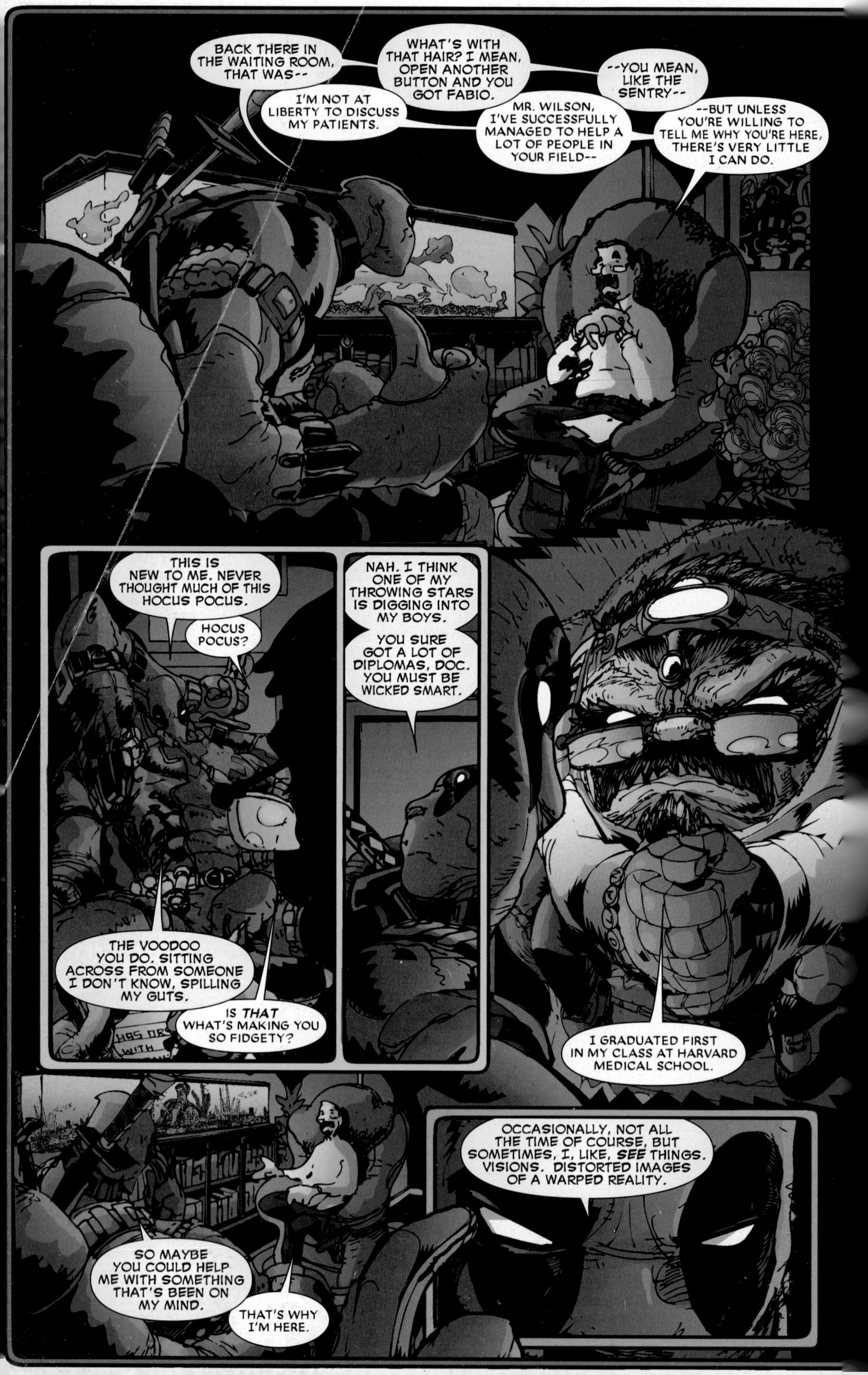

BACK THERE IN THE WAITING ROOM, THAT WAS--
I'M NOT AT LIBERTY TO DISCUSS MY PATIENTS.
WHAT'S WITH THAT HAIR? I MEAN, OPEN ANOTHER BUTTON AND YOU GOT FABIO.
--YOU MEAN, LIKE THE SENTRY--
MR. WILSON, I'VE SUCCESSFULLY MANAGED TO HELP A LOT OF PEOPLE IN YOUR FIELD--
--BUT UNLESS YOU'RE WILLING TO TELL ME WHY YOU'RE HERE, THERE'S VERY LITTLE I CAN DO.
THIS IS NEW TO ME. NEVER THOUGHT MUCH OF THIS HOCUS POCUS.
HOCUS POCUS?
THE VOODOO YOU DO. SITTING ACROSS FROM SOMEONE I DON'T KNOW, SPILLING MY GUTS.
IS *THAT* WHAT'S MAKING YOU SO FIDGETY?
NAH. I THINK ONE OF MY THROWING STARS IS DIGGING INTO MY BOYS.
YOU SURE GOT A LOT OF DIPLOMAS, DOC. YOU MUST BE WICKED SMART.
I GRADUATED FIRST IN MY CLASS AT HARVARD MEDICAL SCHOOL.
SO MAYBE YOU COULD HELP ME WITH SOMETHING THAT'S BEEN ON MY MIND.
THAT'S WHY I'M HERE.
OCCASIONALLY, NOT ALL THE TIME OF COURSE, BUT SOMETIMES, I, LIKE, *SEE* THINGS. VISIONS. DISTORTED IMAGES OF A WARPED REALITY.

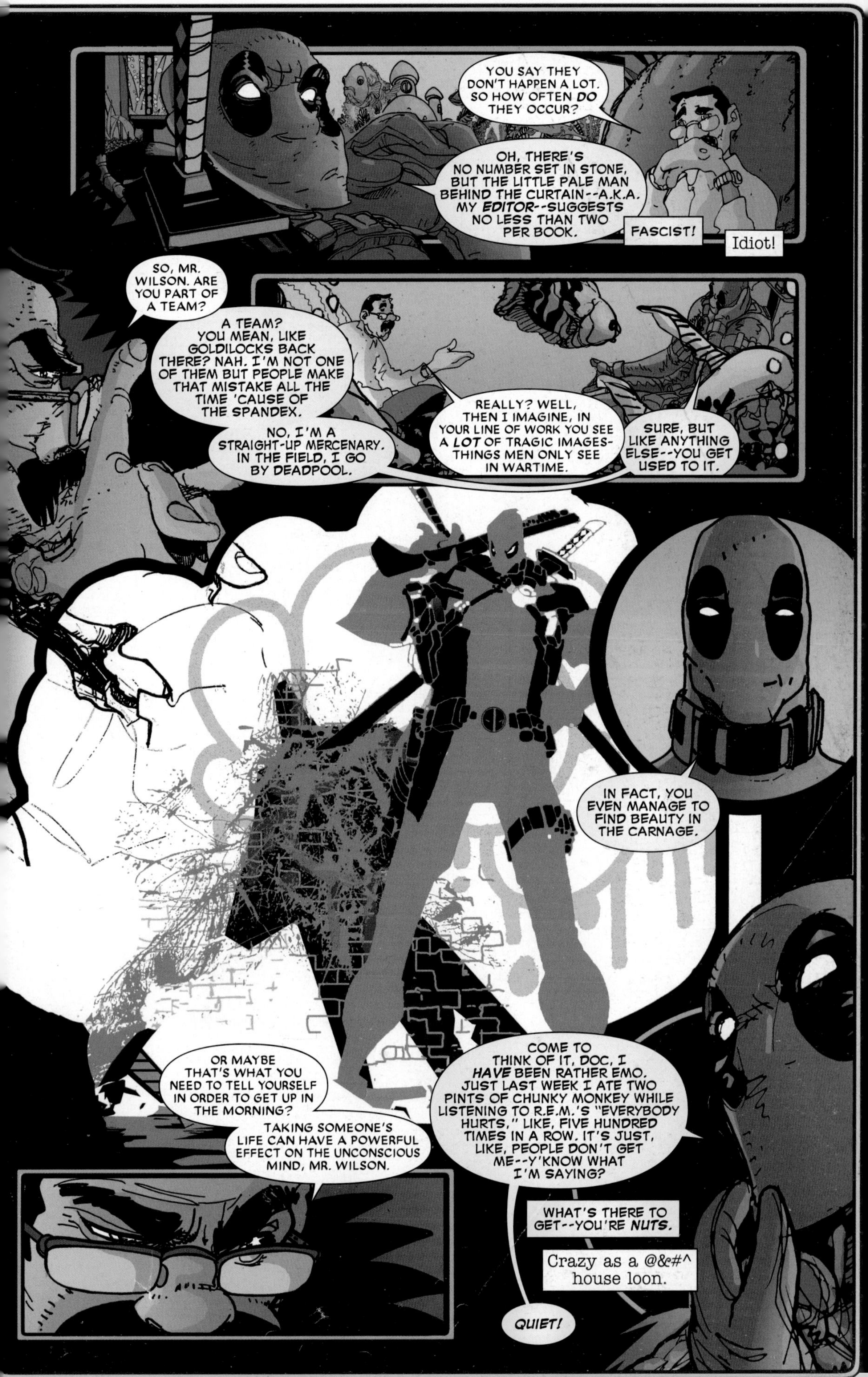
YOU SAY THEY DON'T HAPPEN A LOT. SO HOW OFTEN DO THEY OCCUR?
OH, THERE'S NO NUMBER SET IN STONE, BUT THE LITTLE PALE MAN BEHIND THE CURTAIN--A.K.A. MY EDITOR--SUGGESTS NO LESS THAN TWO PER BOOK.
FASCIST!
Idiot!
SO, MR. WILSON. ARE YOU PART OF A TEAM?
A TEAM? YOU MEAN, LIKE GOLDILOCKS BACK THERE? NAH. I'M NOT ONE OF THEM BUT PEOPLE MAKE THAT MISTAKE ALL THE TIME 'CAUSE OF THE SPANDEX.
NO, I'M A STRAIGHT-UP MERCENARY. IN THE FIELD, I GO BY DEADPOOL.
REALLY? WELL, THEN I IMAGINE, IN YOUR LINE OF WORK YOU SEE A LOT OF TRAGIC IMAGES-THINGS MEN ONLY SEE IN WARTIME.
SURE, BUT LIKE ANYTHING ELSE--YOU GET USED TO IT.
IN FACT, YOU EVEN MANAGE TO FIND BEAUTY IN THE CARNAGE.
OR MAYBE THAT'S WHAT YOU NEED TO TELL YOURSELF IN ORDER TO GET UP IN THE MORNING?
TAKING SOMEONE'S LIFE CAN HAVE A POWERFUL EFFECT ON THE UNCONSCIOUS MIND, MR. WILSON.
COME TO THINK OF IT, DOC, I HAVE BEEN RATHER EMO. JUST LAST WEEK I ATE TWO PINTS OF CHUNKY MONKEY WHILE LISTENING TO R.E.M.'S "EVERYBODY HURTS," LIKE, FIVE HUNDRED TIMES IN A ROW. IT'S JUST, LIKE, PEOPLE DON'T GET ME--Y'KNOW WHAT I'M SAYING?
WHAT'S THERE TO GET--YOU'RE NUTS.
Crazy as a @&#^ house loon.
QUIET!

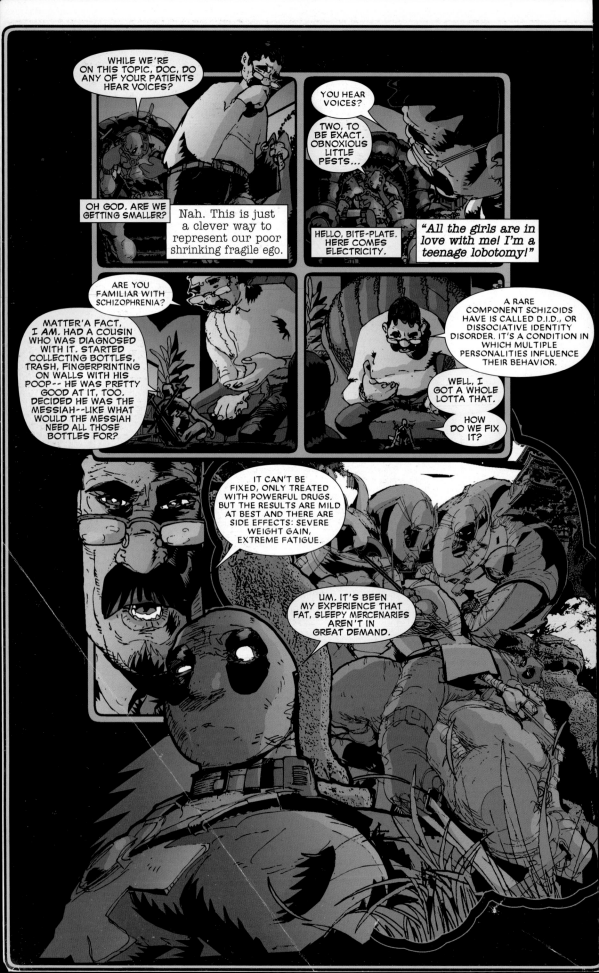

WHILE WE'RE ON THIS TOPIC, DOC, DO ANY OF YOUR PATIENTS HEAR VOICES?

YOU HEAR VOICES?

TWO, TO BE EXACT. OBNOXIOUS LITTLE PESTS...

OH GOD. ARE WE GETTING SMALLER?

Nah. This is just a clever way to represent our poor shrinking fragile ego.

HELLO, BITE-PLATE. HERE COMES ELECTRICITY.

"All the girls are in love with me! I'm a teenage lobotomy!"

ARE YOU FAMILIAR WITH SCHIZOPHRENIA?

MATTER'A FACT, I AM. HAD A COUSIN WHO WAS DIAGNOSED WITH IT. STARTED COLLECTING BOTTLES, TRASH, FINGERPRINTING ON WALLS WITH HIS POOP-- HE WAS PRETTY GOOD AT IT, TOO. DECIDED HE WAS THE MESSIAH--LIKE WHAT WOULD THE MESSIAH NEED ALL THOSE BOTTLES FOR?

A RARE COMPONENT SCHIZOIDS HAVE IS CALLED D.I.D., OR DISSOCIATIVE IDENTITY DISORDER. IT'S A CONDITION IN WHICH MULTIPLE PERSONALITIES INFLUENCE THEIR BEHAVIOR.

WELL, I GOT A WHOLE LOTTA THAT.

HOW DO WE FIX IT?

IT CAN'T BE FIXED, ONLY TREATED WITH POWERFUL DRUGS. BUT THE RESULTS ARE MILD AT BEST AND THERE ARE SIDE EFFECTS: SEVERE WEIGHT GAIN, EXTREME FATIGUE.

UM. IT'S BEEN MY EXPERIENCE THAT FAT, SLEEPY MERCENARIES AREN'T IN GREAT DEMAND.

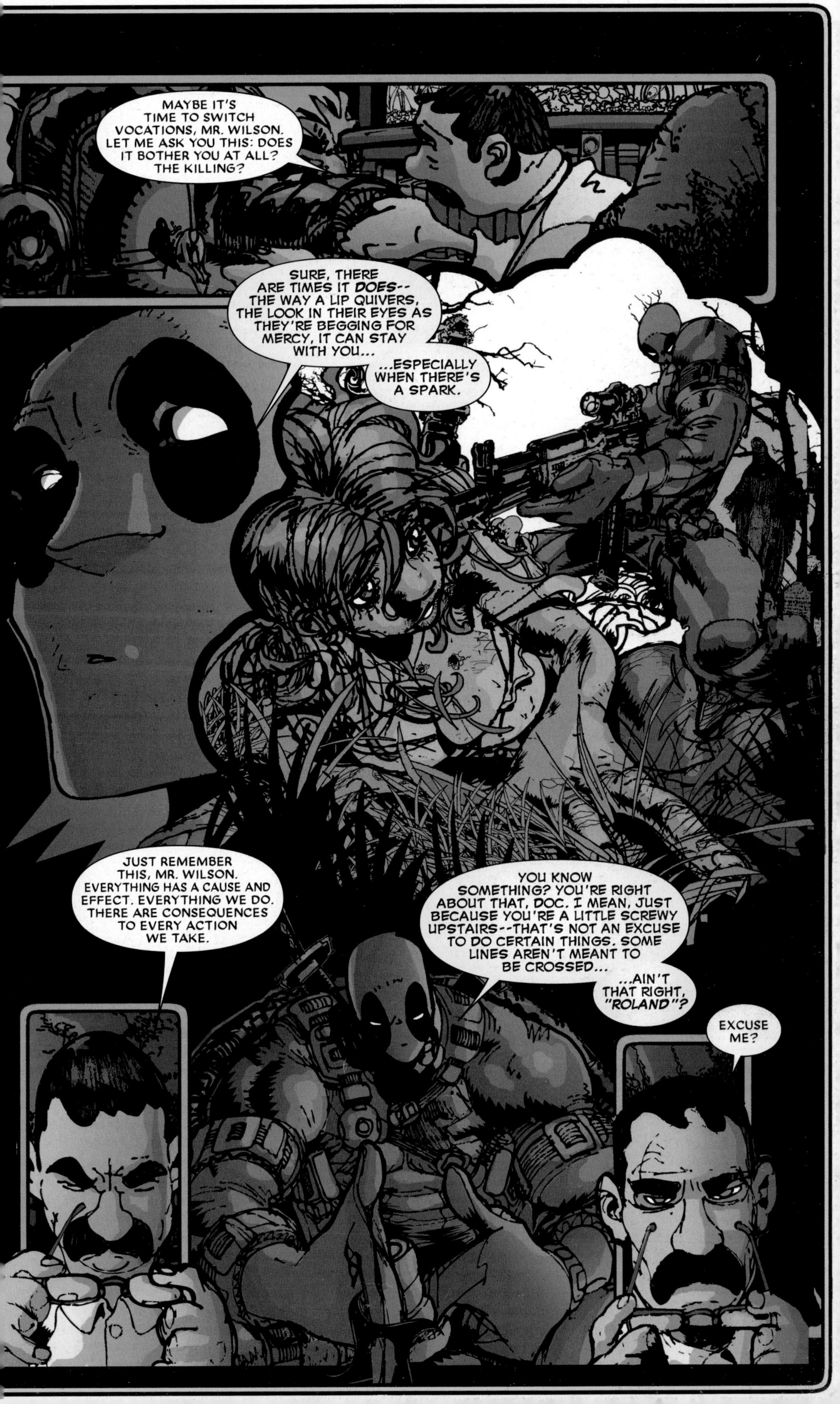

MAYBE IT'S TIME TO SWITCH VOCATIONS, MR. WILSON. LET ME ASK YOU THIS: DOES IT BOTHER YOU AT ALL? THE KILLING?
SURE, THERE ARE TIMES IT DOES--THE WAY A LIP QUIVERS, THE LOOK IN THEIR EYES AS THEY'RE BEGGING FOR MERCY, IT CAN STAY WITH YOU...
...ESPECIALLY WHEN THERE'S A SPARK.
JUST REMEMBER THIS, MR. WILSON. EVERYTHING HAS A CAUSE AND EFFECT. EVERYTHING WE DO. THERE ARE CONSEQUENCES TO EVERY ACTION WE TAKE.
YOU KNOW SOMETHING? YOU'RE RIGHT ABOUT THAT, DOC. I MEAN, JUST BECAUSE YOU'RE A LITTLE SCREWY UPSTAIRS--THAT'S NOT AN EXCUSE TO DO CERTAIN THINGS. SOME LINES AREN'T MEANT TO BE CROSSED...
...AIN'T THAT RIGHT, "ROLAND"?
EXCUSE ME?

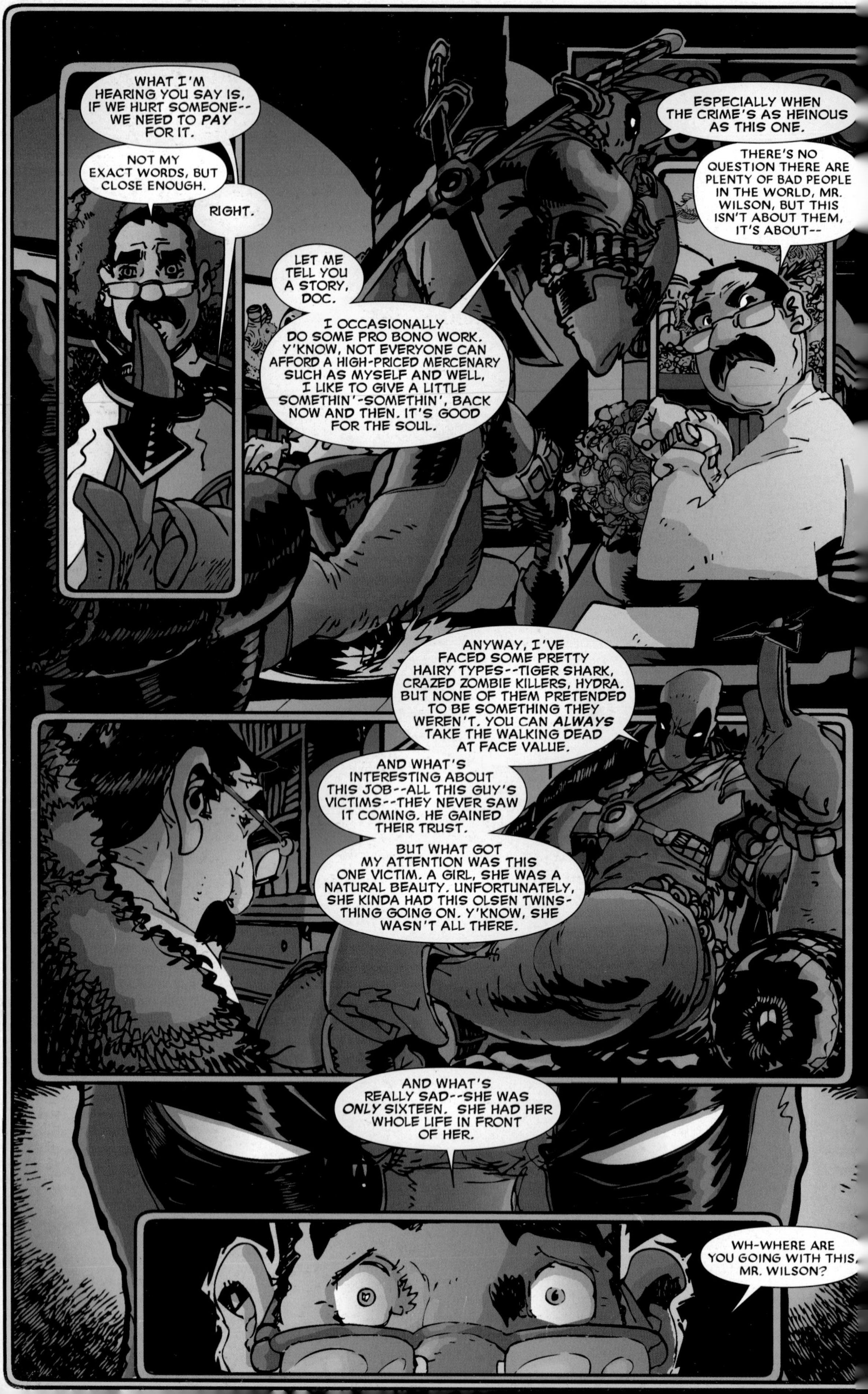
WHAT I'M HEARING YOU SAY IS, IF WE HURT SOMEONE-- WE NEED TO PAY FOR IT.
NOT MY EXACT WORDS, BUT CLOSE ENOUGH.
RIGHT.
ESPECIALLY WHEN THE CRIME'S AS HEINOUS AS THIS ONE.
THERE'S NO QUESTION THERE ARE PLENTY OF BAD PEOPLE IN THE WORLD, MR. WILSON, BUT THIS ISN'T ABOUT THEM, IT'S ABOUT--
LET ME TELL YOU A STORY, DOC.
I OCCASIONALLY DO SOME PRO BONO WORK. Y'KNOW, NOT EVERYONE CAN AFFORD A HIGH-PRICED MERCENARY SUCH AS MYSELF AND WELL, I LIKE TO GIVE A LITTLE SOMETHIN'-SOMETHIN', BACK NOW AND THEN. IT'S GOOD FOR THE SOUL.
ANYWAY, I'VE FACED SOME PRETTY HAIRY TYPES--TIGER SHARK, CRAZED ZOMBIE KILLERS, HYDRA. BUT NONE OF THEM PRETENDED TO BE SOMETHING THEY WEREN'T. YOU CAN ALWAYS TAKE THE WALKING DEAD AT FACE VALUE.
AND WHAT'S INTERESTING ABOUT THIS JOB--ALL THIS GUY'S VICTIMS--THEY NEVER SAW IT COMING. HE GAINED THEIR TRUST.
BUT WHAT GOT MY ATTENTION WAS THIS ONE VICTIM. A GIRL, SHE WAS A NATURAL BEAUTY. UNFORTUNATELY, SHE KINDA HAD THIS OLSEN TWINS-THING GOING ON. Y'KNOW, SHE WASN'T ALL THERE.
AND WHAT'S REALLY SAD--SHE WAS ONLY SIXTEEN. SHE HAD HER WHOLE LIFE IN FRONT OF HER.
WH-WHERE ARE YOU GOING WITH THIS, MR. WILSON?

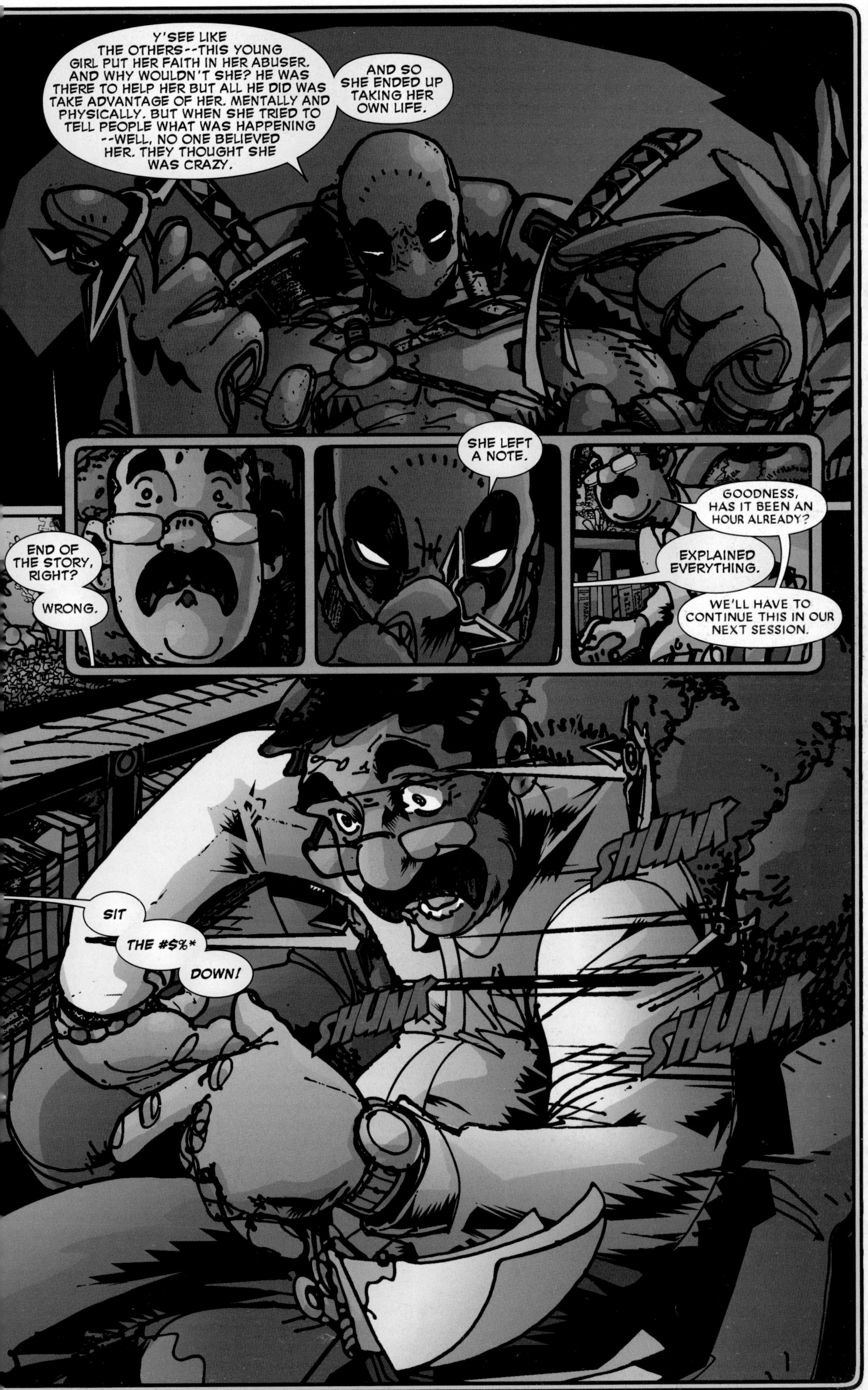
Y'SEE LIKE THE OTHERS--THIS YOUNG GIRL PUT HER FAITH IN HER ABUSER. AND WHY WOULDN'T SHE? HE WAS THERE TO HELP HER BUT ALL HE DID WAS TAKE ADVANTAGE OF HER. MENTALLY AND PHYSICALLY. BUT WHEN SHE TRIED TO TELL PEOPLE WHAT WAS HAPPENING --WELL, NO ONE BELIEVED HER. THEY THOUGHT SHE WAS CRAZY.
AND SO SHE ENDED UP TAKING HER OWN LIFE.
END OF THE STORY, RIGHT?
WRONG.
SHE LEFT A NOTE.
EXPLAINED EVERYTHING.
GOODNESS, HAS IT BEEN AN HOUR ALREADY?
WE'LL HAVE TO CONTINUE THIS IN OUR NEXT SESSION.
SIT
THE #$%*
DOWN!
SHUNK
SHUNK
SHUNK

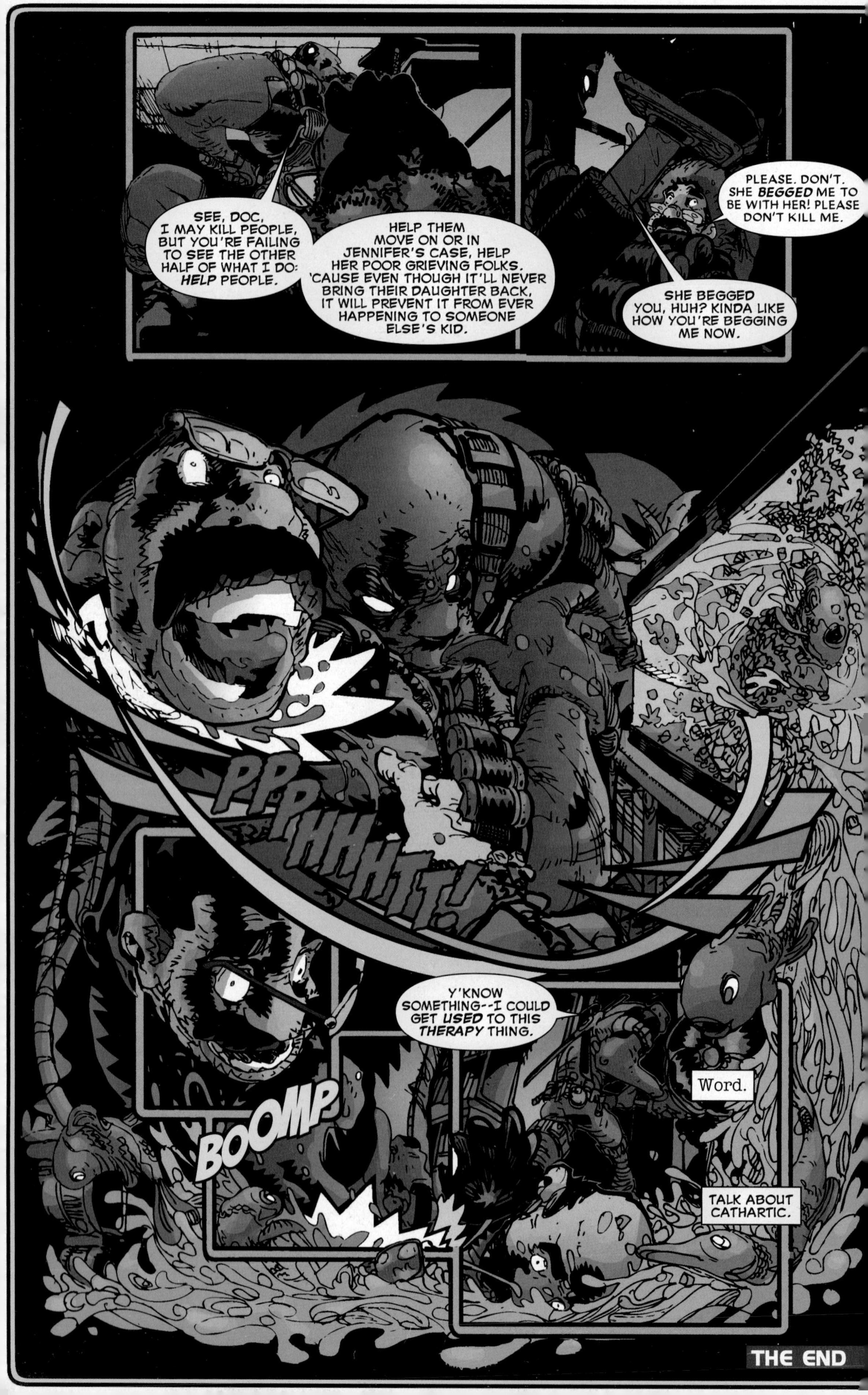
SEE, DOC, I MAY KILL PEOPLE, BUT YOU'RE FAILING TO SEE THE OTHER HALF OF WHAT I DO: HELP PEOPLE.
HELP THEM MOVE ON OR IN JENNIFER'S CASE, HELP HER POOR GRIEVING FOLKS. 'CAUSE EVEN THOUGH IT'LL NEVER BRING THEIR DAUGHTER BACK, IT WILL PREVENT IT FROM EVER HAPPENING TO SOMEONE ELSE'S KID.
PLEASE. DON'T. SHE BEGGED ME TO BE WITH HER! PLEASE DON'T KILL ME.
SHE BEGGED YOU, HUH? KINDA LIKE HOW YOU'RE BEGGING ME NOW.
PPPHHHATTT!
Y'KNOW SOMETHING--I COULD GET USED TO THIS THERAPY THING.
Word.
BOOMP
TALK ABOUT CATHARTIC.
THE END

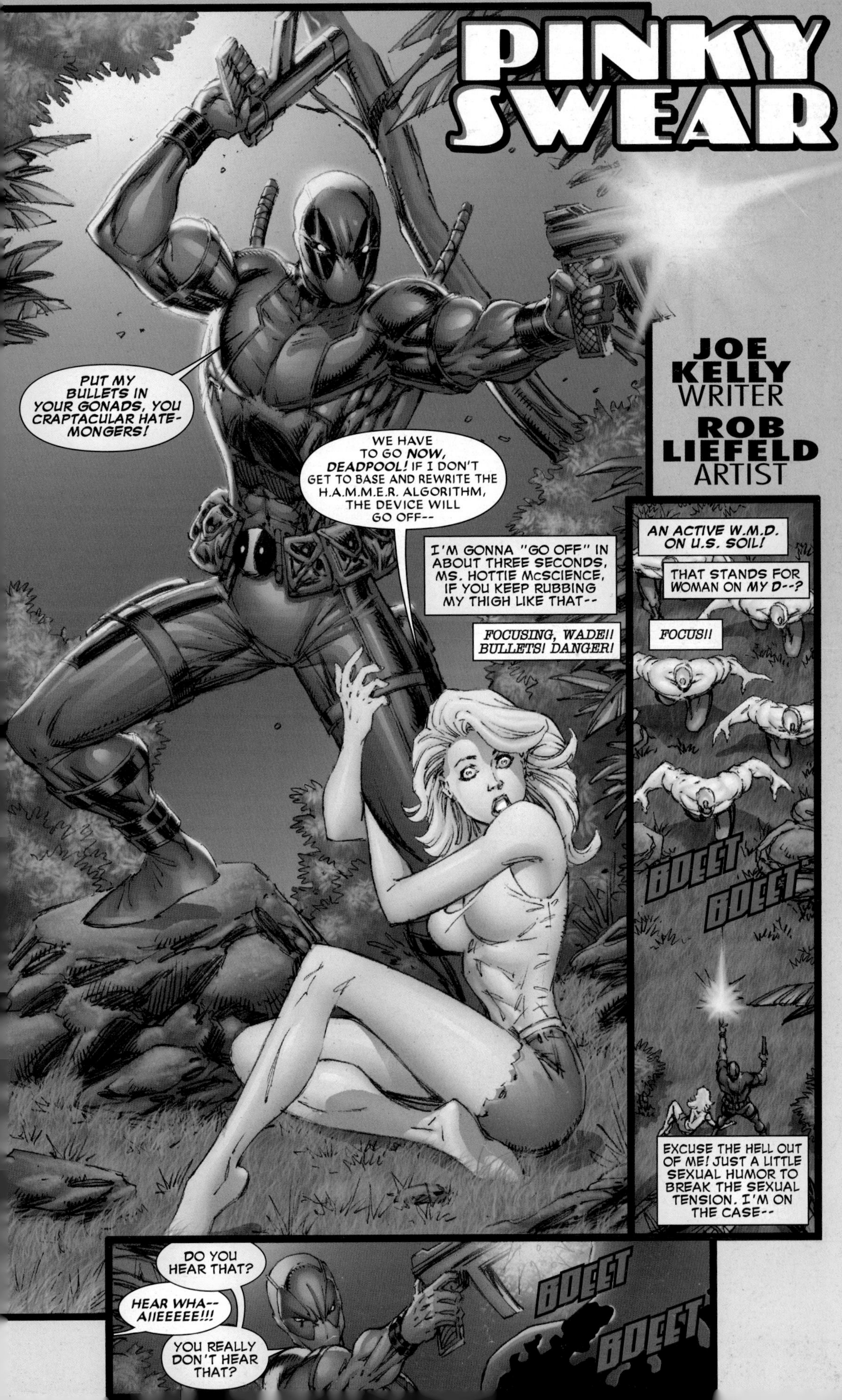

PINKY SWEAR
JOE KELLY WRITER
ROB LIEFELD ARTIST
PUT MY BULLETS IN YOUR GONADS, YOU CRAPTACULAR HATE-MONGERS!
WE HAVE TO GO NOW, DEADPOOL! IF I DON'T GET TO BASE AND REWRITE THE H.A.M.M.E.R. ALGORITHM, THE DEVICE WILL GO OFF--
I'M GONNA "GO OFF" IN ABOUT THREE SECONDS, MS. HOTTIE McSCIENCE, IF YOU KEEP RUBBING MY THIGH LIKE THAT--
FOCUSING, WADE!! BULLETS! DANGER!
AN ACTIVE W.M.D. ON U.S. SOIL!
THAT STANDS FOR WOMAN ON MY D--?
FOCUS!!
BDEET
BDEET
EXCUSE THE HELL OUT OF ME! JUST A LITTLE SEXUAL HUMOR TO BREAK THE SEXUAL TENSION. I'M ON THE CASE--
DO YOU HEAR THAT?
HEAR WHA-- AIIEEEEE!!!
YOU REALLY DON'T HEAR THAT?
BDEET
BDEET

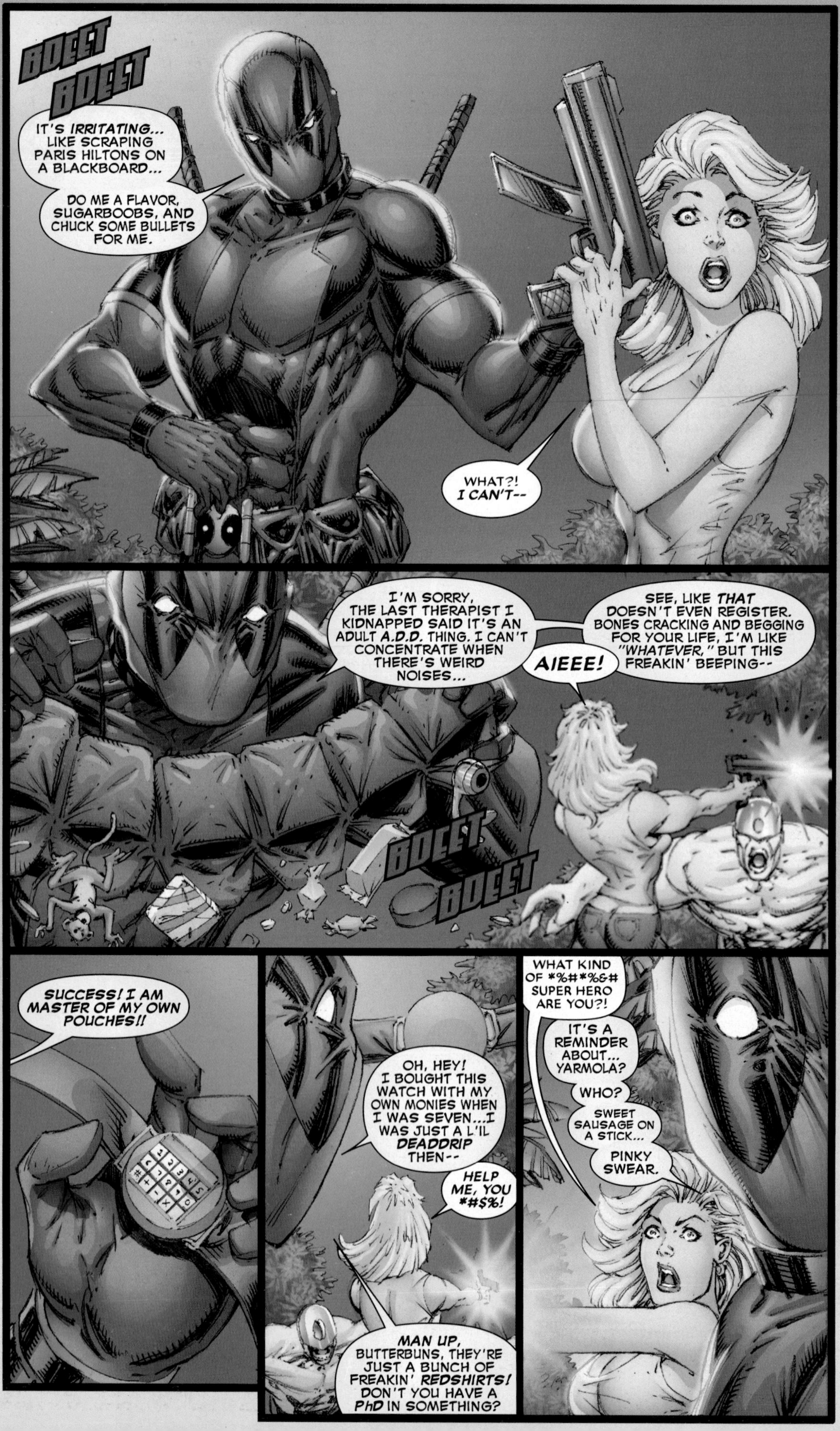
BDEET BDEET
IT'S *IRRITATING*... LIKE SCRAPING PARIS HILTONS ON A BLACKBOARD...
DO ME A FLAVOR, SUGARBOOBS, AND CHUCK SOME BULLETS FOR ME.
WHAT?! *I CAN'T*--
I'M SORRY, THE LAST THERAPIST I KIDNAPPED SAID IT'S AN ADULT *A.D.D.* THING. I CAN'T CONCENTRATE WHEN THERE'S WEIRD NOISES...
SEE, LIKE *THAT* DOESN'T EVEN REGISTER. BONES CRACKING AND BEGGING FOR YOUR LIFE, I'M LIKE "*WHATEVER*," BUT THIS FREAKIN' BEEPING--
AIEEE!
BDEET BDEET
SUCCESS! I AM MASTER OF MY OWN POUCHES!!
OH, HEY! I BOUGHT THIS WATCH WITH MY OWN MONIES WHEN I WAS SEVEN...I WAS JUST A L'IL *DEADDRIP* THEN--
HELP ME, YOU *#$%!
MAN UP, BUTTERBUNS, THEY'RE JUST A BUNCH OF FREAKIN' *REDSHIRTS!* DON'T YOU HAVE A *PhD* IN SOMETHING?
WHAT KIND OF *%#*%&# SUPER HERO ARE YOU?!
IT'S A REMINDER ABOUT... YARMOLA?
WHO?
SWEET SAUSAGE ON A STICK...
PINKY SWEAR.

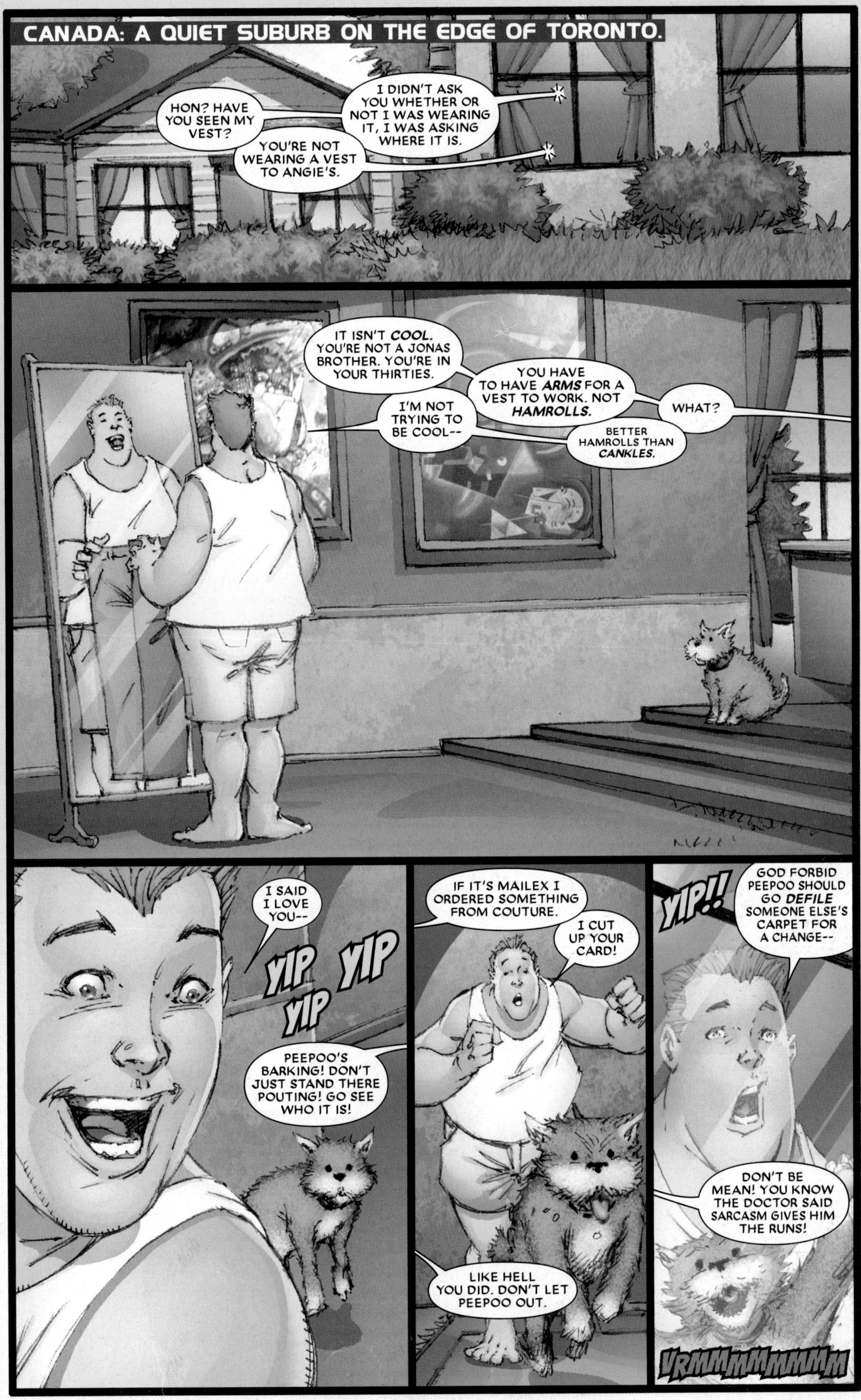
CANADA: A QUIET SUBURB ON THE EDGE OF TORONTO.
HON? HAVE YOU SEEN MY VEST?
YOU'RE NOT WEARING A VEST TO ANGIE'S.
I DIDN'T ASK YOU WHETHER OR NOT I WAS WEARING IT, I WAS ASKING WHERE IT IS.
IT ISN'T COOL. YOU'RE NOT A JONAS BROTHER. YOU'RE IN YOUR THIRTIES.
I'M NOT TRYING TO BE COOL--
YOU HAVE TO HAVE ARMS FOR A VEST TO WORK. NOT HAMROLLS.
BETTER HAMROLLS THAN CANKLES.
WHAT?
I SAID I LOVE YOU--
YIP YIP YIP
PEEPOO'S BARKING! DON'T JUST STAND THERE POUTING! GO SEE WHO IT IS!
IF IT'S MAILEX I ORDERED SOMETHING FROM COUTURE.
I CUT UP YOUR CARD!
LIKE HELL YOU DID. DON'T LET PEEPOO OUT.
YIP!!
GOD FORBID PEEPOO SHOULD GO DEFILE SOMEONE ELSE'S CARPET FOR A CHANGE--
DON'T BE MEAN! YOU KNOW THE DOCTOR SAID SARCASM GIVES HIM THE RUNS!
VRMMMMMMMMM

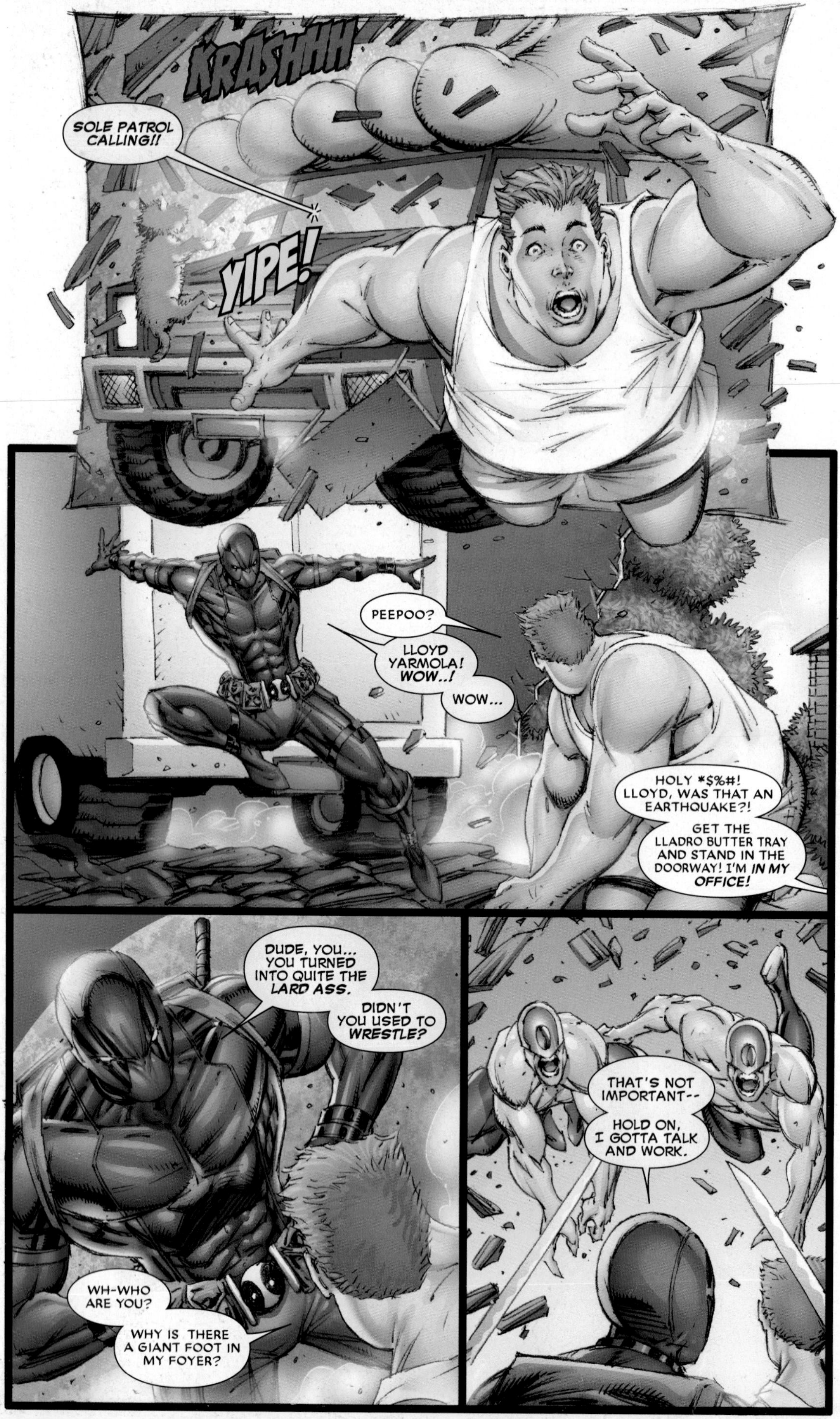
KRASHHH
SOLE PATROL CALLING!!
YIPE!
PEEPOO?
LLOYD YARMOLA! WOW..!
WOW...
HOLY *$%#! LLOYD, WAS THAT AN EARTHQUAKE?!
GET THE LLADRO BUTTER TRAY AND STAND IN THE DOORWAY! I'M IN MY OFFICE!
DUDE, YOU... YOU TURNED INTO QUITE THE LARD ASS.
DIDN'T YOU USED TO WRESTLE?
WH-WHO ARE YOU?
WHY IS THERE A GIANT FOOT IN MY FOYER?
THAT'S NOT IMPORTANT--
HOLD ON, I GOTTA TALK AND WORK.

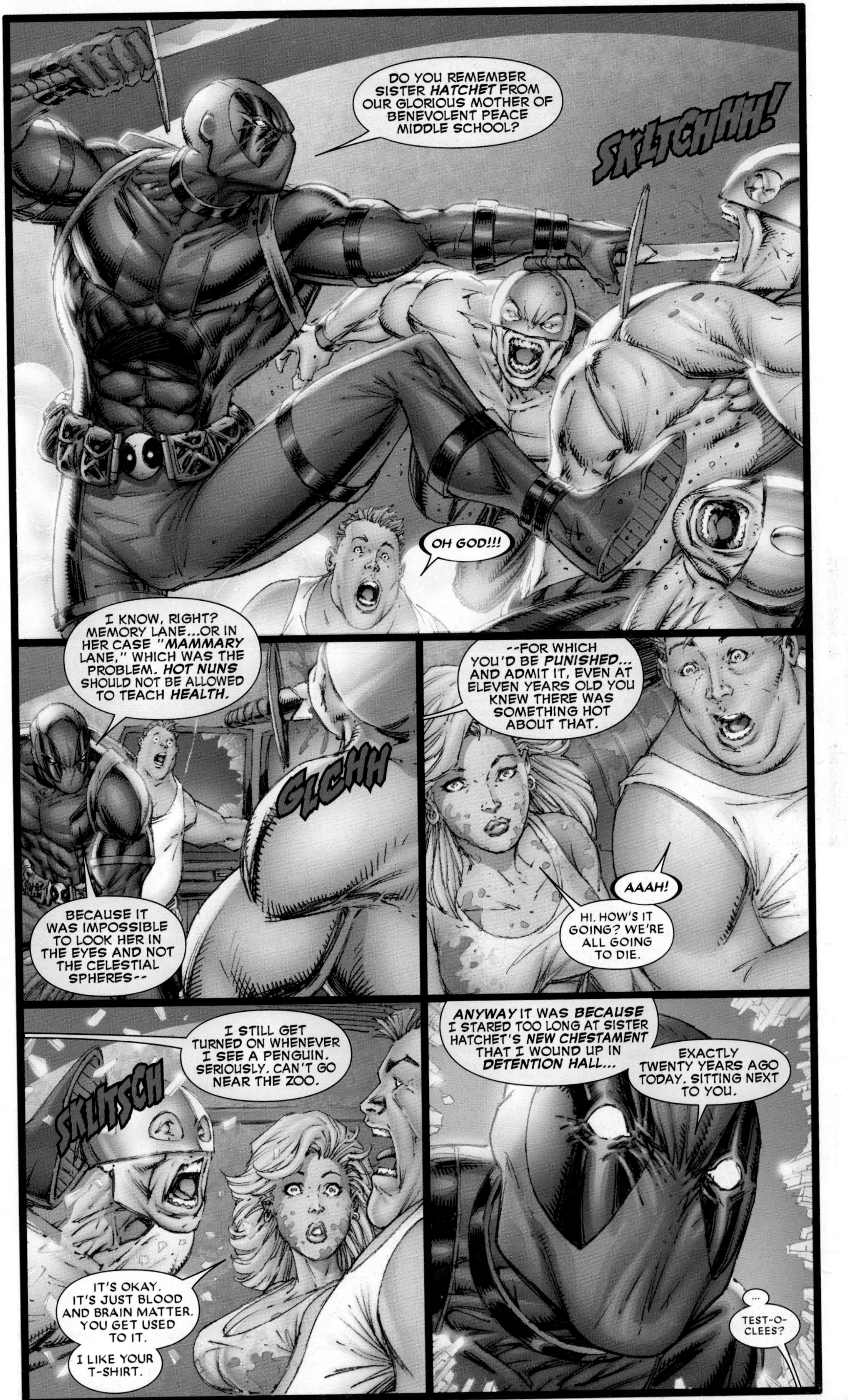
DO YOU REMEMBER SISTER *HATCHET* FROM OUR GLORIOUS MOTHER OF BENEVOLENT PEACE MIDDLE SCHOOL?
SKLTCHHH!
OH GOD!!!
I KNOW, RIGHT? MEMORY LANE...OR IN HER CASE *"MAMMARY LANE,"* WHICH WAS THE PROBLEM. *HOT NUNS* SHOULD NOT BE ALLOWED TO TEACH *HEALTH.*
GLCHH
BECAUSE IT WAS IMPOSSIBLE TO LOOK HER IN THE EYES AND NOT THE CELESTIAL SPHERES--
--FOR WHICH YOU'D BE *PUNISHED*... AND ADMIT IT, EVEN AT ELEVEN YEARS OLD YOU KNEW THERE WAS SOMETHING HOT ABOUT THAT.
AAAH!
HI. HOW'S IT GOING? WE'RE ALL GOING TO DIE.
I STILL GET TURNED ON WHENEVER I SEE A PENGUIN. SERIOUSLY. CAN'T GO NEAR THE ZOO.
SKLITSCH
IT'S OKAY. IT'S JUST BLOOD AND BRAIN MATTER. YOU GET USED TO IT.
I LIKE YOUR T-SHIRT.
ANYWAY IT WAS *BECAUSE* I STARED TOO LONG AT SISTER HATCHET'S *NEW CHESTAMENT* THAT I WOUND UP IN *DETENTION HALL...*
EXACTLY TWENTY YEARS AGO TODAY. SITTING NEXT TO YOU.
...
TEST-O-CLEES?

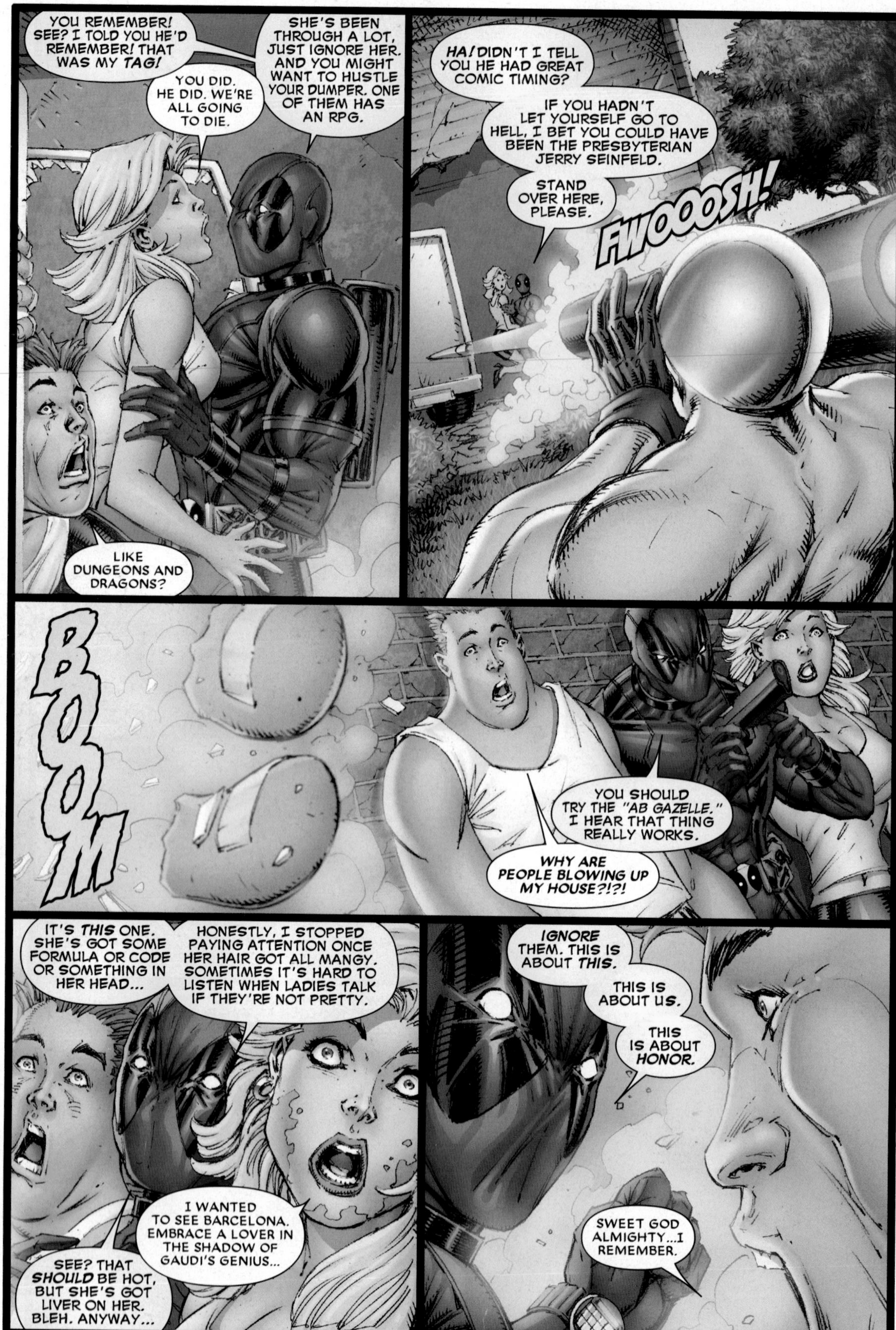

YOU REMEMBER! SEE? I TOLD YOU HE'D REMEMBER! THAT WAS MY *TAG!*
SHE'S BEEN THROUGH A LOT, JUST IGNORE HER. AND YOU MIGHT WANT TO HUSTLE YOUR DUMPER. ONE OF THEM HAS AN RPG.
YOU DID. HE DID. WE'RE ALL GOING TO DIE.
LIKE DUNGEONS AND DRAGONS?
HA! DIDN'T I TELL YOU HE HAD GREAT COMIC TIMING?
IF YOU HADN'T LET YOURSELF GO TO HELL, I BET YOU COULD HAVE BEEN THE PRESBYTERIAN JERRY SEINFELD.
STAND OVER HERE, PLEASE.
FWOOOSH!
BOOM
YOU SHOULD TRY THE *"AB GAZELLE."* I HEAR THAT THING REALLY WORKS.
WHY ARE PEOPLE BLOWING UP MY HOUSE?!?!
IT'S *THIS* ONE. SHE'S GOT SOME FORMULA OR CODE OR SOMETHING IN HER HEAD...
HONESTLY, I STOPPED PAYING ATTENTION ONCE HER HAIR GOT ALL MANGY. SOMETIMES IT'S HARD TO LISTEN WHEN LADIES TALK IF THEY'RE NOT PRETTY.
I WANTED TO SEE BARCELONA. EMBRACE A LOVER IN THE SHADOW OF GAUDI'S GENIUS...
SEE? THAT *SHOULD* BE HOT, BUT SHE'S GOT LIVER ON HER. BLEH. ANYWAY...
IGNORE THEM. THIS IS ABOUT *THIS.*
THIS IS ABOUT U*S.*
THIS IS ABOUT *HONOR.*
SWEET GOD ALMIGHTY...I REMEMBER.

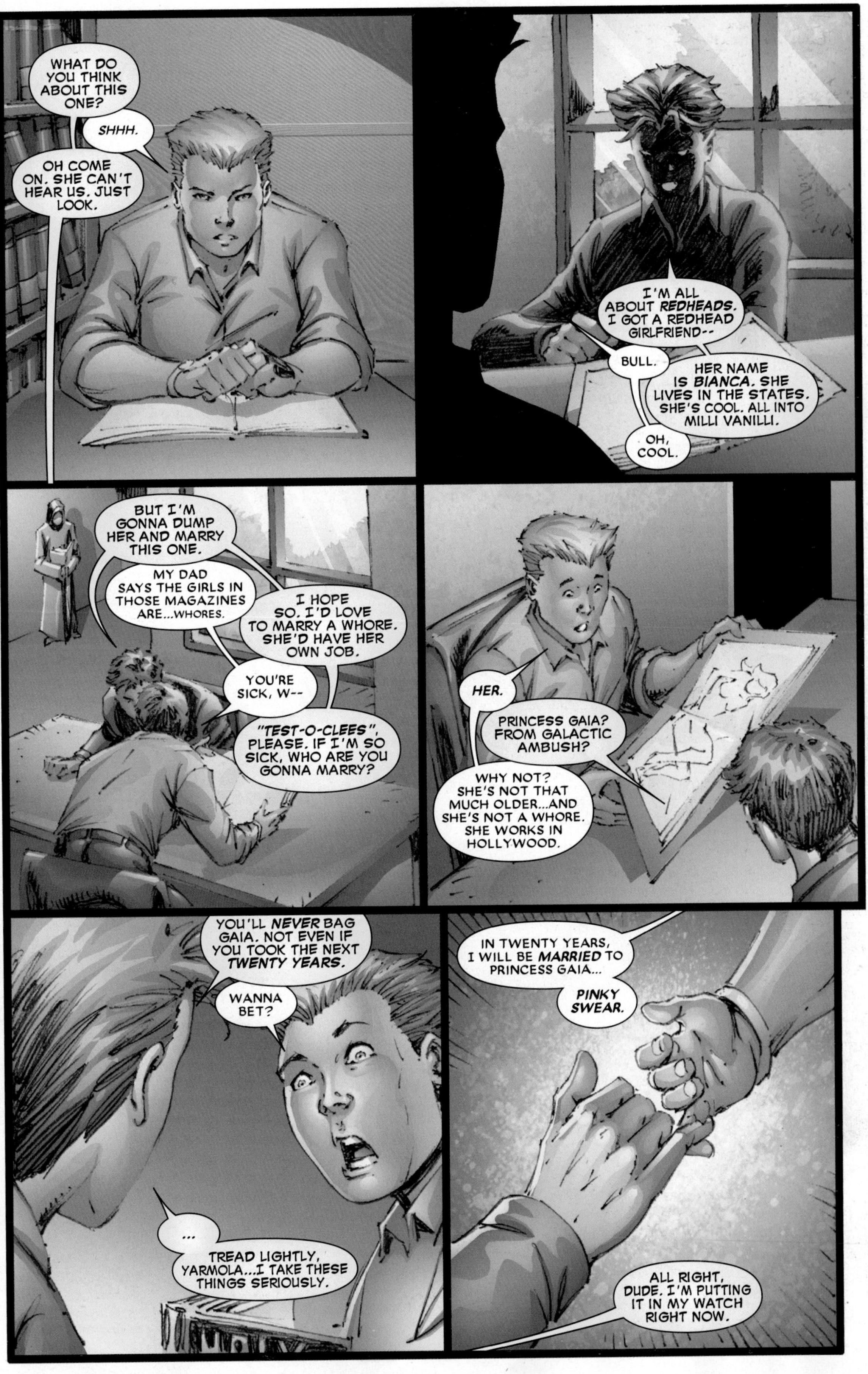
WHAT DO YOU THINK ABOUT THIS ONE?
SHHH.
OH COME ON. SHE CAN'T HEAR US. JUST LOOK.
I'M ALL ABOUT REDHEADS. I GOT A REDHEAD GIRLFRIEND--
BULL.
HER NAME IS BIANCA. SHE LIVES IN THE STATES. SHE'S COOL. ALL INTO MILLI VANILLI.
OH, COOL.
BUT I'M GONNA DUMP HER AND MARRY THIS ONE.
MY DAD SAYS THE GIRLS IN THOSE MAGAZINES ARE...WHORES.
I HOPE SO. I'D LOVE TO MARRY A WHORE. SHE'D HAVE HER OWN JOB.
YOU'RE SICK, W--
"TEST-O-CLEES", PLEASE. IF I'M SO SICK, WHO ARE YOU GONNA MARRY?
HER.
PRINCESS GAIA? FROM GALACTIC AMBUSH?
WHY NOT? SHE'S NOT THAT MUCH OLDER...AND SHE'S NOT A WHORE. SHE WORKS IN HOLLYWOOD.
YOU'LL NEVER BAG GAIA. NOT EVEN IF YOU TOOK THE NEXT TWENTY YEARS.
WANNA BET?
...
TREAD LIGHTLY, YARMOLA...I TAKE THESE THINGS SERIOUSLY.
IN TWENTY YEARS, I WILL BE MARRIED TO PRINCESS GAIA...
PINKY SWEAR.
ALL RIGHT, DUDE. I'M PUTTING IT IN MY WATCH RIGHT NOW.

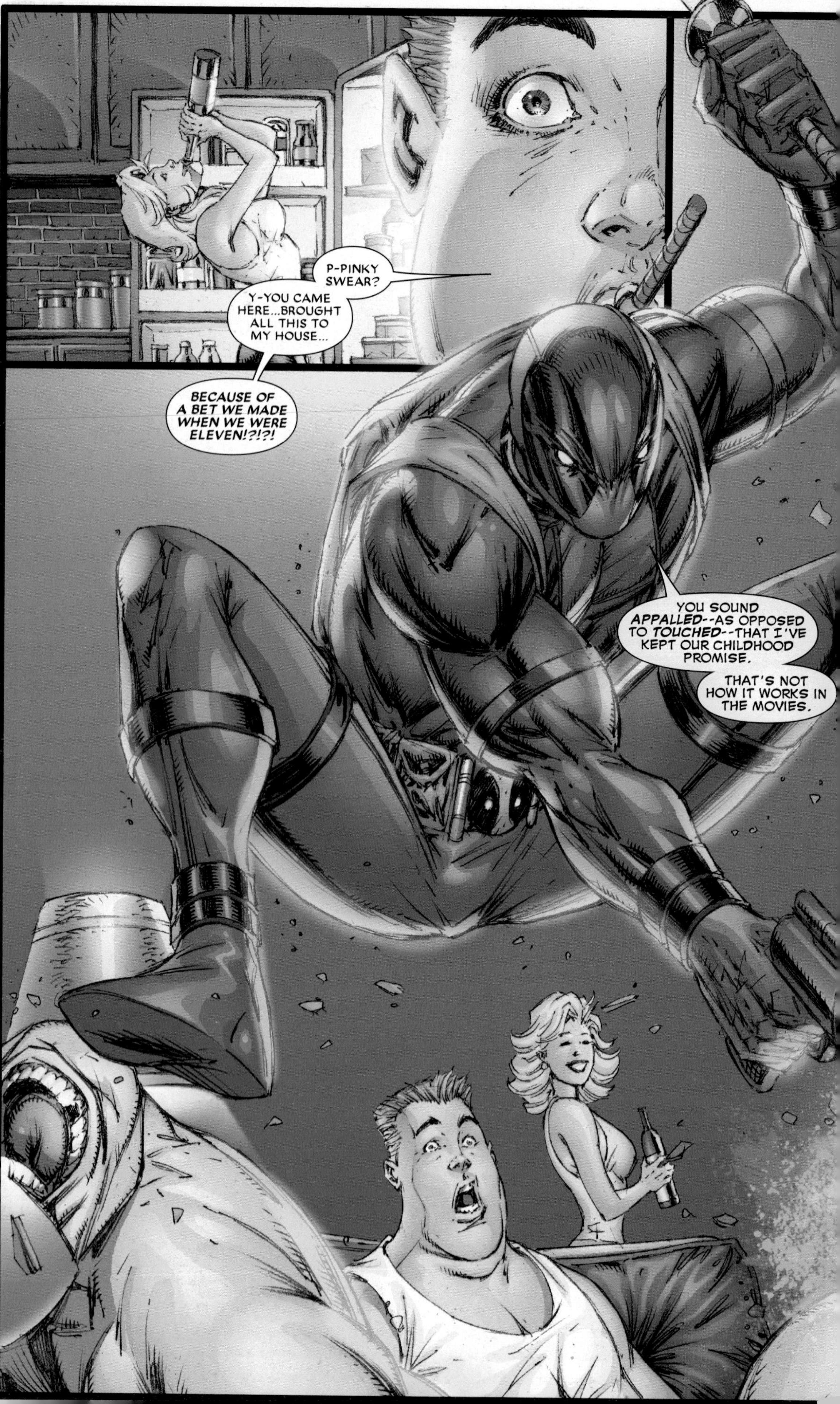
P-PINKY SWEAR?
Y-YOU CAME HERE...BROUGHT ALL THIS TO MY HOUSE...
BECAUSE OF A BET WE MADE WHEN WE WERE ELEVEN!?!?!
YOU SOUND APPALLED--AS OPPOSED TO TOUCHED--THAT I'VE KEPT OUR CHILDHOOD PROMISE.
THAT'S NOT HOW IT WORKS IN THE MOVIES.

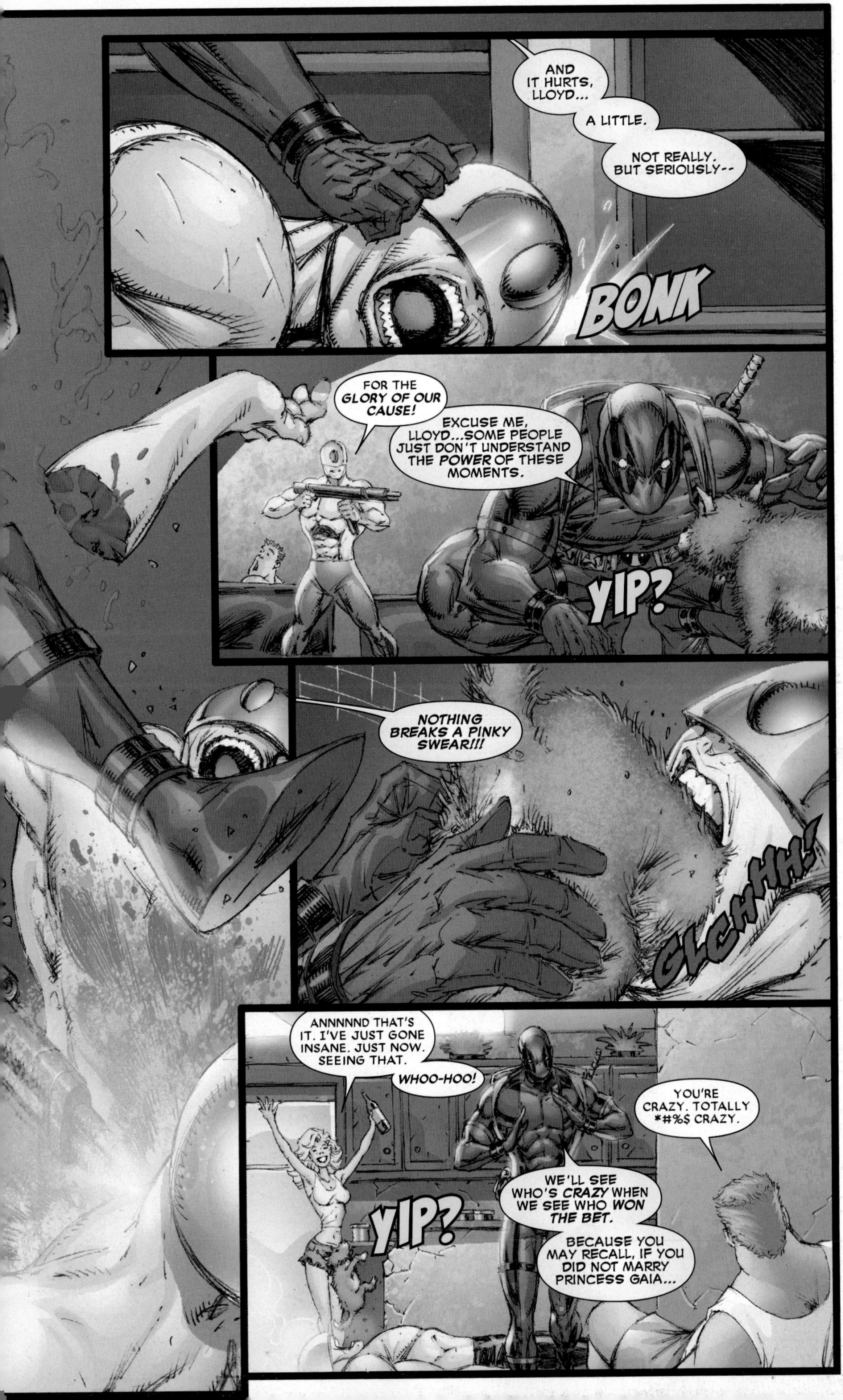
AND IT HURTS, LLOYD...
A LITTLE.
NOT REALLY. BUT SERIOUSLY--
BONK
FOR THE GLORY OF OUR CAUSE!
EXCUSE ME, LLOYD...SOME PEOPLE JUST DON'T UNDERSTAND THE POWER OF THESE MOMENTS.
YIP?
NOTHING BREAKS A PINKY SWEAR!!!
GLCHHH!
ANNNNND THAT'S IT. I'VE JUST GONE INSANE. JUST NOW. SEEING THAT.
WHOO-HOO!
YOU'RE CRAZY. TOTALLY *#%$ CRAZY.
WE'LL SEE WHO'S CRAZY WHEN WE SEE WHO WON THE BET.
YIP?
BECAUSE YOU MAY RECALL, IF YOU DID NOT MARRY PRINCESS GAIA...

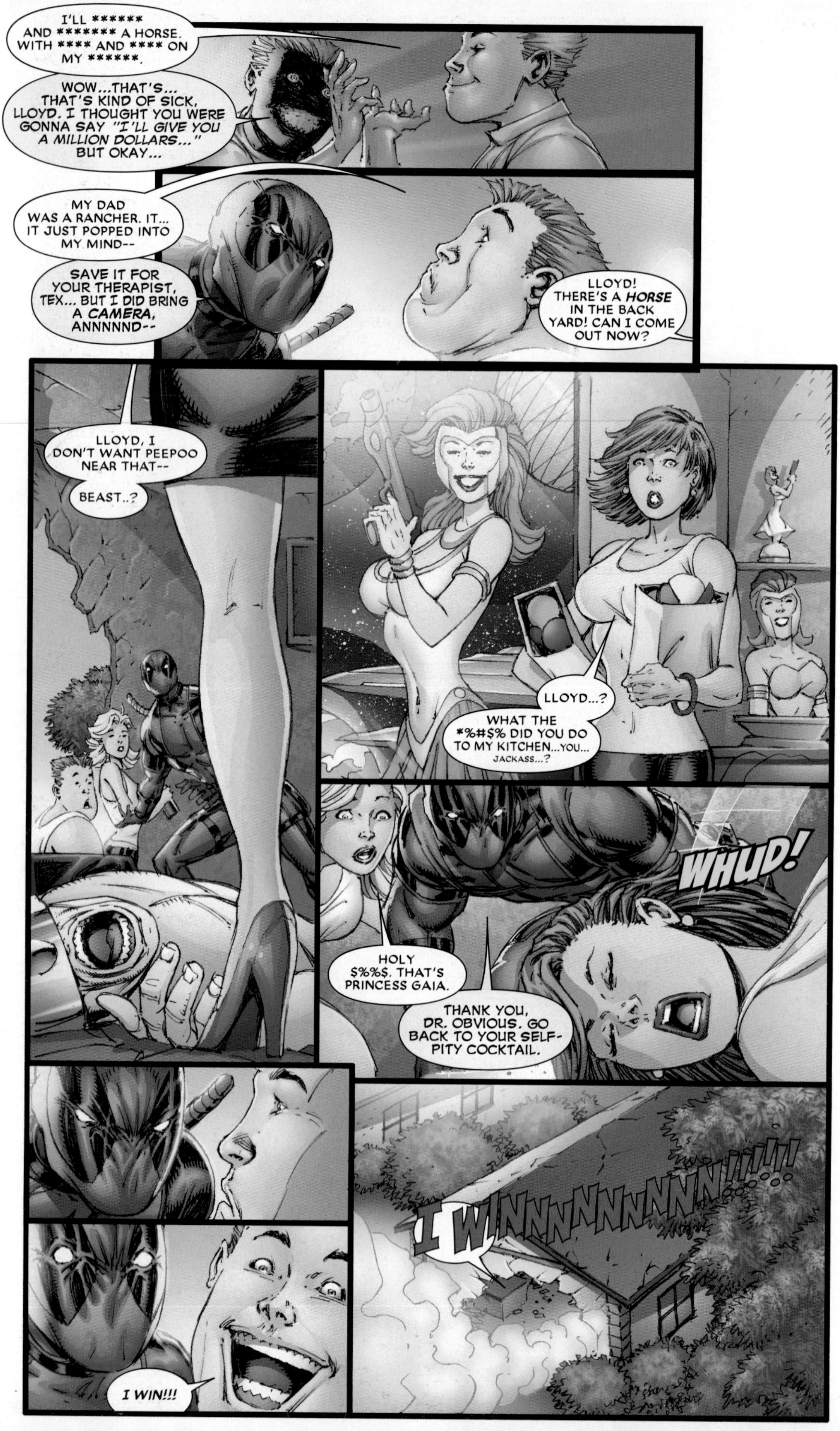
I'LL ****** AND ******* A HORSE. WITH **** AND **** ON MY ******.
WOW...THAT'S... THAT'S KIND OF SICK, LLOYD. I THOUGHT YOU WERE GONNA SAY "I'LL GIVE YOU A MILLION DOLLARS..." BUT OKAY...
MY DAD WAS A RANCHER. IT... IT JUST POPPED INTO MY MIND--
SAVE IT FOR YOUR THERAPIST, TEX... BUT I DID BRING A CAMERA, ANNNNND--
LLOYD! THERE'S A HORSE IN THE BACK YARD! CAN I COME OUT NOW?
LLOYD, I DON'T WANT PEEPOO NEAR THAT--
BEAST..?
LLOYD...?
WHAT THE *%#$% DID YOU DO TO MY KITCHEN...YOU... JACKASS...?
WHUD!
HOLY $%%$. THAT'S PRINCESS GAIA.
THANK YOU, DR. OBVIOUS. GO BACK TO YOUR SELF-PITY COCKTAIL.
I WIN!!!
I WINNNNNNNNNN!!!!!!

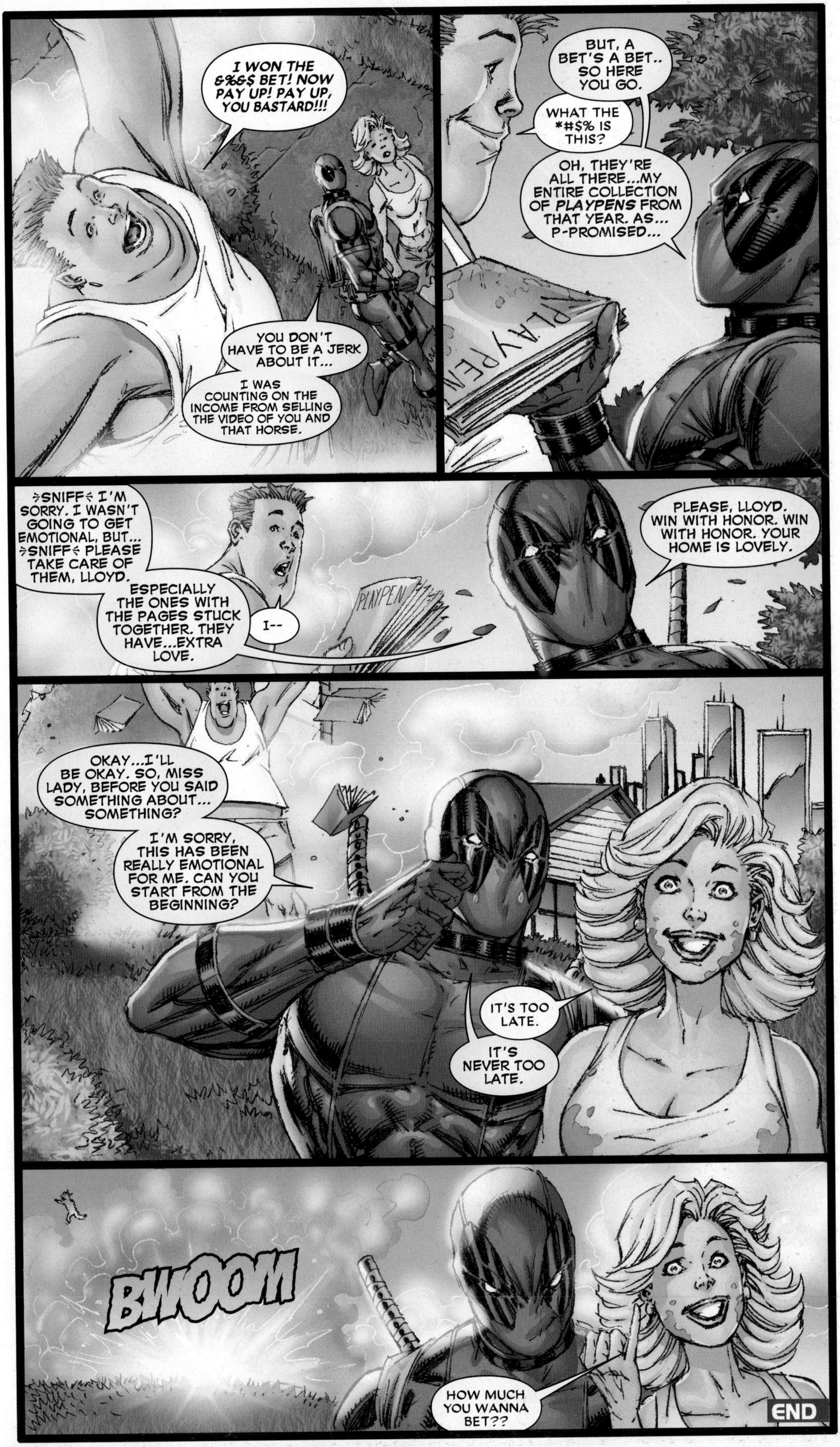
I WON THE &%&$ BET! NOW PAY UP! PAY UP, YOU BASTARD!!!
YOU DON'T HAVE TO BE A JERK ABOUT IT...
I WAS COUNTING ON THE INCOME FROM SELLING THE VIDEO OF YOU AND THAT HORSE.
BUT, A BET'S A BET.. SO HERE YOU GO.
WHAT THE *#$% IS THIS?
OH, THEY'RE ALL THERE...MY ENTIRE COLLECTION OF PLAYPENS FROM THAT YEAR. AS... P-PROMISED...
PLAYPEN
≠SNIFF≠ I'M SORRY. I WASN'T GOING TO GET EMOTIONAL, BUT... ≠SNIFF≠ PLEASE TAKE CARE OF THEM, LLOYD.
ESPECIALLY THE ONES WITH THE PAGES STUCK TOGETHER. THEY HAVE...EXTRA LOVE.
I--
PLAYPEN
PLEASE, LLOYD. WIN WITH HONOR. WIN WITH HONOR. YOUR HOME IS LOVELY.
OKAY...I'LL BE OKAY. SO, MISS LADY, BEFORE YOU SAID SOMETHING ABOUT... SOMETHING?
I'M SORRY, THIS HAS BEEN REALLY EMOTIONAL FOR ME. CAN YOU START FROM THE BEGINNING?
IT'S TOO LATE.
IT'S NEVER TOO LATE.
BWOOM
HOW MUCH YOU WANNA BET??
END

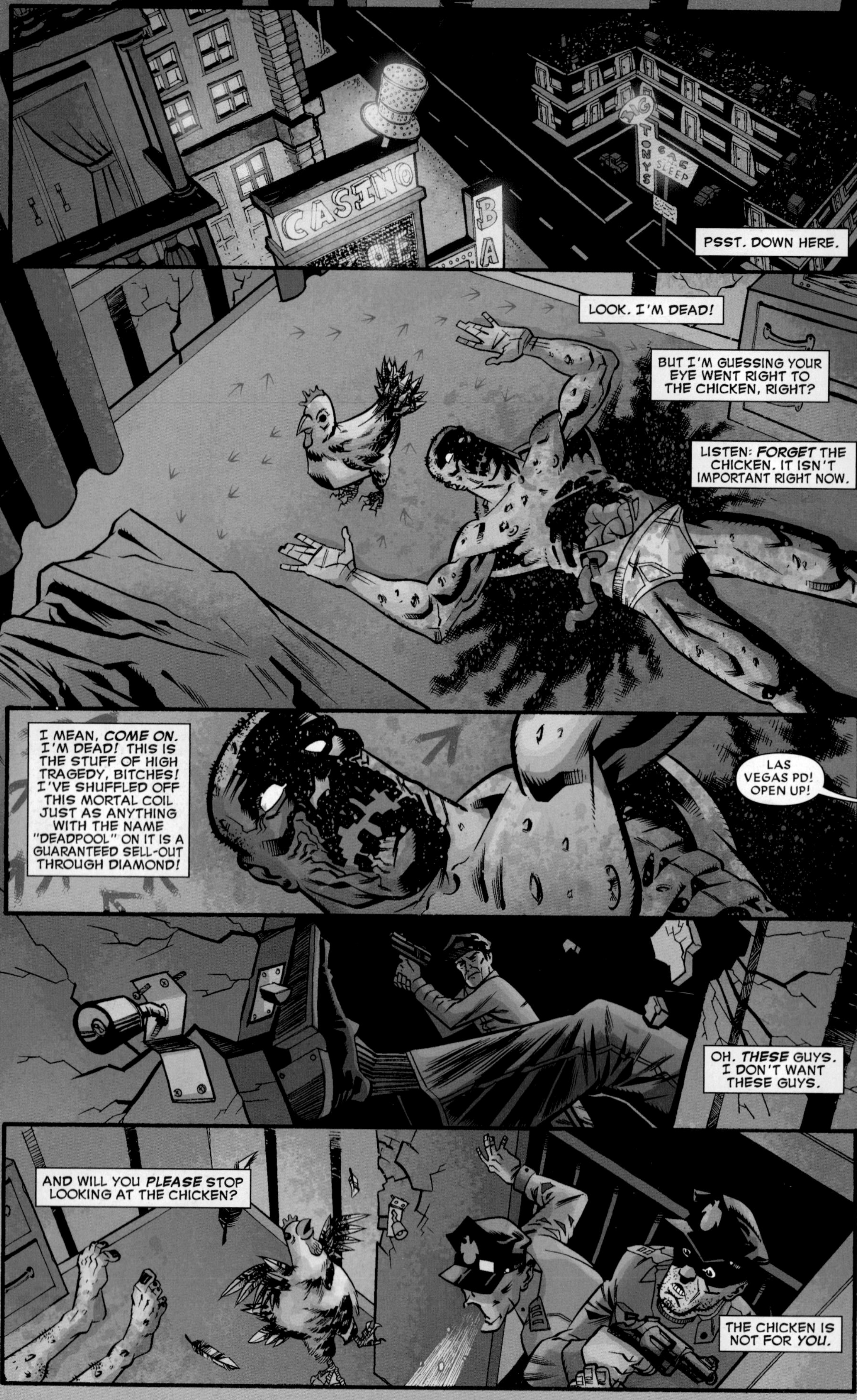
CASINO
BIG TONY'S
GAS SLEEP
PSST. DOWN HERE.
LOOK. I'M DEAD!
BUT I'M GUESSING YOUR EYE WENT RIGHT TO THE CHICKEN, RIGHT?
LISTEN: *FORGET* THE CHICKEN. IT ISN'T IMPORTANT RIGHT NOW.
I MEAN, *COME ON*. I'M *DEAD!* THIS IS THE STUFF OF HIGH TRAGEDY, BITCHES! I'VE SHUFFLED OFF THIS MORTAL COIL JUST AS ANYTHING WITH THE NAME "DEADPOOL" ON IT IS A GUARANTEED SELL-OUT THROUGH DIAMOND!
LAS VEGAS PD! OPEN UP!
OH. *THESE* GUYS. I DON'T WANT THESE GUYS.
AND WILL YOU *PLEASE* STOP LOOKING AT THE CHICKEN?
THE CHICKEN IS NOT FOR *YOU*.

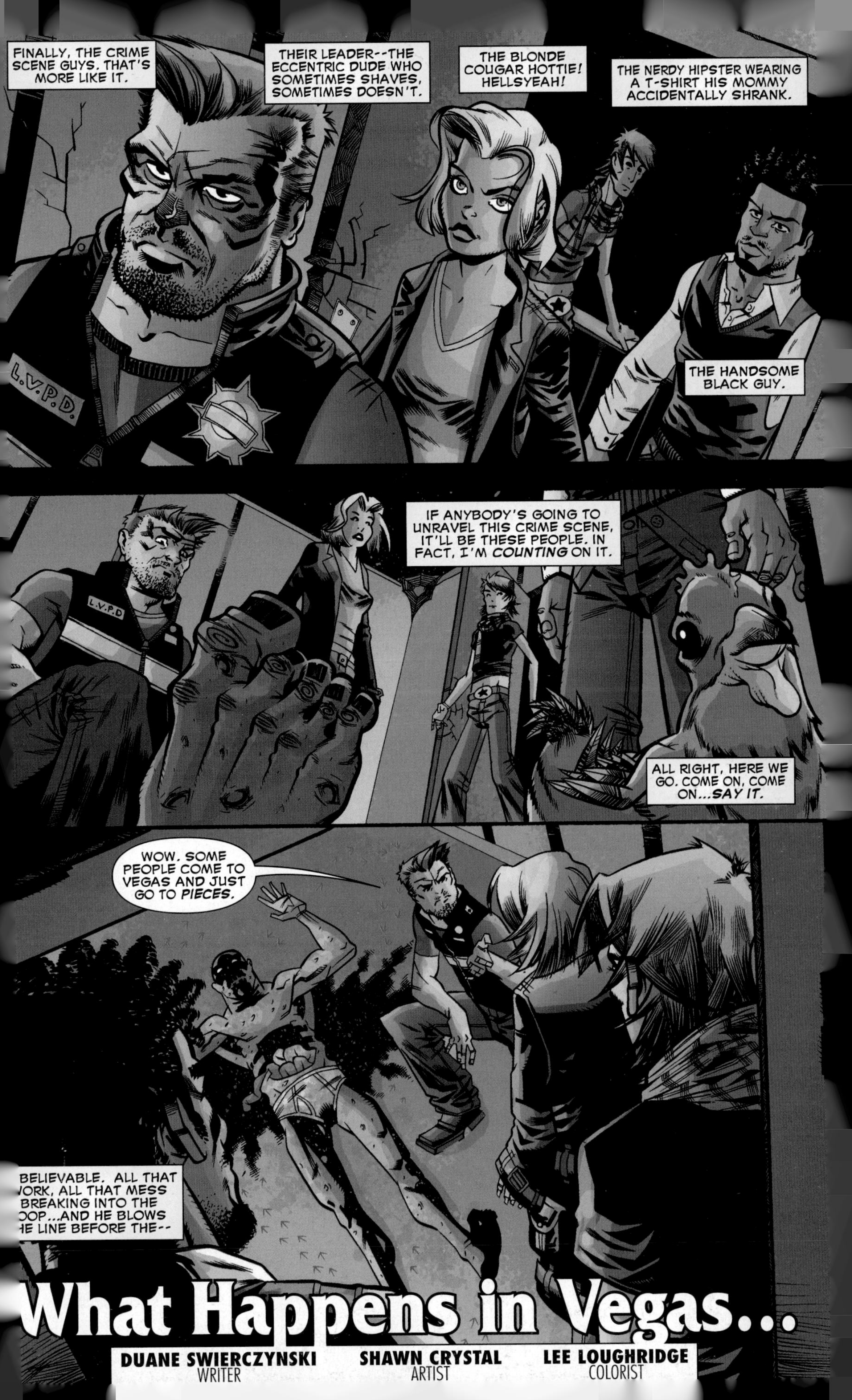
FINALLY, THE CRIME SCENE GUYS. THAT'S MORE LIKE IT.
THEIR LEADER--THE ECCENTRIC DUDE WHO SOMETIMES SHAVES, SOMETIMES DOESN'T.
THE BLONDE COUGAR HOTTIE! HELLSYEAH!
THE NERDY HIPSTER WEARING A T-SHIRT HIS MOMMY ACCIDENTALLY SHRANK.
THE HANDSOME BLACK GUY.
L.V.P.D.
L.V.P.D
IF ANYBODY'S GOING TO UNRAVEL THIS CRIME SCENE, IT'LL BE THESE PEOPLE. IN FACT, I'M COUNTING ON IT.
ALL RIGHT, HERE WE GO. COME ON, COME ON...SAY IT.
WOW. SOME PEOPLE COME TO VEGAS AND JUST GO TO PIECES.
BELIEVABLE. ALL THAT ORK, ALL THAT MESS BREAKING INTO THE OOP...AND HE BLOWS HE LINE BEFORE THE--
What Happens in Vegas...
DUANE SWIERCZYNSKI WRITER
SHAWN CRYSTAL ARTIST
LEE LOUGHRIDGE COLORIST

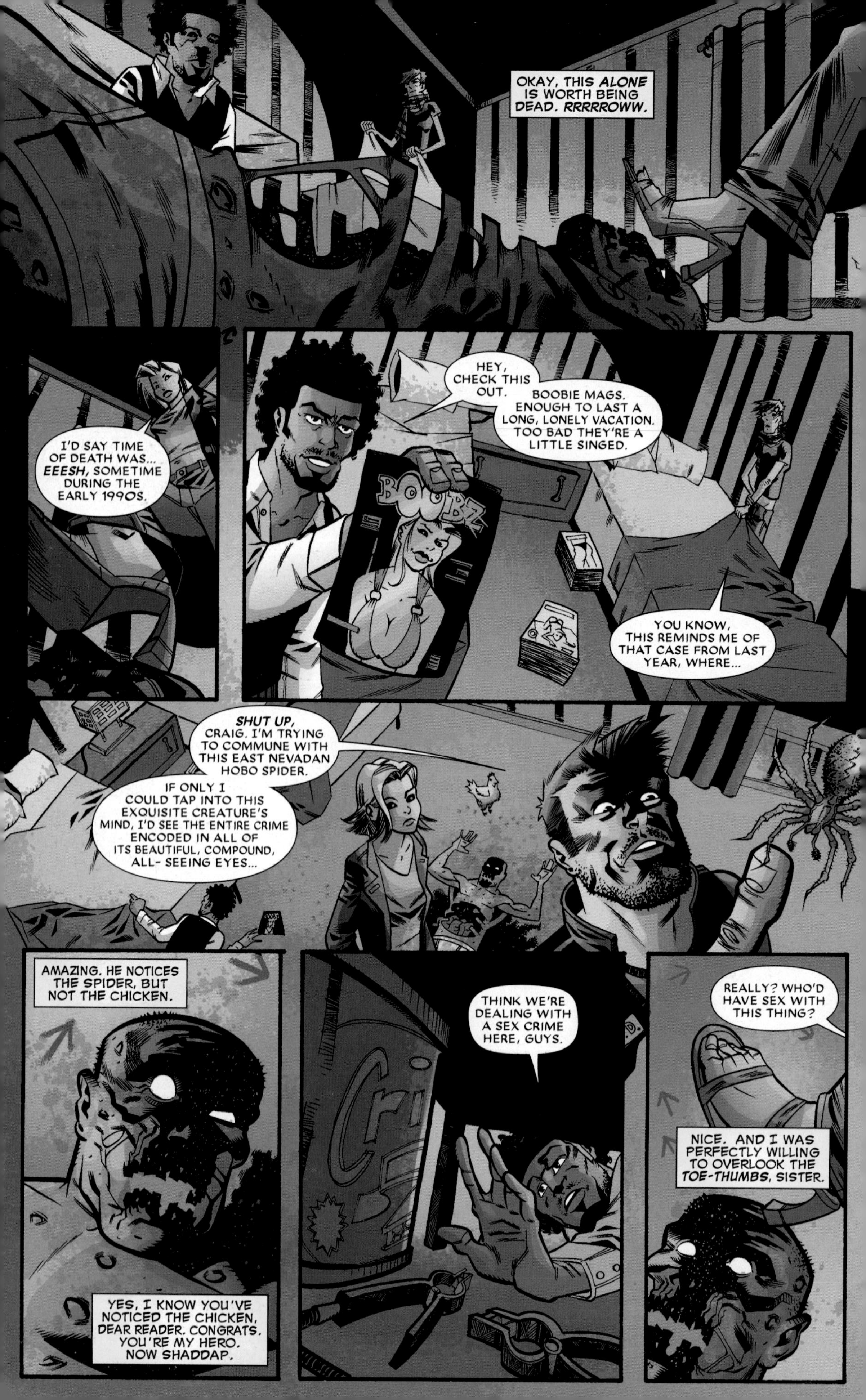
OKAY, THIS ALONE IS WORTH BEING DEAD. RRRRROWW.
I'D SAY TIME OF DEATH WAS... EEESH, SOMETIME DURING THE EARLY 1990S.
HEY, CHECK THIS OUT.
BOOBIE MAGS. ENOUGH TO LAST A LONG, LONELY VACATION. TOO BAD THEY'RE A LITTLE SINGED.
BOOBZ
YOU KNOW, THIS REMINDS ME OF THAT CASE FROM LAST YEAR, WHERE...
SHUT UP, CRAIG. I'M TRYING TO COMMUNE WITH THIS EAST NEVADAN HOBO SPIDER.
IF ONLY I COULD TAP INTO THIS EXQUISITE CREATURE'S MIND, I'D SEE THE ENTIRE CRIME ENCODED IN ALL OF ITS BEAUTIFUL, COMPOUND, ALL- SEEING EYES...
AMAZING. HE NOTICES THE SPIDER, BUT NOT THE CHICKEN.
YES, I KNOW YOU'VE NOTICED THE CHICKEN, DEAR READER. CONGRATS. YOU'RE MY HERO. NOW SHADDAP.
THINK WE'RE DEALING WITH A SEX CRIME HERE, GUYS.
REALLY? WHO'D HAVE SEX WITH THIS THING?
NICE. AND I WAS PERFECTLY WILLING TO OVERLOOK THE TOE-THUMBS, SISTER.

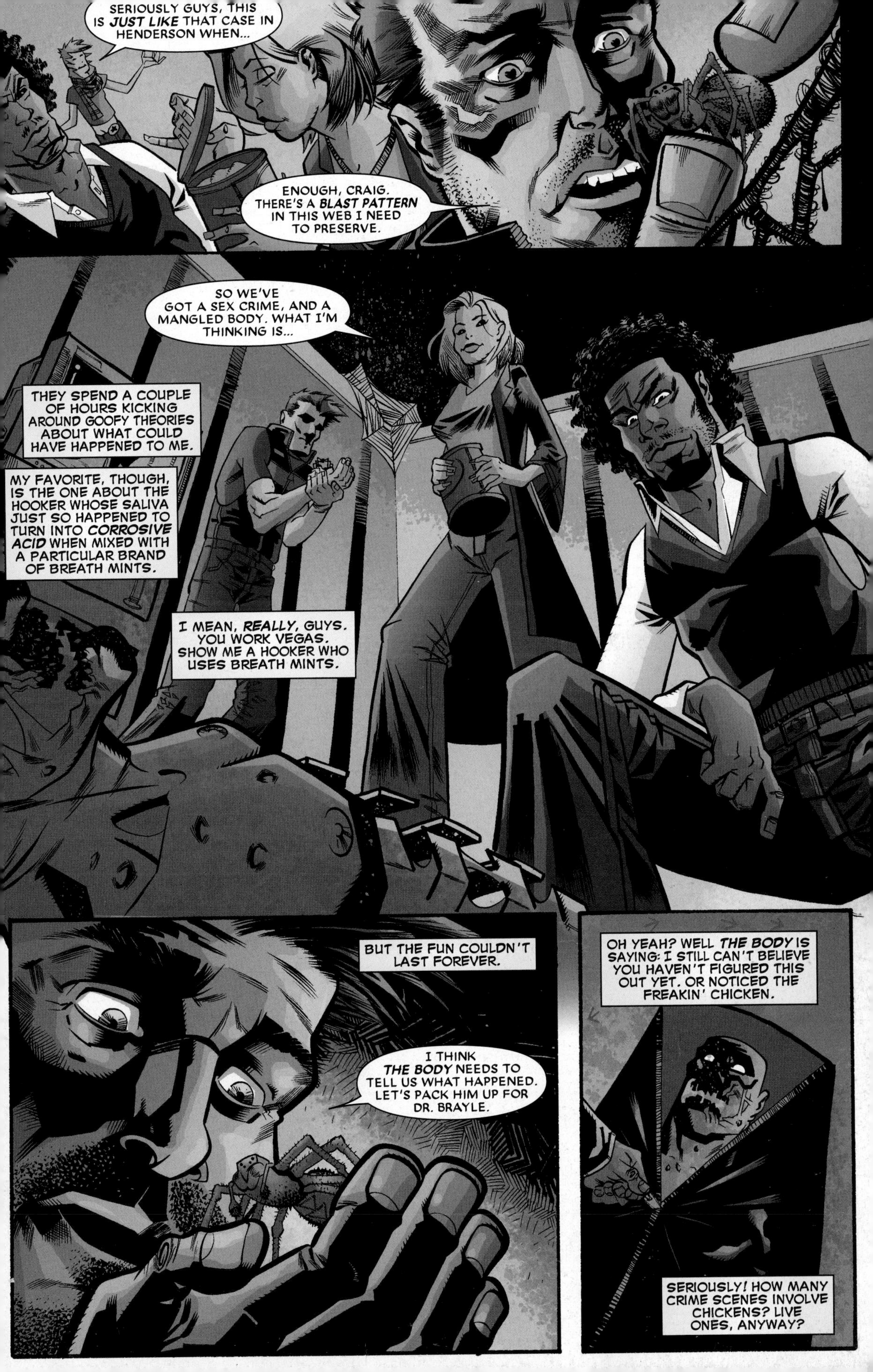
SERIOUSLY GUYS, THIS IS JUST LIKE THAT CASE IN HENDERSON WHEN...
ENOUGH, CRAIG. THERE'S A BLAST PATTERN IN THIS WEB I NEED TO PRESERVE.
SO WE'VE GOT A SEX CRIME, AND A MANGLED BODY. WHAT I'M THINKING IS...
THEY SPEND A COUPLE OF HOURS KICKING AROUND GOOFY THEORIES ABOUT WHAT COULD HAVE HAPPENED TO ME.
MY FAVORITE, THOUGH, IS THE ONE ABOUT THE HOOKER WHOSE SALIVA JUST SO HAPPENED TO TURN INTO CORROSIVE ACID WHEN MIXED WITH A PARTICULAR BRAND OF BREATH MINTS.
I MEAN, REALLY, GUYS. YOU WORK VEGAS. SHOW ME A HOOKER WHO USES BREATH MINTS.
BUT THE FUN COULDN'T LAST FOREVER.
I THINK THE BODY NEEDS TO TELL US WHAT HAPPENED. LET'S PACK HIM UP FOR DR. BRAYLE.
OH YEAH? WELL THE BODY IS SAYING: I STILL CAN'T BELIEVE YOU HAVEN'T FIGURED THIS OUT YET. OR NOTICED THE FREAKIN' CHICKEN.
SERIOUSLY! HOW MANY CRIME SCENES INVOLVE CHICKENS? LIVE ONES, ANYWAY?

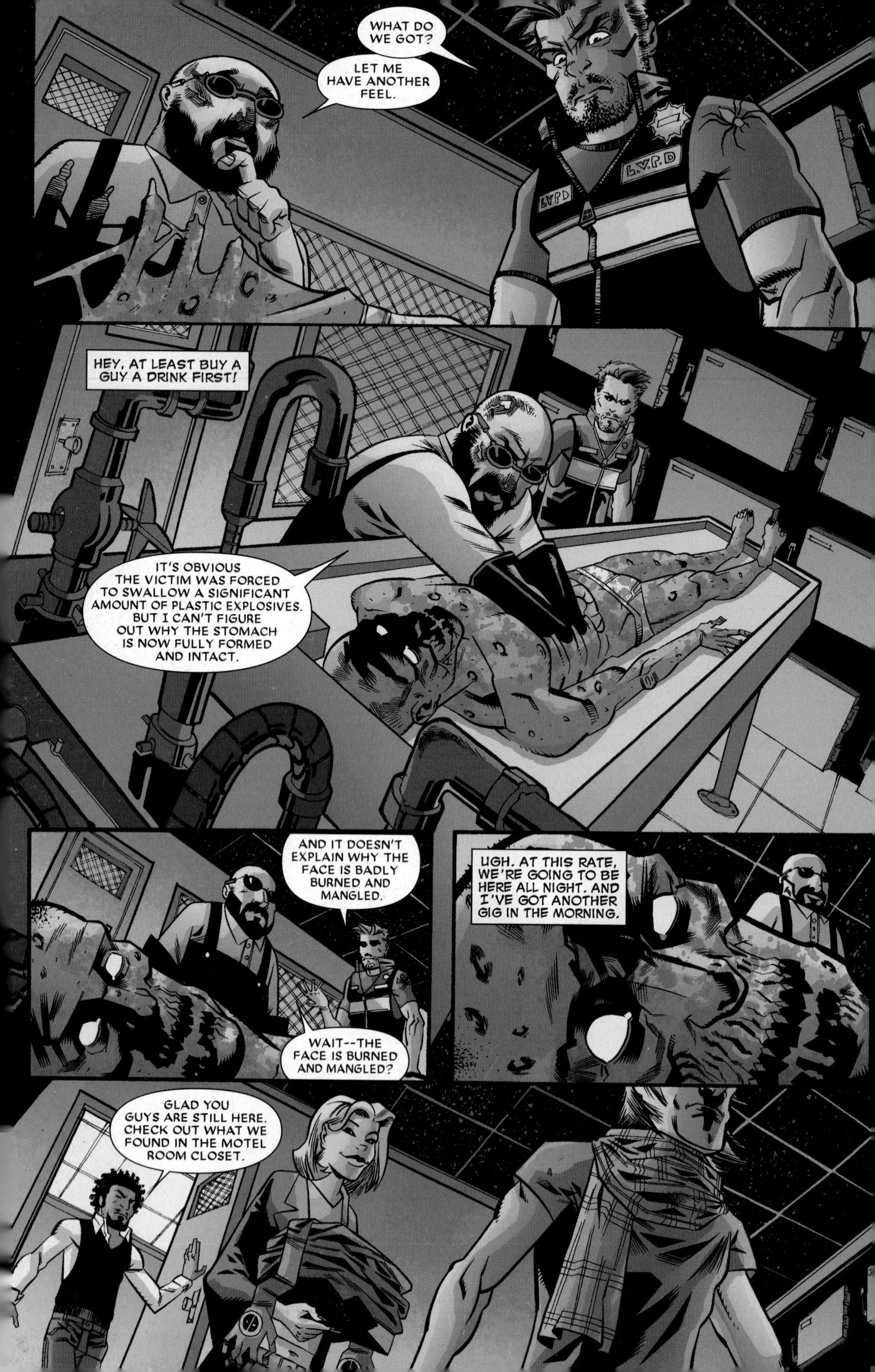
WHAT DO WE GOT?
LET ME HAVE ANOTHER FEEL.
HEY, AT LEAST BUY A GUY A DRINK FIRST!
IT'S OBVIOUS THE VICTIM WAS FORCED TO SWALLOW A SIGNIFICANT AMOUNT OF PLASTIC EXPLOSIVES. BUT I CAN'T FIGURE OUT WHY THE STOMACH IS NOW FULLY FORMED AND INTACT.
AND IT DOESN'T EXPLAIN WHY THE FACE IS BADLY BURNED AND MANGLED.
WAIT--THE FACE IS BURNED AND MANGLED?
UGH. AT THIS RATE, WE'RE GOING TO BE HERE ALL NIGHT. AND I'VE GOT ANOTHER GIG IN THE MORNING.
GLAD YOU GUYS ARE STILL HERE. CHECK OUT WHAT WE FOUND IN THE MOTEL ROOM CLOSET.

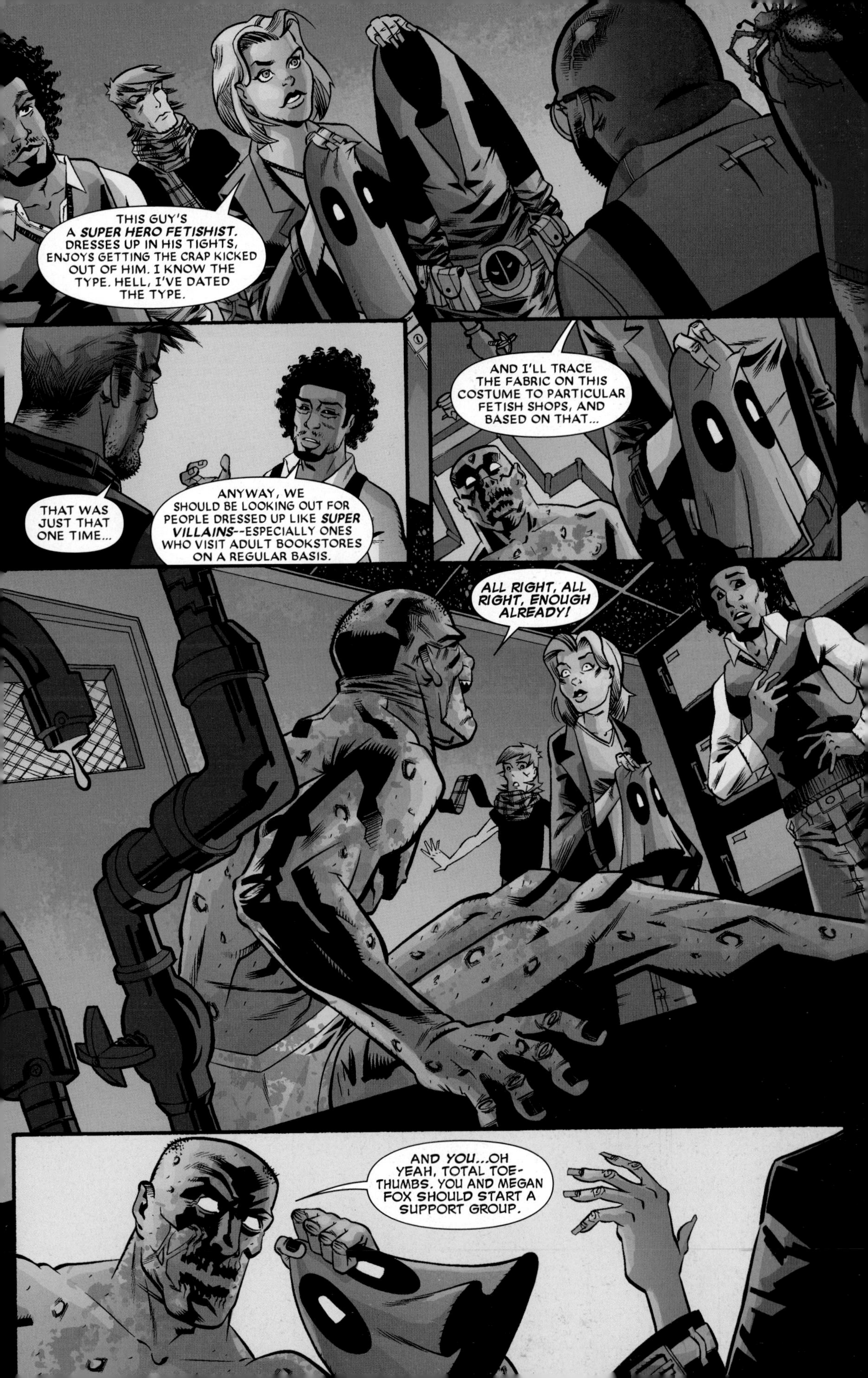
THIS GUY'S A SUPER HERO FETISHIST. DRESSES UP IN HIS TIGHTS, ENJOYS GETTING THE CRAP KICKED OUT OF HIM. I KNOW THE TYPE. HELL, I'VE DATED THE TYPE.
THAT WAS JUST THAT ONE TIME...
ANYWAY, WE SHOULD BE LOOKING OUT FOR PEOPLE DRESSED UP LIKE SUPER VILLAINS--ESPECIALLY ONES WHO VISIT ADULT BOOKSTORES ON A REGULAR BASIS.
AND I'LL TRACE THE FABRIC ON THIS COSTUME TO PARTICULAR FETISH SHOPS, AND BASED ON THAT...
ALL RIGHT, ALL RIGHT, ENOUGH ALREADY!
AND YOU...OH YEAH, TOTAL TOE-THUMBS. YOU AND MEGAN FOX SHOULD START A SUPPORT GROUP.

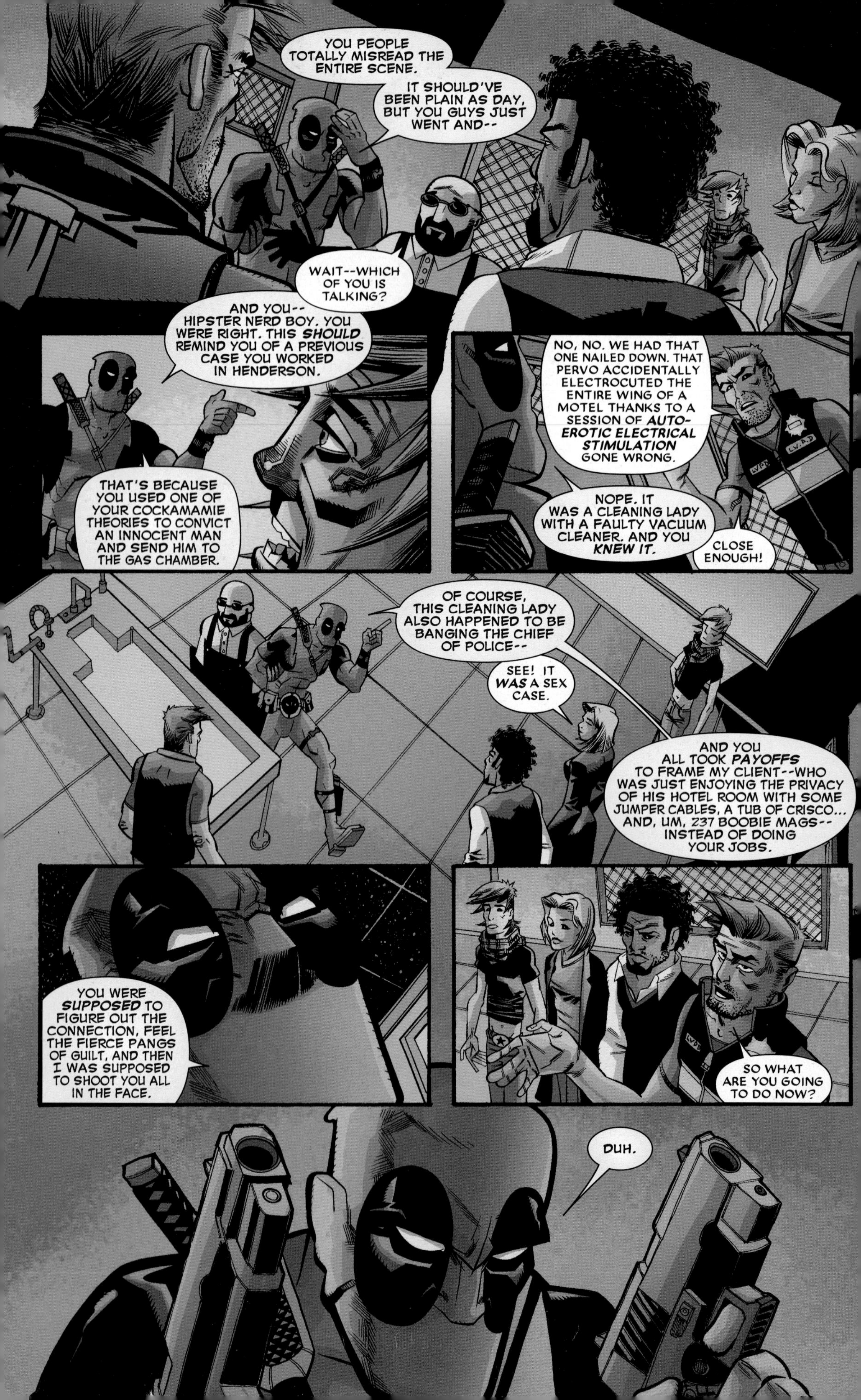
YOU PEOPLE TOTALLY MISREAD THE ENTIRE SCENE.
IT SHOULD'VE BEEN PLAIN AS DAY, BUT YOU GUYS JUST WENT AND--
WAIT--WHICH OF YOU IS TALKING?
AND YOU-- HIPSTER NERD BOY. YOU WERE RIGHT. THIS SHOULD REMIND YOU OF A PREVIOUS CASE YOU WORKED IN HENDERSON.
THAT'S BECAUSE YOU USED ONE OF YOUR COCKAMAMIE THEORIES TO CONVICT AN INNOCENT MAN AND SEND HIM TO THE GAS CHAMBER.
NO, NO. WE HAD THAT ONE NAILED DOWN. THAT PERVO ACCIDENTALLY ELECTROCUTED THE ENTIRE WING OF A MOTEL THANKS TO A SESSION OF AUTO-EROTIC ELECTRICAL STIMULATION GONE WRONG.
NOPE. IT WAS A CLEANING LADY WITH A FAULTY VACUUM CLEANER. AND YOU KNEW IT.
CLOSE ENOUGH!
OF COURSE, THIS CLEANING LADY ALSO HAPPENED TO BE BANGING THE CHIEF OF POLICE--
SEE! IT WAS A SEX CASE.
AND YOU ALL TOOK PAYOFFS TO FRAME MY CLIENT--WHO WAS JUST ENJOYING THE PRIVACY OF HIS HOTEL ROOM WITH SOME JUMPER CABLES, A TUB OF CRISCO... AND, UM, 237 BOOBIE MAGS-- INSTEAD OF DOING YOUR JOBS.
YOU WERE SUPPOSED TO FIGURE OUT THE CONNECTION, FEEL THE FIERCE PANGS OF GUILT, AND THEN I WAS SUPPOSED TO SHOOT YOU ALL IN THE FACE.
SO WHAT ARE YOU GOING TO DO NOW?
DUH.

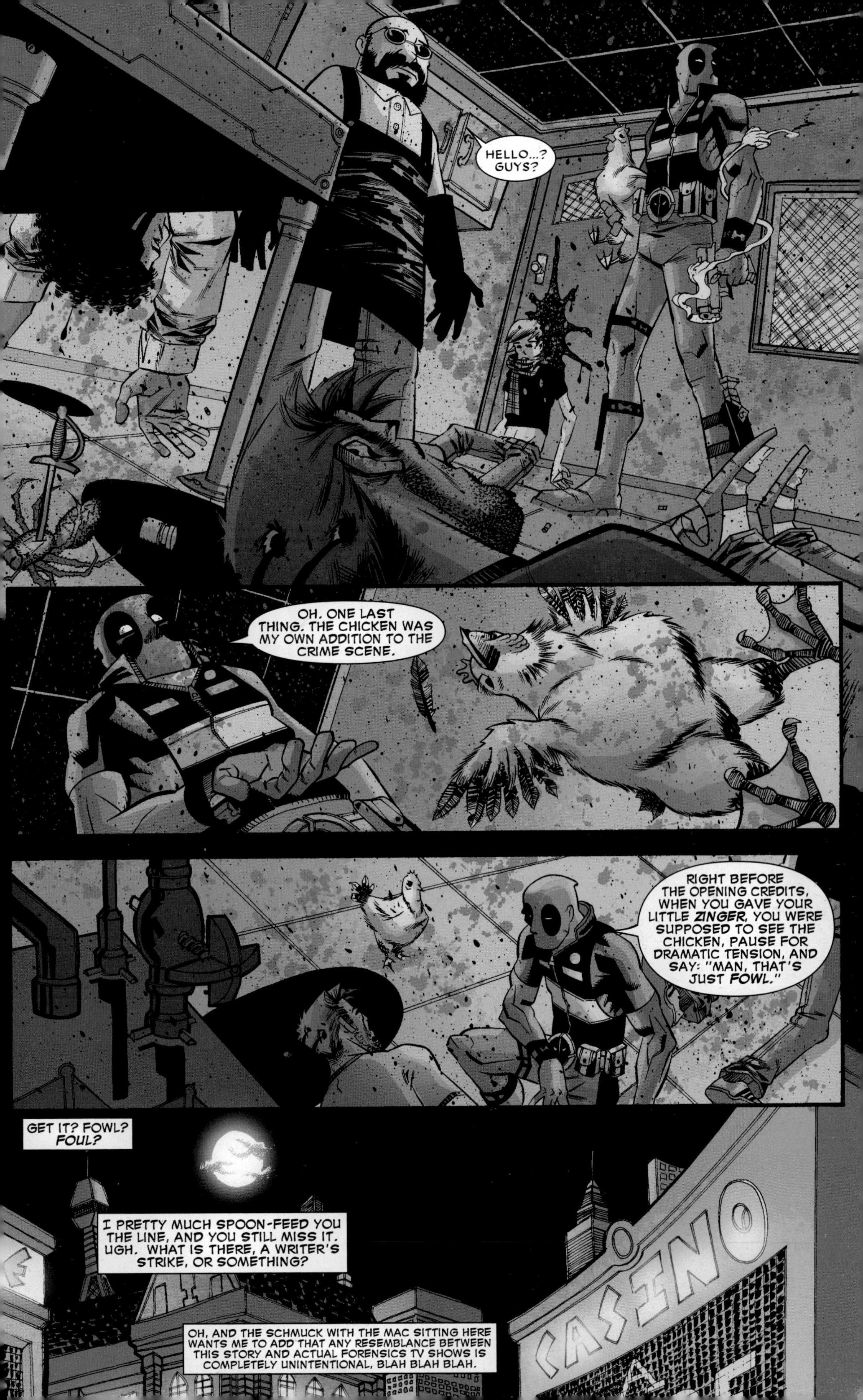
HELLO...? GUYS?
OH. ONE LAST THING. THE CHICKEN WAS MY OWN ADDITION TO THE CRIME SCENE.
RIGHT BEFORE THE OPENING CREDITS, WHEN YOU GAVE YOUR LITTLE ZINGER, YOU WERE SUPPOSED TO SEE THE CHICKEN, PAUSE FOR DRAMATIC TENSION, AND SAY: "MAN, THAT'S JUST FOWL."
GET IT? FOWL? FOUL?
I PRETTY MUCH SPOON-FEED YOU THE LINE, AND YOU STILL MISS IT. UGH. WHAT IS THERE, A WRITER'S STRIKE, OR SOMETHING?
OH, AND THE SCHMUCK WITH THE MAC SITTING HERE WANTS ME TO ADD THAT ANY RESEMBLANCE BETWEEN THIS STORY AND ACTUAL FORENSICS TV SHOWS IS COMPLETELY UNINTENTIONAL, BLAH BLAH BLAH.
CASINO

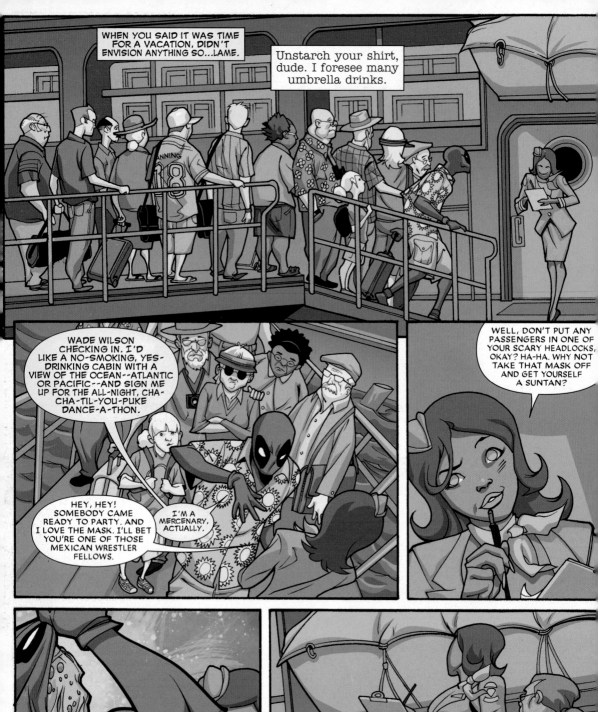

WHEN YOU SAID IT WAS TIME FOR A VACATION, DIDN'T ENVISION ANYTHING SO...LAME.

Unstarch your shirt, dude. I foresee many umbrella drinks.

WADE WILSON CHECKING IN. I'D LIKE A NO-SMOKING, YES-DRINKING CABIN WITH A VIEW OF THE OCEAN--ATLANTIC OR PACIFIC--AND SIGN ME UP FOR THE ALL-NIGHT, CHA-CHA-TIL-YOU-PUKE DANCE-A-THON.

HEY, HEY! SOMEBODY CAME READY TO PARTY. AND I LOVE THE MASK. I'LL BET YOU'RE ONE OF THOSE MEXICAN WRESTLER FELLOWS.

I'M A MERCENARY, ACTUALLY.

WELL, DON'T PUT ANY PASSENGERS IN ONE OF YOUR SCARY HEADLOCKS, OKAY? HA-HA. WHY NOT TAKE THAT MASK OFF AND GET YOURSELF A SUNTAN?

I GUESS A LITTLE SUN MIGHT BE NICE, AND--

PUT IT BACK ON! PUT IT BACK ON!

I'D LIKE TO BE ON THE OTHER SIDE OF THE SHIP FROM HIM, PLEASE.

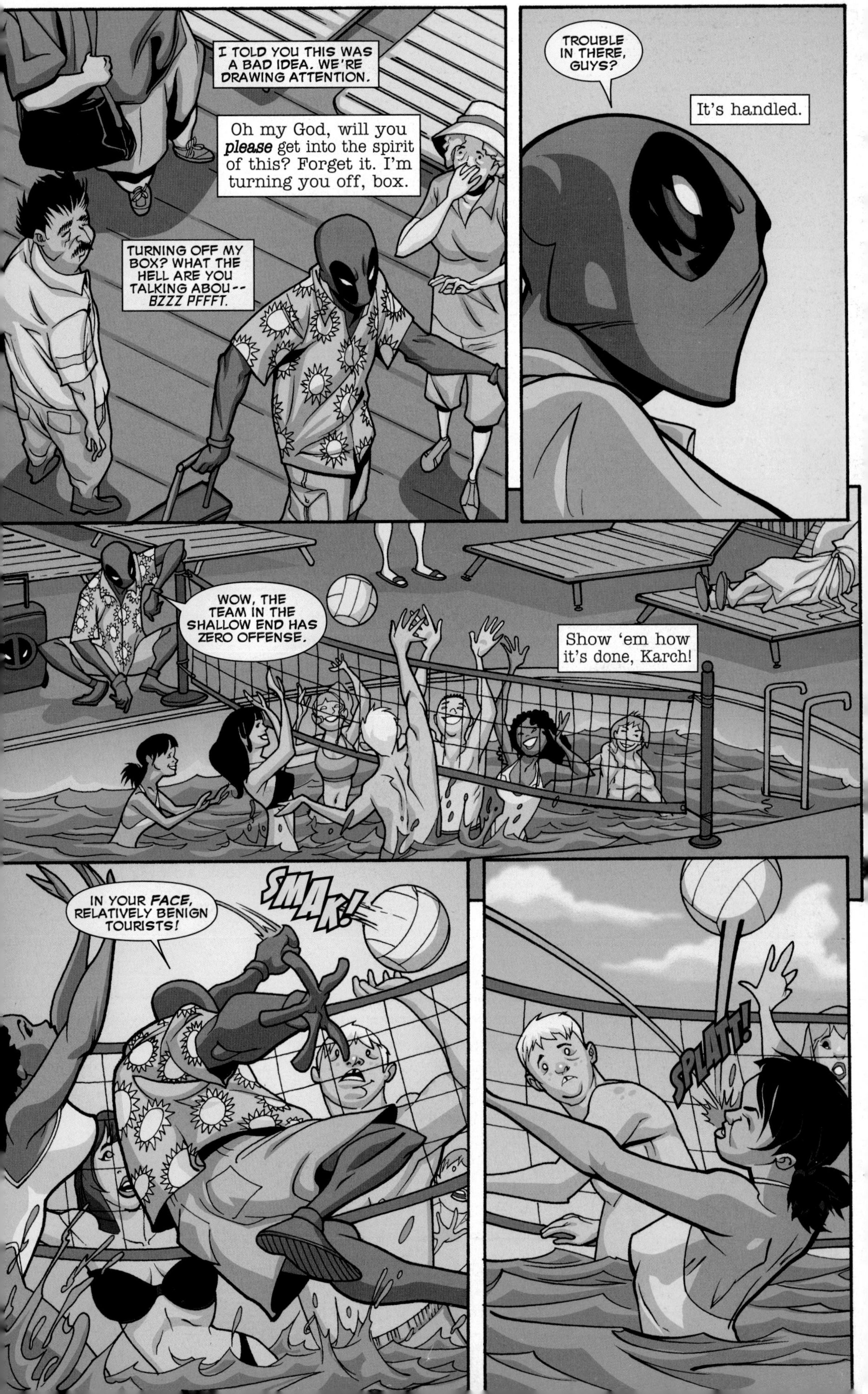
I TOLD YOU THIS WAS A BAD IDEA. WE'RE DRAWING ATTENTION.
Oh my God, will you *please* get into the spirit of this? Forget it. I'm turning you off, box.
TURNING OFF MY BOX? WHAT THE HELL ARE YOU TALKING ABOU-- *BZZZ PFFFT.*
TROUBLE IN THERE, GUYS?
It's handled.
WOW, THE TEAM IN THE SHALLOW END HAS ZERO OFFENSE.
Show 'em how it's done, Karch!
IN YOUR *FACE*, RELATIVELY BENIGN TOURISTS!
SMAK!
SPLATT!

MOMMY MOMMY MOMMY!

THAT'S RIGHT! DON'T BRING THAT WEAK D INTO MY HOUSE. OH NO YOU DI-IN'T.

KNOCK IT OFF, PINHEAD. I'M TRYING TO RELAX.

WHAT'S YOUR DAMAGE, HEATHER? I'M JUST GETTING MY VACATION ON.

NO, YOU'RE ANNOYING THE HELL OUT OF EVERYONE. AND YOU'RE DRIPPING ON MY COPY OF TWILIGHT.

MAN, YOU WANT TO THROW DOWN, JUST SAY THE WORD.

I DON'T WANT TO THROW ANYTHING, YOU SIMPLETON. I JUST WANT TO RELAX. WHY DON'T YOU GO PLAY SHUFFLEBOARD OR SOMETHING?

Dude, we could totally rule shuffleboard.

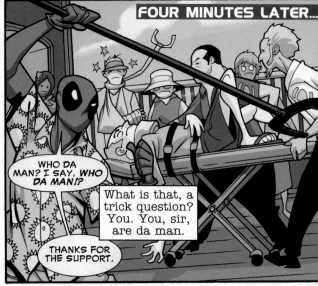

FOUR MINUTES LATER...

WHO DA MAN? I SAY, WHO DA MAN!?

What is that, a trick question? You. You, sir, are da man.

THANKS FOR THE SUPPORT.

MR. WILSON, PLEASE! DON'T SHUFFLE SO... ZEALOUSLY.

HEY, THERE WAS FIVE BUCKS RIDING ON THAT MATCH.

MAYBE PING-PONG IS MORE YOUR THING.

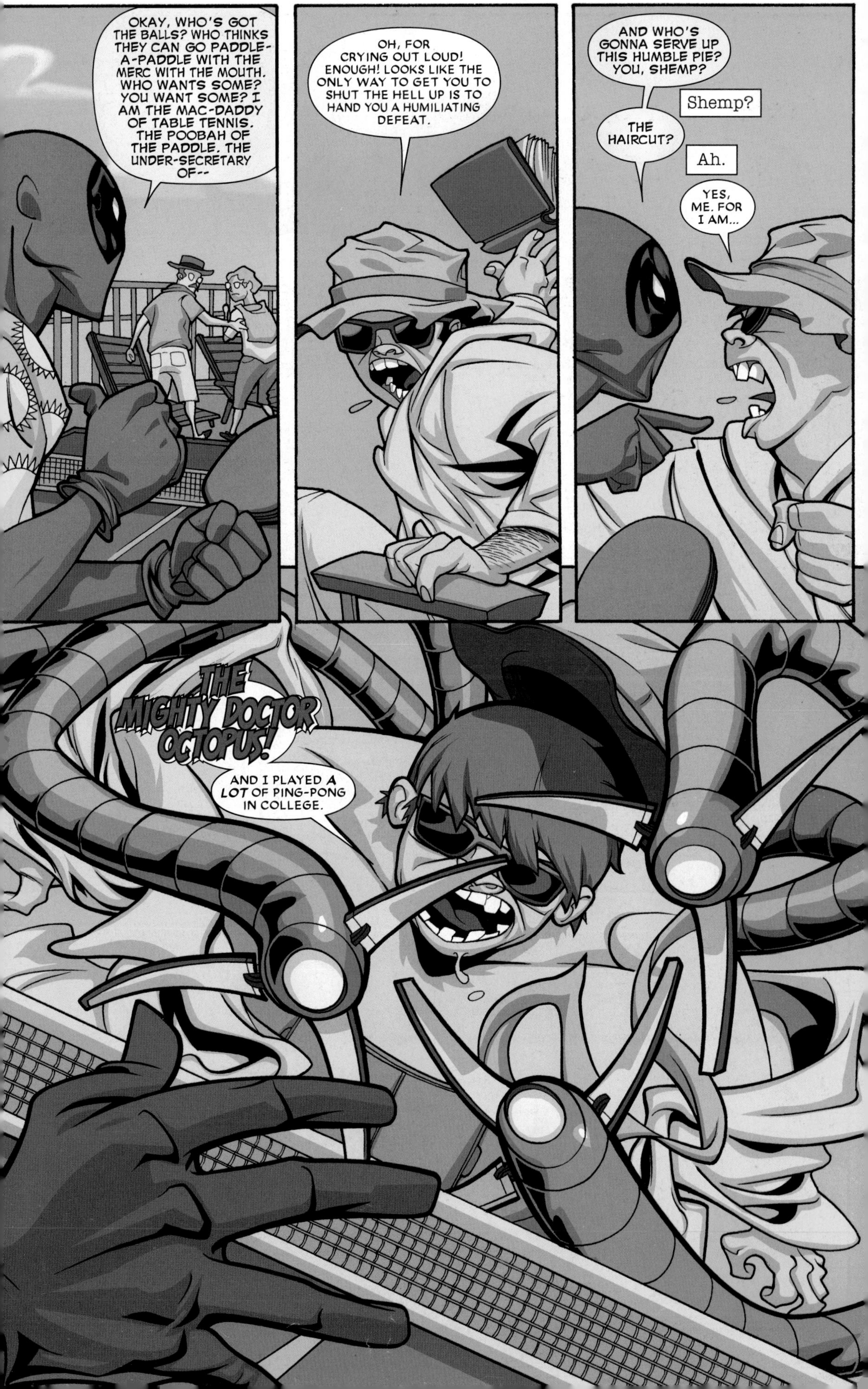
OKAY, WHO'S GOT THE BALLS? WHO THINKS THEY CAN GO PADDLE-A-PADDLE WITH THE MERC WITH THE MOUTH. WHO WANTS SOME? YOU WANT SOME? I AM THE MAC-DADDY OF TABLE TENNIS. THE POOBAH OF THE PADDLE. THE UNDER-SECRETARY OF--
OH, FOR CRYING OUT LOUD! ENOUGH! LOOKS LIKE THE ONLY WAY TO GET YOU TO SHUT THE HELL UP IS TO HAND YOU A HUMILIATING DEFEAT.
AND WHO'S GONNA SERVE UP THIS HUMBLE PIE? YOU, SHEMP?
Shemp?
THE HAIRCUT?
Ah.
YES, ME. FOR I AM...
THE MIGHTY DOCTOR OCTOPUS!
AND I PLAYED A LOT OF PING-PONG IN COLLEGE.

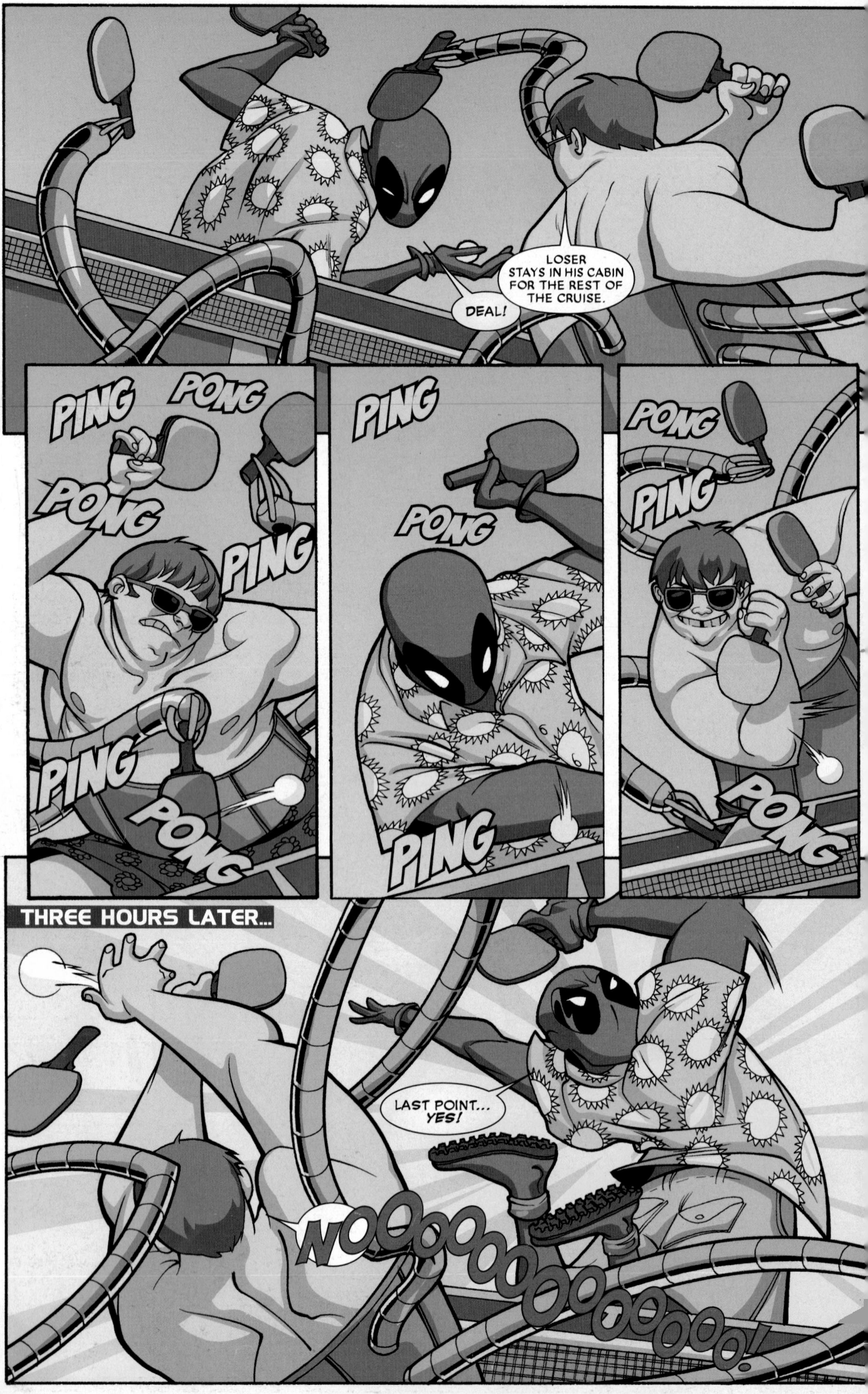
LOSER STAYS IN HIS CABIN FOR THE REST OF THE CRUISE.
DEAL!
PING
PONG
PONG
PING
PING
PONG
PING
PONG
PING
PONG
PING
PONG
THREE HOURS LATER...
LAST POINT... YES!
NOOOOOOOOOOOOOOOOO!

HA! I RULE, AND YOU SUCK EGGS.
I THINK YOU'RE LOOKING TO GET HIT IN THAT FAMOUS MOUTH OF YOURS.
YEAH, RIGHT! LUCKY FOR YOU THE VACATION CODE KEEPS ME FROM LAYING A SMACKDOWN ON YOU RIGHT HERE AND NOW.
Vacation code?
YOU KNOW. NO SUPERS SHALL RUIN A VACATION BY THROWING DOWN WITH OTHER SUPERS. YOU GOT TO AGREE TO THE VACATION CODE. IT'S THE CORNERSTONE OF OUR CIVILIZATION.
TWENTY MINUTES LATER...
YOU'RE TELLING ME THERE'S NOT A VACATION CODE?
OH, SHUT UP.
BZZZZZZPFFFT-AH-HA. I'M BACK. NOW AS I WAS SAYING-OH, MY GOD, WHAT THE HELL HAPPENED!?
Great Balls of Thunder on the Deep Blue Sea
VICTOR GISCHLER WRITER
SANFORD GREENE PENCILER
NATHAN MASSENGILL INKER
DAVE McCAIG COLORIST

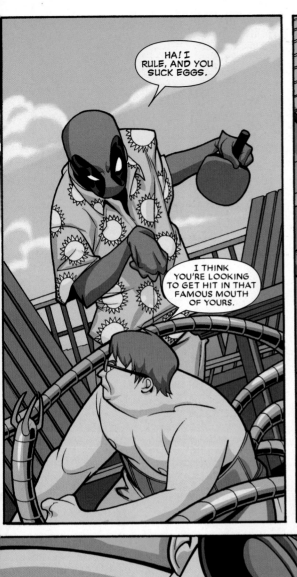

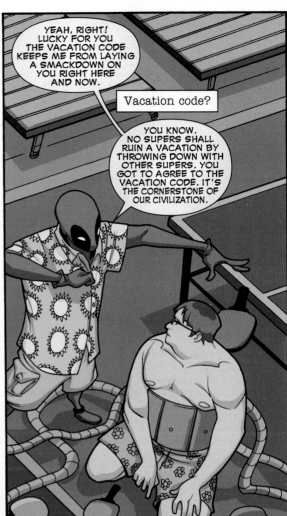

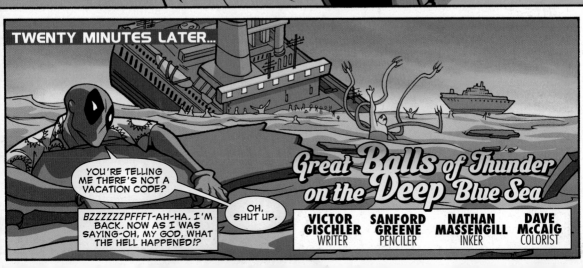

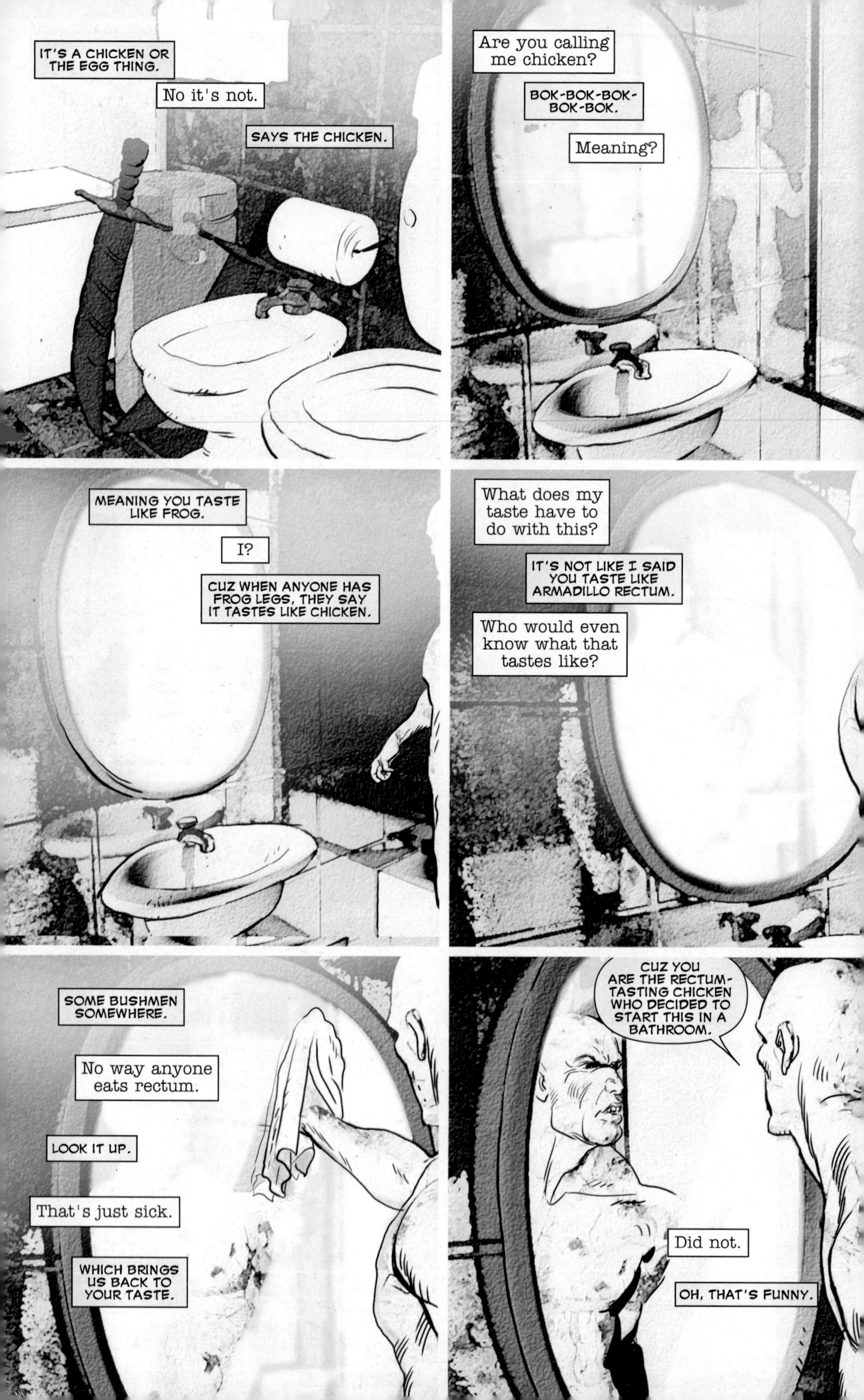
IT'S A CHICKEN OR THE EGG THING.
No it's not.
SAYS THE CHICKEN.
Are you calling me chicken?
BOK-BOK-BOK-BOK-BOK.
Meaning?
MEANING YOU TASTE LIKE FROG.
I?
CUZ WHEN ANYONE HAS FROG LEGS, THEY SAY IT TASTES LIKE CHICKEN.
What does my taste have to do with this?
IT'S NOT LIKE I SAID YOU TASTE LIKE ARMADILLO RECTUM.
Who would even know what that tastes like?
SOME BUSHMEN SOMEWHERE.
No way anyone eats rectum.
LOOK IT UP.
That's just sick.
WHICH BRINGS US BACK TO YOUR TASTE.
CUZ YOU ARE THE RECTUM-TASTING CHICKEN WHO DECIDED TO START THIS IN A BATHROOM.
Did not.
OH, THAT'S FUNNY.

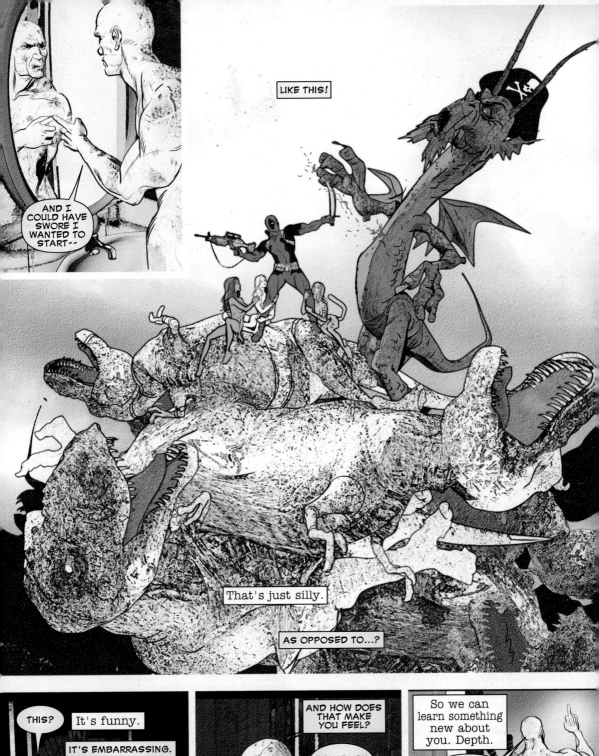

AND I COULD HAVE SWORE I WANTED TO START--

LIKE THIS!

That's just silly.

AS OPPOSED TO...?

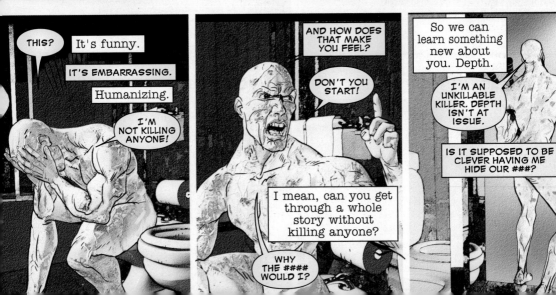

THIS? It's funny.

IT'S EMBARRASSING.

Humanizing.

I'M NOT KILLING ANYONE!

AND HOW DOES THAT MAKE YOU FEEL?

DON'T YOU START!

I mean, can you get through a whole story without killing anyone?

WHY THE #### WOULD I?

So we can learn something new about you. Depth.

I'M AN UNKILLABLE KILLER. DEPTH ISN'T AT ISSUE.

IS IT SUPPOSED TO BE CLEVER HAVING ME HIDE OUR ###?

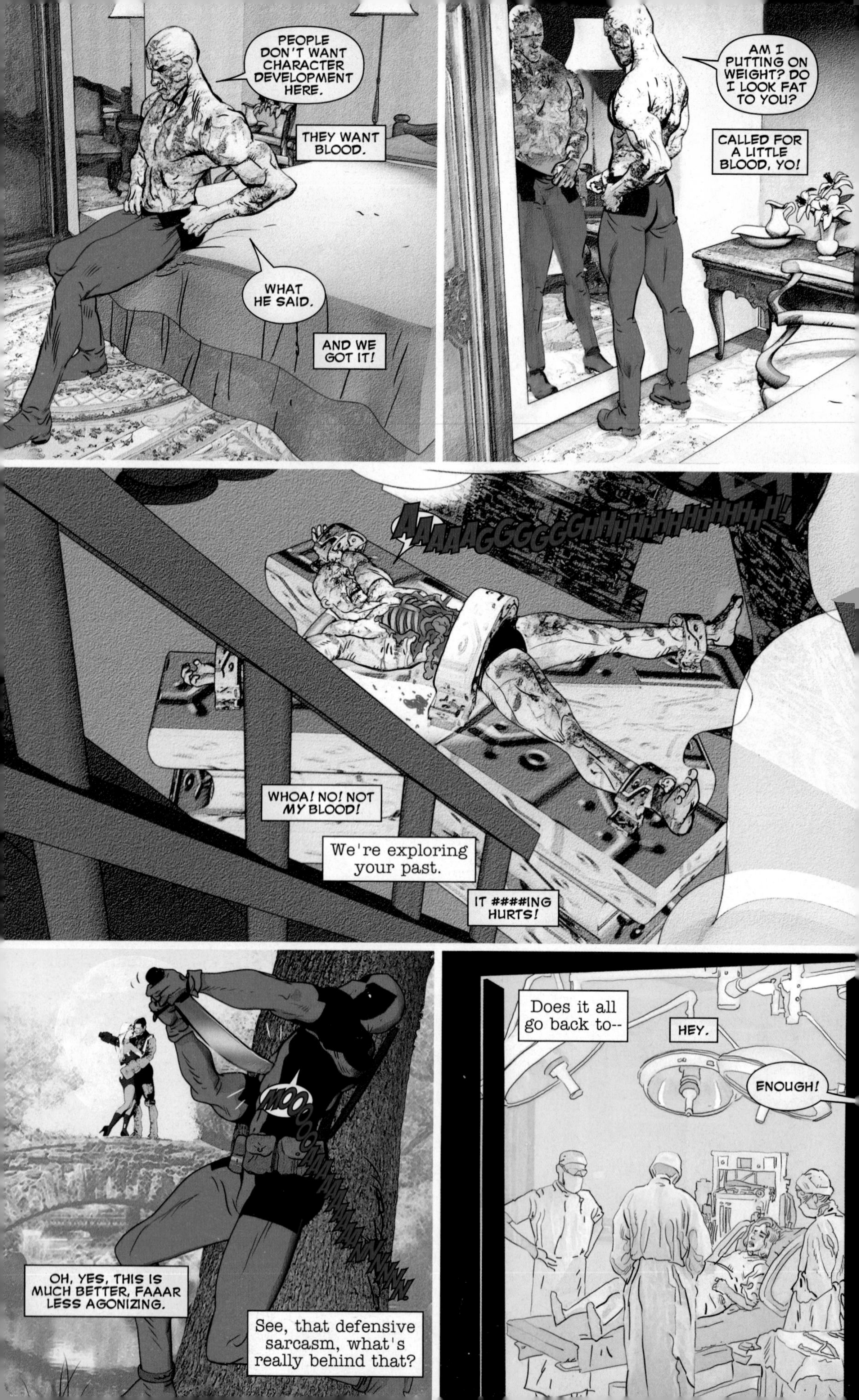
PEOPLE DON'T WANT CHARACTER DEVELOPMENT HERE.
THEY WANT BLOOD.
WHAT HE SAID.
AND WE GOT IT!
AM I PUTTING ON WEIGHT? DO I LOOK FAT TO YOU?
CALLED FOR A LITTLE BLOOD, YO!
AAAAAGGGGGGHHHHHHHHHHHHHH!
WHOA! NO! NOT MY BLOOD!
We're exploring your past.
IT ####ING HURTS!
MOOOOOAAAAAANNNNN.
OH, YES, THIS IS MUCH BETTER, FAAAR LESS AGONIZING.
See, that defensive sarcasm, what's really behind that?
Does it all go back to--
HEY.
ENOUGH!

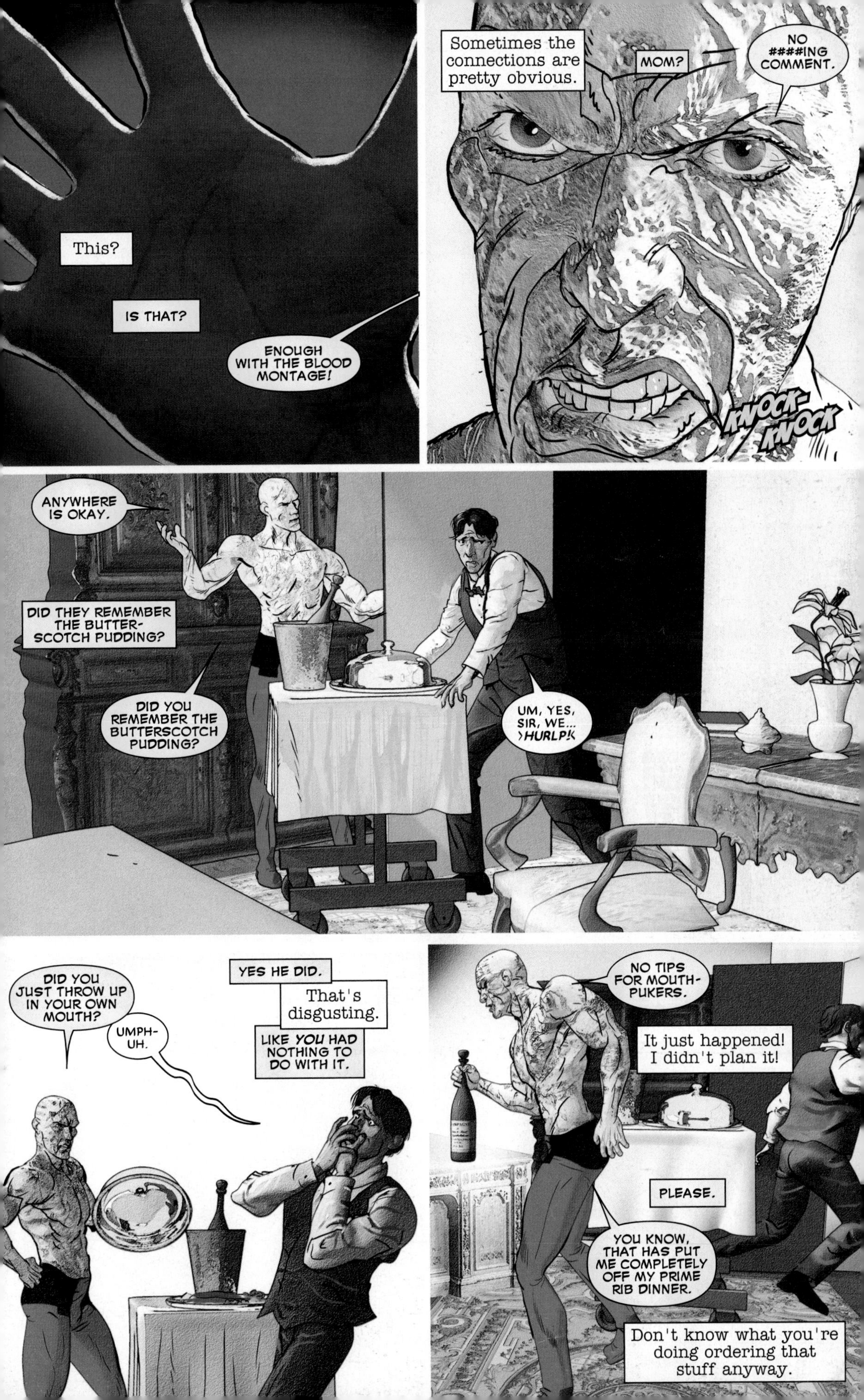
This?
IS THAT?
ENOUGH WITH THE BLOOD MONTAGE!
Sometimes the connections are pretty obvious.
MOM?
NO ####ING COMMENT.
KNOCK-KNOCK
ANYWHERE IS OKAY.
DID THEY REMEMBER THE BUTTER-SCOTCH PUDDING?
DID YOU REMEMBER THE BUTTERSCOTCH PUDDING?
UM, YES, SIR, WE... >HURLP!<
DID YOU JUST THROW UP IN YOUR OWN MOUTH?
UMPH-UH.
YES HE DID.
That's disgusting.
LIKE YOU HAD NOTHING TO DO WITH IT.
NO TIPS FOR MOUTH-PUKERS.
It just happened! I didn't plan it!
PLEASE.
YOU KNOW, THAT HAS PUT ME COMPLETELY OFF MY PRIME RIB DINNER.
Don't know what you're doing ordering that stuff anyway.

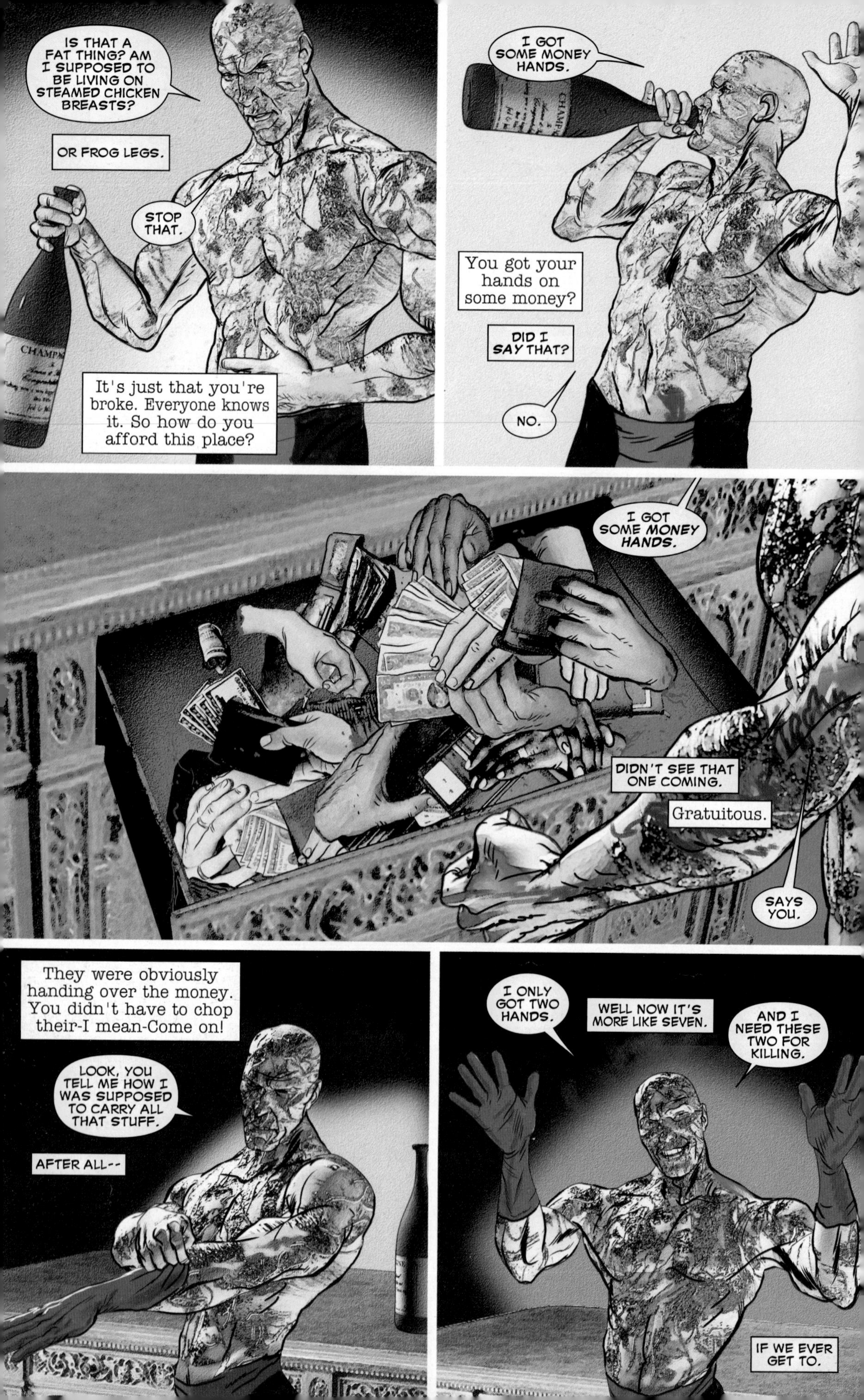
IS THAT A FAT THING? AM I SUPPOSED TO BE LIVING ON STEAMED CHICKEN BREASTS?
OR FROG LEGS.
STOP THAT.
It's just that you're broke. Everyone knows it. So how do you afford this place?
I GOT SOME MONEY HANDS.
You got your hands on some money?
DID I SAY THAT?
NO.
I GOT SOME MONEY HANDS.
DIDN'T SEE THAT ONE COMING.
Gratuitous.
SAYS YOU.
They were obviously handing over the money. You didn't have to chop their-I mean-Come on!
LOOK, YOU TELL ME HOW I WAS SUPPOSED TO CARRY ALL THAT STUFF.
AFTER ALL--
I ONLY GOT TWO HANDS.
WELL NOW IT'S MORE LIKE SEVEN.
AND I NEED THESE TWO FOR KILLING.
IF WE EVER GET TO.

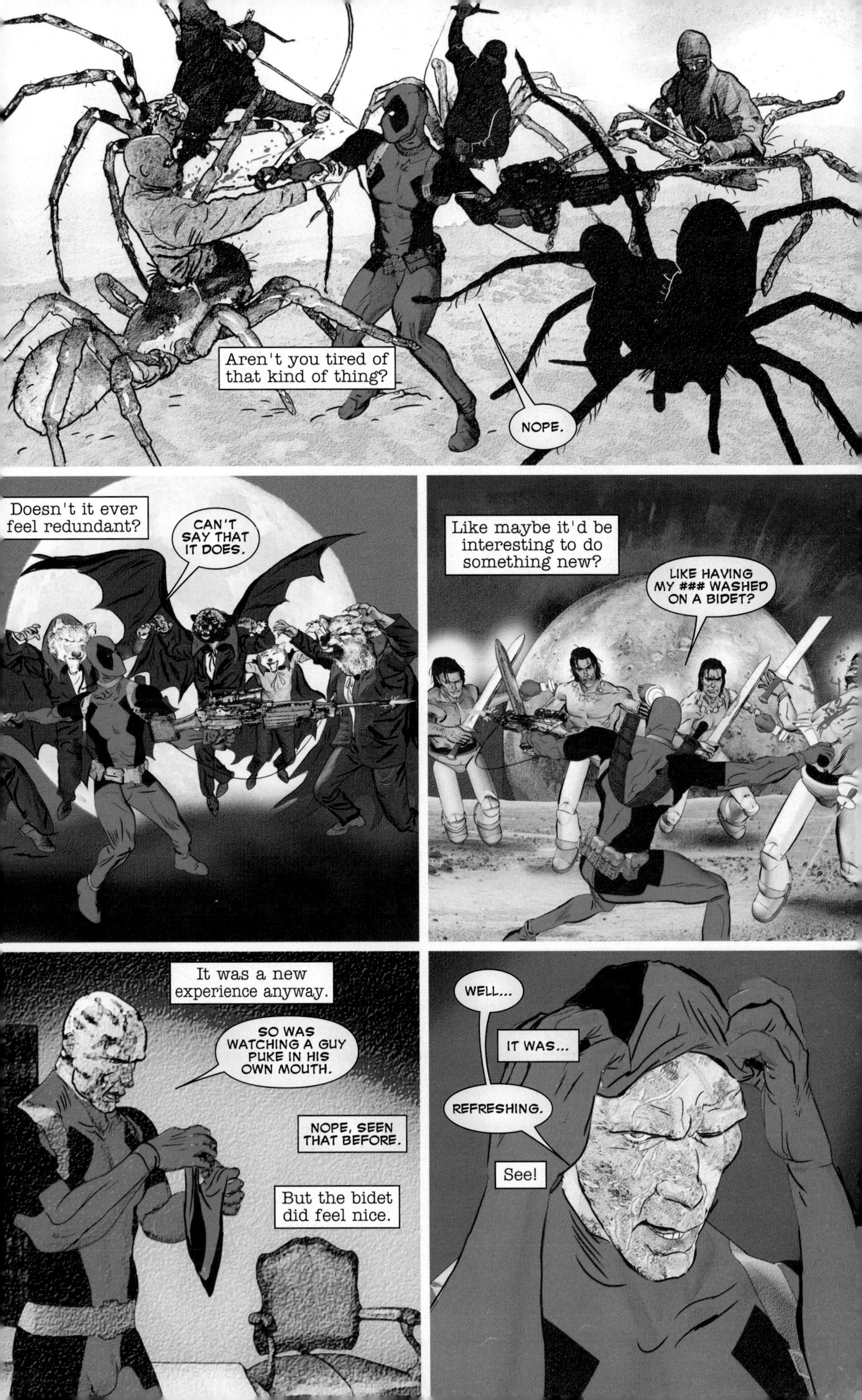
Aren't you tired of that kind of thing?
NOPE.
Doesn't it ever feel redundant?
CAN'T SAY THAT IT DOES.
Like maybe it'd be interesting to do something new?
LIKE HAVING MY ### WASHED ON A BIDET?
It was a new experience anyway.
SO WAS WATCHING A GUY PUKE IN HIS OWN MOUTH.
NOPE, SEEN THAT BEFORE.
But the bidet did feel nice.
WELL...
IT WAS...
REFRESHING.
See!

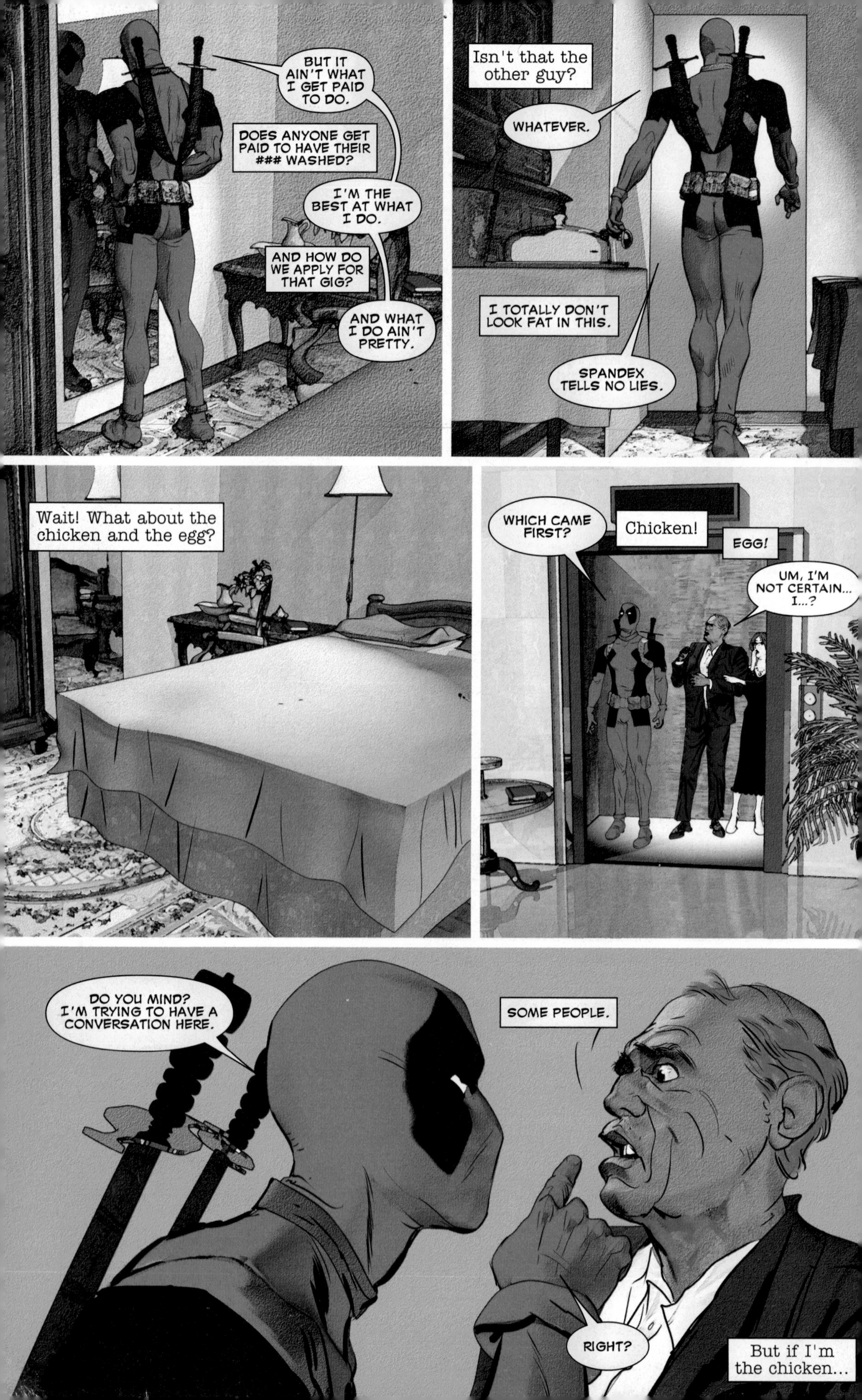
BUT IT AIN'T WHAT I GET PAID TO DO.
DOES ANYONE GET PAID TO HAVE THEIR ### WASHED?
I'M THE BEST AT WHAT I DO.
AND HOW DO WE APPLY FOR THAT GIG?
AND WHAT I DO AIN'T PRETTY.
Isn't that the other guy?
WHATEVER.
I TOTALLY DON'T LOOK FAT IN THIS.
SPANDEX TELLS NO LIES.
Wait! What about the chicken and the egg?
WHICH CAME FIRST?
Chicken!
EGG!
UM, I'M NOT CERTAIN... I...?
DO YOU MIND? I'M TRYING TO HAVE A CONVERSATION HERE.
SOME PEOPLE.
RIGHT?
But if I'm the chicken...

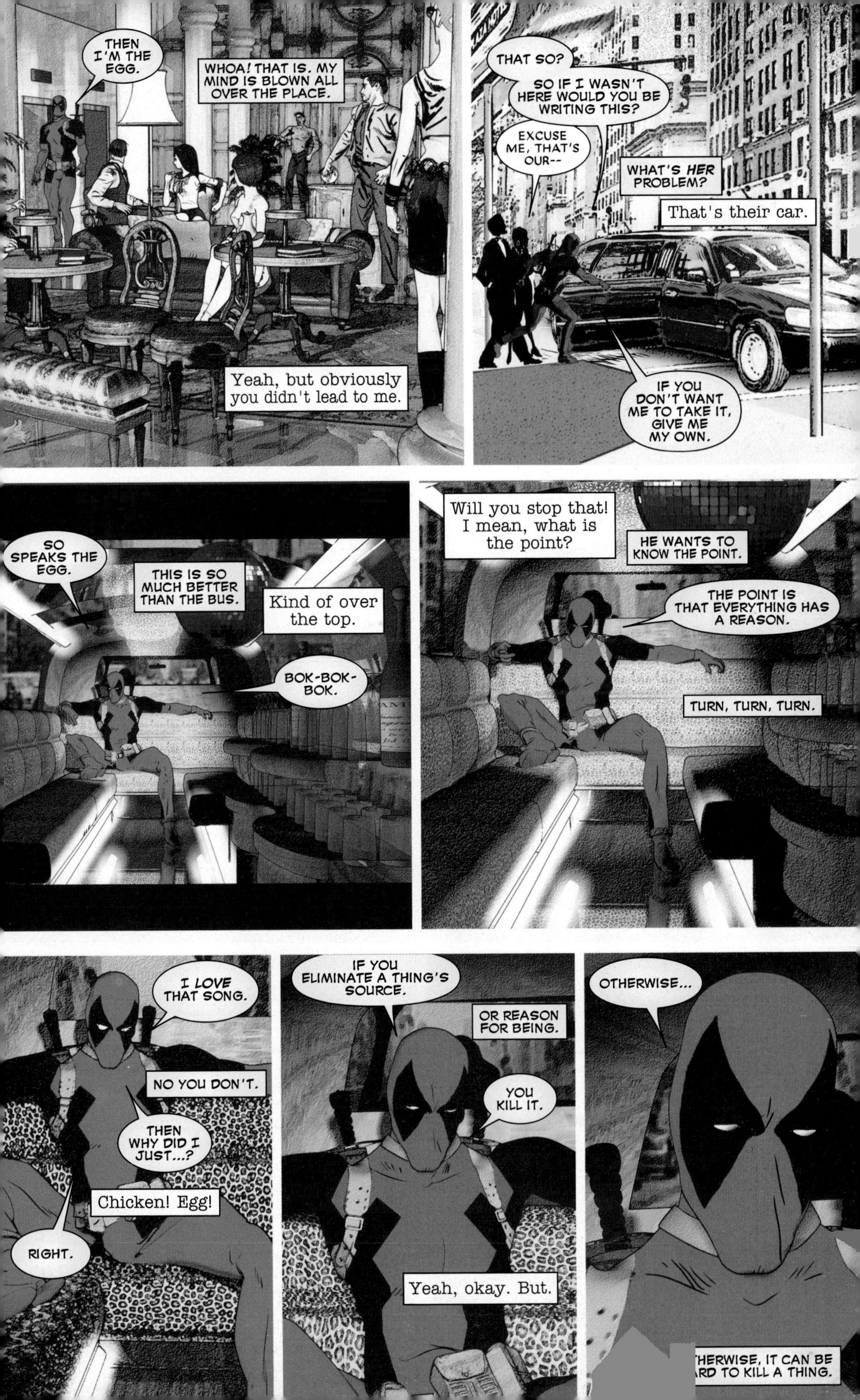
THEN I'M THE EGG.
WHOA! THAT IS. MY MIND IS BLOWN ALL OVER THE PLACE.
Yeah, but obviously you didn't lead to me.
THAT SO?
SO IF I WASN'T HERE WOULD YOU BE WRITING THIS?
EXCUSE ME, THAT'S OUR--
WHAT'S HER PROBLEM?
That's their car.
IF YOU DON'T WANT ME TO TAKE IT, GIVE ME MY OWN.
SO SPEAKS THE EGG.
THIS IS SO MUCH BETTER THAN THE BUS.
Kind of over the top.
BOK-BOK-BOK.
Will you stop that! I mean, what is the point?
HE WANTS TO KNOW THE POINT.
THE POINT IS THAT EVERYTHING HAS A REASON.
TURN, TURN, TURN.
I LOVE THAT SONG.
NO YOU DON'T.
THEN WHY DID I JUST...?
Chicken! Egg!
RIGHT.
IF YOU ELIMINATE A THING'S SOURCE.
OR REASON FOR BEING.
YOU KILL IT.
Yeah, okay. But.
OTHERWISE...
THERWISE, IT CAN BE
ARD TO KILL A THING.

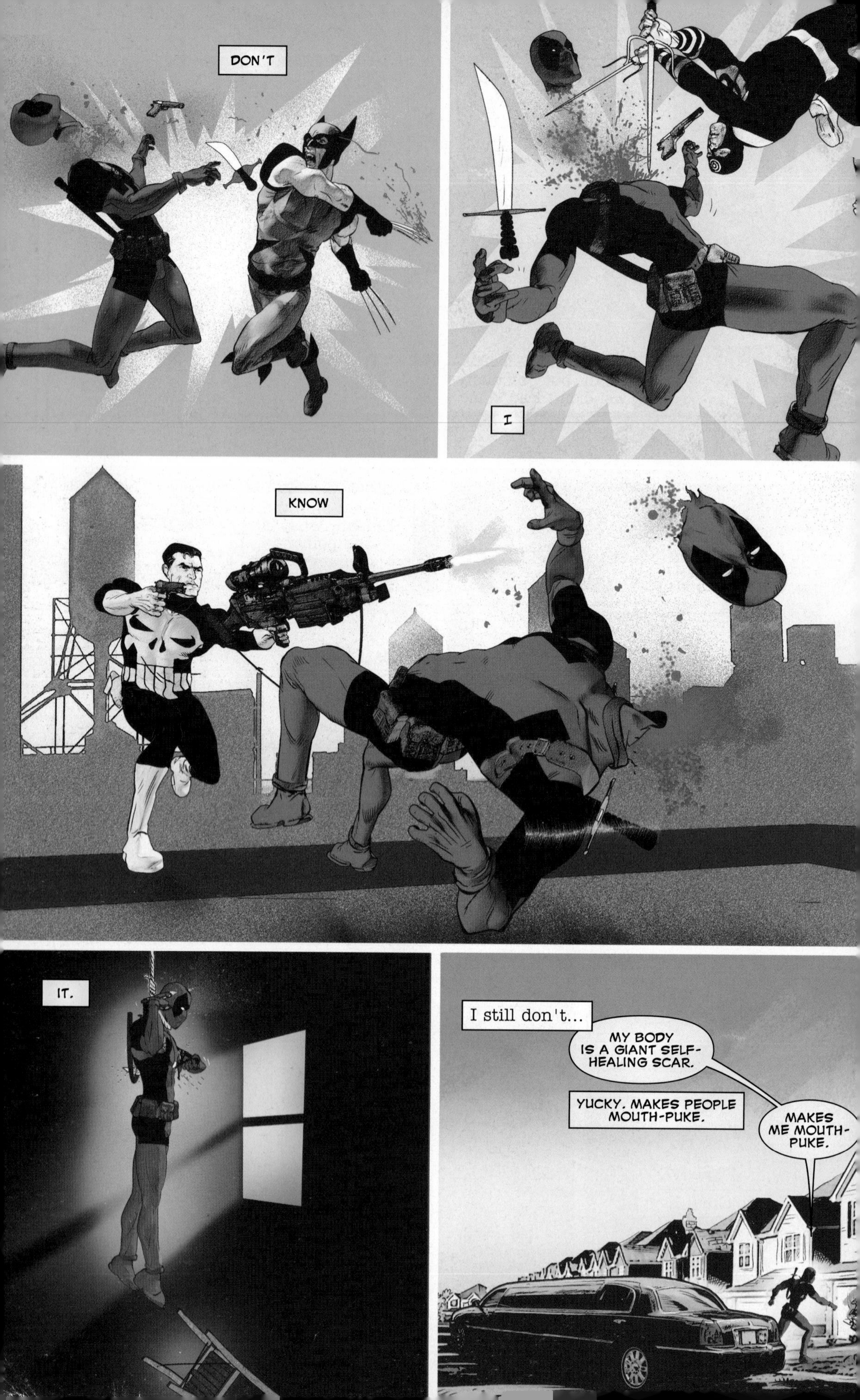
DON'T
I
KNOW
IT.
I still don't...
MY BODY IS A GIANT SELF-HEALING SCAR.
YUCKY. MAKES PEOPLE MOUTH-PUKE.
MAKES ME MOUTH-PUKE.

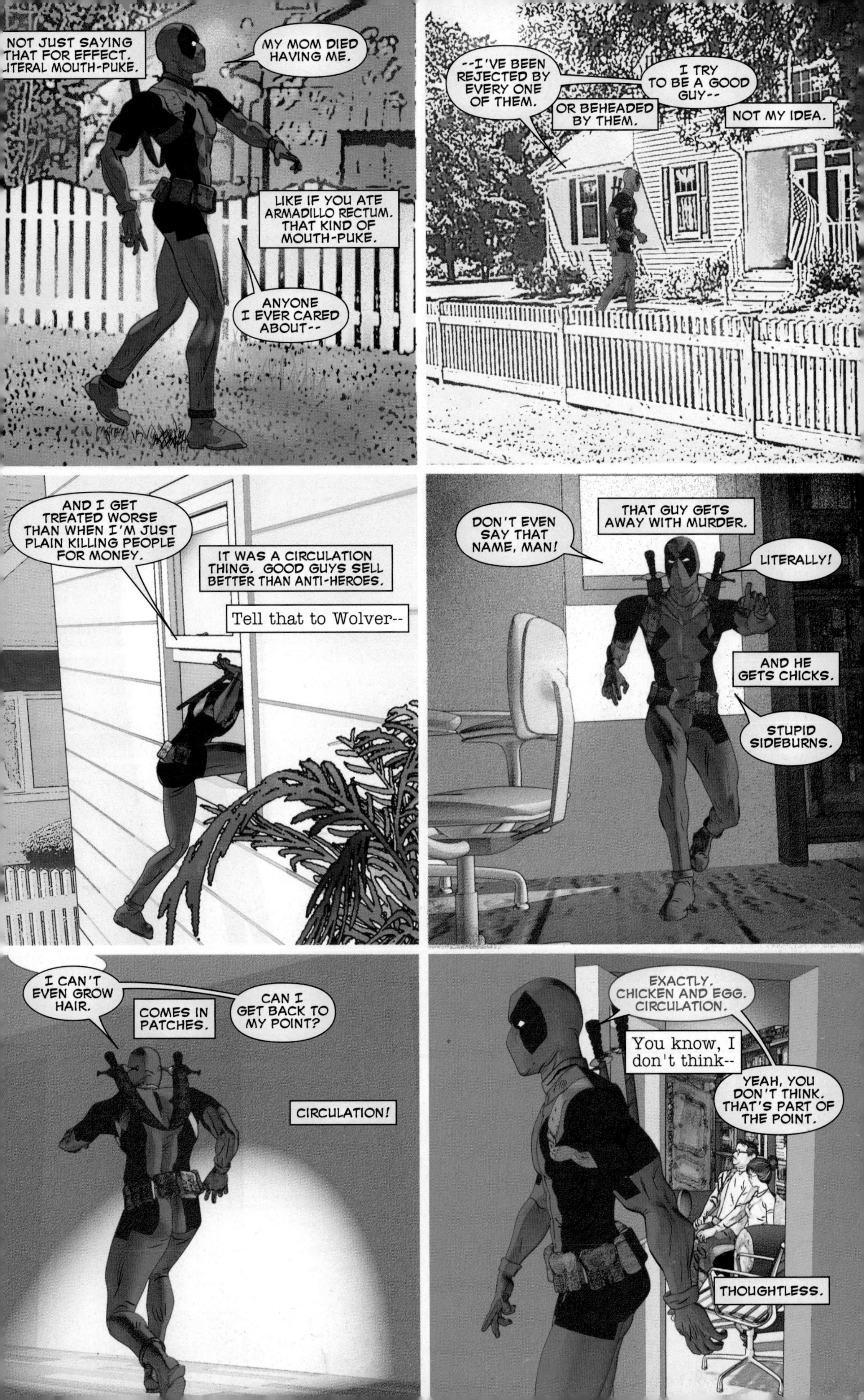
NOT JUST SAYING THAT FOR EFFECT. LITERAL MOUTH-PUKE.
MY MOM DIED HAVING ME.
LIKE IF YOU ATE ARMADILLO RECTUM. THAT KIND OF MOUTH-PUKE.
ANYONE I EVER CARED ABOUT--
--I'VE BEEN REJECTED BY EVERY ONE OF THEM.
I TRY TO BE A GOOD GUY--
OR BEHEADED BY THEM.
NOT MY IDEA.
AND I GET TREATED WORSE THAN WHEN I'M JUST PLAIN KILLING PEOPLE FOR MONEY.
IT WAS A CIRCULATION THING. GOOD GUYS SELL BETTER THAN ANTI-HEROES.
Tell that to Wolver--
DON'T EVEN SAY THAT NAME, MAN!
THAT GUY GETS AWAY WITH MURDER.
LITERALLY!
AND HE GETS CHICKS.
STUPID SIDEBURNS.
I CAN'T EVEN GROW HAIR.
COMES IN PATCHES.
CAN I GET BACK TO MY POINT?
CIRCULATION!
EXACTLY. CHICKEN AND EGG. CIRCULATION.
You know, I don't think--
YEAH, YOU DON'T THINK. THAT'S PART OF THE POINT.
THOUGHTLESS.

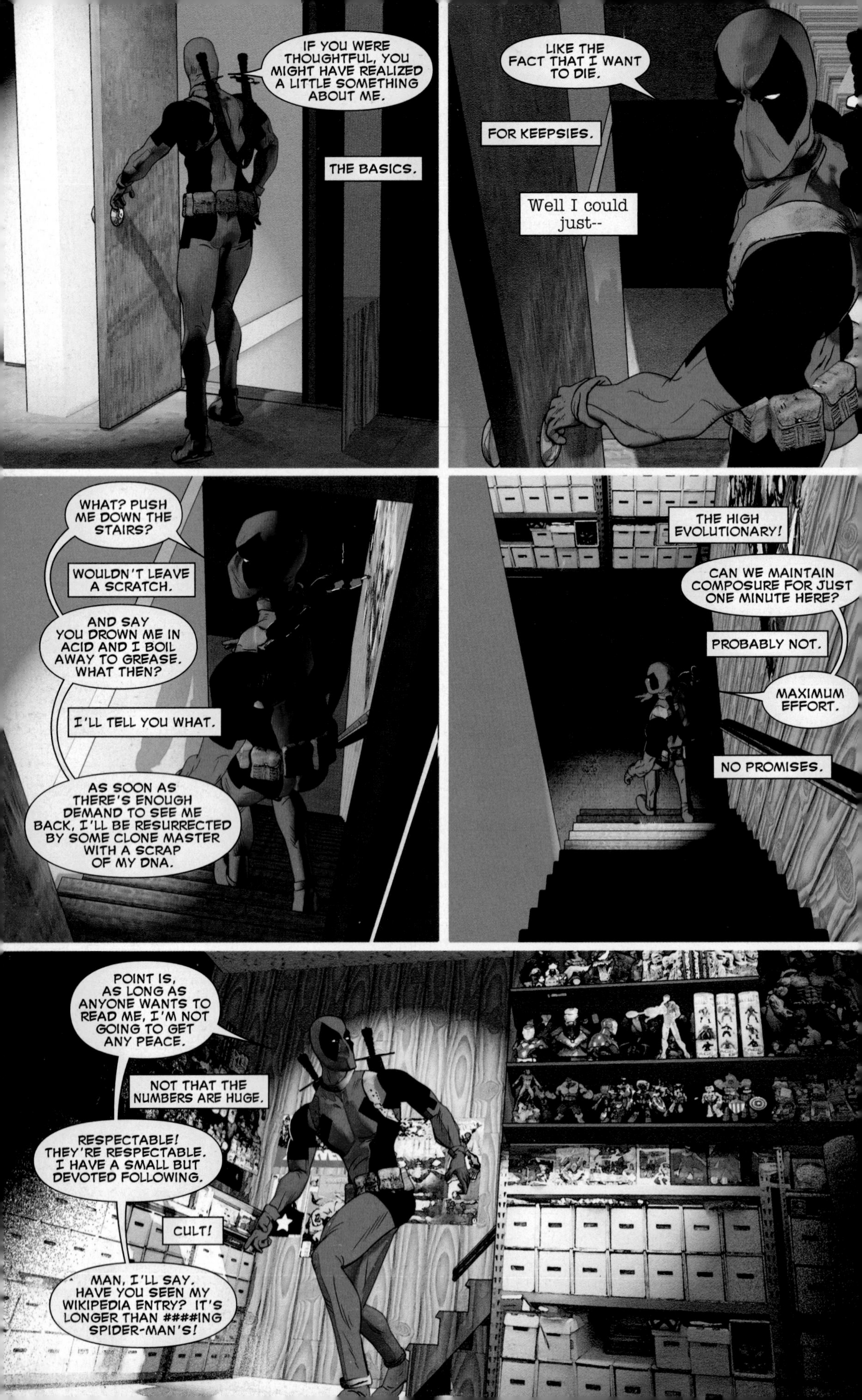

IF YOU WERE THOUGHTFUL, YOU MIGHT HAVE REALIZED A LITTLE SOMETHING ABOUT ME.
THE BASICS.
LIKE THE FACT THAT I WANT TO DIE.
FOR KEEPSIES.
Well I could just--
WHAT? PUSH ME DOWN THE STAIRS?
WOULDN'T LEAVE A SCRATCH.
AND SAY YOU DROWN ME IN ACID AND I BOIL AWAY TO GREASE. WHAT THEN?
I'LL TELL YOU WHAT.
AS SOON AS THERE'S ENOUGH DEMAND TO SEE ME BACK, I'LL BE RESURRECTED BY SOME CLONE MASTER WITH A SCRAP OF MY DNA.
THE HIGH EVOLUTIONARY!
CAN WE MAINTAIN COMPOSURE FOR JUST ONE MINUTE HERE?
PROBABLY NOT.
MAXIMUM EFFORT.
NO PROMISES.
POINT IS, AS LONG AS ANYONE WANTS TO READ ME, I'M NOT GOING TO GET ANY PEACE.
NOT THAT THE NUMBERS ARE HUGE.
RESPECTABLE! THEY'RE RESPECTABLE. I HAVE A SMALL BUT DEVOTED FOLLOWING.
CULT!
MAN, I'LL SAY. HAVE YOU SEEN MY WIKIPEDIA ENTRY? IT'S LONGER THAN ####ING SPIDER-MAN'S!

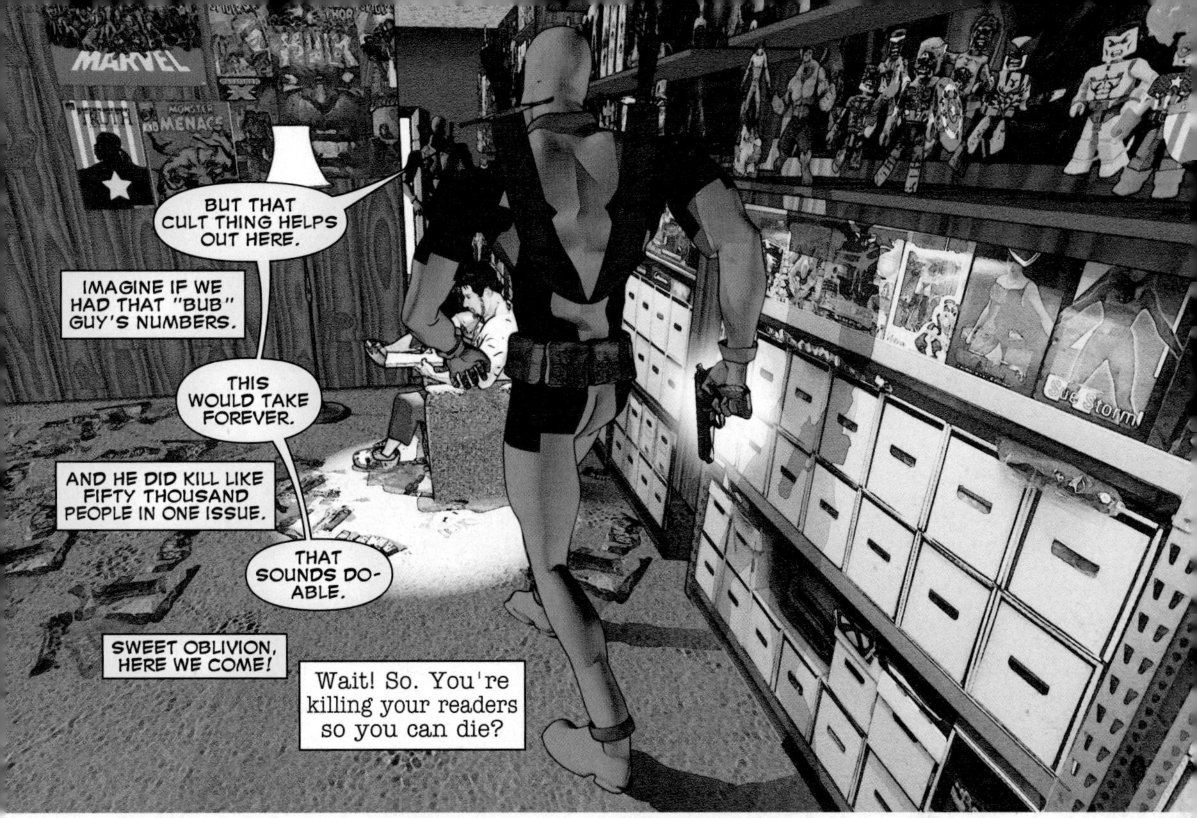
MARVEL
BUT THAT CULT THING HELPS OUT HERE.
IMAGINE IF WE HAD THAT "BUB" GUY'S NUMBERS.
THIS WOULD TAKE FOREVER.
AND HE DID KILL LIKE FIFTY THOUSAND PEOPLE IN ONE ISSUE.
THAT SOUNDS DO-ABLE.
SWEET OBLIVION, HERE WE COME!
Wait! So. You're killing your readers so you can die?
Sue Storm

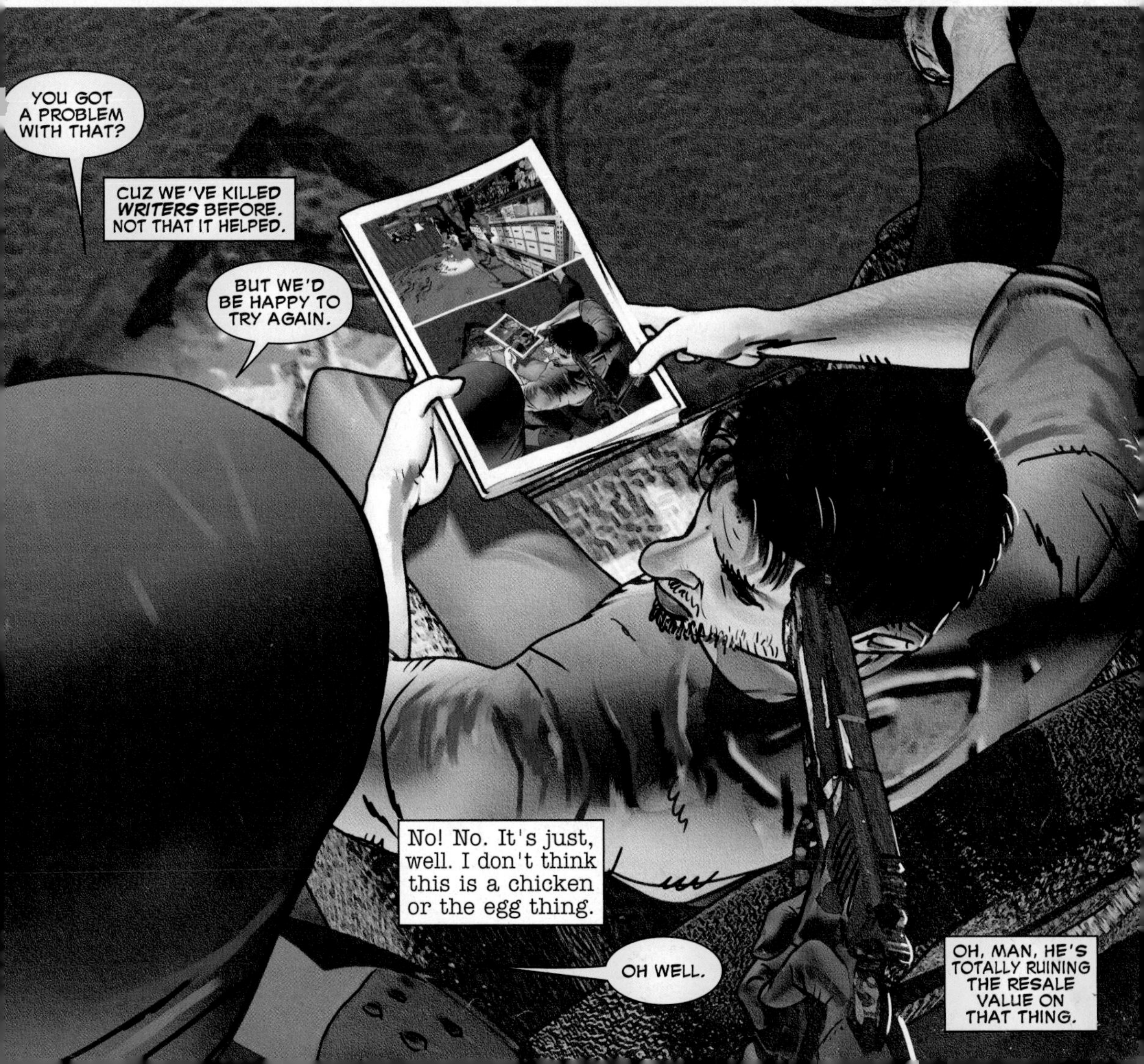
YOU GOT A PROBLEM WITH THAT?
CUZ WE'VE KILLED *WRITERS* BEFORE. NOT THAT IT HELPED.
BUT WE'D BE HAPPY TO TRY AGAIN.
No! No. It's just, well. I don't think this is a chicken or the egg thing.
OH WELL.
OH, MAN, HE'S TOTALLY RUINING THE RESALE VALUE ON THAT THING.

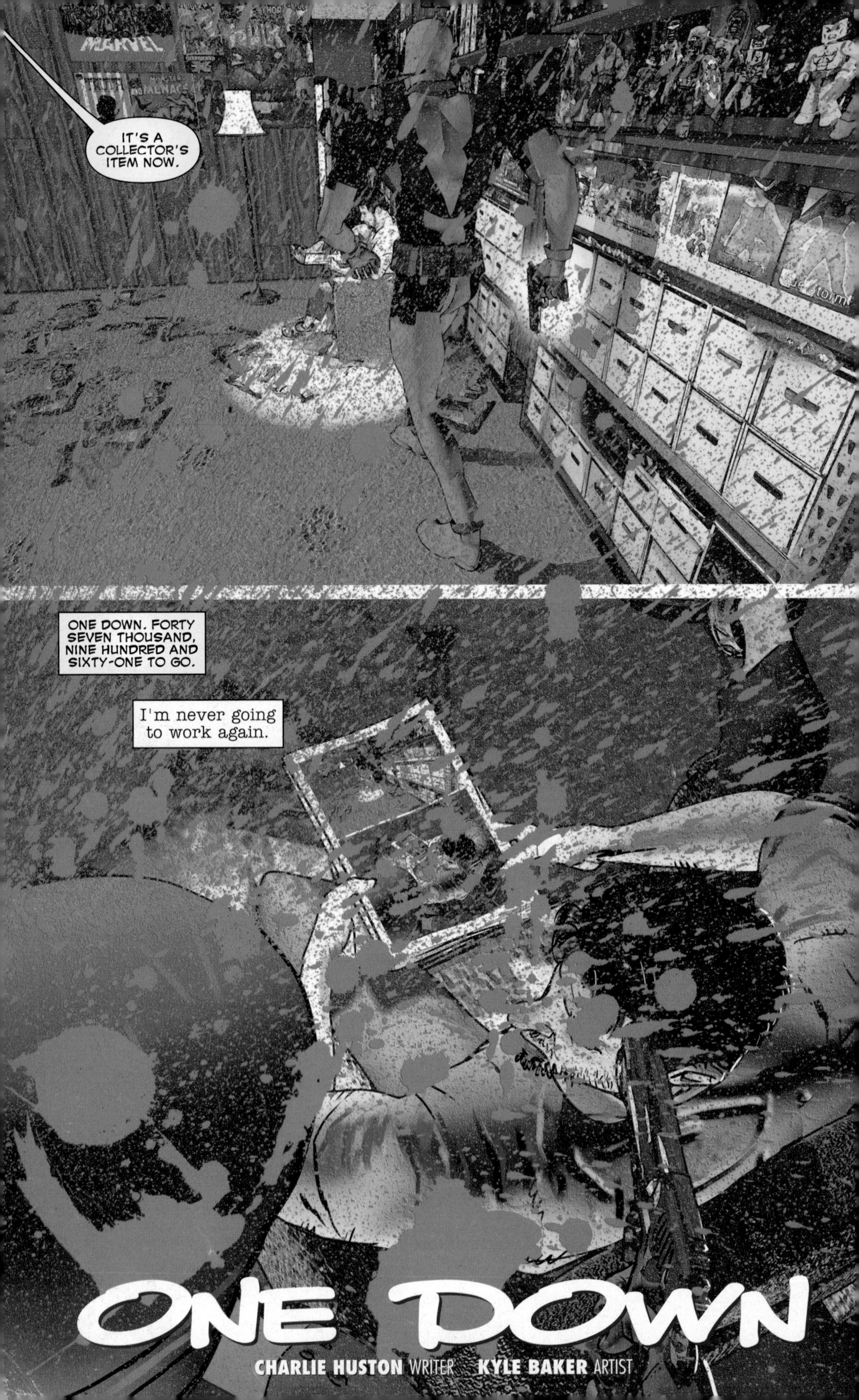
IT'S A COLLECTOR'S ITEM NOW.
ONE DOWN. FORTY SEVEN THOUSAND, NINE HUNDRED AND SIXTY-ONE TO GO.
I'm never going to work again.
ONE DOWN
CHARLIE HUSTON WRITER KYLE BAKER ARTIST

DEADPOOL 900

Cover Gallery 1-100

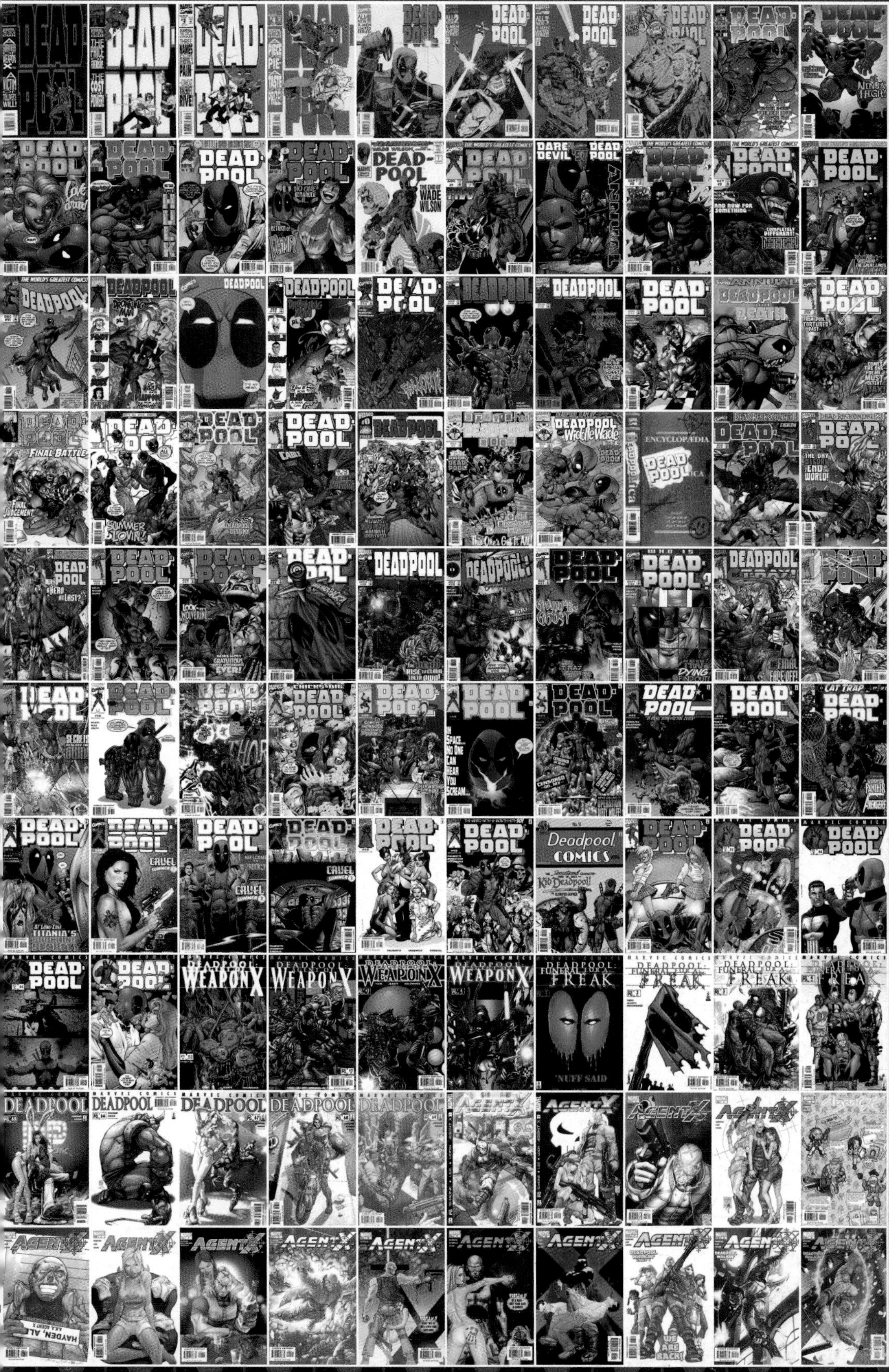

DEADPOOL 900

Cover Gallery 101-200

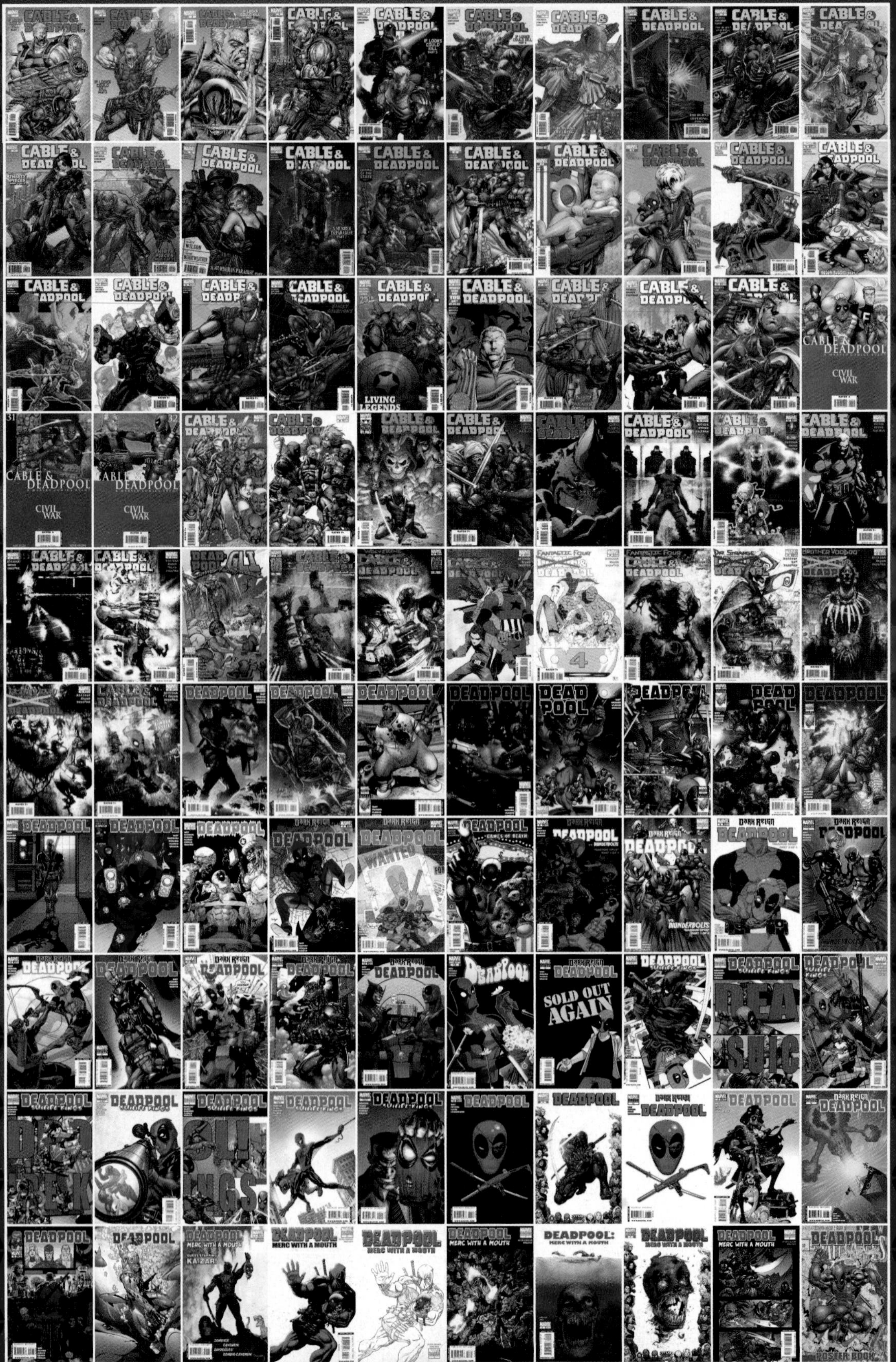
CABLE & DEADPOOL
CIVIL WAR
LIVING LEGENDS
SOLD OUT AGAIN
DEADPOOL
MERC WITH A MOUTH
ROSTER BOOK

DEADPOOL 900
Cover Gallery 201-900

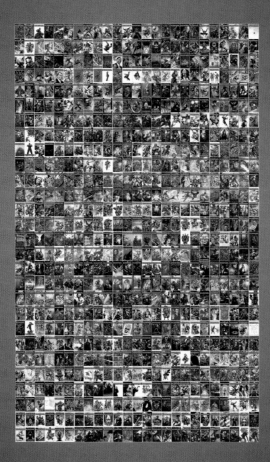

Design: Spring Hoteling • Production: Ryan Devall • Special Thanks to Jeph York

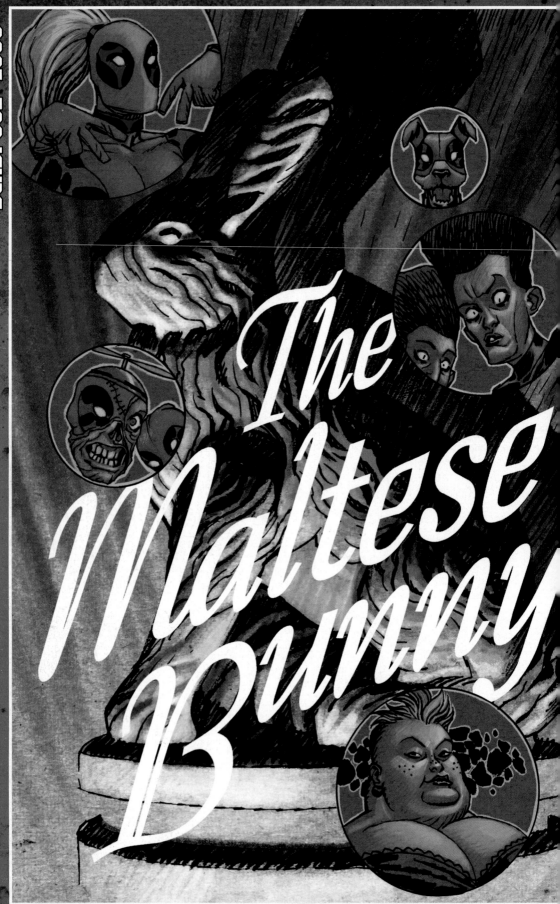

The Maltese Bunny

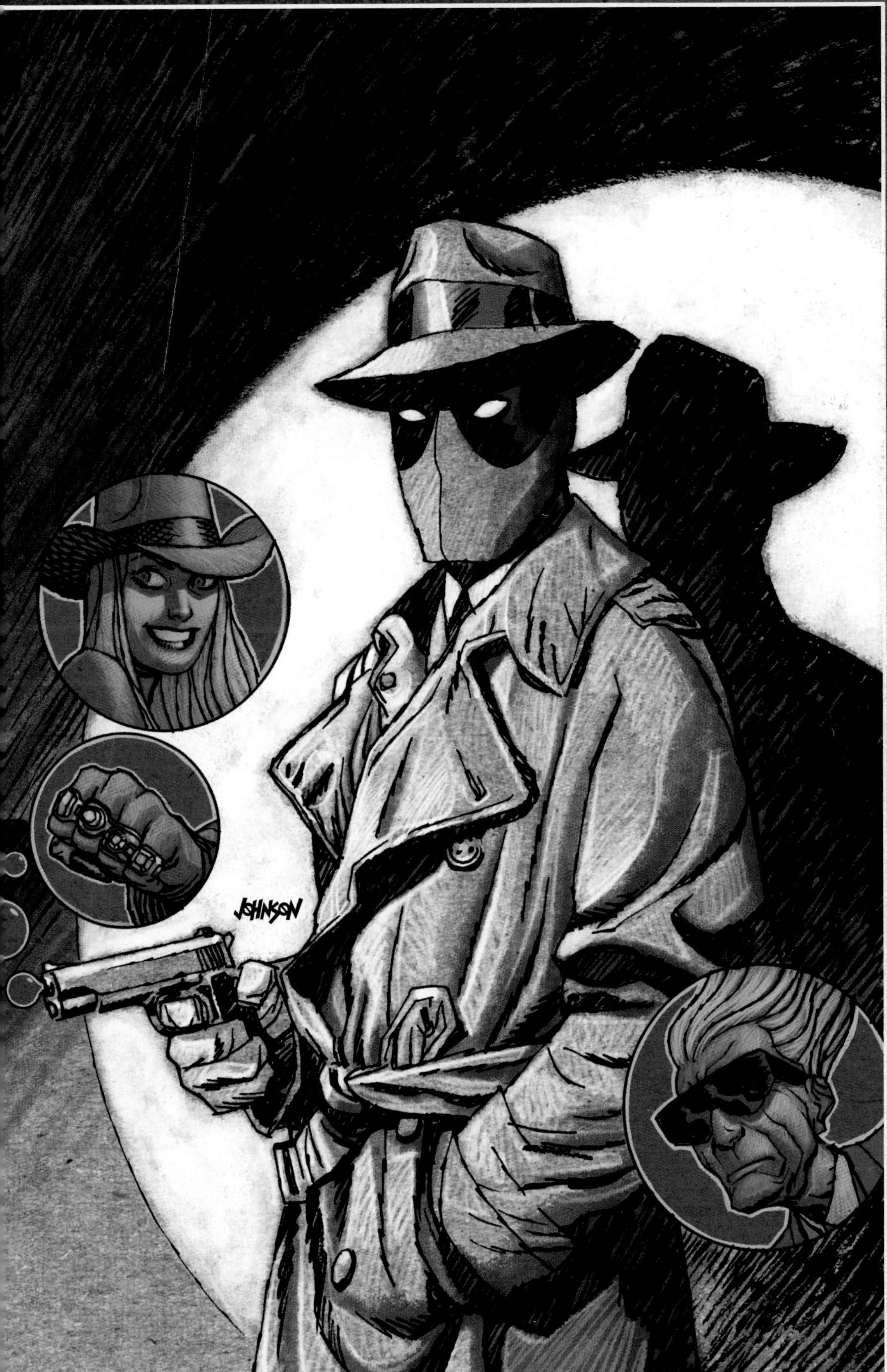
JOHNSON

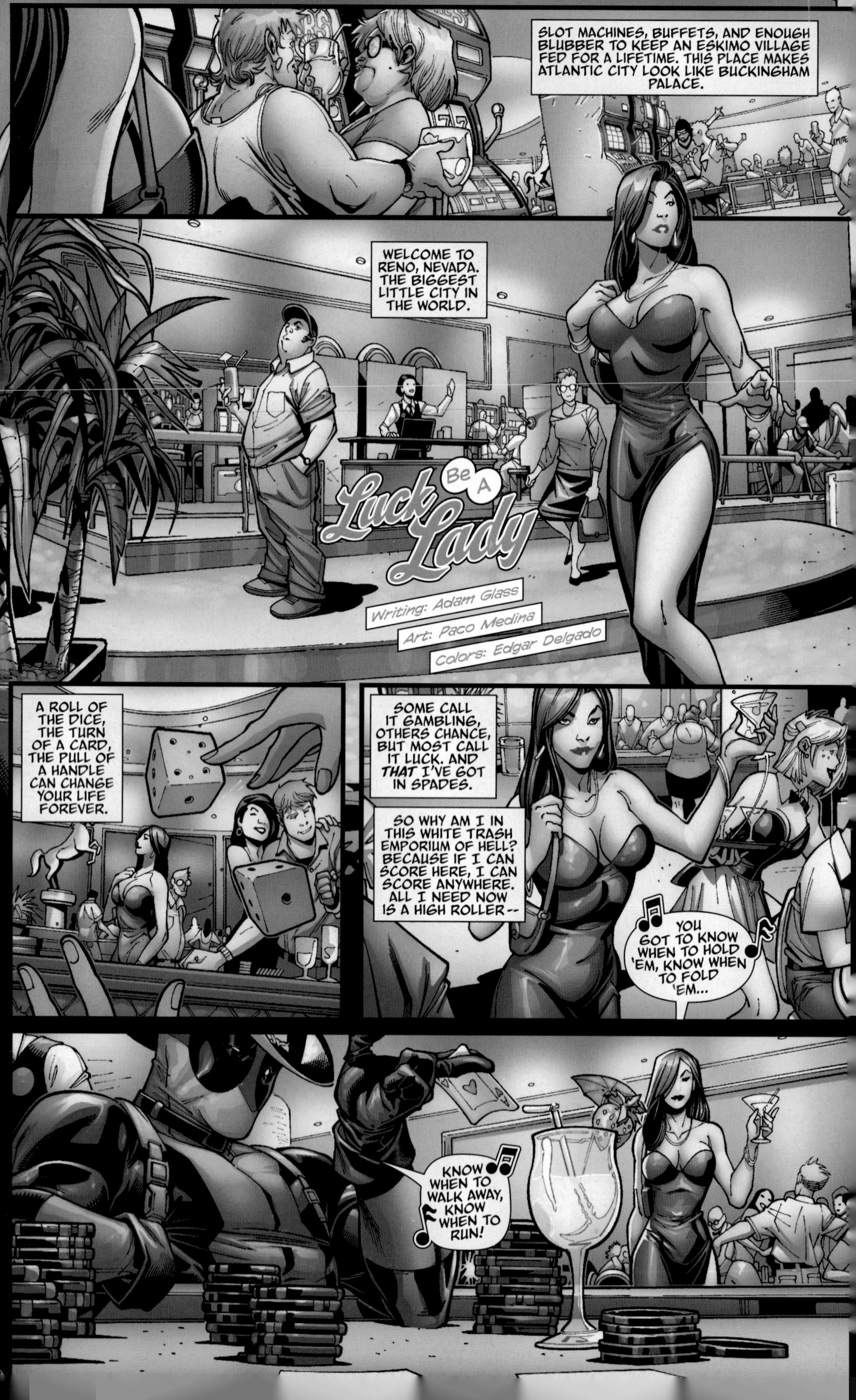
SLOT MACHINES, BUFFETS, AND ENOUGH BLUBBER TO KEEP AN ESKIMO VILLAGE FED FOR A LIFETIME. THIS PLACE MAKES ATLANTIC CITY LOOK LIKE BUCKINGHAM PALACE.
WELCOME TO RENO, NEVADA. THE BIGGEST LITTLE CITY IN THE WORLD.
Luck Be A Lady
Writing: Adam Glass
Art: Paco Medina
Colors: Edgar Delgado
A ROLL OF THE DICE, THE TURN OF A CARD, THE PULL OF A HANDLE CAN CHANGE YOUR LIFE FOREVER.
SOME CALL IT GAMBLING, OTHERS CHANCE, BUT MOST CALL IT LUCK. AND *THAT* I'VE GOT IN SPADES.
SO WHY AM I IN THIS WHITE TRASH EMPORIUM OF HELL? BECAUSE IF I CAN SCORE HERE, I CAN SCORE ANYWHERE. ALL I NEED NOW IS A HIGH ROLLER--
YOU GOT TO KNOW WHEN TO HOLD 'EM, KNOW WHEN TO FOLD 'EM...
KNOW WHEN TO WALK AWAY, KNOW WHEN TO RUN!

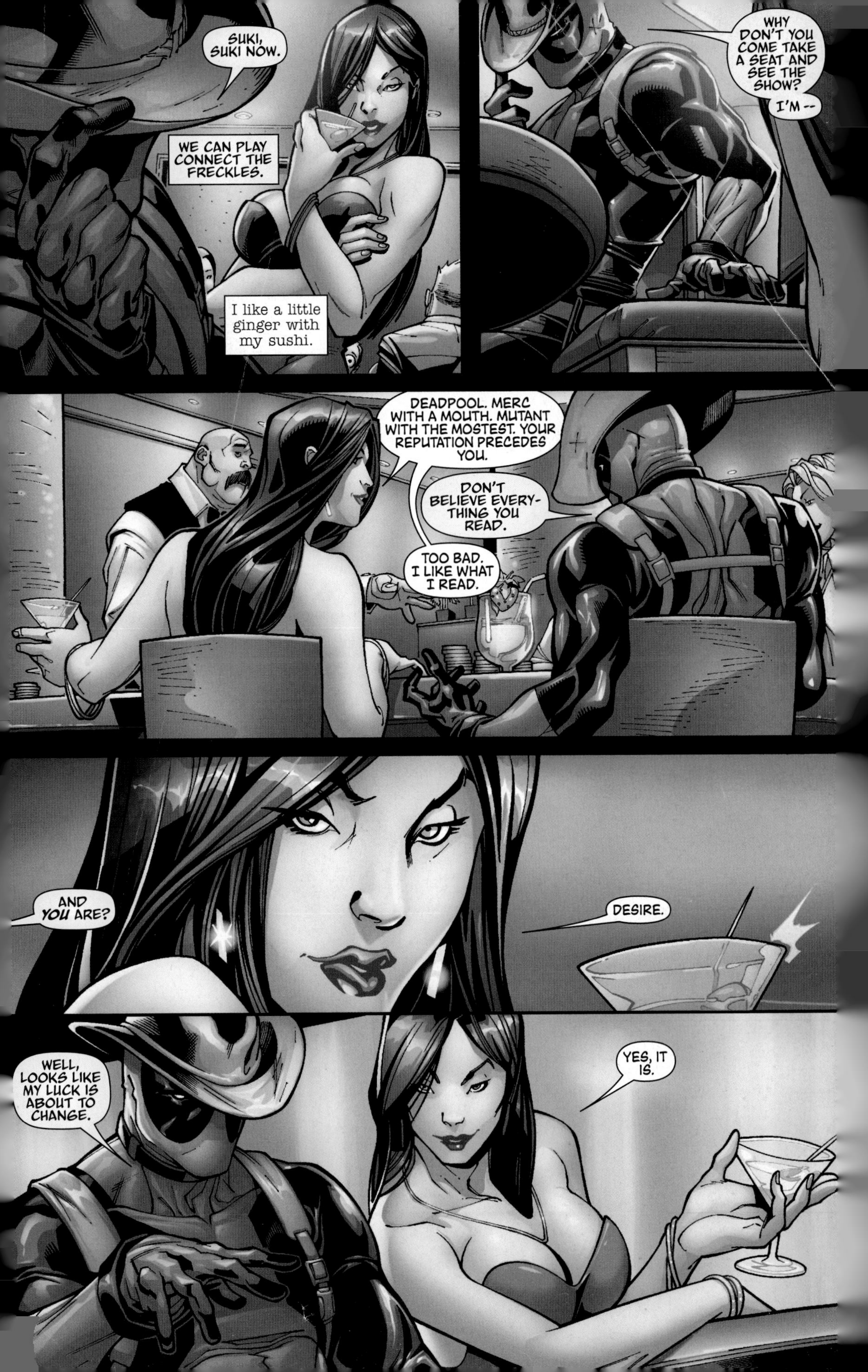
SUKI, SUKI NOW.
WE CAN PLAY CONNECT THE FRECKLES.
I like a little ginger with my sushi.
WHY DON'T YOU COME TAKE A SEAT AND SEE THE SHOW?
I'M --
DEADPOOL. MERC WITH A MOUTH. MUTANT WITH THE MOSTEST. YOUR REPUTATION PRECEDES YOU.
DON'T BELIEVE EVERY-THING YOU READ.
TOO BAD. I LIKE WHAT I READ.
AND YOU ARE?
DESIRE.
WELL, LOOKS LIKE MY LUCK IS ABOUT TO CHANGE.
YES, IT IS.

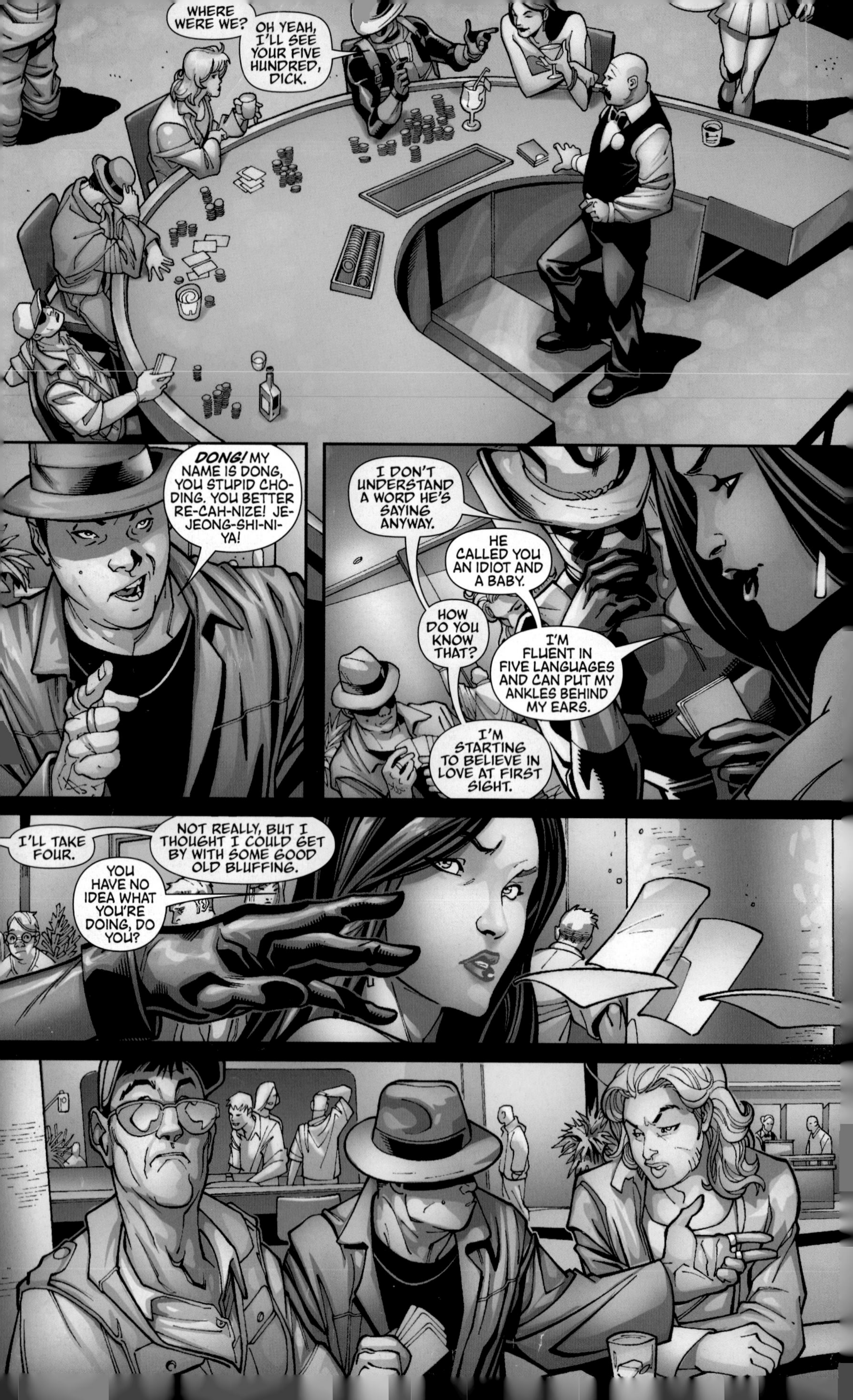
WHERE WERE WE?
OH YEAH, I'LL SEE YOUR FIVE HUNDRED, DICK.
DONG! MY NAME IS DONG, YOU STUPID CHO-DING. YOU BETTER RE-CAH-NIZE! JE-JEONG-SHI-NI-YA!
I DON'T UNDERSTAND A WORD HE'S SAYING ANYWAY.
HE CALLED YOU AN IDIOT AND A BABY.
HOW DO YOU KNOW THAT?
I'M FLUENT IN FIVE LANGUAGES AND CAN PUT MY ANKLES BEHIND MY EARS.
I'M STARTING TO BELIEVE IN LOVE AT FIRST SIGHT.
I'LL TAKE FOUR.
YOU HAVE NO IDEA WHAT YOU'RE DOING, DO YOU?
NOT REALLY, BUT I THOUGHT I COULD GET BY WITH SOME GOOD OLD BLUFFING.

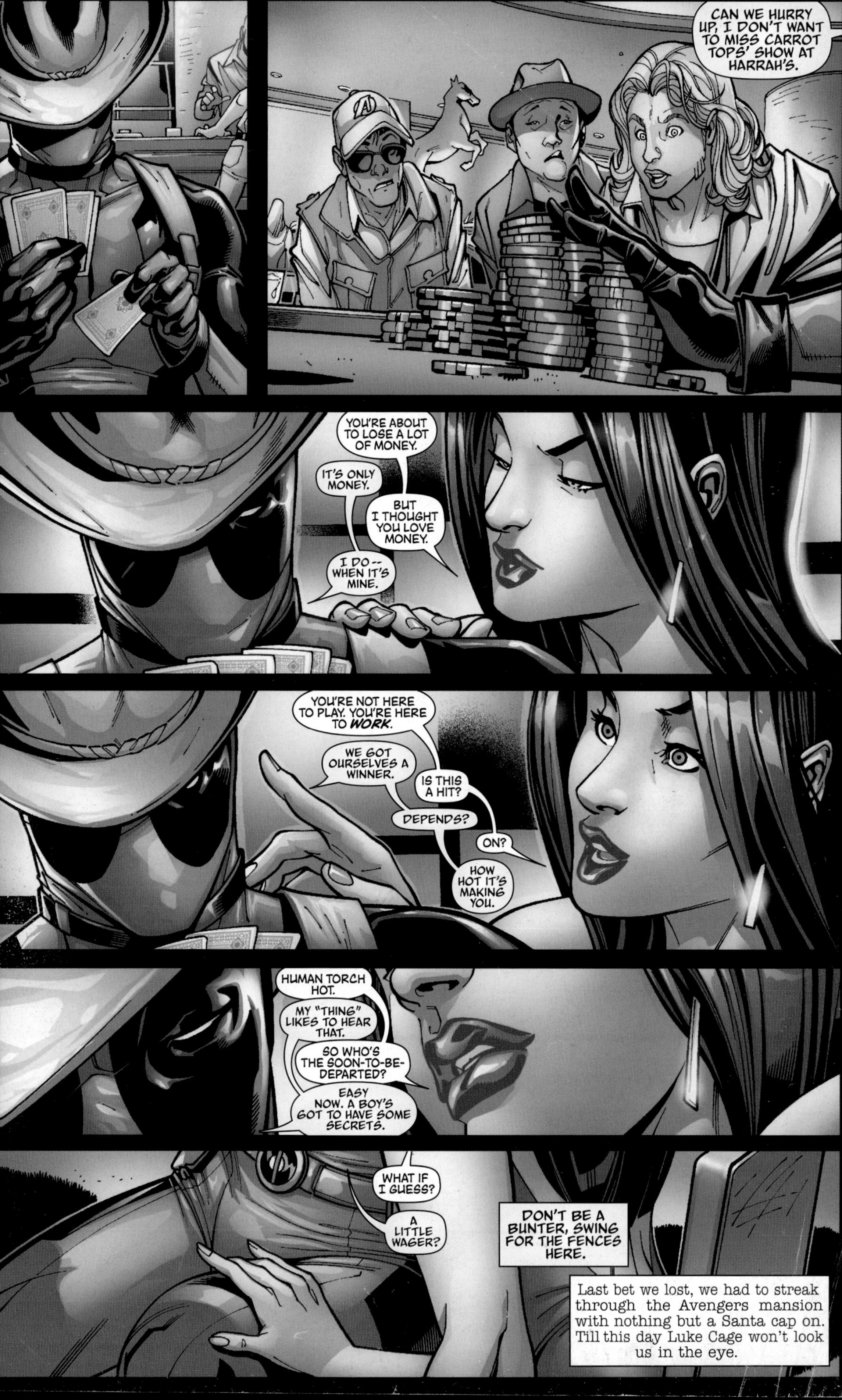

CAN WE HURRY UP, I DON'T WANT TO MISS CARROT TOPS' SHOW AT HARRAH'S.
YOU'RE ABOUT TO LOSE A LOT OF MONEY.
IT'S ONLY MONEY.
BUT I THOUGHT YOU LOVE MONEY.
I DO-- WHEN IT'S MINE.
YOU'RE NOT HERE TO PLAY. YOU'RE HERE TO WORK.
WE GOT OURSELVES A WINNER.
IS THIS A HIT?
DEPENDS?
ON?
HOW HOT IT'S MAKING YOU.
HUMAN TORCH HOT.
MY "THING" LIKES TO HEAR THAT.
SO WHO'S THE SOON-TO-BE-DEPARTED?
EASY NOW. A BOY'S GOT TO HAVE SOME SECRETS.
WHAT IF I GUESS?
A LITTLE WAGER?
DON'T BE A BUNTER, SWING FOR THE FENCES HERE.
Last bet we lost, we had to streak through the Avengers mansion with nothing but a Santa cap on. Till this day Luke Cage won't look us in the eye.

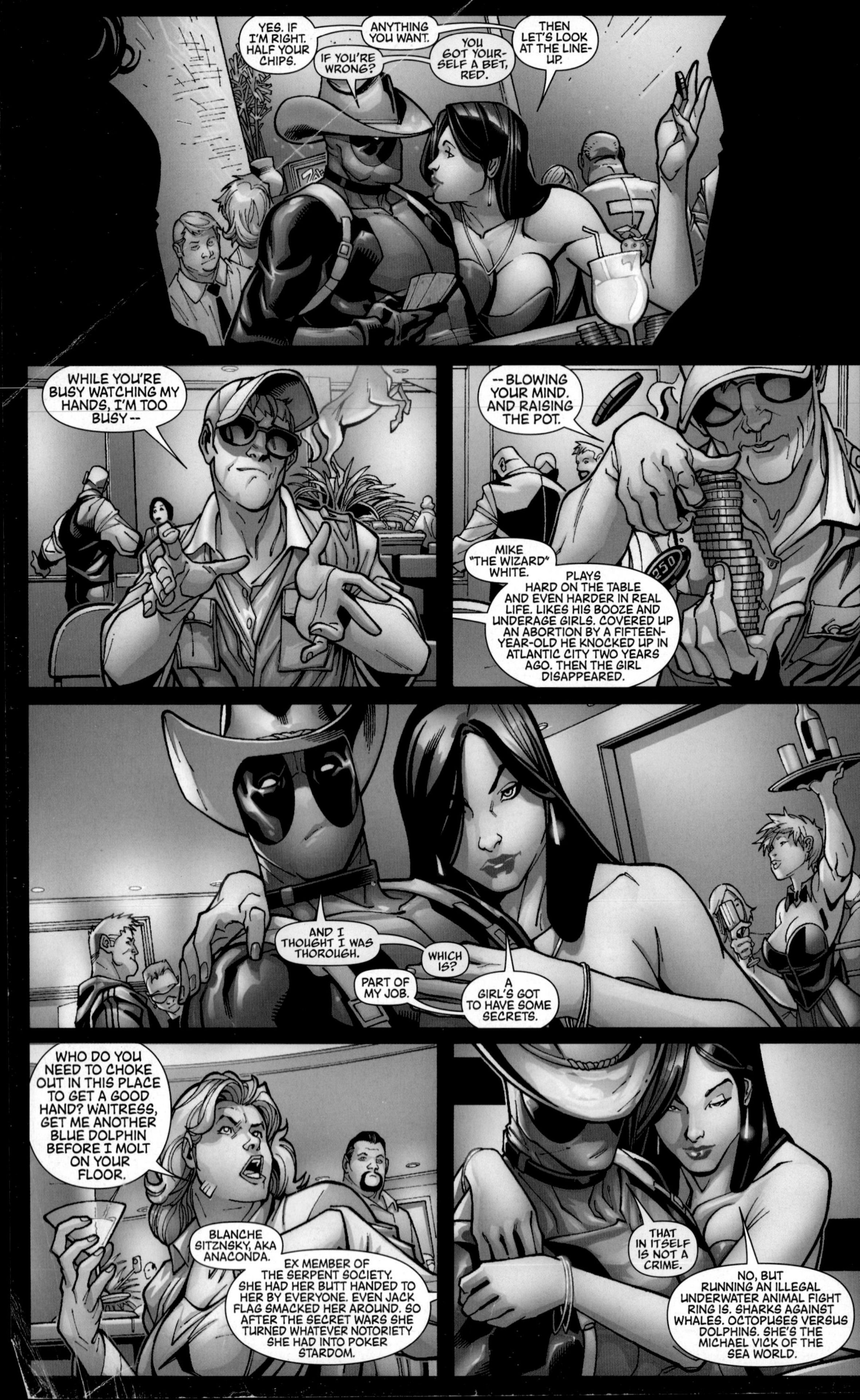
YES. IF I'M RIGHT. HALF YOUR CHIPS.
ANYTHING YOU WANT.
IF YOU'RE WRONG?
YOU GOT YOURSELF A BET, RED.
THEN LET'S LOOK AT THE LINE-UP.
WHILE YOU'RE BUSY WATCHING MY HANDS, I'M TOO BUSY --
-- BLOWING YOUR MIND. AND RAISING THE POT.
MIKE "THE WIZARD" WHITE.
PLAYS HARD ON THE TABLE AND EVEN HARDER IN REAL LIFE. LIKES HIS BOOZE AND UNDERAGE GIRLS. COVERED UP AN ABORTION BY A FIFTEEN-YEAR-OLD HE KNOCKED UP IN ATLANTIC CITY TWO YEARS AGO. THEN THE GIRL DISAPPEARED.
AND I THOUGHT I WAS THOROUGH.
WHICH IS?
PART OF MY JOB.
A GIRL'S GOT TO HAVE SOME SECRETS.
WHO DO YOU NEED TO CHOKE OUT IN THIS PLACE TO GET A GOOD HAND? WAITRESS, GET ME ANOTHER BLUE DOLPHIN BEFORE I MOLT ON YOUR FLOOR.
BLANCHE SITZNSKY, AKA ANACONDA.
EX MEMBER OF THE SERPENT SOCIETY. SHE HAD HER BUTT HANDED TO HER BY EVERYONE. EVEN JACK FLAG SMACKED HER AROUND. SO AFTER THE SECRET WARS SHE TURNED WHATEVER NOTORIETY SHE HAD INTO POKER STARDOM.
THAT IN ITSELF IS NOT A CRIME.
NO, BUT RUNNING AN ILLEGAL UNDERWATER ANIMAL FIGHT RING IS. SHARKS AGAINST WHALES. OCTOPUSES VERSUS DOLPHINS. SHE'S THE MICHAEL VICK OF THE SEA WORLD.

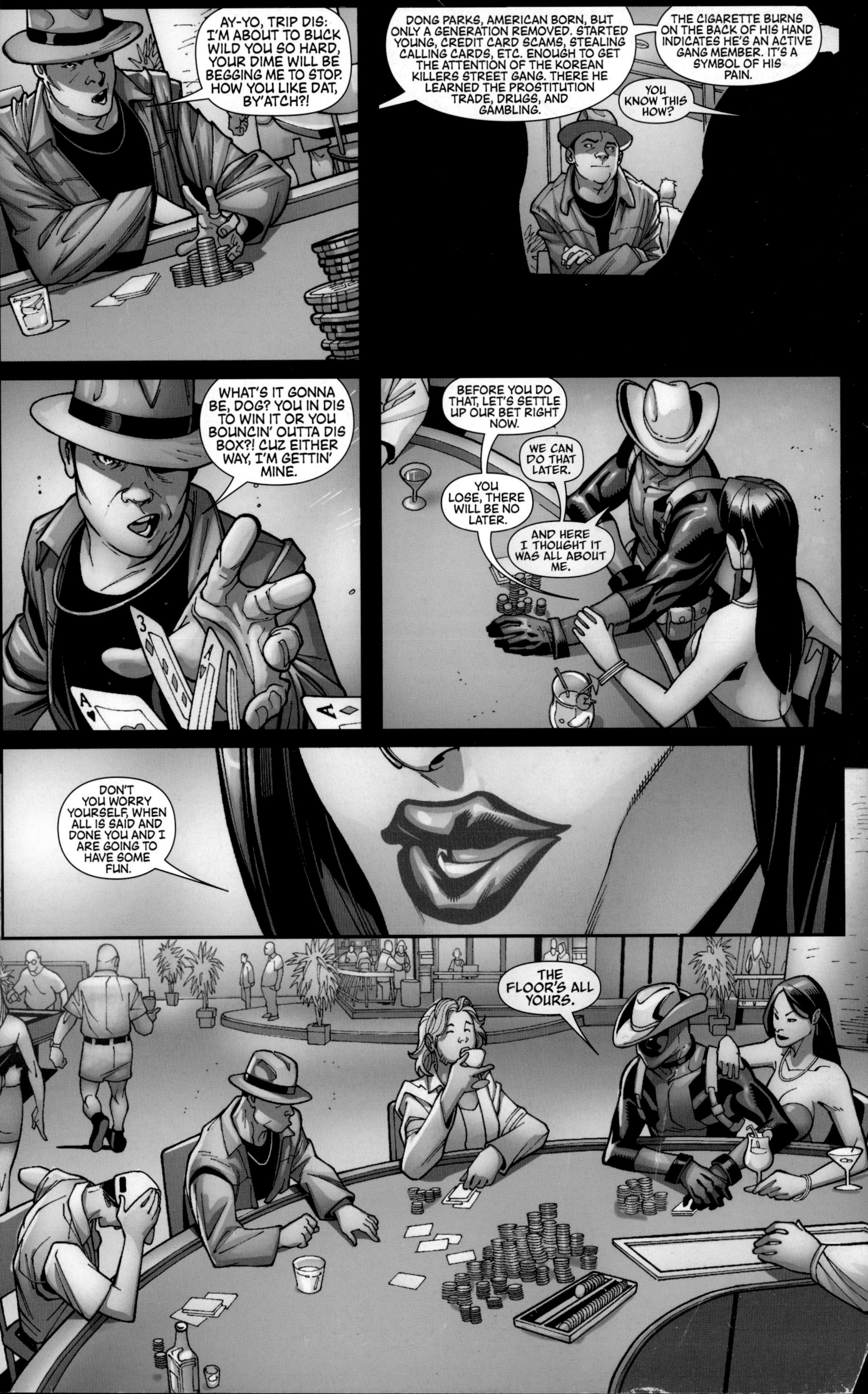
AY-YO, TRIP DIS: I'M ABOUT TO BUCK WILD YOU SO HARD, YOUR DIME WILL BE BEGGING ME TO STOP. HOW YOU LIKE DAT, BY'ATCH?!
DONG PARKS, AMERICAN BORN, BUT ONLY A GENERATION REMOVED. STARTED YOUNG, CREDIT CARD SCAMS, STEALING CALLING CARDS, ETC. ENOUGH TO GET THE ATTENTION OF THE KOREAN KILLERS STREET GANG. THERE HE LEARNED THE PROSTITUTION TRADE, DRUGS, AND GAMBLING.
THE CIGARETTE BURNS ON THE BACK OF HIS HAND INDICATES HE'S AN ACTIVE GANG MEMBER. IT'S A SYMBOL OF HIS PAIN.
YOU KNOW THIS HOW?
WHAT'S IT GONNA BE, DOG? YOU IN DIS TO WIN IT OR YOU BOUNCIN' OUTTA DIS BOX?! CUZ EITHER WAY, I'M GETTIN' MINE.
BEFORE YOU DO THAT, LET'S SETTLE UP OUR BET RIGHT NOW.
WE CAN DO THAT LATER.
YOU LOSE, THERE WILL BE NO LATER.
AND HERE I THOUGHT IT WAS ALL ABOUT ME.
DON'T YOU WORRY YOURSELF, WHEN ALL IS SAID AND DONE YOU AND I ARE GOING TO HAVE SOME FUN.
THE FLOOR'S ALL YOURS.

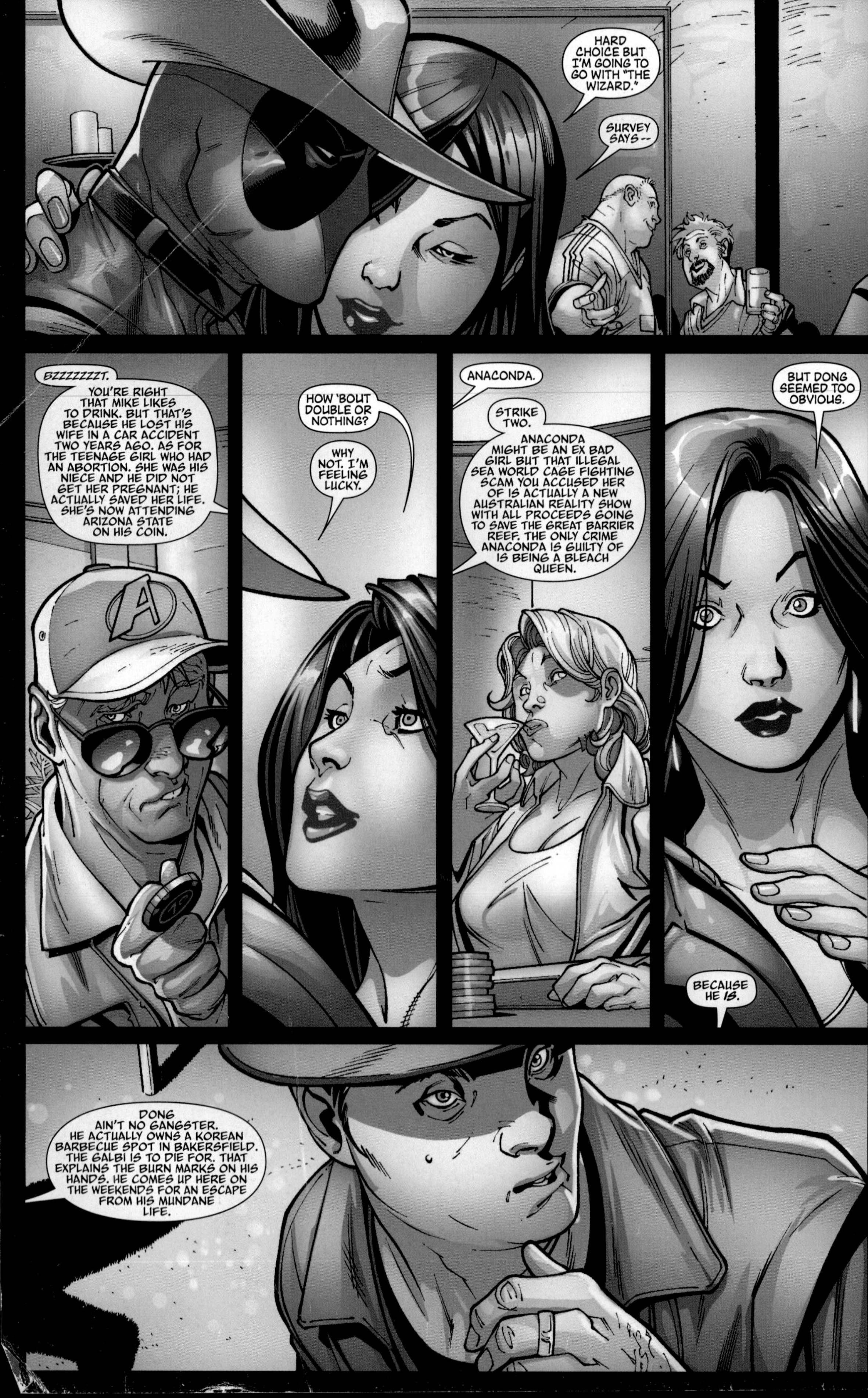

HARD CHOICE BUT I'M GOING TO GO WITH "THE WIZARD."
SURVEY SAYS --
BZZZZZZZT.
YOU'RE RIGHT THAT MIKE LIKES TO DRINK. BUT THAT'S BECAUSE HE LOST HIS WIFE IN A CAR ACCIDENT TWO YEARS AGO. AS FOR THE TEENAGE GIRL WHO HAD AN ABORTION. SHE WAS HIS NIECE AND HE DID NOT GET HER PREGNANT; HE ACTUALLY SAVED HER LIFE. SHE'S NOW ATTENDING ARIZONA STATE ON HIS COIN.
HOW 'BOUT DOUBLE OR NOTHING?
WHY NOT. I'M FEELING LUCKY.
ANACONDA.
STRIKE TWO.
ANACONDA MIGHT BE AN EX BAD GIRL BUT THAT ILLEGAL SEA WORLD CAGE FIGHTING SCAM YOU ACCUSED HER OF IS ACTUALLY A NEW AUSTRALIAN REALITY SHOW WITH ALL PROCEEDS GOING TO SAVE THE GREAT BARRIER REEF. THE ONLY CRIME ANACONDA IS GUILTY OF IS BEING A BLEACH QUEEN.
BUT DONG SEEMED TOO OBVIOUS.
BECAUSE HE IS.
DONG AIN'T NO GANGSTER. HE ACTUALLY OWNS A KOREAN BARBECUE SPOT IN BAKERSFIELD. THE GALBI IS TO DIE FOR. THAT EXPLAINS THE BURN MARKS ON HIS HANDS. HE COMES UP HERE ON THE WEEKENDS FOR AN ESCAPE FROM HIS MUNDANE LIFE.

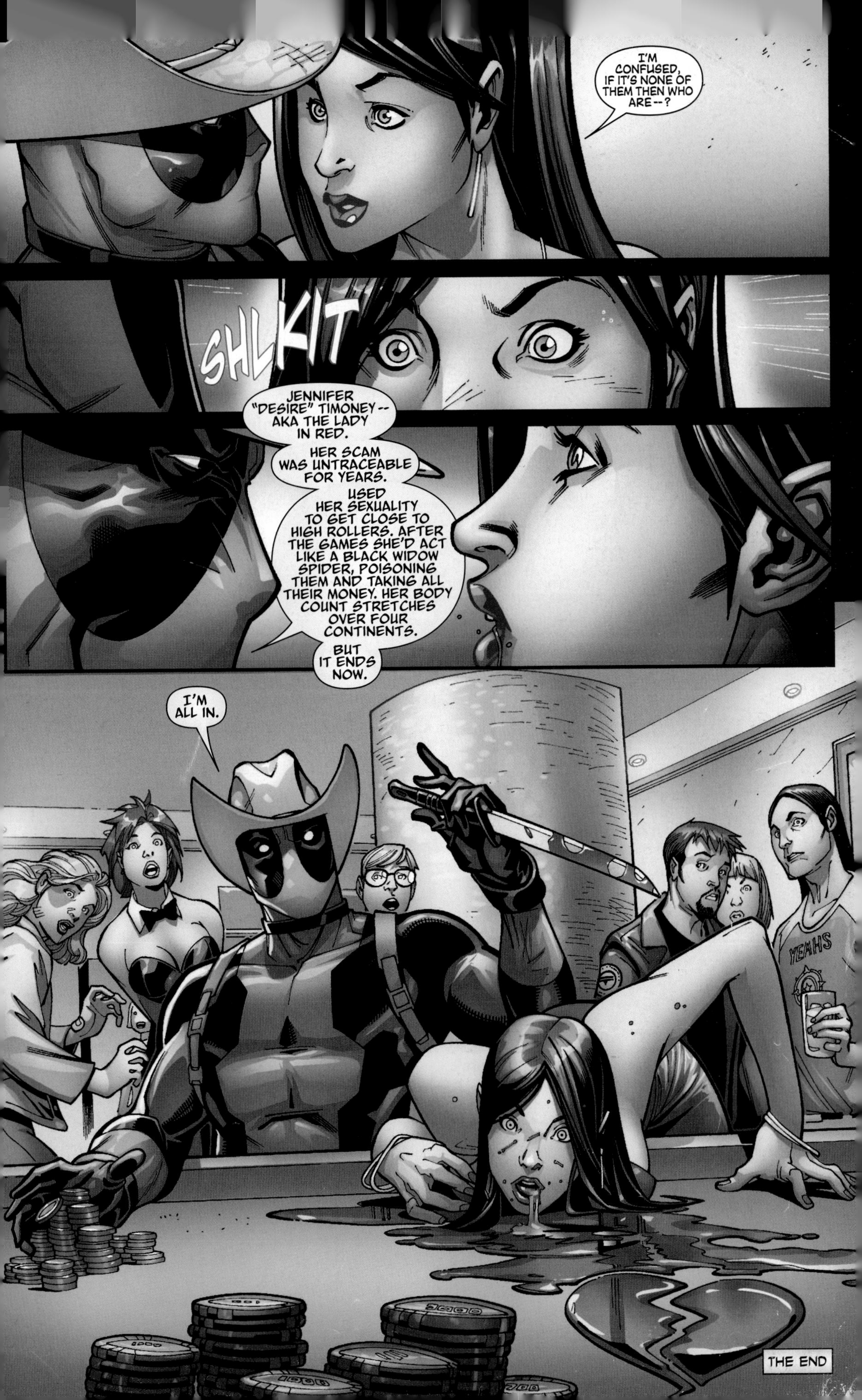

I'M CONFUSED, IF IT'S NONE OF THEM THEN WHO ARE--?
SHLKIT
JENNIFER "DESIRE" TIMONEY-- AKA THE LADY IN RED.
HER SCAM WAS UNTRACEABLE FOR YEARS.
USED HER SEXUALITY TO GET CLOSE TO HIGH ROLLERS. AFTER THE GAMES SHE'D ACT LIKE A BLACK WIDOW SPIDER, POISONING THEM AND TAKING ALL THEIR MONEY. HER BODY COUNT STRETCHES OVER FOUR CONTINENTS.
BUT IT ENDS NOW.
I'M ALL IN.
YEAHS
THE END

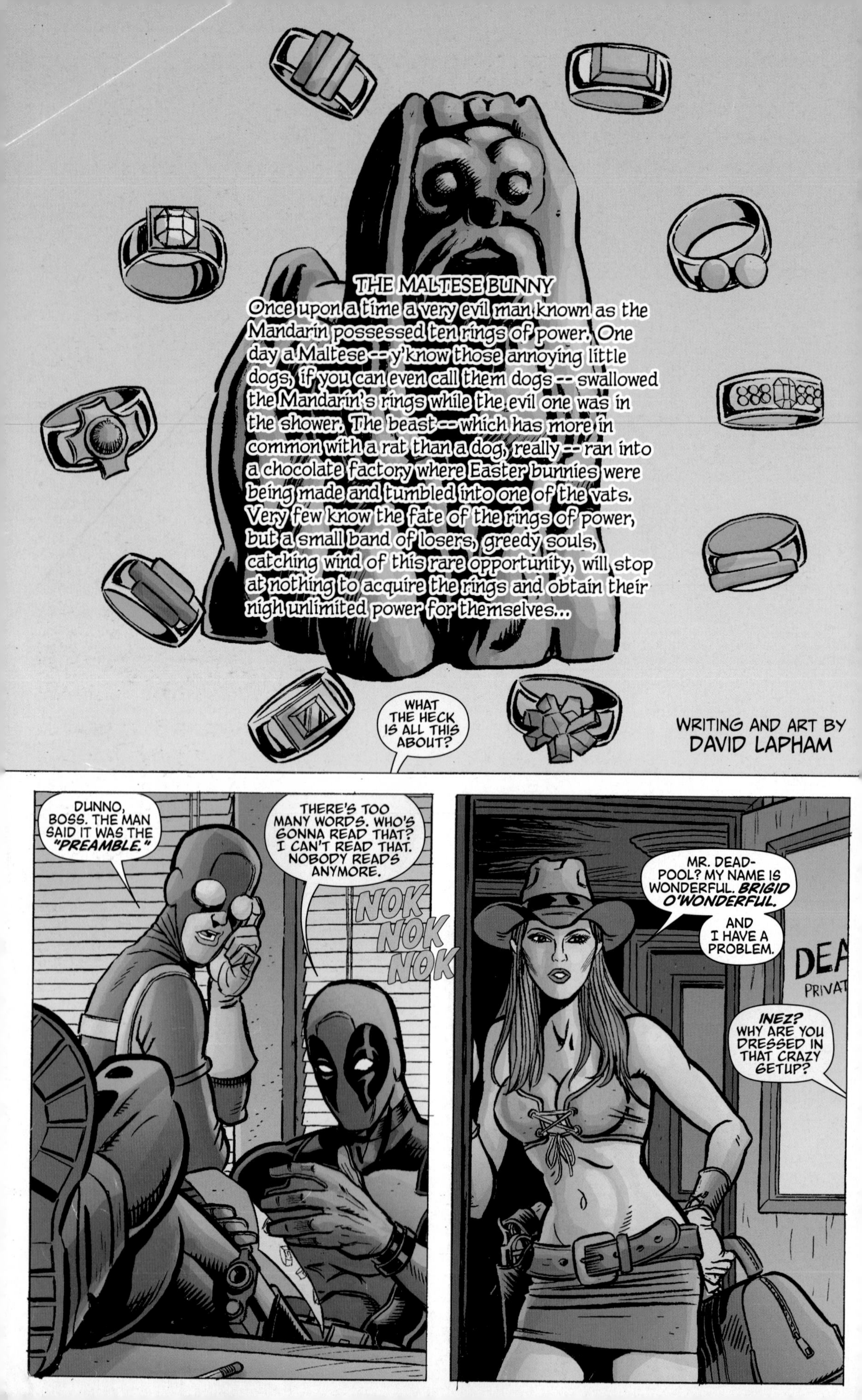
THE MALTESE BUNNY
Once upon a time a very evil man known as the Mandarin possessed ten rings of power. One day a Maltese -- y'know those annoying little dogs, if you can even call them dogs -- swallowed the Mandarin's rings while the evil one was in the shower. The beast -- which has more in common with a rat than a dog, really -- ran into a chocolate factory where Easter bunnies were being made and tumbled into one of the vats. Very few know the fate of the rings of power, but a small band of losers, greedy souls, catching wind of this rare opportunity, will stop at nothing to acquire the rings and obtain their nigh unlimited power for themselves...
WHAT THE HECK IS ALL THIS ABOUT?
WRITING AND ART BY DAVID LAPHAM
DUNNO, BOSS. THE MAN SAID IT WAS THE "PREAMBLE."
THERE'S TOO MANY WORDS. WHO'S GONNA READ THAT? I CAN'T READ THAT. NOBODY READS ANYMORE.
NOK NOK NOK
MR. DEAD-POOL? MY NAME IS WONDERFUL. BRIGID O'WONDERFUL.
AND I HAVE A PROBLEM.
DEA
PRIVAT
INEZ? WHY ARE YOU DRESSED IN THAT CRAZY GETUP?

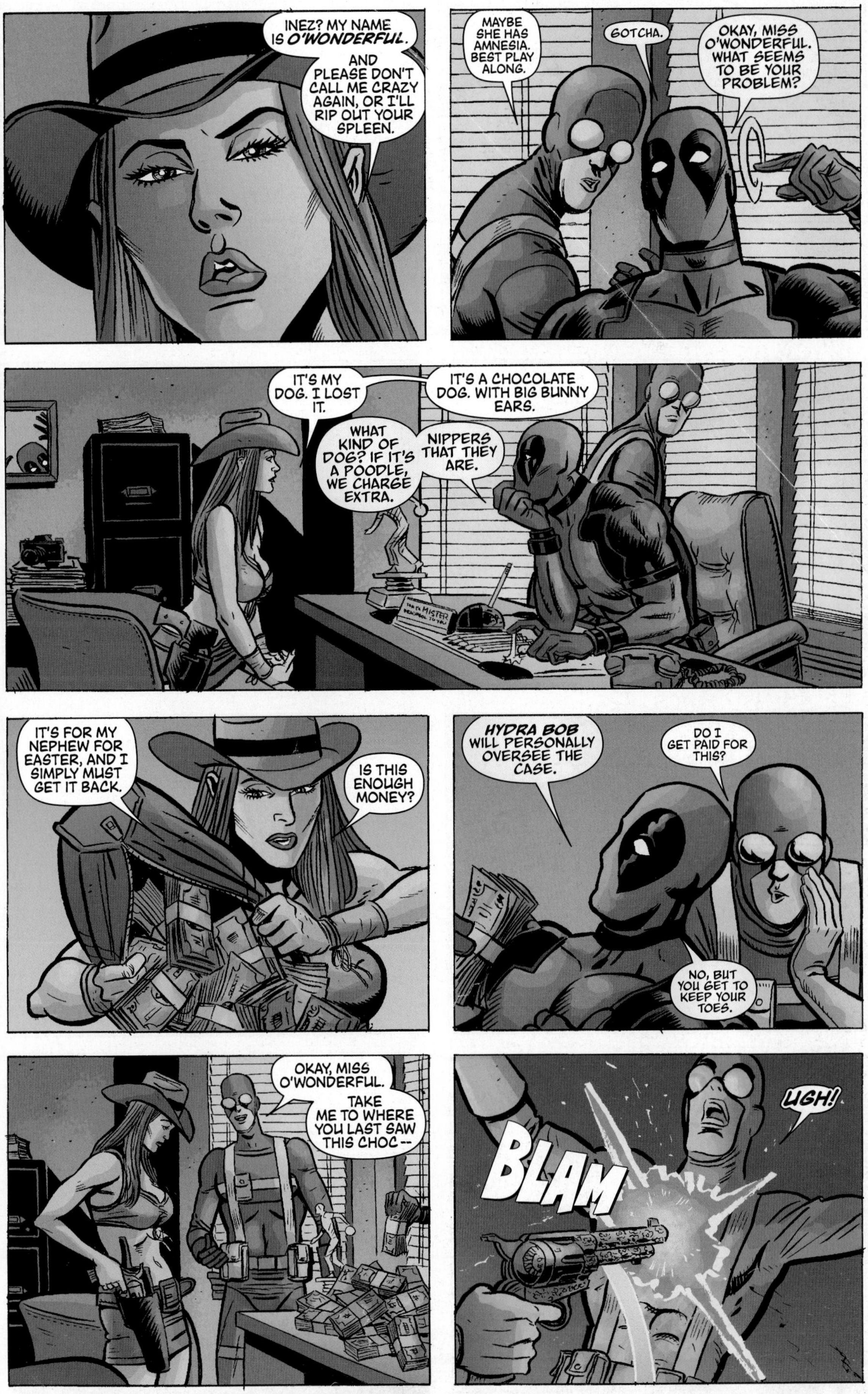
INEZ? MY NAME IS O'WONDERFUL.
AND PLEASE DON'T CALL ME CRAZY AGAIN, OR I'LL RIP OUT YOUR SPLEEN.
MAYBE SHE HAS AMNESIA. BEST PLAY ALONG.
GOTCHA.
OKAY, MISS O'WONDERFUL. WHAT SEEMS TO BE YOUR PROBLEM?
IT'S MY DOG. I LOST IT.
IT'S A CHOCOLATE DOG. WITH BIG BUNNY EARS.
WHAT KIND OF DOG? IF IT'S A POODLE, WE CHARGE EXTRA.
NIPPERS THAT THEY ARE.
IT'S FOR MY NEPHEW FOR EASTER, AND I SIMPLY MUST GET IT BACK.
IS THIS ENOUGH MONEY?
HYDRA BOB WILL PERSONALLY OVERSEE THE CASE.
DO I GET PAID FOR THIS?
NO, BUT YOU GET TO KEEP YOUR TOES.
OKAY, MISS O'WONDERFUL.
TAKE ME TO WHERE YOU LAST SAW THIS CHOC --
UGH!
BLAM

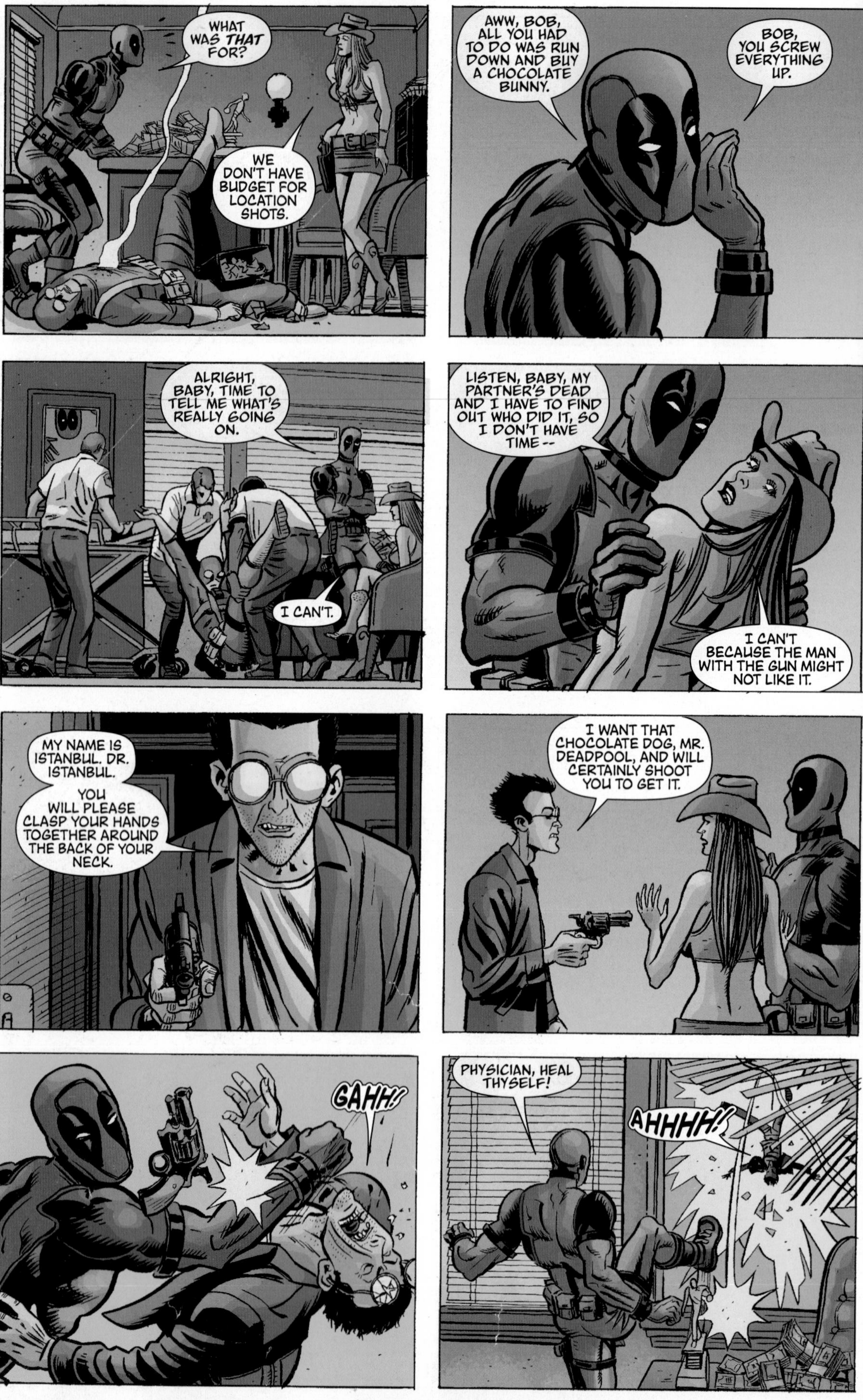
WHAT WAS THAT FOR?
WE DON'T HAVE BUDGET FOR LOCATION SHOTS.
AWW, BOB, ALL YOU HAD TO DO WAS RUN DOWN AND BUY A CHOCOLATE BUNNY.
BOB, YOU SCREW EVERYTHING UP.
ALRIGHT, BABY, TIME TO TELL ME WHAT'S REALLY GOING ON.
I CAN'T.
LISTEN, BABY, MY PARTNER'S DEAD AND I HAVE TO FIND OUT WHO DID IT, SO I DON'T HAVE TIME --
I CAN'T BECAUSE THE MAN WITH THE GUN MIGHT NOT LIKE IT.
MY NAME IS ISTANBUL. DR. ISTANBUL.
YOU WILL PLEASE CLASP YOUR HANDS TOGETHER AROUND THE BACK OF YOUR NECK.
I WANT THAT CHOCOLATE DOG, MR. DEADPOOL, AND WILL CERTAINLY SHOOT YOU TO GET IT.
GAHH!
PHYSICIAN, HEAL THYSELF!
AHHHH!

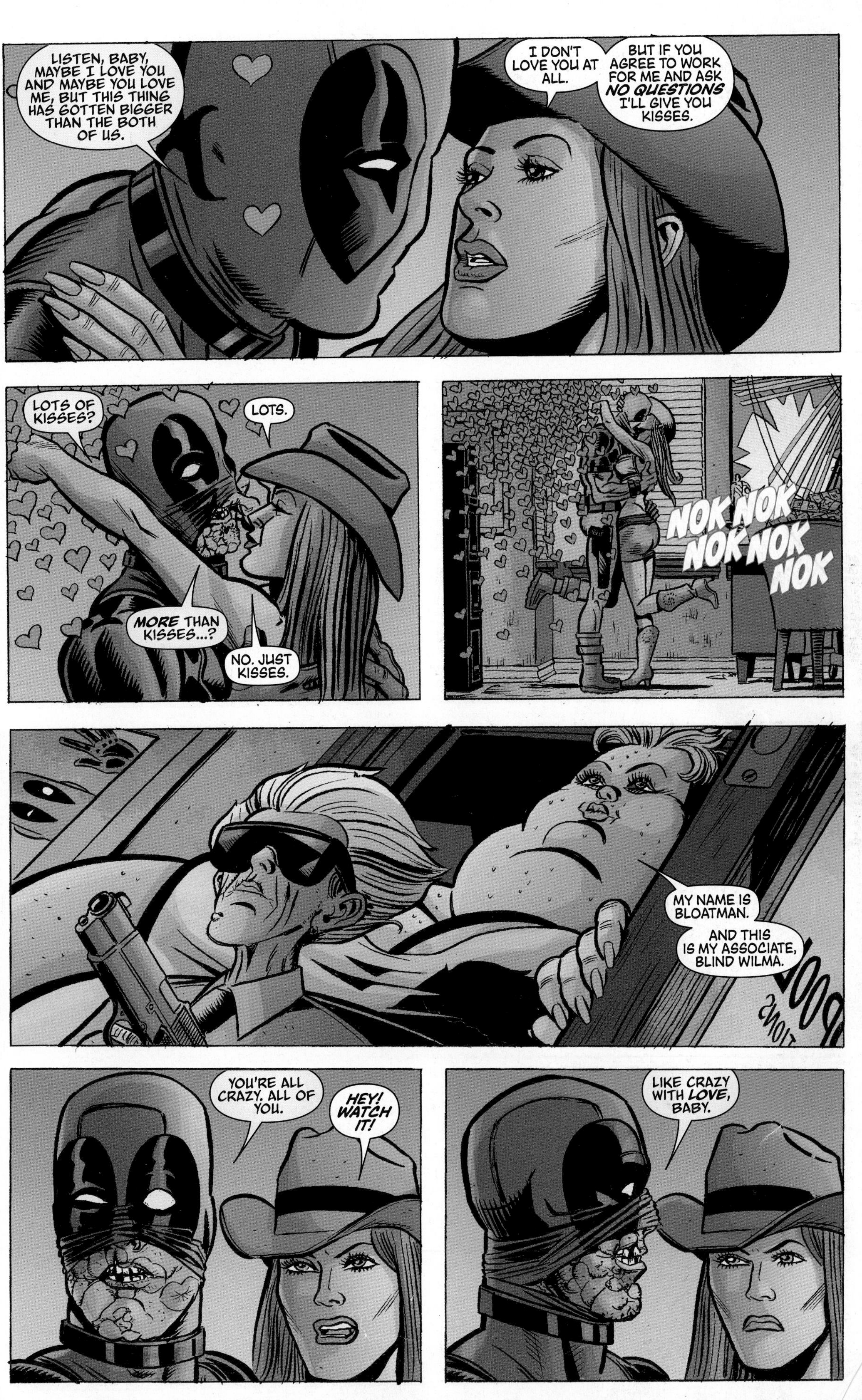
LISTEN, BABY, MAYBE I LOVE YOU AND MAYBE YOU LOVE ME, BUT THIS THING HAS GOTTEN BIGGER THAN THE BOTH OF US.
I DON'T LOVE YOU AT ALL.
BUT IF YOU AGREE TO WORK FOR ME AND ASK NO QUESTIONS I'LL GIVE YOU KISSES.
LOTS OF KISSES?
LOTS.
MORE THAN KISSES...?
NO. JUST KISSES.
NOK NOK NOK NOK NOK
MY NAME IS BLOATMAN.
AND THIS IS MY ASSOCIATE, BLIND WILMA.
YOU'RE ALL CRAZY. ALL OF YOU.
HEY! WATCH IT!
LIKE CRAZY WITH LOVE, BABY.

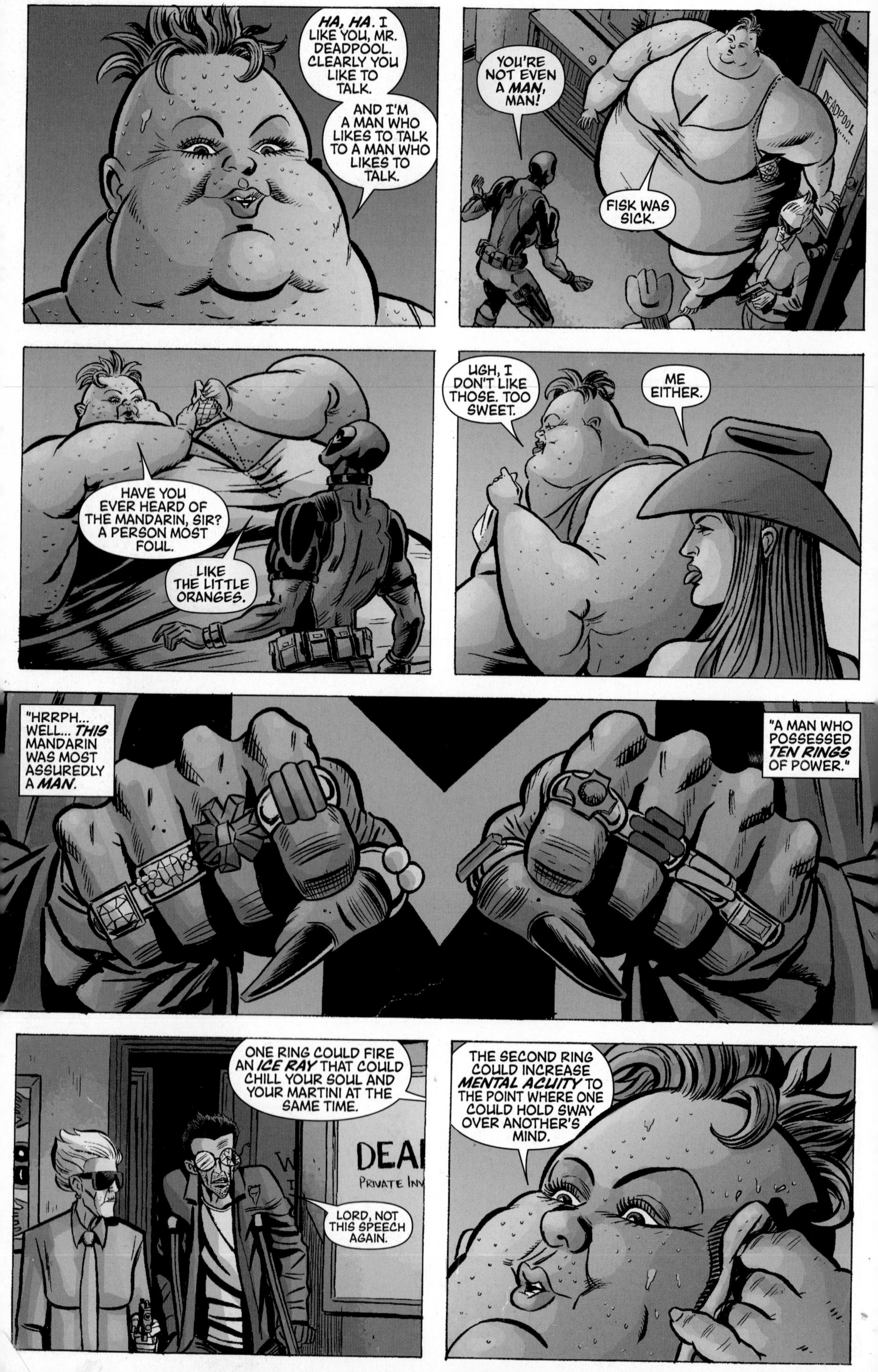
HA, HA. I LIKE YOU, MR. DEADPOOL. CLEARLY YOU LIKE TO TALK.
AND I'M A MAN WHO LIKES TO TALK TO A MAN WHO LIKES TO TALK.
YOU'RE NOT EVEN A MAN, MAN!
DEADPOOL
FISK WAS SICK.
HAVE YOU EVER HEARD OF THE MANDARIN, SIR? A PERSON MOST FOUL.
LIKE THE LITTLE ORANGES.
UGH, I DON'T LIKE THOSE. TOO SWEET.
ME EITHER.
"HRRPH... WELL... THIS MANDARIN WAS MOST ASSUREDLY A MAN.
"A MAN WHO POSSESSED TEN RINGS OF POWER."
ONE RING COULD FIRE AN ICE RAY THAT COULD CHILL YOUR SOUL AND YOUR MARTINI AT THE SAME TIME.
LORD, NOT THIS SPEECH AGAIN.
THE SECOND RING COULD INCREASE MENTAL ACUITY TO THE POINT WHERE ONE COULD HOLD SWAY OVER ANOTHER'S MIND.

YET A THIRD COULD PRODUCE ENOUGH *ELECTRICITY* TO POWER A SMALL CITY.

YOU *LOVE* ME...

STOP TOUCHING ME.

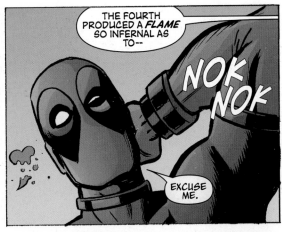

THE FOURTH PRODUCED A *FLAME* SO INFERNAL AS TO--

NOK NOK

EXCUSE ME.

BOB? YOU'RE NOT DEAD?

JUST A SCRATCH, BOSS, BUT LOOK WHAT SOME SEA CAPTAIN RANDOMLY DROPPED OFF FOR ME AT THE HOSPITAL.

IT'S THE DOG -- BUNNY -- THING!

LOOK, BOB. TRAGICALLY, I'M GOING TO HAVE TO PIN YOUR MURDER ON MY SOON-TO-BE FIANCÉ.

IT'S PROBABLY BEST IF YOU STAY DEAD...

AHHHHHHH!

...NINE. *DISINTEGRATION.* TRUE AND COMPLETE. I HAVE NEVER HEARD TELL OF RETURN FROM IT.

HEH, HEH... *HAH... HAGHHH...* EXCUSE ME. NOW THE FINAL RING --

STOP ALL THE JAB-JAB-JABBERING. I HAVE THE DOG!

DEADPOOL PRIVATE INVEST

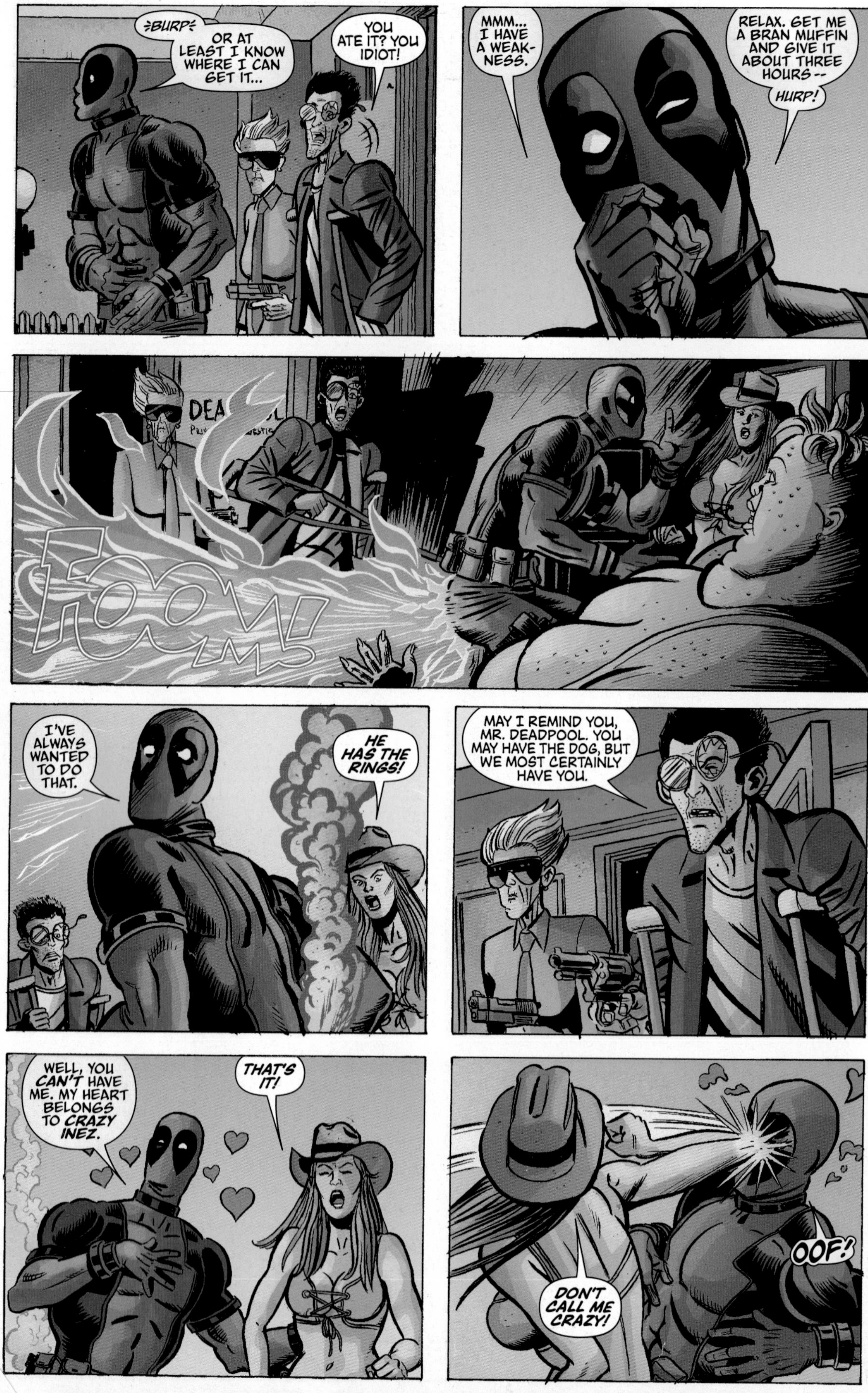

BURP
OR AT LEAST I KNOW WHERE I CAN GET IT...
YOU ATE IT? YOU IDIOT!
MMM... I HAVE A WEAKNESS.
RELAX. GET ME A BRAN MUFFIN AND GIVE IT ABOUT THREE HOURS --
HURP!
FOOOM!
I'VE ALWAYS WANTED TO DO THAT.
HE HAS THE RINGS!
MAY I REMIND YOU, MR. DEADPOOL. YOU MAY HAVE THE DOG, BUT WE MOST CERTAINLY HAVE YOU.
WELL, YOU CAN'T HAVE ME. MY HEART BELONGS TO CRAZY INEZ.
THAT'S IT!
OOF!
DON'T CALL ME CRAZY!

HE HAS THE RINGS?!
OF COURSE HE HAS THEM YOU IDIOT. YOU FOOL.
DID YOU THINK HE HAD HEMORRHOIDS!
LET'S GET HIM.
DEADPOOL
GIVE ME THOSE RINGS!
BRAAAAAAAT
AGH! DISINTEGRATION...
NOW THAT'S POWER.
HEY, BABY...
HAVE ANY WEDDING PLANS THIS WEEKEND?
YOU JUST MADE THE BIGGEST MISTAKE OF YOUR LIFE, PAL.
ARE YOU KIDDING?

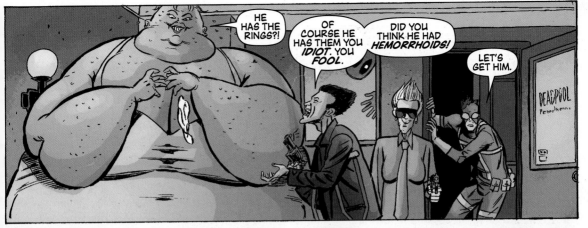

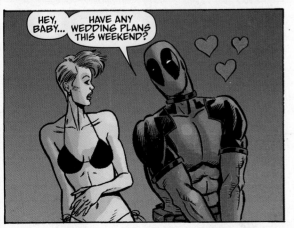

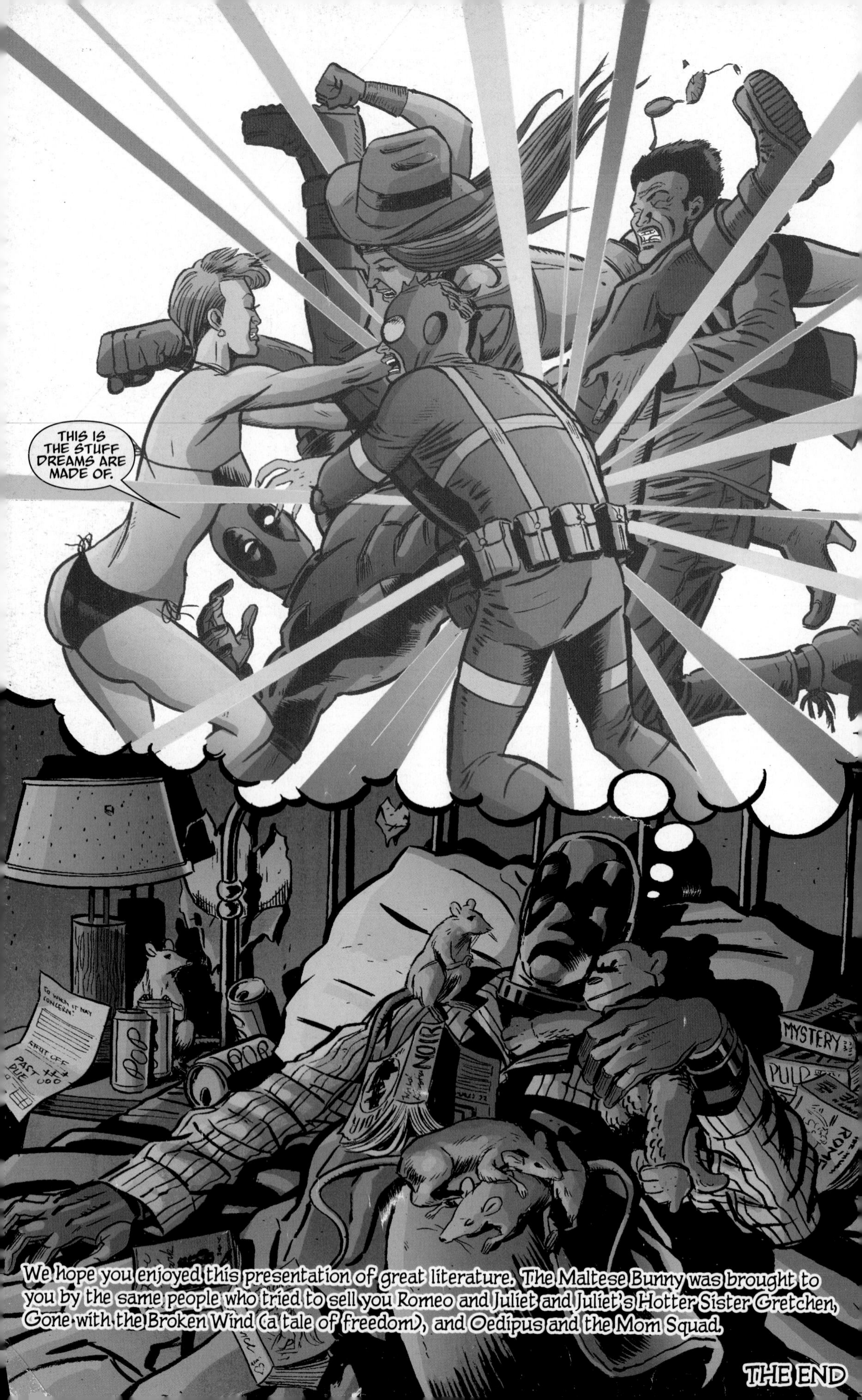
THIS IS THE STUFF DREAMS ARE MADE OF.
TO WHOM IT MAY CONCERN:
SHUT OFF
PAST DUE
POP
POP
NOIR
MYSTERY
PULP
We hope you enjoyed this presentation of great literature. The Maltese Bunny was brought to you by the same people who tried to sell you Romeo and Juliet and Juliet's Hotter Sister Gretchen, Gone with the Broken Wind (a tale of freedom), and Oedipus and the Mom Squad.
THE END

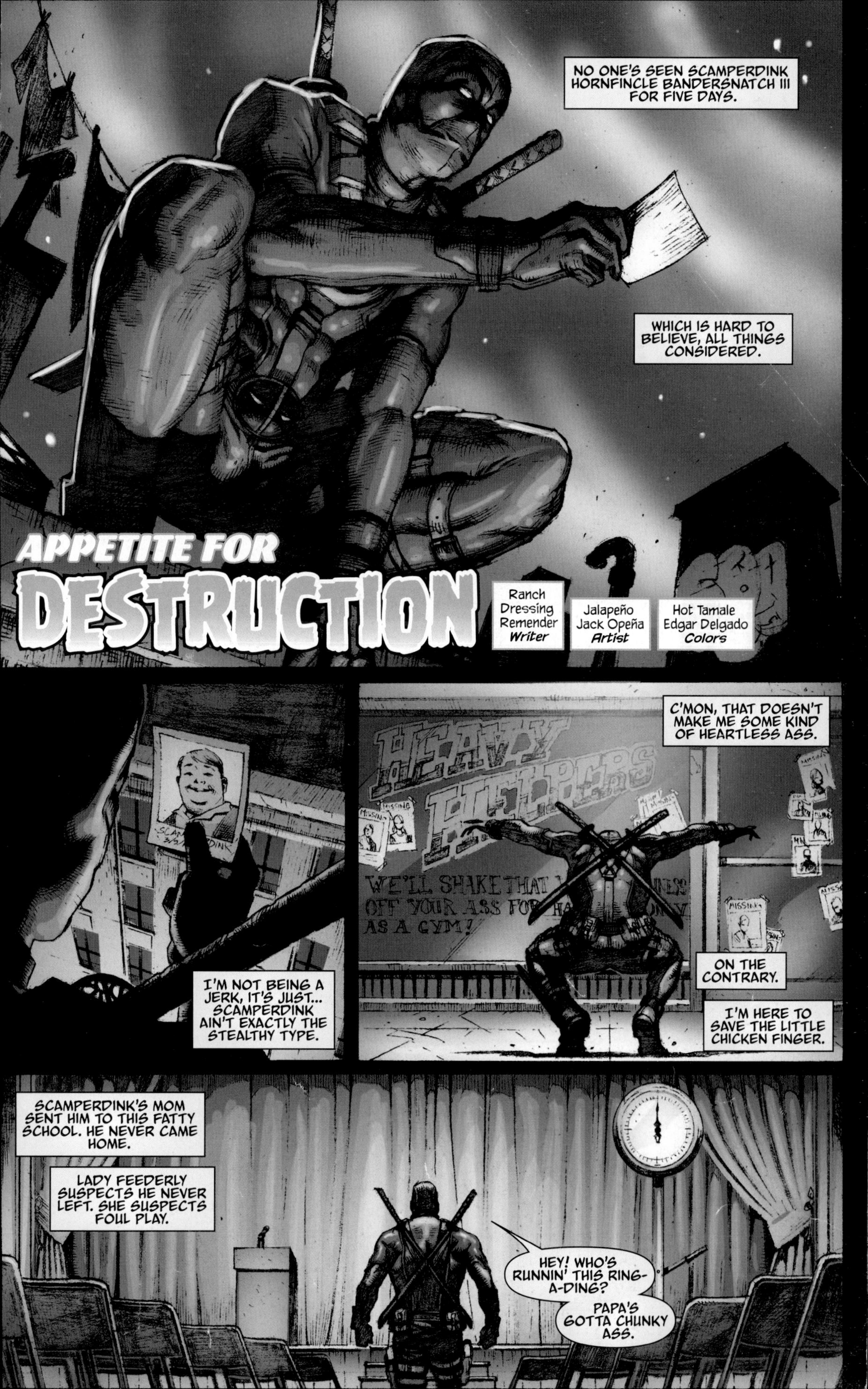
NO ONE'S SEEN SCAMPERDINK HORNFINCLE BANDERSNATCH III FOR FIVE DAYS.
WHICH IS HARD TO BELIEVE, ALL THINGS CONSIDERED.
APPETITE FOR DESTRUCTION
Ranch Dressing Remender Writer
Jalapeño Jack Opeña Artist
Hot Tamale Edgar Delgado Colors
I'M NOT BEING A JERK, IT'S JUST... SCAMPERDINK AIN'T EXACTLY THE STEALTHY TYPE.
C'MON, THAT DOESN'T MAKE ME SOME KIND OF HEARTLESS ASS.
HEAVY HELPERS
WE'LL SHAKE THAT
OFF YOUR ASS FOR
AS A GYM!
MISSING
ON THE CONTRARY.
I'M HERE TO SAVE THE LITTLE CHICKEN FINGER.
SCAMPERDINK'S MOM SENT HIM TO THIS FATTY SCHOOL. HE NEVER CAME HOME.
LADY FEEDERLY SUSPECTS HE NEVER LEFT. SHE SUSPECTS FOUL PLAY.
HEY! WHO'S RUNNIN' THIS RING-A-DING?
PAPA'S GOTTA CHUNKY ASS.

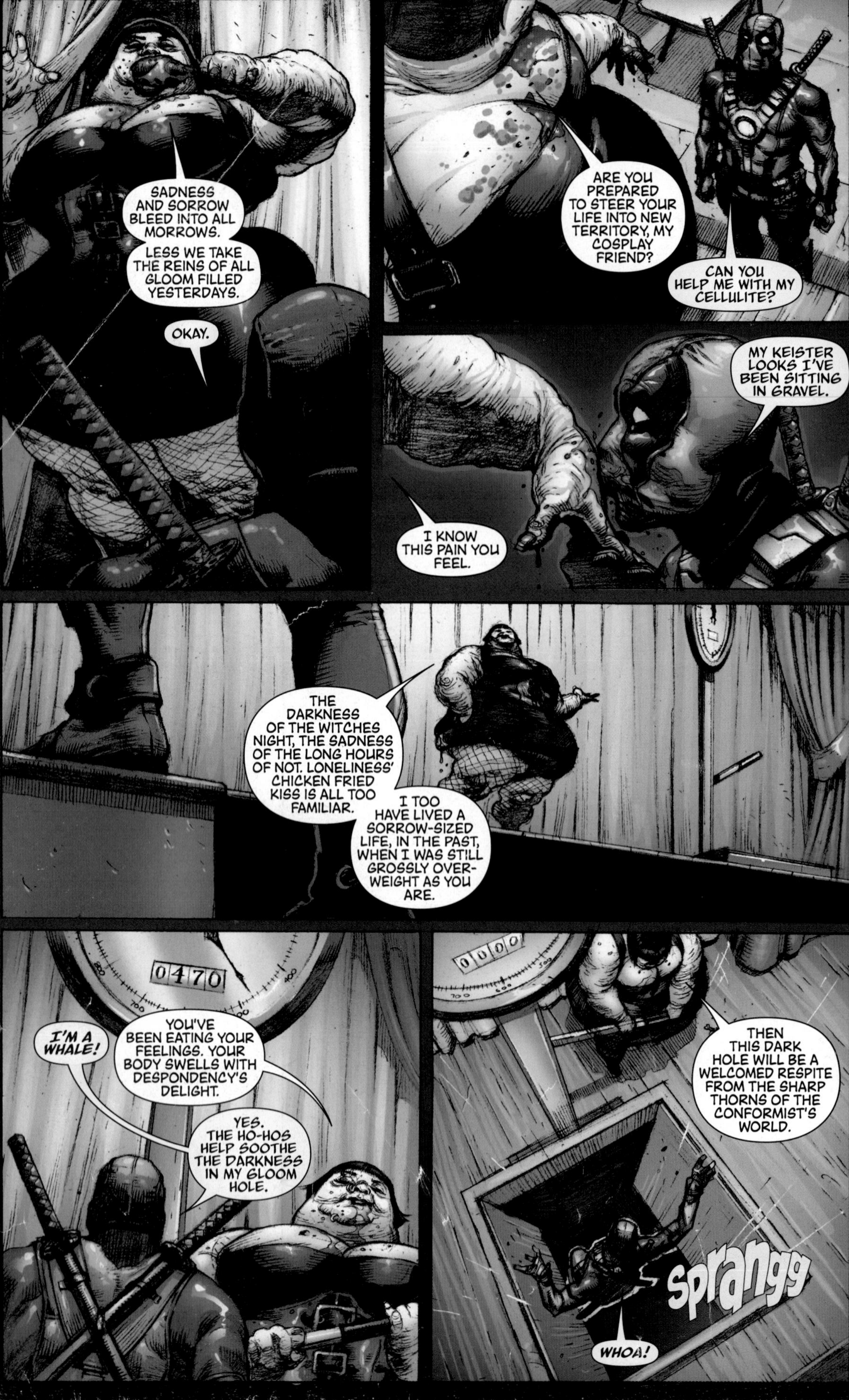
SADNESS AND SORROW BLEED INTO ALL MORROWS.
LESS WE TAKE THE REINS OF ALL GLOOM FILLED YESTERDAYS.
OKAY.
ARE YOU PREPARED TO STEER YOUR LIFE INTO NEW TERRITORY, MY COSPLAY FRIEND?
CAN YOU HELP ME WITH MY CELLULITE?
MY KEISTER LOOKS I'VE BEEN SITTING IN GRAVEL.
I KNOW THIS PAIN YOU FEEL.
THE DARKNESS OF THE WITCHES NIGHT, THE SADNESS OF THE LONG HOURS OF NOT. LONELINESS' CHICKEN FRIED KISS IS ALL TOO FAMILIAR.
I TOO HAVE LIVED A SORROW-SIZED LIFE, IN THE PAST, WHEN I WAS STILL GROSSLY OVER-WEIGHT AS YOU ARE.
0470
YOU'VE BEEN EATING YOUR FEELINGS. YOUR BODY SWELLS WITH DESPONDENCY'S DELIGHT.
I'M A WHALE!
YES. THE HO-HOS HELP SOOTHE THE DARKNESS IN MY GLOOM HOLE.
0000
THEN THIS DARK HOLE WILL BE A WELCOMED RESPITE FROM THE SHARP THORNS OF THE CONFORMIST'S WORLD.
SPRANGG
WHOA!

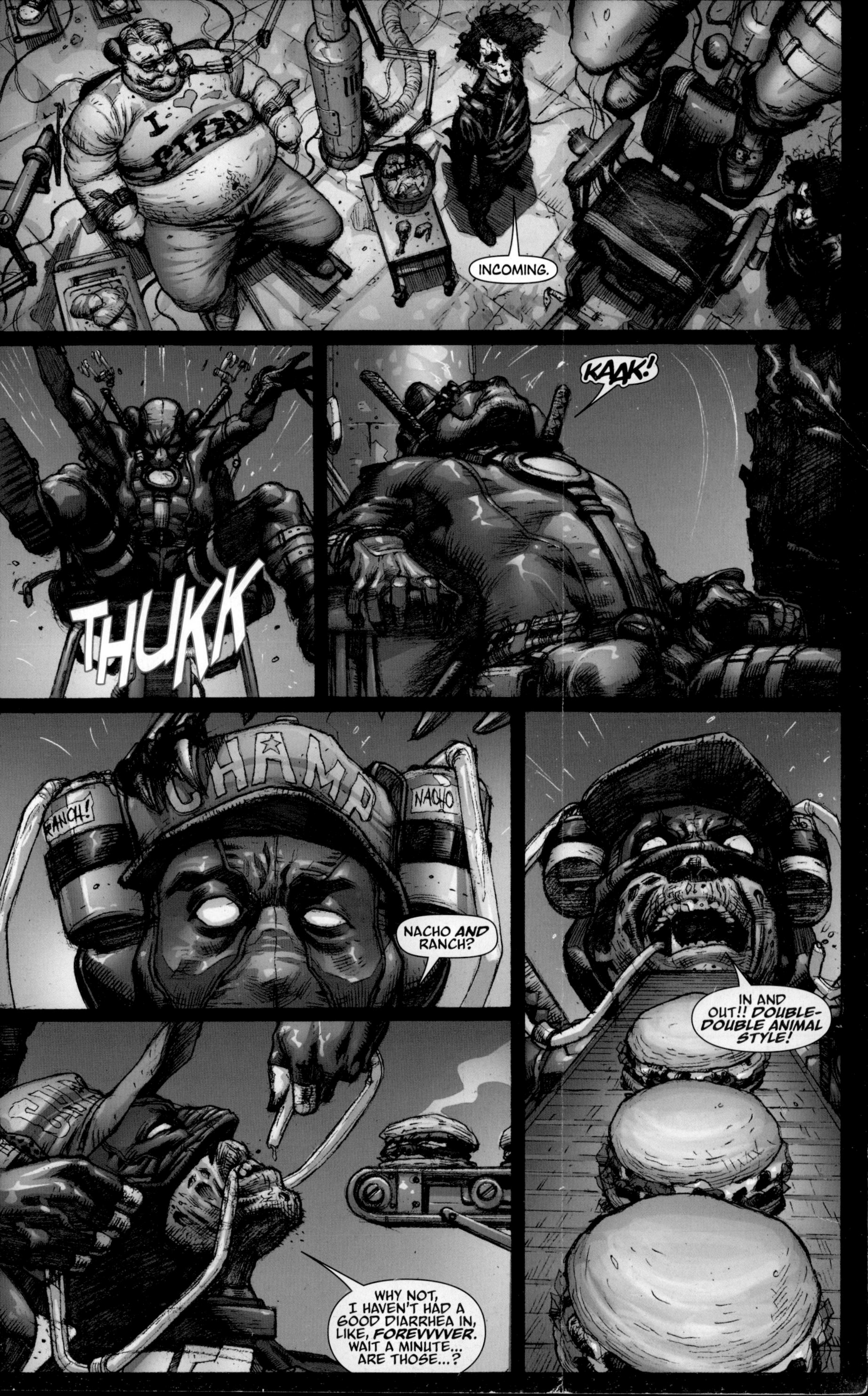
I ♥ PIZZA
INCOMING.
THUKK
KAAK!
CHAMP
RANCH!
NACHO
NACHO AND RANCH?
IN AND OUT!! DOUBLE-DOUBLE ANIMAL STYLE!
WHY NOT, I HAVEN'T HAD A GOOD DIARRHEA IN, LIKE, FOREVVVVER. WAIT A MINUTE... ARE THOSE...?

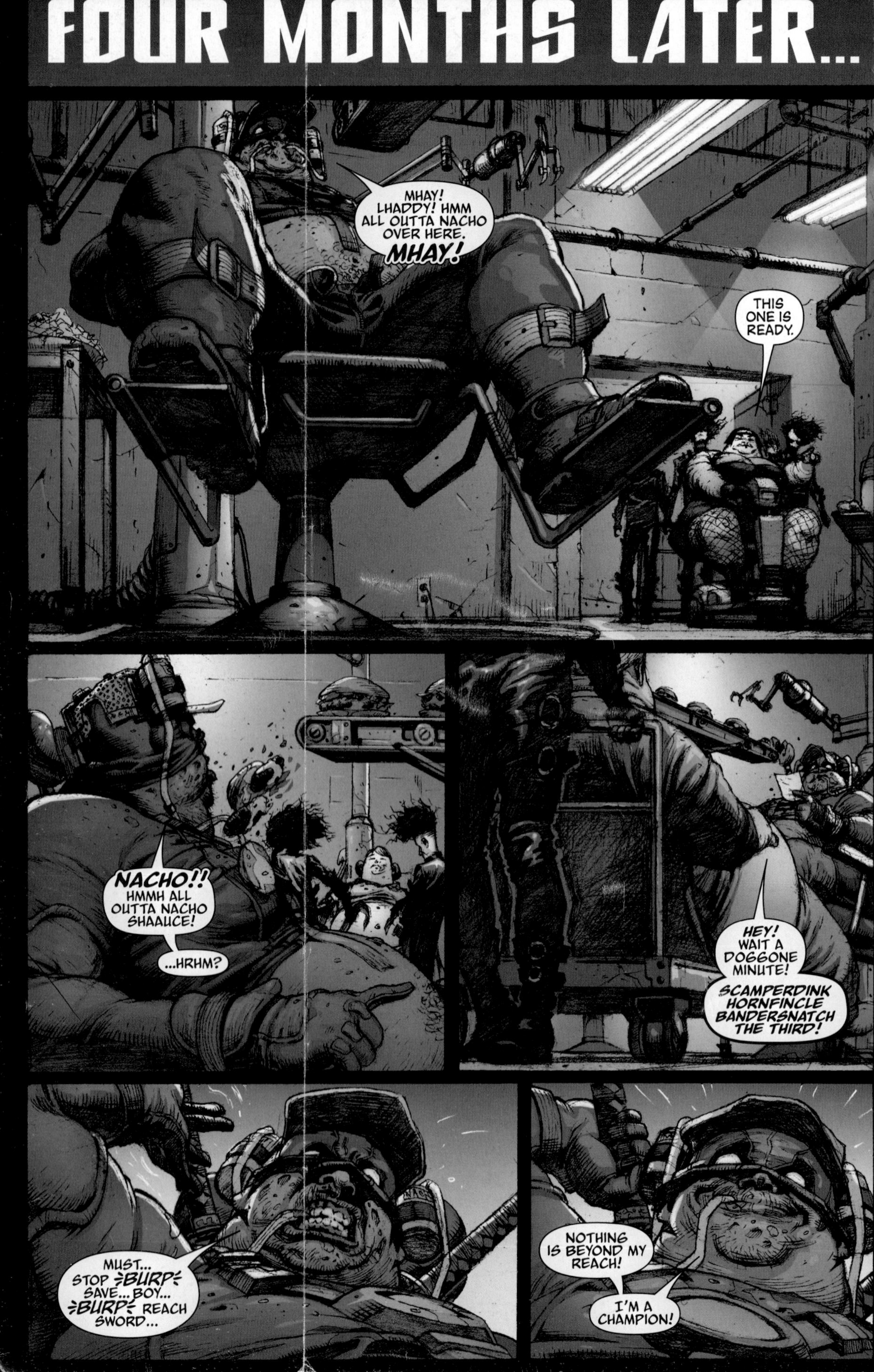
FOUR MONTHS LATER...
MHAY! LHADDY! HMM ALL OUTTA NACHO OVER HERE. MHAY!
THIS ONE IS READY.
NACHO!! HMMH ALL OUTTA NACHO SHAAUCE!
...HRHM?
HEY! WAIT A DOGGONE MINUTE! SCAMPERDINK HORNFINCLE BANDERSNATCH THE THIRD!
MUST... STOP BURP SAVE... BOY... BURP REACH SWORD...
NOTHING IS BEYOND MY REACH!
I'M A CHAMPION!

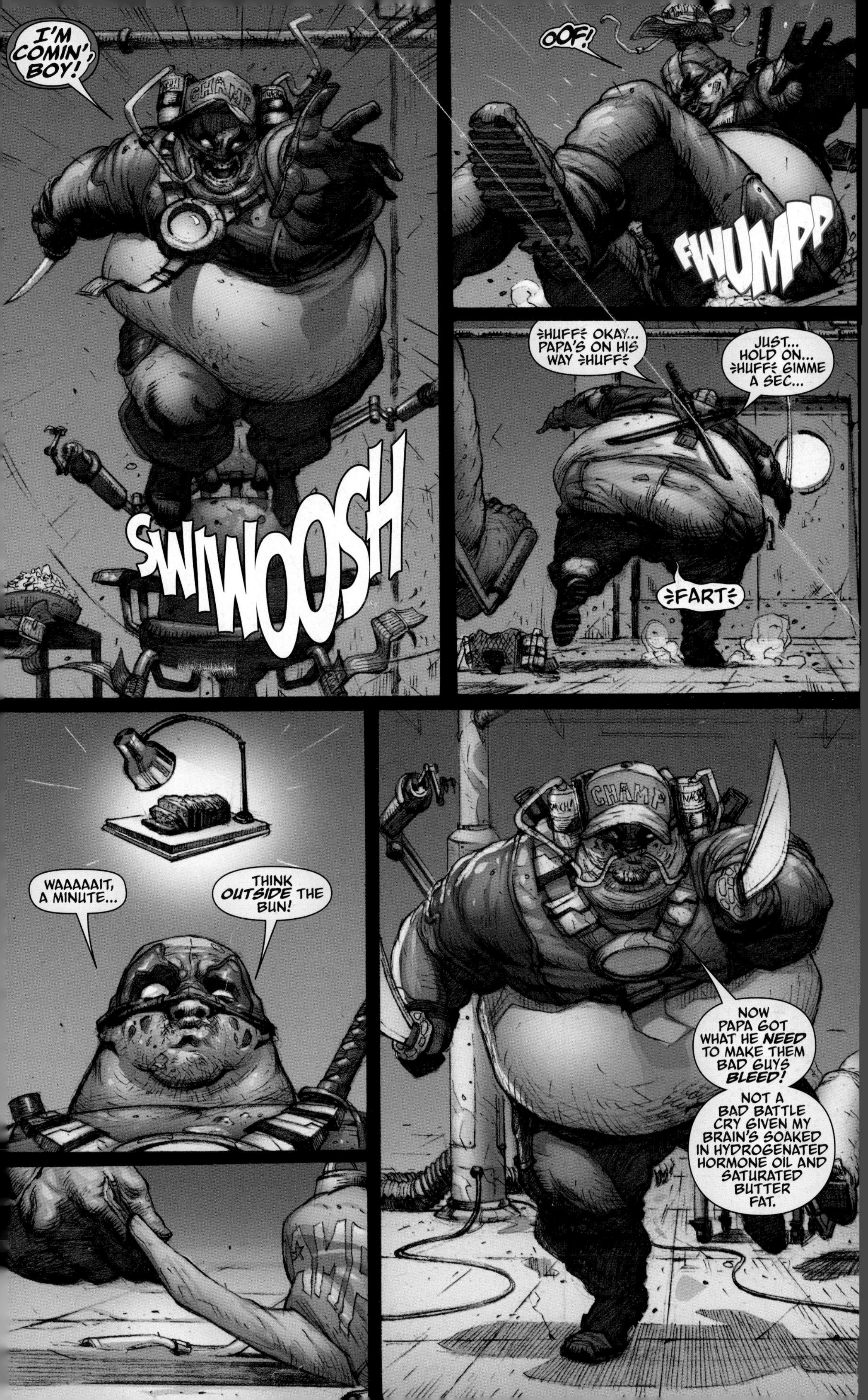
I'M COMIN', BOY!
SWIWOOSH
OOF!
FWUMPP
≑HUFF≑ OKAY... PAPA'S ON HIS WAY ≑HUFF≑
JUST... HOLD ON... ≑HUFF≑ GIMME A SEC...
≑FART≑
WAAAAAIT, A MINUTE...
THINK *OUTSIDE* THE BUN!
NOW PAPA GOT WHAT HE *NEED* TO MAKE THEM BAD GUYS *BLEED!*
NOT A BAD BATTLE CRY GIVEN MY BRAIN'S SOAKED IN HYDROGENATED HORMONE OIL AND SATURATED BUTTER FAT.

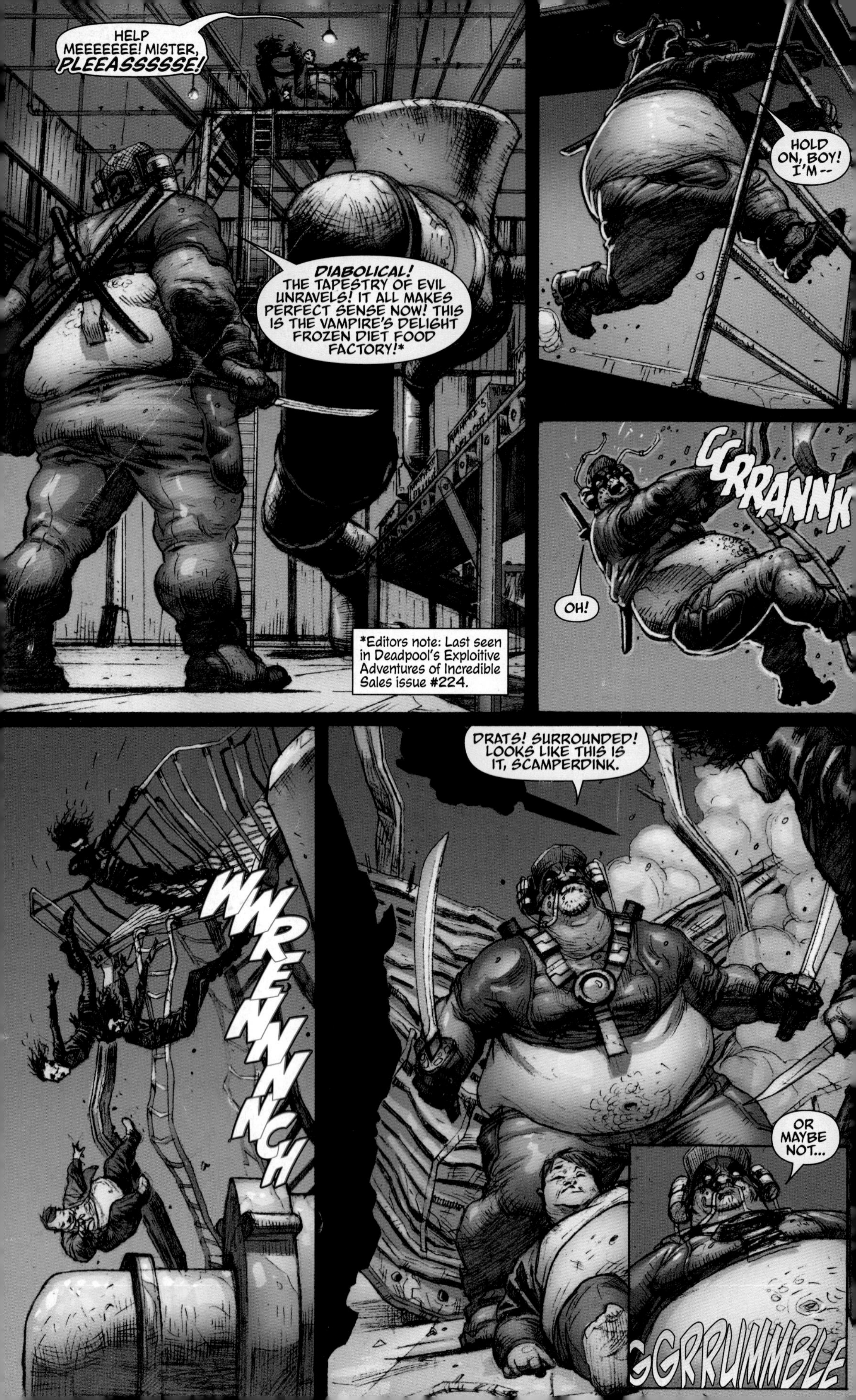
HELP MEEEEEEE! MISTER, PLEEASSSSSE!
DIABOLICAL! THE TAPESTRY OF EVIL UNRAVELS! IT ALL MAKES PERFECT SENSE NOW! THIS IS THE VAMPIRE'S DELIGHT FROZEN DIET FOOD FACTORY!*
*Editors note: Last seen in Deadpool's Exploitive Adventures of Incredible Sales issue #224.
HOLD ON, BOY! I'M --
GGRRANNK
OH!
WWRENNNNCH
DRATS! SURROUNDED! LOOKS LIKE THIS IS IT, SCAMPERDINK.
OR MAYBE NOT...
GGRRUMMBLE

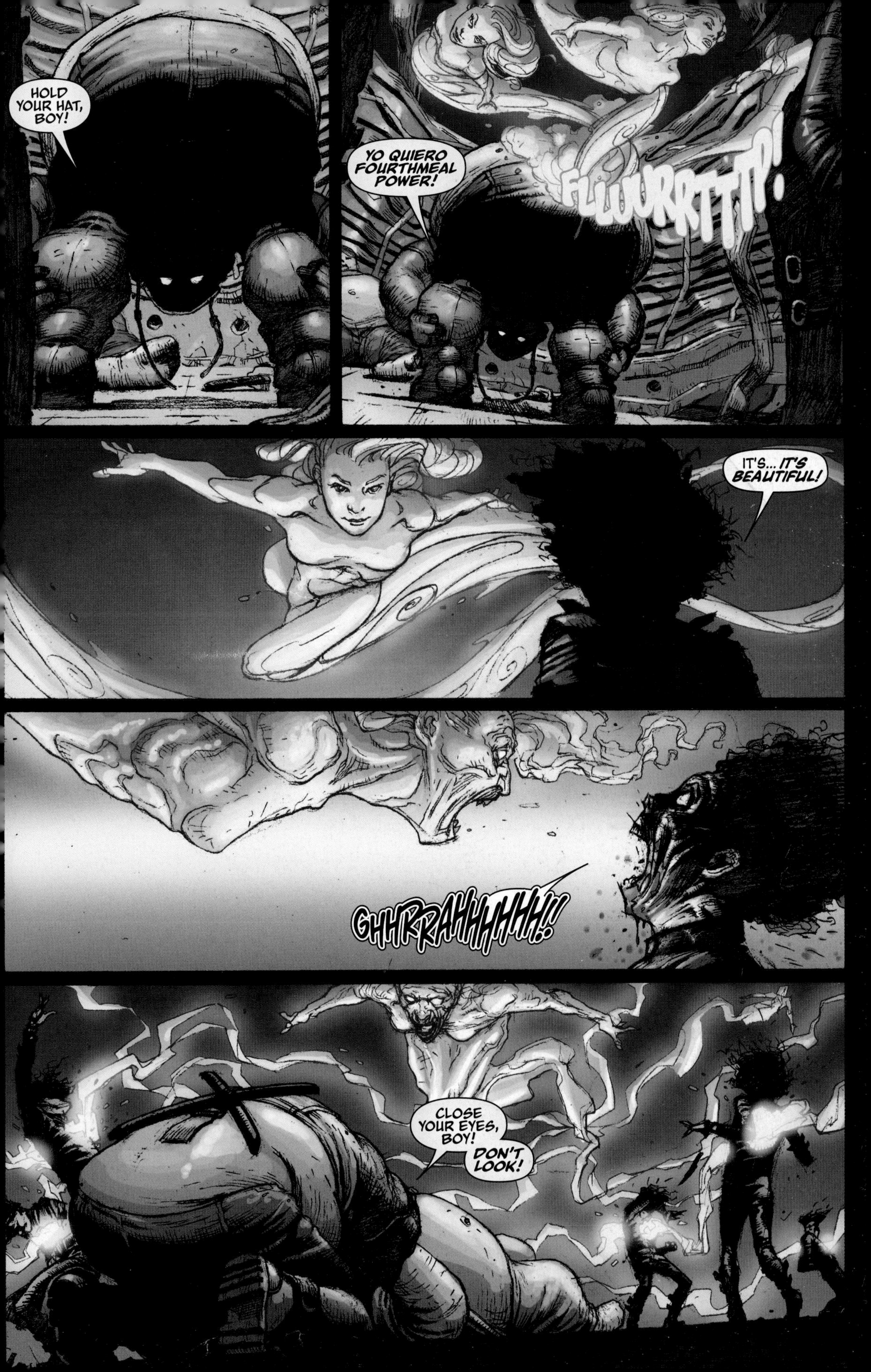
HOLD YOUR HAT, BOY!
YO QUIERO FOURTHMEAL POWER!
FLLUURRTTTP!
IT'S... IT'S BEAUTIFUL!
GHHRRAHHHHHH!!
CLOSE YOUR EYES, BOY!
DON'T LOOK!

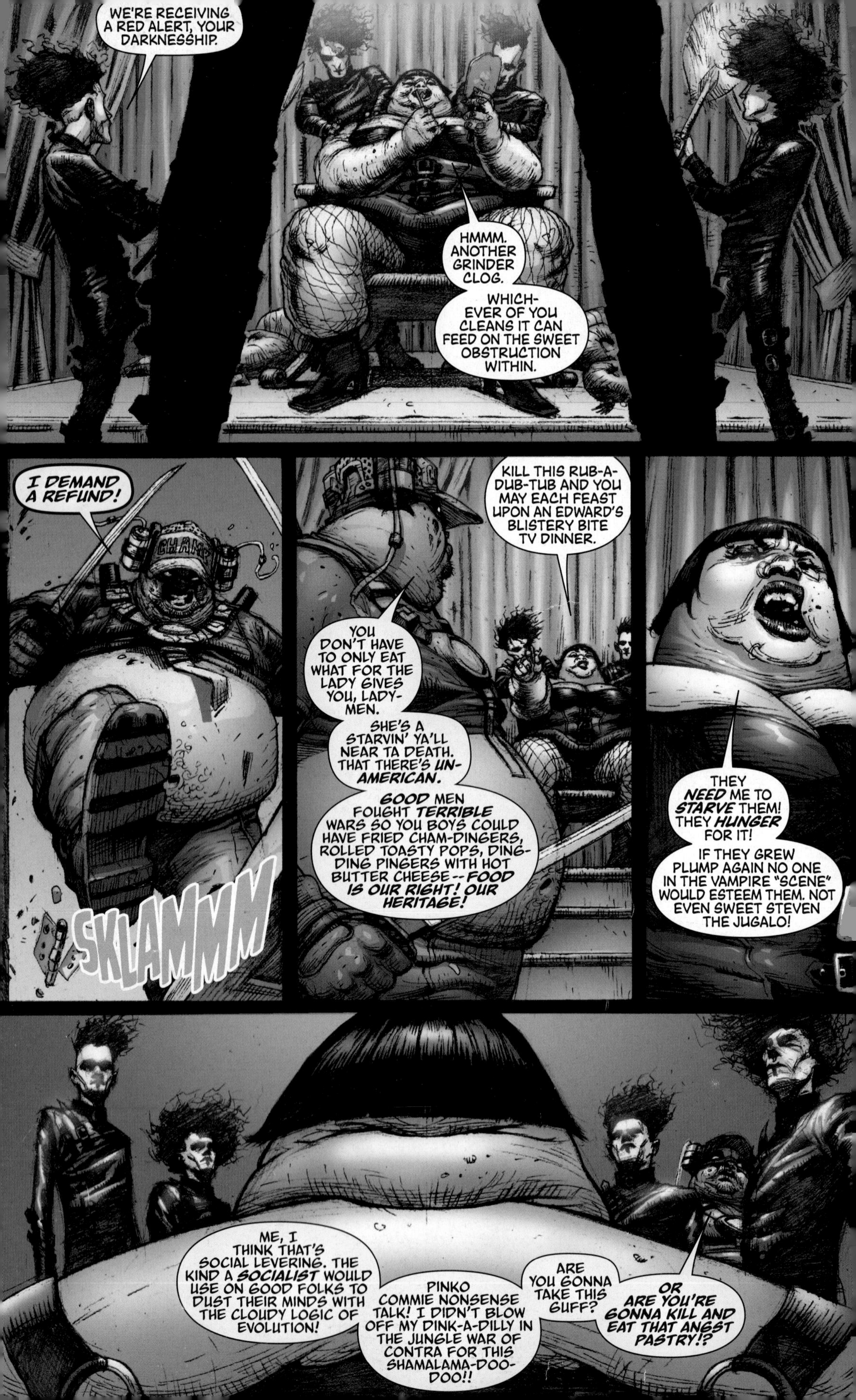
WE'RE RECEIVING A RED ALERT, YOUR DARKNESSSHIP.
HMMM. ANOTHER GRINDER CLOG.
WHICH-EVER OF YOU CLEANS IT CAN FEED ON THE SWEET OBSTRUCTION WITHIN.
I DEMAND A REFUND!
SKLAMMM
KILL THIS RUB-A-DUB-TUB AND YOU MAY EACH FEAST UPON AN EDWARD'S BLISTERY BITE TV DINNER.
YOU DON'T HAVE TO ONLY EAT WHAT FOR THE LADY GIVES YOU, LADY-MEN.
SHE'S A STARVIN' YA'LL NEAR TA DEATH. THAT THERE'S UN-AMERICAN.
GOOD MEN FOUGHT TERRIBLE WARS SO YOU BOYS COULD HAVE FRIED CHAM-DINGERS, ROLLED TOASTY POPS, DING-DING PINGERS WITH HOT BUTTER CHEESE -- FOOD IS OUR RIGHT! OUR HERITAGE!
THEY NEED ME TO STARVE THEM! THEY HUNGER FOR IT!
IF THEY GREW PLUMP AGAIN NO ONE IN THE VAMPIRE "SCENE" WOULD ESTEEM THEM. NOT EVEN SWEET STEVEN THE JUGALO!
ME, I THINK THAT'S SOCIAL LEVERING. THE KIND A SOCIALIST WOULD USE ON GOOD FOLKS TO DUST THEIR MINDS WITH THE CLOUDY LOGIC OF EVOLUTION!
PINKO COMMIE NONSENSE TALK! I DIDN'T BLOW OFF MY DINK-A-DILLY IN THE JUNGLE WAR OF CONTRA FOR THIS SHAMALAMA-DOO-DOO!!
ARE YOU GONNA TAKE THIS GUFF?
OR ARE YOU'RE GONNA KILL AND EAT THAT ANGST PASTRY!?

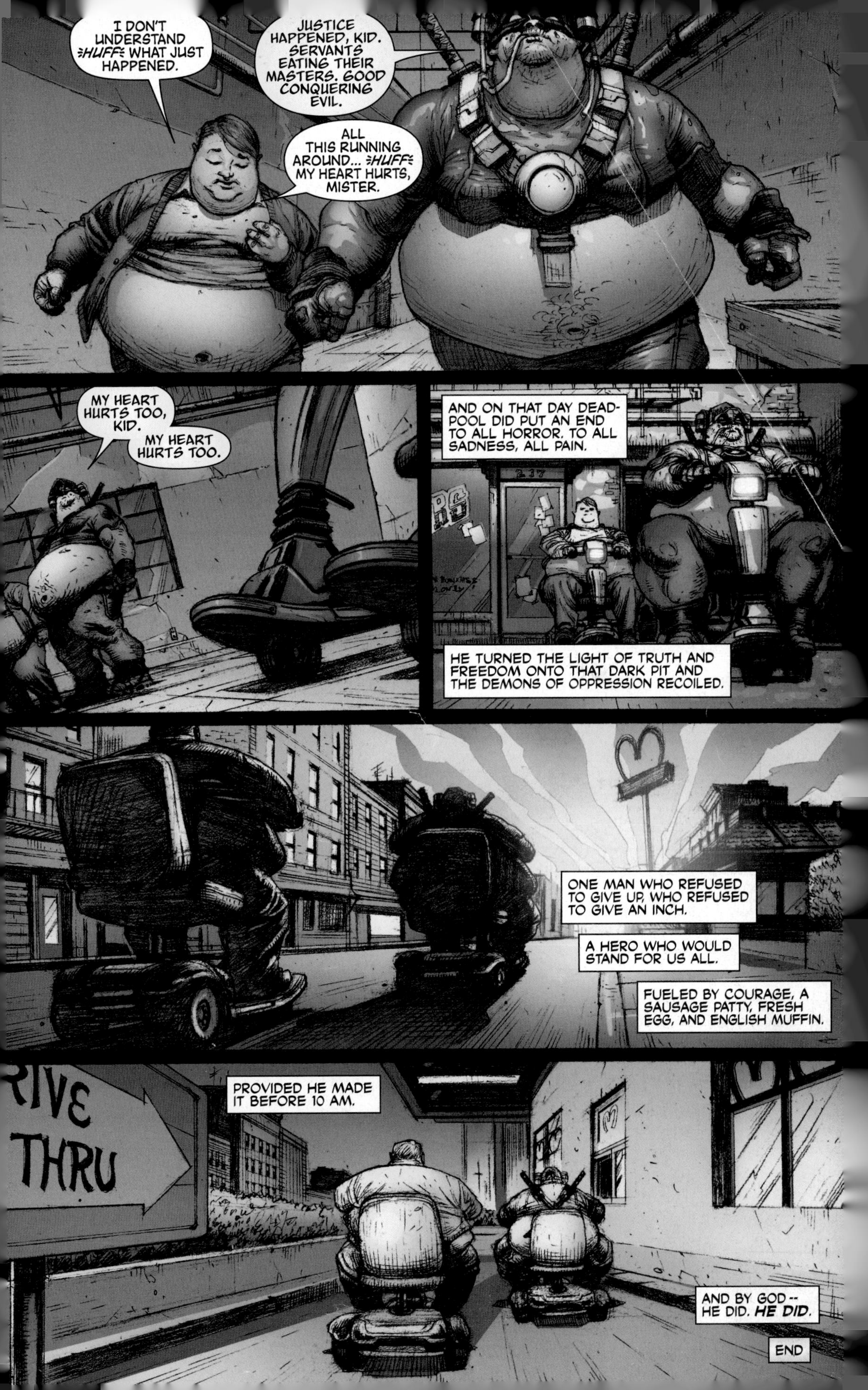
I DON'T UNDERSTAND *HUFF* WHAT JUST HAPPENED.
JUSTICE HAPPENED, KID. SERVANTS EATING THEIR MASTERS. GOOD CONQUERING EVIL.
ALL THIS RUNNING AROUND... *HUFF* MY HEART HURTS, MISTER.
MY HEART HURTS TOO, KID.
MY HEART HURTS TOO.
AND ON THAT DAY DEAD-POOL DID PUT AN END TO ALL HORROR. TO ALL SADNESS, ALL PAIN.
HE TURNED THE LIGHT OF TRUTH AND FREEDOM ONTO THAT DARK PIT AND THE DEMONS OF OPPRESSION RECOILED.
ONE MAN WHO REFUSED TO GIVE UP, WHO REFUSED TO GIVE AN INCH.
A HERO WHO WOULD STAND FOR US ALL.
FUELED BY COURAGE, A SAUSAGE PATTY, FRESH EGG, AND ENGLISH MUFFIN.
PROVIDED HE MADE IT BEFORE 10 AM.
RIVE THRU
AND BY GOD -- HE DID. ***HE DID.***
END

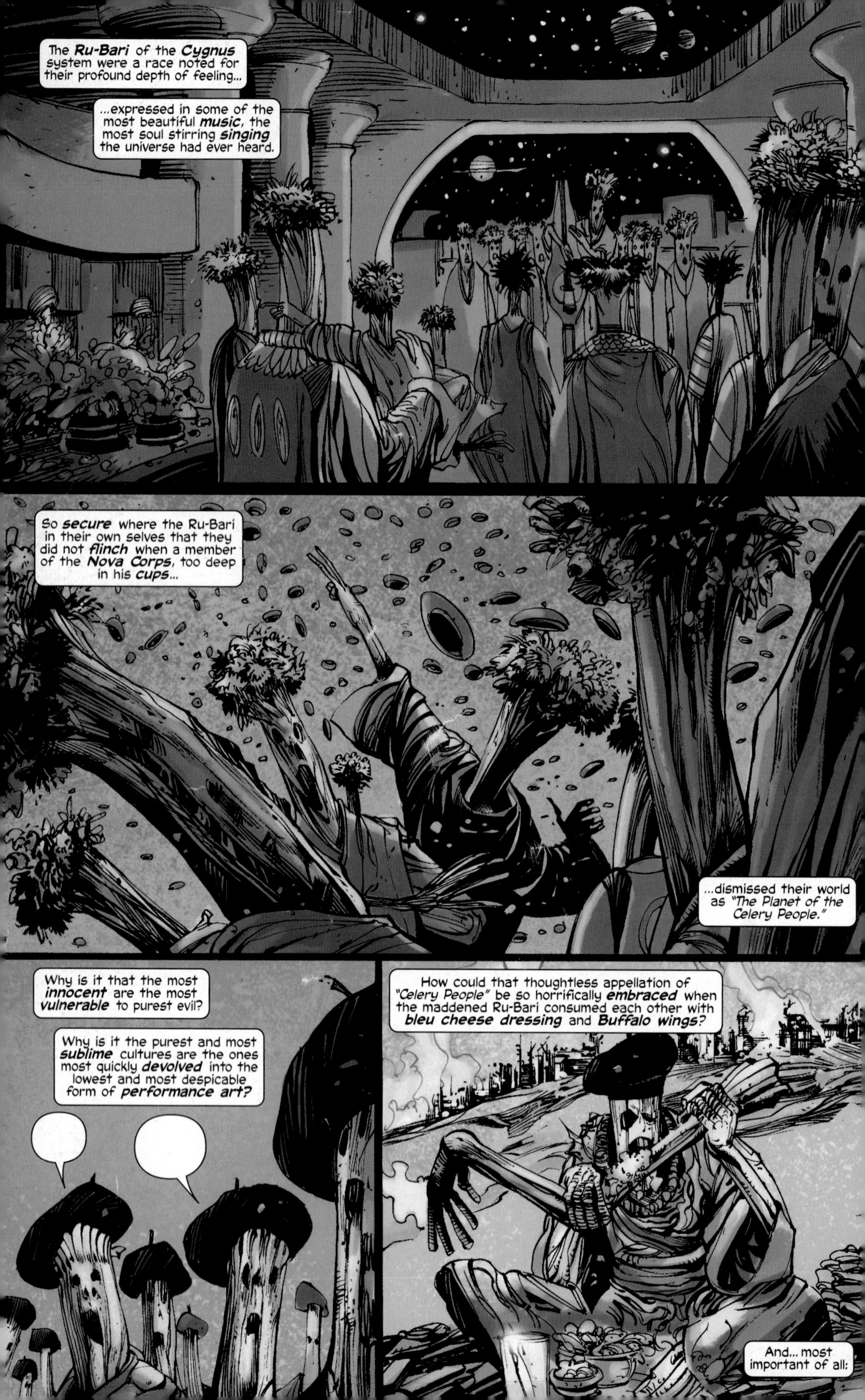
The Ru-Bari of the Cygnus system were a race noted for their profound depth of feeling...
...expressed in some of the most beautiful music, the most soul stirring singing the universe had ever heard.
So secure where the Ru-Bari in their own selves that they did not flinch when a member of the Nova Corps, too deep in his cups...
...dismissed their world as "The Planet of the Celery People."
Why is it that the most innocent are the most vulnerable to purest evil?
Why is it the purest and most sublime cultures are the ones most quickly devolved into the lowest and most despicable form of performance art?
How could that thoughtless appellation of "Celery People" be so horrifically embraced when the maddened Ru-Bari consumed each other with bleu cheese dressing and Buffalo wings?
And... most important of all:

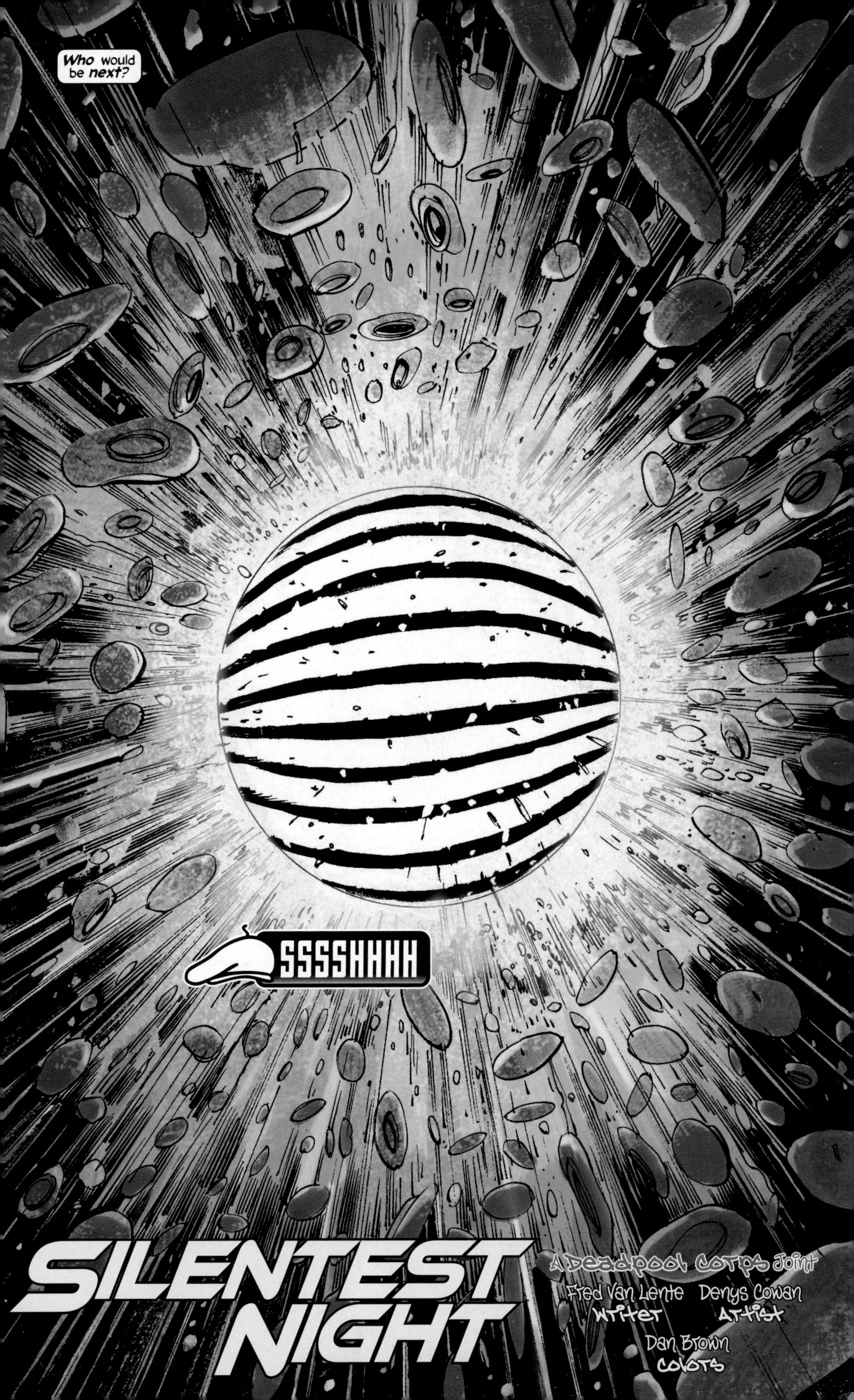
Who would be next?
SSSSHHHH
SILENTEST NIGHT
A Deadpool Corps Joint
Fred Van Lente Writer
Denys Cowan Artist
Dan Brown Colors

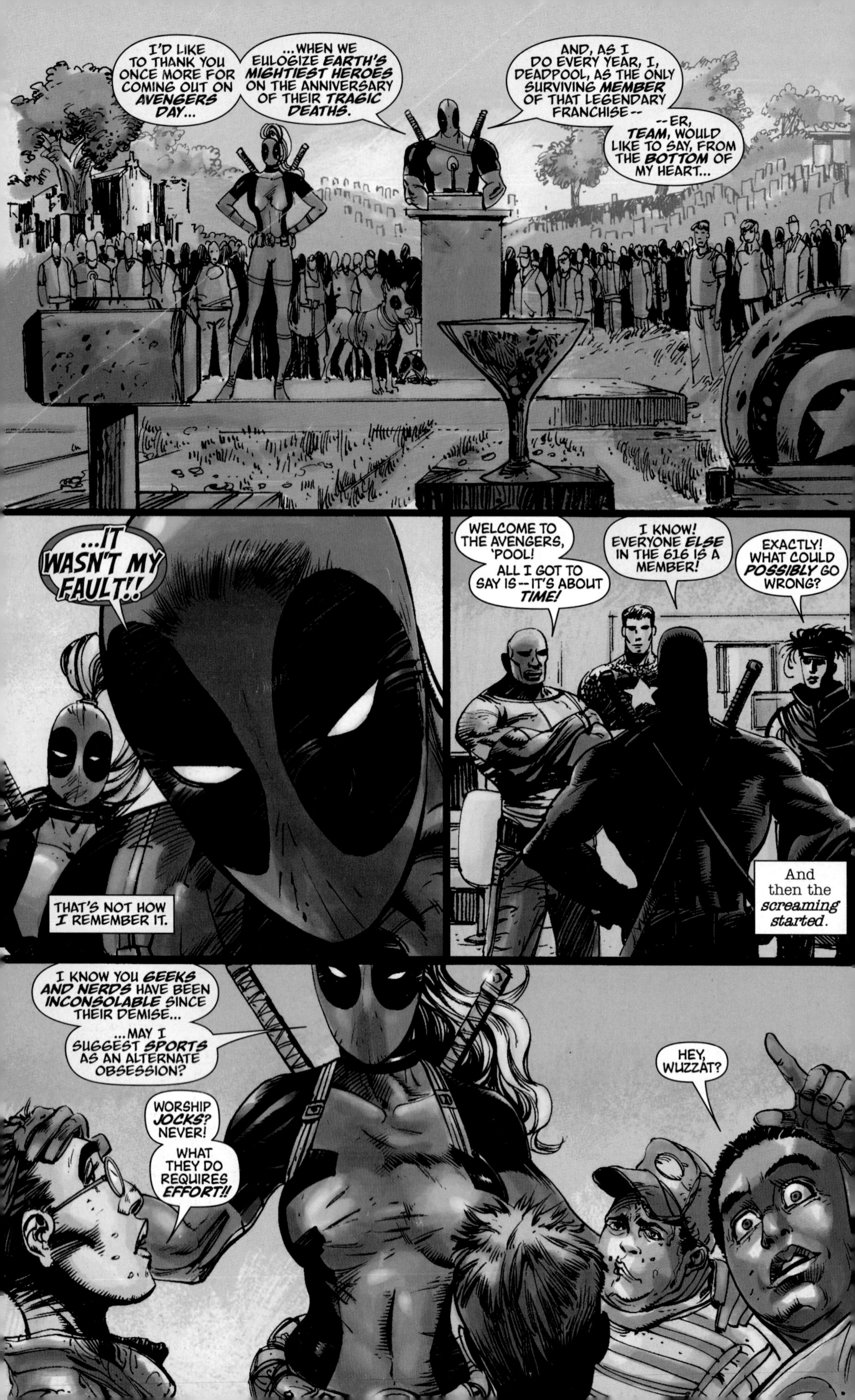

I'D LIKE TO THANK YOU ONCE MORE FOR COMING OUT ON AVENGERS DAY...
...WHEN WE EULOGIZE EARTH'S MIGHTIEST HEROES ON THE ANNIVERSARY OF THEIR TRAGIC DEATHS.
AND, AS I DO EVERY YEAR, I, DEADPOOL, AS THE ONLY SURVIVING MEMBER OF THAT LEGENDARY FRANCHISE--
--ER, TEAM, WOULD LIKE TO SAY, FROM THE BOTTOM OF MY HEART...
...IT WASN'T MY FAULT!!
THAT'S NOT HOW I REMEMBER IT.
WELCOME TO THE AVENGERS, 'POOL!
ALL I GOT TO SAY IS--IT'S ABOUT TIME!
I KNOW! EVERYONE ELSE IN THE 616 IS A MEMBER!
EXACTLY! WHAT COULD POSSIBLY GO WRONG?
And then the screaming started.
I KNOW YOU GEEKS AND NERDS HAVE BEEN INCONSOLABLE SINCE THEIR DEMISE...
...MAY I SUGGEST SPORTS AS AN ALTERNATE OBSESSION?
WORSHIP JOCKS? NEVER!
WHAT THEY DO REQUIRES EFFORT!!
HEY, WUZZAT?

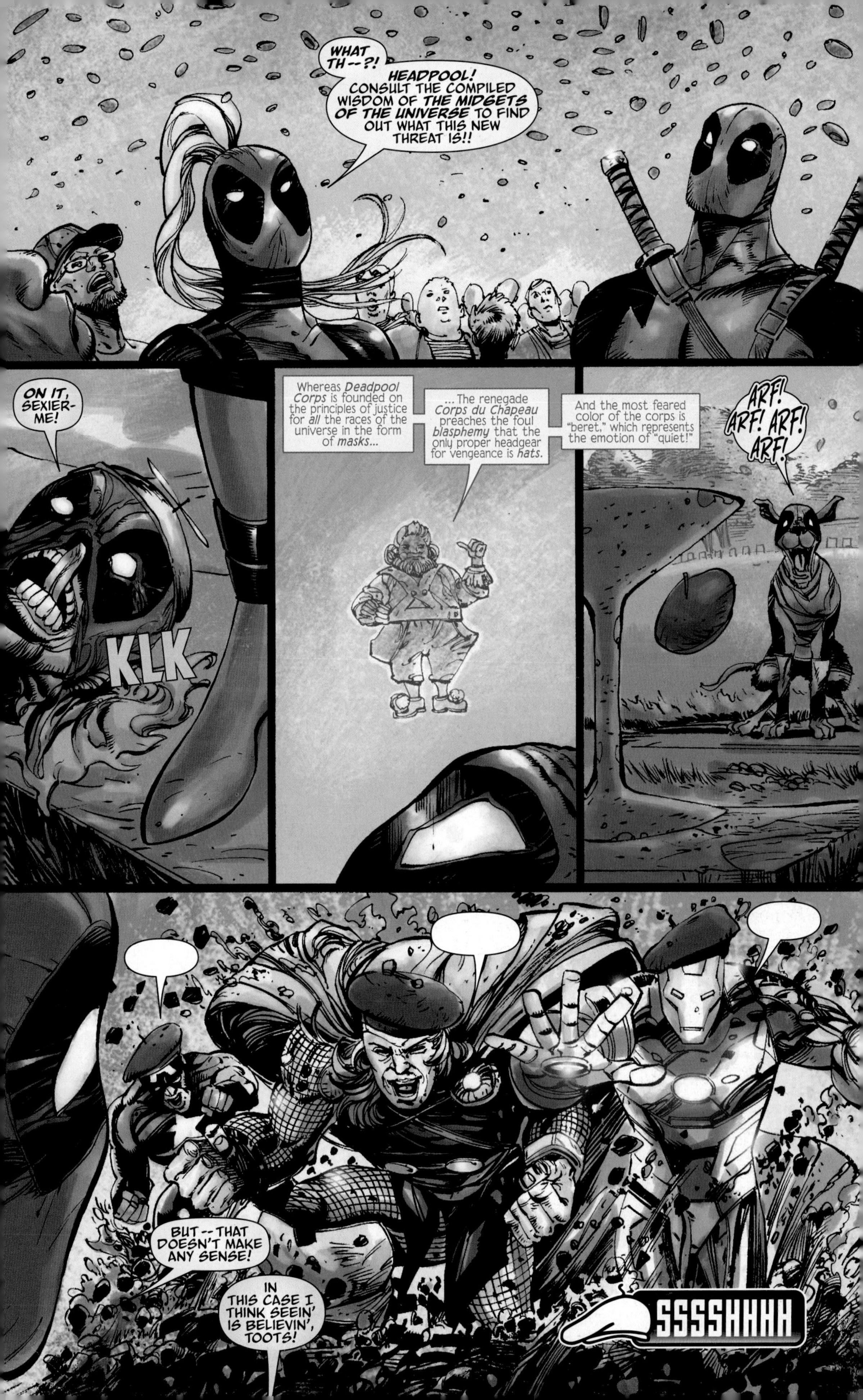
WHAT TH--?!
HEADPOOL! CONSULT THE COMPILED WISDOM OF THE MIDGETS OF THE UNIVERSE TO FIND OUT WHAT THIS NEW THREAT IS!!
ON IT, SEXIER-ME!
KLK
Whereas Deadpool Corps is founded on the principles of justice for all the races of the universe in the form of masks...
...The renegade Corps du Chapeau preaches the foul blasphemy that the only proper headgear for vengeance is hats.
And the most feared color of the corps is "beret," which represents the emotion of "quiet!"
ARF! ARF! ARF! ARF!
BUT--THAT DOESN'T MAKE ANY SENSE!
IN THIS CASE I THINK SEEIN' IS BELIEVIN', TOOTS!
SSSSHHHH

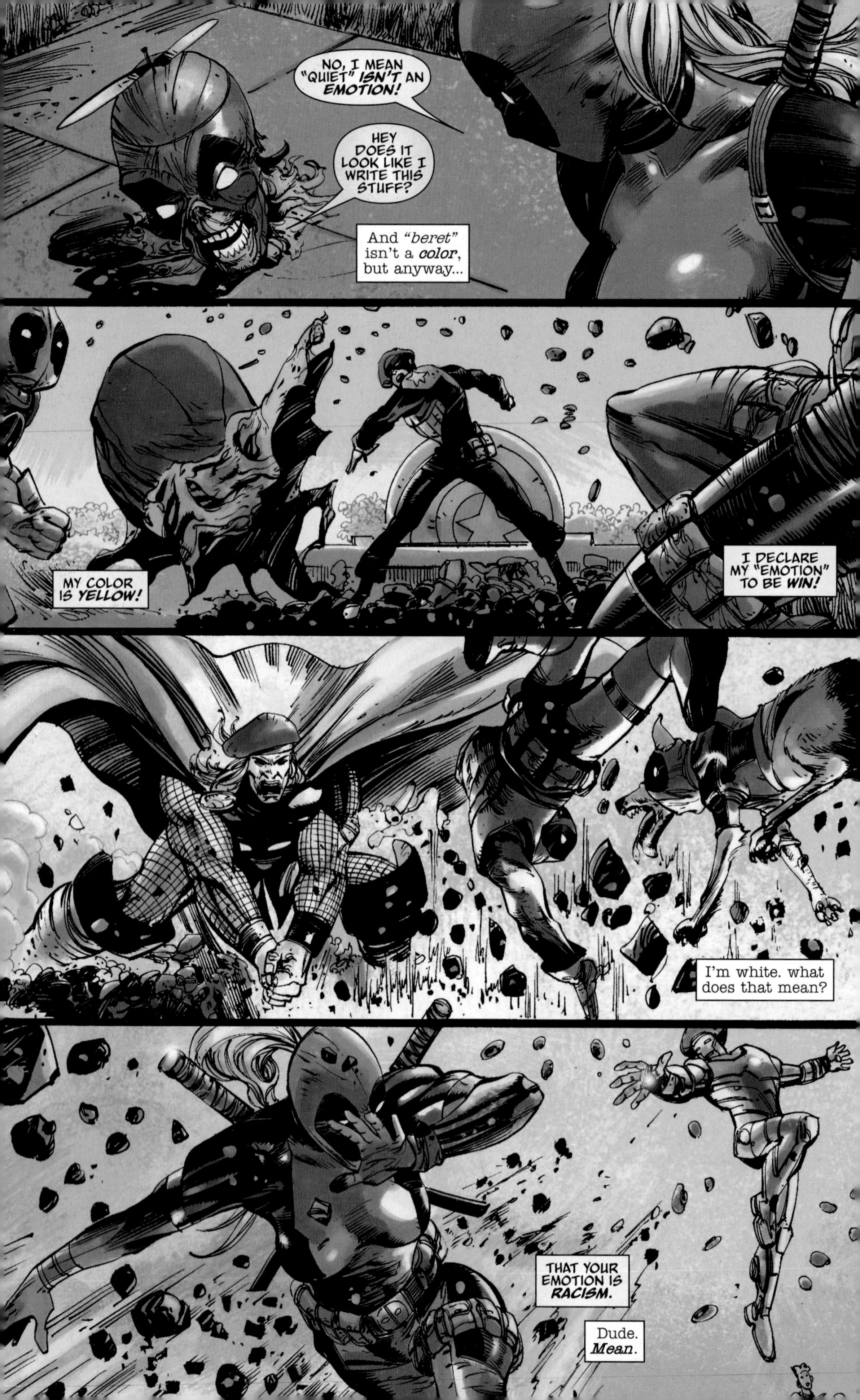
NO, I MEAN "QUIET" ISN'T AN EMOTION!
HEY DOES IT LOOK LIKE I WRITE THIS STUFF?
And "beret" isn't a color, but anyway...
MY COLOR IS YELLOW!
I DECLARE MY "EMOTION" TO BE WIN!
I'm white. what does that mean?
THAT YOUR EMOTION IS RACISM.
Dude. Mean.

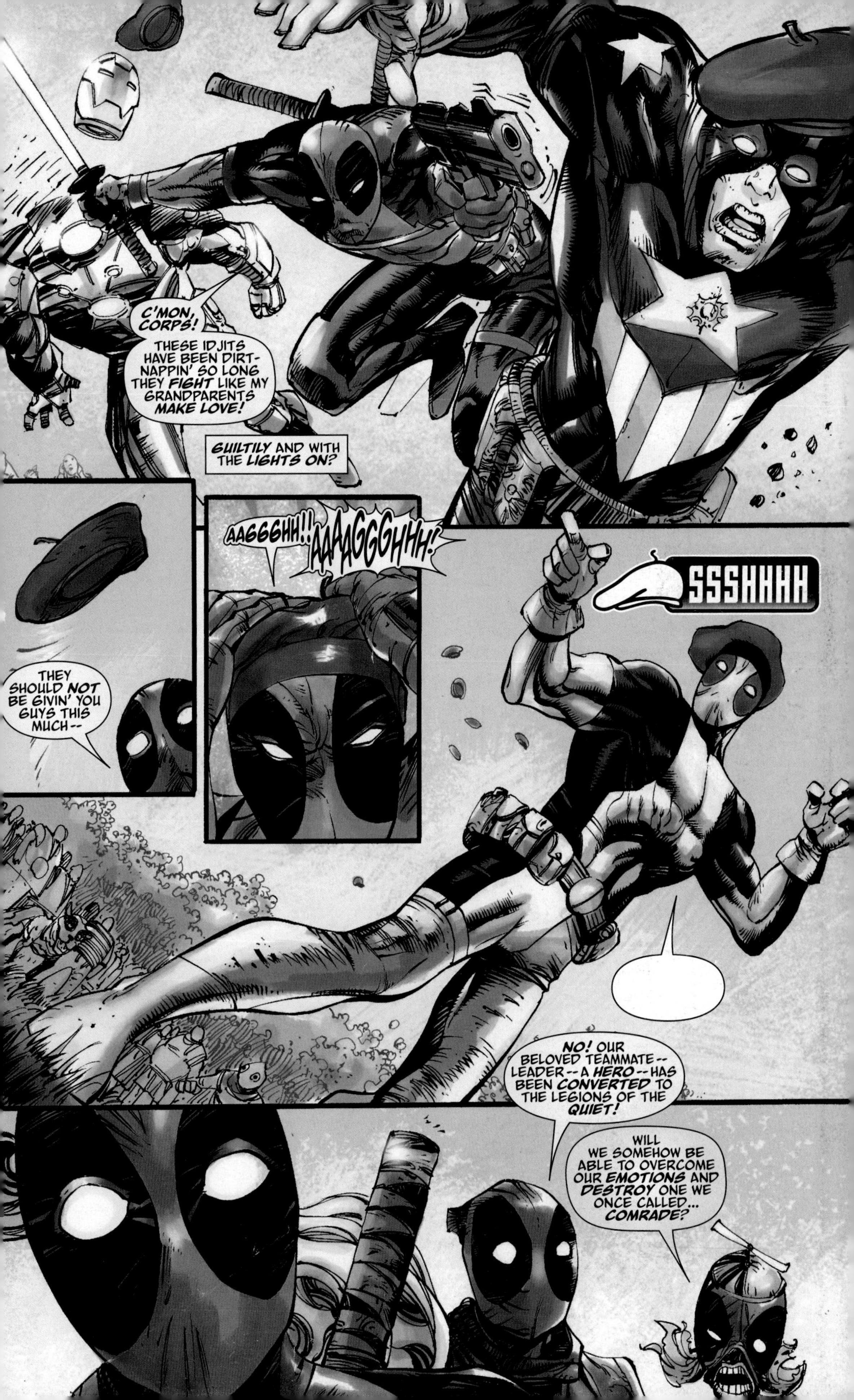

C'MON, CORPS!
THESE IDJITS HAVE BEEN DIRT-NAPPIN' SO LONG THEY FIGHT LIKE MY GRANDPARENTS MAKE LOVE!
GUILTILY AND WITH THE LIGHTS ON?
THEY SHOULD NOT BE GIVIN' YOU GUYS THIS MUCH--
AAGGGHH!!
AAAAGGGHHH!
SSSHHHH
NO! OUR BELOVED TEAMMATE--LEADER--A HERO--HAS BEEN CONVERTED TO THE LEGIONS OF THE QUIET!
WILL WE SOMEHOW BE ABLE TO OVERCOME OUR EMOTIONS AND DESTROY ONE WE ONCE CALLED... COMRADE?

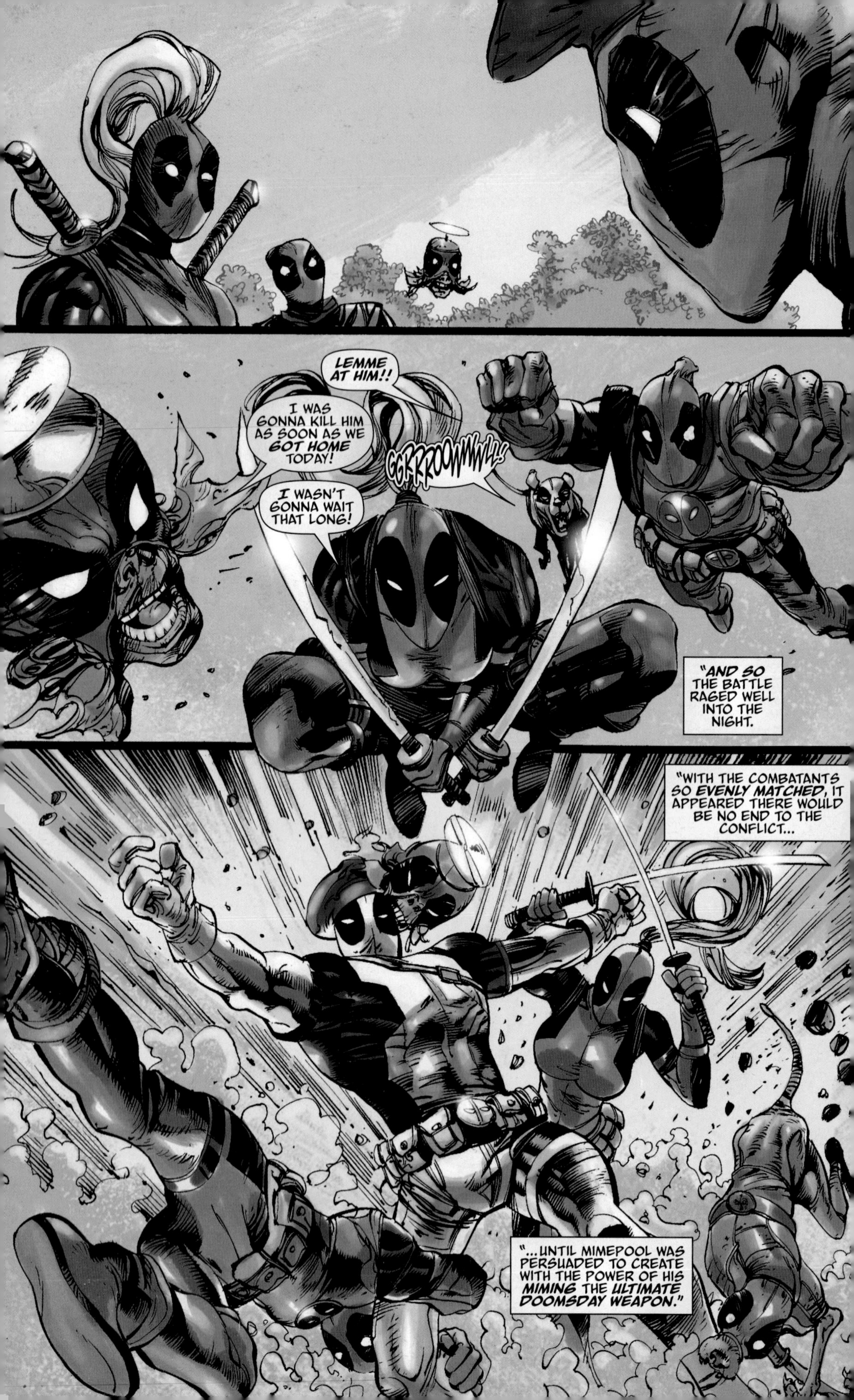
LEMME AT HIM!!
I WAS GONNA KILL HIM AS SOON AS WE GOT HOME TODAY!
GGRRROOWWWLL!
I WASN'T GONNA WAIT THAT LONG!
"AND SO THE BATTLE RAGED WELL INTO THE NIGHT.
"WITH THE COMBATANTS SO EVENLY MATCHED, IT APPEARED THERE WOULD BE NO END TO THE CONFLICT...
"...UNTIL MIMEPOOL WAS PERSUADED TO CREATE WITH THE POWER OF HIS MIMING THE ULTIMATE DOOMSDAY WEAPON."

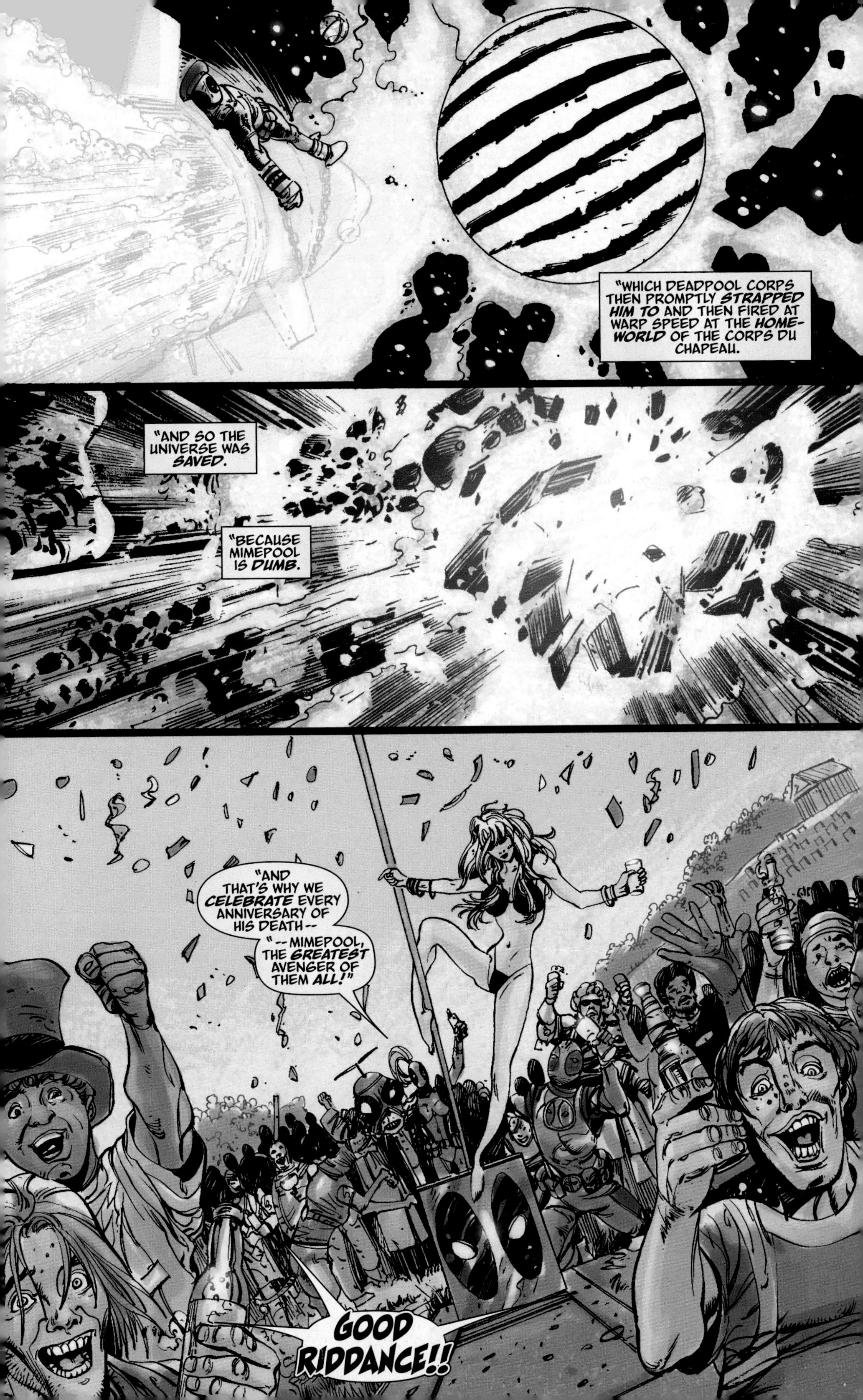
"WHICH DEADPOOL CORPS THEN PROMPTLY STRAPPED HIM TO AND THEN FIRED AT WARP SPEED AT THE HOME-WORLD OF THE CORPS DU CHAPEAU.
"AND SO THE UNIVERSE WAS SAVED.
"BECAUSE MIMEPOOL IS DUMB.
"AND THAT'S WHY WE CELEBRATE EVERY ANNIVERSARY OF HIS DEATH --
"-- MIMEPOOL, THE GREATEST AVENGER OF THEM ALL!"
GOOD RIDDANCE!!

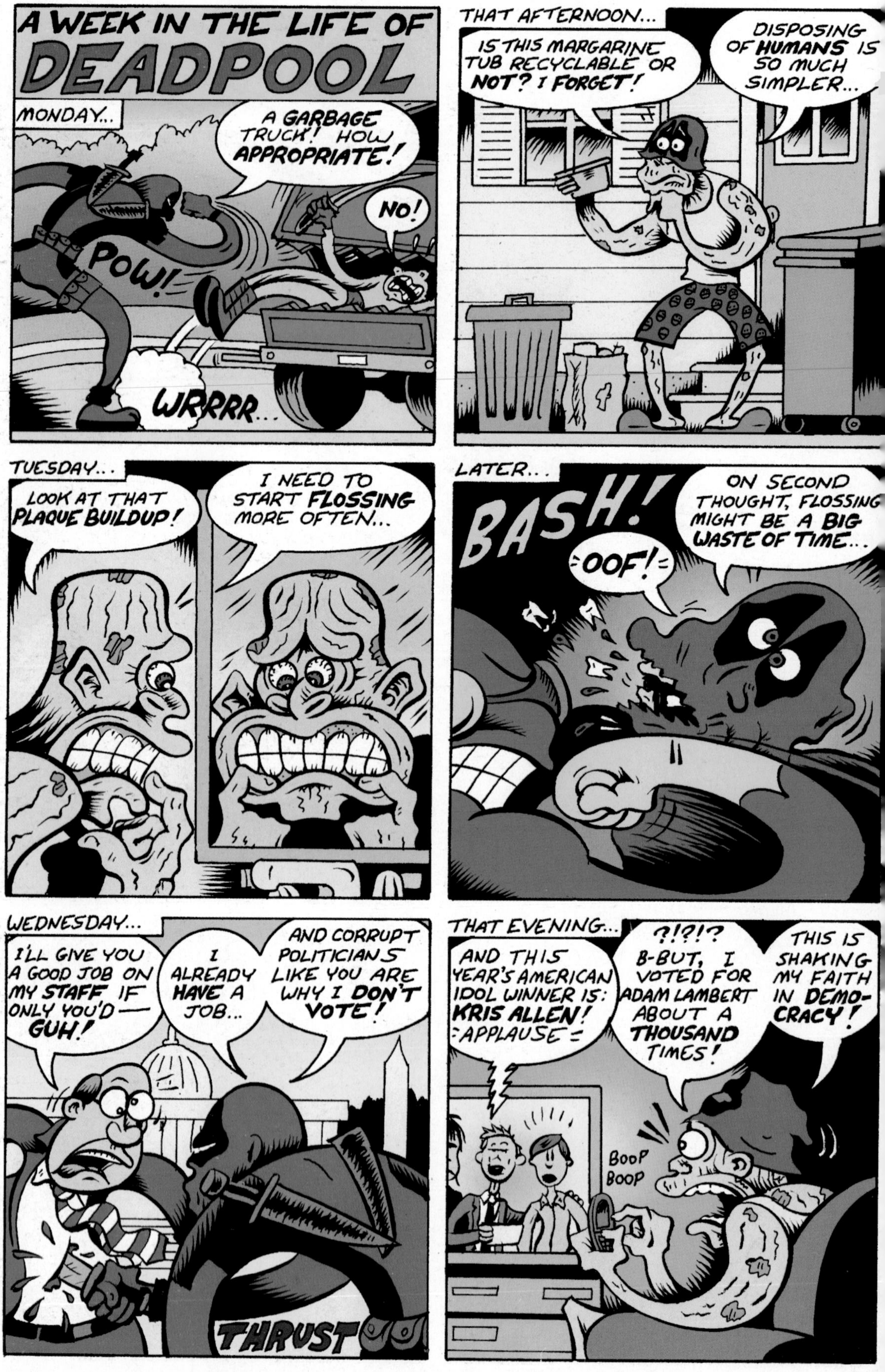
A WEEK IN THE LIFE OF
DEADPOOL
MONDAY...
A GARBAGE TRUCK! HOW APPROPRIATE!
NO!
POW!
WRRRR...
THAT AFTERNOON...
IS THIS MARGARINE TUB RECYCLABLE OR NOT? I FORGET!
DISPOSING OF HUMANS IS SO MUCH SIMPLER...
TUESDAY...
LOOK AT THAT PLAQUE BUILDUP!
I NEED TO START FLOSSING MORE OFTEN...
LATER...
BASH!
OOF!
ON SECOND THOUGHT, FLOSSING MIGHT BE A BIG WASTE OF TIME...
WEDNESDAY...
I'LL GIVE YOU A GOOD JOB ON MY STAFF IF ONLY YOU'D— GUH!
I ALREADY HAVE A JOB...
AND CORRUPT POLITICIANS LIKE YOU ARE WHY I DON'T VOTE!
THRUST
THAT EVENING...
AND THIS YEAR'S AMERICAN IDOL WINNER IS: KRIS ALLEN! =APPLAUSE=
?!?!?
B-BUT, I VOTED FOR ADAM LAMBERT ABOUT A THOUSAND TIMES!
BOOP BOOP
THIS IS SHAKING MY FAITH IN DEMOCRACY!

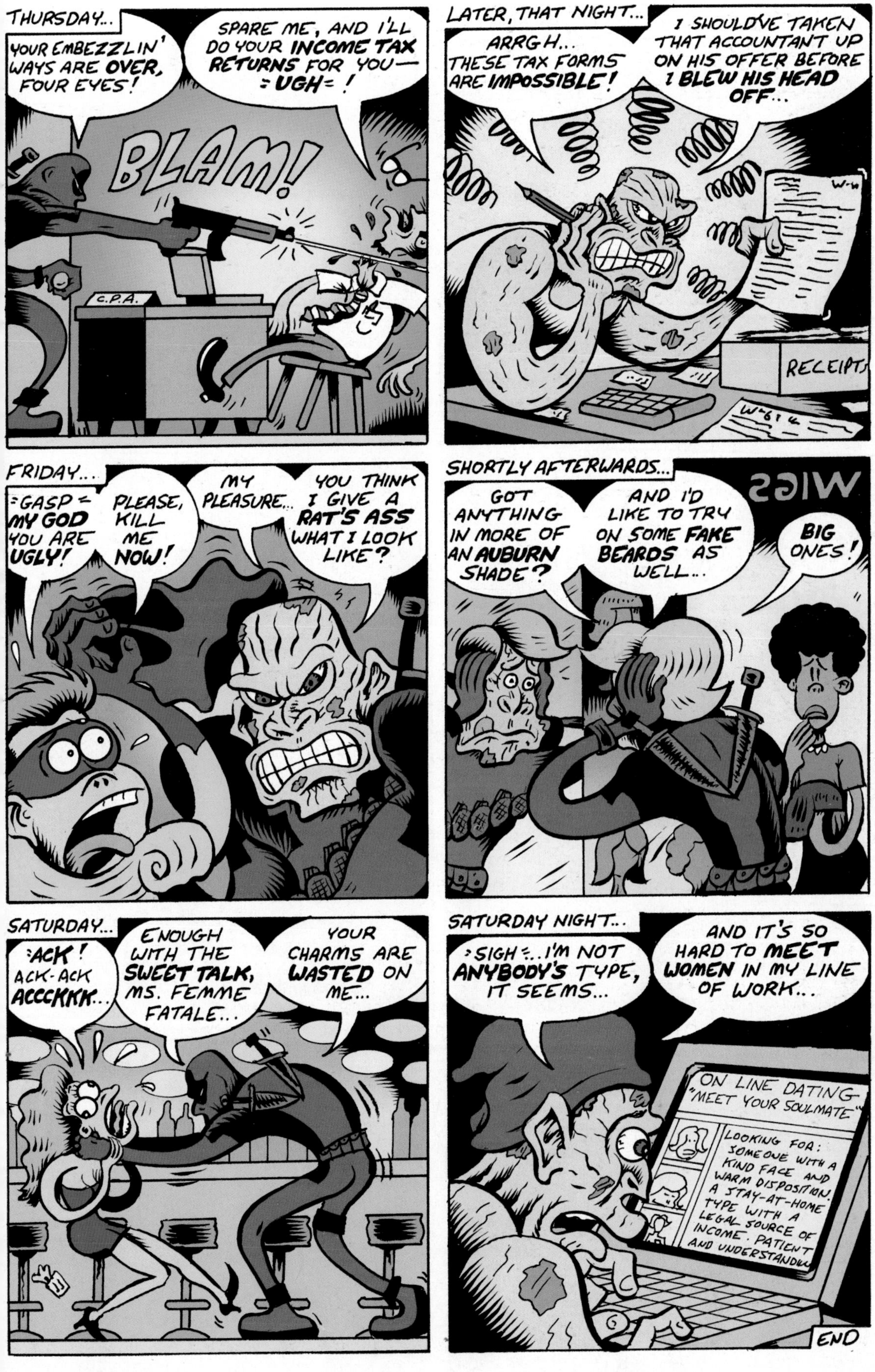
THURSDAY...
YOUR EMBEZZLIN' WAYS ARE OVER, FOUR EYES!
SPARE ME, AND I'LL DO YOUR INCOME TAX RETURNS FOR YOU— =UGH= !
BLAM!
C.P.A.
LATER, THAT NIGHT...
ARRGH... THESE TAX FORMS ARE IMPOSSIBLE!
I SHOULD'VE TAKEN THAT ACCOUNTANT UP ON HIS OFFER BEFORE I BLEW HIS HEAD OFF...
RECEIPTS
FRIDAY...
=GASP= MY GOD YOU ARE UGLY!
PLEASE, KILL ME NOW!
MY PLEASURE...
YOU THINK I GIVE A RAT'S ASS WHAT I LOOK LIKE?
SHORTLY AFTERWARDS...
WIGS
GOT ANYTHING IN MORE OF AN AUBURN SHADE?
AND I'D LIKE TO TRY ON SOME FAKE BEARDS AS WELL...
BIG ONES!
SATURDAY...
=ACK! ACK-ACK ACCCKKK...
ENOUGH WITH THE SWEET TALK, MS. FEMME FATALE...
YOUR CHARMS ARE WASTED ON ME...
SATURDAY NIGHT...
=SIGH=...I'M NOT ANYBODY'S TYPE, IT SEEMS...
AND IT'S SO HARD TO MEET WOMEN IN MY LINE OF WORK...
ON LINE DATING
"MEET YOUR SOULMATE"
LOOKING FOR: SOMEONE WITH A KIND FACE AND WARM DISPOSITION. A STAY-AT-HOME TYPE WITH A LEGAL SOURCE OF INCOME. PATIENT AND UNDERSTANDI
END

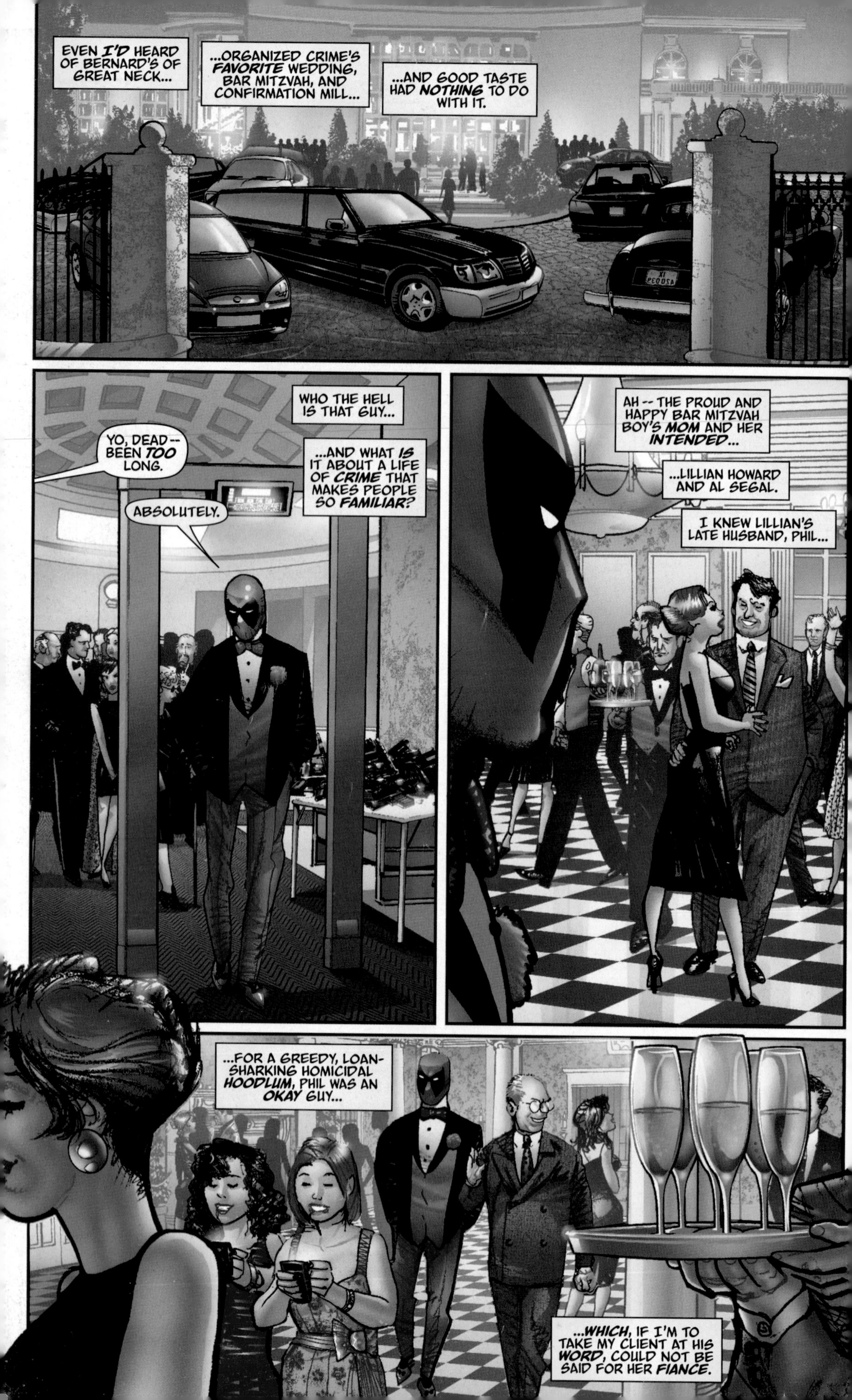
EVEN I'D HEARD OF BERNARD'S OF GREAT NECK...
...ORGANIZED CRIME'S FAVORITE WEDDING, BAR MITZVAH, AND CONFIRMATION MILL...
...AND GOOD TASTE HAD NOTHING TO DO WITH IT.
WHO THE HELL IS THAT GUY...
YO, DEAD -- BEEN TOO LONG.
...AND WHAT IS IT ABOUT A LIFE OF CRIME THAT MAKES PEOPLE SO FAMILIAR?
ABSOLUTELY.
AH -- THE PROUD AND HAPPY BAR MITZVAH BOY'S MOM AND HER INTENDED...
...LILLIAN HOWARD AND AL SEGAL.
I KNEW LILLIAN'S LATE HUSBAND, PHIL...
...FOR A GREEDY, LOAN-SHARKING HOMICIDAL HOODLUM, PHIL WAS AN OKAY GUY...
...WHICH, IF I'M TO TAKE MY CLIENT AT HIS WORD, COULD NOT BE SAID FOR HER FIANCE.

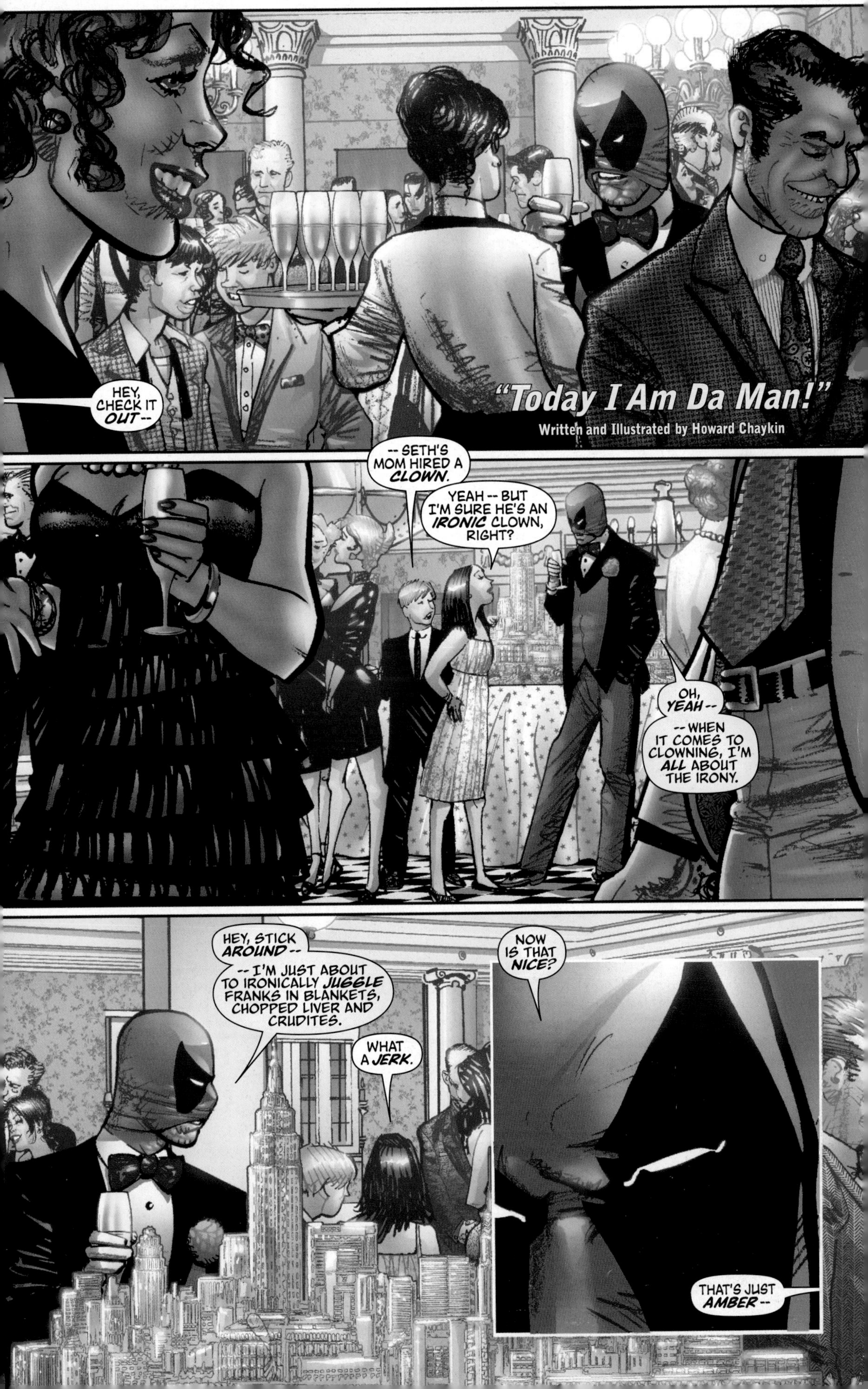

HEY, CHECK IT OUT--
"Today I Am Da Man!"
Written and Illustrated by Howard Chaykin
-- SETH'S MOM HIRED A CLOWN.
YEAH -- BUT I'M SURE HE'S AN IRONIC CLOWN, RIGHT?
OH, YEAH --
-- WHEN IT COMES TO CLOWNING, I'M ALL ABOUT THE IRONY.
HEY, STICK AROUND --
-- I'M JUST ABOUT TO IRONICALLY JUGGLE FRANKS IN BLANKETS, CHOPPED LIVER AND CRUDITES.
WHAT A JERK.
NOW IS THAT NICE?
THAT'S JUST AMBER --

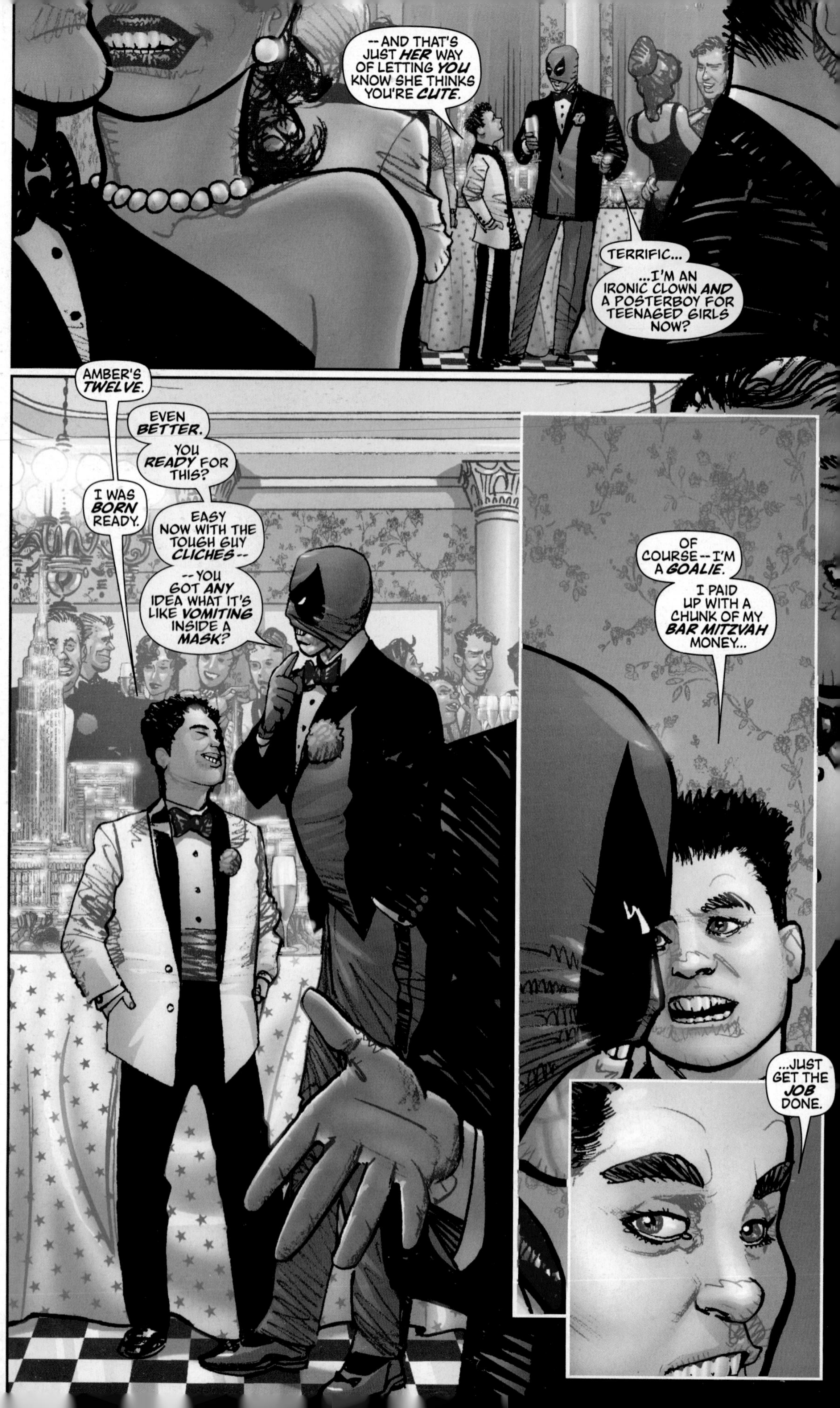

--AND THAT'S JUST HER WAY OF LETTING YOU KNOW SHE THINKS YOU'RE CUTE.
TERRIFIC...
...I'M AN IRONIC CLOWN AND A POSTERBOY FOR TEENAGED GIRLS NOW?
AMBER'S TWELVE.
EVEN BETTER.
YOU READY FOR THIS?
I WAS BORN READY.
EASY NOW WITH THE TOUGH GUY CLICHES--
--YOU GOT ANY IDEA WHAT IT'S LIKE VOMITING INSIDE A MASK?
OF COURSE--I'M A GOALIE.
I PAID UP WITH A CHUNK OF MY BAR MITZVAH MONEY...
...JUST GET THE JOB DONE.

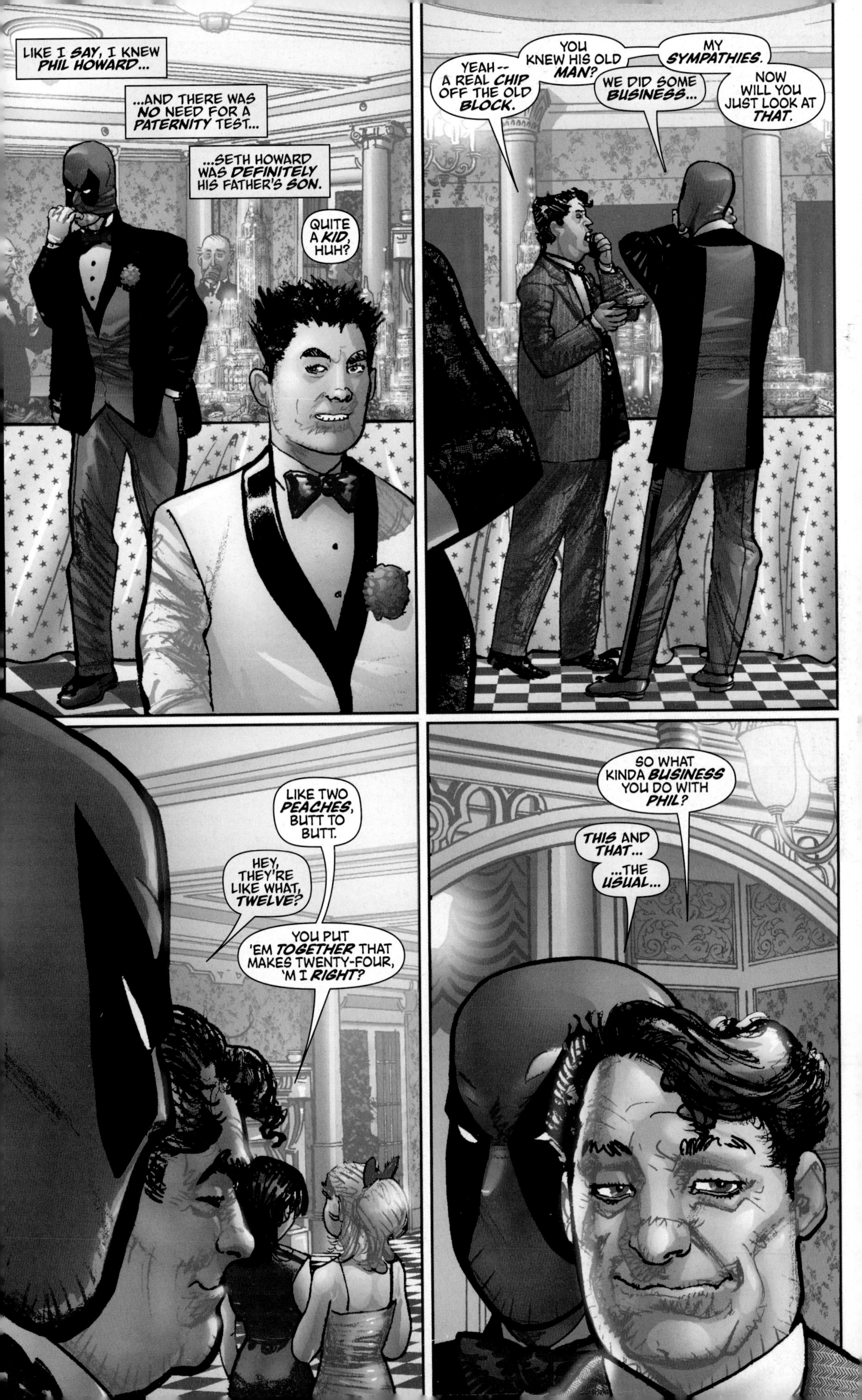
LIKE I SAY, I KNEW PHIL HOWARD...
...AND THERE WAS NO NEED FOR A PATERNITY TEST...
...SETH HOWARD WAS DEFINITELY HIS FATHER'S SON.
QUITE A KID, HUH?
YEAH -- A REAL CHIP OFF THE OLD BLOCK.
YOU KNEW HIS OLD MAN?
WE DID SOME BUSINESS...
MY SYMPATHIES.
NOW WILL YOU JUST LOOK AT THAT.
LIKE TWO PEACHES, BUTT TO BUTT.
HEY, THEY'RE LIKE WHAT, TWELVE?
YOU PUT 'EM TOGETHER THAT MAKES TWENTY-FOUR, 'M I RIGHT?
SO WHAT KINDA BUSINESS YOU DO WITH PHIL?
THIS AND THAT...
...THE USUAL...

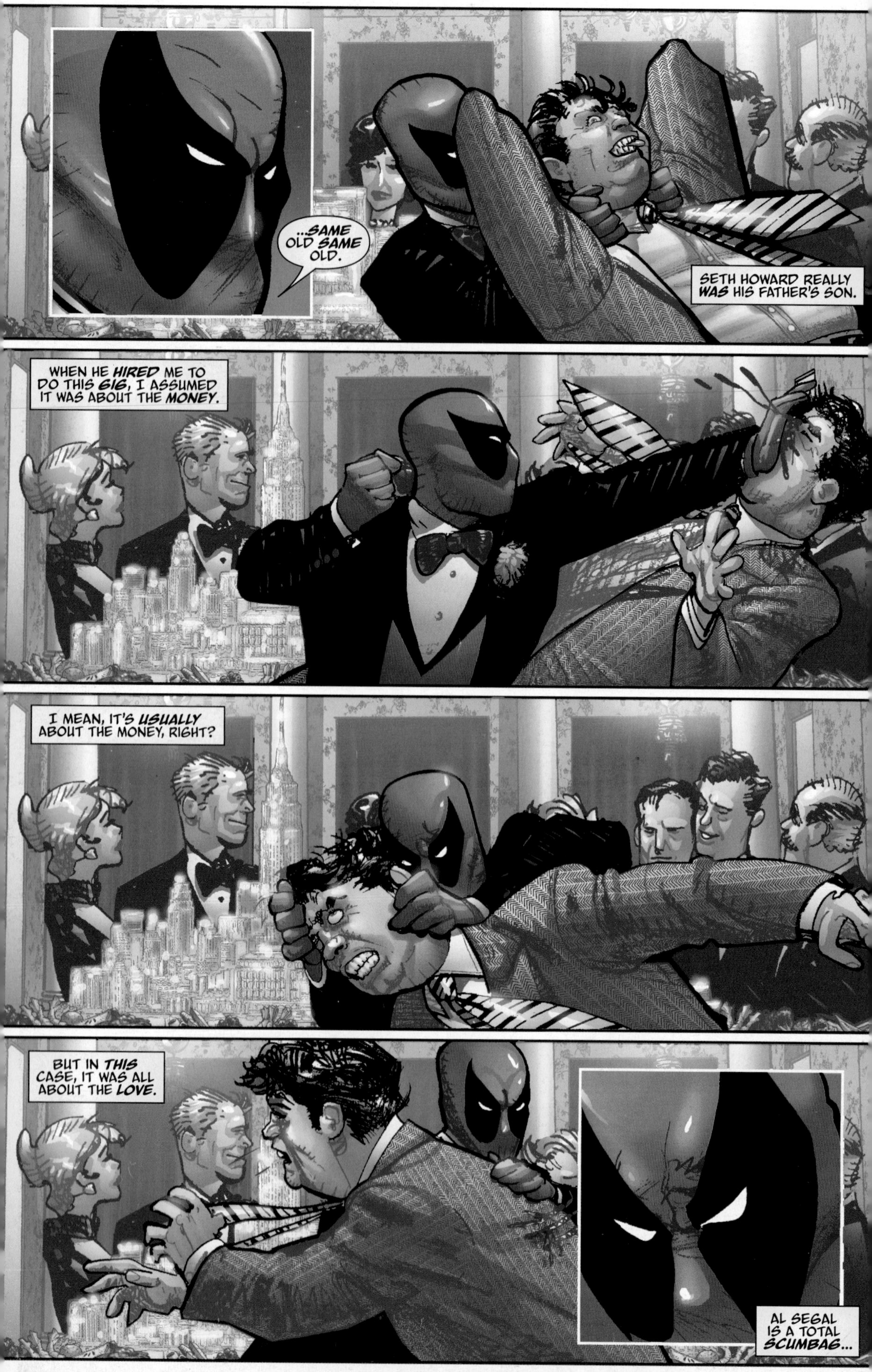
...SAME OLD SAME OLD.
SETH HOWARD REALLY WAS HIS FATHER'S SON.
WHEN HE HIRED ME TO DO THIS GIG, I ASSUMED IT WAS ABOUT THE MONEY.
I MEAN, IT'S USUALLY ABOUT THE MONEY, RIGHT?
BUT IN THIS CASE, IT WAS ALL ABOUT THE LOVE.
AL SEGAL IS A TOTAL SCUMBAG...

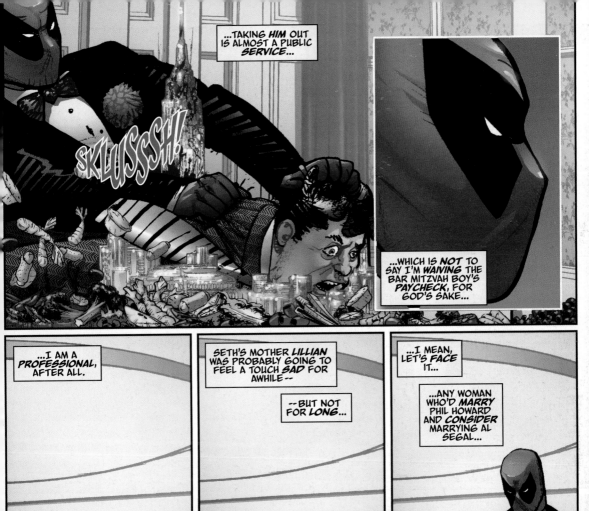

...TAKING *HIM* OUT IS ALMOST A PUBLIC *SERVICE*...

SKLUSSSH!

...WHICH IS *NOT* TO SAY I'M *WAIVING* THE BAR MITZVAH BOY'S *PAYCHECK*, FOR GOD'S SAKE...

...I AM A *PROFESSIONAL*, AFTER ALL.

'EY -- WHAT'D THE IRONIC CLOWN DO TO *AL*?

SETH'S MOTHER *LILLIAN* WAS PROBABLY GOING TO FEEL A TOUCH *SAD* FOR AWHILE --

-- BUT NOT FOR *LONG*...

CHANNGGK-CHANGGKK!

...I MEAN, LET'S *FACE* IT...

...ANY WOMAN WHO'D *MARRY* PHIL HOWARD AND *CONSIDER* MARRYING AL SEGAL...

BRATA-BLAMABRAKA-CHANGKK!

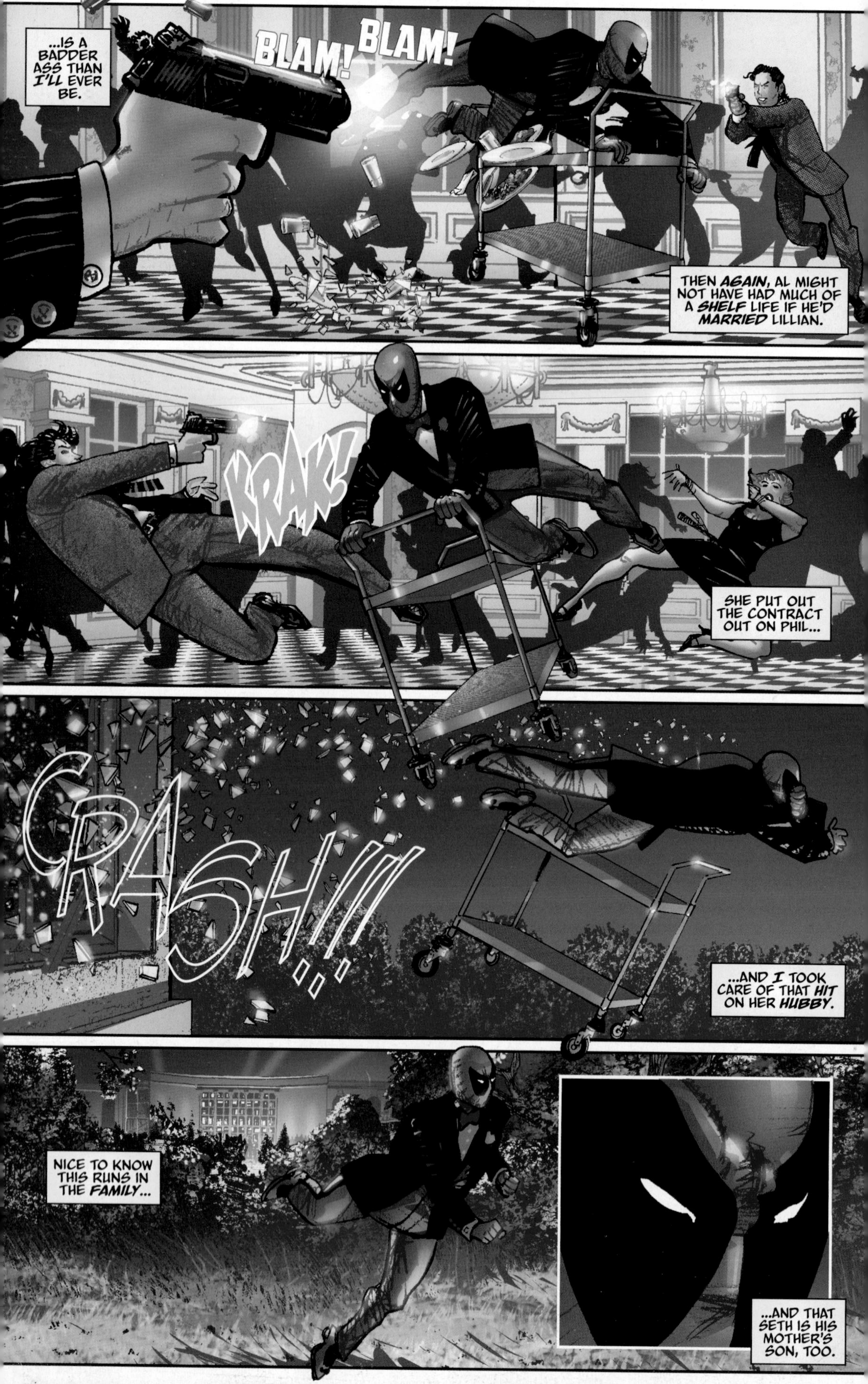
...IS A BADDER ASS THAN I'LL EVER BE.
BLAM!
BLAM!
THEN AGAIN, AL MIGHT NOT HAVE HAD MUCH OF A SHELF LIFE IF HE'D MARRIED LILLIAN.
KRAK!
SHE PUT OUT THE CONTRACT OUT ON PHIL...
CRASH!!!
...AND I TOOK CARE OF THAT HIT ON HER HUBBY.
NICE TO KNOW THIS RUNS IN THE FAMILY...
...AND THAT SETH IS HIS MOTHER'S SON, TOO.

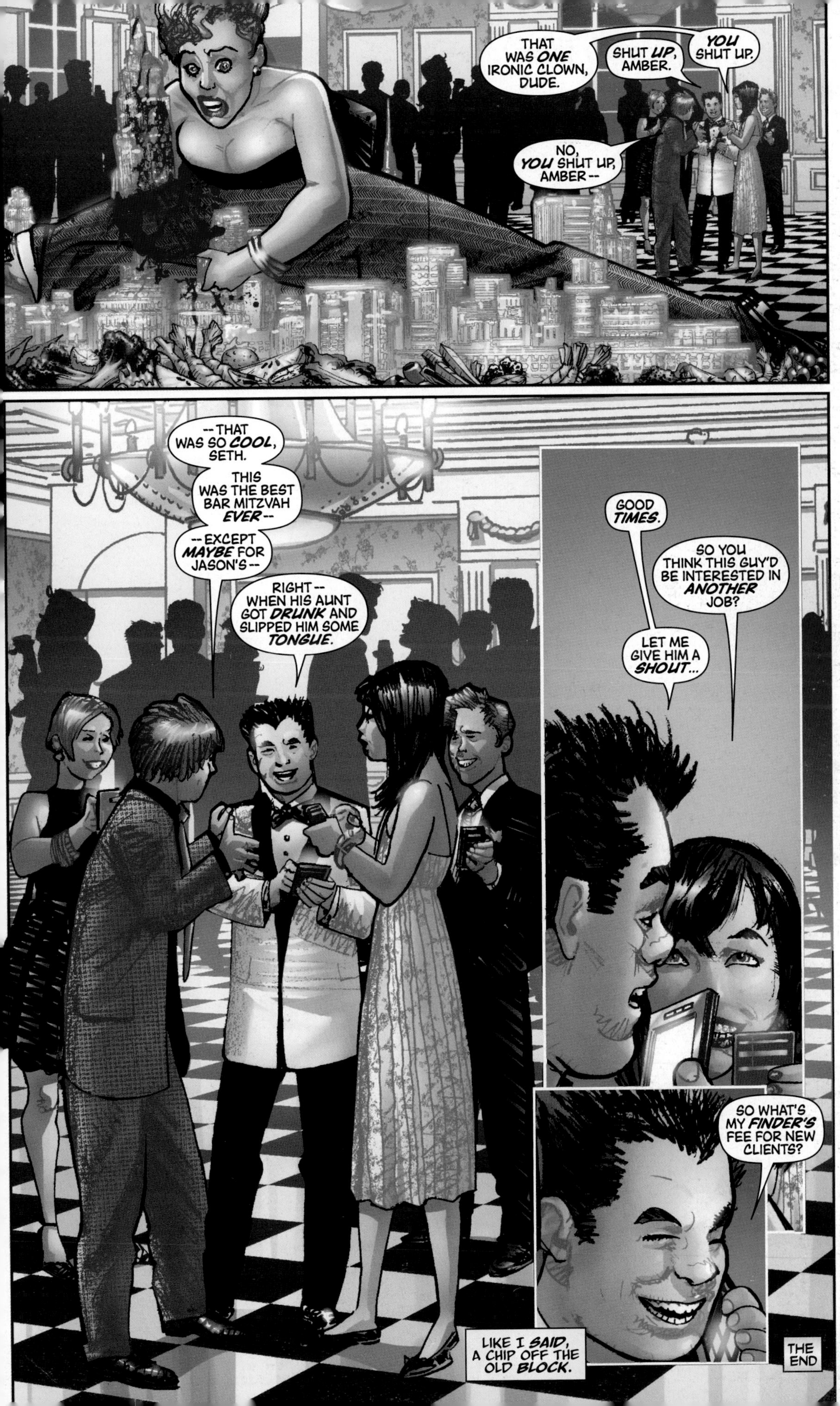
THAT WAS ONE IRONIC CLOWN, DUDE.
SHUT UP, AMBER.
YOU SHUT UP.
NO, YOU SHUT UP, AMBER --
-- THAT WAS SO COOL, SETH.
THIS WAS THE BEST BAR MITZVAH EVER --
-- EXCEPT MAYBE FOR JASON'S --
RIGHT -- WHEN HIS AUNT GOT DRUNK AND SLIPPED HIM SOME TONGUE.
GOOD TIMES.
SO YOU THINK THIS GUY'D BE INTERESTED IN ANOTHER JOB?
LET ME GIVE HIM A SHOUT...
SO WHAT'S MY FINDER'S FEE FOR NEW CLIENTS?
LIKE I SAID, A CHIP OFF THE OLD BLOCK.
THE END

MARVEL BROMANCE COMICS PRESENTS:

"NO LONGER IN A RELATIONSHIP"

WRITTEN AND ILLUSTRATED BY TIM HAMILTON

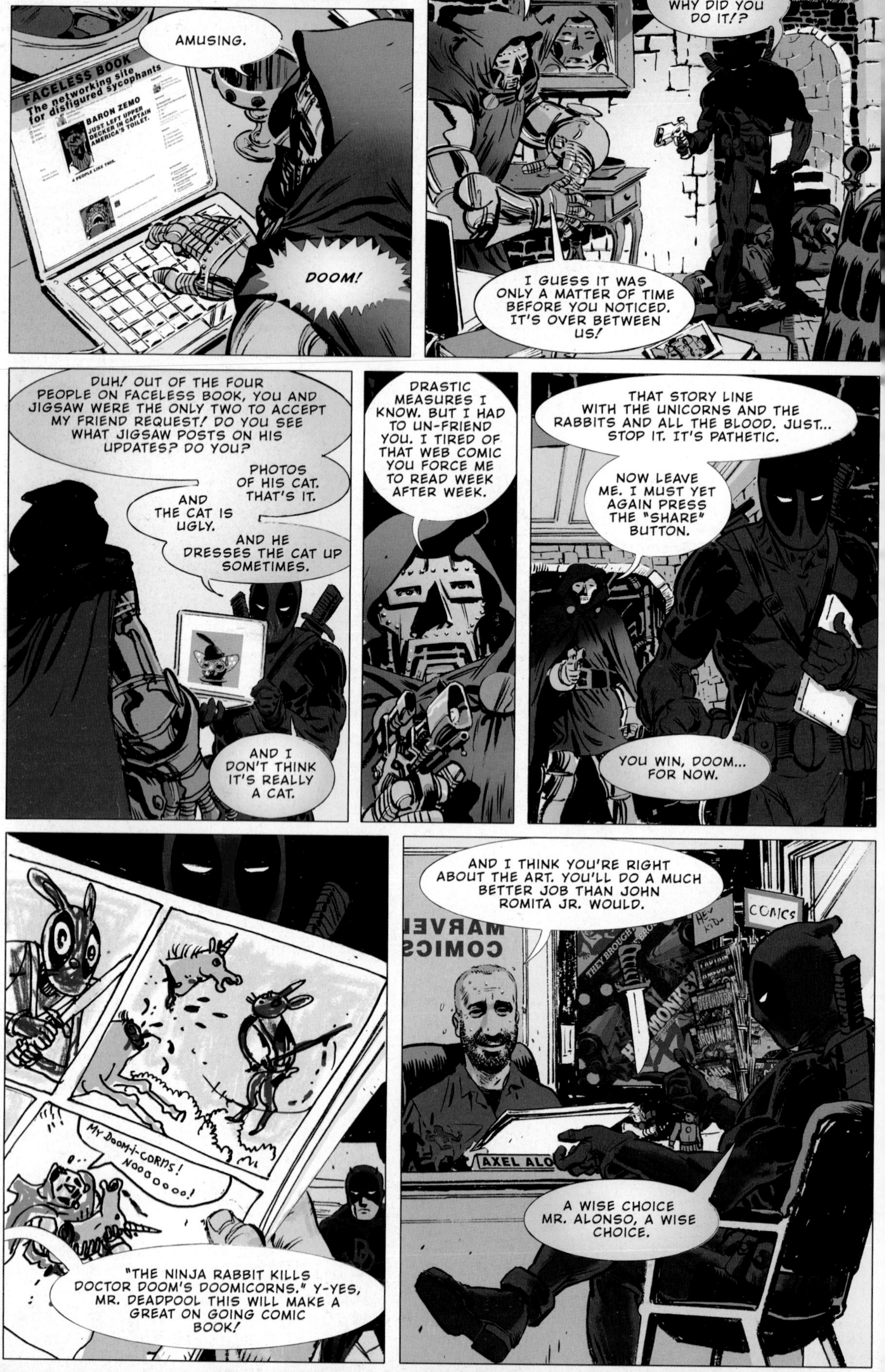

FACELESS BOOK
The networking site for disfigured sycophants
BARON ZEMO
JUST LEFT UPPER DECKER IN CAPTAIN AMERICA'S TOILET.
4 PEOPLE LIKE THIS.
AMUSING.
DOOM!
DEADPOOL!
WHY DOOM?! WHY DID YOU DO IT!?
I GUESS IT WAS ONLY A MATTER OF TIME BEFORE YOU NOTICED. IT'S OVER BETWEEN US!
DUH! OUT OF THE FOUR PEOPLE ON FACELESS BOOK, YOU AND JIGSAW WERE THE ONLY TWO TO ACCEPT MY FRIEND REQUEST! DO YOU SEE WHAT JIGSAW POSTS ON HIS UPDATES? DO YOU?
PHOTOS OF HIS CAT. THAT'S IT.
AND THE CAT IS UGLY.
AND HE DRESSES THE CAT UP SOMETIMES.
AND I DON'T THINK IT'S REALLY A CAT.
DRASTIC MEASURES I KNOW. BUT I HAD TO UN-FRIEND YOU. I TIRED OF THAT WEB COMIC YOU FORCE ME TO READ WEEK AFTER WEEK.
THAT STORY LINE WITH THE UNICORNS AND THE RABBITS AND ALL THE BLOOD. JUST... STOP IT. IT'S PATHETIC.
NOW LEAVE ME. I MUST YET AGAIN PRESS THE "SHARE" BUTTON.
YOU WIN, DOOM... FOR NOW.
MY DOOM-I-CORNS! NOOOOOOO!
"THE NINJA RABBIT KILLS DOCTOR DOOM'S DOOMICORNS." Y-YES, MR. DEADPOOL THIS WILL MAKE A GREAT ON GOING COMIC BOOK!
AND I THINK YOU'RE RIGHT ABOUT THE ART. YOU'LL DO A MUCH BETTER JOB THAN JOHN ROMITA JR. WOULD.
COMICS
A WISE CHOICE MR. ALONSO, A WISE CHOICE.

CANADA, MAN!

Writing: Rob Williams • Art: Phil Bond • Colors: Tomislav Tikuiin

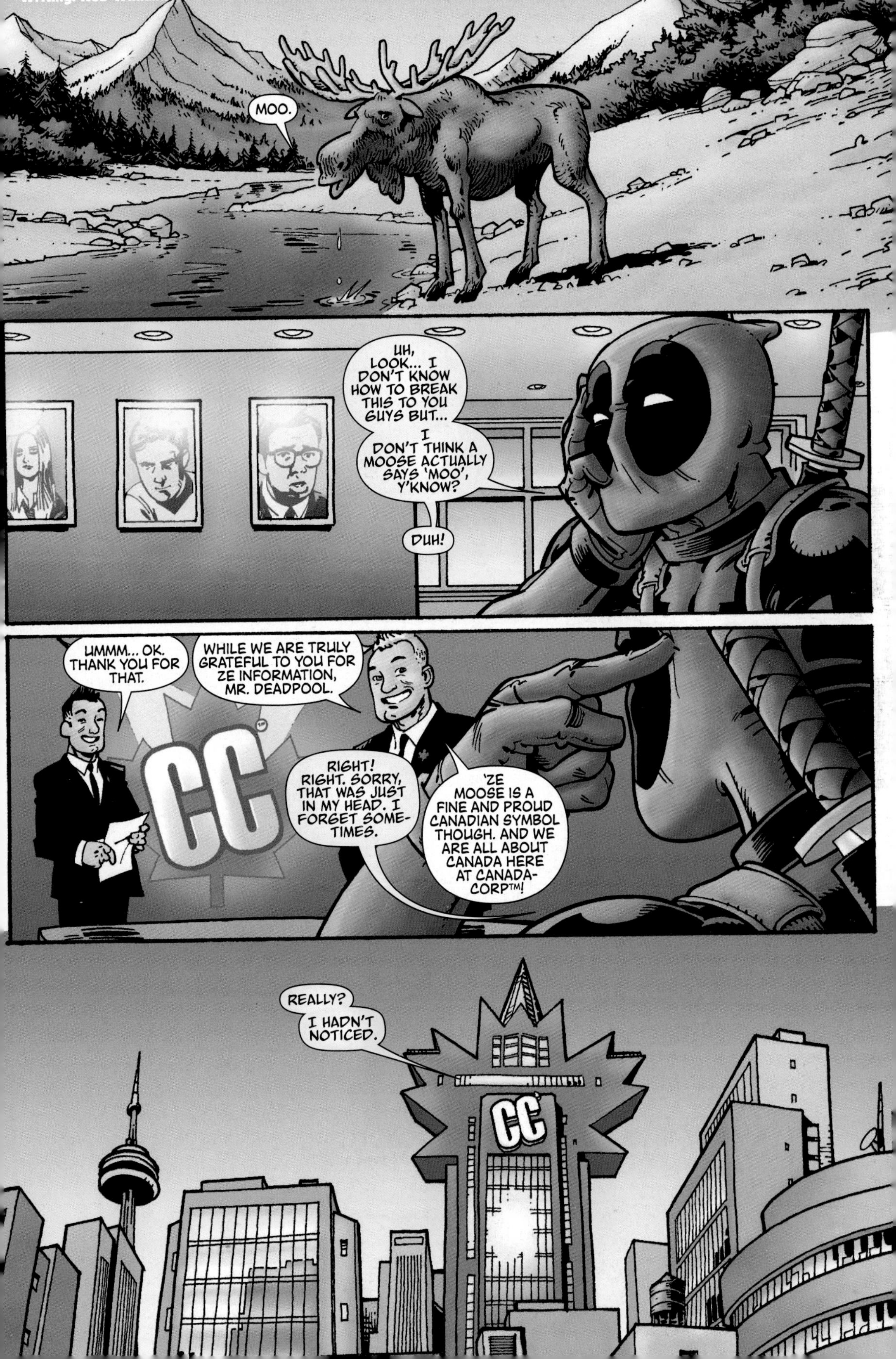
MOO.
UH, LOOK... I DON'T KNOW HOW TO BREAK THIS TO YOU GUYS BUT...
I DON'T THINK A MOOSE ACTUALLY SAYS 'MOO', Y'KNOW?
DUH!
UMMM... OK. THANK YOU FOR THAT.
WHILE WE ARE TRULY GRATEFUL TO YOU FOR ZE INFORMATION, MR. DEADPOOL.
CC
RIGHT! RIGHT. SORRY, THAT WAS JUST IN MY HEAD. I FORGET SOME-TIMES.
'ZE MOOSE IS A FINE AND PROUD CANADIAN SYMBOL THOUGH. AND WE ARE ALL ABOUT CANADA HERE AT CANADA-CORP™!
REALLY? I HADN'T NOTICED.
CC

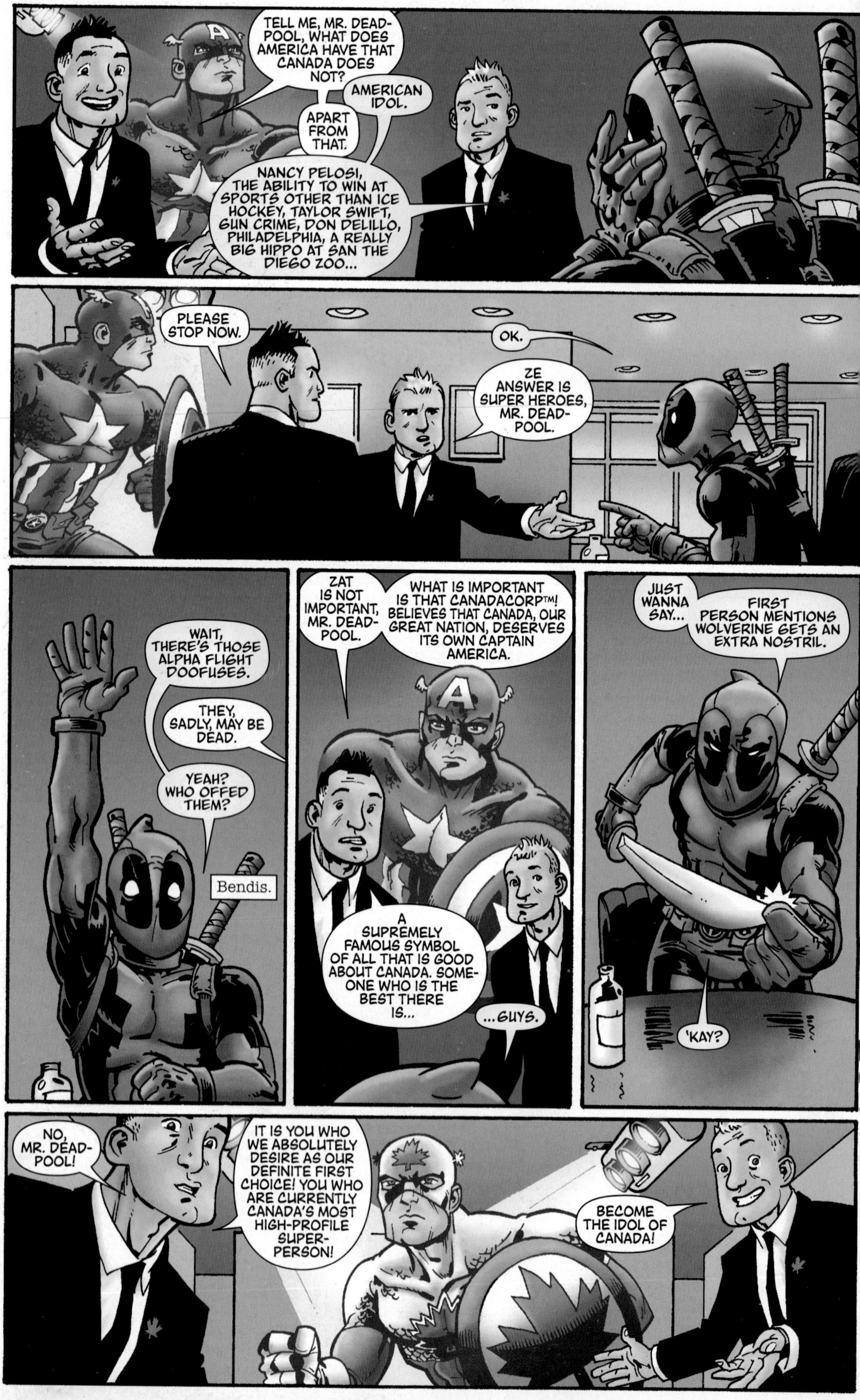
TELL ME, MR. DEAD-POOL, WHAT DOES AMERICA HAVE THAT CANADA DOES NOT?
AMERICAN IDOL.
APART FROM THAT.
NANCY PELOSI, THE ABILITY TO WIN AT SPORTS OTHER THAN ICE HOCKEY, TAYLOR SWIFT, GUN CRIME, DON DELILLO, PHILADELPHIA, A REALLY BIG HIPPO AT SAN THE DIEGO ZOO...
PLEASE STOP NOW.
OK.
ZE ANSWER IS SUPER HEROES, MR. DEAD-POOL.
WAIT, THERE'S THOSE ALPHA FLIGHT DOOFUSES.
THEY, SADLY, MAY BE DEAD.
YEAH? WHO OFFED THEM?
Bendis.
ZAT IS NOT IMPORTANT, MR. DEAD-POOL.
WHAT IS IMPORTANT IS THAT CANADACORP™! BELIEVES THAT CANADA, OUR GREAT NATION, DESERVES ITS OWN CAPTAIN AMERICA.
A SUPREMELY FAMOUS SYMBOL OF ALL THAT IS GOOD ABOUT CANADA. SOME-ONE WHO IS THE BEST THERE IS...
...GUYS.
JUST WANNA SAY...
FIRST PERSON MENTIONS WOLVERINE GETS AN EXTRA NOSTRIL.
'KAY?
NO, MR. DEAD-POOL!
IT IS YOU WHO WE ABSOLUTELY DESIRE AS OUR DEFINITE FIRST CHOICE! YOU WHO ARE CURRENTLY CANADA'S MOST HIGH-PROFILE SUPER-PERSON!
BECOME THE IDOL OF CANADA!

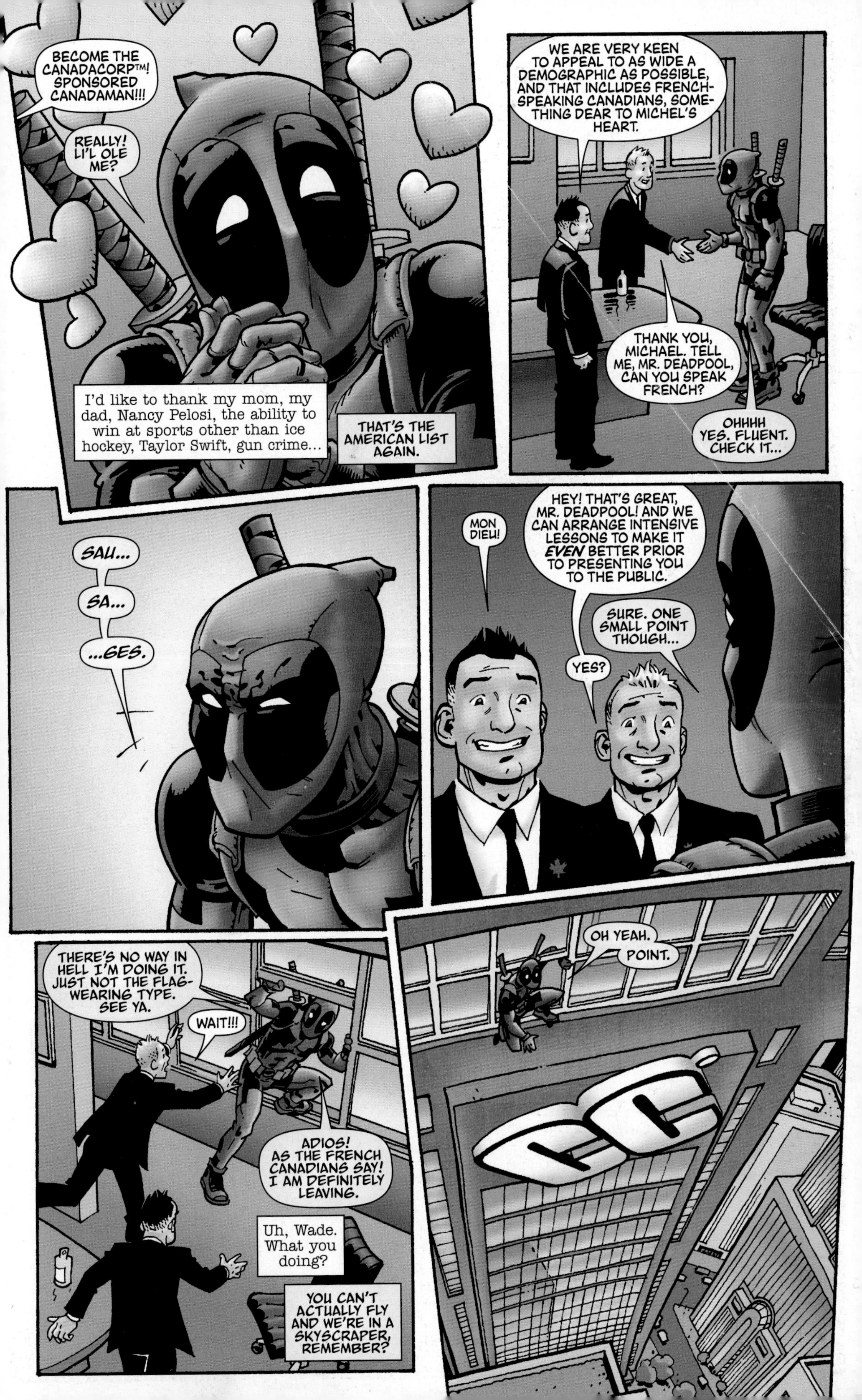

BECOME THE CANADACORP™! SPONSORED CANADAMAN!!!
REALLY! LI'L OLE ME?
I'd like to thank my mom, my dad, Nancy Pelosi, the ability to win at sports other than ice hockey, Taylor Swift, gun crime...
THAT'S THE AMERICAN LIST AGAIN.
WE ARE VERY KEEN TO APPEAL TO AS WIDE A DEMOGRAPHIC AS POSSIBLE, AND THAT INCLUDES FRENCH-SPEAKING CANADIANS, SOMETHING DEAR TO MICHEL'S HEART.
THANK YOU, MICHAEL. TELL ME, MR. DEADPOOL, CAN YOU SPEAK FRENCH?
OHHHH YES. FLUENT. CHECK IT...
SAU...
SA...
...GES.
MON DIEU!
HEY! THAT'S GREAT, MR. DEADPOOL! AND WE CAN ARRANGE INTENSIVE LESSONS TO MAKE IT EVEN BETTER PRIOR TO PRESENTING YOU TO THE PUBLIC.
SURE. ONE SMALL POINT THOUGH...
YES?
THERE'S NO WAY IN HELL I'M DOING IT. JUST NOT THE FLAG-WEARING TYPE. SEE YA.
WAIT!!!
ADIOS! AS THE FRENCH CANADIANS SAY! I AM DEFINITELY LEAVING.
Uh, Wade. What you doing?
YOU CAN'T ACTUALLY FLY AND WE'RE IN A SKYSCRAPER, REMEMBER?
OH YEAH.
POINT.

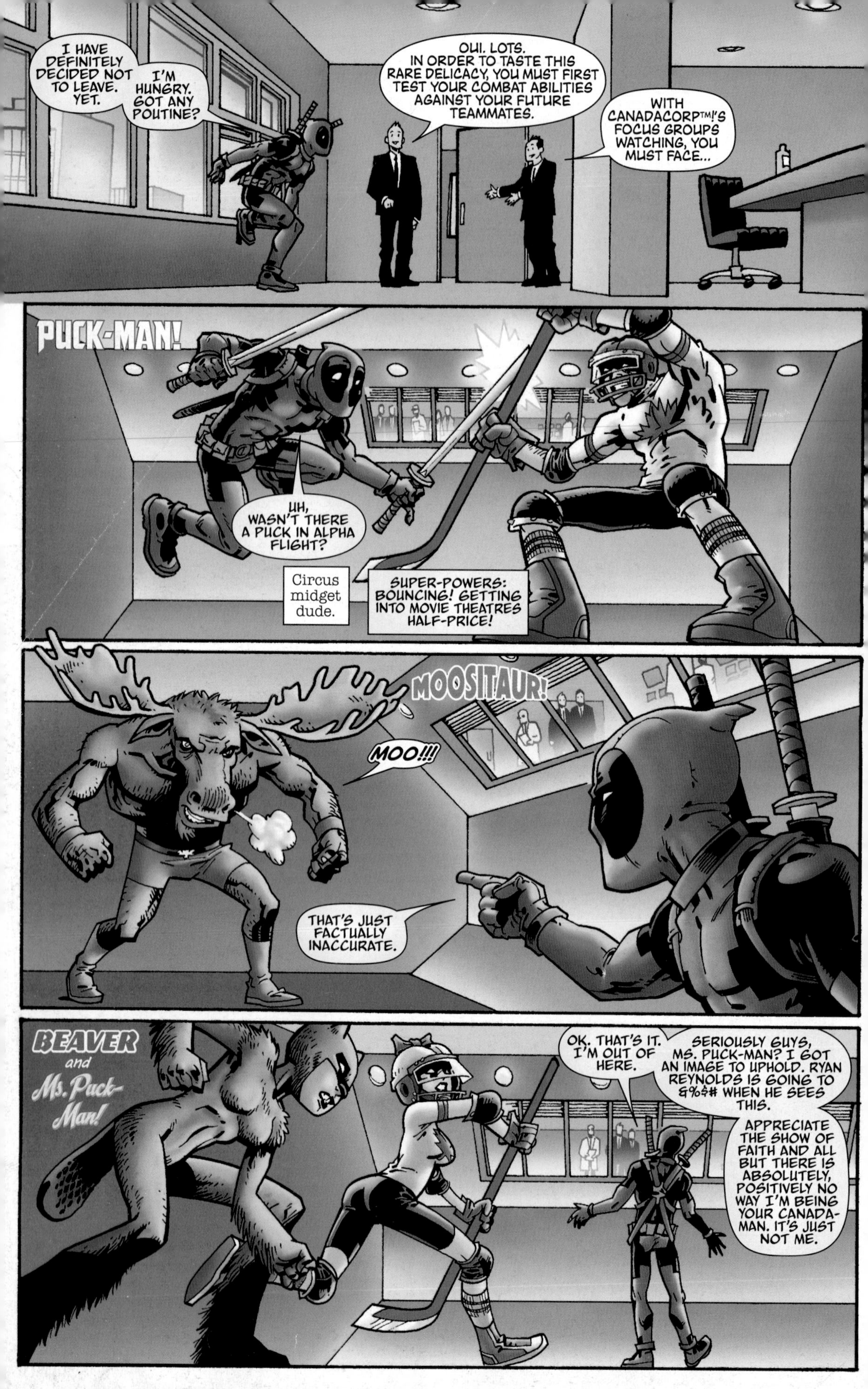
I HAVE DEFINITELY DECIDED NOT TO LEAVE. YET.
I'M HUNGRY. GOT ANY POUTINE?
OUI. LOTS. IN ORDER TO TASTE THIS RARE DELICACY, YOU MUST FIRST TEST YOUR COMBAT ABILITIES AGAINST YOUR FUTURE TEAMMATES.
WITH CANADACORP™!'S FOCUS GROUPS WATCHING, YOU MUST FACE...
PUCK-MAN!
UH, WASN'T THERE A PUCK IN ALPHA FLIGHT?
Circus midget dude.
SUPER-POWERS: BOUNCING! GETTING INTO MOVIE THEATRES HALF-PRICE!
MOOSITAUR!
MOO!!!
THAT'S JUST FACTUALLY INACCURATE.
BEAVER and Ms. Puck-Man!
OK. THAT'S IT. I'M OUT OF HERE.
SERIOUSLY GUYS, MS. PUCK-MAN? I GOT AN IMAGE TO UPHOLD. RYAN REYNOLDS IS GOING TO &%$# WHEN HE SEES THIS.
APPRECIATE THE SHOW OF FAITH AND ALL BUT THERE IS ABSOLUTELY, POSITIVELY NO WAY I'M BEING YOUR CANADA-MAN. IT'S JUST NOT ME.

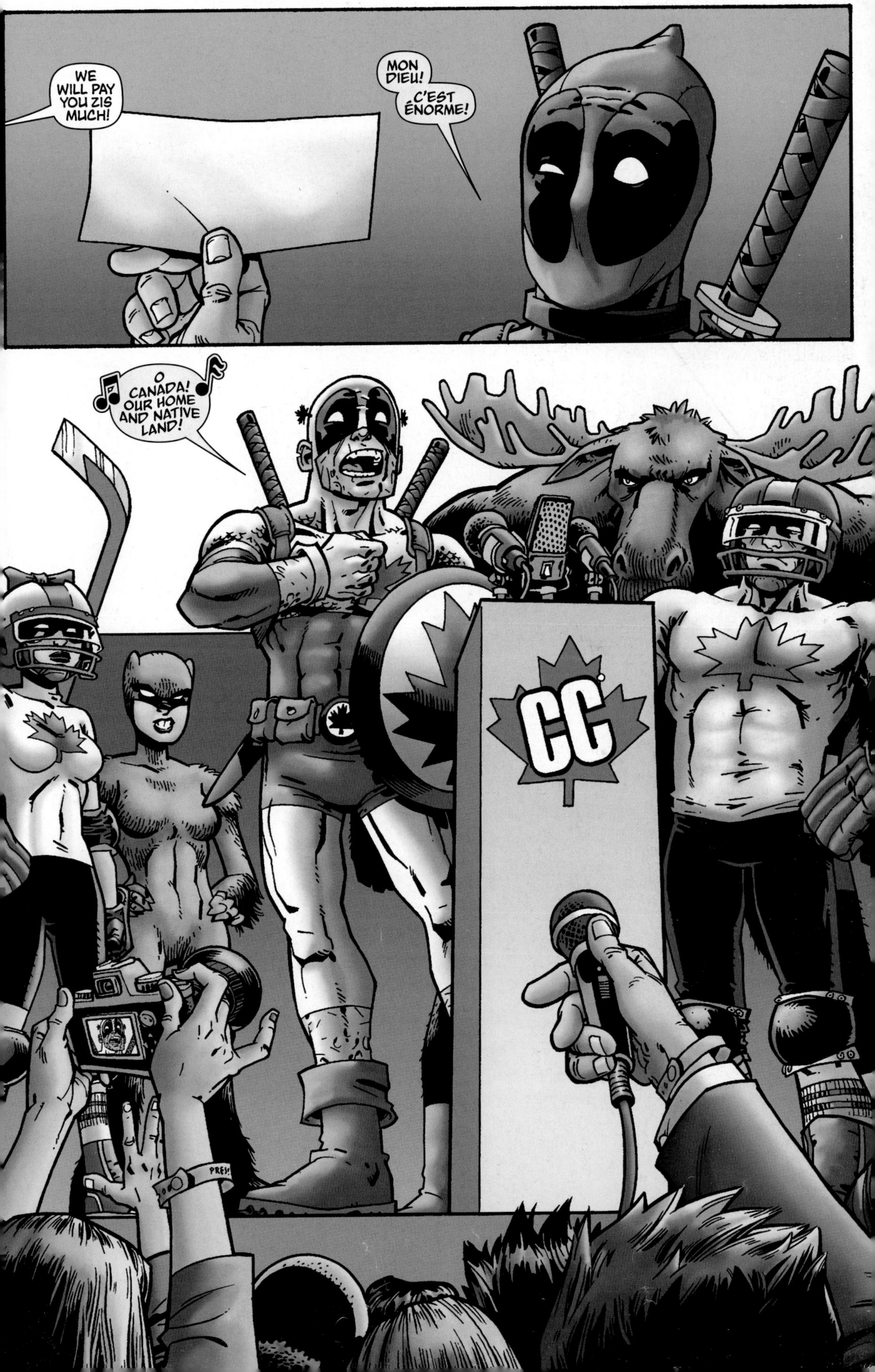
WE WILL PAY YOU ZIS MUCH!
MON DIEU! C'EST ÉNORME!
O CANADA! OUR HOME AND NATIVE LAND!
CC

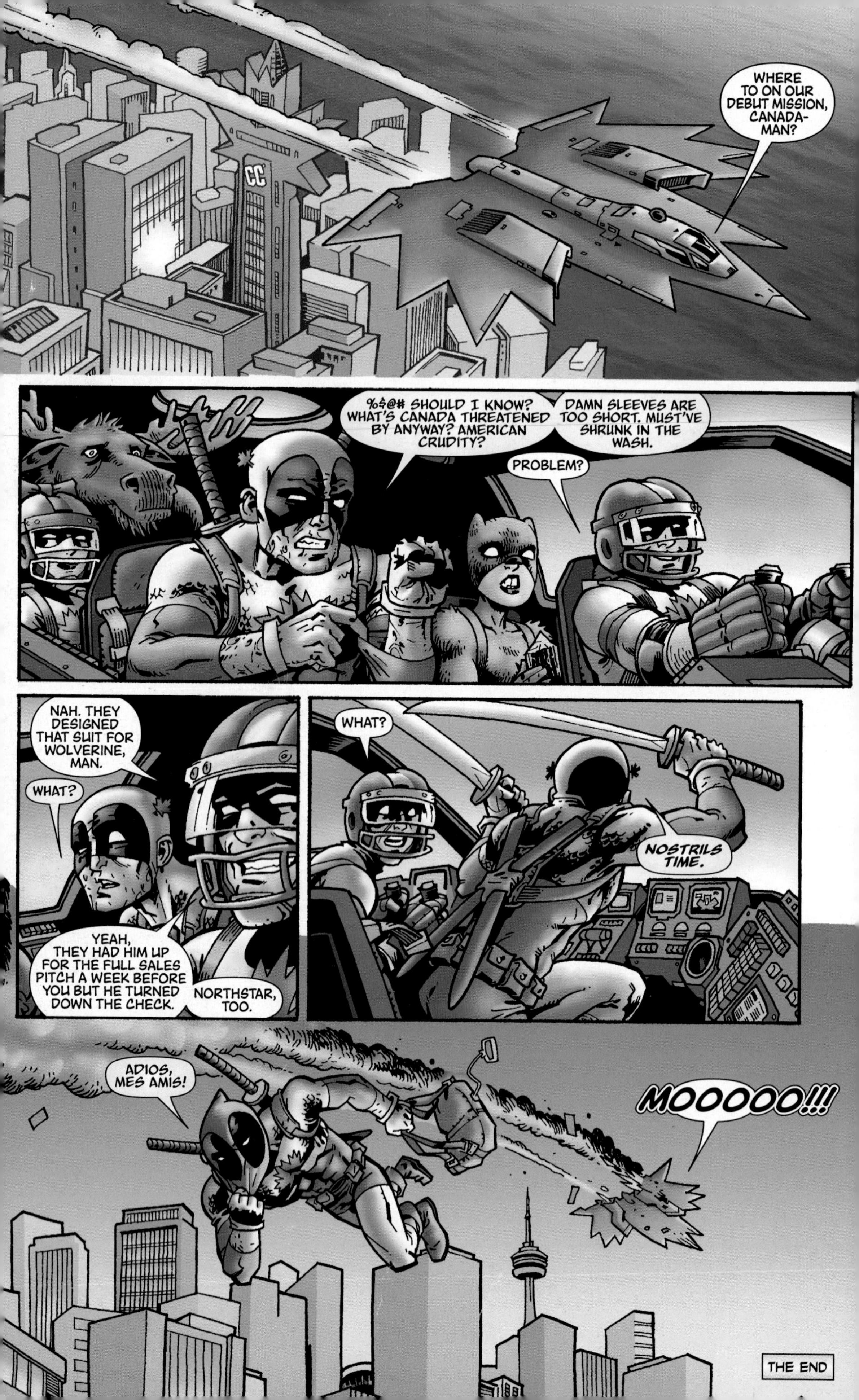
WHERE TO ON OUR DEBUT MISSION, CANADA-MAN?
%$@# SHOULD I KNOW? WHAT'S CANADA THREATENED BY ANYWAY? AMERICAN CRUDITY?
DAMN SLEEVES ARE TOO SHORT. MUST'VE SHRUNK IN THE WASH.
PROBLEM?
NAH. THEY DESIGNED THAT SUIT FOR WOLVERINE, MAN.
WHAT?
YEAH, THEY HAD HIM UP FOR THE FULL SALES PITCH A WEEK BEFORE YOU BUT HE TURNED DOWN THE CHECK.
NORTHSTAR, TOO.
WHAT?
NOSTRILS TIME.
ADIOS, MES AMIS!
MOOOOO!!!
THE END

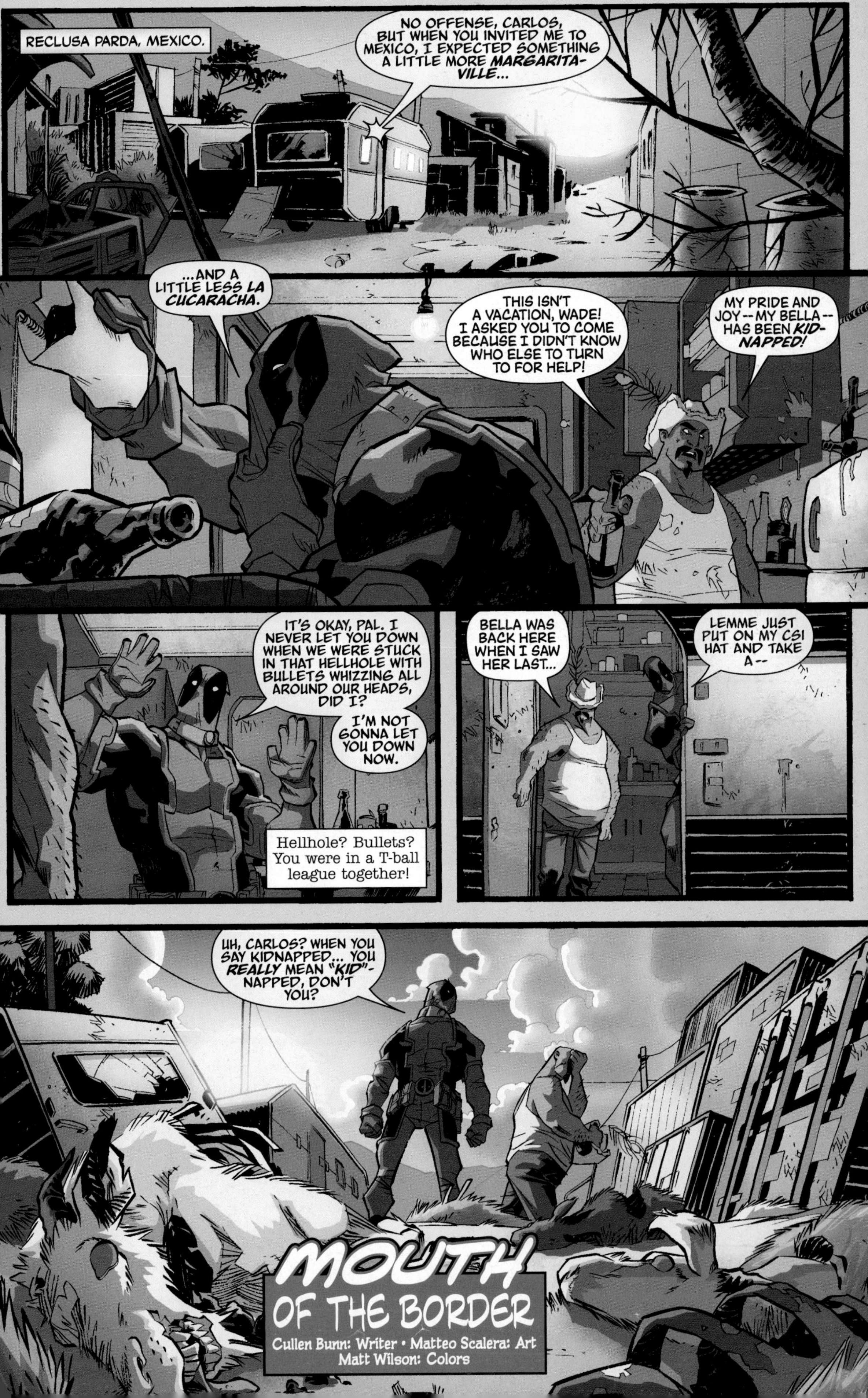
RECLUSA PARDA, MEXICO.
NO OFFENSE, CARLOS, BUT WHEN YOU INVITED ME TO MEXICO, I EXPECTED SOMETHING A LITTLE MORE MARGARITA-VILLE...
...AND A LITTLE LESS LA CUCARACHA.
THIS ISN'T A VACATION, WADE! I ASKED YOU TO COME BECAUSE I DIDN'T KNOW WHO ELSE TO TURN TO FOR HELP!
MY PRIDE AND JOY -- MY BELLA -- HAS BEEN KID-NAPPED!
IT'S OKAY, PAL. I NEVER LET YOU DOWN WHEN WE WERE STUCK IN THAT HELLHOLE WITH BULLETS WHIZZING ALL AROUND OUR HEADS, DID I?
I'M NOT GONNA LET YOU DOWN NOW.
Hellhole? Bullets? You were in a T-ball league together!
BELLA WAS BACK HERE WHEN I SAW HER LAST...
LEMME JUST PUT ON MY CSI HAT AND TAKE A --
UH, CARLOS? WHEN YOU SAY KIDNAPPED... YOU REALLY MEAN "KID"-NAPPED, DON'T YOU?
MOUTH OF THE BORDER
Cullen Bunn: Writer • Matteo Scalera: Art
Matt Wilson: Colors

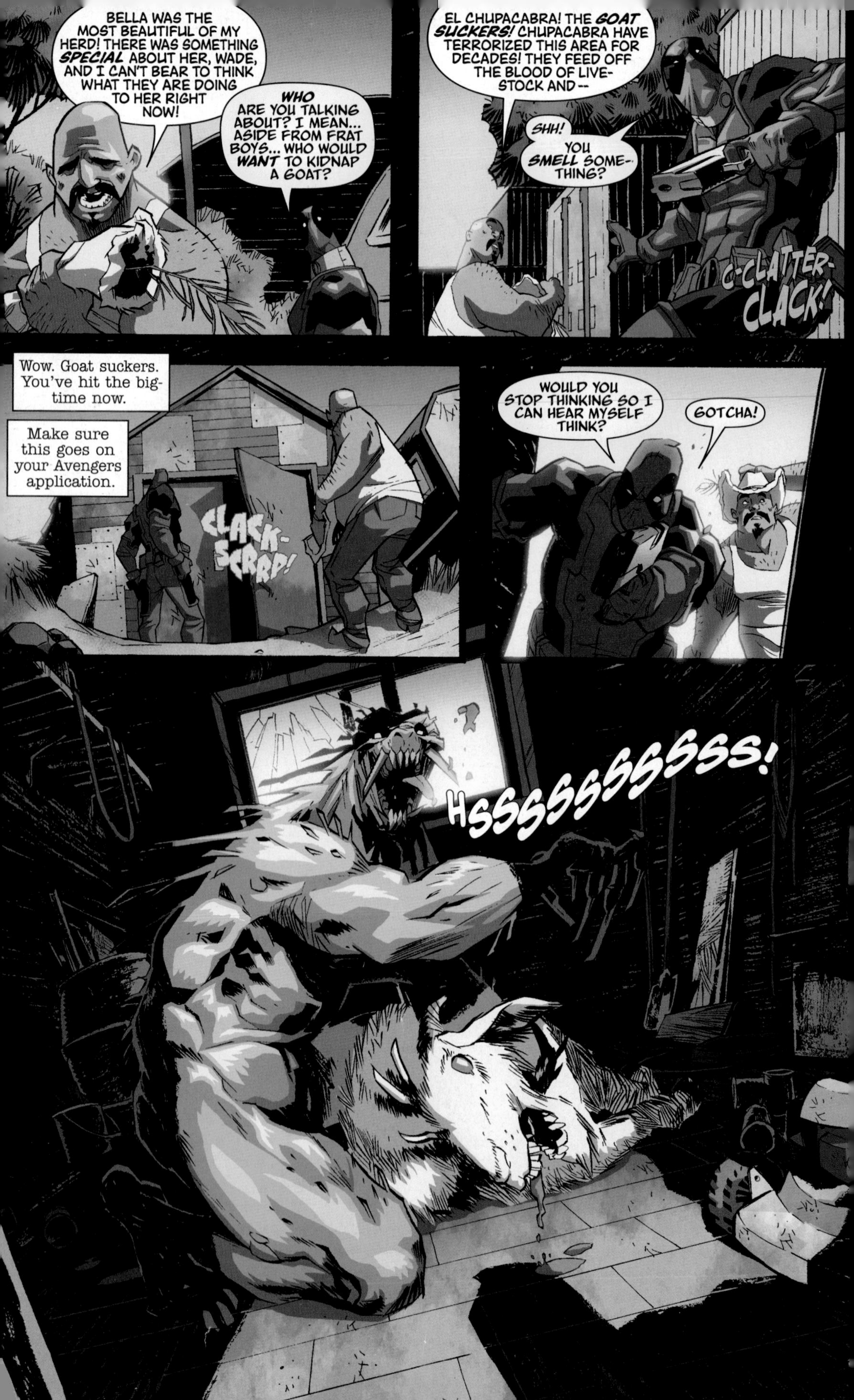
BELLA WAS THE MOST BEAUTIFUL OF MY HERD! THERE WAS SOMETHING SPECIAL ABOUT HER, WADE, AND I CAN'T BEAR TO THINK WHAT THEY ARE DOING TO HER RIGHT NOW!
WHO ARE YOU TALKING ABOUT? I MEAN... ASIDE FROM FRAT BOYS... WHO WOULD WANT TO KIDNAP A GOAT?
EL CHUPACABRA! THE GOAT SUCKERS! CHUPACABRA HAVE TERRORIZED THIS AREA FOR DECADES! THEY FEED OFF THE BLOOD OF LIVE-STOCK AND --
SHH!
YOU SMELL SOME-THING?
C-CLATTER-CLACK!
Wow. Goat suckers. You've hit the big-time now.
Make sure this goes on your Avengers application.
CLACK-SCRRP!
WOULD YOU STOP THINKING SO I CAN HEAR MYSELF THINK?
GOTCHA!
HSSSSSSSSSSS!

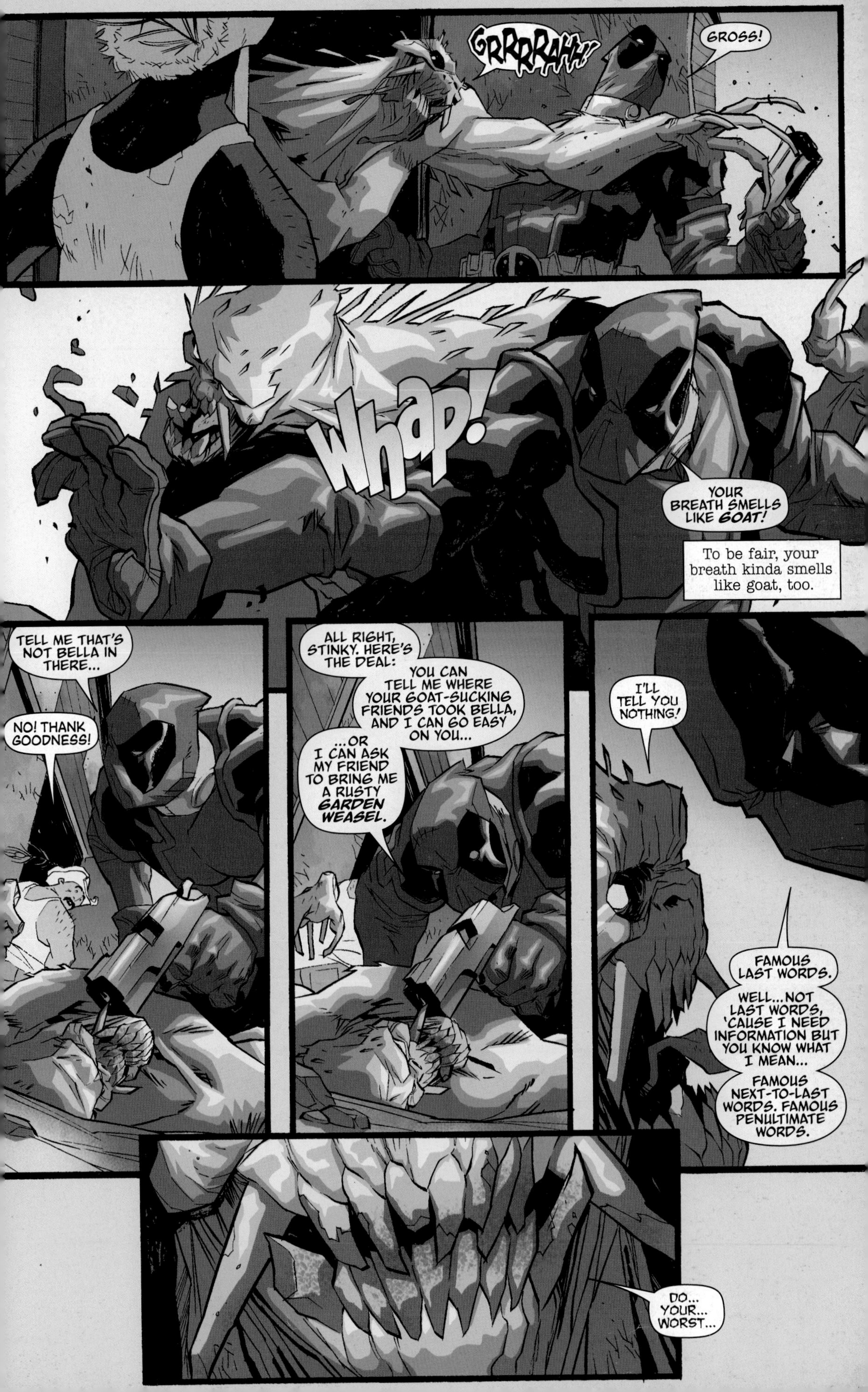
GRRRRAHH!
GROSS!
WHAP!
YOUR BREATH SMELLS LIKE *GOAT!*
To be fair, your breath kinda smells like goat, too.
TELL ME THAT'S NOT BELLA IN THERE...
NO! THANK GOODNESS!
ALL RIGHT, STINKY. HERE'S THE DEAL:
YOU CAN TELL ME WHERE YOUR GOAT-SUCKING FRIENDS TOOK BELLA, AND I CAN GO EASY ON YOU...
...OR I CAN ASK MY FRIEND TO BRING ME A RUSTY *GARDEN WEASEL.*
I'LL TELL YOU NOTHING!
FAMOUS LAST WORDS.
WELL...NOT LAST WORDS, 'CAUSE I NEED INFORMATION BUT YOU KNOW WHAT I MEAN...
FAMOUS NEXT-TO-LAST WORDS. FAMOUS PENULTIMATE WORDS.
DO... YOUR... WORST...

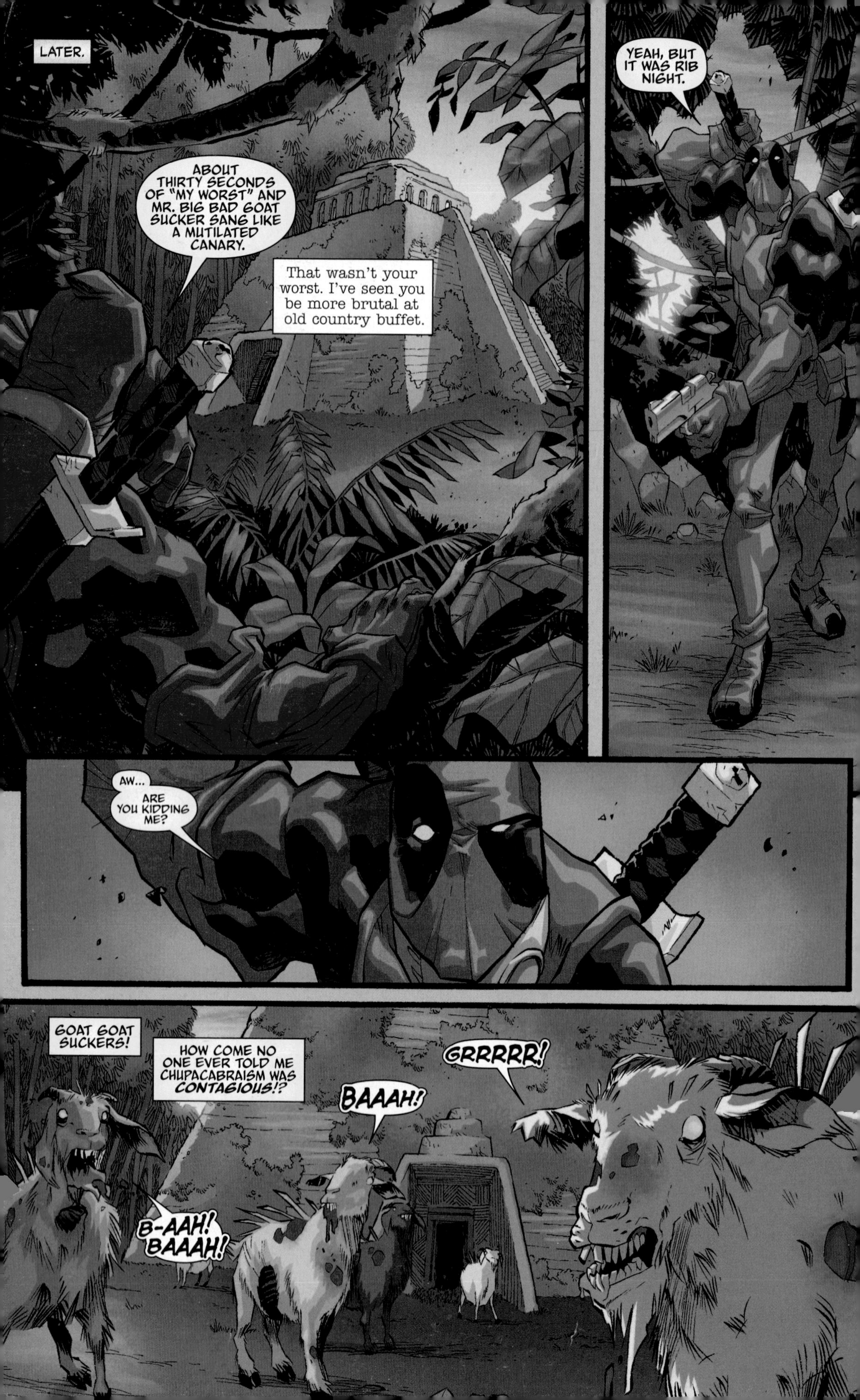
LATER.
ABOUT THIRTY SECONDS OF "MY WORST" AND MR. BIG BAD GOAT SUCKER SANG LIKE A MUTILATED CANARY.
That wasn't your worst. I've seen you be more brutal at old country buffet.
YEAH, BUT IT WAS RIB NIGHT.
AW... ARE YOU KIDDING ME?
GOAT GOAT SUCKERS!
HOW COME NO ONE EVER TOLD ME CHUPACABRAISM WAS CONTAGIOUS!?
GRRRRR!
BAAAH!
B-AAH! BAAAH!

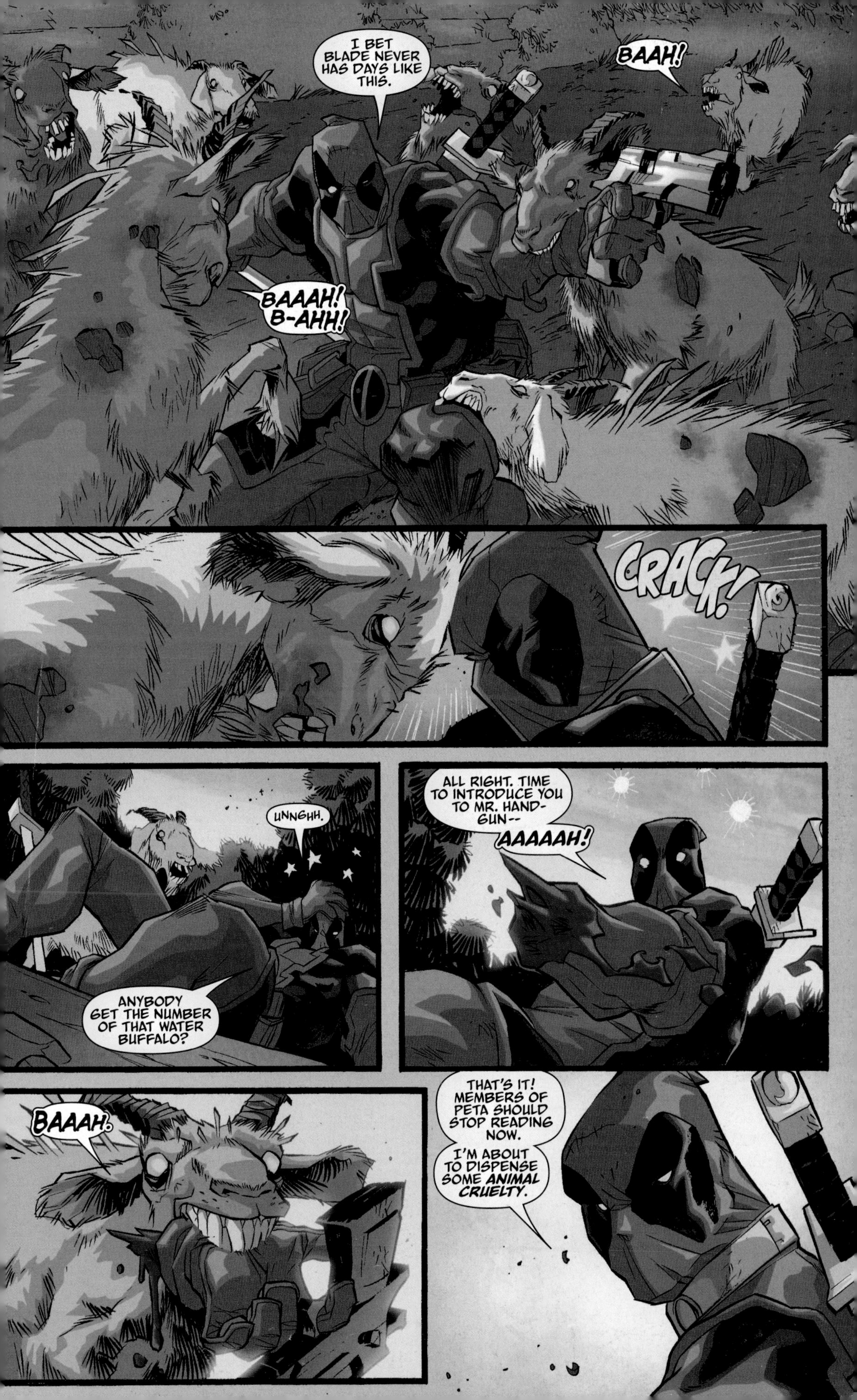
I BET BLADE NEVER HAS DAYS LIKE THIS.
BAAH!
BAAAH! B-AHH!
CRACK!
UNNGHH.
ANYBODY GET THE NUMBER OF THAT WATER BUFFALO?
ALL RIGHT. TIME TO INTRODUCE YOU TO MR. HAND-GUN--
AAAAAH!
BAAAH.
THAT'S IT! MEMBERS OF PETA SHOULD STOP READING NOW.
I'M ABOUT TO DISPENSE SOME *ANIMAL CRUELTY*.

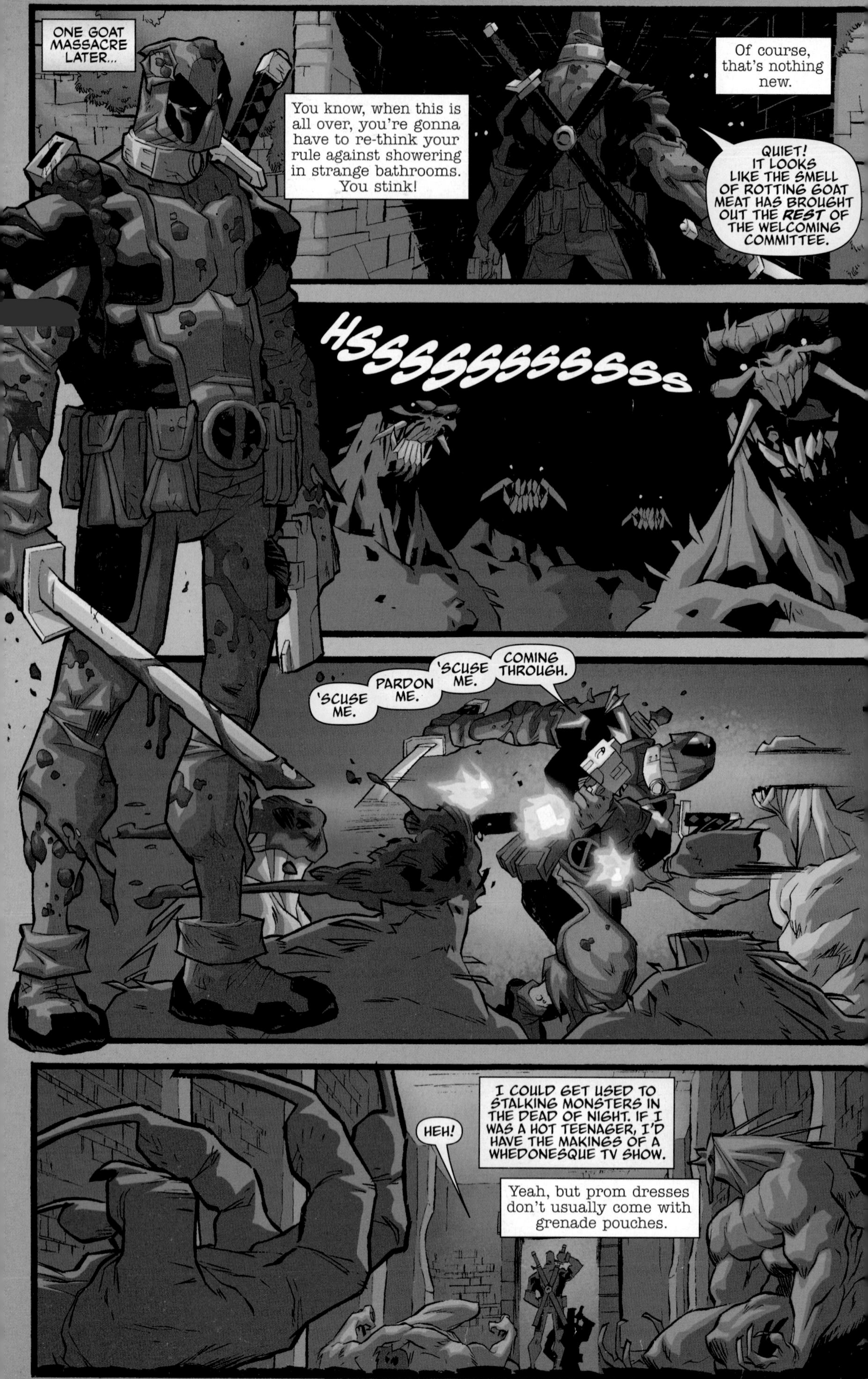

ONE GOAT MASSACRE LATER...
You know, when this is all over, you're gonna have to re-think your rule against showering in strange bathrooms. You stink!
Of course, that's nothing new.
QUIET! IT LOOKS LIKE THE SMELL OF ROTTING GOAT MEAT HAS BROUGHT OUT THE REST OF THE WELCOMING COMMITTEE.
HSSSSSSSSSSSs
'SCUSE ME.
PARDON ME.
'SCUSE ME.
COMING THROUGH.
HEH!
I COULD GET USED TO STALKING MONSTERS IN THE DEAD OF NIGHT. IF I WAS A HOT TEENAGER, I'D HAVE THE MAKINGS OF A WHEDONESQUE TV SHOW.
Yeah, but prom dresses don't usually come with grenade pouches.

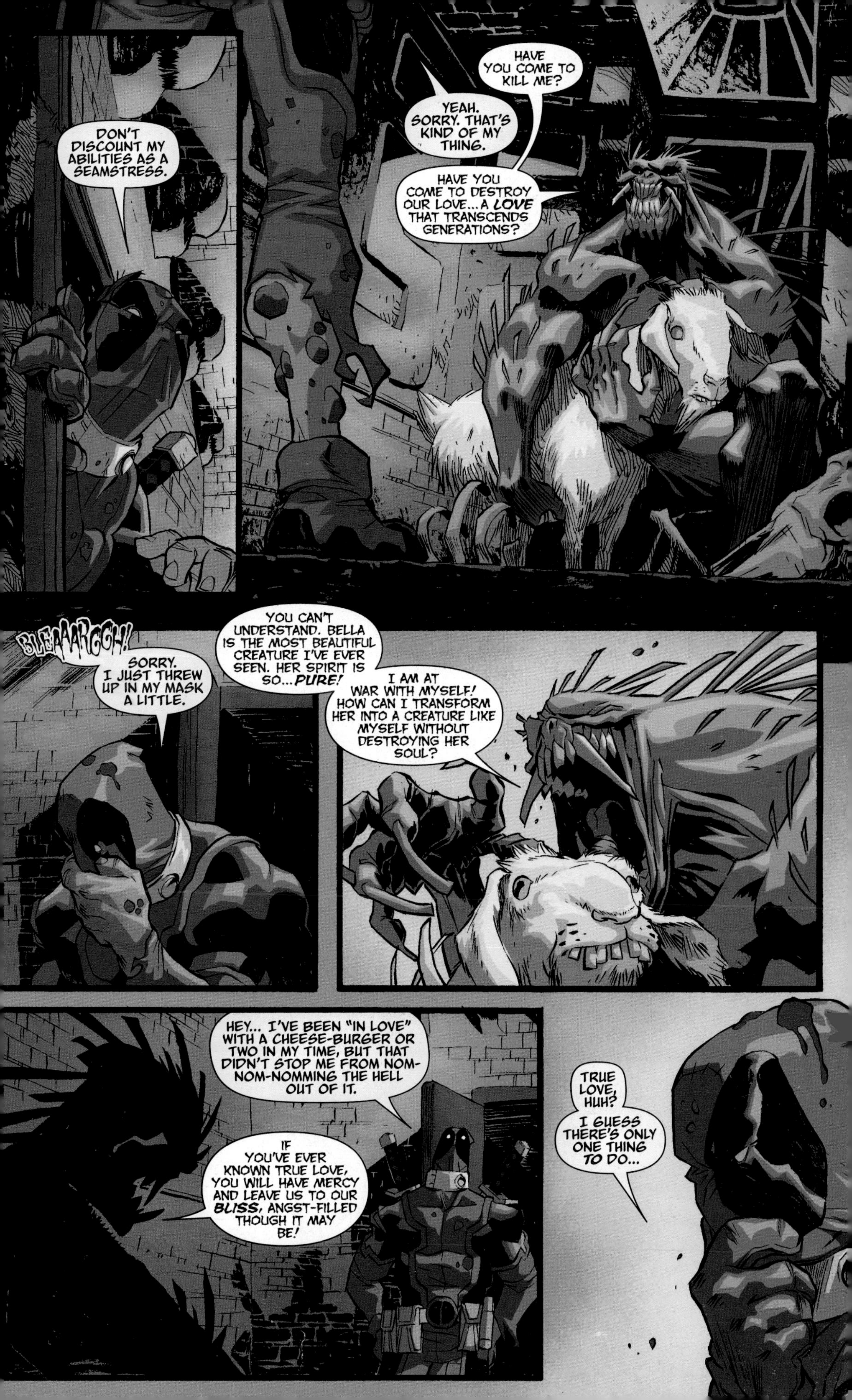
DON'T DISCOUNT MY ABILITIES AS A SEAMSTRESS.
HAVE YOU COME TO KILL ME?
YEAH. SORRY. THAT'S KIND OF MY THING.
HAVE YOU COME TO DESTROY OUR LOVE...A LOVE THAT TRANSCENDS GENERATIONS?
BLEAAARGGH!
SORRY. I JUST THREW UP IN MY MASK A LITTLE.
YOU CAN'T UNDERSTAND. BELLA IS THE MOST BEAUTIFUL CREATURE I'VE EVER SEEN. HER SPIRIT IS SO...PURE!
I AM AT WAR WITH MYSELF! HOW CAN I TRANSFORM HER INTO A CREATURE LIKE MYSELF WITHOUT DESTROYING HER SOUL?
HEY... I'VE BEEN "IN LOVE" WITH A CHEESE-BURGER OR TWO IN MY TIME, BUT THAT DIDN'T STOP ME FROM NOM-NOM-NOMMING THE HELL OUT OF IT.
IF YOU'VE EVER KNOWN TRUE LOVE, YOU WILL HAVE MERCY AND LEAVE US TO OUR BLISS, ANGST-FILLED THOUGH IT MAY BE!
TRUE LOVE, HUH?
I GUESS THERE'S ONLY ONE THING TO DO...

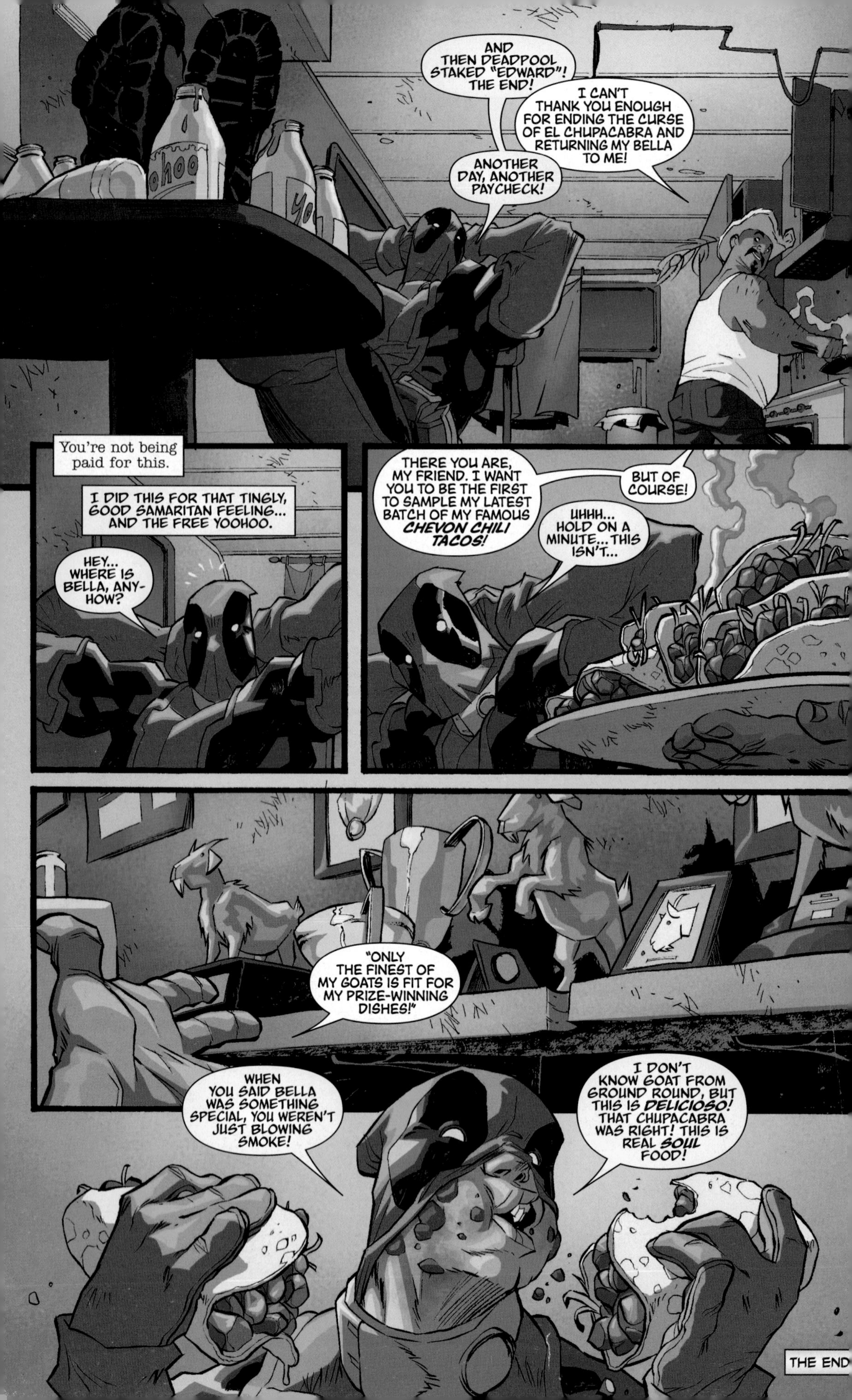
AND THEN DEADPOOL STAKED "EDWARD"! THE END!
ANOTHER DAY, ANOTHER PAYCHECK!
I CAN'T THANK YOU ENOUGH FOR ENDING THE CURSE OF EL CHUPACABRA AND RETURNING MY BELLA TO ME!
You're not being paid for this.
I DID THIS FOR THAT TINGLY, GOOD SAMARITAN FEELING... AND THE FREE YOOHOO.
HEY... WHERE IS BELLA, ANYHOW?
THERE YOU ARE, MY FRIEND. I WANT YOU TO BE THE FIRST TO SAMPLE MY LATEST BATCH OF MY FAMOUS CHEVON CHILI TACOS!
BUT OF COURSE!
UHHH... HOLD ON A MINUTE... THIS ISN'T...
"ONLY THE FINEST OF MY GOATS IS FIT FOR MY PRIZE-WINNING DISHES!"
WHEN YOU SAID BELLA WAS SOMETHING SPECIAL, YOU WEREN'T JUST BLOWING SMOKE!
I DON'T KNOW GOAT FROM GROUND ROUND, BUT THIS IS DELICIOSO! THAT CHUPACABRA WAS RIGHT! THIS IS REAL SOUL FOOD!
THE END

DEADPOOL IN "TOO MANY DEADPOOLS"

ANOTHER CONTRACT SUCCESSFULLY TERMINATED!

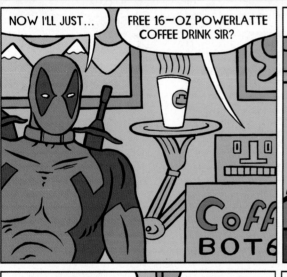

NOW I'LL JUST...

FREE 16-OZ POWERLATTE COFFEE DRINK SIR?

DON'T MIND IF I DO!

HERE— HAVE TWO!

THOSE WERE GREAT! NOW I'LL JUST...

DO YOU NEED TO URINATE, SIR?

NOW THAT YOU MENTION IT...

THIS RESTROOM IS FREE, SIR!

MENS

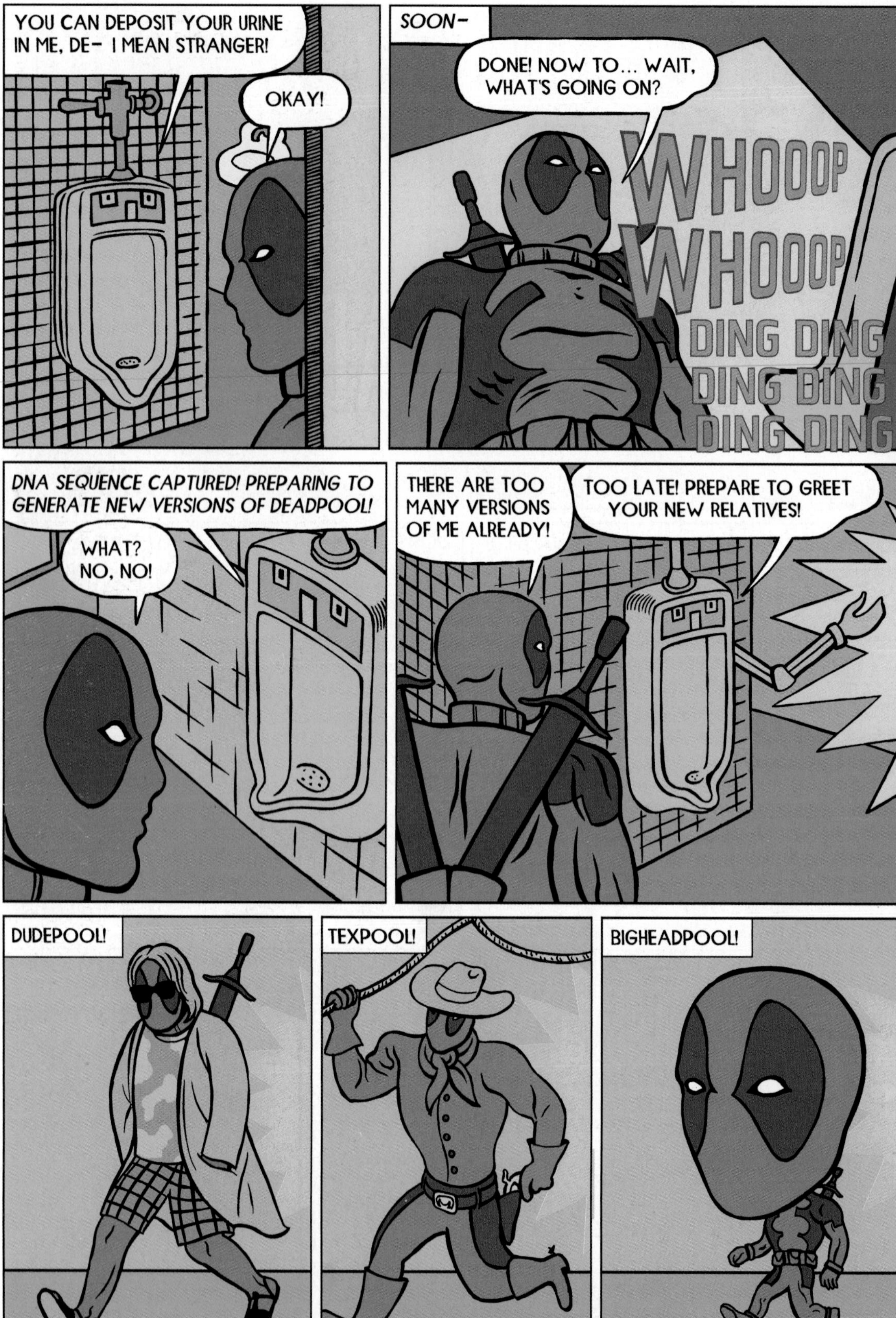
YOU CAN DEPOSIT YOUR URINE IN ME, DE– I MEAN STRANGER!
OKAY!
SOON–
DONE! NOW TO... WAIT, WHAT'S GOING ON?
WHOOOP
WHOOOP
DING DING
DING DING
DING DING
DNA SEQUENCE CAPTURED! PREPARING TO GENERATE NEW VERSIONS OF DEADPOOL!
WHAT? NO, NO!
THERE ARE TOO MANY VERSIONS OF ME ALREADY!
TOO LATE! PREPARE TO GREET YOUR NEW RELATIVES!
DUDEPOOL!
TEXPOOL!
BIGHEADPOOL!

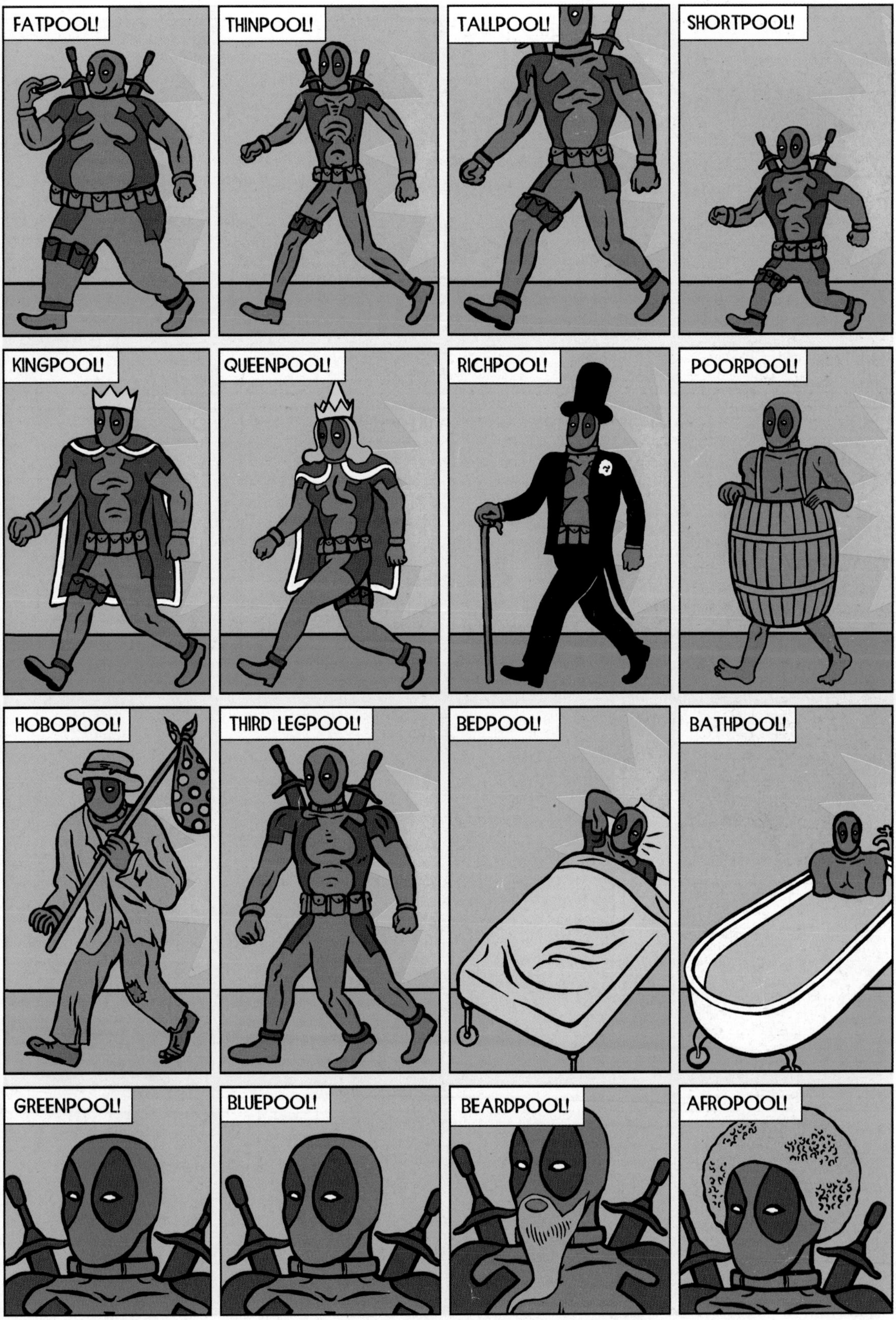
FATPOOL!
THINPOOL!
TALLPOOL!
SHORTPOOL!
KINGPOOL!
QUEENPOOL!
RICHPOOL!
POORPOOL!
HOBOPOOL!
THIRD LEGPOOL!
BEDPOOL!
BATHPOOL!
GREENPOOL!
BLUEPOOL!
BEARDPOOL!
AFROPOOL!

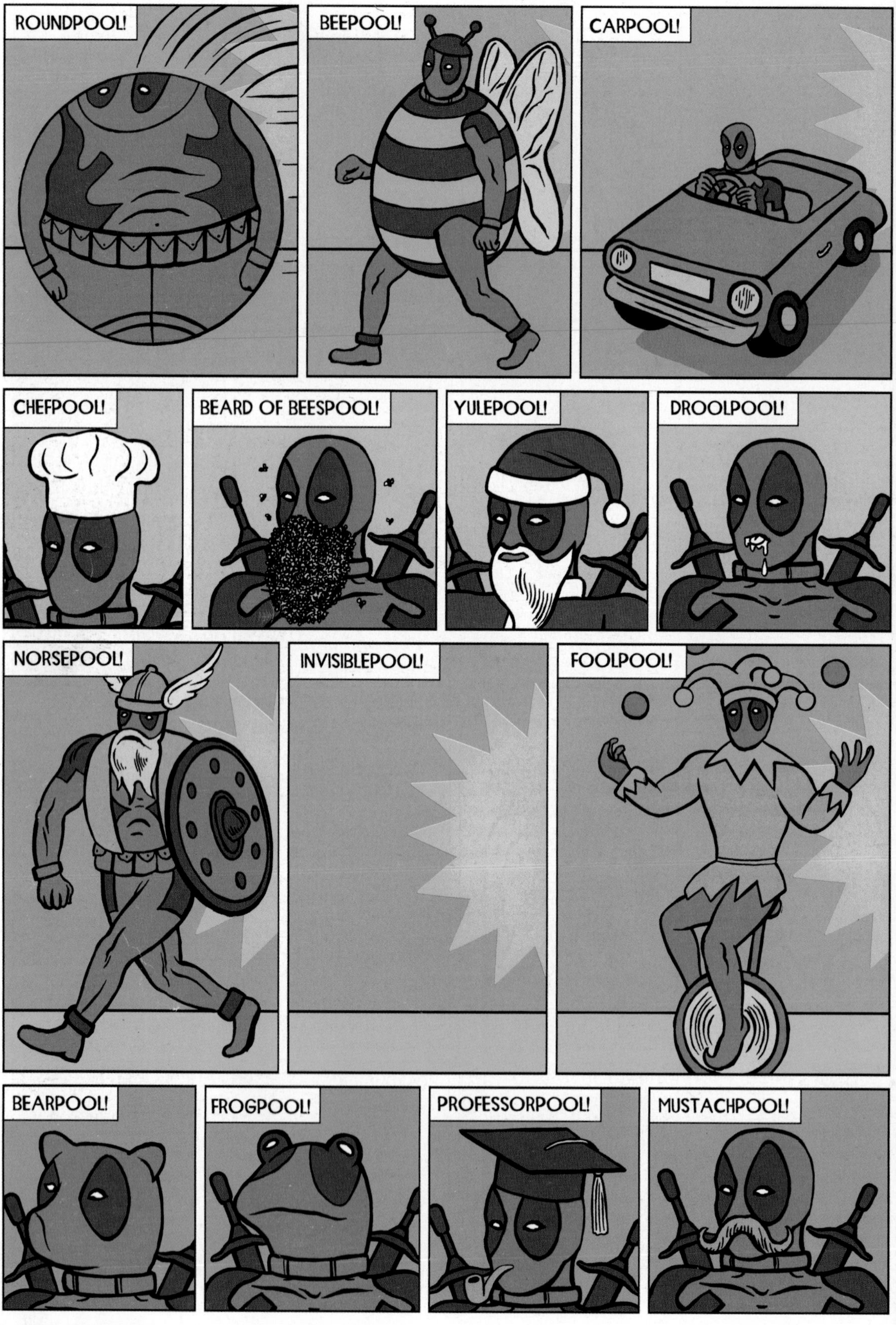
ROUNDPOOL!
BEEPOOL!
CARPOOL!
CHEFPOOL!
BEARD OF BEESPOOL!
YULEPOOL!
DROOLPOOL!
NORSEPOOL!
INVISIBLEPOOL!
FOOLPOOL!
BEARPOOL!
FROGPOOL!
PROFESSORPOOL!
MUSTACHPOOL!

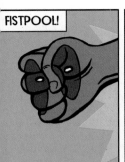

FISTPOOL!

BUTTPOOL!

AND STICKPOOL!

LAME!!

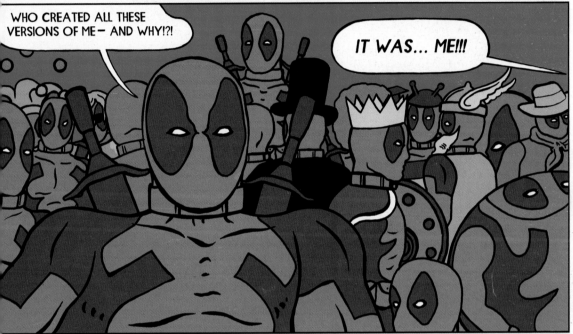

WHO CREATED ALL THESE VERSIONS OF ME— AND WHY!?!

IT WAS... ME!!!

HOT—PANTS ZEUS!

WHO?

I COME FROM AN ALTERNATE UNIVERSE... WHERE THE GREEK GODS WEAR HOT PANTS!

AND I CREATED ALL THESE VERSIONS OF DEADPOOL TO...

FIGHT!!!!!!

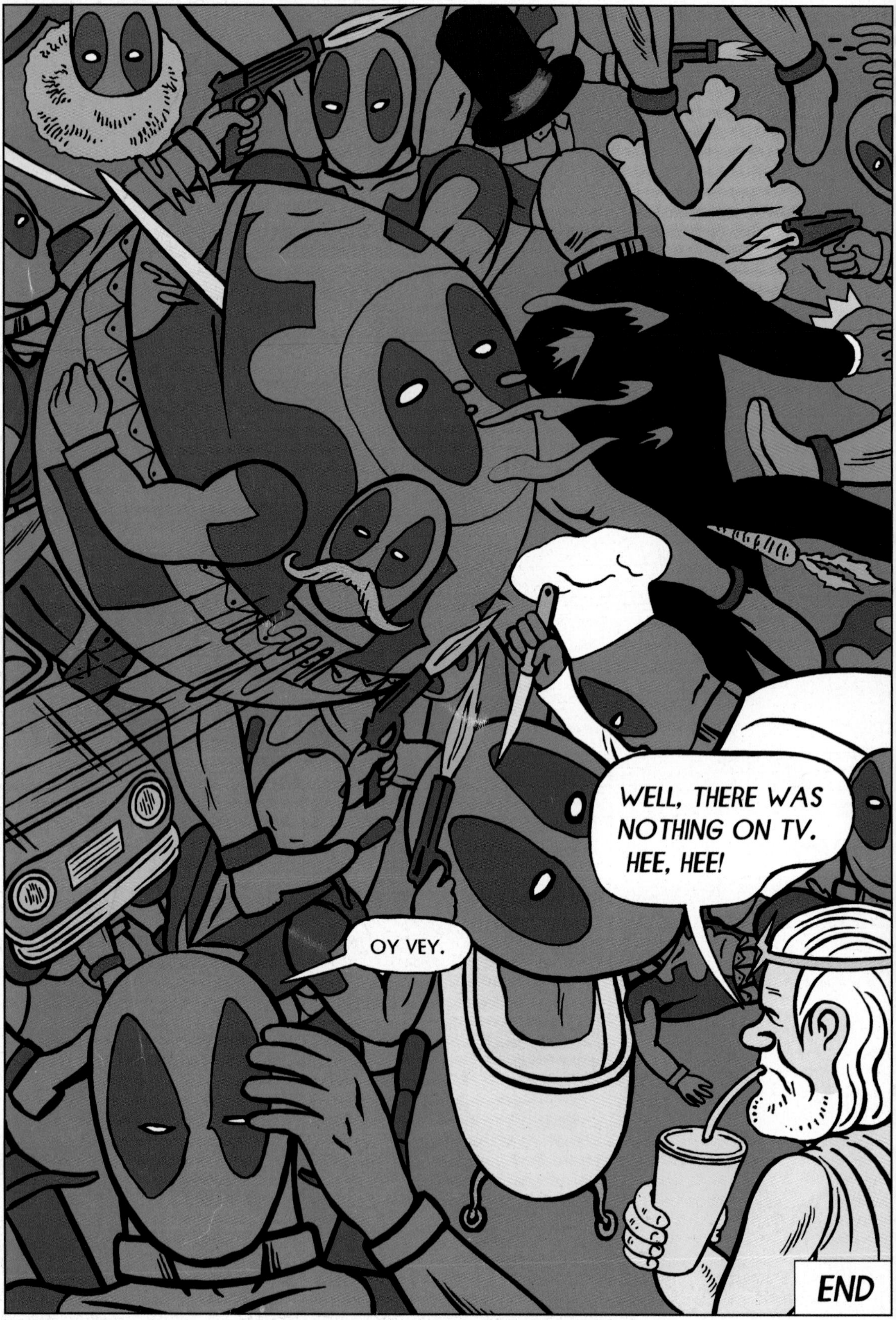
WELL, THERE WAS NOTHING ON TV. HEE, HEE!
OY VEY.
END

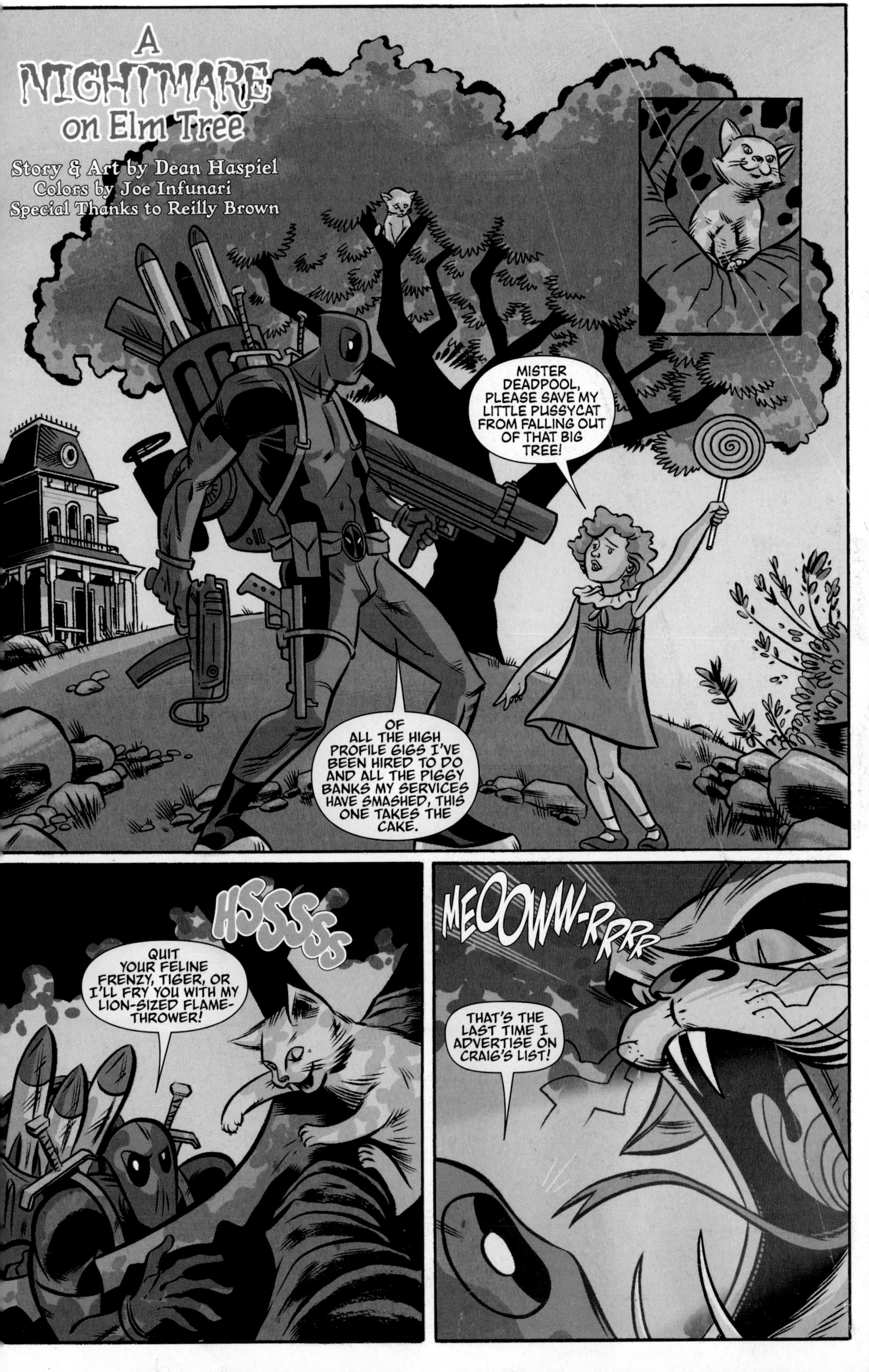
A NIGHTMARE on Elm Tree
Story & Art by Dean Haspiel
Colors by Joe Infunari
Special Thanks to Reilly Brown
MISTER DEADPOOL, PLEASE SAVE MY LITTLE PUSSYCAT FROM FALLING OUT OF THAT BIG TREE!
OF ALL THE HIGH PROFILE GIGS I'VE BEEN HIRED TO DO AND ALL THE PIGGY BANKS MY SERVICES HAVE SMASHED, THIS ONE TAKES THE CAKE.
HSSSSS
QUIT YOUR FELINE FRENZY, TIGER, OR I'LL FRY YOU WITH MY LION-SIZED FLAME-THROWER!
MEOOWW-RRRR
THAT'S THE LAST TIME I ADVERTISE ON CRAIG'S LIST!

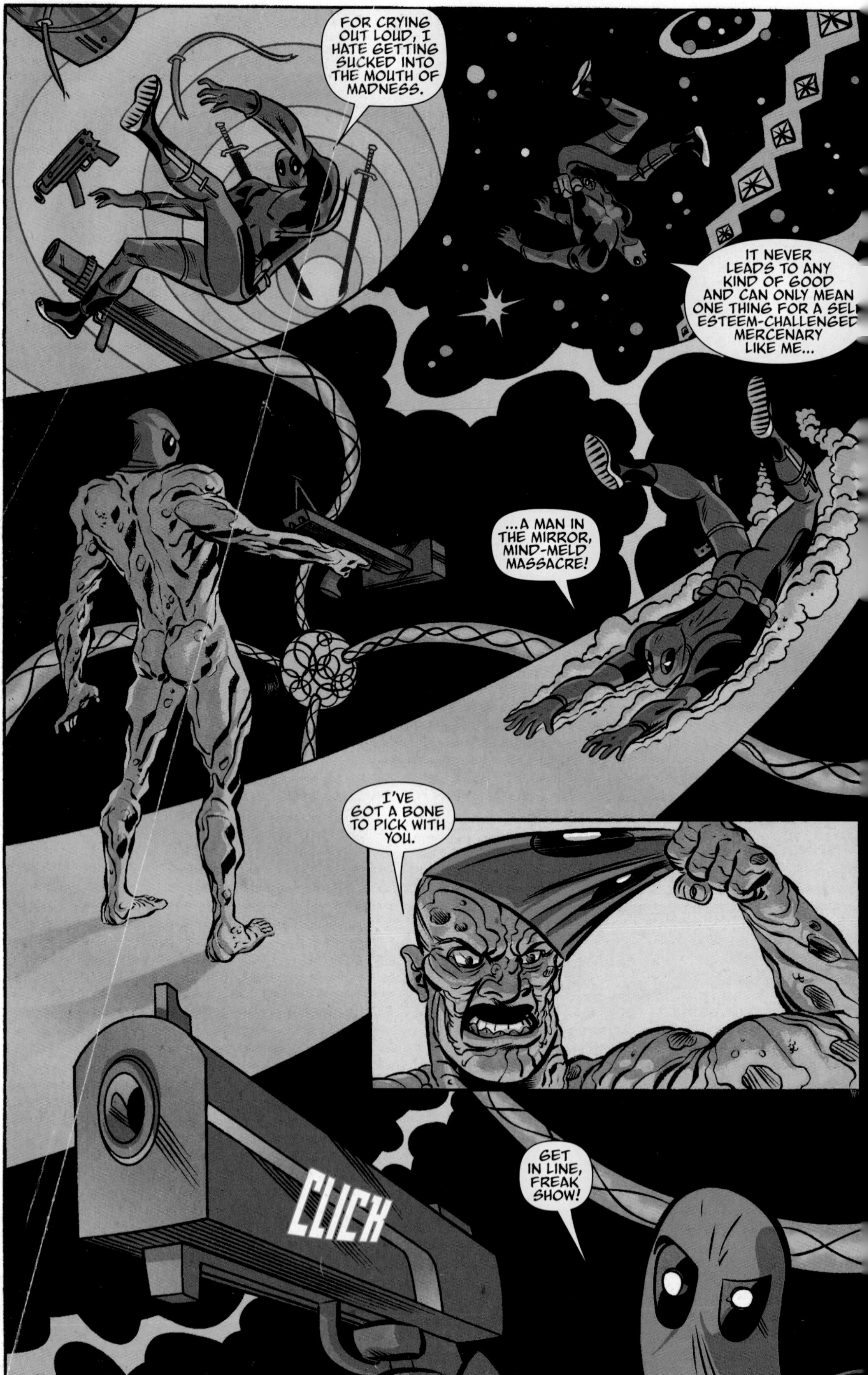
FOR CRYING OUT LOUD, I HATE GETTING SUCKED INTO THE MOUTH OF MADNESS.
IT NEVER LEADS TO ANY KIND OF GOOD AND CAN ONLY MEAN ONE THING FOR A SEL ESTEEM-CHALLENGED MERCENARY LIKE ME...
...A MAN IN THE MIRROR, MIND-MELD MASSACRE!
I'VE GOT A BONE TO PICK WITH YOU.
CLICK
GET IN LINE, FREAK SHOW!

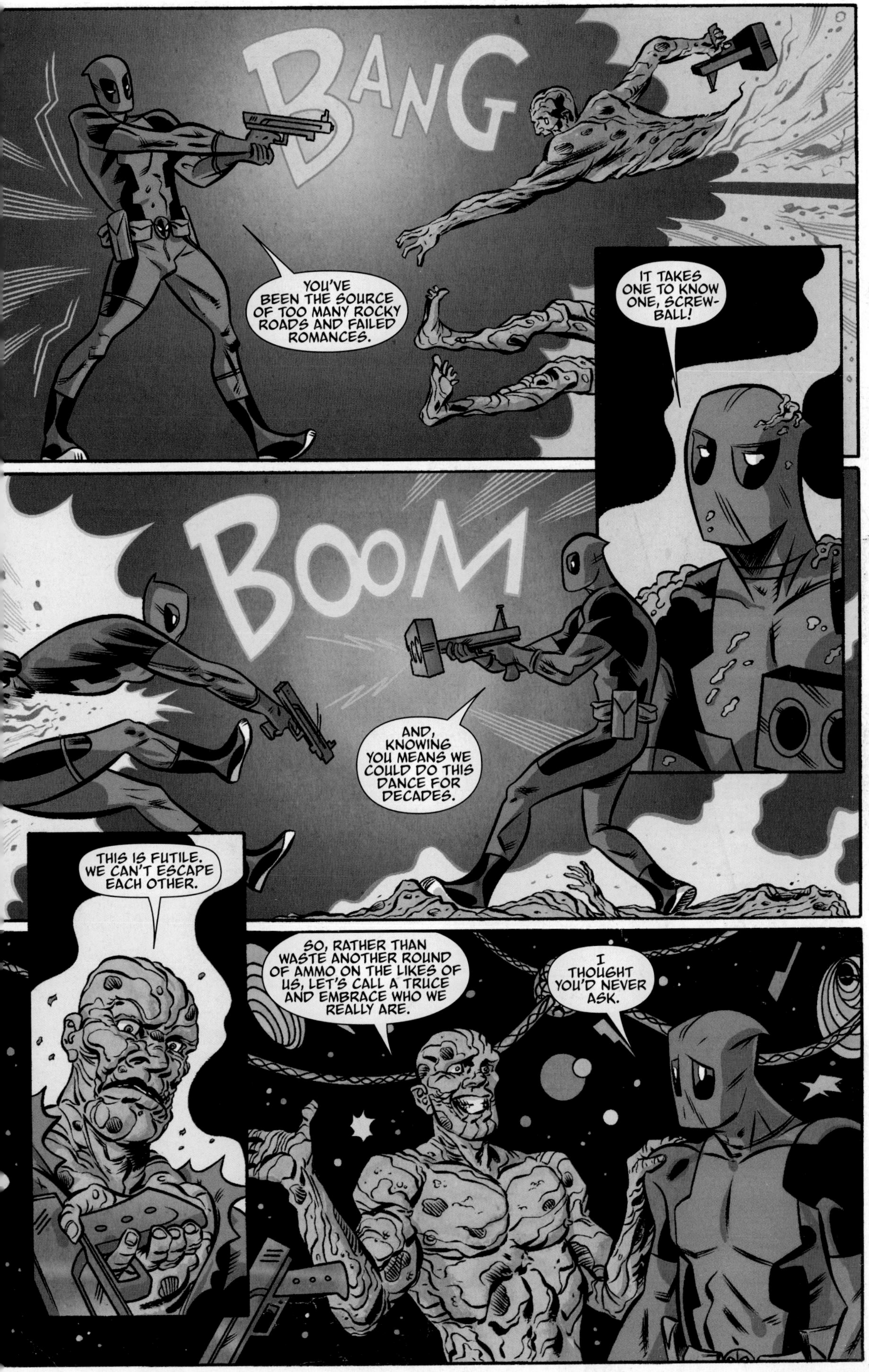
BANG
YOU'VE BEEN THE SOURCE OF TOO MANY ROCKY ROADS AND FAILED ROMANCES.
IT TAKES ONE TO KNOW ONE, SCREW-BALL!
BOOM
AND, KNOWING YOU MEANS WE COULD DO THIS DANCE FOR DECADES.
THIS IS FUTILE. WE CAN'T ESCAPE EACH OTHER.
SO, RATHER THAN WASTE ANOTHER ROUND OF AMMO ON THE LIKES OF US, LET'S CALL A TRUCE AND EMBRACE WHO WE REALLY ARE.
I THOUGHT YOU'D NEVER ASK.

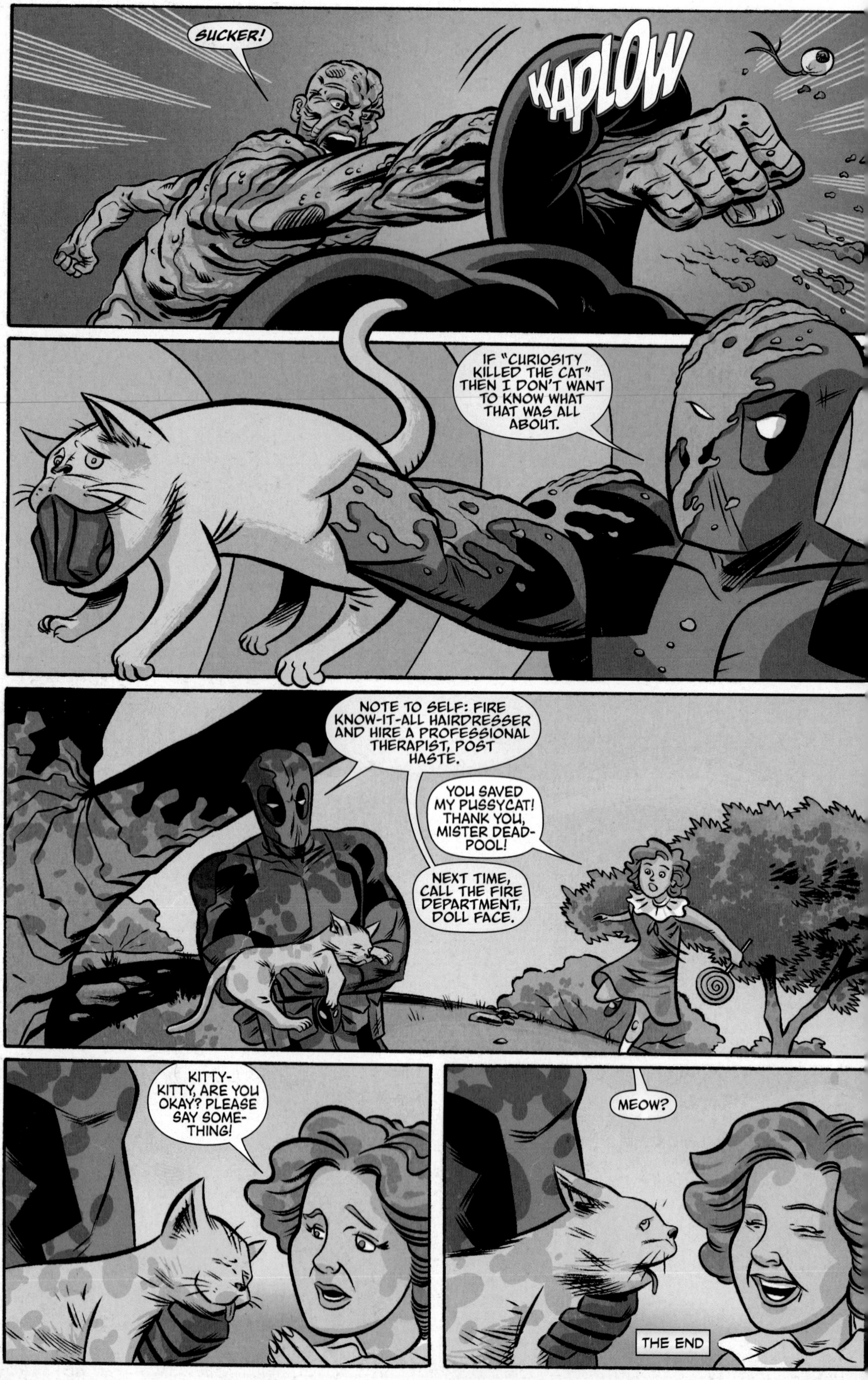
SUCKER!
KAPLOW
IF "CURIOSITY KILLED THE CAT" THEN I DON'T WANT TO KNOW WHAT THAT WAS ALL ABOUT.
NOTE TO SELF: FIRE KNOW-IT-ALL HAIRDRESSER AND HIRE A PROFESSIONAL THERAPIST, POST HASTE.
YOU SAVED MY PUSSYCAT! THANK YOU, MISTER DEAD-POOL!
NEXT TIME, CALL THE FIRE DEPARTMENT, DOLL FACE.
KITTY-KITTY, ARE YOU OKAY? PLEASE SAY SOME-THING!
MEOW?
THE END

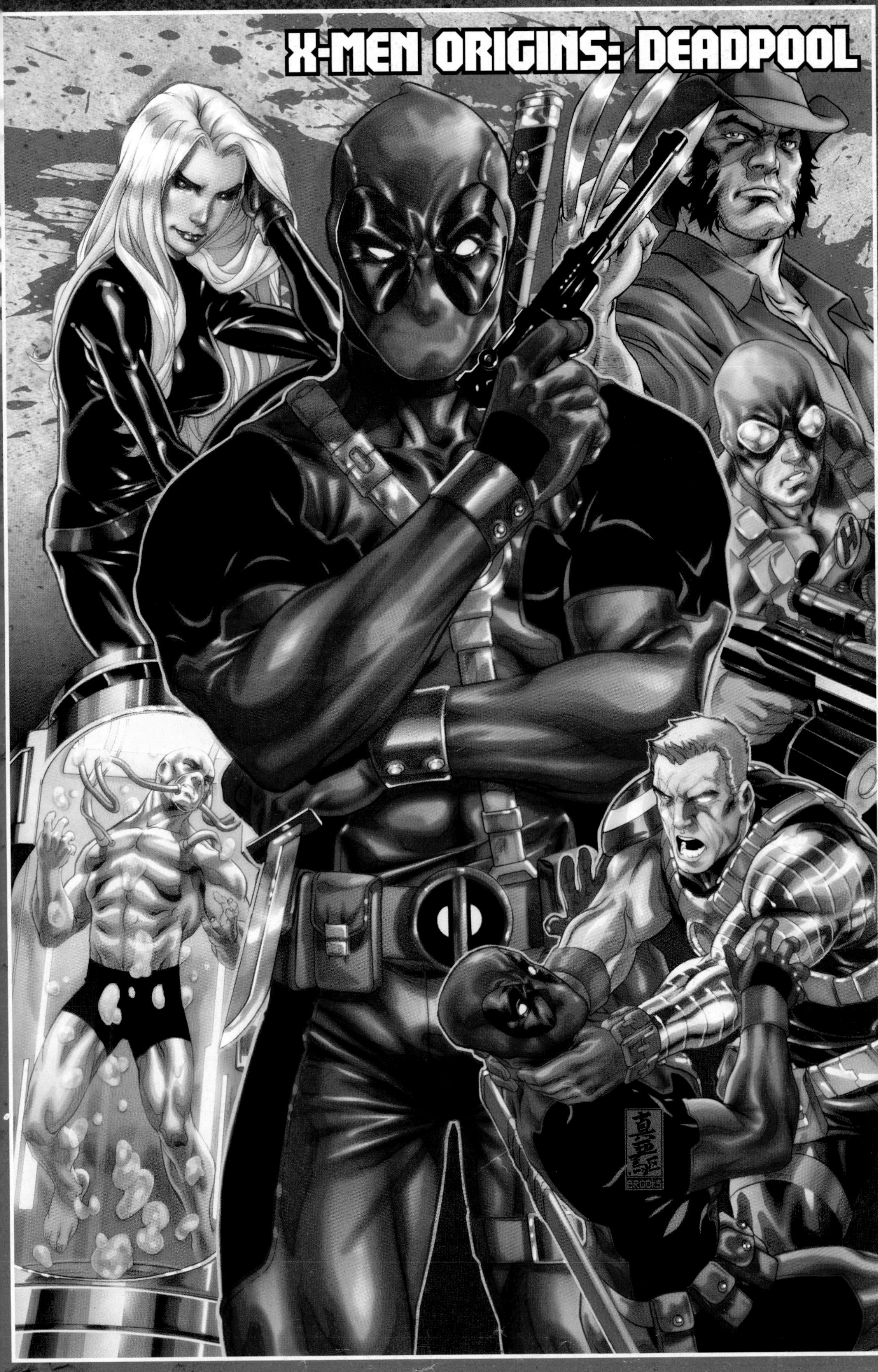
X-MEN ORIGINS: DEADPOOL
BROOKS

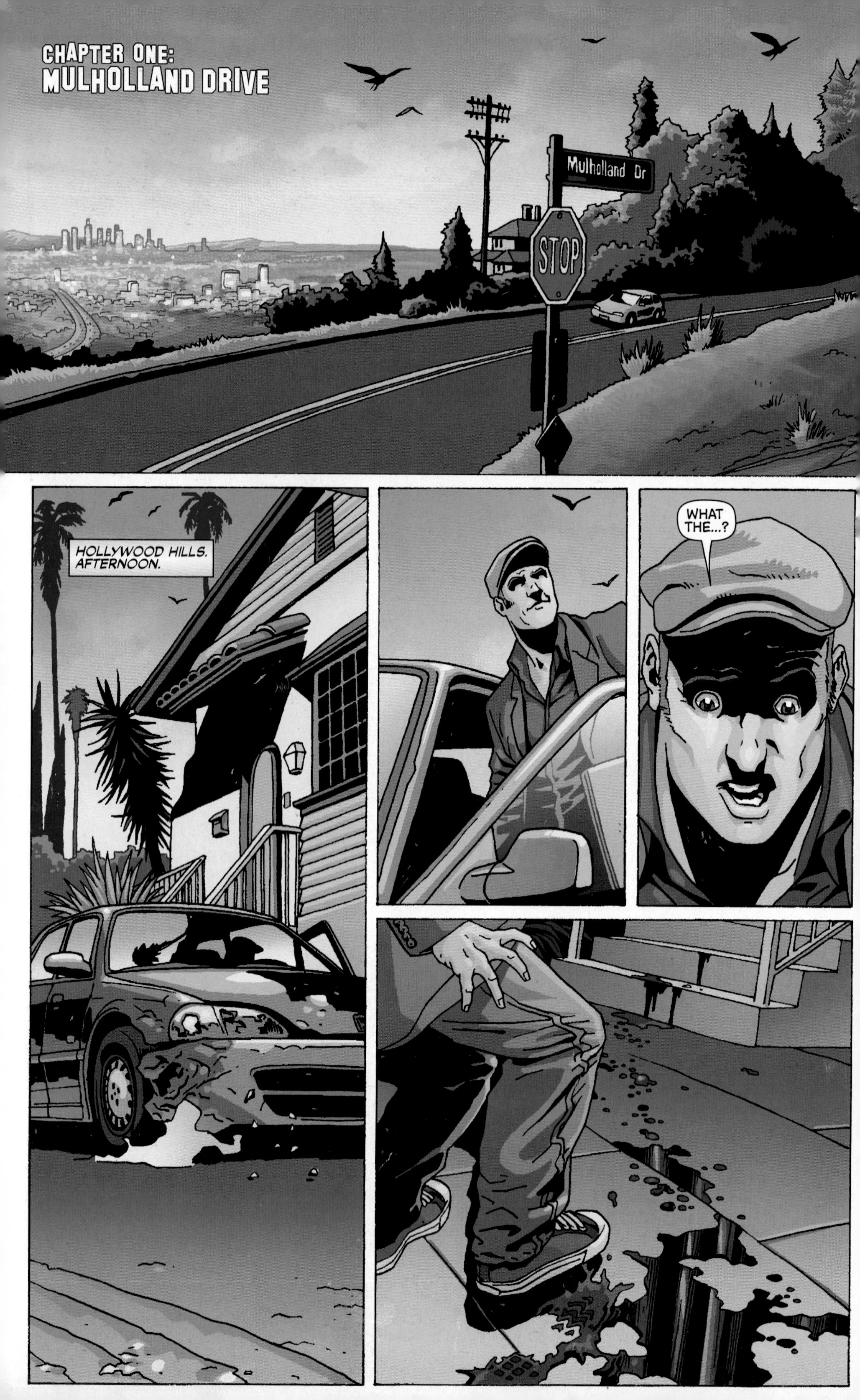
CHAPTER ONE:
MULHOLLAND DRIVE
Mulholland Dr
STOP
HOLLYWOOD HILLS. AFTERNOON.
WHAT THE...?

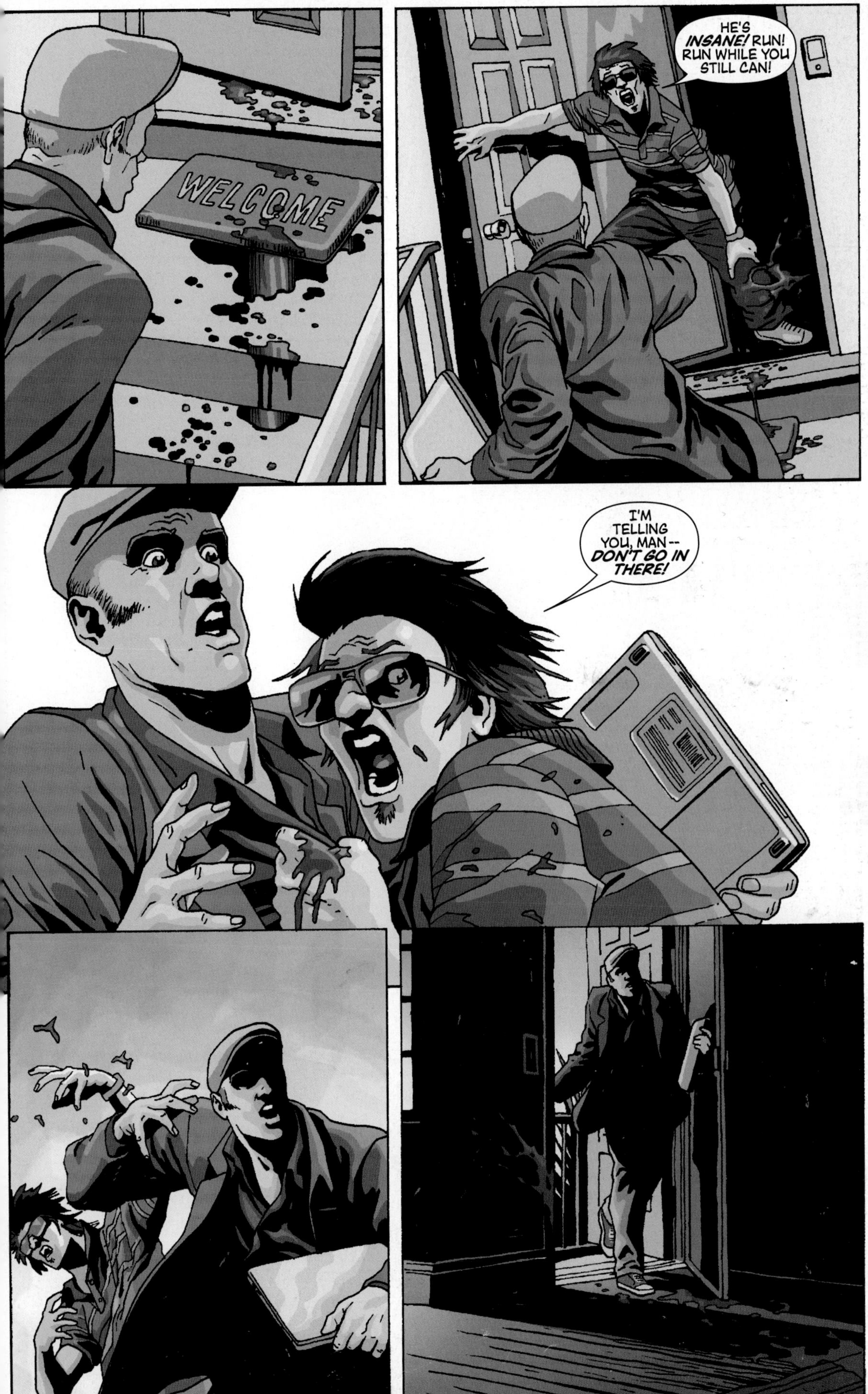
WELCOME
HE'S INSANE! RUN! RUN WHILE YOU STILL CAN!
I'M TELLING YOU, MAN-- DON'T GO IN THERE!

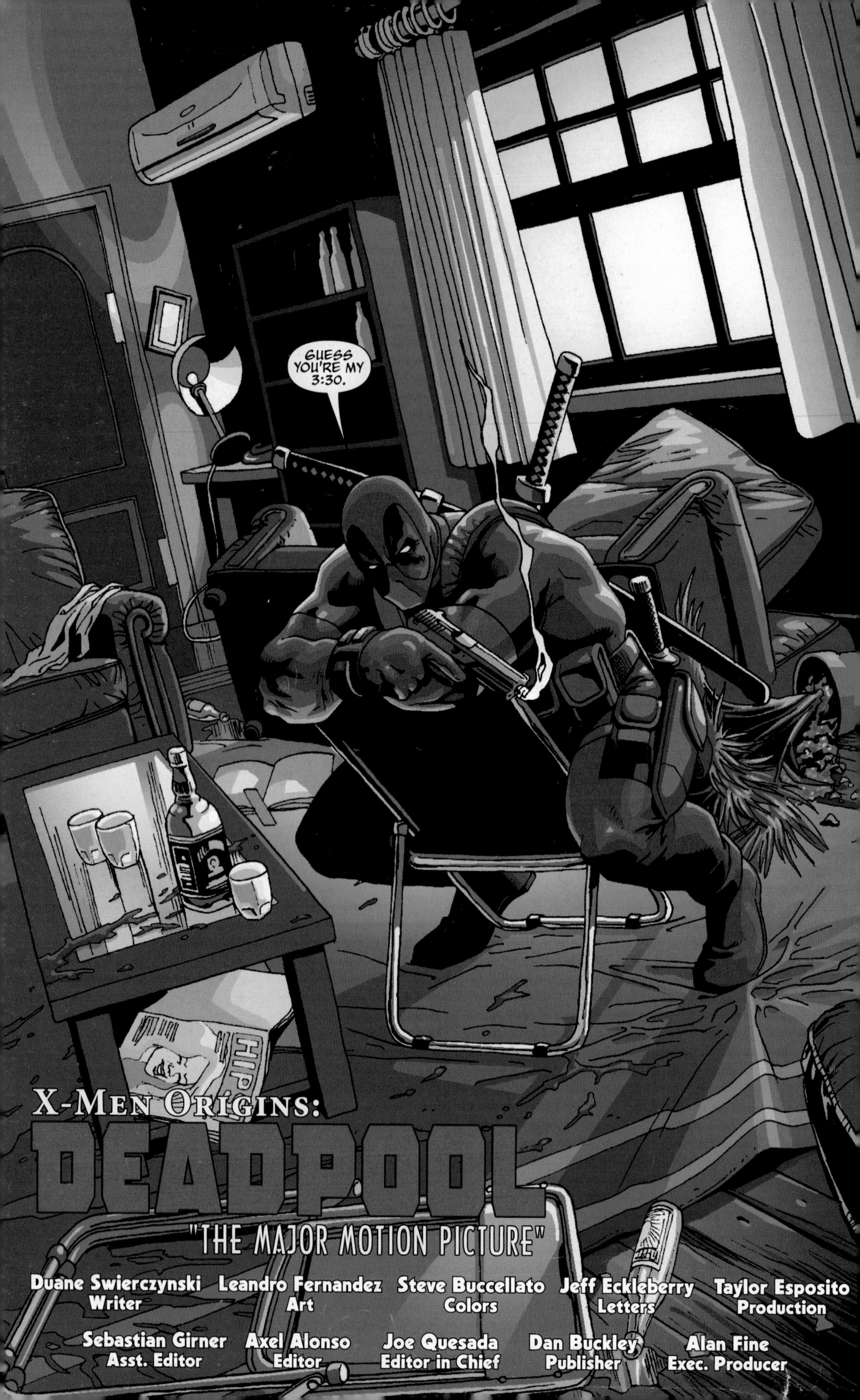
GUESS YOU'RE MY 3:30.
X-MEN ORIGINS:
DEADPOOL
"THE MAJOR MOTION PICTURE"
Duane Swierczynski Writer
Leandro Fernandez Art
Steve Buccellato Colors
Jeff Eckleberry Letters
Taylor Esposito Production
Sebastian Girner Asst. Editor
Axel Alonso Editor
Joe Quesada Editor in Chief
Dan Buckley Publisher
Alan Fine Exec. Producer

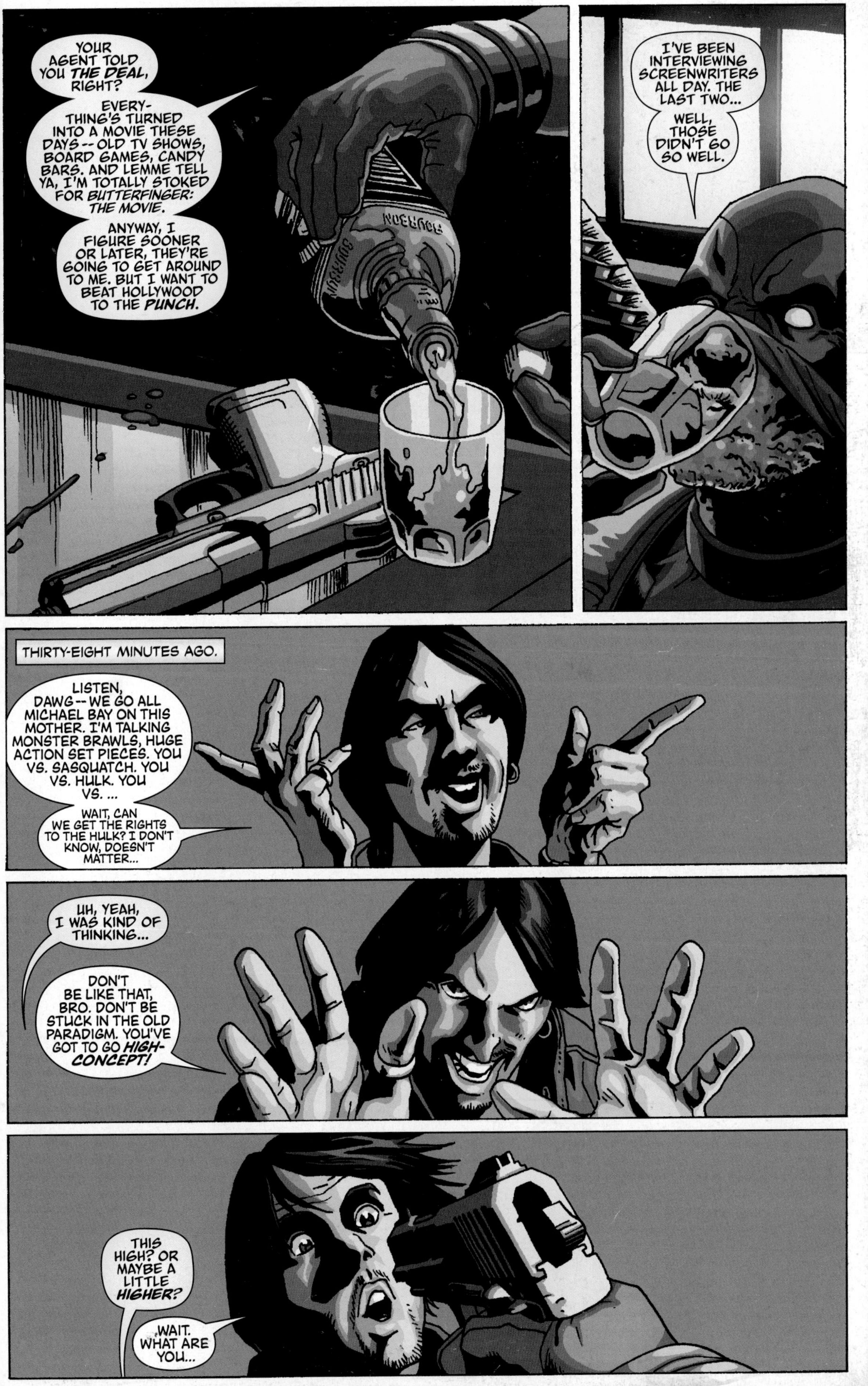
YOUR AGENT TOLD YOU THE DEAL, RIGHT?
EVERY-THING'S TURNED INTO A MOVIE THESE DAYS -- OLD TV SHOWS, BOARD GAMES, CANDY BARS. AND LEMME TELL YA, I'M TOTALLY STOKED FOR BUTTERFINGER: THE MOVIE.
ANYWAY, I FIGURE SOONER OR LATER, THEY'RE GOING TO GET AROUND TO ME. BUT I WANT TO BEAT HOLLYWOOD TO THE PUNCH.
BOURBON
I'VE BEEN INTERVIEWING SCREENWRITERS ALL DAY. THE LAST TWO...
WELL, THOSE DIDN'T GO SO WELL.
THIRTY-EIGHT MINUTES AGO.
LISTEN, DAWG -- WE GO ALL MICHAEL BAY ON THIS MOTHER. I'M TALKING MONSTER BRAWLS, HUGE ACTION SET PIECES. YOU VS. SASQUATCH. YOU VS. HULK. YOU VS. ...
WAIT, CAN WE GET THE RIGHTS TO THE HULK? I DON'T KNOW, DOESN'T MATTER...
UH, YEAH, I WAS KIND OF THINKING...
DON'T BE LIKE THAT, BRO. DON'T BE STUCK IN THE OLD PARADIGM. YOU'VE GOT TO GO HIGH-CONCEPT!
THIS HIGH? OR MAYBE A LITTLE HIGHER?
WAIT. WHAT ARE YOU...

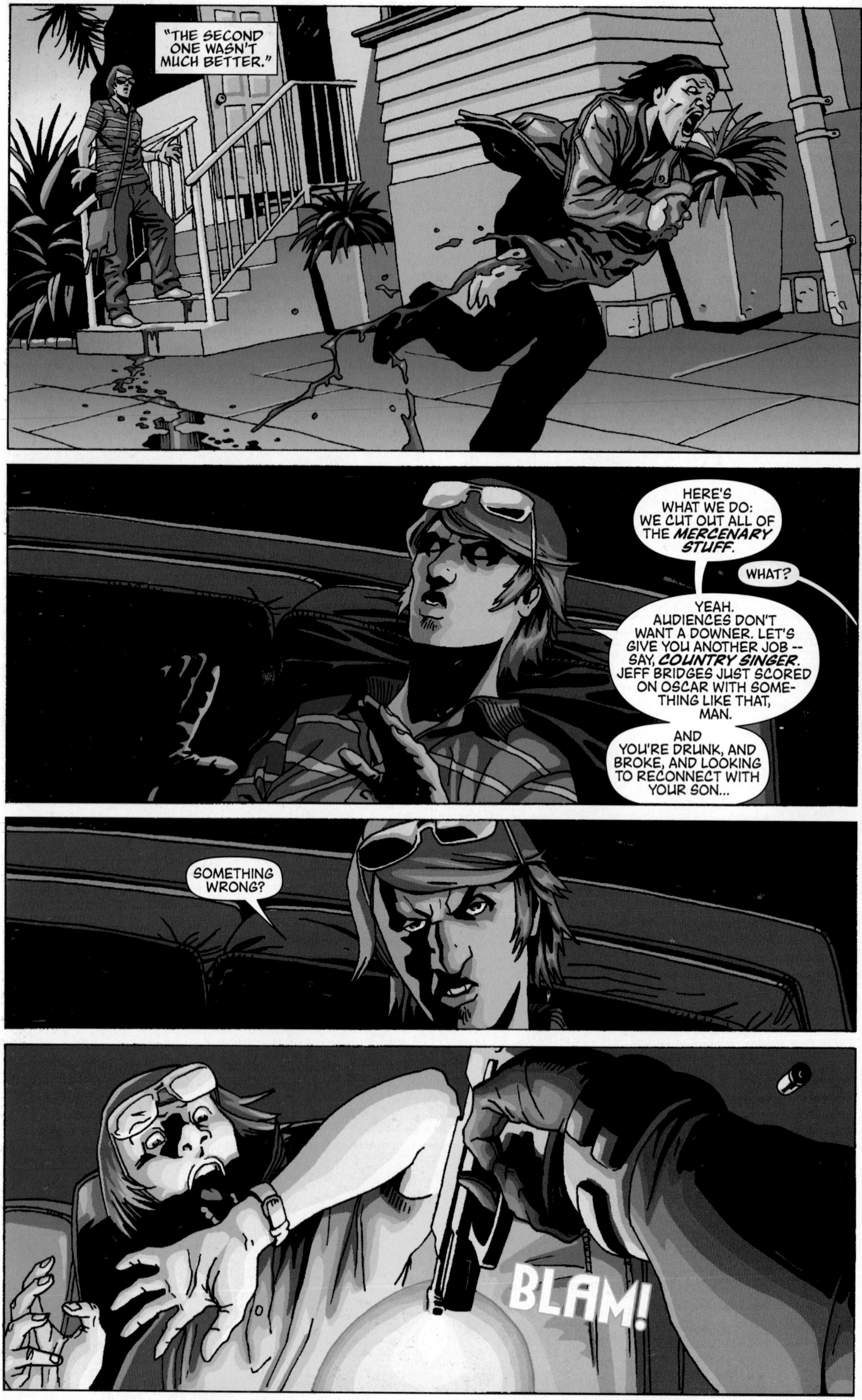
"THE SECOND ONE WASN'T MUCH BETTER."
HERE'S WHAT WE DO: WE CUT OUT ALL OF THE *MERCENARY STUFF*.
WHAT?
YEAH. AUDIENCES DON'T WANT A DOWNER. LET'S GIVE YOU ANOTHER JOB -- SAY, *COUNTRY SINGER*. JEFF BRIDGES JUST SCORED ON OSCAR WITH SOMETHING LIKE THAT, MAN.
AND YOU'RE DRUNK, AND BROKE, AND LOOKING TO RECONNECT WITH YOUR SON...
SOMETHING WRONG?
BLAM!

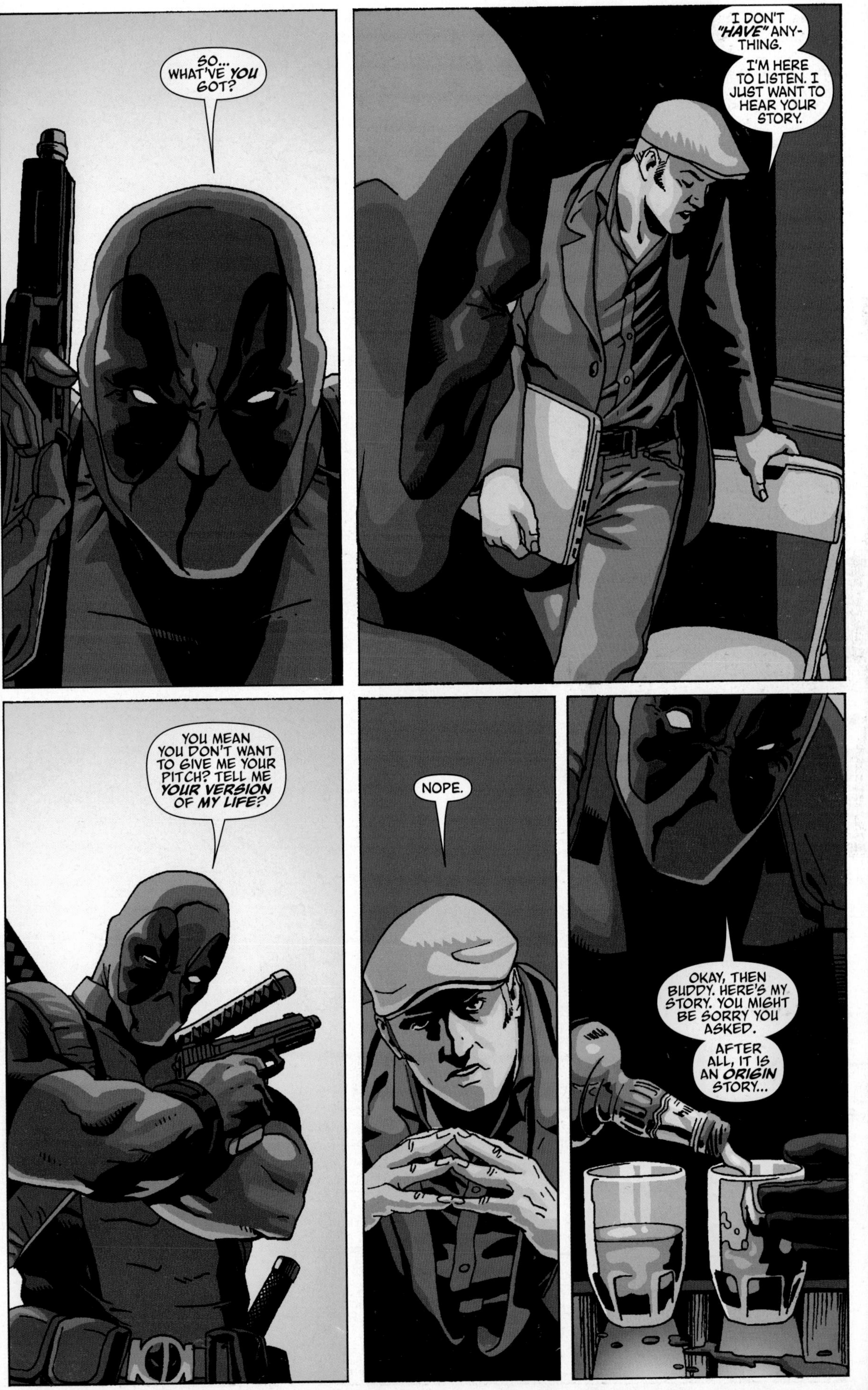
SO... WHAT'VE YOU GOT?
I DON'T "HAVE" ANY-THING.
I'M HERE TO LISTEN. I JUST WANT TO HEAR YOUR STORY.
YOU MEAN YOU DON'T WANT TO GIVE ME YOUR PITCH? TELL ME YOUR VERSION OF MY LIFE?
NOPE.
OKAY, THEN BUDDY. HERE'S MY STORY. YOU MIGHT BE SORRY YOU ASKED.
AFTER ALL, IT IS AN ORIGIN STORY...

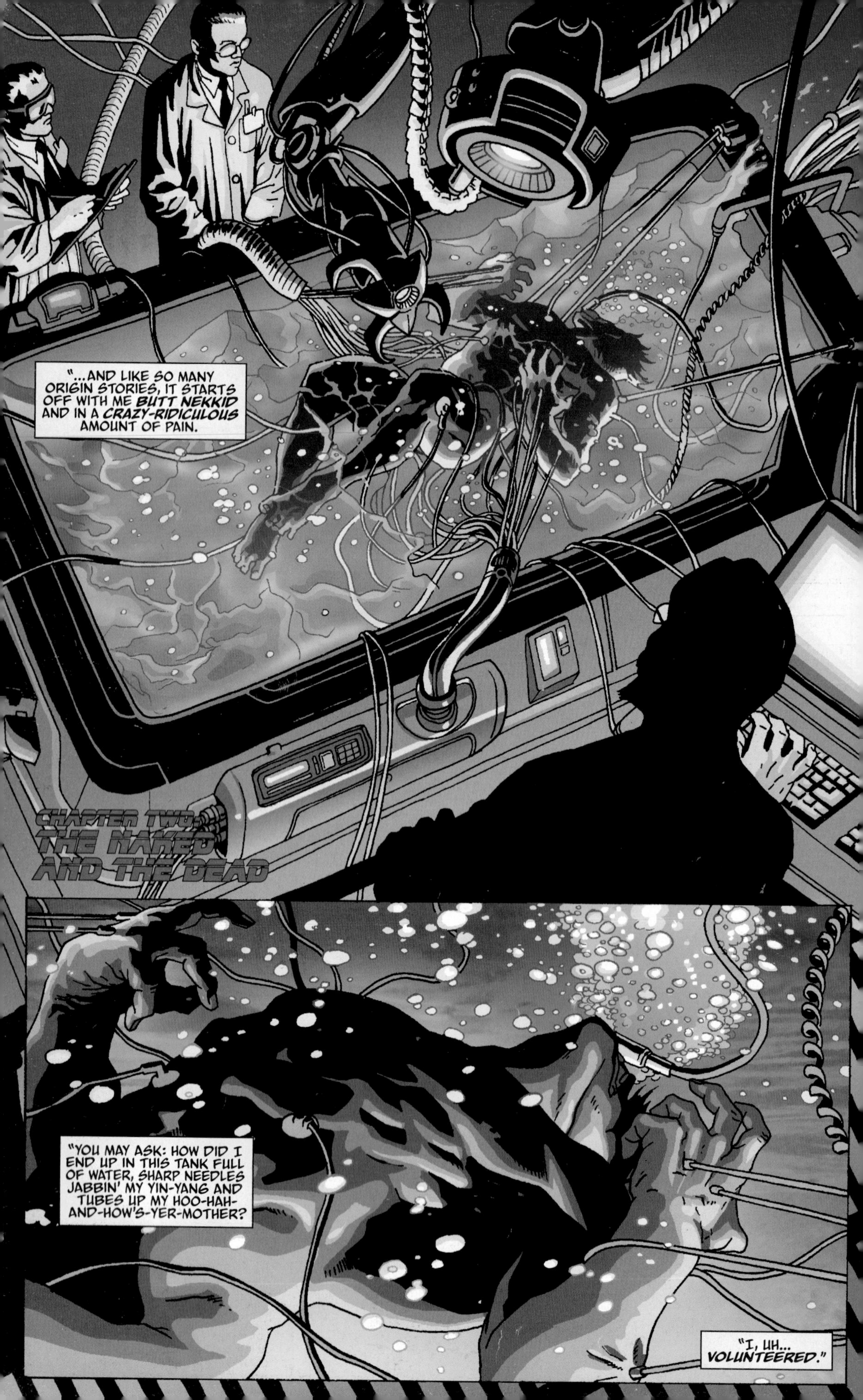
"...AND LIKE SO MANY ORIGIN STORIES, IT STARTS OFF WITH ME BUTT NEKKID AND IN A CRAZY-RIDICULOUS AMOUNT OF PAIN.
CHAPTER TWO: THE NAKED AND THE DEAD
"YOU MAY ASK: HOW DID I END UP IN THIS TANK FULL OF WATER, SHARP NEEDLES JABBIN' MY YIN-YANG AND TUBES UP MY HOO-HAH-AND-HOW'S-YER-MOTHER?
"I, UH... VOLUNTEERED."

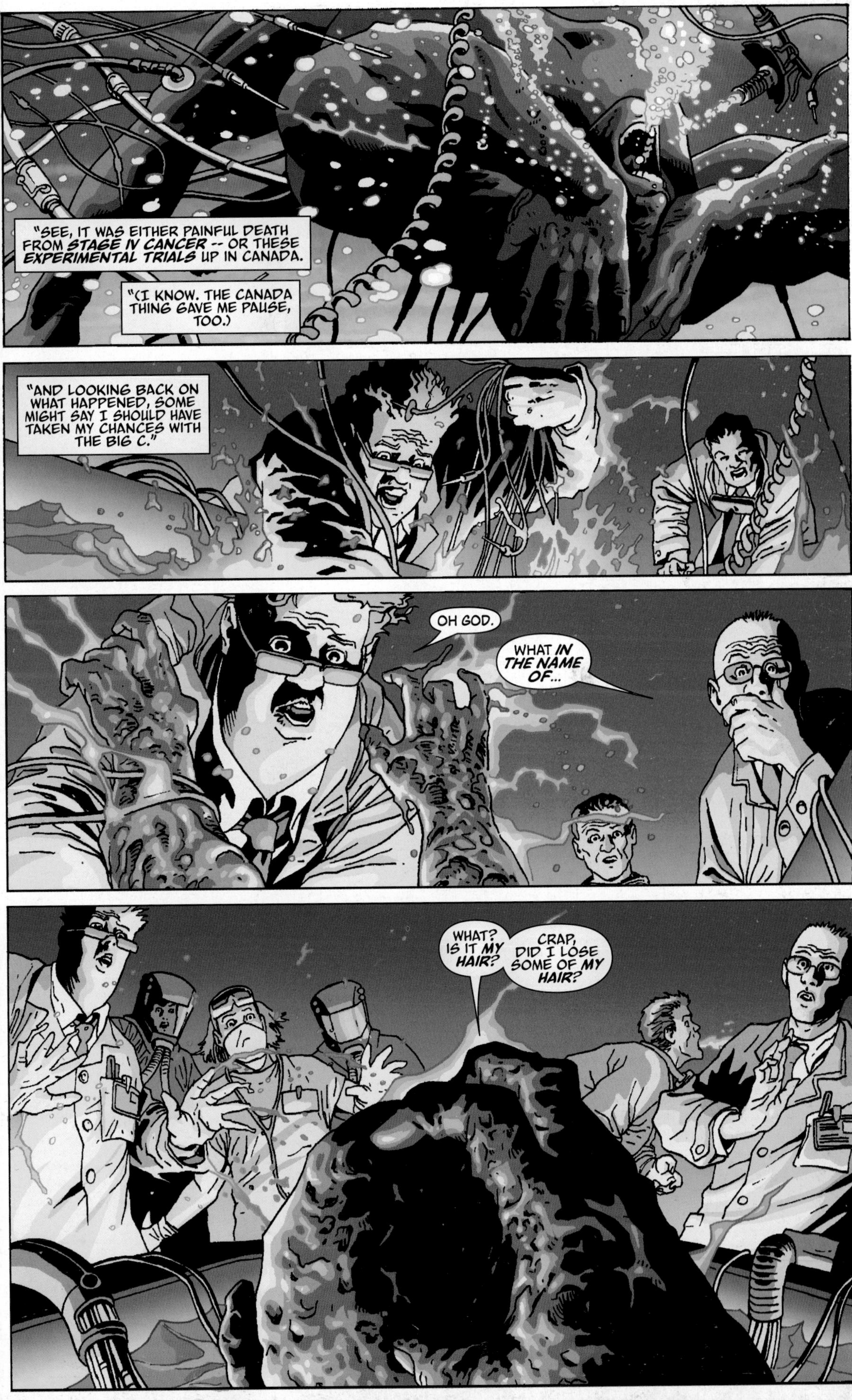
"SEE, IT WAS EITHER PAINFUL DEATH FROM STAGE IV CANCER -- OR THESE EXPERIMENTAL TRIALS UP IN CANADA.
"(I KNOW. THE CANADA THING GAVE ME PAUSE, TOO.)
"AND LOOKING BACK ON WHAT HAPPENED, SOME MIGHT SAY I SHOULD HAVE TAKEN MY CHANCES WITH THE BIG C."
OH GOD.
WHAT IN THE NAME OF...
WHAT? IS IT MY HAIR?
CRAP, DID I LOSE SOME OF MY HAIR?

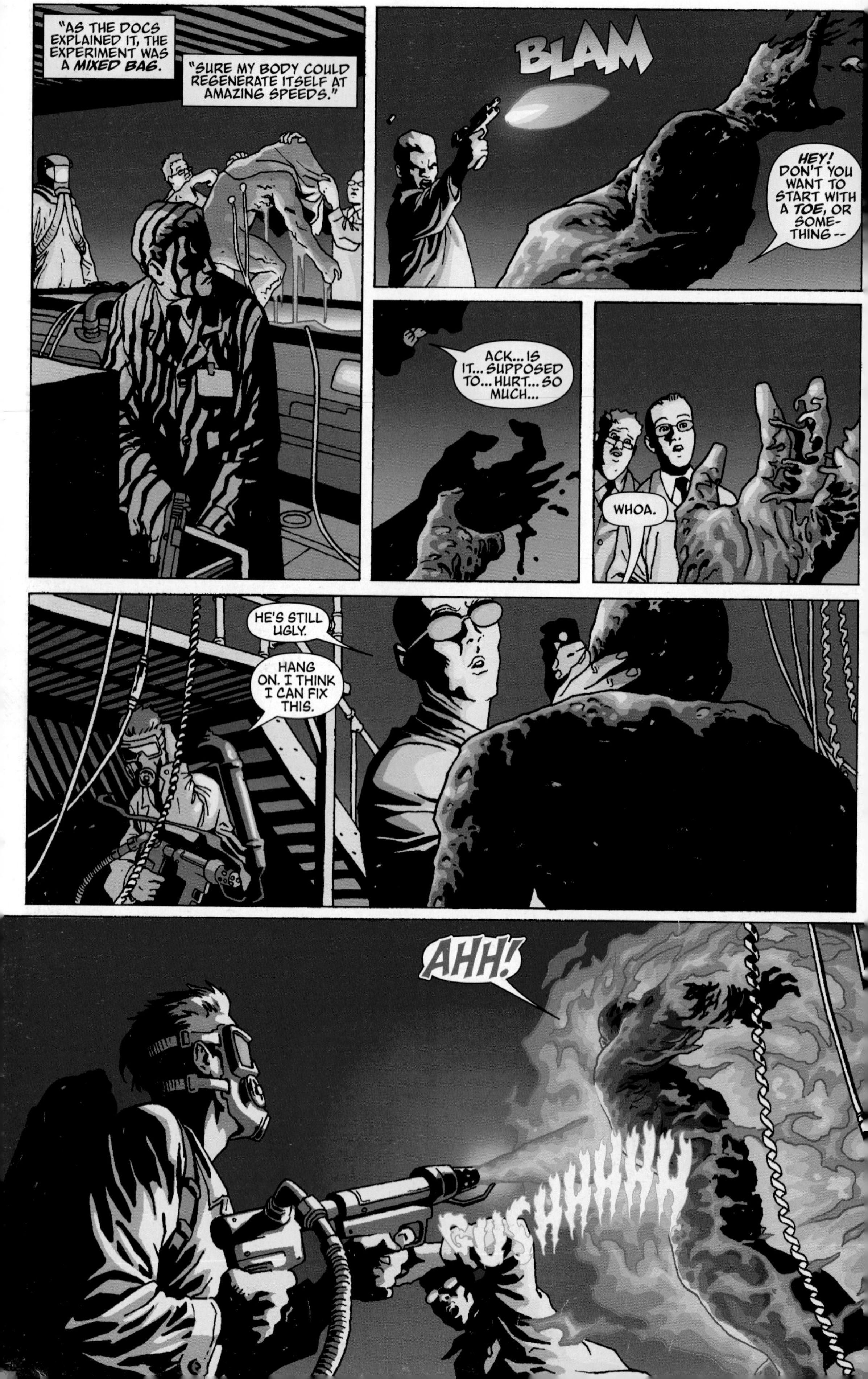
"AS THE DOCS EXPLAINED IT, THE EXPERIMENT WAS A *MIXED BAG*.
"SURE MY BODY COULD REGENERATE ITSELF AT AMAZING SPEEDS."
BLAM
HEY! DON'T YOU WANT TO START WITH A *TOE*, OR SOME-THING --
ACK... IS IT... SUPPOSED TO... HURT... SO MUCH...
WHOA.
HE'S STILL UGLY.
HANG ON. I THINK I CAN FIX THIS.
AHH!
GUSHHHHH

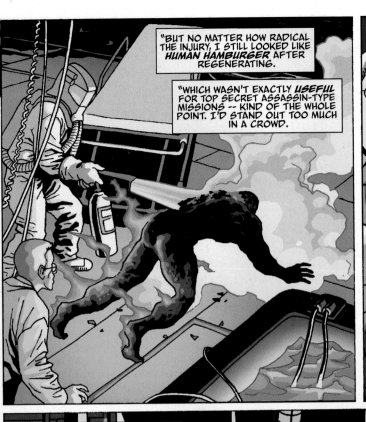

"BUT NO MATTER HOW RADICAL THE INJURY, I STILL LOOKED LIKE *HUMAN HAMBURGER* AFTER REGENERATING.

"WHICH WASN'T EXACTLY *USEFUL* FOR TOP SECRET ASSASSIN-TYPE MISSIONS -- KIND OF THE WHOLE POINT. I'D STAND OUT TOO MUCH IN A CROWD.

"THEY TOLD ME NOT TO WORRY. WHILE THEY SORTED IT OUT, I COULD CHILL OUT AT A *RESORT* TO RECOVER.

"AND IT WAS A REAL *CLUB MED.*

"IF BY CLUB MED YOU MEAN *CLUB FAILED MED*-ICAL EXPERIMENTS.

"ROTTING AWAY IN MY CELL, I REALIZED I SIGNED ON FOR A FATE WORSE THAN CANCER. AT LEAST CANCER ENDS. THIS WENT ON AND ON... POTENTIALLY *FOREVER.*

"I HAD TO FIND A WAY OUT."

OW MY SKIN. OW MY SKIN OW MY SKIN. OW MY SKIN. OW MY SKIN HURTS. OW MY SKIN...

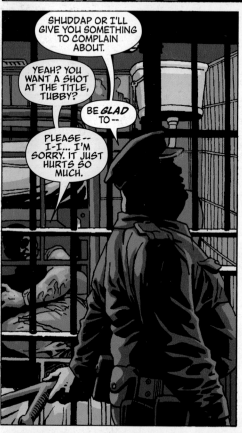

SHUDDAP OR I'LL GIVE YOU SOMETHING TO COMPLAIN ABOUT.

YEAH? YOU WANT A SHOT AT THE TITLE, TUBBY?

BE *GLAD* TO --

PLEASE -- I-I... I'M SORRY. IT JUST HURTS SO MUCH.

BUT SERIOUSLY -- DO YOU HAVE ANY VASELINE HANDY? YOU KNOW, THE KIND YOU USE ON YOUR *STRETCH MARKS?*

OKAY, FREAK -- IT'S ON. WAIT UNTIL YOU SEE HOW MUCH YOUR SKIN CAN *REALLY* HURT.

"AH, BULLIES. THEY CAN'T RESIST KICKIN' THE SNOT OUT OF THE LITTLE GUY."

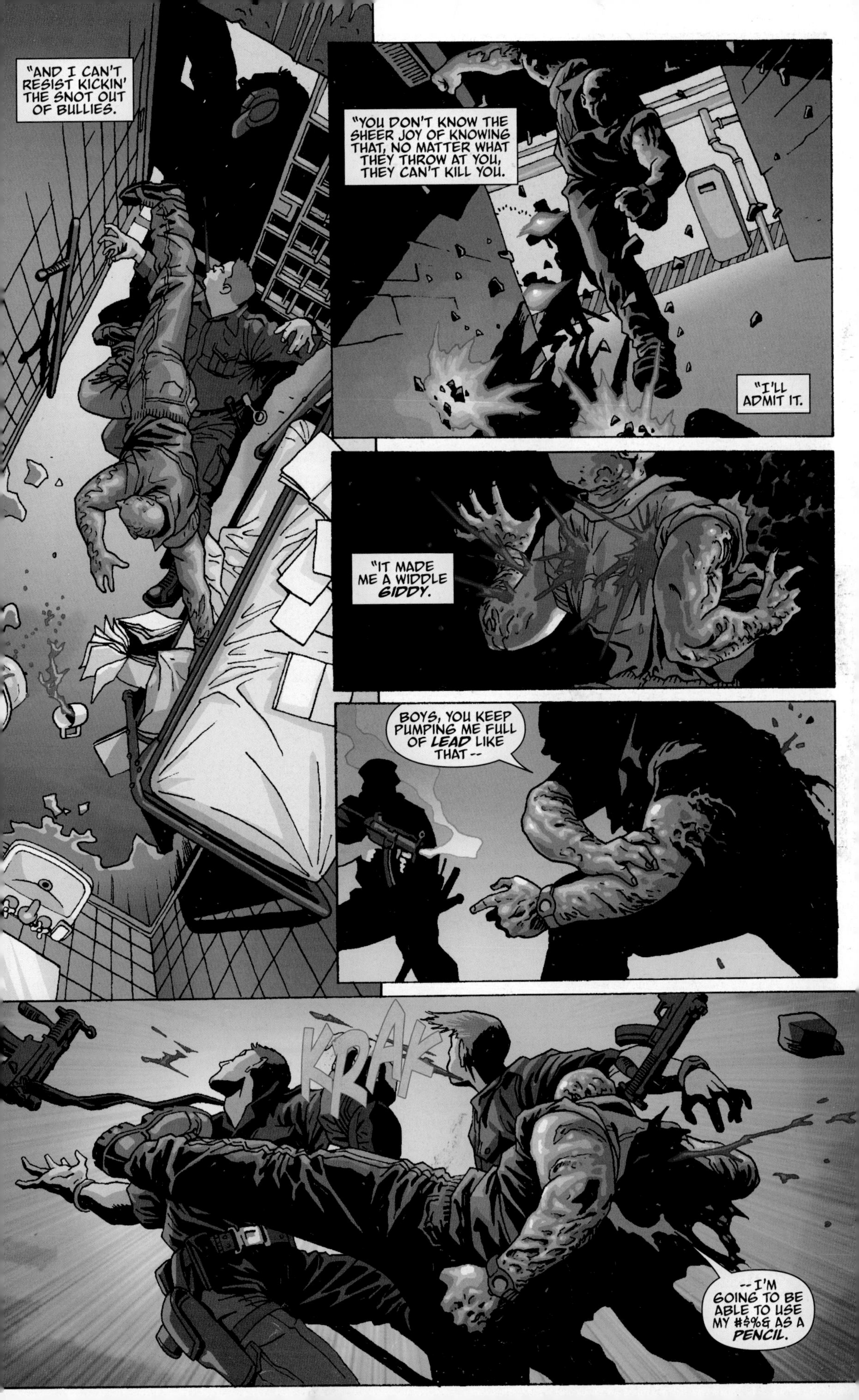
"AND I CAN'T RESIST KICKIN' THE SNOT OUT OF BULLIES.
"YOU DON'T KNOW THE SHEER JOY OF KNOWING THAT, NO MATTER WHAT THEY THROW AT YOU, THEY CAN'T KILL YOU.
"I'LL ADMIT IT.
"IT MADE ME A WIDDLE GIDDY.
BOYS, YOU KEEP PUMPING ME FULL OF LEAD LIKE THAT --
KRAK
--I'M GOING TO BE ABLE TO USE MY #$%& AS A PENCIL.

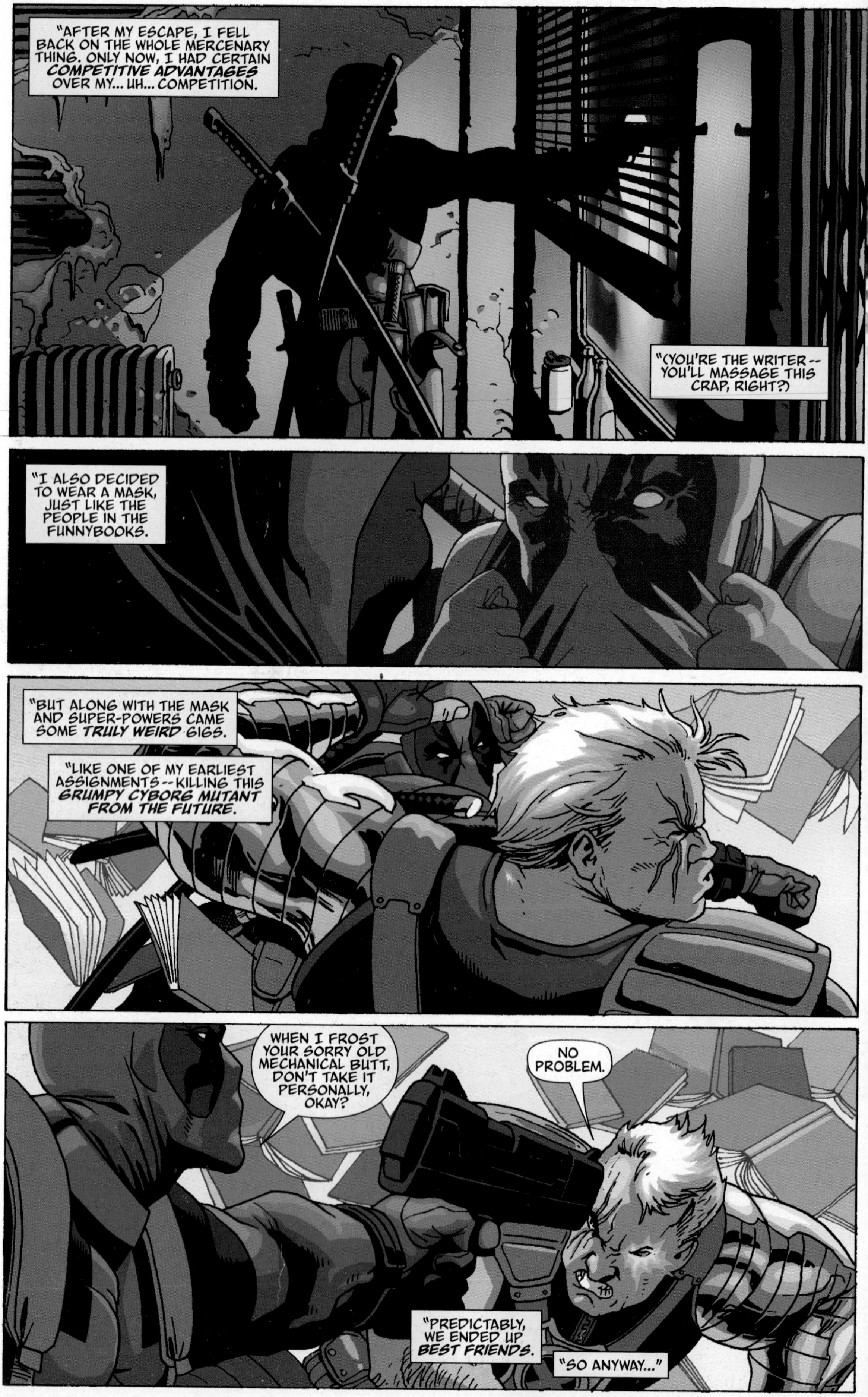
"AFTER MY ESCAPE, I FELL BACK ON THE WHOLE MERCENARY THING. ONLY NOW, I HAD CERTAIN *COMPETITIVE ADVANTAGES* OVER MY... UH... COMPETITION.
"(YOU'RE THE WRITER -- YOU'LL MASSAGE THIS CRAP, RIGHT?)
"I ALSO DECIDED TO WEAR A MASK, JUST LIKE THE PEOPLE IN THE FUNNYBOOKS.
"BUT ALONG WITH THE MASK AND SUPER-POWERS CAME SOME *TRULY WEIRD* GIGS.
"LIKE ONE OF MY EARLIEST ASSIGNMENTS -- KILLING THIS *GRUMPY CYBORG MUTANT FROM THE FUTURE*.
WHEN I FROST YOUR SORRY OLD MECHANICAL BUTT, DON'T TAKE IT PERSONALLY, OKAY?
NO PROBLEM.
"PREDICTABLY, WE ENDED UP *BEST FRIENDS*.
"SO ANYWAY..."

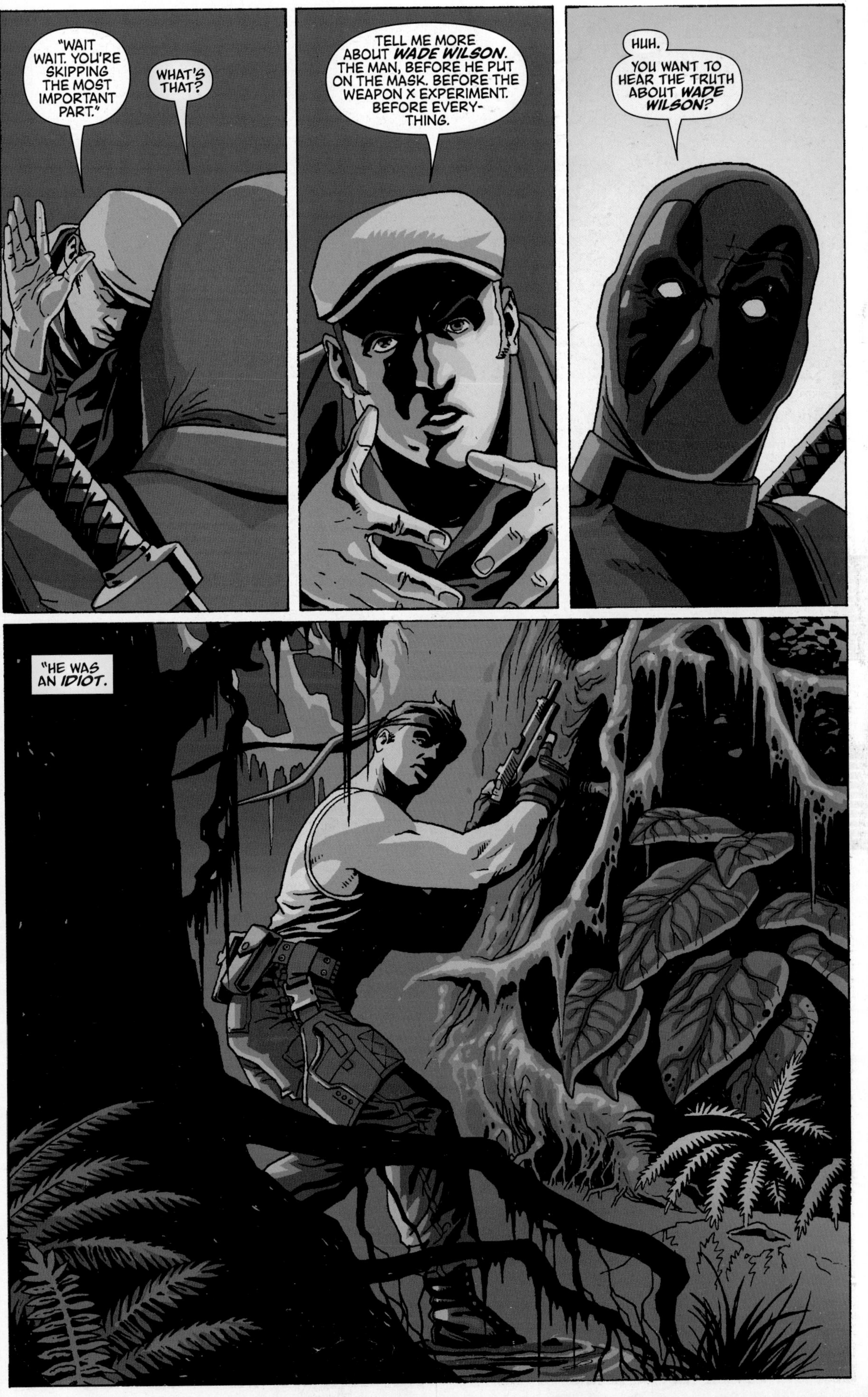
"WAIT WAIT. YOU'RE SKIPPING THE MOST IMPORTANT PART."
WHAT'S THAT?
TELL ME MORE ABOUT WADE WILSON. THE MAN, BEFORE HE PUT ON THE MASK. BEFORE THE WEAPON X EXPERIMENT. BEFORE EVERY-THING.
HUH.
YOU WANT TO HEAR THE TRUTH ABOUT WADE WILSON?
"HE WAS AN IDIOT.

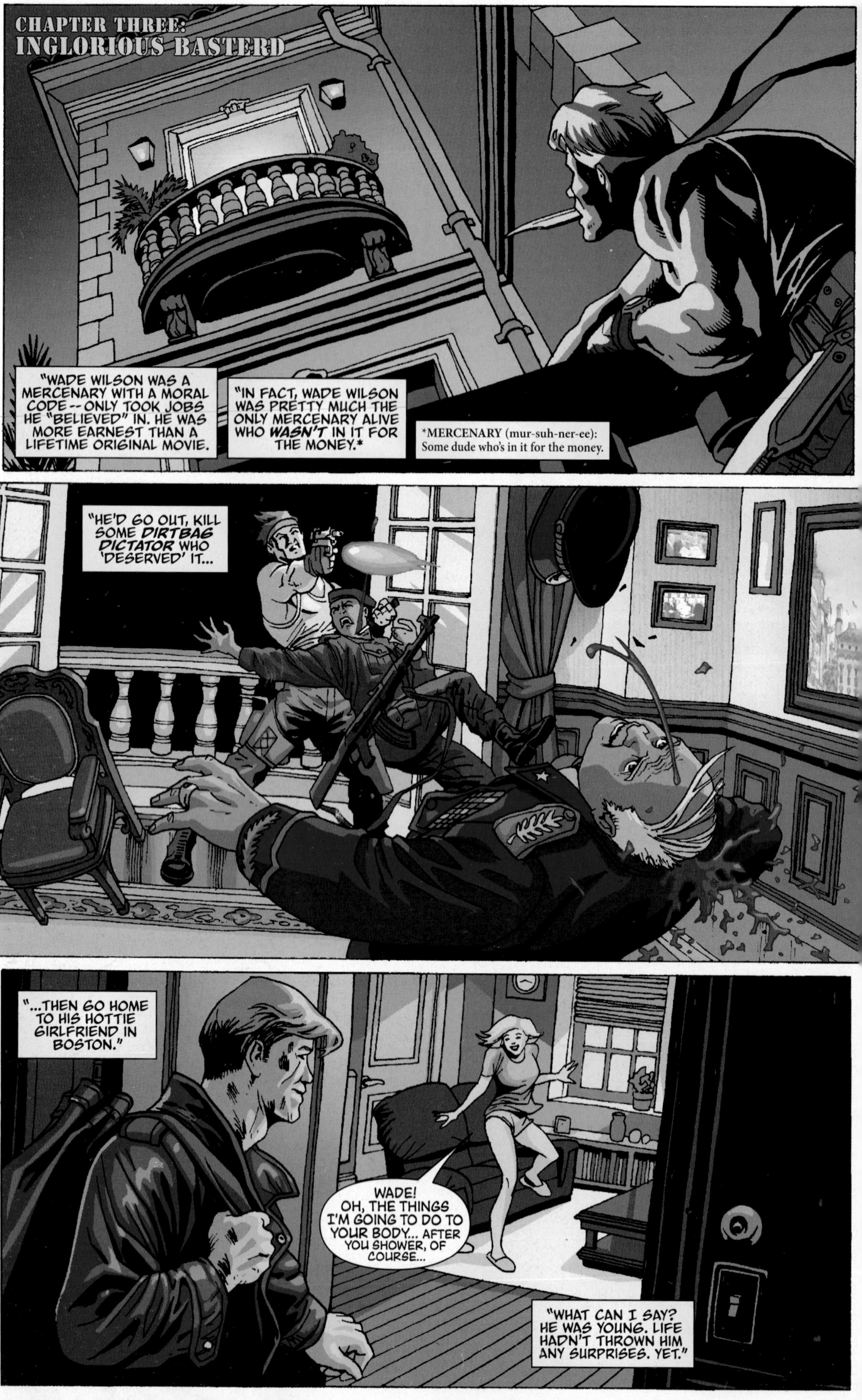
CHAPTER THREE:
INGLORIOUS BASTERD
"WADE WILSON WAS A MERCENARY WITH A MORAL CODE -- ONLY TOOK JOBS HE "BELIEVED" IN. HE WAS MORE EARNEST THAN A LIFETIME ORIGINAL MOVIE.
"IN FACT, WADE WILSON WAS PRETTY MUCH THE ONLY MERCENARY ALIVE WHO WASN'T IN IT FOR THE MONEY.*
*MERCENARY (mur-suh-ner-ee): Some dude who's in it for the money.
"HE'D GO OUT, KILL SOME DIRTBAG DICTATOR WHO 'DESERVED' IT...
"...THEN GO HOME TO HIS HOTTIE GIRLFRIEND IN BOSTON."
WADE! OH, THE THINGS I'M GOING TO DO TO YOUR BODY... AFTER YOU SHOWER, OF COURSE...
"WHAT CAN I SAY? HE WAS YOUNG. LIFE HADN'T THROWN HIM ANY SURPRISES. YET."

IS THIS ALL OF THE MAIL?

HOW ABOUT YOU **OPEN** ME?

SERIOUSLY, NESS... ANYTHING FROM NYU MEDICAL, BY CHANCE?

I'LL EVEN LET YOU CANCEL MY STAMP...

HERE IT IS. JUST ONE SEC, BABE...

OKAY, I CHANGED MY MIND. YOU DON'T HAVE TO SHOWER.

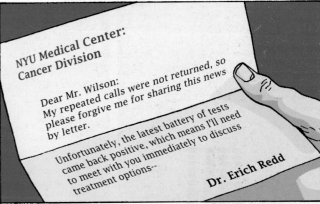

NYU Medical Center: Cancer Division

Dear Mr. Wilson:
My repeated calls were not returned, so please forgive me for sharing this news by letter.

Unfortunately, the latest battery of tests came back positive, which means I'll need to meet with you immediately to discuss treatment options--

Dr. Erich Redd

WADE? WHAT **IS** IT?

YOU DON'T UNDERSTAND -- I **WANT** TO HELP YOU THROUGH THIS. YOU ARE **NOT** A BURDEN.

I'M NOT GOING TO LET YOU WATCH ME DIE.

YOU'RE DAMNED RIGHT, I'M NOT -- BECAUSE I'M GOING TO HELP YOU **BEAT** THIS THING!

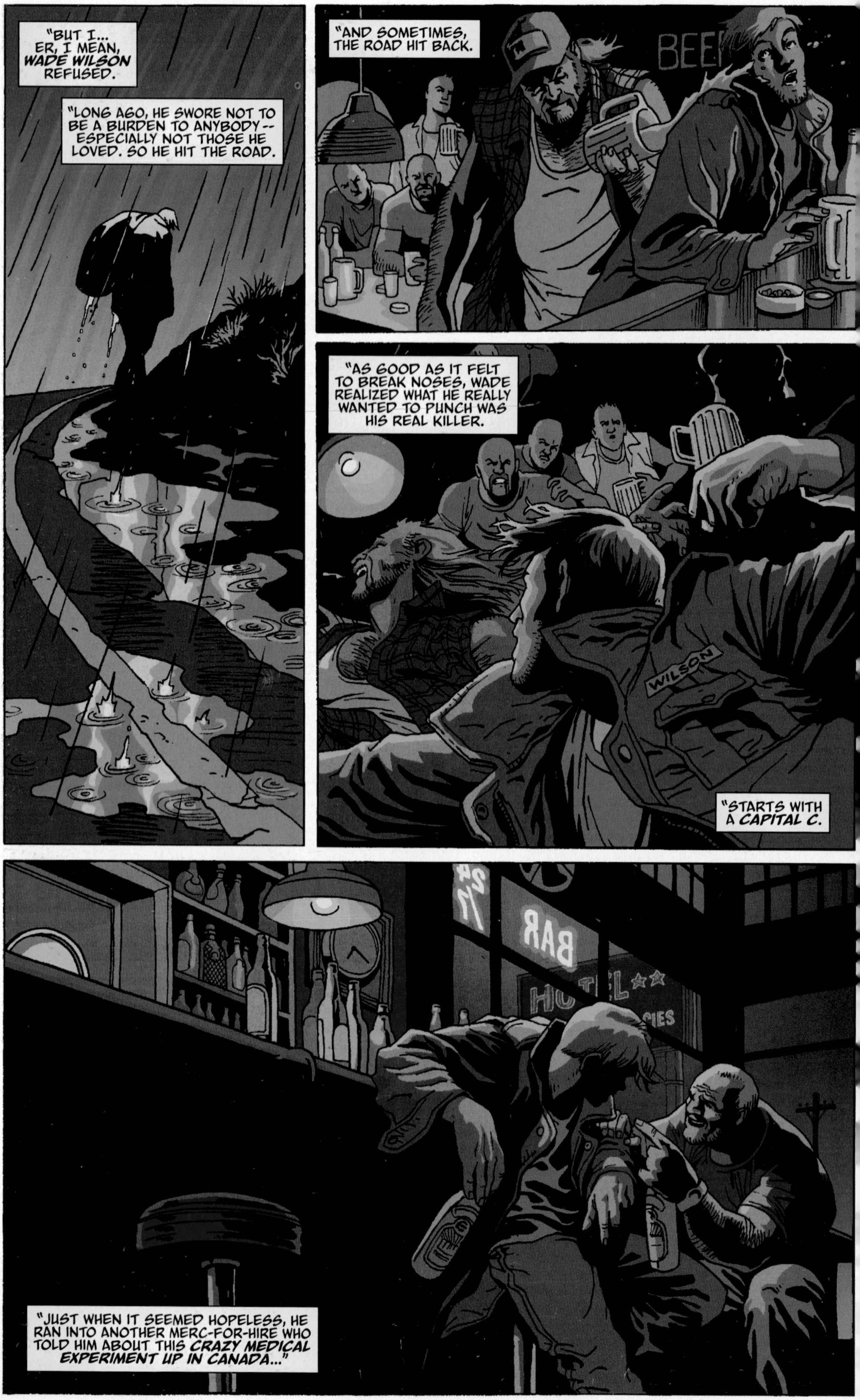
"BUT I... ER, I MEAN, WADE WILSON REFUSED.
"LONG AGO, HE SWORE NOT TO BE A BURDEN TO ANYBODY -- ESPECIALLY NOT THOSE HE LOVED. SO HE HIT THE ROAD.
"AND SOMETIMES, THE ROAD HIT BACK.
"AS GOOD AS IT FELT TO BREAK NOSES, WADE REALIZED WHAT HE REALLY WANTED TO PUNCH WAS HIS REAL KILLER.
WILSON
"STARTS WITH A CAPITAL C.
BAR
"JUST WHEN IT SEEMED HOPELESS, HE RAN INTO ANOTHER MERC-FOR-HIRE WHO TOLD HIM ABOUT THIS CRAZY MEDICAL EXPERIMENT UP IN CANADA..."

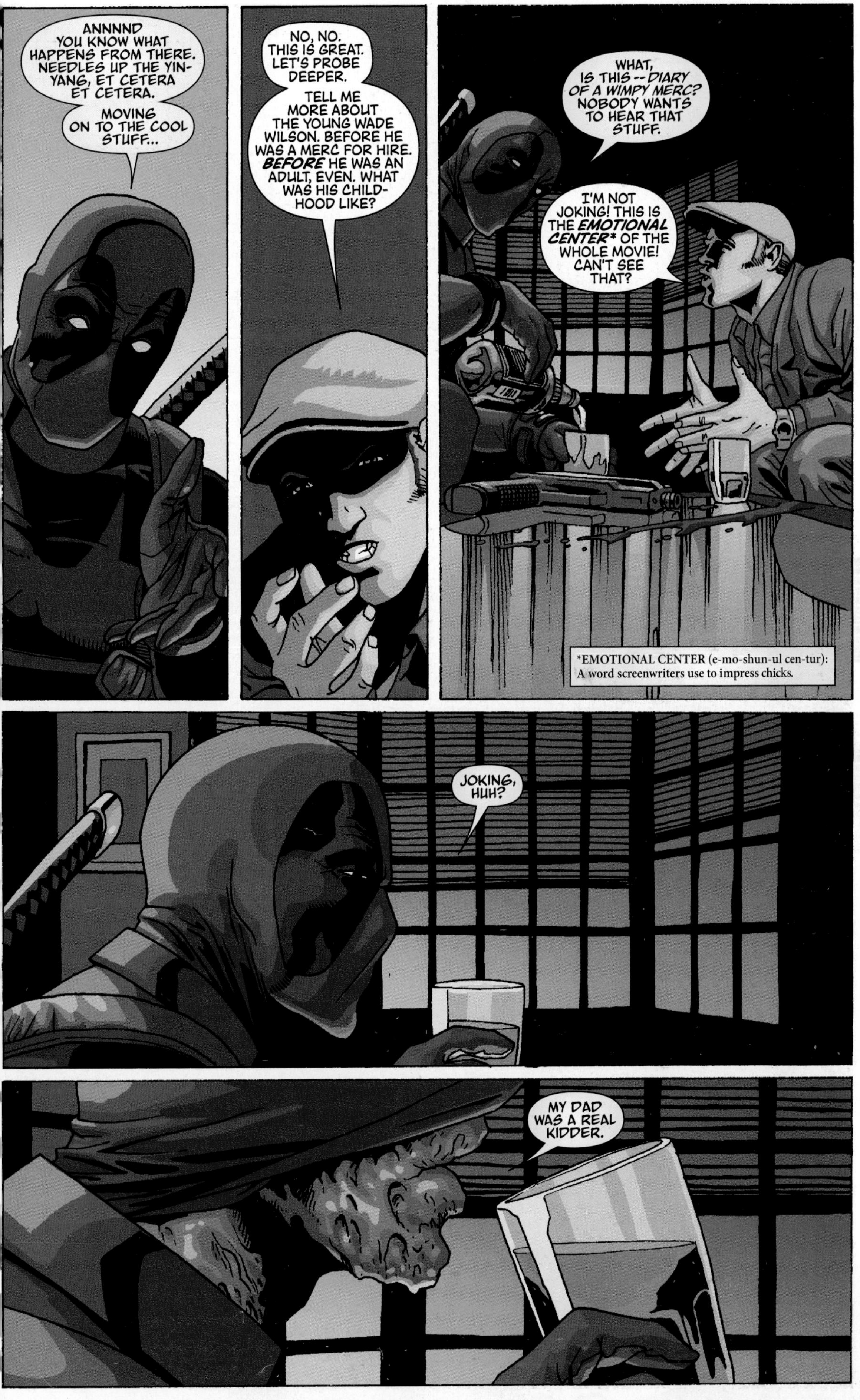
ANNNND YOU KNOW WHAT HAPPENS FROM THERE. NEEDLES UP THE YIN-YANG, ET CETERA ET CETERA.
MOVING ON TO THE COOL STUFF...
NO, NO. THIS IS GREAT. LET'S PROBE DEEPER.
TELL ME MORE ABOUT THE YOUNG WADE WILSON. BEFORE HE WAS A MERC FOR HIRE. BEFORE HE WAS AN ADULT, EVEN. WHAT WAS HIS CHILD-HOOD LIKE?
WHAT, IS THIS -- DIARY OF A WIMPY MERC? NOBODY WANTS TO HEAR THAT STUFF.
I'M NOT JOKING! THIS IS THE EMOTIONAL CENTER* OF THE WHOLE MOVIE! CAN'T SEE THAT?
*EMOTIONAL CENTER (e-mo-shun-ul cen-tur): A word screenwriters use to impress chicks.
JOKING, HUH?
MY DAD WAS A REAL KIDDER.

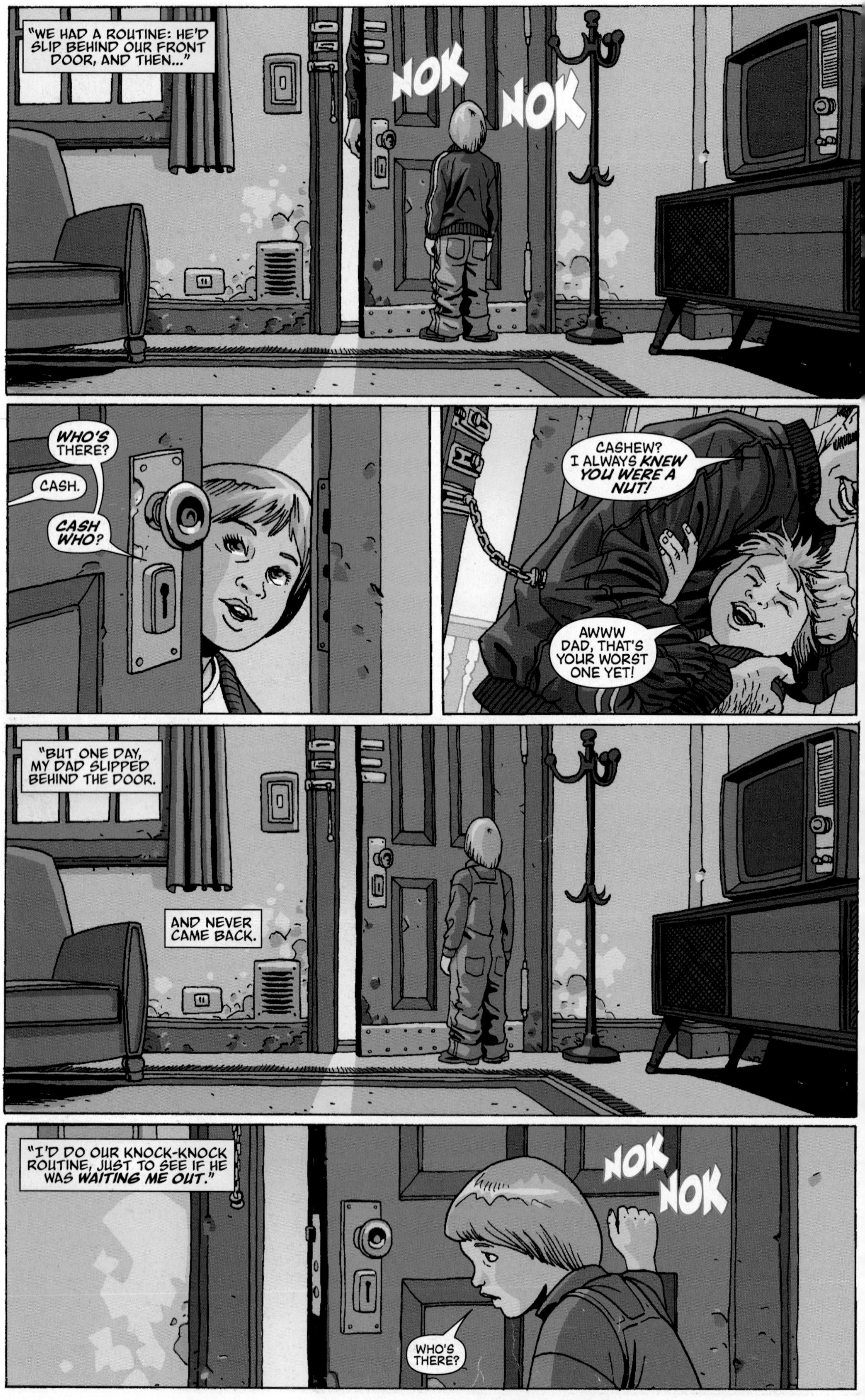
"WE HAD A ROUTINE: HE'D SLIP BEHIND OUR FRONT DOOR, AND THEN..."
NOK NOK
WHO'S THERE?
CASH.
CASH WHO?
CASHEW? I ALWAYS KNEW YOU WERE A NUT!
AWWW DAD, THAT'S YOUR WORST ONE YET!
"BUT ONE DAY, MY DAD SLIPPED BEHIND THE DOOR.
AND NEVER CAME BACK.
"I'D DO OUR KNOCK-KNOCK ROUTINE, JUST TO SEE IF HE WAS WAITING ME OUT."
NOK NOK
WHO'S THERE?

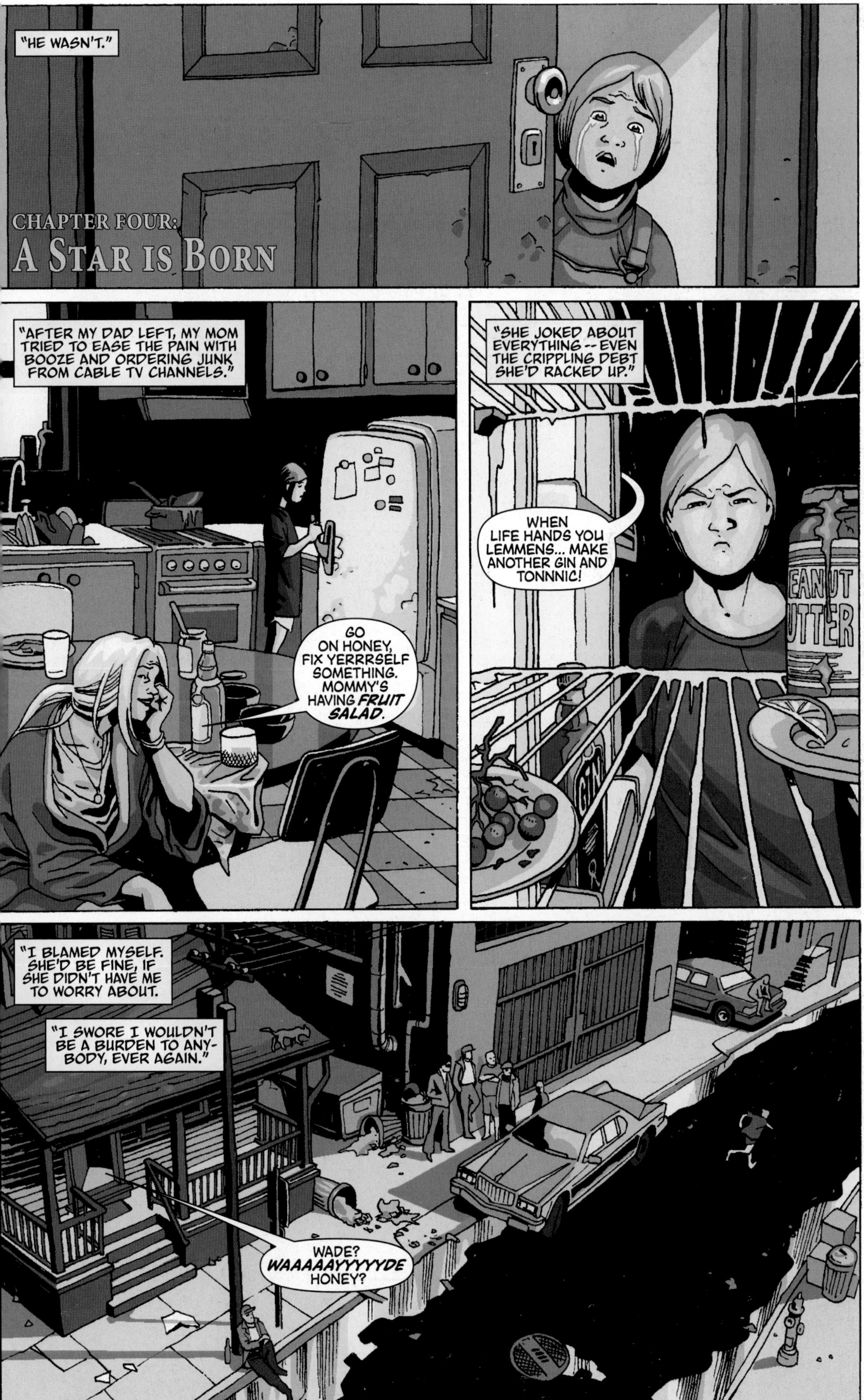
"HE WASN'T."
CHAPTER FOUR:
A STAR IS BORN
"AFTER MY DAD LEFT, MY MOM TRIED TO EASE THE PAIN WITH BOOZE AND ORDERING JUNK FROM CABLE TV CHANNELS."
GO ON HONEY, FIX YERRRSELF SOMETHING. MOMMY'S HAVING *FRUIT SALAD*.
"SHE JOKED ABOUT EVERYTHING -- EVEN THE CRIPPLING DEBT SHE'D RACKED UP."
WHEN LIFE HANDS YOU LEMMENS... MAKE ANOTHER GIN AND TONNNIC!
"I BLAMED MYSELF. SHE'D BE FINE, IF SHE DIDN'T HAVE ME TO WORRY ABOUT.
"I SWORE I WOULDN'T BE A BURDEN TO ANYBODY, EVER AGAIN."
WADE? ***WAAAAAYYYYYDE*** HONEY?

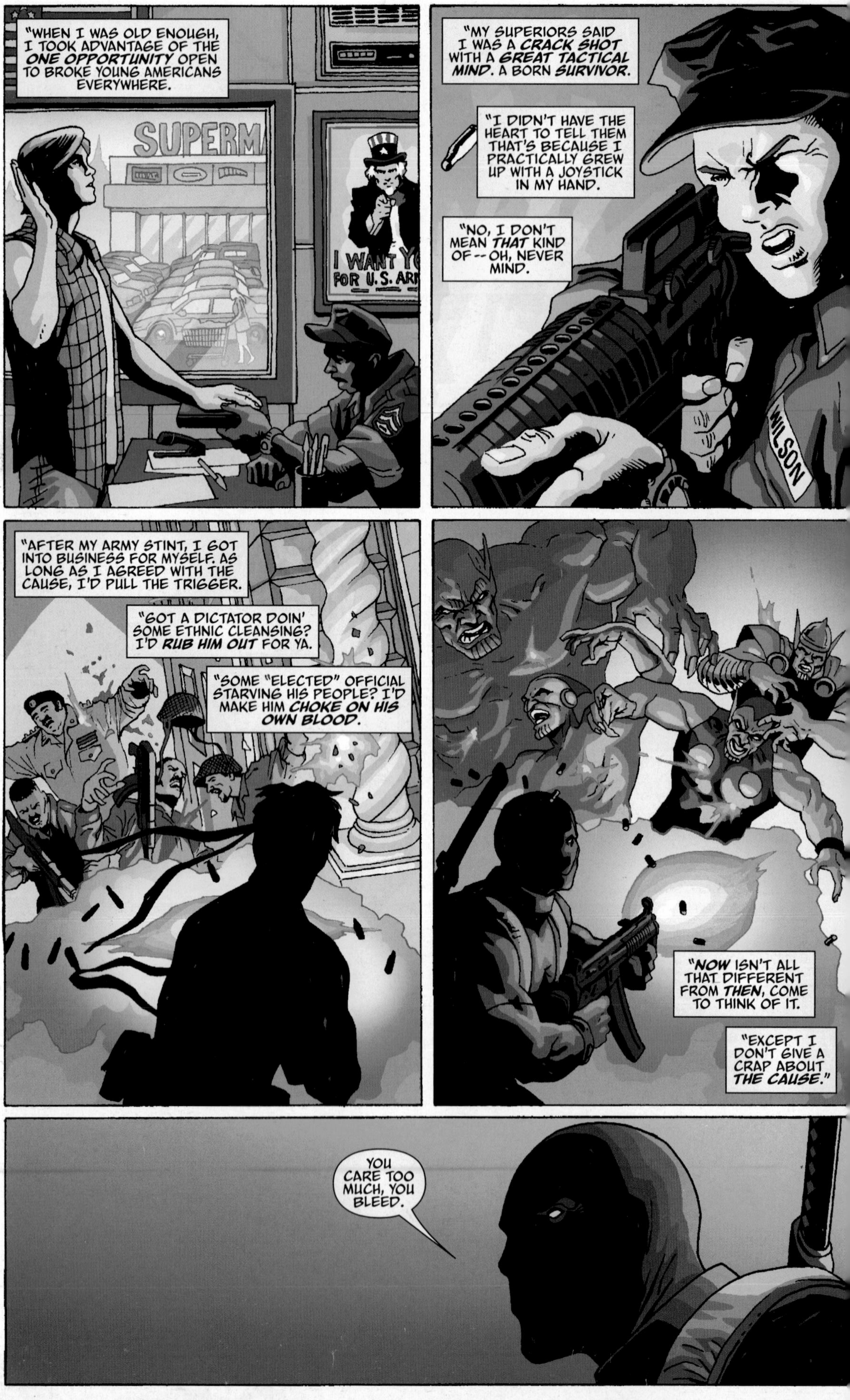
"WHEN I WAS OLD ENOUGH, I TOOK ADVANTAGE OF THE ONE OPPORTUNITY OPEN TO BROKE YOUNG AMERICANS EVERYWHERE.
SUPERM
I WANT YO
FOR U.S. AR
"MY SUPERIORS SAID I WAS A CRACK SHOT WITH A GREAT TACTICAL MIND. A BORN SURVIVOR.
"I DIDN'T HAVE THE HEART TO TELL THEM THAT'S BECAUSE I PRACTICALLY GREW UP WITH A JOYSTICK IN MY HAND.
"NO, I DON'T MEAN THAT KIND OF -- OH, NEVER MIND.
WILSON
"AFTER MY ARMY STINT, I GOT INTO BUSINESS FOR MYSELF. AS LONG AS I AGREED WITH THE CAUSE, I'D PULL THE TRIGGER.
"GOT A DICTATOR DOIN' SOME ETHNIC CLEANSING? I'D RUB HIM OUT FOR YA.
"SOME "ELECTED" OFFICIAL STARVING HIS PEOPLE? I'D MAKE HIM CHOKE ON HIS OWN BLOOD.
"NOW ISN'T ALL THAT DIFFERENT FROM THEN, COME TO THINK OF IT.
"EXCEPT I DON'T GIVE A CRAP ABOUT THE CAUSE."
YOU CARE TOO MUCH, YOU BLEED.

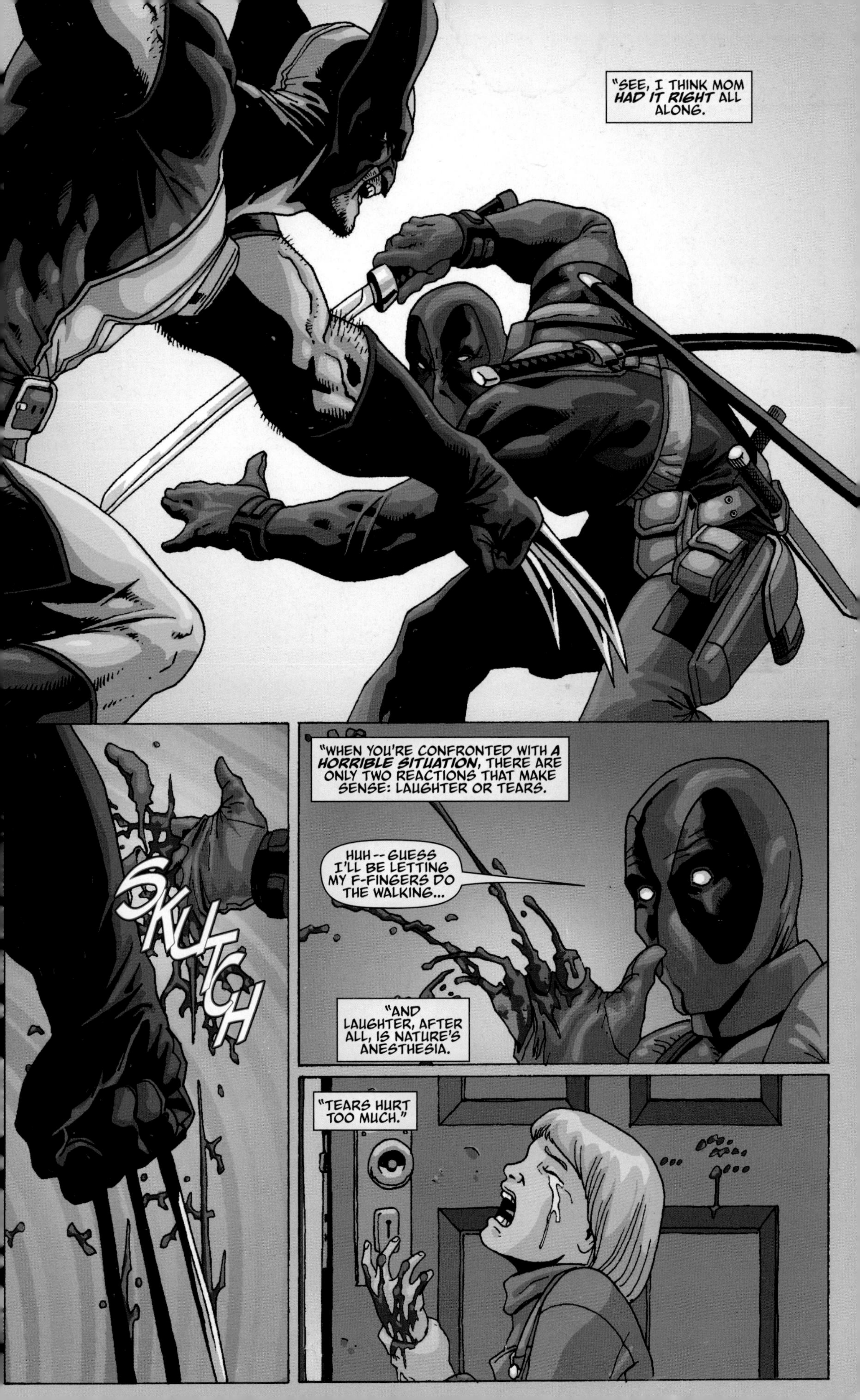
"SEE, I THINK MOM HAD IT RIGHT ALL ALONG.
SKUTCH
"WHEN YOU'RE CONFRONTED WITH A HORRIBLE SITUATION, THERE ARE ONLY TWO REACTIONS THAT MAKE SENSE: LAUGHTER OR TEARS.
HUH--GUESS I'LL BE LETTING MY F-FINGERS DO THE WALKING...
"AND LAUGHTER, AFTER ALL, IS NATURE'S ANESTHESIA.
"TEARS HURT TOO MUCH."

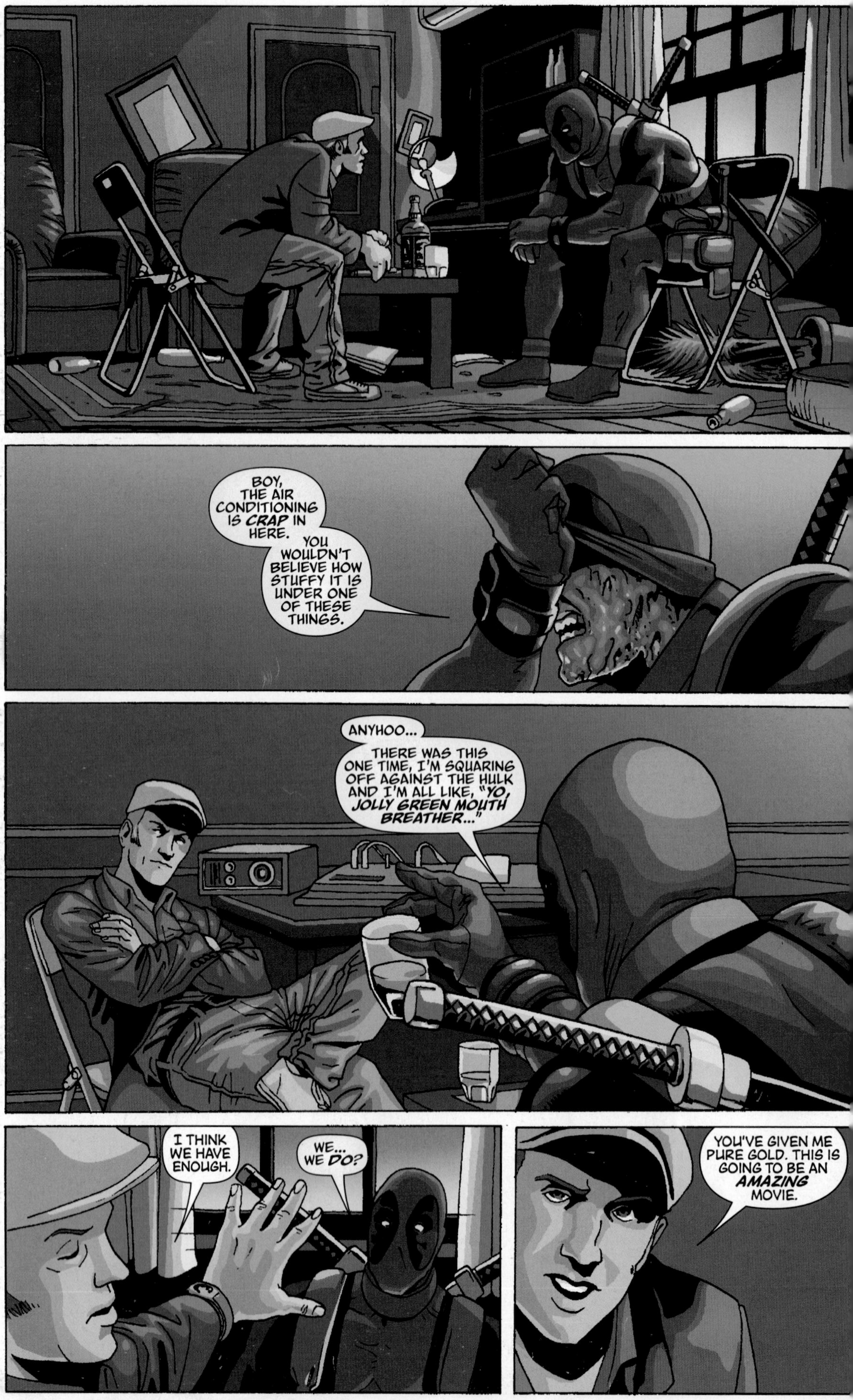
BOY, THE AIR CONDITIONING IS CRAP IN HERE.
YOU WOULDN'T BELIEVE HOW STUFFY IT IS UNDER ONE OF THESE THINGS.
ANYHOO...
THERE WAS THIS ONE TIME, I'M SQUARING OFF AGAINST THE HULK AND I'M ALL LIKE, "YO, JOLLY GREEN MOUTH BREATHER..."
I THINK WE HAVE ENOUGH.
WE... WE DO?
YOU'VE GIVEN ME PURE GOLD. THIS IS GOING TO BE AN AMAZING MOVIE.

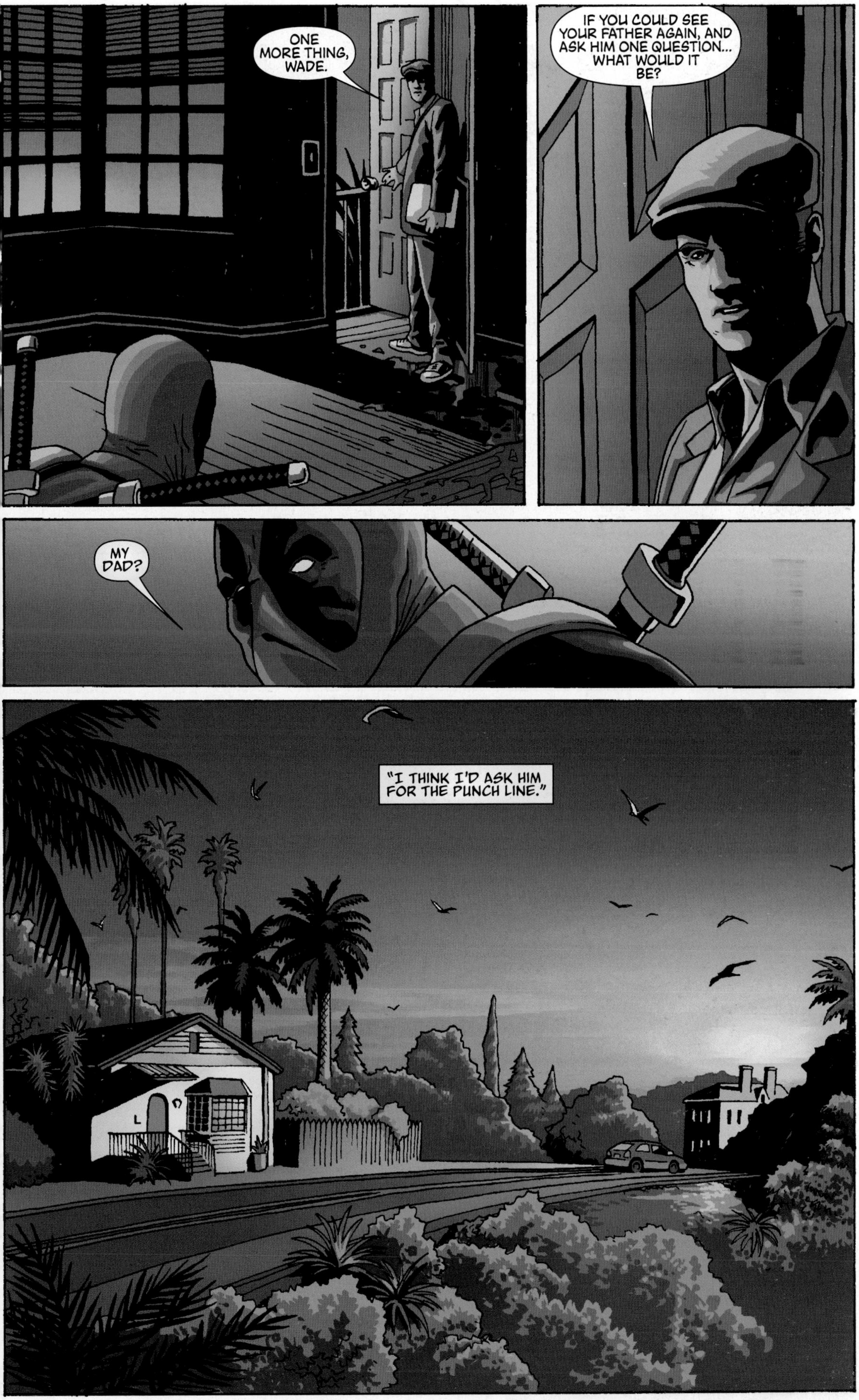
ONE MORE THING, WADE.
IF YOU COULD SEE YOUR FATHER AGAIN, AND ASK HIM ONE QUESTION... WHAT WOULD IT BE?
MY DAD?
"I THINK I'D ASK HIM FOR THE PUNCH LINE."

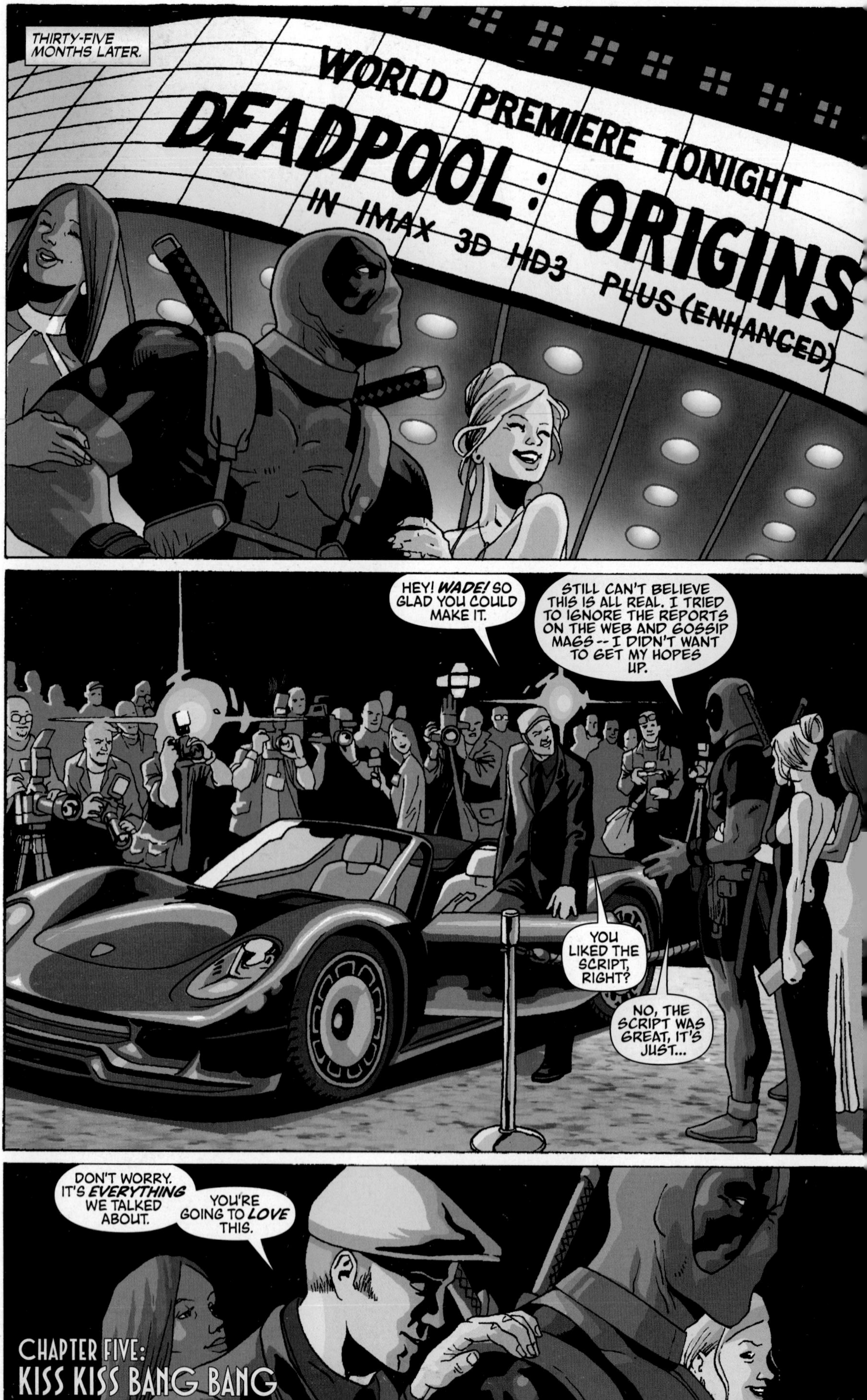
THIRTY-FIVE MONTHS LATER.
WORLD PREMIERE TONIGHT
DEADPOOL: ORIGINS
IN IMAX 3D HD3 PLUS (ENHANCED)
HEY! WADE! SO GLAD YOU COULD MAKE IT.
STILL CAN'T BELIEVE THIS IS ALL REAL. I TRIED TO IGNORE THE REPORTS ON THE WEB AND GOSSIP MAGS -- I DIDN'T WANT TO GET MY HOPES UP.
YOU LIKED THE SCRIPT, RIGHT?
NO, THE SCRIPT WAS GREAT, IT'S JUST...
DON'T WORRY. IT'S EVERYTHING WE TALKED ABOUT.
YOU'RE GOING TO LOVE THIS.
CHAPTER FIVE:
KISS KISS BANG BANG

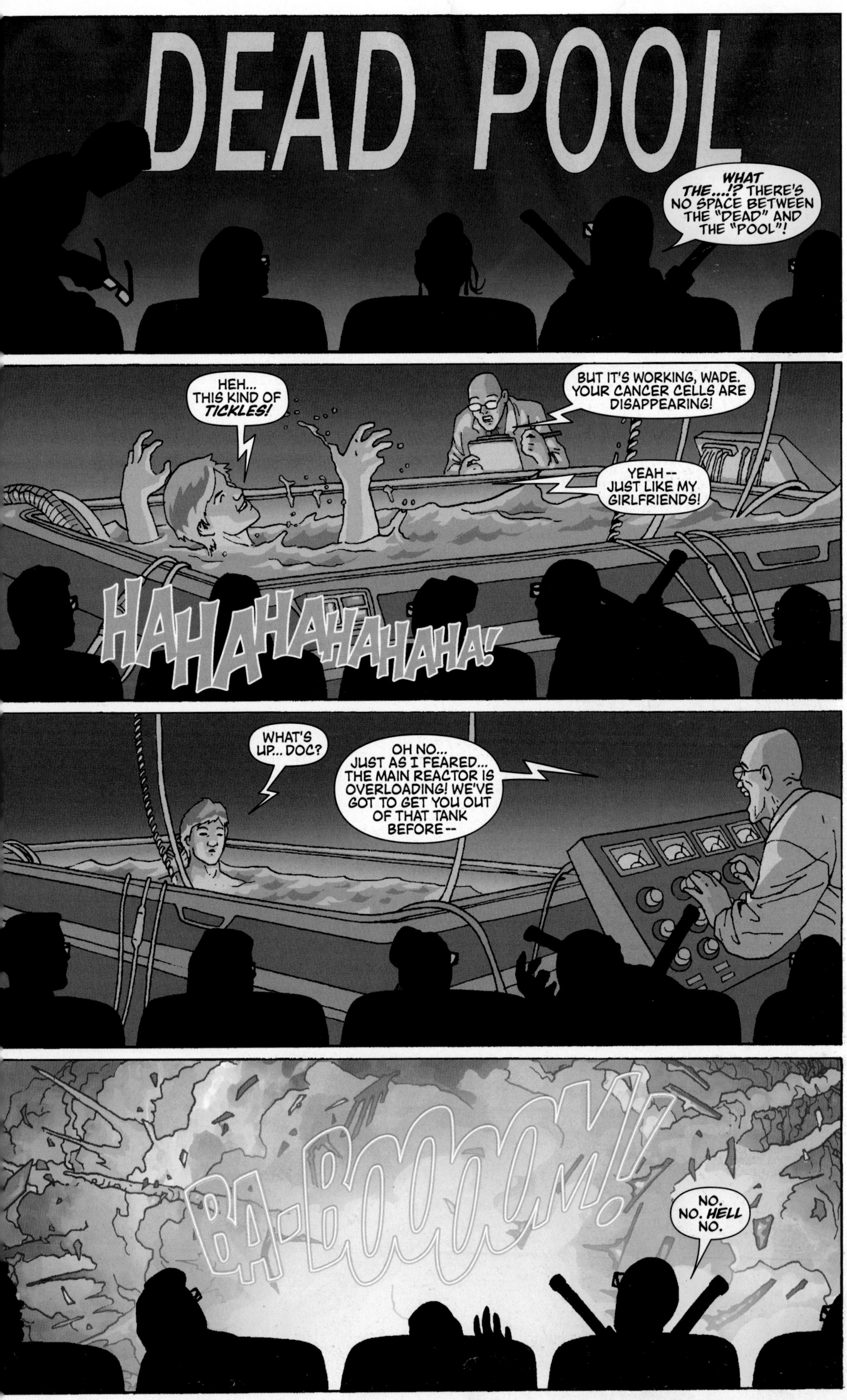
DEAD POOL
WHAT THE...!? THERE'S NO SPACE BETWEEN THE "DEAD" AND THE "POOL"!
HEH... THIS KIND OF TICKLES!
BUT IT'S WORKING, WADE. YOUR CANCER CELLS ARE DISAPPEARING!
YEAH -- JUST LIKE MY GIRLFRIENDS!
HAHAHAHAHAHAHA!
WHAT'S UP... DOC?
OH NO... JUST AS I FEARED... THE MAIN REACTOR IS OVERLOADING! WE'VE GOT TO GET YOU OUT OF THAT TANK BEFORE --
BA-BOOOOOM!
NO. NO. HELL NO.

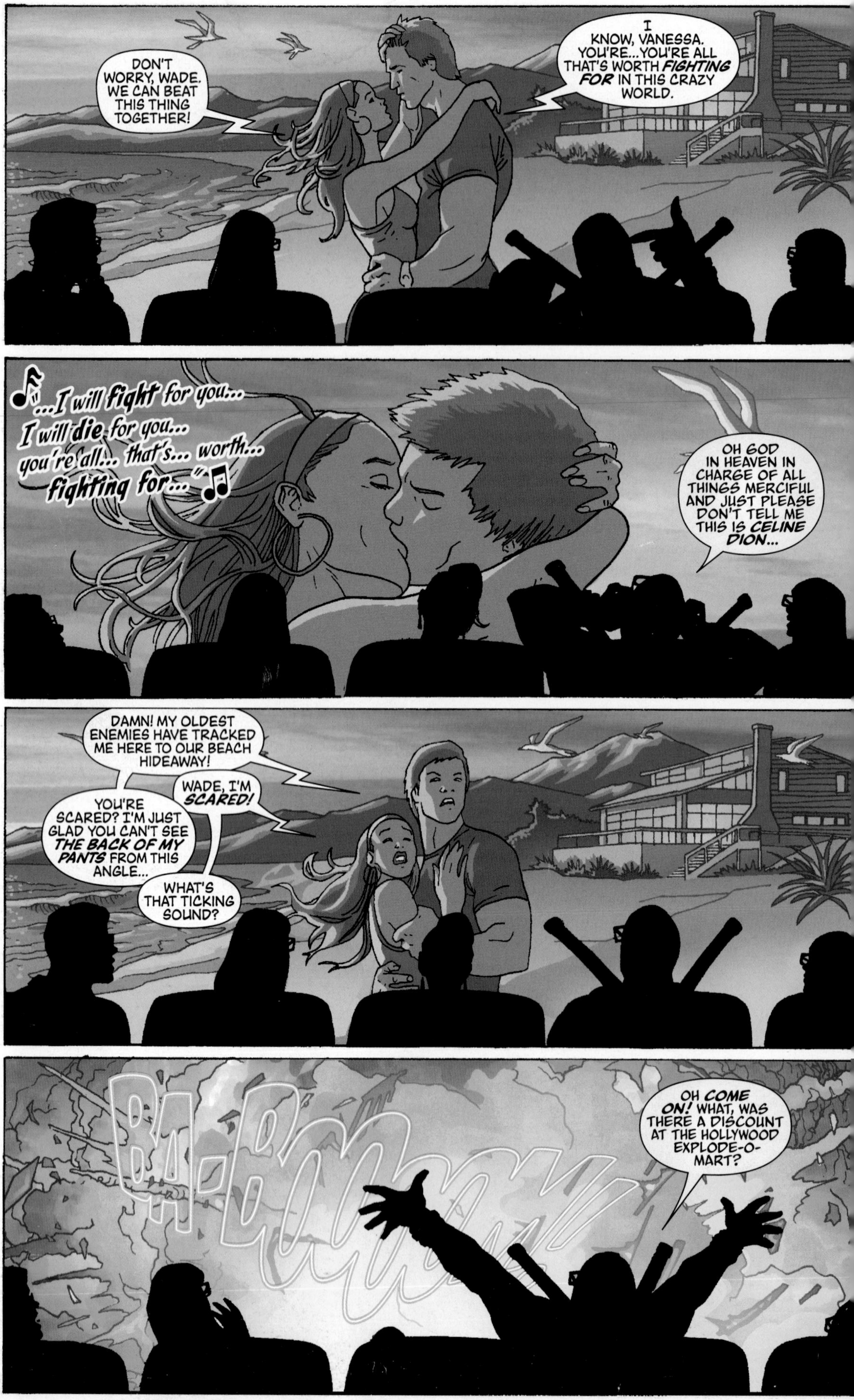
DON'T WORRY, WADE. WE CAN BEAT THIS THING TOGETHER!
I KNOW, VANESSA. YOU'RE... YOU'RE ALL THAT'S WORTH FIGHTING FOR IN THIS CRAZY WORLD.
"...I will fight for you... I will die for you... you're all... that's... worth... fighting for..."
OH GOD IN HEAVEN IN CHARGE OF ALL THINGS MERCIFUL AND JUST PLEASE DON'T TELL ME THIS IS CELINE DION...
DAMN! MY OLDEST ENEMIES HAVE TRACKED ME HERE TO OUR BEACH HIDEAWAY!
WADE, I'M SCARED!
YOU'RE SCARED? I'M JUST GLAD YOU CAN'T SEE THE BACK OF MY PANTS FROM THIS ANGLE...
WHAT'S THAT TICKING SOUND?
BA-BOOOOM!
OH COME ON! WHAT, WAS THERE A DISCOUNT AT THE HOLLYWOOD EXPLODE-O-MART?

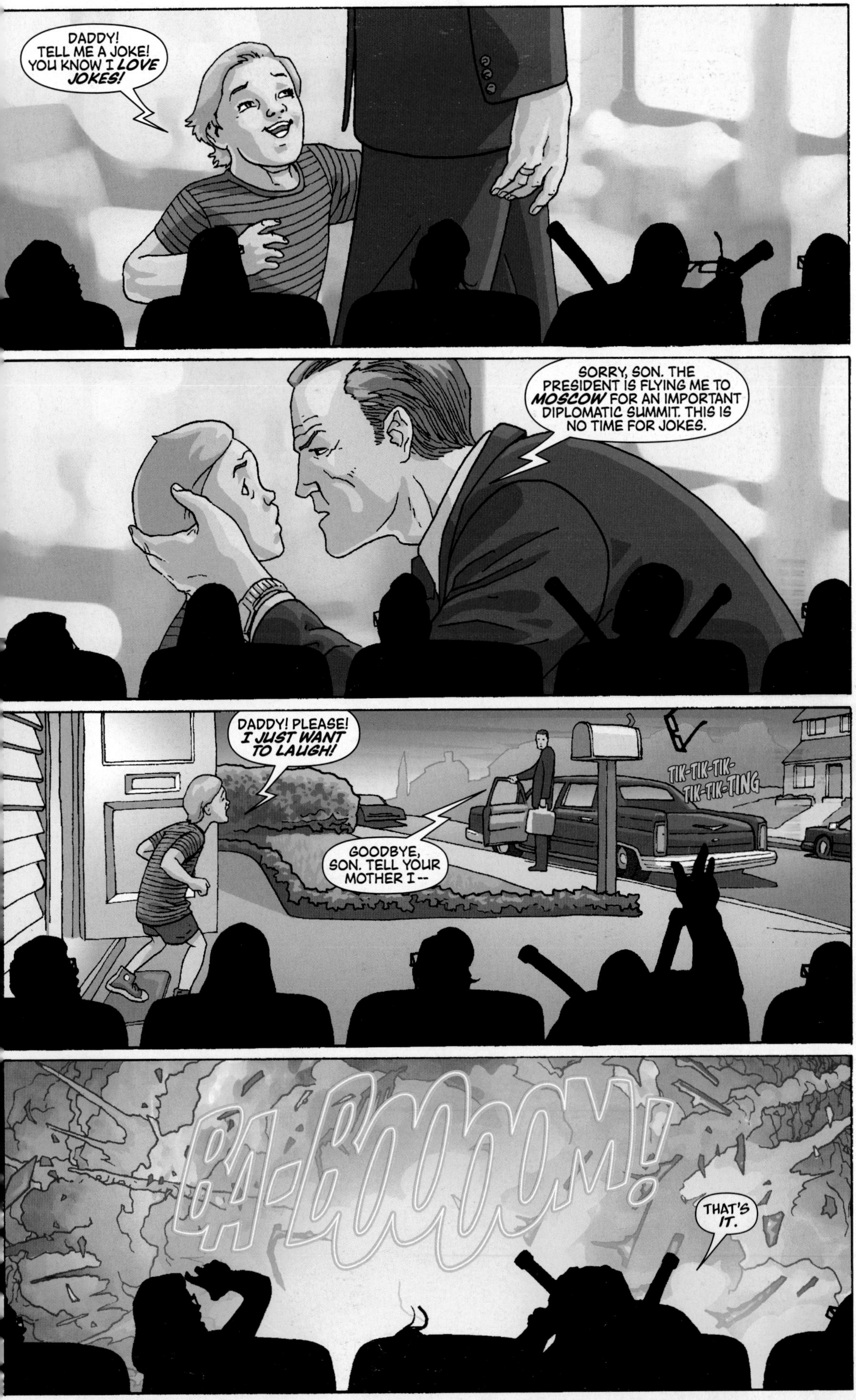
DADDY! TELL ME A JOKE! YOU KNOW I *LOVE JOKES!*
SORRY, SON. THE PRESIDENT IS FLYING ME TO *MOSCOW* FOR AN IMPORTANT DIPLOMATIC SUMMIT. THIS IS NO TIME FOR JOKES.
DADDY! PLEASE! *I JUST WANT TO LAUGH!*
GOODBYE, SON. TELL YOUR MOTHER I --
TIK-TIK-TIK-TIK-TIK-TING
BA-BOOOOOM!
THAT'S *IT.*

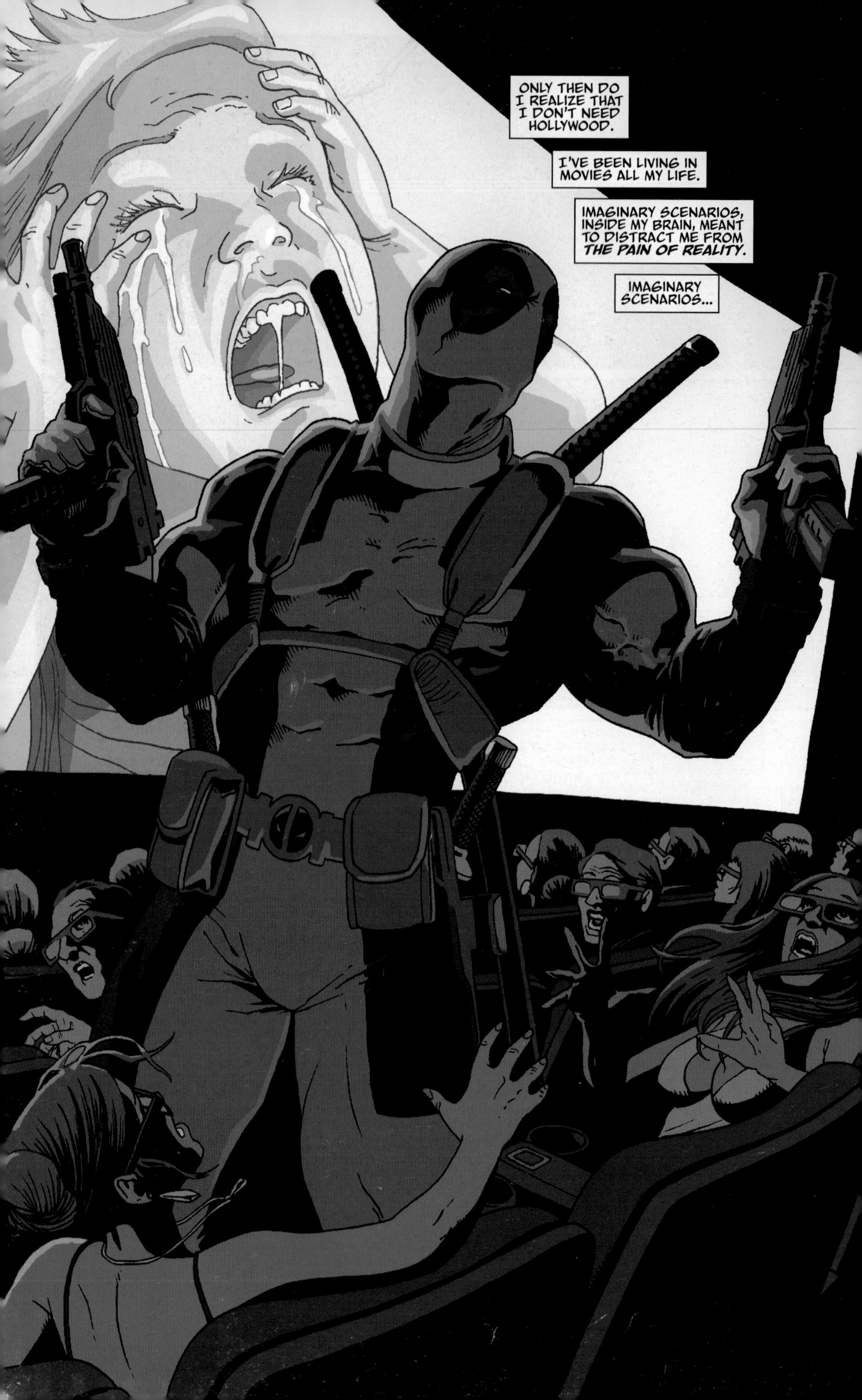
ONLY THEN DO I REALIZE THAT I DON'T NEED HOLLYWOOD.
I'VE BEEN LIVING IN MOVIES ALL MY LIFE.
IMAGINARY SCENARIOS, INSIDE MY BRAIN, MEANT TO DISTRACT ME FROM *THE PAIN OF REALITY*.
IMAGINARY SCENARIOS...

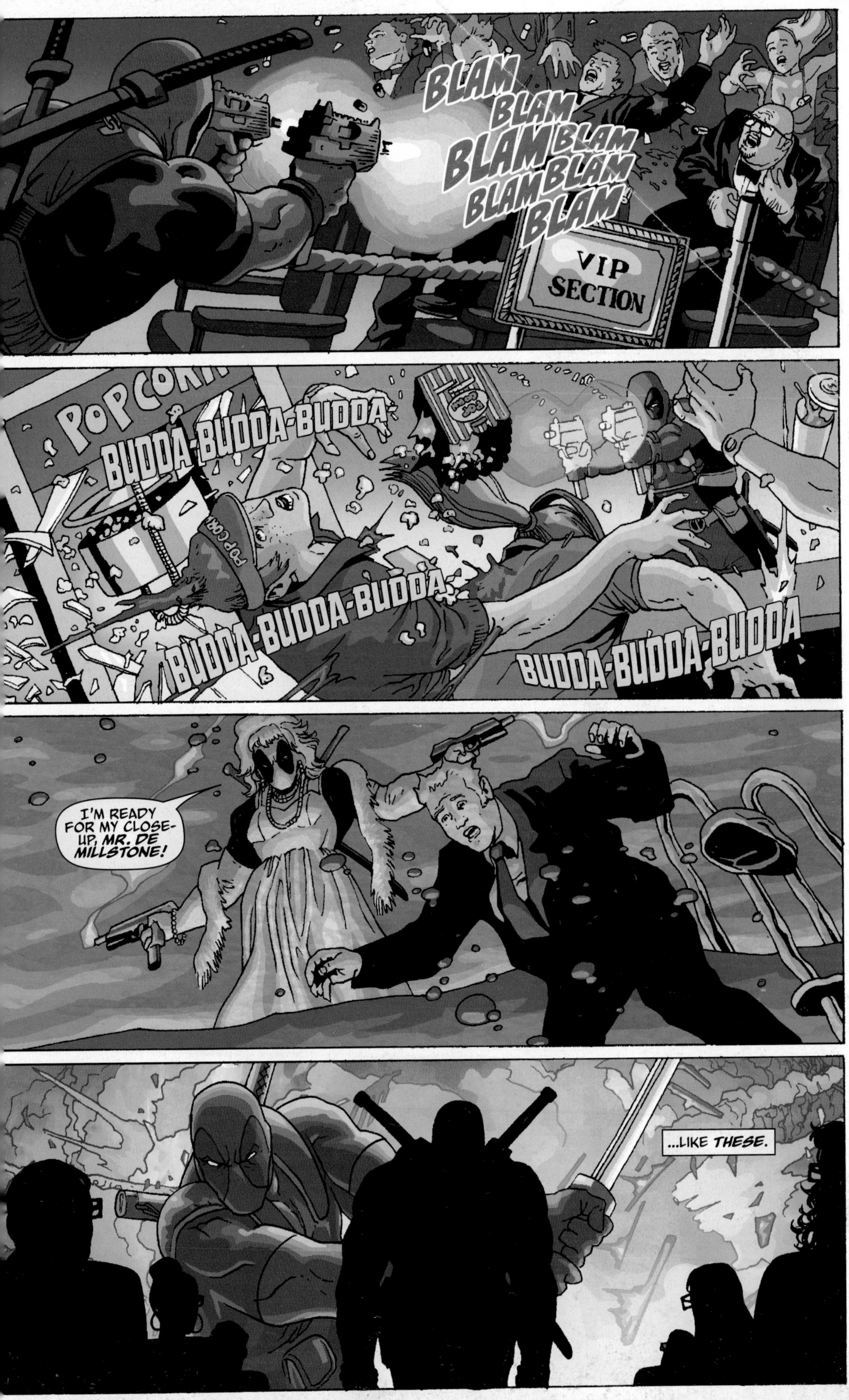
BLAM BLAM BLAM BLAM BLAM BLAM BLAM
VIP SECTION
POPCORN
BUDDA-BUDDA-BUDDA
BUDDA-BUDDA-BUDDA
BUDDA-BUDDA-BUDDA
I'M READY FOR MY CLOSE-UP, MR. DE MILLSTONE!
...LIKE THESE.

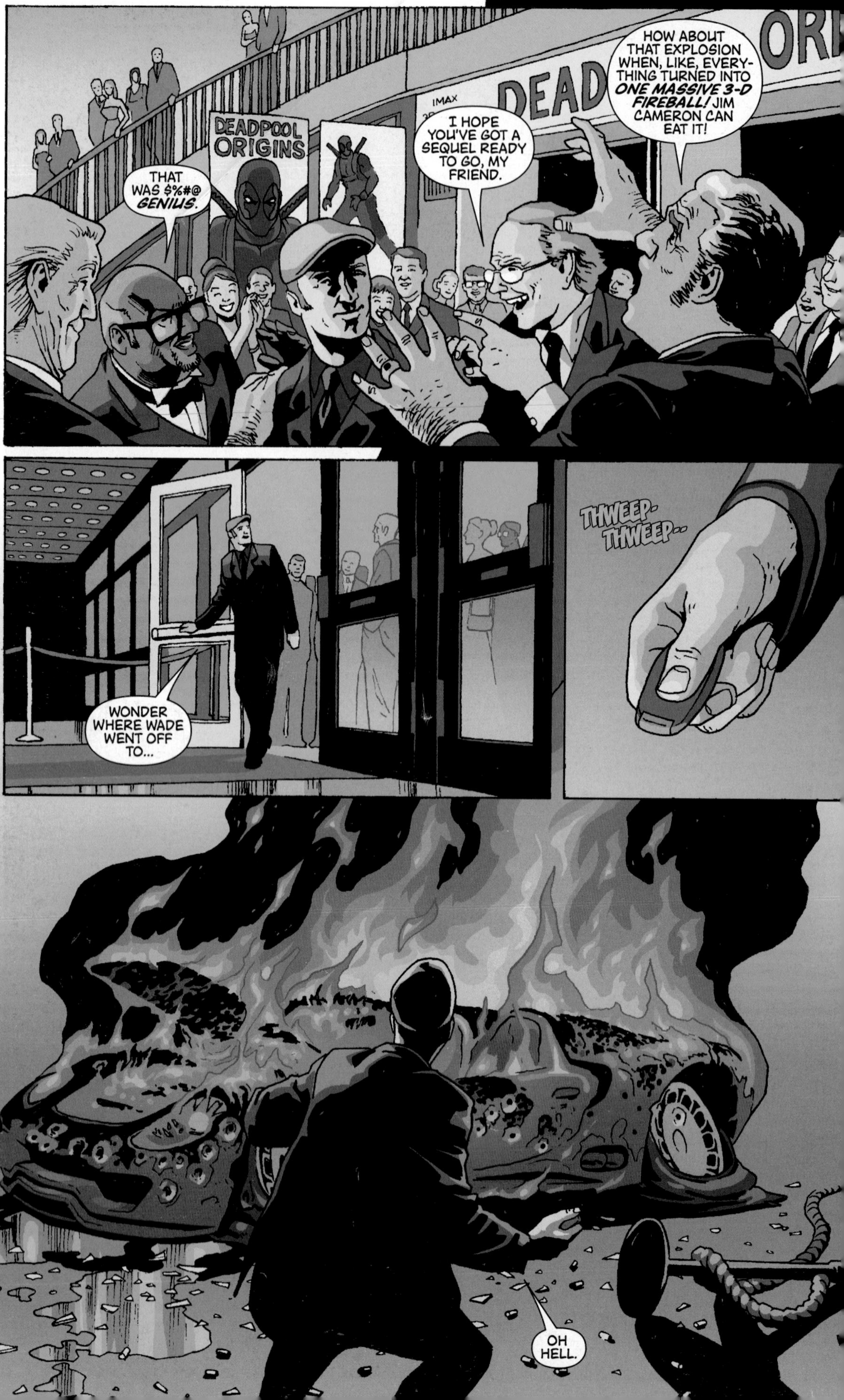
DEADPOOL ORIGINS
IMAX
THAT WAS $%#@ GENIUS.
I HOPE YOU'VE GOT A SEQUEL READY TO GO, MY FRIEND.
HOW ABOUT THAT EXPLOSION WHEN, LIKE, EVERYTHING TURNED INTO ONE MASSIVE 3-D FIREBALL! JIM CAMERON CAN EAT IT!
WONDER WHERE WADE WENT OFF TO...
THWEEP-THWEEP..
OH HELL.

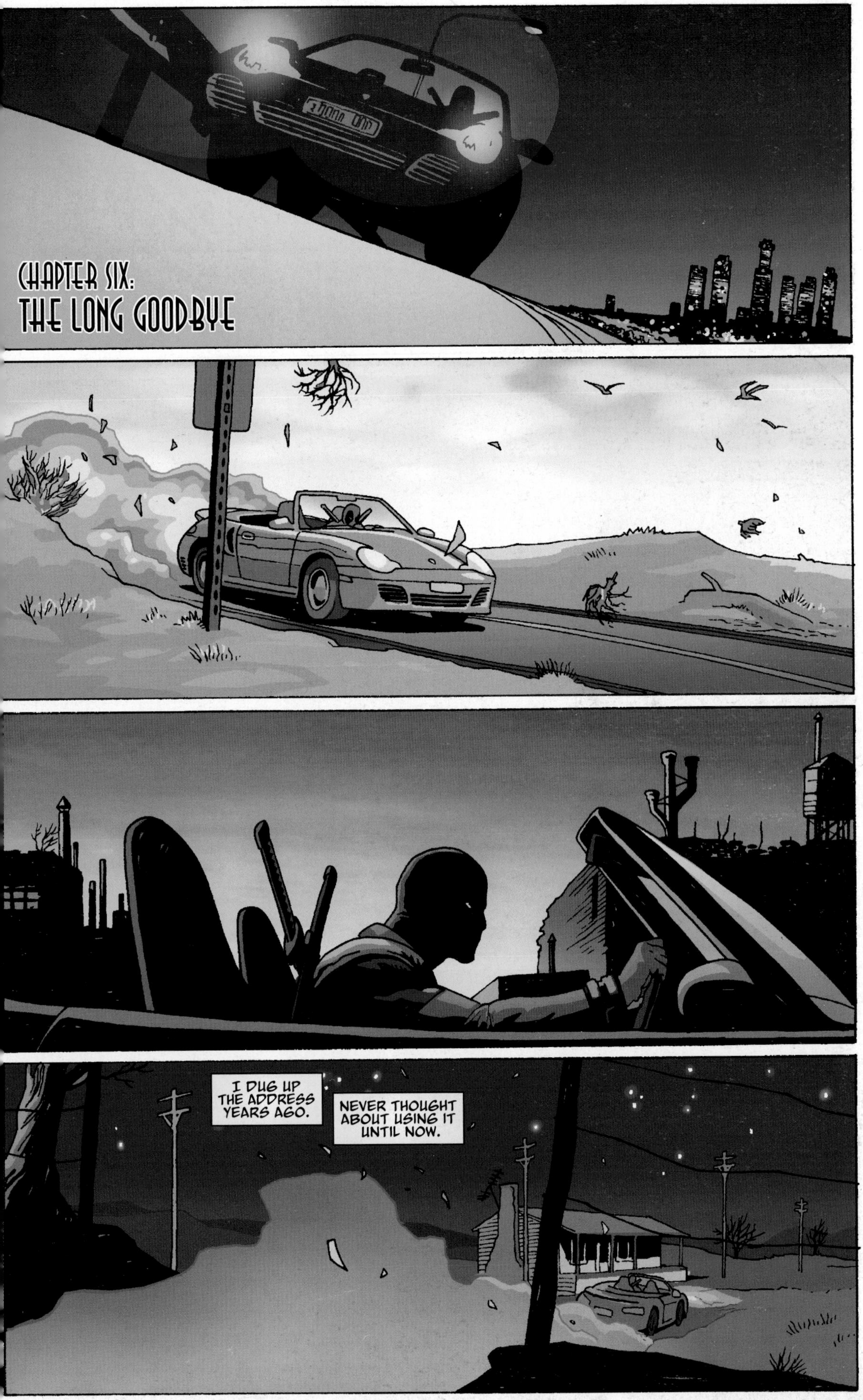
CHAPTER SIX:
THE LONG GOODBYE
I DUG UP THE ADDRESS YEARS AGO.
NEVER THOUGHT ABOUT USING IT UNTIL NOW.

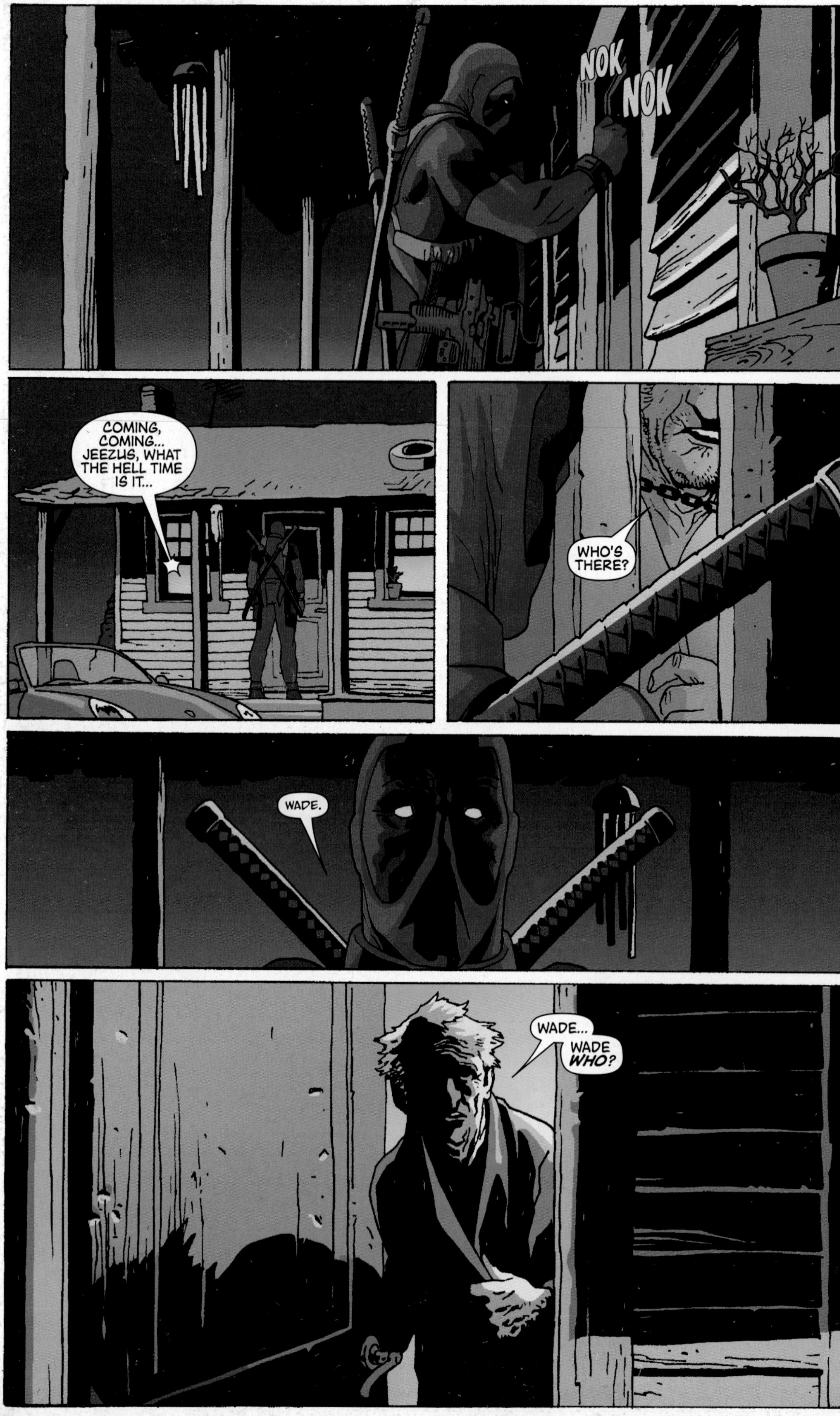
NOK NOK
COMING, COMING... JEEZUS, WHAT THE HELL TIME IS IT...
WHO'S THERE?
WADE.
WADE... WADE *WHO?*

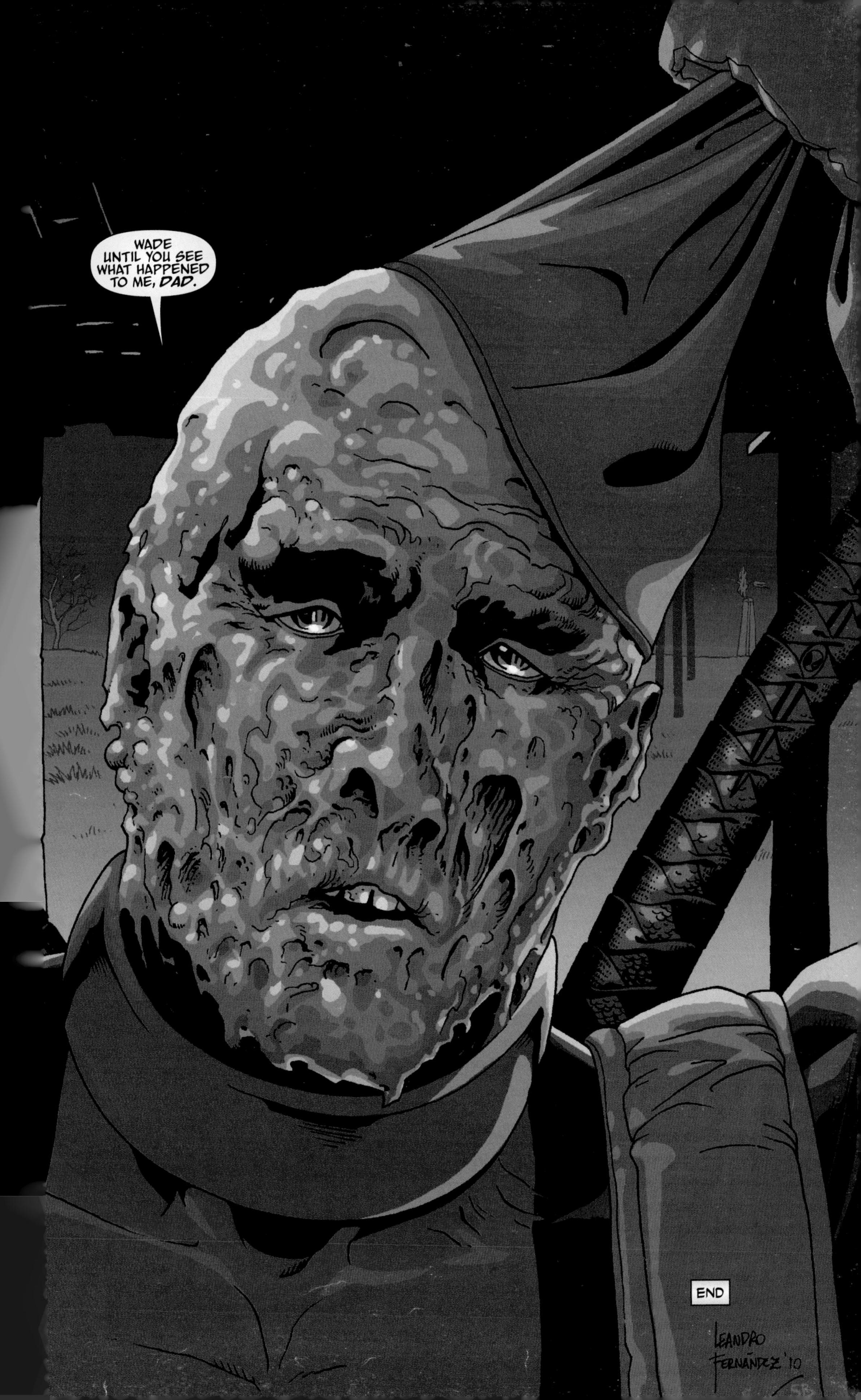
WADE UNTIL YOU SEE WHAT HAPPENED TO ME, DAD.
END
LEANDRO FERNÁNDEZ '10

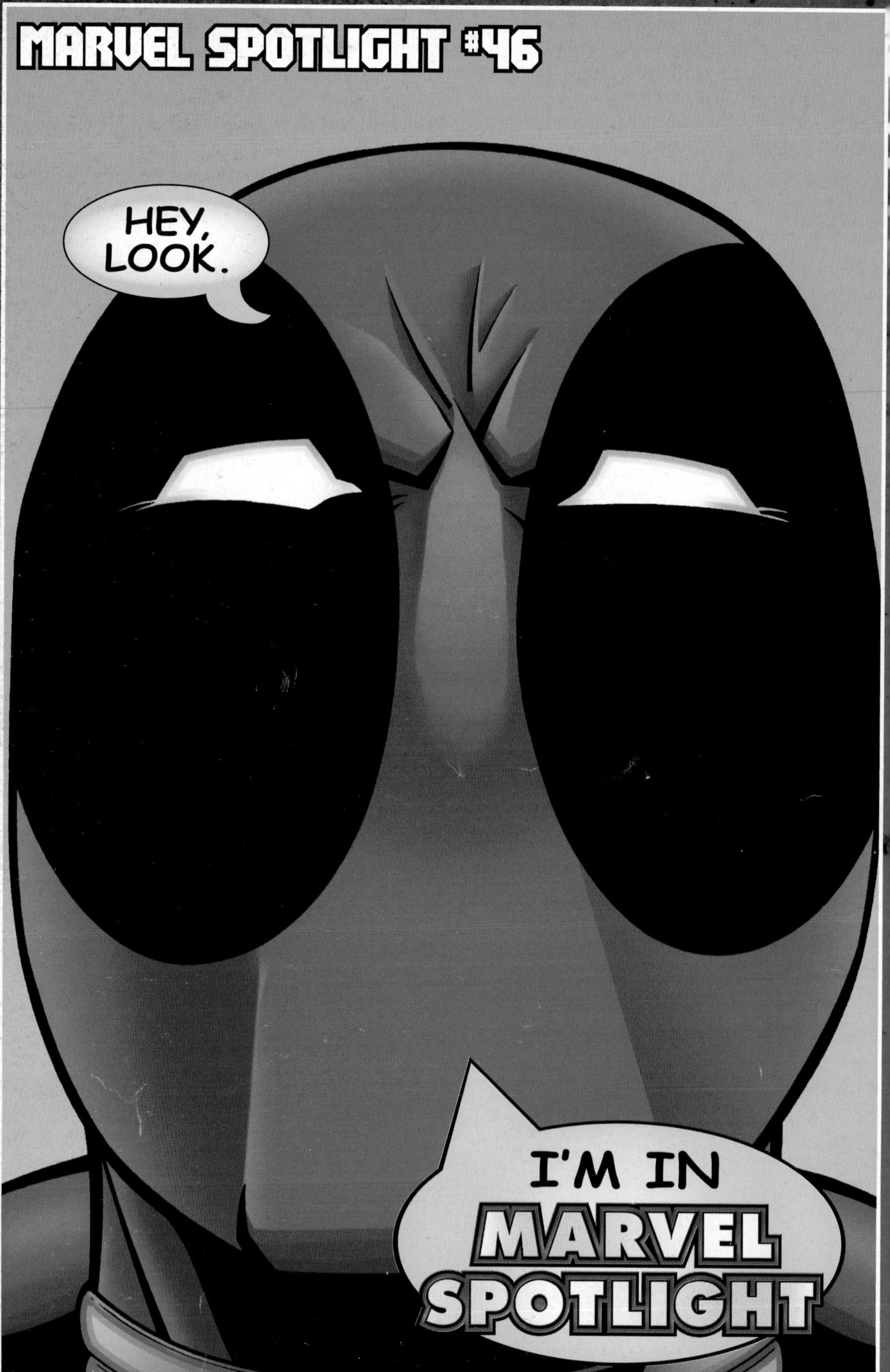
MARVEL SPOTLIGHT #46
HEY, LOOK.
I'M IN MARVEL SPOTLIGHT

LOOK, PA! IT'S ME! DEADPOOL!

In 1991, Rob Liefeld Created One Of Marvel's Biggest Big Shots, Deadpool! (And He Hasn't Lived It Down Since!)

By Jess Harrold

When comic fans think of the 1990s, more likely than not they're picturing Rob Liefeld's art in their heads. Rob took the artistic reins for Marvel's motley band of *New Mutants* just as the decade began, and within a year had propelled the book up the sales charts and transformed it into the multi-million-selling phenomenon that was *X-Force*. By then one of the industry's highest profile stars, he left Marvel to form Image Comics with other luminaries such as Todd McFarlane, Erik Larsen and Marc Silvestri. But in that relatively short time, Rob had bequeathed the House of Ideas two of its newest, brightest stars. Cable may have hogged the limelight at first, the success of *New Mutants* and *X-Force* largely borne upon his notoriously broad shoulders. But a very different character, a an irreverent contrast to Cable's grim and gritty demeanor, has now hacked and slashed his way all the way to the top – none other than Deadpool. The regenerating degenerate waltzed right into *New Mutants* #98, making light work of the team and poking fun at his target, Cable. The Marvel Universe has not been the same since. And Rob – very much the proud father – wouldn't have it any other way. Back drawing the character for the upcoming *Deadpool* #900 special, Rob was all too happy to give *Spotlight* the lowdown on the craziest of all his creations.

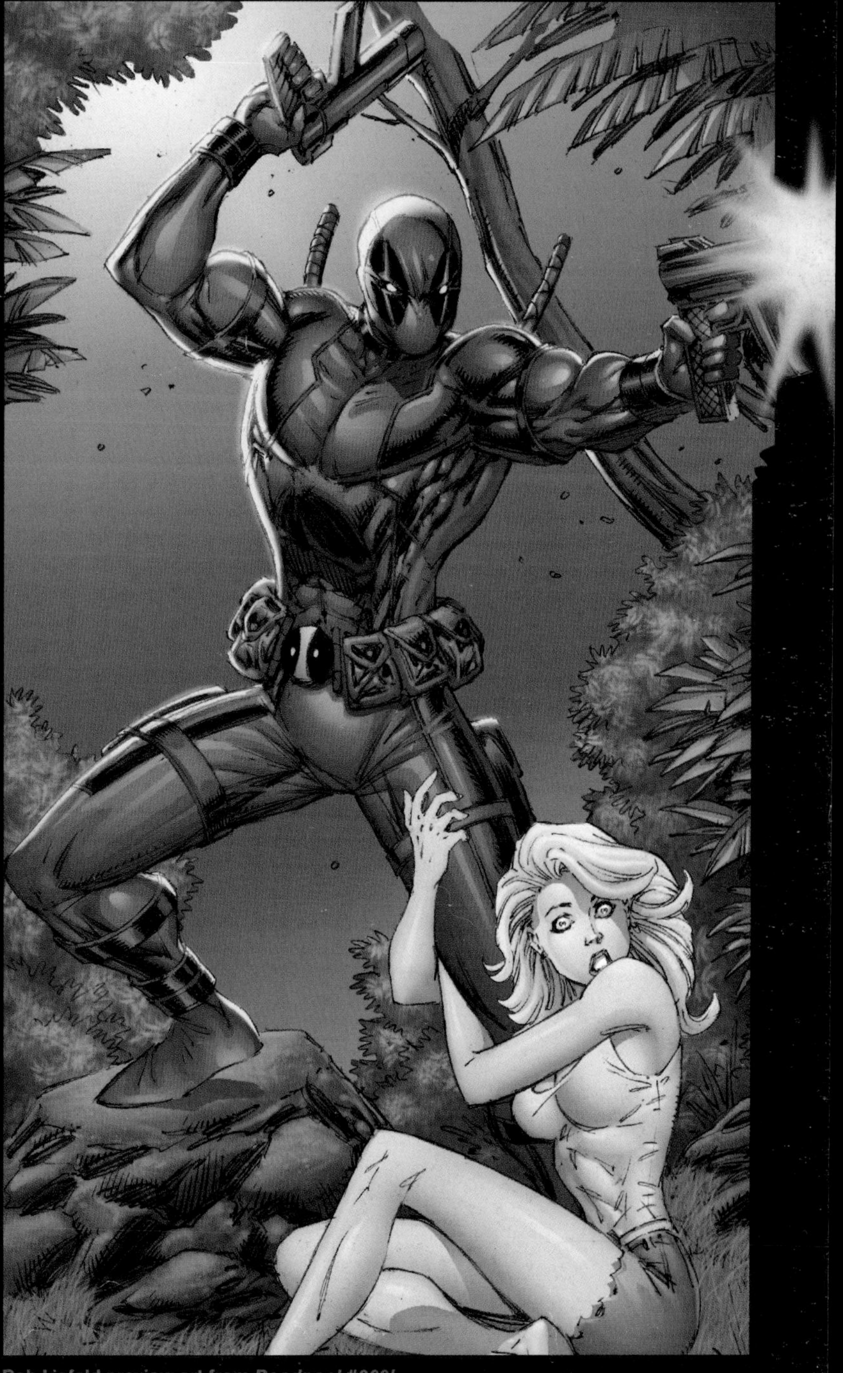

Rob Liefeld preview art from *Deadpool #900!*

SPOTLIGHT: When you introduced Deadpool in *New Mutants* #98 did you have any idea exactly what you were unleashing on the Marvel Universe?

ROB: I thought he would be well received, but not to the extent that he has taken off. When I looked at the final pages of his first appearance, I thought, "Well, he looks cool, he's funny, he has a cool name and he takes out the entire New Mutants team all by himself, so he has a nice introduction..." But I wasn't prepared for the fan frenzy that ensued. X-Editor Bob Harras called me a few days after his first appearance and said: "We have to do more Deadpool, the fans LOVE him!" Which is why he appeared in a fact file in *New Mutants* #100, a trading card in *X-Force* #1 and had a huge role in *X-Force* #2 and then issue #10.

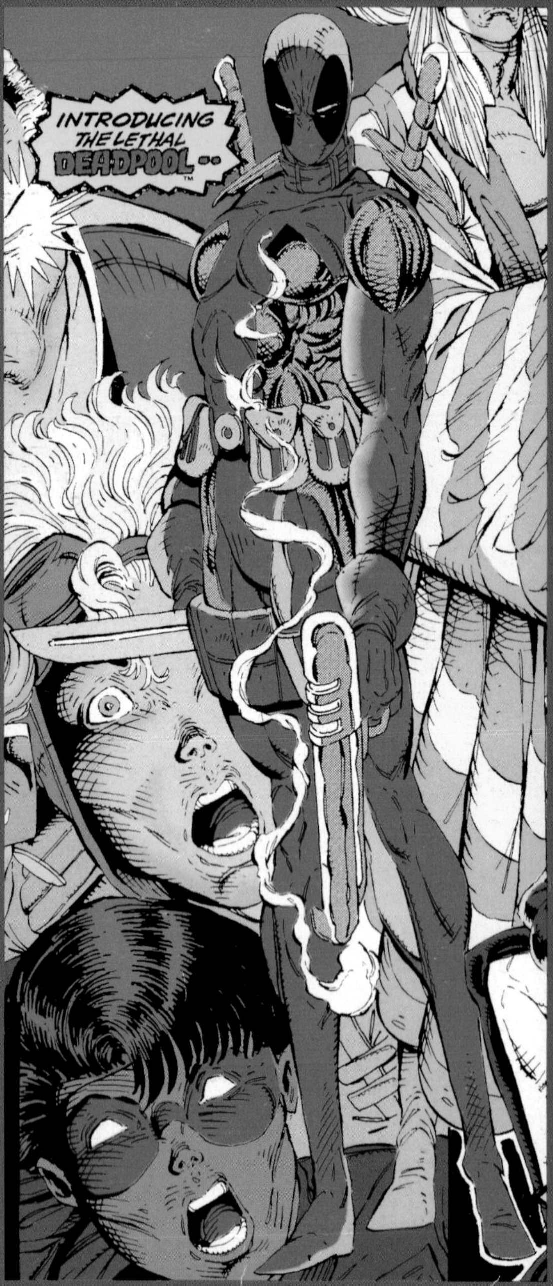
INTRODUCING THE LETHAL DEADPOOL --

Cover art from *New Mutants #98* by Liefeld, Deadpool's first appearance!

SPOTLIGHT: Now, 18 years later, Deadpool has matured – well, maybe *matured* isn't the right word – into one of the major players at Marvel. Is it something you take professional pride in, adding your own patch to the great Marvel quilt like that?

ROB: Of course! I take great pride in everything I create and when they reach the pinnacle of popularity, such as Cable and now Deadpool, it is remarkably satisfying.

SPOTLIGHT: When you measure Deadpool against your other Marvel creations like Cable, as well as your work elsewhere, how high does he rate in your personal list of achievements in comics?

ROB: Right now he's tops! How could he not be?

SPOTLIGHT: Are you someone who invests a lot personally in your characters? Do you find yourself reading later comics by other creators and going, "He would never say that?"

"I was out to create the anti-Spider-Man."

– Rob Liefeld, on his inspiration for Deadpool.

ROB: I follow all of it. It's great to see what directions and turns that other writers and artists take with the characters. Even when they took his costume off and Deadpool became Agent X and his popularity ebbed, I still enjoyed the approach.

SPOTLIGHT: With that in mind, what's your opinion on the direction Deadpool has taken over the years? Who do you think "got" him the best?

ROB: Well, the powers that be have returned to the tried and true formula of violence and action paired with humor that made Deadpool so popular at the outset. I think that Joe Kelly and Daniel Way are the two writers that have maximized Deadpool's voice. But everyone from Jimmy Palmiotti to Gail Simone, Michael Benson, Mark Waid and others have certainly done excellent work.

SPOTLIGHT: Casting our minds back to those halcyon '90s days, can you remember much about the day you first came up with Deadpool? Caffeine high, sugar rush?

ROB: Lots of Mountain Dew, definitely! I was out to create the anti-Spider Man. There's a lot of Spidey in there! I've always stated that I was envious of Todd McFarlane drawing Spider-Man and his cool mask. I set out to duplicate that somewhat with the big eye motif and made sure Deadpool was leaner, agile, bouncy – like Spidey. Then I gave him an arsenal of weapons and we made him a smartass and the next thing you know we had hit the jackpot!

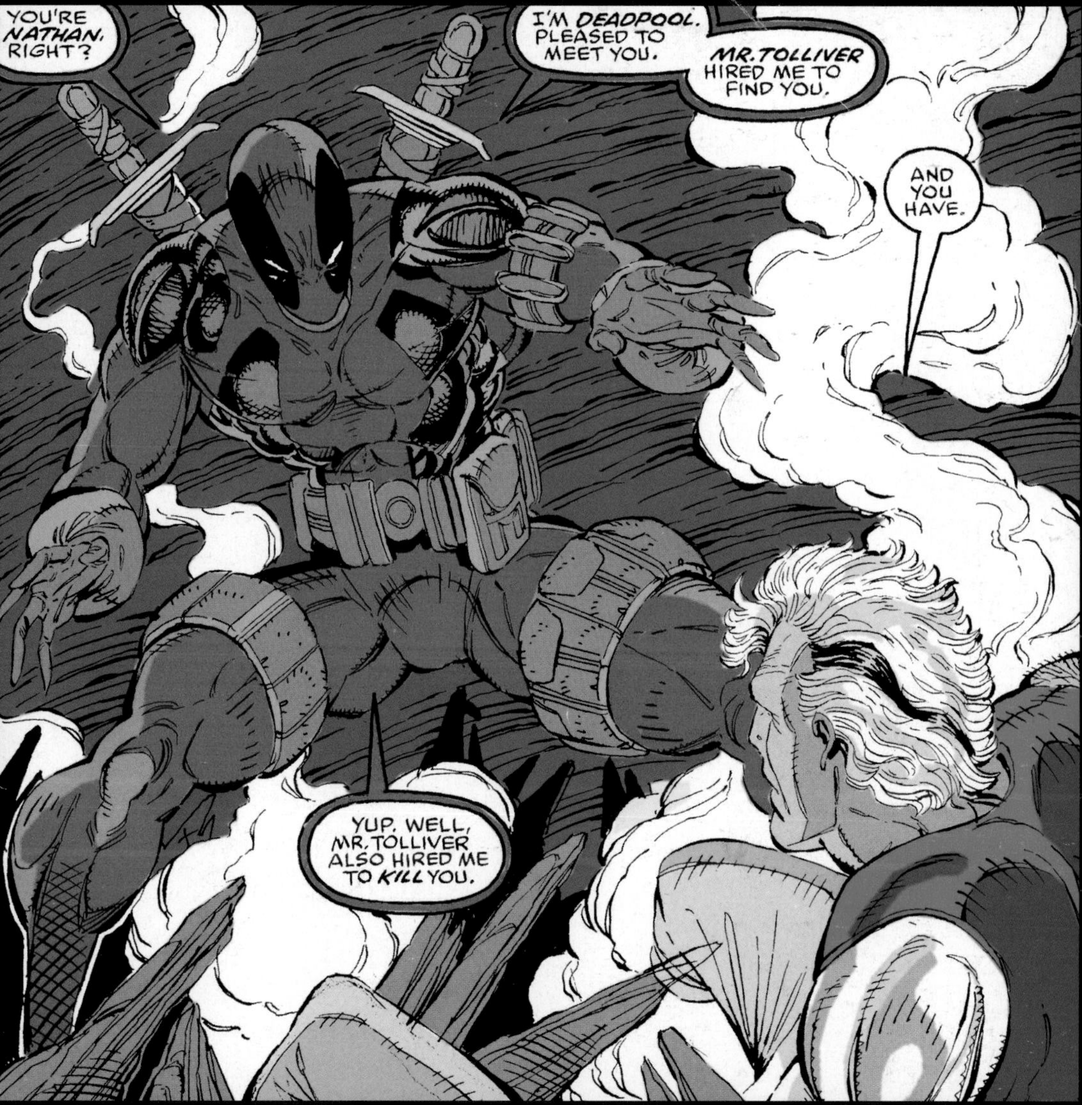
YOU'RE NATHAN, RIGHT?
I'M DEADPOOL. PLEASED TO MEET YOU.
MR. TOLLIVER HIRED ME TO FIND YOU.
AND YOU HAVE.
YUP. WELL, MR. TOLLIVER ALSO HIRED ME TO KILL YOU.

CONTRACT FOR CABLE: Deadpool is out for Cable's blood in *NM #98*. (Art by Liefeld.)

SPOTLIGHT: As for his personality, his fast lip and wisecracks to distract opponents also brings a certain wallcrawler to mind. Do you think Wade has much in common with Peter?

ROB: Well, no, Deadpool is a tortured product of an aborted Weapon X experiment. He's a mental madman, closer to the Joker wrapped in the body of a deadly killer who believes he has nothing to lose. Other than his ability to crack jokes, he's nothing like Peter Parker.

SPOTLIGHT: Speaking of jokes, he's cracking wise right from word go in his debut, telling Cable: "Let me put you out of my misery." But what was your favorite Deadpool crack?

ROB: Too many to mention. I think he's always got something funny to say.

SPOTLIGHT: And in that same issue, Cable and X-Force are desperate to shut him up. Nate just about breaks his jaw, and when he gets mailed back to Tolliver he's been gagged. Did it amuse you when they did much the same to Ryan Reynolds in *X-Men Origins: Wolverine*?

ROB: Oh yeah, I loved him in the Wolverine movie. People approached me all summer asking, "What did you think?" And I said, well, it was a good start. It's true to the comics in that he's still an aborted product of Weapon X and it gives him the foundation to create his own mythos in film just as he did in the comics. It speaks to how popular he is that so many fans were frustrated that he wasn't in the film more prominently. Had they put him in his costume at the end credits, people would have freaked and they would have added many more millions to their grosses.

SPOTLIGHT: Now, you're a creator who, shall we say, divides opinion amongst fans. And Deadpool

Speech bubbles in image:

"COULD BE BETTER. COULD BE WORSE."

"WE WERE DOING OKAY AGAINST DEADPOOL!"

"YEAH, SURE--AND YOU DIDN'T NEED ANY HELP, DID YOU?"

"LET'S NOT SPEND TOO MUCH TIME TRYING TO TAKE THE CREDIT FOR THIS PUNK'S CAPTURE."

"WHAT DO WE DO WITH YOU NOW, DEADPOOL?"

"Y'KNOW, I'VE ALWAYS WANTED THE CHANCE TO REHABILITATE MYSELF--YOU KNOW, SOMEWHERE NICE..."

"...HOW ABOUT A PRISON IN THE BAHAMAS?"

BEST BUDDIES: Cable won the first battle but has arguably lost the war against his relentlessly wisecracking pal, Deadpool! (Art from *NM #98* by Liefeld.)

SPOTLIGHT: You mentioned Joe Kelly earlier, and he is certainly one of the writers who has had the most impact on the character. Now you're working on his return to the character in the landmark *Deadpool* #900. Have you enjoyed reacquainting yourself with Wade, and working with Joe?

ROB: Oh yeah! Joe is great and this story in *Deadpool* #900 is so funny. He gave me what any Deadpool collaborator would want: guns, action, babes and great gags! I hope the fans enjoy it.

SPOTLIGHT: I heard a little Tweet that we're finally gonna see what's inside those pouches...

ROB: Yes, Joe has Deadpool empty out the contents of his pouches and the stuff he described was pretty funny. Especially the little monkey!

isn't exactly universally popular in the Marvel Universe. We have to ask: How much of you is there in Deadpool? Are you more like Wade in real life, or Cable?

ROB: I'm certainly more like Wade. I'm a wiseacre as well and I'm always upbeat in the face of conflict. I'm not as grim as Cable.

SPOTLIGHT: Your good pal and Deadpool co-creator Fabian Nicieza teamed them up in *Cable and Deadpool* – what is it that makes them two great tastes that taste great together?

ROB: They counterbalance each other perfectly; they are the "Odd Couple." Great balance, classic "opposites attract."

SPOTLIGHT: Wade's origin has been explored quite a bit by other creators – how closely does it fit with what you had in mind when you created him? Had you figured out a whole backstory?

ROB: He was always a bitter product of Weapon X, a bad experiment, thus the connection with the whole program. He fled the Weapon X program and used his skills and abilities and enhancements to bolster himself as a mercenary. There was no love interest or daddy issues or other details other than that. By tying into the Weapon X program I thought there was plenty of material to mine.

SPOTLIGHT: We'll look out for it! Even including #900, you've actually written and drawn Deadpool surprisingly few times. Do you still have that one big Deadpool story you're itching to tell some day?

ROB: Yes, I do have one great Deadpool story I'd love to tell. It's called *Deadpool: Big Shot* and hopefully I'll get a chance to share it someday soon.

SPOTLIGHT: Lastly, if Deadpool were to ask you one question, what would it be? And how would you answer it?

ROB: He'd say, "Dad, what the hell were you thinking when you unleashed me on the world?" I would just shrug.

Look out, Rob. You answer with a shrug, 'Pool might reply with a slug! (Hey, don't blame us! We didn't invent the guy.) As it is we're mighty thankful your refrigerator wasn't empty of Mountain Dew on that fateful day you created Deadpool, and we'll definitely be looking out for your "one big Deadpool story" one day. Until then, we'll gladly take your story with Joe Kelly in DEADPOOL #900, due in October! •

DEADPOOL FROM THE OLD SCHOOL

Writer Joe Kelly Revisits An Old Friend In Deadpool #900

By Jess Harrold

Back in 1997, the Marvel Universe was holding out for some heroes. Captain America, Iron Man, the Avengers and the Fantastic Four had fallen victim to Onslaught, their titles all taking place on a brand new Earth during the Heroes Reborn event. Stepping up to the plate in their absence? Alpha Flight, Ka-Zar and…Wade Wilson?!? Drawn away from the dark side by – what else? – a woman, everyone's favorite sassin' assassin, Deadpool, burst into his first ongoing series in a quest for redemption that would see him swear off killing and be declared a Messiah. And, at the helm, ensuring Deadpool was a merc with more mouth than ever was fresh young scribe Joe Kelly.

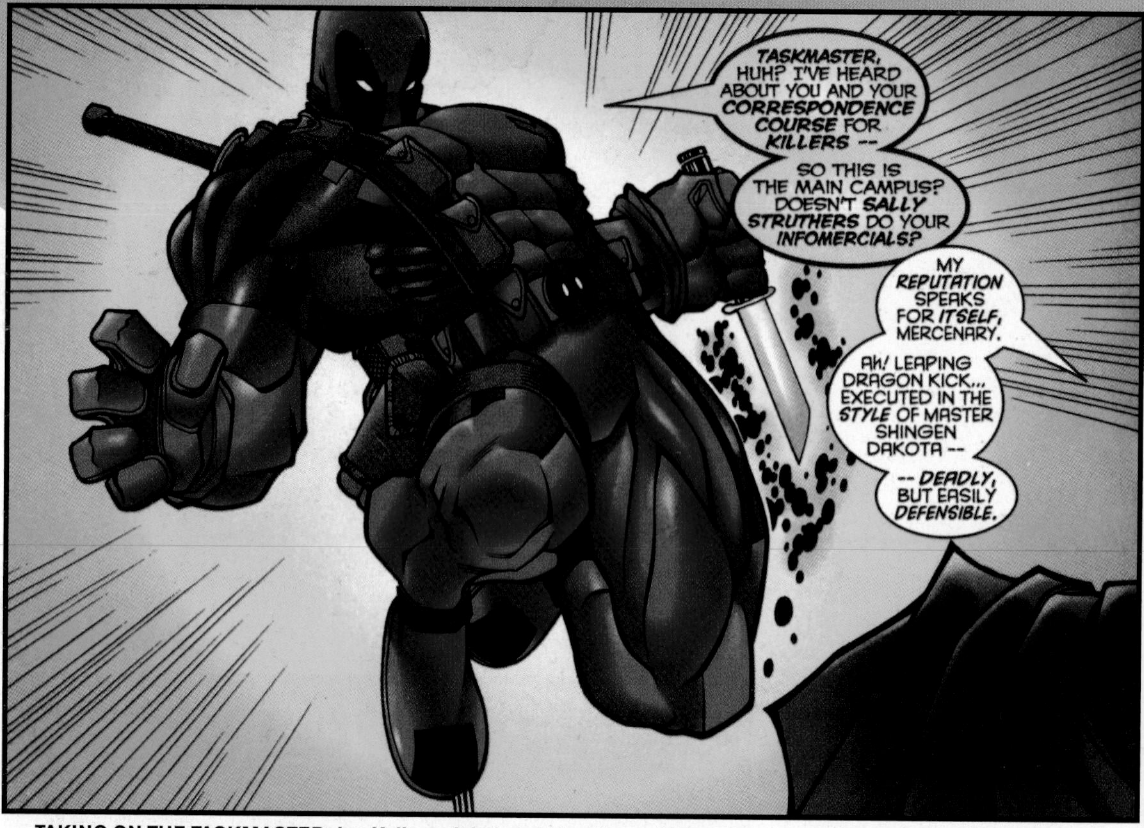
TASKMASTER, HUH? I'VE HEARD ABOUT YOU AND YOUR CORRESPONDENCE COURSE FOR KILLERS --
SO THIS IS THE MAIN CAMPUS? DOESN'T SALLY STRUTHERS DO YOUR INFOMERCIALS?
MY REPUTATION SPEAKS FOR ITSELF, MERCENARY.
AH! LEAPING DRAGON KICK... EXECUTED IN THE STYLE OF MASTER SHINGEN DAKOTA --
-- DEADLY, BUT EASILY DEFENSIBLE.

TAKING ON THE TASKMASTER: Joe Kelly can't help yukking it up with Deadpool, especially in a fight! (Art from *Deadpool* #2 by Ed McGuinness.)

In a three-year run that blended madcap humor, soul-searching pathos and some genuinely harrowing scenes, Joe built a platform for a career that has gone from strength to strength. He's written *X-Men*, *Action Comics* and *JLA*, and now he's a major player in the *Amazing Spider-Man* Web-Heads. Somewhere along the line he found time to co-create the cartoon sensation that is *Ben 10*. But you won't find blind, old-lady hostages on Cartoon Network. For that you'll need Joe's fan-favorite *Deadpool* comics, currently being collected for your convenience in *Deadpool Classic* trades. *Spotlight* locked Joe in the Deadhut and threatened him with The Box until he spilled all the details on his time with the character, and their upcoming reacquaintance in the pages of *Amazing Spider-Man* #611 and the very special *Deadpool* #900. Then we tickled him until he revealed the secret history of Blind Al!

SPOTLIGHT: Your very first ongoing series was *Deadpool* with Ed McGuinness – are you the luckiest man in comics?

JOE: *(Laughter.)* Definitely. My entire career is based on being at the right place at the right time so I'm very grateful about the way the universe has thrown things at me up to this point!

"It allowed me to have my mental diarrhea for Deadpool!" – Writer Joe Kelly on the approach of his 1997 *Deadpool* series.

SPOTLIGHT: It was the right time for 'Pool too. His series started during *Heroes Reborn*, when there was a vacuum for heroes on Marvel Earth. While titles like *Alpha Flight*, *Ka-Zar* and *Maverick* were short-lived, *Deadpool* and *Thunderbolts* are still around to this day. Did that dreaded "C-word", cancellation, rear its head a lot back then?

JOE: Oh sure, but not until we were well into it. The irony is that we started the book believing we were gonna be cancelled within six or seven issues, so when editor Matt Idelson and I sat down to work out the series we kind of felt, let's just make this book different, have fun, do what the heck we want because it's gonna be gone. We might as well go out in a blaze of glory. And since everybody else thought it would be cancelled, nobody really paid attention and we got to do whatever we wanted. I think the threat of cancellation was our strength at the beginning. But it wasn't until around the time we left that the numbers were on the edge. One month they'd say you're going to be cancelled, the next month they'd say, "We got a lot of fan letters so you can stay." This went on for four or five months and I just couldn't plan out stories that way. If that had not happened, there's an excellent chance I would have stayed on the book at least another year, if not longer. I sort of

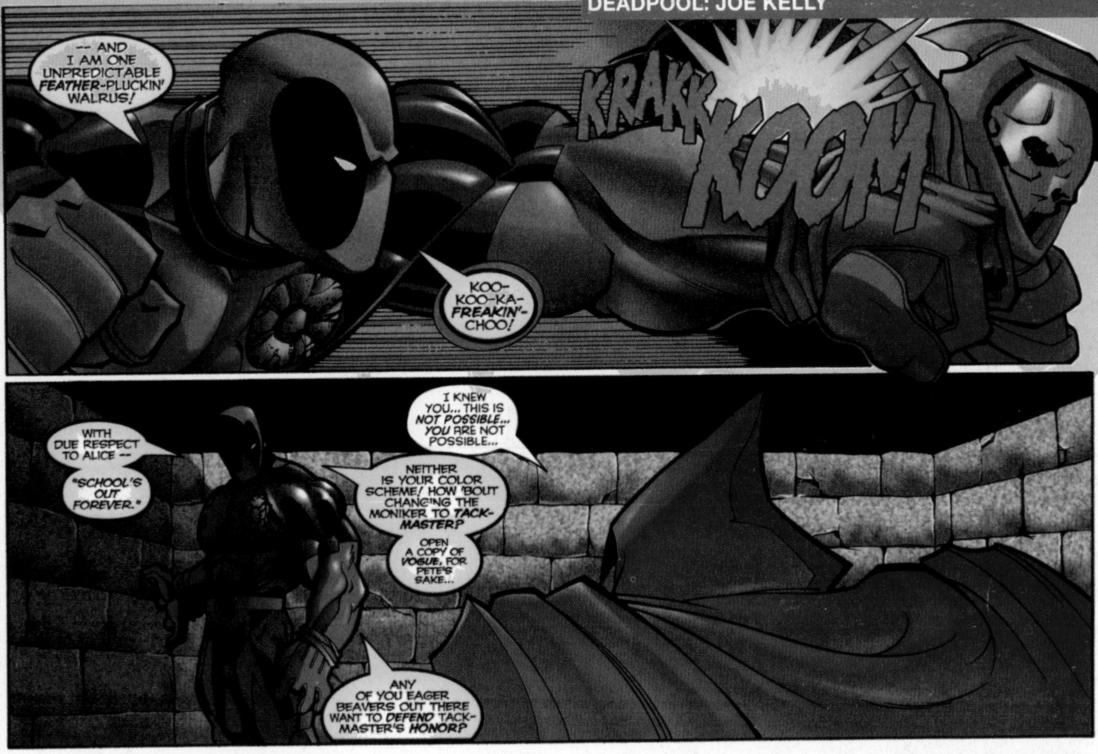
-- AND I AM ONE UNPREDICTABLE FEATHER-PLUCKIN' WALRUS!
KRAKK
KOOM
KOO-KOO-KA-FREAKIN'-CHOO!
WITH DUE RESPECT TO ALICE --
"SCHOOL'S OUT FOREVER."
I KNEW YOU... THIS IS NOT POSSIBLE... YOU ARE NOT POSSIBLE...
NEITHER IS YOUR COLOR SCHEME! HOW 'BOUT CHANGING THE MONIKER TO TACK-MASTER?
OPEN A COPY OF VOGUE, FOR PETE'S SAKE...
ANY OF YOU EAGER BEAVERS OUT THERE WANT TO DEFEND TACK-MASTER'S HONOR?

forget that it started during *Heroes Reborn*. But the initial pitch for *Deadpool* had him actually carrying Franklin Richard's ball around for the whole year, like he didn't know he had the entire universe in his possession. He was bouncing it, abusing it for twelve issues, and couldn't figure out why everybody wanted to kill him. But that was tossed out because it was too big for our little book that would inevitably be cancelled!

SPOTLIGHT: 'Pool had already had a few appearances and a couple of limited series under his belt, but it was your run that fully fleshed out his character, particularly his more heroic side, and explored his history. Were you told how to play the character, or given an "untold origin" you had to stick to?

JOE: Y'know, I was really lucky. Matt and I went through the series the guys had done before, which were very cool and we really liked. We obviously wanted to keep the humor, and keep it as dark as possible, but after that point it was really open. We were allowed to mess around. Even to the point where, although I know it was subsequently changed, we got it where he wasn't really Wade Wilson and had stolen that identity. With the back story, you just go, OK, he was with Weapon X, we don't know exactly when that was…It's a big playground, and you know it's already half there, but you find your own corner and build your jungle gym there. That's how we did it.

SPOTLIGHT: You mentioned keeping the humor of his early appearances – you dialed that up to 11.

JOE: Well, thank you. I love comedy and especially dark comedy. I want the pendulum always to swing between hilarious and dark within the same story as often as possible. It keeps the reader off balance. Those are the kind of movies I respond to. In comics, we have that conceit where you can say an awful lot in one panel. While a guy is flying through the air kicking somebody in the face, you can have five balloons. It allowed me to have my mental diarrhea for Deadpool! I love that stuff. And I guess at the time, a lot of the books were so serious. So, to be that little light where it's, like, I'm gonna do dark stories and I have an anti-hero, but you know you're gonna get stupid jokes and other comedy from month to month, really helped.

SPOTLIGHT: Does it take longer to script when you have so many one-liners and gags?

JOE: Writing for me as a process really is one of two things – it's either extremely easy or extremely hard; there's no middle ground. With *Deadpool*, if I was on and I was channeling his voice the right way it would flow, and I would be laughing. But sometimes it's like pulling teeth. It can really kill me, because I know I want it to be funny, and my expectations are high. Sometimes it's, like, am I the only one who's gonna find this funny, or did I already run this joke? That's the beauty of having a good editor, and Matt was always fantastic to bounce stuff off. He'd make suggestions and if something weren't funny we'd cut it. He would call me if I was repeating myself. Or was going soft, or too rough!

SPOTLIGHT: Did you carry a notebook around to record jokes when they came to you?

JOE: I'm pretty good: If I get struck with an idea, I repeat it over and over until I can get to a pad. It would be easier to carry a pad, but I don't. When I was writing *Deadpool*, I spent a lot of time trolling the internet and collecting, like, "Your mother…"

jokes. I have a huge file of "Yo mama's so fat..." If I couldn't think of something off the top of my head I could always go to the "Yo mama" file. Even if I didn't rip them off directly, it would inspire something. I was definitely collecting humor at that point. I had a lot on tap when I was writing *Deadpool*. Not so much when I was writing *Superman*; then I was a lot more honest, compassionate...

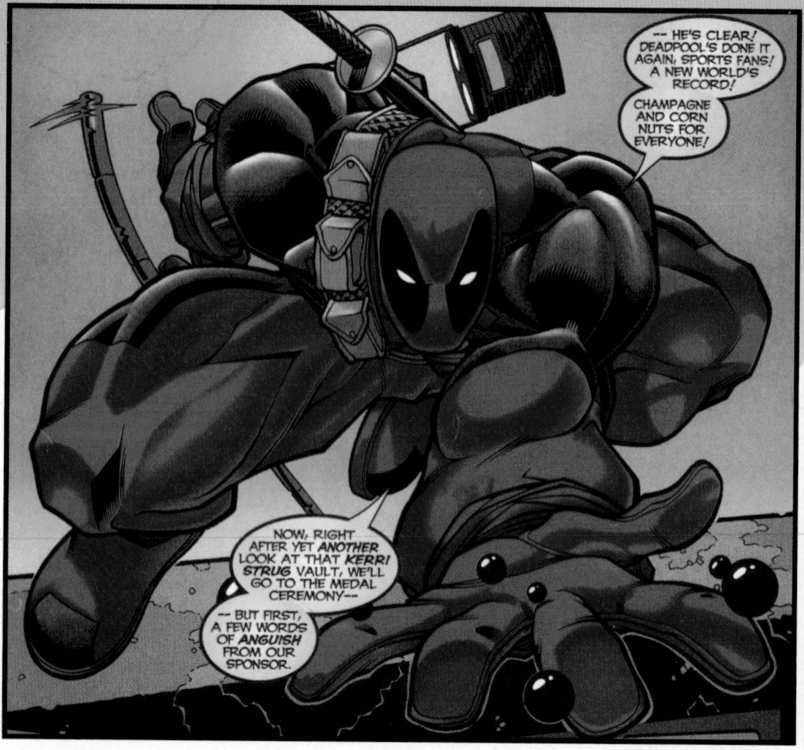

-- HE'S CLEAR! DEADPOOL'S DONE IT AGAIN, SPORTS FANS! A NEW WORLD'S RECORD!
CHAMPAGNE AND CORN NUTS FOR EVERYONE!
NOW, RIGHT AFTER YET ANOTHER LOOK AT THAT KERRI STRUG VAULT, WE'LL GO TO THE MEDAL CEREMONY--
-- BUT FIRST, A FEW WORDS OF ANGUISH FROM OUR SPONSOR.

SPOTLIGHT: Do you find the characters get in your head that way when you're immersed in them?

JOE: I think so, yeah. Sometimes I'm more aware of it than others. Deadpool was one of those great characters that I always felt a really strong emotional connection to. He was my baby. So to sculpt this world where no matter what he did he was gonna screw up, whether it was his own bad intentions or bad nature or just the world at large putting him in horrible positions, I could spend a lot of time really crafting that. Other than creator-owned books I haven't had that since. I'm amazed at guys like Geoff Johns who can carve out their world, and a big world at that, that takes a lot of effort. To have that on *Deadpool* was a really precious thing and I do miss it some days. I like that kind of immersion, but when I get it, I'm, like, "*I wish I had more projects*!" Freelancers are a superstitious and cowardly lot!

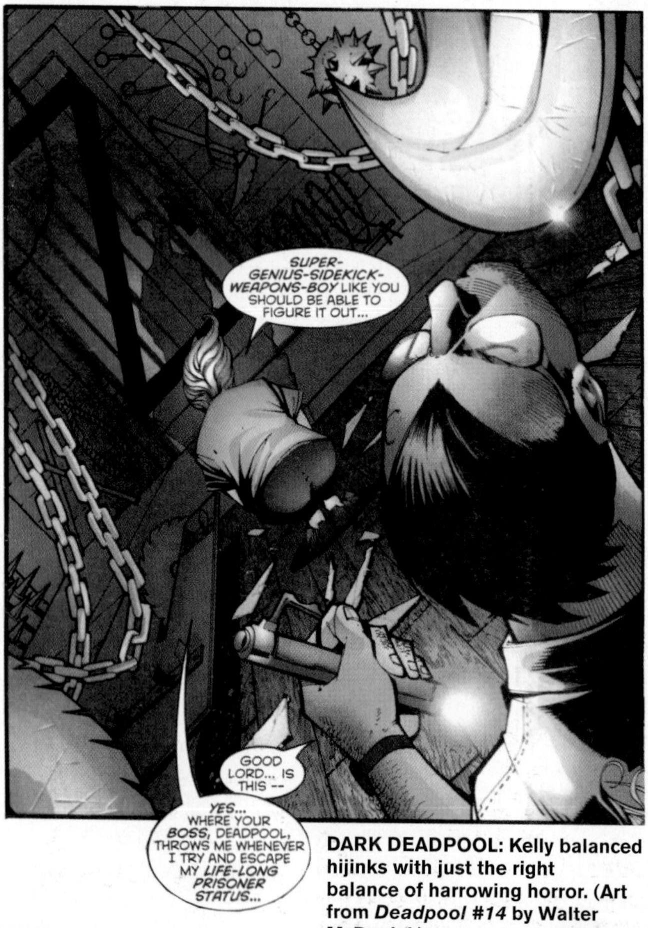

SUPER-GENIUS-SIDEKICK-WEAPONS-BOY LIKE YOU SHOULD BE ABLE TO FIGURE IT OUT...
GOOD LORD... IS THIS --
YES... WHERE YOUR BOSS, DEADPOOL, THROWS ME WHENEVER I TRY AND ESCAPE MY LIFE-LONG PRISONER STATUS...

DARK DEADPOOL: Kelly balanced hijinks with just the right balance of harrowing horror. (Art from *Deadpool #14* by Walter McDaniel.)

JOE: I went back to stuff from my childhood. As dark as *Deadpool* is, all that *Bugs Bunny* and Warner Bros. stuff really did have an influence on me. Also Robin Williams just in general, and probably – and embarrassingly so – Mork from Ork in particular. Robin's stand-up had that chaotic nature.

SPOTLIGHT: I see Bruce Willis' *Moonlighting* character David Addison at his most self-destructive...

JOE: Oh yeah. I would not have picked that off the top of my head, but that was definitely a favorite show of mine. I'm trying to think who else...certainly Tarantino, he was very big when I was writing that book. That sort of writing style was really part of it. I've always been influenced by the Coen Brothers and other surrealistic artist/playwrights. I think that really helps a lot for comics, especially with a character like Deadpool, just that permission to mess around with the story and the audience; to take a road that is completely unexpected.

SPOTLIGHT: And who would have thought

twelve years ago we'd see Deadpool on the silver screen?

JOE: That was really cool. Ryan Reynolds has been gunning for that role for a really long time. A bunch of years ago another journalist I know contacted me after talking to him about *Blade: Trinity*. He was like, dude, do you know that Ryan Reynolds is all over Deadpool, and just wants to be Deadpool? I thought that was cool. To see it finally happening was great.

SPOTLIGHT: You were blessed with a succession of great artists, from Ed to Pete Woods to Walter McDaniel, each of whom brought tremendous expression to Deadpool's ostensibly featureless mask.

JOE: When we had Ed on the book, it was amazing how dark you could get without feeling dark. When we worked with Walter, because his style is so much darker, all of a sudden it was like, wow, Deadpool's really scary. The Blind Al issue comes to mind, with him killing the dogs and stuff. If Ed had drawn that it would have had such a different feel. Matt and I actually ended up having to ratchet some of the stories back a little for our own comfort zone, but we also really exploited how real it would look, knowing that when we want to upset people we've got the guy who can do it. It's the clearest example in my career of how the art directly impacts upon the story. That was a great lesson to have. Pete was maybe a little bit closer to the Ed side on the cartooniness, but his storytelling has always been out of the park, and he could really carry the acting extremely well on all the characters. Everybody did a great job on that book. I tend to write a detailed script and I was always extremely happy with the pages I got back. Like you said, I was the luckiest guy in comics – great artists to work with on a fantastic character.

"I've always thought that a fight between Spidey and Deadpool devolves into a mama joke contest." – Kelly

DEADPOOL: JOE KELLY

SPOTLIGHT: You mentioned the darkness in there, a lot of which came from Wade's treatment of Blind Al. That was a pretty complex relationship you developed – Stockholm Syndrome to the Nth Degree. That really helped show the reader that Wade was not your average super hero.

JOE: Absolutely. My primary thesis for Deadpool is that this was a guy who really was broken and sincerely believed he wanted to do something better, but was constitutionally incapable of being better. That was his internal conflict. He really did think he could be a good person if life was a little different, but he just couldn't. The idea was to surround him with people who would complement those extremes. I try to build in a lot of long story relationships and reveals. Al was probably the best example of that. We never got around to the stories that were gonna explain why she was the way she was. In my version, in a different world, she was the one that actually contributed to him getting cancer in the first place. So she was sort of paying for sins she had committed in her youth. This was stuff that we knew from the beginning. The stuff about him not being Wade and taking that name from T-Ray, that came over time. But Deadpool and Al's relationship we had from the beginning. I wanted to do the reversal of "Oh, it's the funny butler. Oh wait, she's a prisoner. Oh wait, she wants to be there because she got him sick…." Those turns have a great pay-off if you can get to them over time.

SPOTLIGHT: Was Al planned to look like Aunt May with the now classic #11 specifically in mind?

JOE: I don't think it's any secret that Deadpool was meant to be Dark Spider-Man. So we said, "Let's have a messed up Aunt May." And because she's the sidekick, let's call her Alfred. We couldn't do that, so that's why she became Blind Al. She's the Aunt May who really would be abused by the dark Spider-Man. That issue was Matt saying, "I think we could *Forrest Gump* Deadpool into a Spidey comic." It was a perfect opportunity to mess with their visuals.

SPOTLIGHT: How fun was that "Gumping" process?

JOE: Oh, it was great. It was not fun for Matt and all the production guys. I think Pete almost went crazy. But it was a blast for me to take that story and mess around with it. We actually had Stan (Lee)'s blessing, which was really cool. It was great to get to do that, so insane. Again, we were in the land of "nobody cares what we're doing" so why the heck not?

ALL RIGHT, AL... I'LL TRY ANYTHING... I'LL COME GET YOU AS SOON --
-- OMIGOD. THERE'S ACTUALLY TWO OF THEM WITH THAT HAIR?
WELL, Uh... GOTTA GO, AL -- I MEAN MAY! LATER --
THERE HE IS, DAD! HE MAY NOT BE MUCH TO LOOK AT, BUT AT LEAST HE DOESN'T SNORE!
GOOD TO MEET YOU, MY BOY! I'VE HEARD SOME FINE THINGS ABOUT YOU! YOU'RE ATTENDING E.S.U. ON A SCIENCE SCHOLARSHIP, AREN'T YOU?
YEAH... I GUESS...
I'VE BEEN ALL OVER THE WORLD, AND I SEEN LOTS OF CRAZY THINGS... BUT THAT HEAD IS TRULY UNNATURAL!
IT IS GROTESQUE... BUT I CANNOT LOOK AWAY! IS IT BRYL CREEM? GRECIAN FORMULA GONE BAD? GENETIC JOKE?
OBVIOUSLY, PETER WOULD NEVER SAY ANY-THING ABOUT THIS... I'VE GOT TO KEEP MY YAP SHUT! BUT... THOSE FUNKY FOLLICLES... PULLING ME IN... MUST... RESIST... URGE... TO MAKE A CRACK --
Uh... NICE HEAD, SIR.

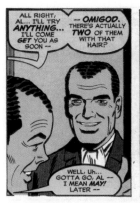

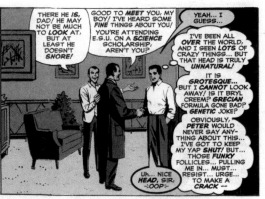

FOLLICLE FOOLISHNESS: Kelly's hilarious "Gumping" of Osborn hair, with Deadpool posing as Peter Parker. (Art from *Deadpool #11* by Pete Woods with John Romita Sr.)

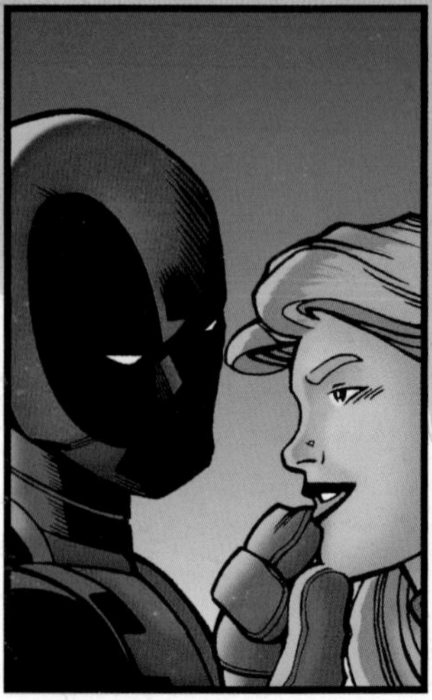

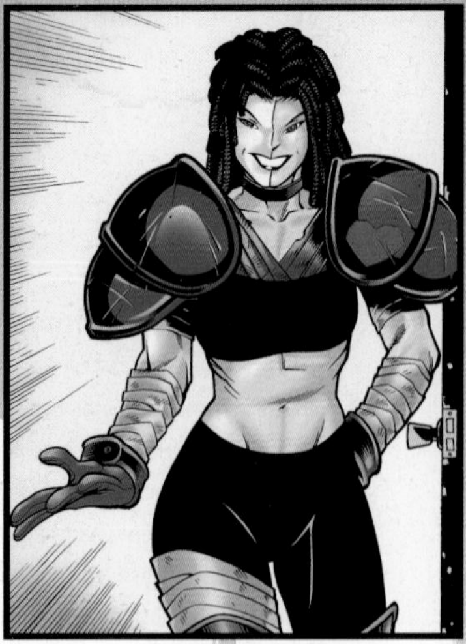

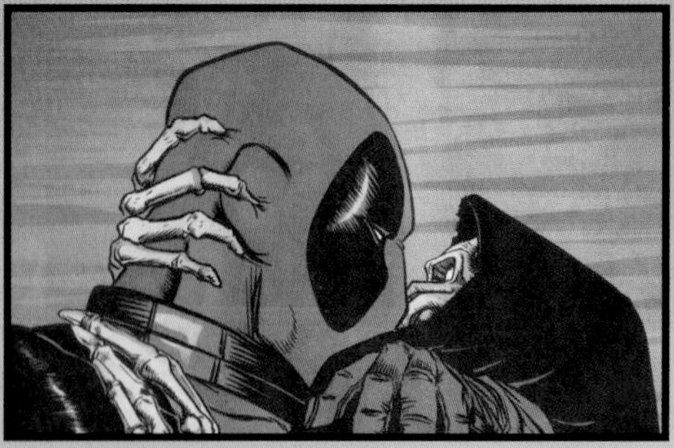

DEADPOOL'S DAMES: Kelly's gaggle of girls included (left to right) Siryn, Typhoid Mary and Death.

SPOTLIGHT: Was it hard to pick which *Amazing Spider-Man* issue to "Gump?"

JOE: Matt had been looking back in the archives and he found this issue where not a lot happens, but the best part about it is this one scene, and when you read it untouched it's just as funny…

SPOTLIGHT: I think I know which one you're going to say…

JOE: Yeah, when MJ walks in. Aunt Anna's like, "Could you help us move these heavy boxes," and she's, like, "Sure, wait a second…I'll start dancing!" Whether she was just meant to be played as an airhead or is literally drugged out of her mind, it was funny, and so ludicrous to us, and we just thought we could make so much of this. (*Amazing Spider-Man* editor) Steve Wacker actually suggested I have to send Spidey into an old *Deadpool* comic. Oh my God, someday we'll pull that off. It's like *Back to the Future III*, or *II*, I don't remember which one…

SPOTLIGHT: Wade and Norman Osborn are bitter rivals these days, but you got to tell the tale of their first meeting in that issue. Tell us the truth, how many hours did you spend just making up Osborn hair jokes for that one?

JOE: *(Laughter.)* That was one of those where I was worried about people actually getting mad. That hair is a comic book conceit that has just stuck. It's so funny to me to see people draw that hair today. There are so many options, but some guys go for the strict cornrow look. To have Deadpool say that out loud, I know a lot of fans were like, "I've been thinking that my entire life, I'm glad somebody's said it…"

SPOTLIGHT: The crossover is an example of something you did from the start – take Wade out of the X box and play with all Marvel's other toys. Do you think it was important to expand his horizons a bit?

JOE: I think so. I'm not always allowed to do it on a mainstream book but, as often as possible, I go in and say let's put the big toys aside for a while and try to build new characters or throw in some unexpected stuff. The hope is that you're gonna find the Kingpin. He started out a Spidey villain, but he became something amazing when you put him with Daredevil. To play around with the dough a little bit and see what comes out of it is important to me. The X stuff is also so complicated; it's nice to get a little breather. In the initial proposal (it's probably good that it never saw the light of day), Deadpool was sent to the oddest corners of the Marvel Universe. We had him fighting Ego the Living Planet, Obnoxio the Clown – really out there characters with no touchstones. Having the right kind of touchstones was the right idea.

SPOTLIGHT: Speaking of touching, Wade had quite a few romantic moments in your run, with three different ladies. Say Siryn, Typhoid Mary and Death are all behind the screen on *The Dating Game* – which one does Wade pick?

JOE: That's an excellent question. Would Death even say anything? Every question would be met with stony silence. If so, he'd probably pick her out of spite. But I think he'd probably end up with Typhoid Mary because he'd think he'd be getting three-for-one.

SPOTLIGHT: Now, Deadpool and Spidey. First time you crossed them over, you didn't even have them meet! That's something you're going to put right during your *Amazing Spider-Man* run, in #611, right?

JOE: Yeah, absolutely. Deadpool is hired to directly interface with Spidey, track him down and mess with his head. Shenanigans ensue. If I was *really* gonna do a hardcore Spidey/Deadpool team-up, I'd do a three-issue story and give it some meat. So I said to Steve, "If it's just a one-off, are you cool with it really being kind of rompy?" And he's like, "I think that's what people want!" So it's a little on the ludicrous side, but it ties into the bigger continuity with Spider-Man and kicks off the Gauntlet story in its way. There's a slow intro into both characters and a contrast of how their internal monologues work – sometimes it's a subtle difference, but mostly it's self-effacing "universe hates me all the time" Peter Parker and Wade Wilson insanity. They're directly duking it out, and I've always thought that a fight between Spidey and Deadpool devolves into a mama joke contest.

SPOTLIGHT: Is Wade Peter without the responsibility?

JOE: That really would be the question for a deeper book. The short answer is absolutely. There's so much I'd like to do with the two characters, there's so much to mine with two guys who suffered and chose to deal with that suffering in drastically different ways. It's like the Batman/Joker relationship; one snapped in a different way and chose to be a bit more productive. Wade became a nihilist. I think that relationship would exist between these two guys, we just need more time to flesh that out. Although there is a moment where Deadpool starts to crack on Spidey's mother and they realize they both have tragic histories.

SPOTLIGHT: Is a deeper team-up something we'll see from you any time soon?

JOE: I would like to do something, it just boils down to "how much time do I have?" This is the first time I've ever gone back to writing a character. It's not a rule; I just don't tend to revisit characters I've written in the past. It's actually kind of intimidating. To be back in that character was definitely fun, but I'm a different writer. It's been a while, it's a challenge.

SPOTLIGHT: You're also revisiting Wade in the pages of the landmark #900. It doesn't seem like 75 years since you wrote #1, does it?

JOE: I've held up pretty well! Axel Alonso asked me to participate but I couldn't do a lead story. It's a little standalone, a 10-pager. If anything it gives you a glimpse into his childhood.

SPOTLIGHT: And it's illustrated by Deadpool co-creator Rob Liefeld. What's that been like?

JOE: Really cool. When I saw the pages I was really happy. He's always been very cool to me. I've said to him, I owe you. He's very nice about *Ben 10*; his kids love it. It's funny, I have very vivid memories of where I was in my life when he did the Spike Lee commercial and really being jealous of him as a human being. Here I am graduating college, not happy with where I was, and this guy's drawing X-Men, what the hell! The fact that my first breakout gig was a character he created, that irony is not lost on me. I'll always appreciate it. It's very cool to finally get to work with him on it.

SPOTLIGHT: And after being out of print for years, your run is getting collected in *Deadpool Classic* trades. Are you getting much feedback from new fans?

JOE: A little bit. San Diego was interesting this year. It's funny how Deadpool really blew up. I had three lady Deadpools show up this year, which I thought was pretty remarkable. One had katanas, guns, the whole bit. Yellow Post-its to be her caption boxes! There's not usually that kind of crossover. I've never seen a female Cap at a con or a lady Iron Man. After seeing them, I thought, hmm, Lady Deadpool…

HE SHOOTS! He scores! Kelly and McGuinness send up the Scarlet Spider/Clone Saga.

SPOTLIGHT: Speaking of female Deadpool fans, I have to tell you, way back in college I showed your *Deadpool* comics to a friend of mine, and she loved them. Obviously, I had to marry her. So I have you (and Deadpool) to thank for my marriage, now going strong in its seventh year!

JOE: Excellent! That is a very cool story. That's the first marriage story I've ever heard. One of the things I've always said about Deadpool fans, and what made it so heartbreaking for me to leave, they are this really voracious fanbase doing everything they could to protect the book. When they knew the book was in danger they were really aggressive about trying to keep it. Deadpool fans are like the best fans in the world. They fall in love with that character and stick with him. Whatever hand I had in shaping that I'm very proud of. I grew up with Spider-Man, I love Spider-Man, but there were many, many years where I did not pick up a Spider-Man comic. Deadpool fans are not like that, they're hardcore!

Speaking of hardcore, it's a dream come true to see Joe's name in the credits for DEADPOOL #900, in stores in October! And don't forget to check out the Joe Kelly tales of yore, available in DEADPOOL CLASSIC VOL. 1-3 trade paperbacks!

DOINK!

THE END

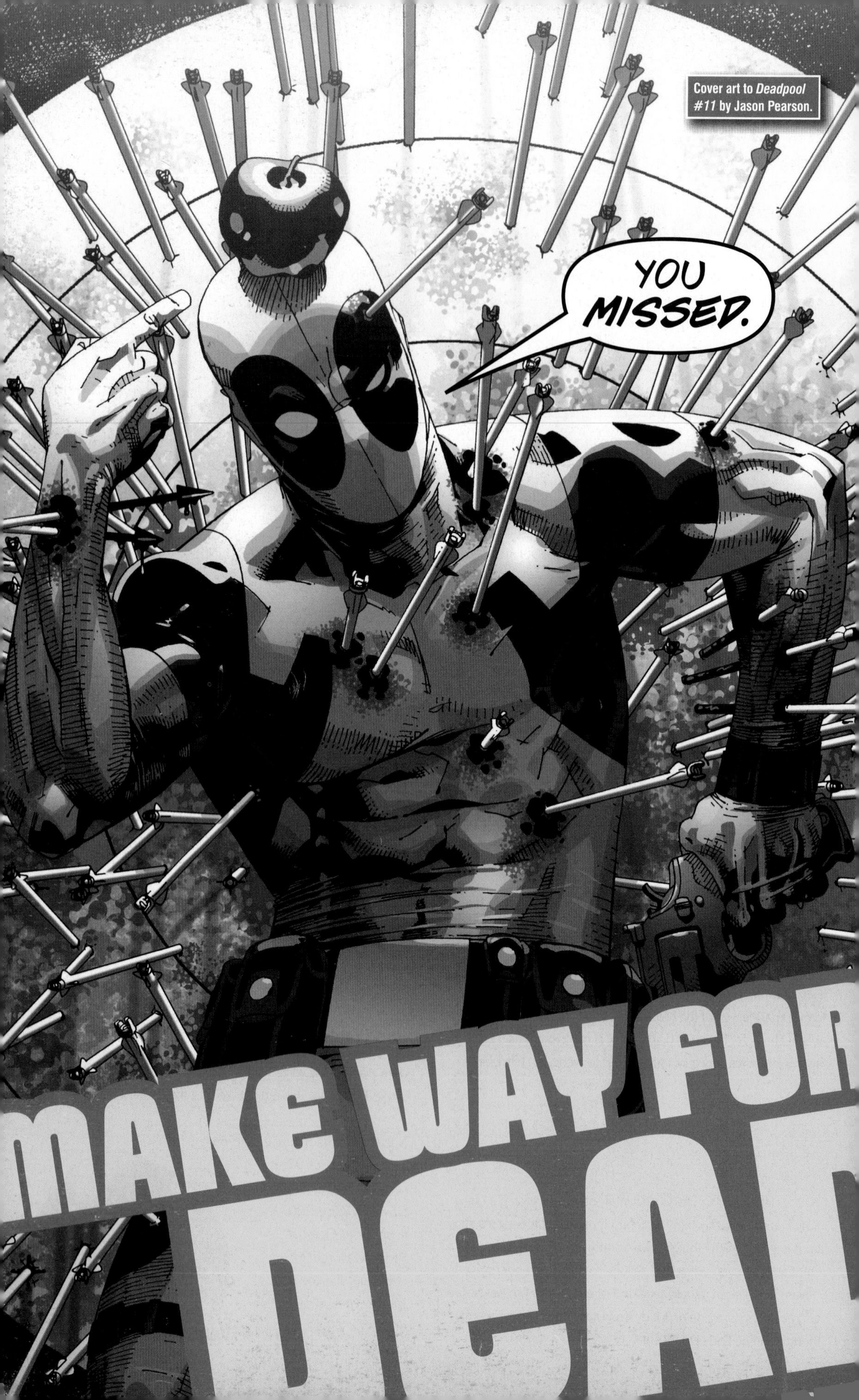
YOU MISSED.
MAKE WAY

Cover art to *Deadpool* #11 by Jason Pearson.

They say writing is all about getting inside the head of the characters. To know what they'd think, how they'd react, and what they'd do in whatever situation they're placed in. ● But what if the character is crazy? ● For many, that might be a risky scenario. But if any comics writer could fit the profile, it'd be writer Daniel Way. The Michigan-born thirty-something has been a familiar face at the House of Ideas in recent years, primarily for writing *Wolverine: Origins* and *Venom*. He's known as a loose cannon by some of the comics press, but that irreverence and skill seems perfectly at home for writing the character of Deadpool (and makes him one of *Spotlight*'s favorite interview subjects!) ● Way first crossed paths with the "Merc With a Mouth" in a five-issue arc of *Wolverine: Origins*, and that pairing provided epic…epic enough to spin off an ongoing series for Deadpool, reteaming Way with artist Paco Medina – who had previously worked with him on *Venom*. Fast forward almost two years and Way is still at the helm, creating some zany moments, unpredictable situations, and a character who isn't afraid to camp it up – while still being one of the deadliest mercenaries in the Marvel U.

SPOTLIGHT: Recently, Deadpool has exploded – figuratively, and in some cases literally – in the Marvel Universe. Three titles, guest-starring in other books and talk of his own movie. Daniel, what do you think of the big surge?

DANIEL: Yeah, Deadpool does seem to be the new black, doesn't he? Obviously, as the writer of the main title, I think that's great – but what really impresses me is that fans are showing such support to a character that, not too long ago, was regarded as a B-lister. Faith in fandom: RENEWED!

SPOTLIGHT: The Merry Marvel Marching Society returns!

DANIEL: (*Laughter.*)

SPOTLIGHT: Well, maybe not. But moving on… in the recent *X-Men Origins: Wolverine* movie, it covered Deadpool when

he was just Wade Wilson. Of course in the comics he's well into his Deadpool ways, but did you think Wade Wilson was in there somewhere?

DANIEL: Deadpool is Wade Wilson's armor against both the world around him and the war within him. If Wade didn't have the Deadpool persona, he'd probably end up like one of those guys you see wandering the streets in a bathrobe and arguing with traffic lights. So to answer your question: yes. Wade Wilson is integral to the character—he's what's under the mask.

SPOTLIGHT: Speaking of movies, it's been said that a Deadpool movie is in the works spinning out of *X-Men Origins: Wolverine*. What would you like to see in a Deadpool movie?

DANIEL: Uhh…Deadpool?

Wolverine: Origins Scribe **DANIEL WAY** Makes Hay With Another Loose Cannon In The MU…Deadpool! BY CHRIS ARRANT

DPOOL!

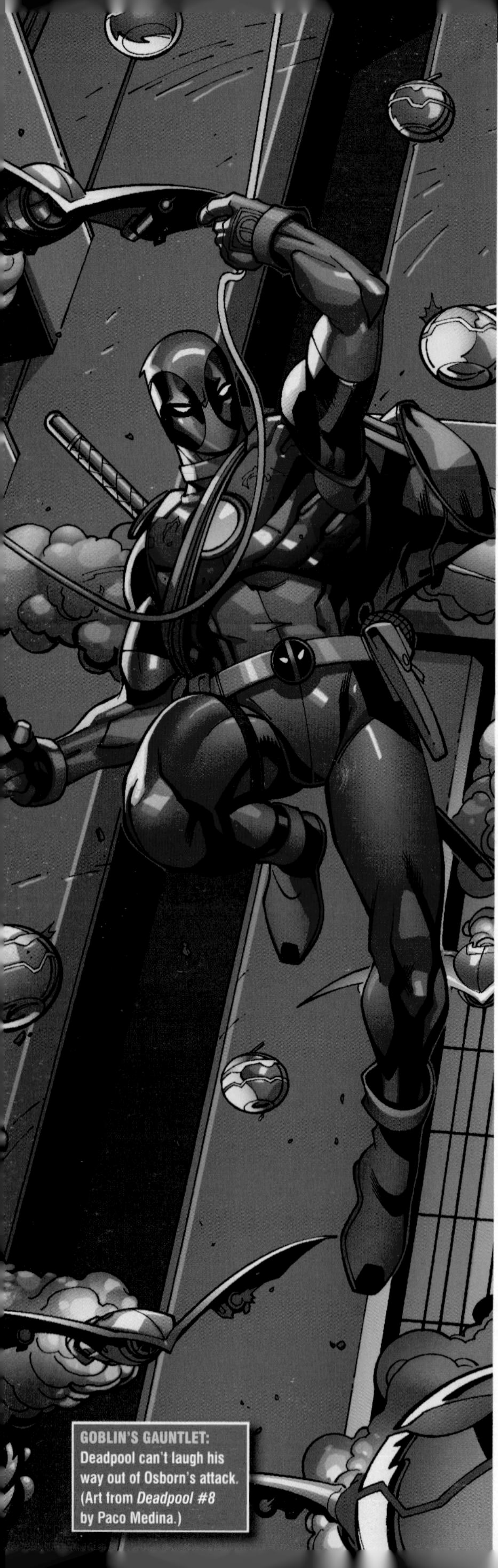

GOBLIN'S GAUNTLET: Deadpool can't laugh his way out of Osborn's attack. (Art from *Deadpool #8* by Paco Medina.)

SPOTLIGHT: Spoken just like someone who has been writing the character for some time! I remember your first big foray into writing the character of Deadpool in a five-issue story arc in *Wolverine: Origins*. Was he someone you'd been looking forward to getting your hands on? What's the big allure of Deadpool for you?

DANIEL: I think I've said this in other interviews, but it really is the most honest answer: Deadpool has no rules. As a writer, that's extremely attractive. I can literally do anything with the character.

SPOTLIGHT: And you've really done a lot with him. In the wake of Dark Reign, Deadpool's been really busy – between Nick Fury, Norman Osborn, the Thunderbolts he's been bouncing around all over. Without getting too messy, let us inside Deadpool's head to tell us what he thinks of the current situation.

DANIEL: He loves it! Deadpool, at his best, is a living, breathing reaction. For the past year (our time), there's been nothing *but* action in his life and it's been, in his opinion, completely rad. The worst thing that could've happened to him, did happen—he got paid off. Or, in his opinion, blown off. So now it's time to get some more action going.

SPOTLIGHT: In the story arc beginning in *Deadpool #15*, "Want You To Want Me," Deadpool questions his mercenary line of work and goes job-hunting. What's not to like about being a merc-for-hire for Deadpool?

DANIEL: It's short-term. Deadpool's looking for that permanent high; he wants to throw himself into a situation that can never resolve itself—that is always in flux. Because that's where he thrives.

SPOTLIGHT: The first place Deadpool goes for a new line of work is San Francisco – no not to run a trolley, but to join the X-Men. That has me scratching my head and ready to laugh out loud – where'd this idea come from, and why would Deadpool be so ... crazy?

DANIEL: The idea comes to him when he sees Cyclops making his "Utopia" speech; in his mind, Cyclops is speaking directly to *him*. In his mind, it all makes perfect sense. Then again, in his mind it would also make perfect sense for him to take up residence on the Island of Misfit Toys. That's our boy Wade!

SPOTLIGHT: Wade, aka Deadpool, is far from your typical character, even in the Marvel U. How is it writing such a non-standard and non-linear type character?

DANIEL: Fun. I mean, like, really, really fun. I think that I've really found an outlet with the character to tell "my" kind of stories and that really...I dunno...feels good.

SPOTLIGHT: You've been on Deadpool going on the double-digits, with no sign of slowing down – what do you see in the future for the title and the character?

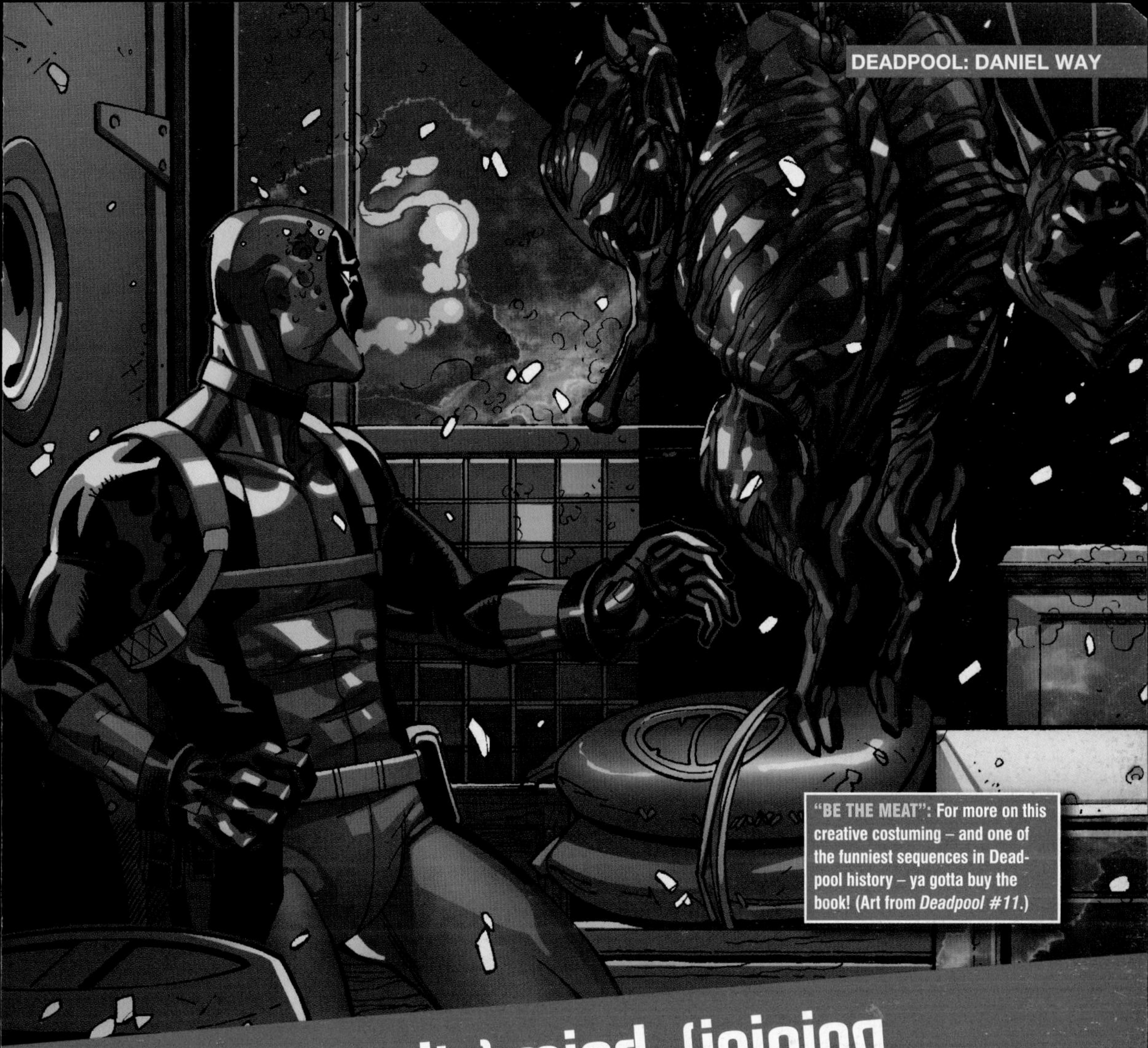

"BE THE MEAT": For more on this creative costuming – and one of the funniest sequences in Deadpool history – ya gotta buy the book! (Art from *Deadpool #11*.)

"In (Deadpool's) mind, (joining the X-Men) makes perfect sense."

– WRITER DANIEL WAY ON HIS POST-UTOPIA PLANS FOR 'POOL.

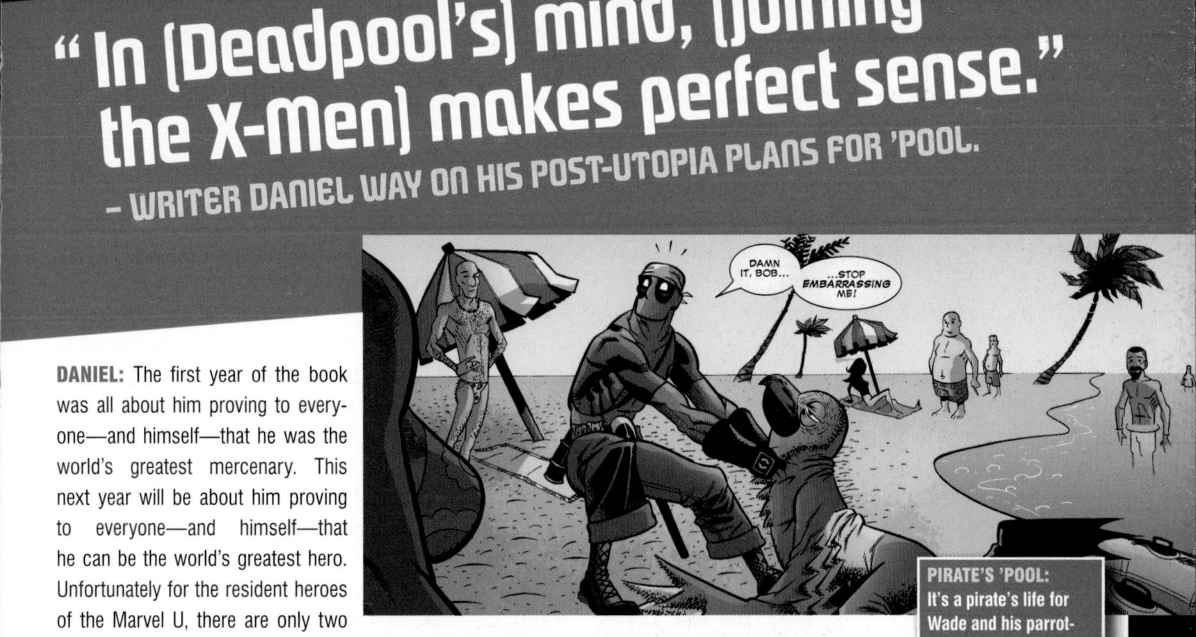
DAMN IT, BOB...
...STOP EMBARRASSING ME!

PIRATE'S 'POOL: It's a pirate's life for Wade and his parrot-costumed pal, Bob, in *Deadpool #13-14*! (Art by Shawn Crystal.)

DANIEL: The first year of the book was all about him proving to everyone—and himself—that he was the world's greatest mercenary. This next year will be about him proving to everyone—and himself—that he can be the world's greatest hero. Unfortunately for the resident heroes of the Marvel U, there are only two ways Deadpool thinks this can be done: 1) Learn from the best, or 2) Kill everyone that's better than him. From the outset, he's going with Plan A – but with Deadpool, you never know when he'll just flip out and go with Plan...U, or something. Because he's just like that. And that's why we love him. ●

Have your faith in Daniel Way renewed every month in* DEADPOOL*! The new storyline, "WANT YOU TO WANT ME", is in stores now with* DEADPOOL #15*!

FUNKY 'POOL MEDINA!

As Artistic Foil To Daniel Way, Penciler **PACO MEDINA** Takes Deadpool To The Edge And Back Again BY CHRIS ARRANT

Deadpool's been one of those lucky characters who attract great artists; from his debut in 1991 under the auspices of Rob Liefeld, on through the hands of Joe Madureira, Ian Churchill, Ed McGuinness, and others, and now he's landed onto the drawing board of Paco Medina. ● After establishing himself with work on everything from Spider-Man to the X-Men Medina first ran into Deadpool in a two-issue arc of *Wolverine: Origins* which co-starred Deadpool. Medina's take, along with writer Daniel Way's scripting, started the drumbeat for a new ongoing series for the hilarious hired gun… and that drumbeat culminated with the new ongoing series in September 2008. ● Medina and Way have now carried on with the series into its double-digits – a nice achievement for the creative tandem in this modern era when teams don't last very long – and the artist took time away from his drawing table to talk about the book. And while he wasn't looking, we got an exclusive look at penciled pages from his run so far on *Deadpool!*

Art from *Deadpool #10* by Paco Medina.

SPOTLIGHT: Paco, you've had good runs on several titles at Marvel, but *Deadpool* seems undoubtedly one of the strangest. What's it like working on the character?

PACO: I would say that rather than being a weird or strange character he is really funny! He has that weird thing of talking to himself with different personalities, making him so incredibly complicated that you never know what he is going to do next. As a penciler it keeps you always at the edge of the drawing table expecting new things. During this year working with *Deadpool*, I've kept myself anticipating every new crazy idea Daniel (Way, series writer) proposes, and it always turns out to be a great experience. I identify myself with Deadpool's crazy personality and I have a great time.

SPOTLIGHT: The character of Deadpool has proven extremely popular in recent movies, with the *X-Men Origins: Wolverine* movie and two other *Deadpool* series going on. What do you think of the character's success?

PACO: I had read some Deadpool stuff and it seemed to me like a character that had never been given attention, I thought. Nobody had explored him a hundred percent.

He is really one of those cult characters; a little bit underground and more for the fans' liking, but if you get to know that this guy can kick Wolverine's butt then I think it was time to put him under the spotlight.

SPOTLIGHT: For this title, you're working with writer Daniel Way. What do you think of the scenes and stories he's had you draw?

PACO: *(Laughter.)* I will say it this way: Sometimes after reading the script I talk over the phone with (series inker) Juan Vlasco, with Juan Mar the translator or with my daughter Monserrat just to tell them what new madness Deadpool has in store. And I do this because I could not have that much fun just by myself. You know, usually I like to see someone's reac-

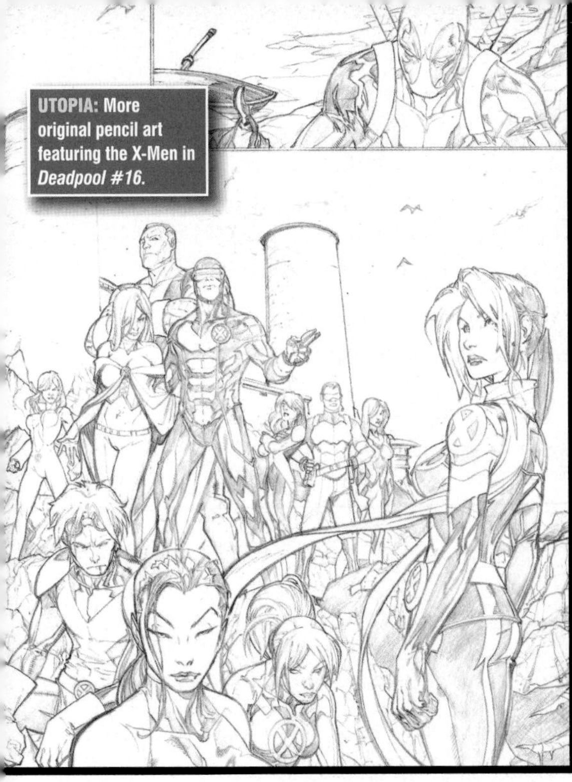

UTOPIA: More original pencil art featuring the X-Men in *Deadpool #16.*

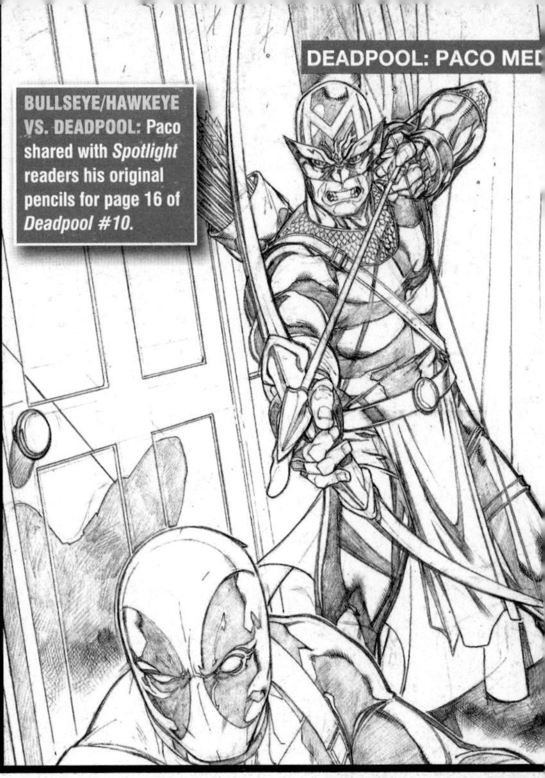

BULLSEYE/HAWKEYE VS. DEADPOOL: Paco shared with *Spotlight* readers his original pencils for page 16 of *Deadpool #10.*

tion before drawing what I have on the table. That makes me feel the possible readers' reaction.

Really I couldn't be more happy, I know Daniel's work from some time ago, when we worked together on *Venom*. And since then I have felt a good chemistry with his writing. I have a great admiration for him and as a penciler I really couldn't ask for more. Daniel asks me to jump, I only ask him "how high?"

SPOTLIGHT: I won't ask you to jump, but I will ask you this – what would you say has been your favorite, or most memorable moment from what you've drawn in *Deadpool* so far?

PACO: Definitely Bullseye. *(Laughter.)* Poor guy. Hey, but the whole series up to this moment has been filled with great moments.... tell me, who else would have thought of fooling the Skrulls that way in the middle of an invasion? Or what about the meat armor...

SPOTLIGHT: *(Laughter.)* Who could forget about the meat armor?

PACO: I don't know what it is, but the great thing of each story is that you never know what he will do. You can expect anything and that is what I enjoy the most.

SPOTLIGHT: I found a real rarity passed on to me by someone at Marvel: a Deadpool Christmas card image you did, which pictures him in a more playful and less, shall we say, *violent* pose than we might typically see him in. How'd it come about?

PACO: Well, it was last Christmas; in the beginning it was something personal for my friends. Let's just say that I painted it and used it to decorate my house door instead of the typical Christmas ornament. After that I sent it as a Christmas card for all my friends and that is how it got to you. And well, who says Deadpool is violent? Deadpool is as cute as a little boy playing with his slingshot...

SPOTLIGHT: *(Laughter.)* Hey, I didn't know you knew the kids in my neighborhood! Paco, your work shows a real enthusiasm for the character, so I have to ask – what do you think of the character of Deadpool himself?

PACO: As I was saying before I feel identified with that part where he talks to himself. I mean, it's not like I'm a psycho artist with multiple personalities! *(Laughter.)* But, trust me, when one spends as much time at the drawing table as I do, one starts to live a second life in the paper. And there's been more than a few times I've noticed myself talking to myself, to scold or congratulate myself. But when I got the first script I loved it, just imagine... first I couldn't stop laughing seeing how this guy did the same thing as me. *(Laughter.)*

I'm really happy with this book. And I'm thankful to my editors Axel Alonso and Jody LeHeup for taking my work to give life to him. Obviously with Daniel, and also it is a luxury to be able to work with friends like (inker and colorist) Juan Vlasco and Marte Gracia, the colorist, my countrymates. (And hey, Deadpool loves to eat tacos!) Or Mr. Jason Pearson's covers, I never imagined working with one of my idols.

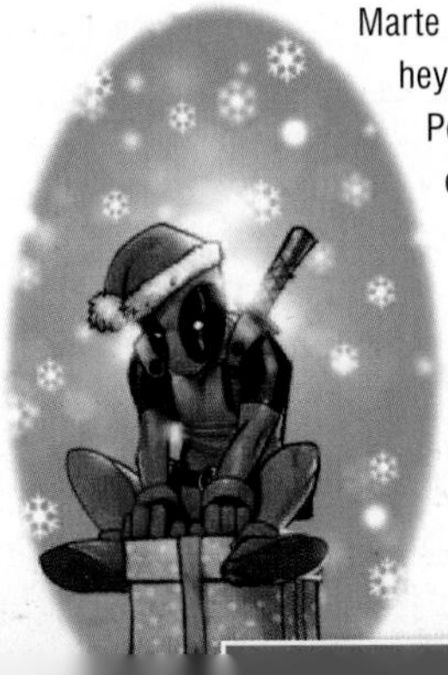

What happens is that the whole *Deadpool* team has this incredible chemistry and that shows beyond the paper! ●

You said it, Paco! We hope the chemistry remains the same as the Way/Medina team continue the ongoing DEADPOOL series!

GAMES OF DEATH AND SUICIDE KINGS

Writer Mike Benson Teams Up With Deadpool For A Trio Of Tales and Team-Ups!

By John Rhett Thomas

In two short years, writer Mike Benson has hopped over from Hollywood, where he has a successful career as a writer and producer for hit shows like The Bernie Mac Show and Entourage, to work in comics, where he's developed quite an entourage of characters that have had great stories told under his tenure. Much like Daniel Way, another fixture on the Deadpool scene (and subject of this issue of Spotlight!), Mike has introduced himself to readers through the anti-heroes and loose cannons of the Marvel super hero set. In Mike's case, the credits roll thusly: Wolverine in the *Chop Shop* one-shot, 16 issues of *Moon Knight*, and three, count 'em, three different Deadpool projects: the gloriously zany *Games of Death* one-shot, the team-up-palooza of *Deadpool: Suicide Kings* mini-series, and now a feature slot in the upcoming *Deadpool Team-Up* series. If this all seems to be too overwhelming for Mike, fear not. He and the little voices in his head got together with *Spotlight* to talk about Deadpool (and the little voices inside *his* head) and some of the other high-water marks in what is turning out to be a fun career in comics!

SPOTLIGHT: So Mike, you came into comics from television screenwriting and producing. What about your experiences on shows like Entourage and The Bernie Mac Show lends itself to comics writing – for instance, when it comes to pitching, meeting deadlines, and pacing your scripts?

MIKE: Deadlines, no doubt. I'm used to a quick turn around. Aside from that, in TV you need to be collaborative and I enjoy that very much. If someone has a better idea than what's on the table, by all means I'll go with it. I try not to let ego get in the way of making the material the best it can be.

SPOTLIGHT: Anytime we talk with someone who has come into comics from another field of writing, we like to establish comic book bona fides. Can you give a little background on the comics you read as a kid, what you liked growing up?

MIKE: First off, as a kid I was a total Marvel zombie. My favorite books were *Moon Knight, The Avengers, Master of Kung Fu, Iron Man* and *Daredevil*. I also really dug *Power Man and Iron Fist*. Those were my main titles, but I collected all things Marvel. Frank Miller was writing his seminal Daredevil run and that just brought the whole

fanboy experience to a whole new level. I also remember being pretty obsessed with anything that Gene Colan and Jack Kirby did. And I'm still pretty obsessed with their art now. I actually own a few pieces.

SPOTLIGHT: Which pieces of art, Mike? *Spotlight* fans wanna know!

I have a couple of Colan *Tomb of Dracula* pages. A beautiful Kirby *New Gods* page. Also, I have a Bob Layton "Demon in a Bottle" recreation cover that Bob gave me as a gift.

SPOTLIGHT: Before we jump into all things Deadpool, can you tell us a little about your first work for Marvel on *Moon Knight*? Had you been reading the Charlie Huston series up to that point?

MIKE: Heck, yeah. At that point I had no idea I'd actually be writing for Marvel, but I was devouring Charlie's MK books. They had a tone and grit I really respond to as a reader, and Charlie is such a talented writer. After reading his comics, I started in on his Joe Pitt novels. But enough about Charlie, let's talk more about me! (*Laughter.*) I'm joking, Charlie's a bud.

SPOTLIGHT: What was the key thing you wanted to do in transitioning from Charlie's storyline to yours?

MIKE: Well, because I wasn't launching the title, because I was taking over the reins, I didn't want to change directions. Moon Knight fans, such as myself, really appreciated what Charlie was doing. There had been a few incarnations of *Moon Knight* that didn't work at all in my opinion. Charlie was staying true to Doug Moench's *Moon Knight* and that's the interpretation I responded to myself. So for me, it was playing out Moon Knight's natural trajectory that Huston set in place. I think that's why we originally got along so well and why Charlie decided to stay on board and work with me. It was a terrific experience. I guess if anything I wanted to dip Moonie's toe into the deep end of the Marvel pool – and that really came to fruition when he went up against the Thunderbolts. I also wanted to keep

> ## "Deadpool at first was a terribly hard character to write."
> – Writer Mike Benson

the book as a team book and use Marlene, Frenchie and the rest of the gang.

SPOTLIGHT: The last arc of Moon Knight introduced the Zapata Brothers (more on them later), guest-starred Punisher, and featured the strikingly moody art of Jefte Palo. All things considered, I think this is one of the best stories published by Marvel in recent years, so to save me the trouble of gushing, can you share what you consider to be the high marks you hit with "Down South?"

MIKE: That's really nice of you to say. Well as you know, MK killed off his Marc Spector persona. And he needed a place to hang his hat and regroup. And so Mexico seemed like one of those places people go to get lost. And because MK was in such a predicament, it gave me the opportunity to tell a much smaller story and put him on the path to being a true hero again, which was always my intention.

That said, I wanted the tone of the arc to feel like a Sam Peckinpah film. Something dark and gritty and Jefte Palo was just the man to deliver on that vision.

SPOTLIGHT: Can you give us a little background on the Zapata Brothers? They were a good element of comic relief in an otherwise bloody, dark story. Are you a fan of lucha libre?

MIKE: I don't know if I'd say I'm a fan as much as I appreciate the look and style. (But I am a fan of *Nacho Libre!*) The Zapata Brothers were characters Axel Alonso and myself created. It's funny, but we set out to create Toltec, who I'd like to explore more, but we just started bantering and came up with a couple of Lucha Libre hitmen. We both got really excited and they eventually became the Zapatas.

SPOTLIGHT: You went for Punisher in both your last arc of *Moon Knight* and the *Deadpool: Suicide Kings* miniseries, both of which showed very different sides of Frank Castle (deadly serious/comic relief). Is he a character you'd like a crack at in a more long-form series?

MIKE: One hundred percent, yes. I really became a fan of Castle – as did many others – when Garth Ennis started writing him. His run on *Punisher* was as important to me as when Frank Miller was doing *Daredevil*. I've never met Garth but I can say without hesitation, he's my favorite comic writer.

MOON KNIGHT: Mike's first ongoing title at Marvel was Moon Knight. The "Down South" arc guest-starred Punisher and featured the menace of Toltec. (Art from *Moon Knight #28* by Jefte Palo.)

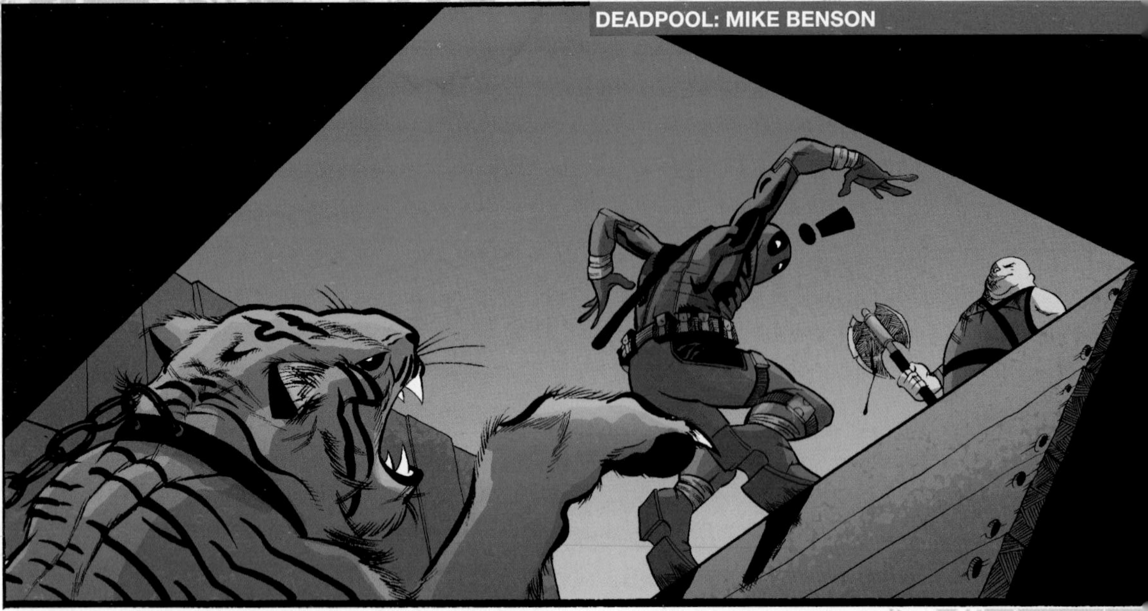

GAMES OF DEATH: One of which included Deadpool's bum getting chewed off by a hungry tiger! (Art from *Deadpool: Games of Death* by Shawn Crystal.)

SPOTLIGHT: So, Moon Knight, Punisher and Deadpool: Who's crazier?

MIKE: I'd say Moon Knight, Deadpool, and then Punisher.

SPOTLIGHT: Wow! I wouldn't have guessed that order. MK tops the list? What's your gut on why?

MIKE: Multiple personalities tops hearing voices and the occasional hallucination.

SPOTLIGHT: Now, picking up on Deadpool, if "Down South" from *Moon Knight* was one of the best series, the *Deadpool: Games of Death* one-shot is one of the most hilarious stand-alone stories. You really brought the funny with that one. I assume that's easier to do with Deadpool than, say, Wolverine?

MIKE: I have to introduce you to my wife and you can tell her how great I am. (*Laughter.*) Actually no. The Wolverine one-shot I did – *Chop Shop* – was one of the easiest books I've written – and one of my favorites, too. Deadpool at first was a terribly hard character to write. I didn't know much about him, so I went back and read everything I could get my hands on. *Games of Death* was a difficult script to write because I didn't have a great feel for the character and so it was really trying to me to find his voice. I look back at the comic and see so many things I would've done differently now. Now I feel much more confident and understand the delicate balance between comedy and action; what works and what doesn't.

"I feel much more confident and understand the delicate balance between comedy and action; what works and what doesn't."

– Benson on writing Deadpool.

SPOTLIGHT: The introduction of the players in the underground reality show was pretty great. Do any of these characters have real life inspirations?

MIKE: Well, they were modeled after action heroes – such as Steven Seagal, DMZ, Claude Van Damme, and the great Chuck Norris.

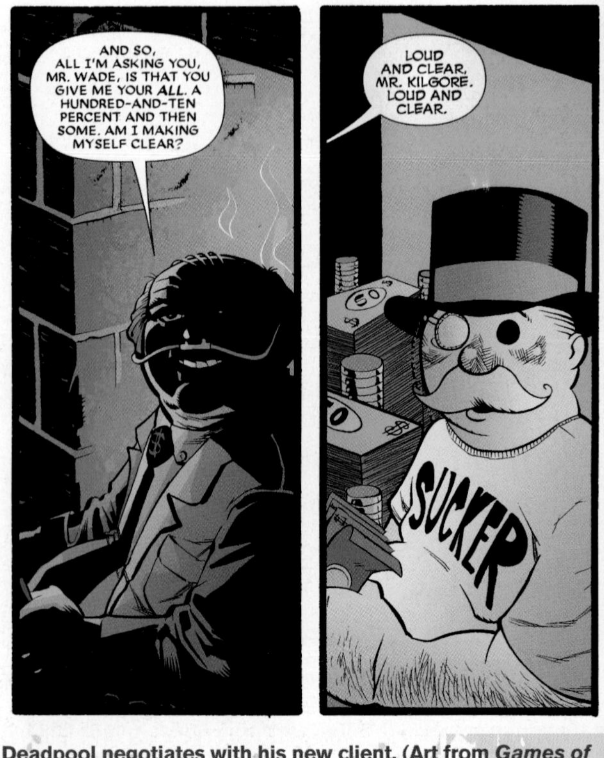
AND SO, ALL I'M ASKING YOU, MR. WADE, IS THAT YOU GIVE ME YOUR ALL. A HUNDRED-AND-TEN PERCENT AND THEN SOME. AM I MAKING MYSELF CLEAR?
LOUD AND CLEAR, MR. KILGORE. LOUD AND CLEAR.
SUCKER

Deadpool negotiates with his new client. (Art from *Games of Death* by Crystal.)

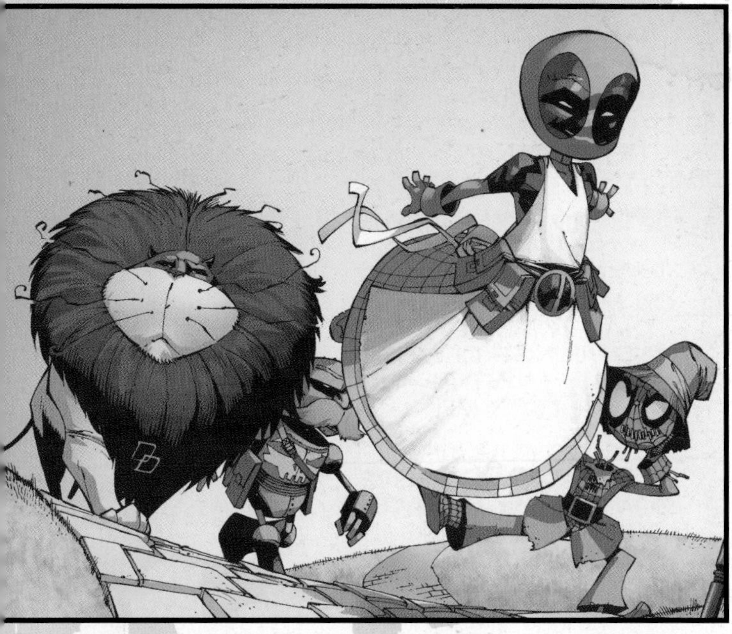

IO PLACE LIKE... HUH? Benson and artist Carlo Barberi send up *Wizard of Oz* with a Skottie Young homage in *Suicide Kings #4*.

SPOTLIGHT: The whole book, with your pacing and Shawn Crystal's slick, stylized art, was pretty hilarious. Does comedy writing come easily to you?

MIKE: Any type of writing for me is hard. However, I think comedy is one of the few things that can't be taught. You're either funny or you're not – and then there are the different levels of funny. I've always been confident that I'm funny and could make people laugh when I wanted to. Writing comedy however is all about how you look at things through your very own lens. Sometimes it just spills out. Other times not so much. When I'm working with my pal Adam Glass, who co-wrote *Suicide Kings* and *Luke Cage Noir*, we both make each other laugh so much that at times it doesn't even feel like work.

SPOTLIGHT: That led into *Suicide Kings*, a five-issue mini that just wrapped up, and also guest-starred Punisher, Daredevil and Spider-Man. Can you talk a little about what you achieved with that series?

MIKE: I think Adam and I accomplished what we wanted to. To have a fun, yet fairly grounded (at least for a DP comic) story.

SPOTLIGHT: Now, you're primed to write an issue of *Deadpool Team-Up*, reuniting with Shawn Crystal. Your association with Deadpool has turned into a nice handful of stories. Are we going to see more from you with Wade Wilson?

MIKE: You sure are. Actually, I'm in the process of breaking out another story with my boy, Adam Glass. It's going to be a lot of fun and a very cool story told from a very different POV.

SPOTLIGHT: You'd mentioned *Luke Cage Noir*, which will be wrapping up as this issue of *Spotlight* hits the stands. What else can readers look forward to with your name on it in the forthcoming months?

SPOTLIGHT: I did a killer Shang-Chi one-shot with Tomm Coker and also a short with Bullseye that I can't say much about but it's pretty cool. Aside from that, I'll be doing a couple of issues of *Amazing Spider-Man* and some more Deadpool books.

There you go, friends, your Spotlight introduction to a future Marvel A-lister. If you haven't read Suicide Kings or Games of Death yet, look no further than the DEADPOOL: SUICIDE KINGS PREMIERE HARDCOVER, in stores now! •

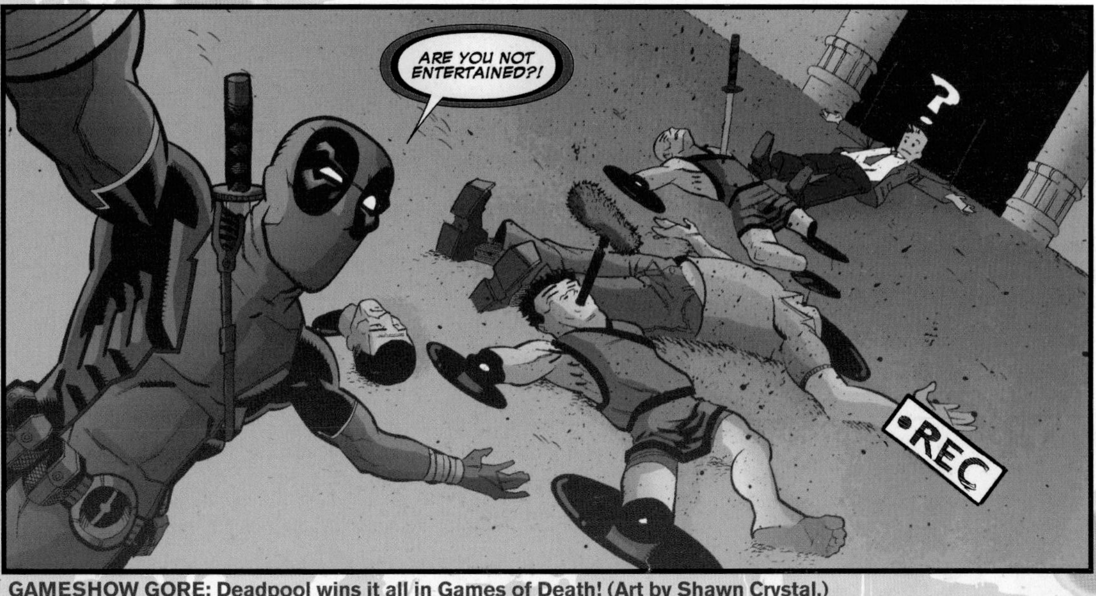
ARE YOU NOT ENTERTAINED?!
?
•REC

GAMESHOW GORE: Deadpool wins it all in Games of Death! (Art by Shawn Crystal.)

COVER GALLERY

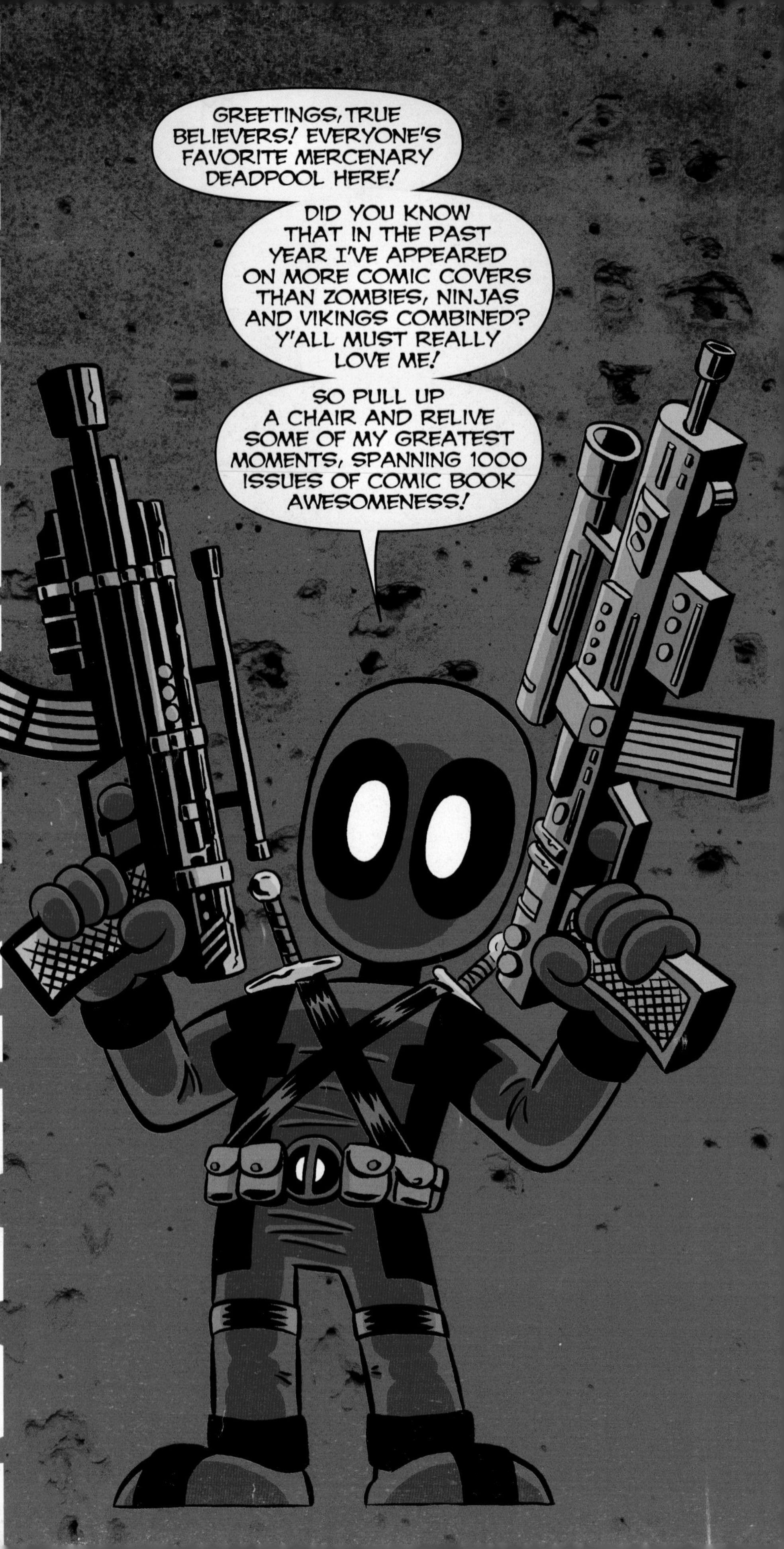
GREETINGS, TRUE BELIEVERS! EVERYONE'S FAVORITE MERCENARY DEADPOOL HERE!
DID YOU KNOW THAT IN THE PAST YEAR I'VE APPEARED ON MORE COMIC COVERS THAN ZOMBIES, NINJAS AND VIKINGS COMBINED? Y'ALL MUST REALLY LOVE ME!
SO PULL UP A CHAIR AND RELIVE SOME OF MY GREATEST MOMENTS, SPANNING 1000 ISSUES OF COMIC BOOK AWESOMENESS!

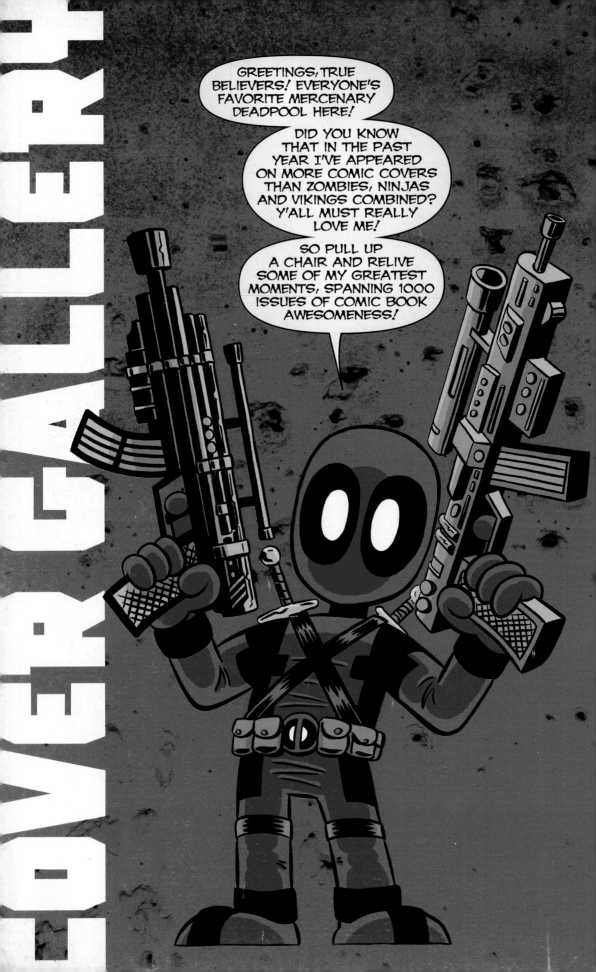

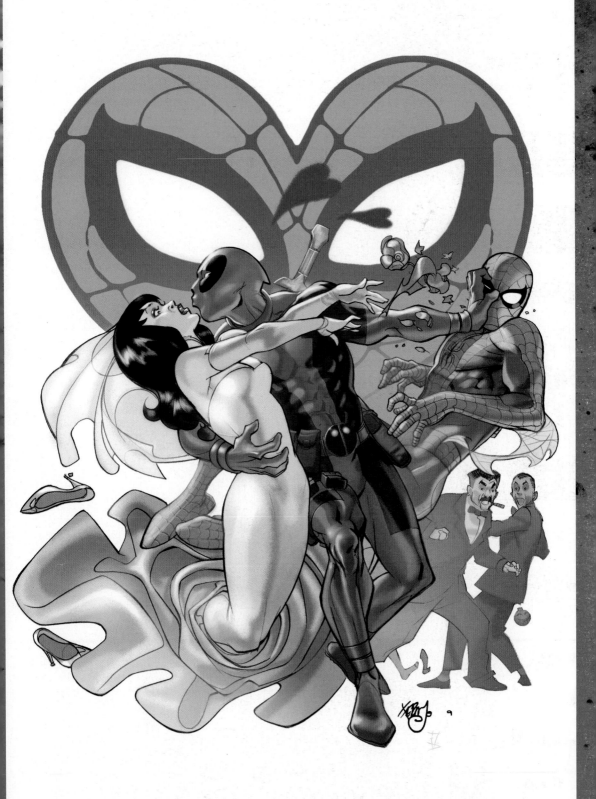

AMAZING SPIDER-MAN #620 DEADPOOL VARIANT
BY PASQUAL FERRY & FABIO D'AURIA

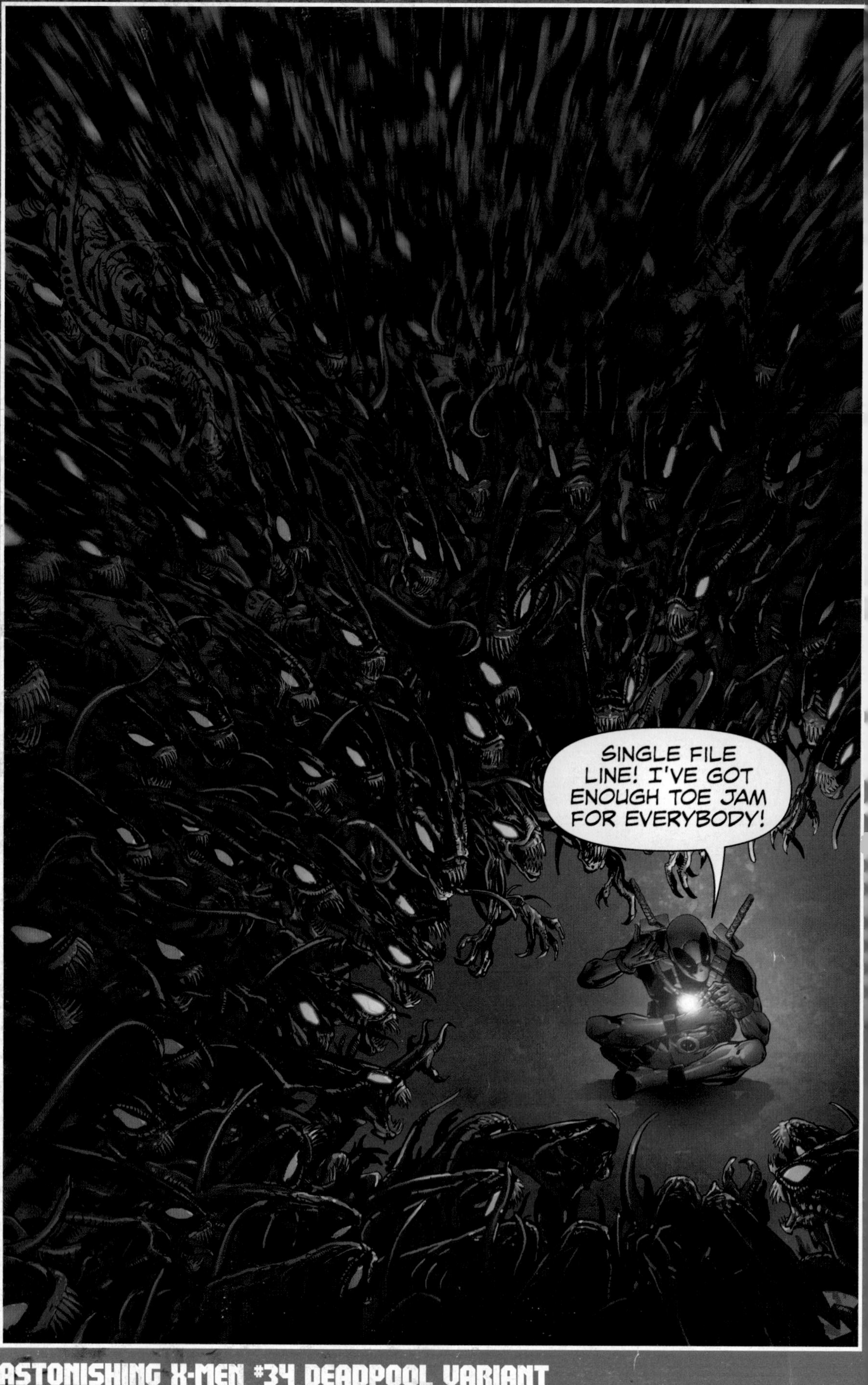
SINGLE FILE LINE! I'VE GOT ENOUGH TOE JAM FOR EVERYBODY!

ASTONISHING X-MEN #34 DEADPOOL VARIANT
BY PHIL JIMENEZ & FRANK D'ARMATA

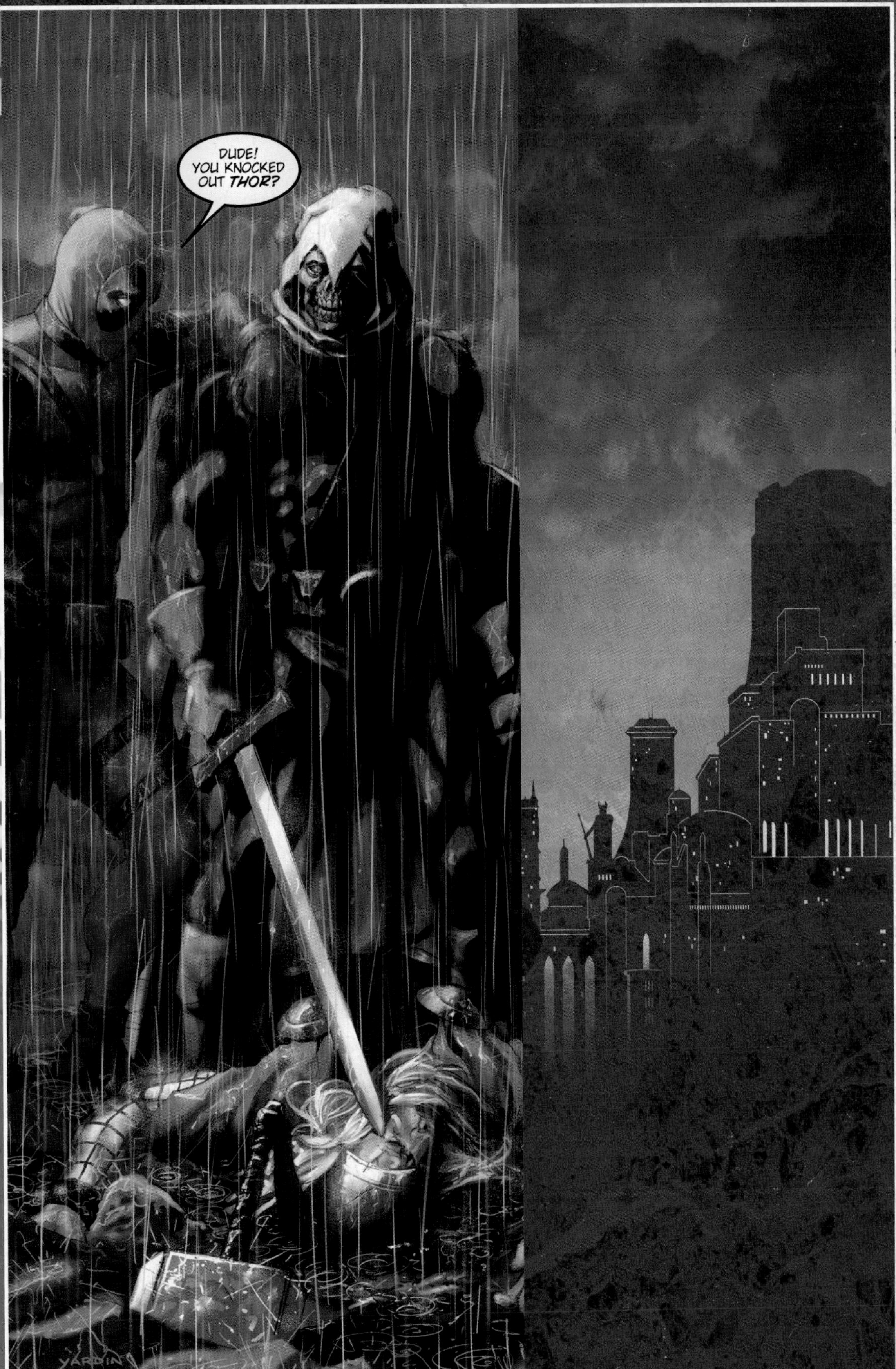
DUDE! YOU KNOCKED OUT THOR?
YARDIN

AVENGERS: THE INITIATIVE #33 DEADPOOL VARIANT
BY DAVID YARDIN

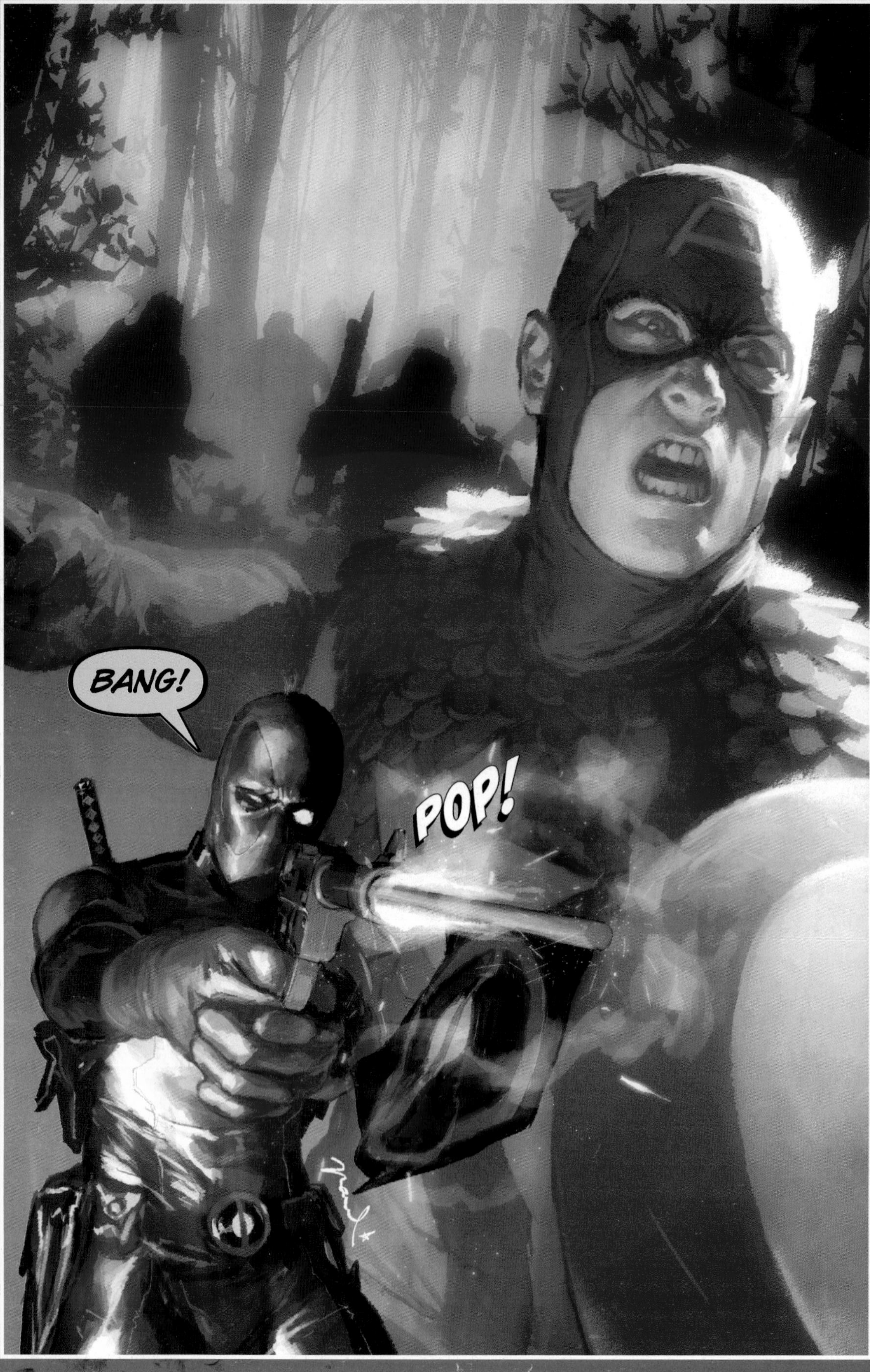
BANG!
POP!

CAPTAIN AMERICA #603 DEADPOOL VARIANT
BY GERALD PAREL

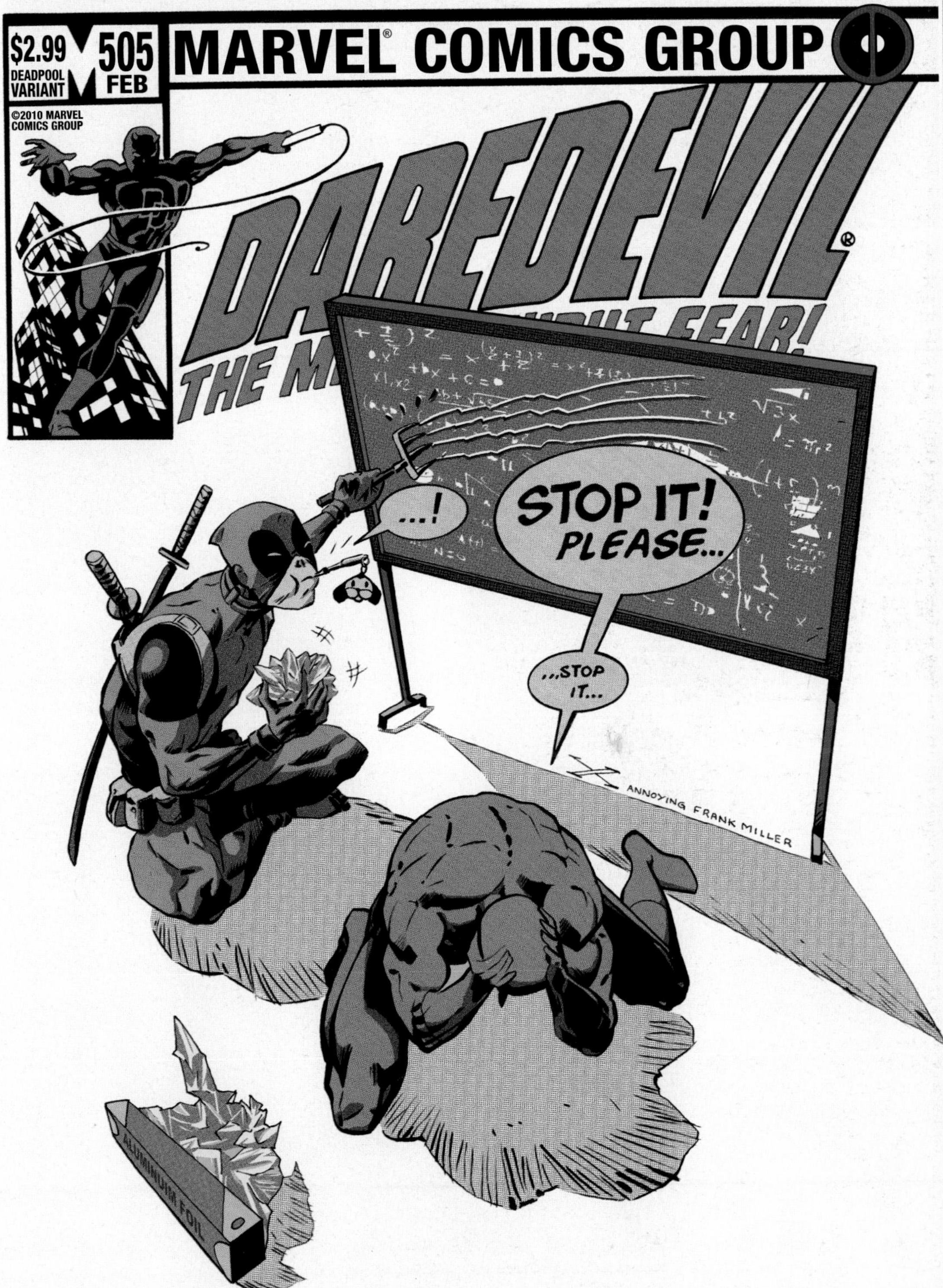
$2.99
DEADPOOL VARIANT
505
FEB
©2010 MARVEL COMICS GROUP
MARVEL® COMICS GROUP
DAREDEVIL®
...!
STOP IT! PLEASE...
...STOP IT...
ANNOYING FRANK MILLER
ALUMINIUM FOIL

DAREDEVIL #505 DEADPOOL VARIANT
BY MAX FIUMARA

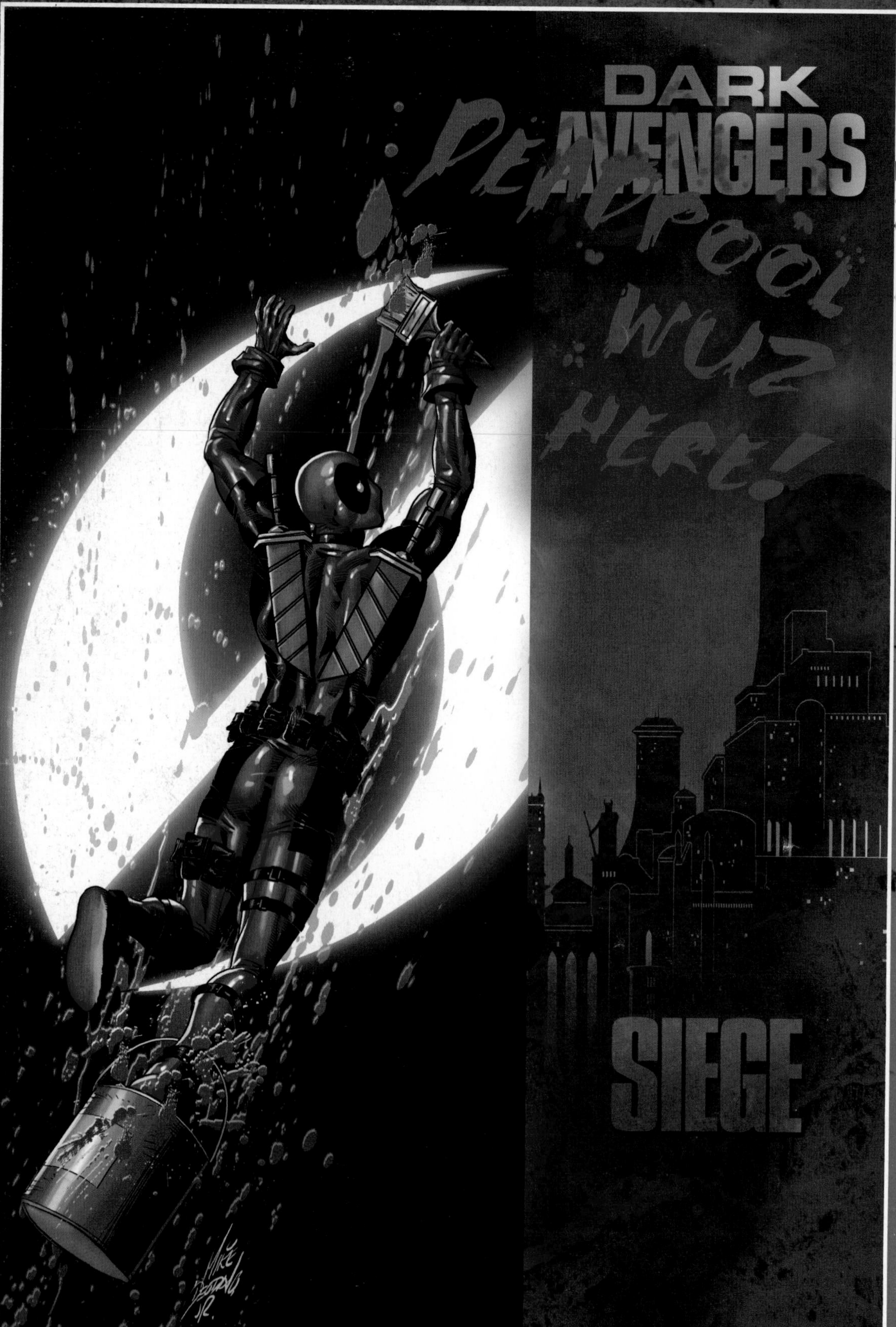
DARK AVENGERS
DEADPOOL WUZ HERE!
SIEGE

DARK AVENGERS #14 DEADPOOL VARIANT
BY MIKE DEODATO JR. WITH RAIN BEREDO

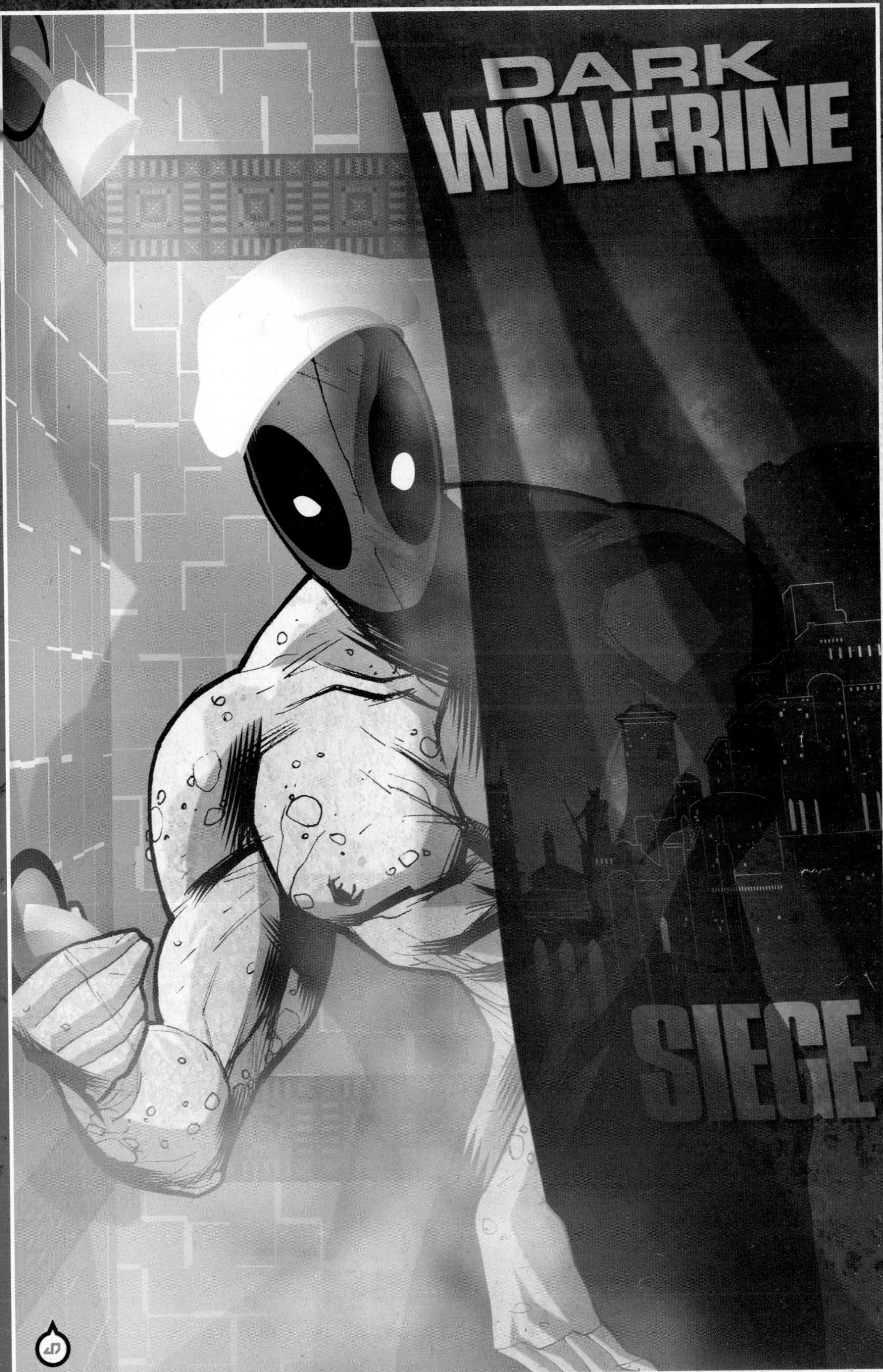
DARK
WOLVERINE
SIEGE

DARK WOLVERINE #83 DEADPOOL VARIANT
BY JUAN DOE

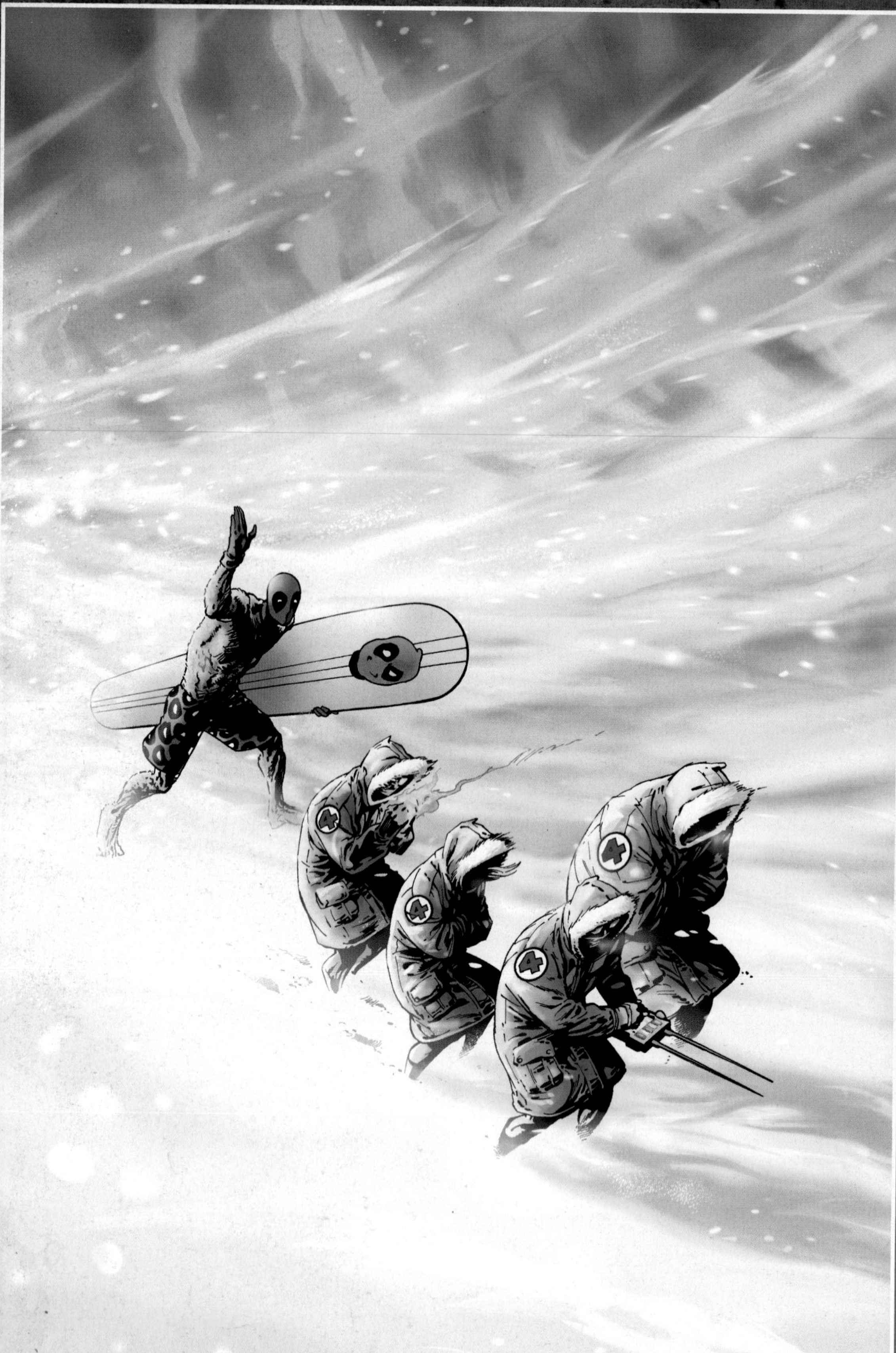

FANTASTIC FOUR #576 DEADPOOL VARIANT

BY ALAN DAVIS, MARK FARMER & JAVIER RODRIGUEZ

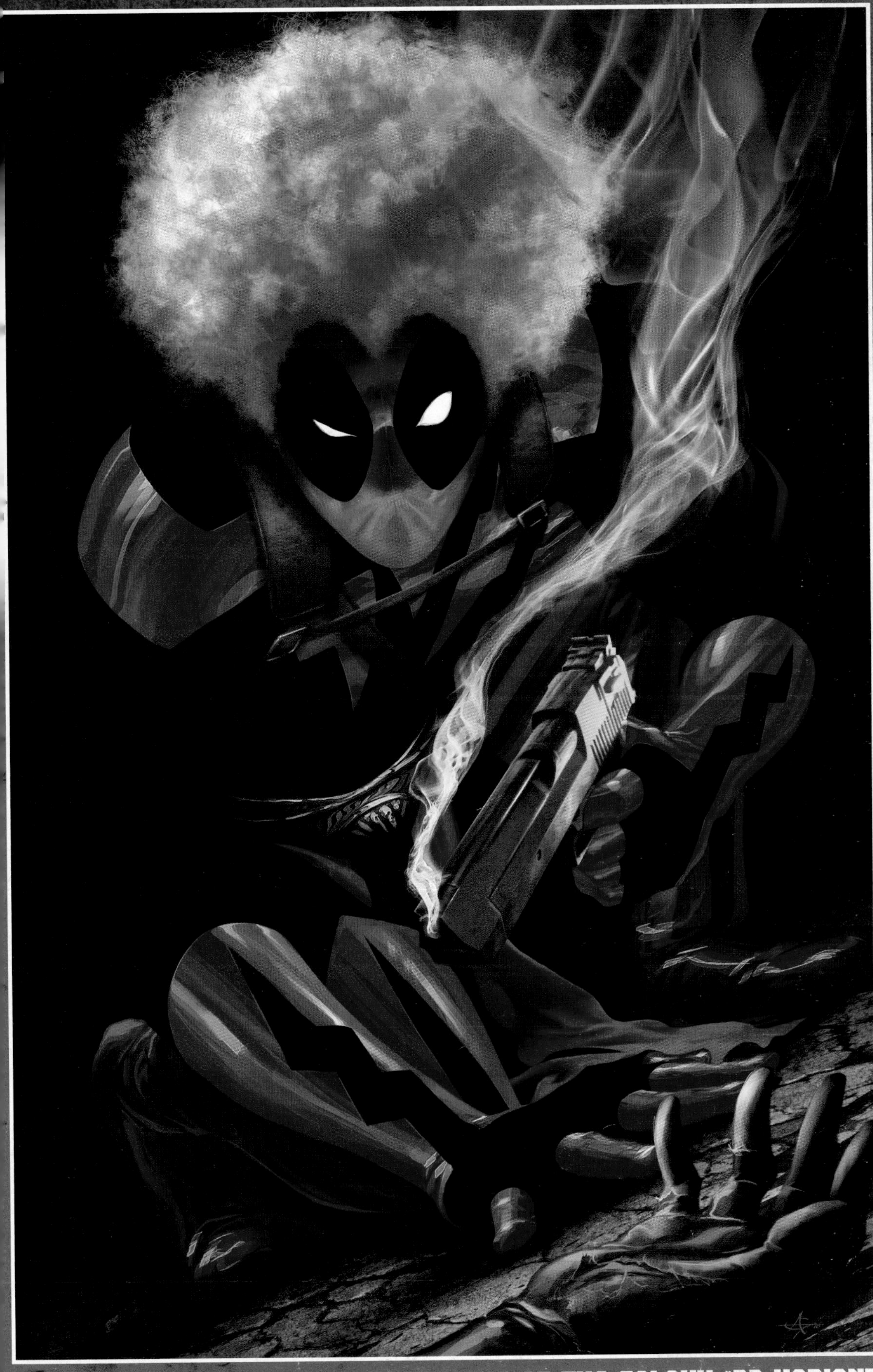

GUARDIANS OF THE GALAXY #23 VARIANT
BY ALEX GARNER

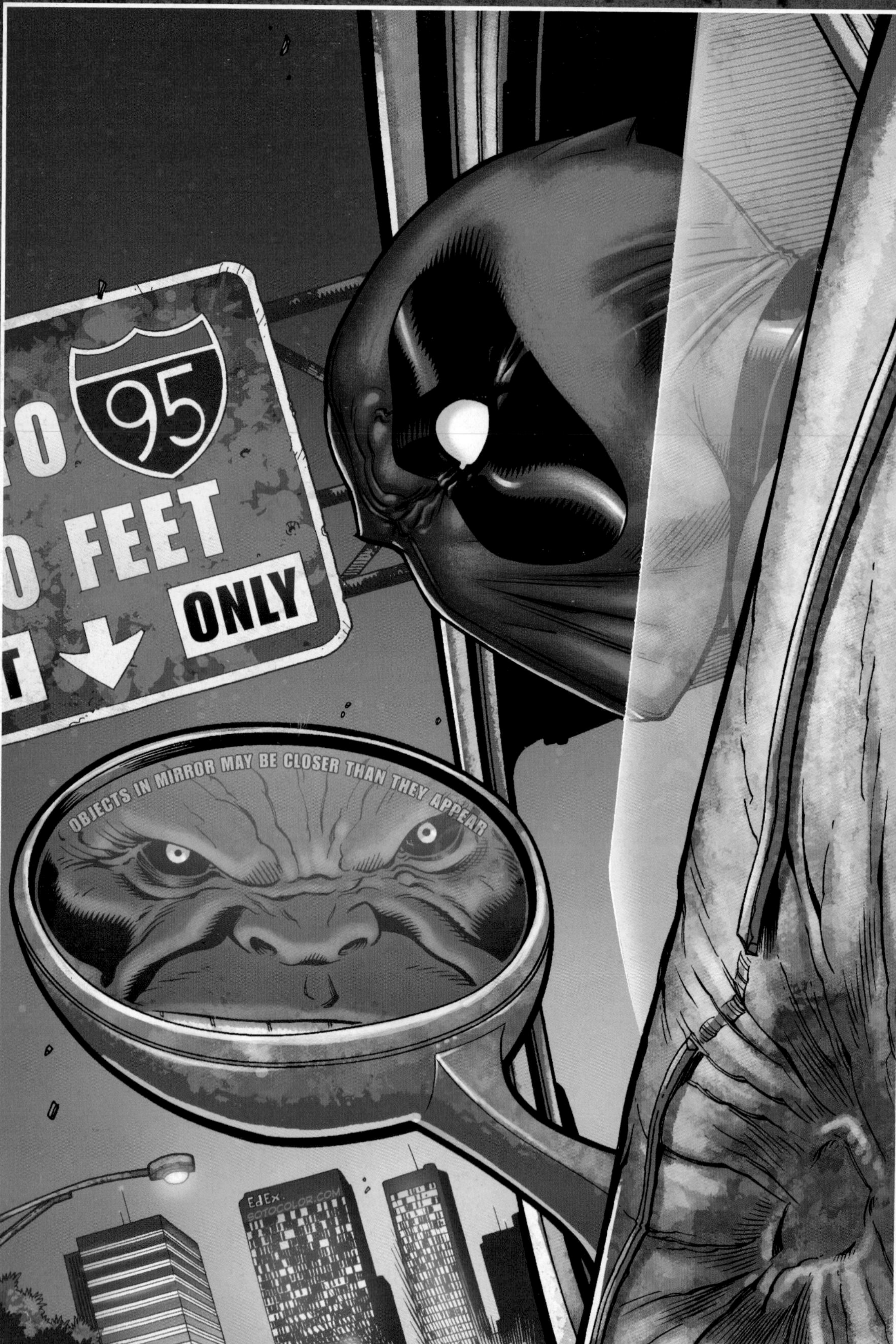

TO 95
O FEET
ONLY
OBJECTS IN MIRROR MAY BE CLOSER THAN THEY APPEAR
EdEx.
SOTOCOLOR.COM

HULK #14 DEADPOOL VARIANT

BY ED McGUINNESS, DEXTER VINES & CHRIS SOTOMAYOR

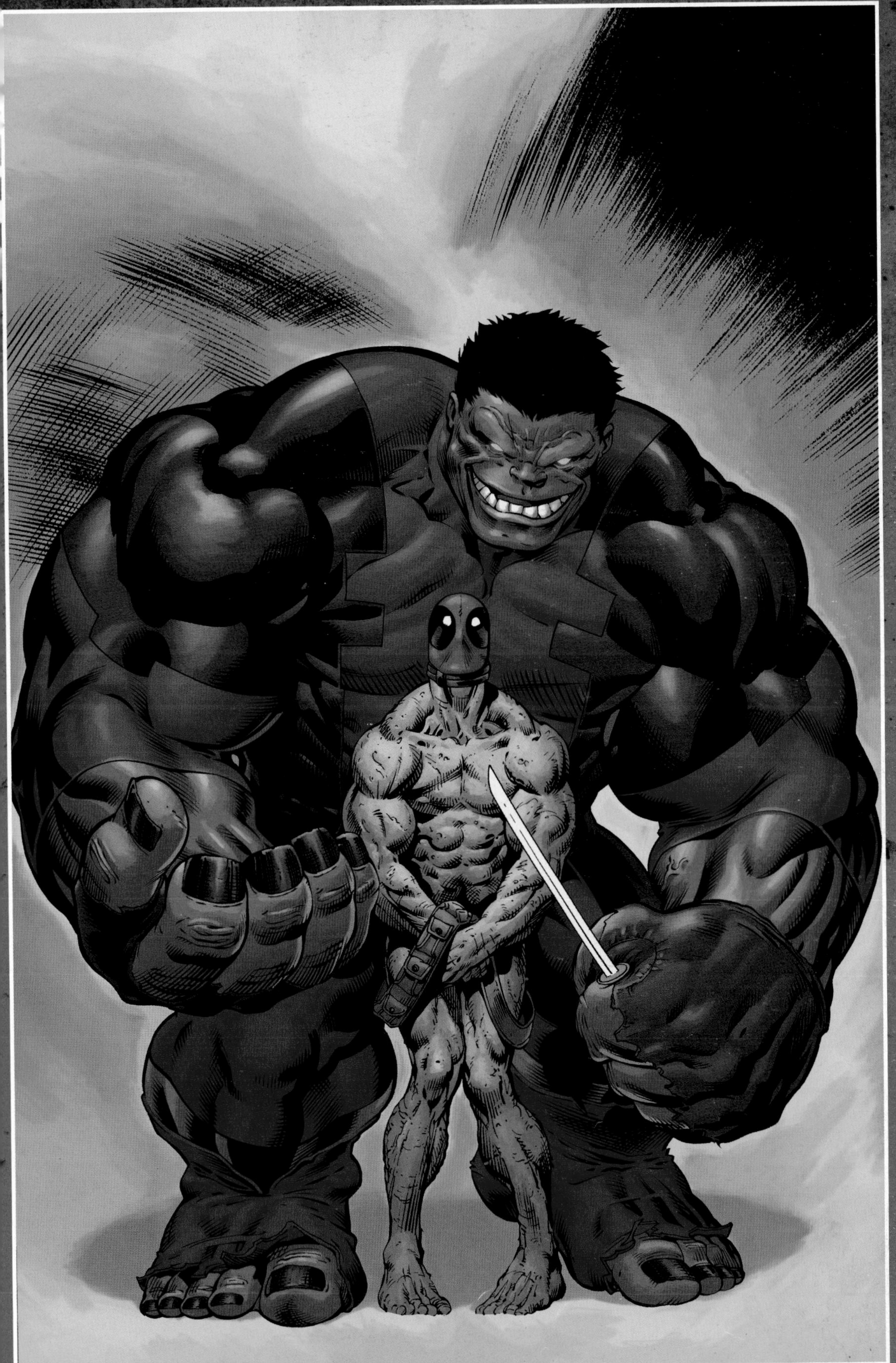

HULK #16 DEADPOOL VARIANT
BY ED McGUINNESS, MARK FARMER & DAVE STEWART

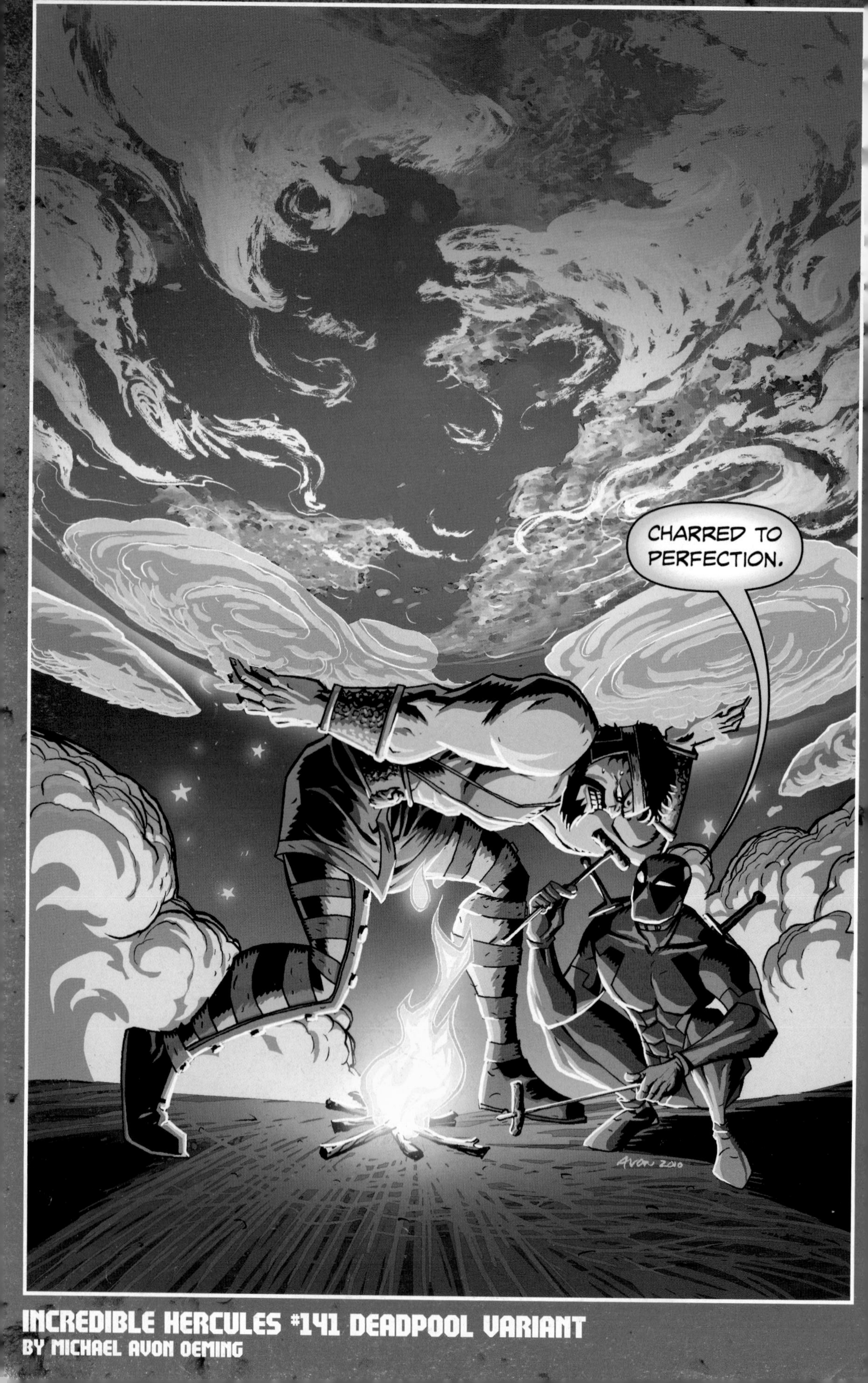
CHARRED TO PERFECTION.
AVON 2010

INCREDIBLE HERCULES #141 DEADPOOL VARIANT
BY MICHAEL AVON OEMING

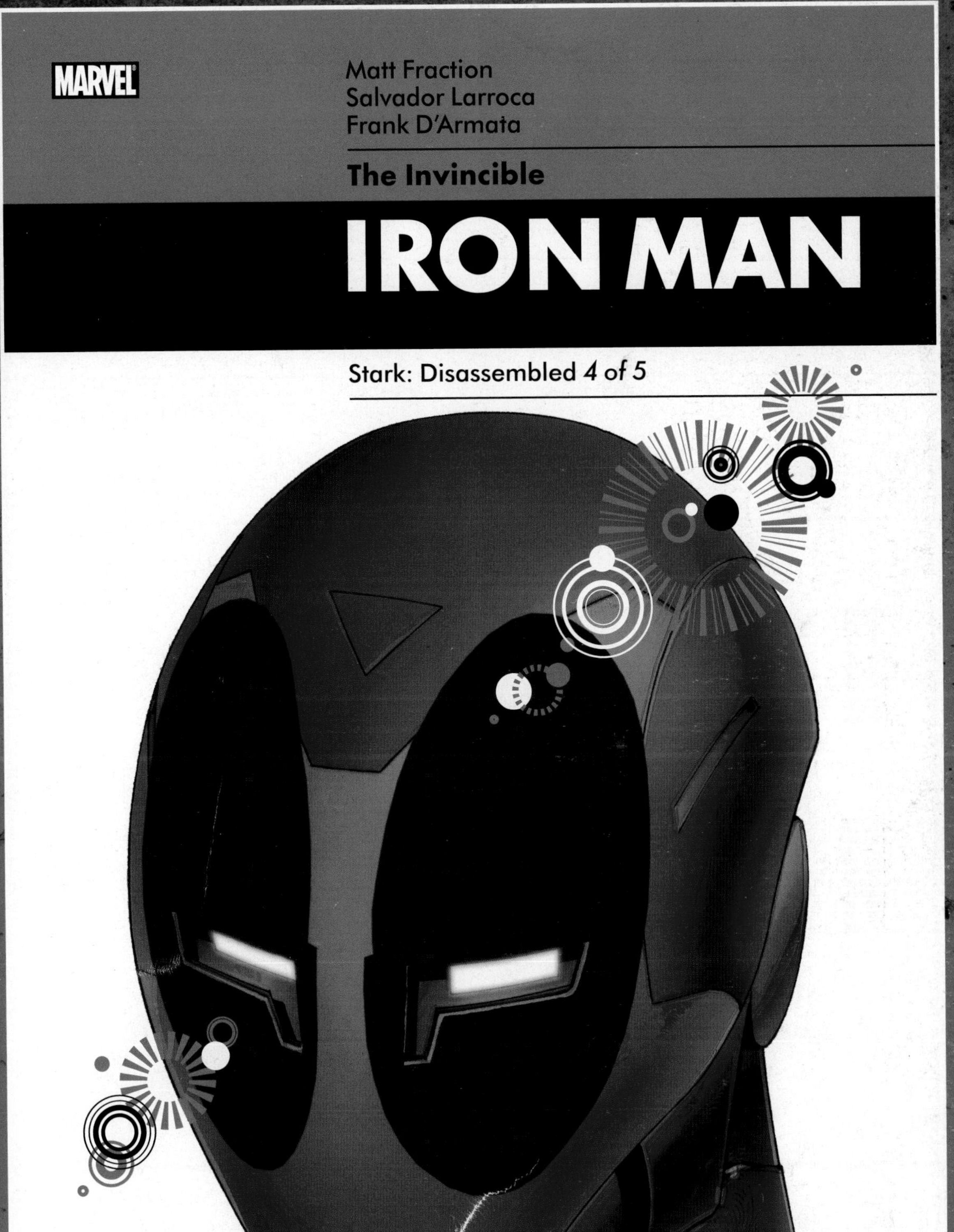
MARVEL
Matt Fraction
Salvador Larroca
Frank D'Armata
The Invincible
IRON MAN
Stark: Disassembled 4 of 5

INVINCIBLE IRON MAN #23 DEADPOOL VARIANT
BY SALVADOR LARROCA, RIAN HUGHES & FRANK D'ARMATA

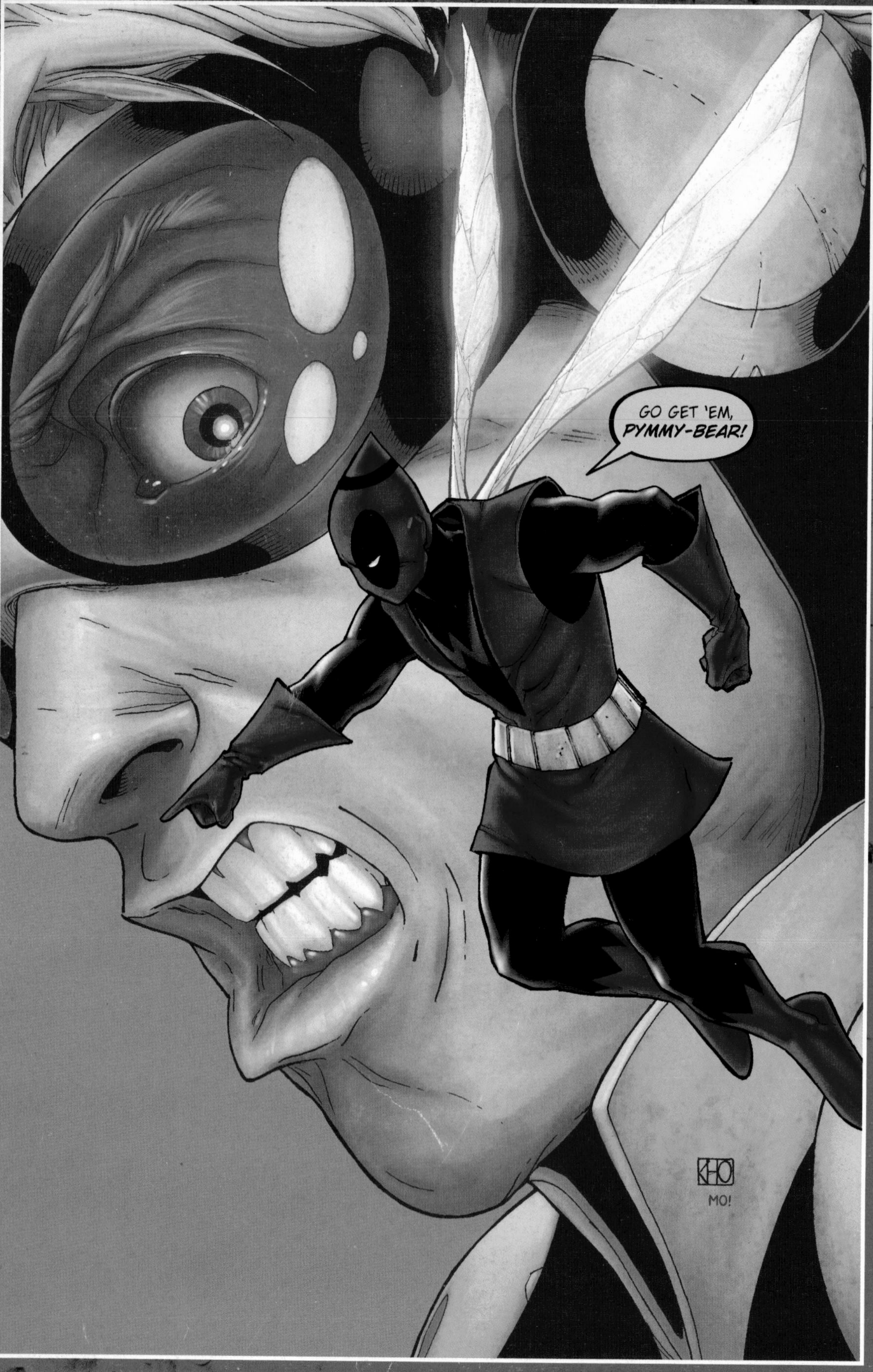
GO GET 'EM, PYMMY-BEAR!
KHO
MO!

MIGHTY AVENGERS #13 DEADPOOL VARIANT
BY KHOI PHAM & MORRY HOLLOWELL

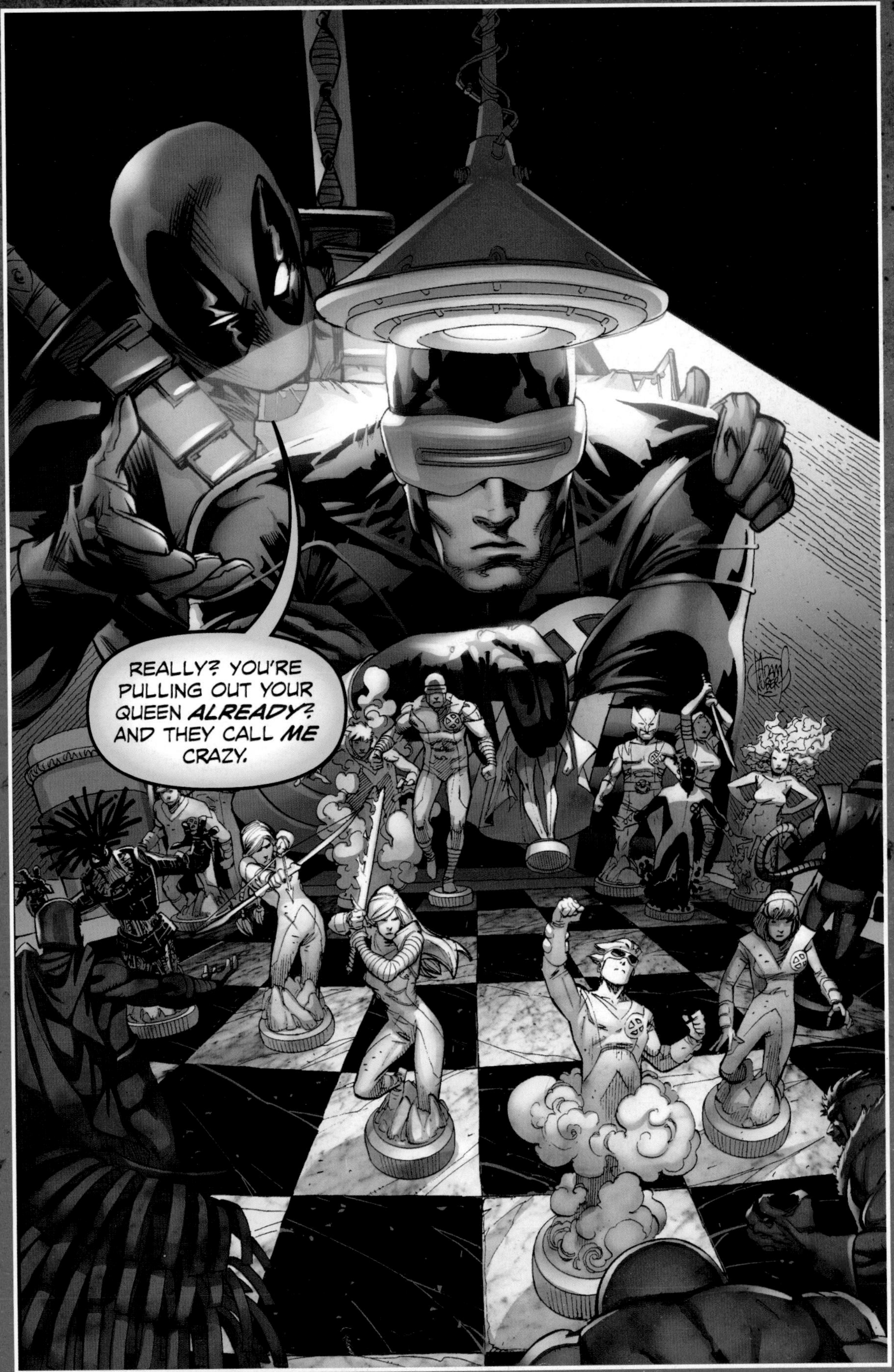
REALLY? YOU'RE PULLING OUT YOUR QUEEN *ALREADY*? AND THEY CALL *ME* CRAZY.
ADAM KUBERT

NEW MUTANTS #10 DEADPOOL VARIANT
BY ADAM KUBERT

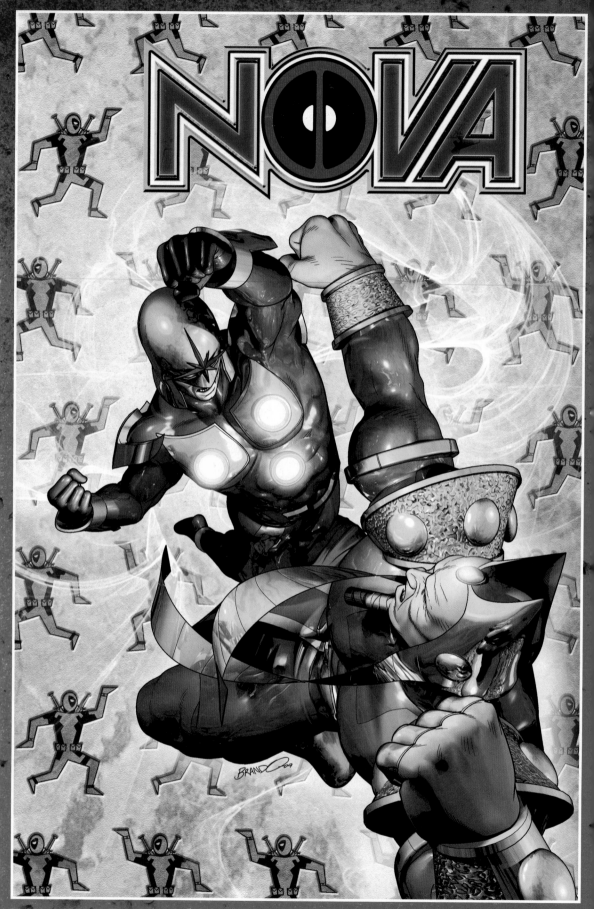

NOVA #34 DEADPOOL VARIANT
BY BRANDON PETERSON

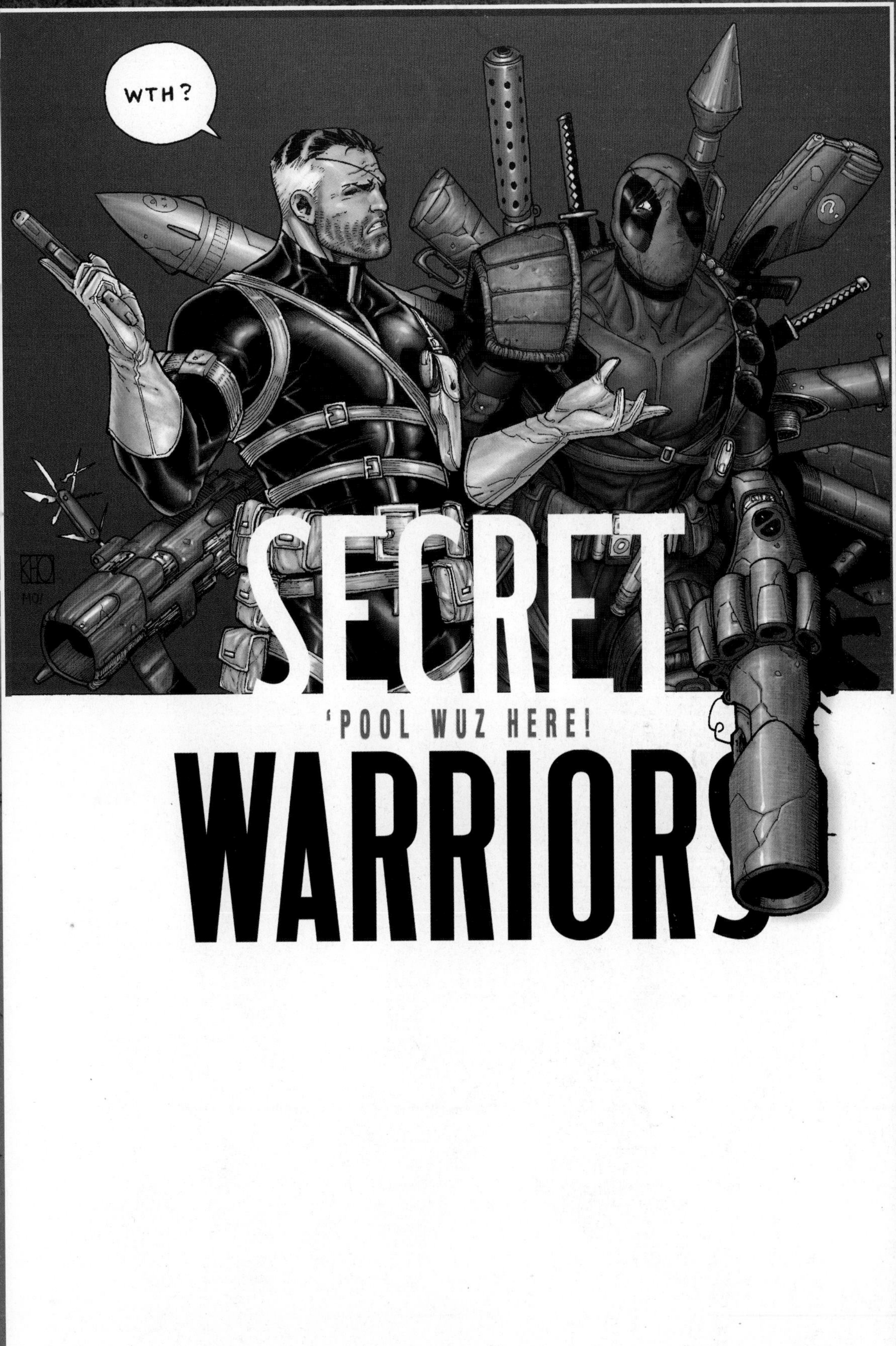
WTH?
SECRET
'POOL WUZ HERE!
WARRIORS

SECRET WARRIORS #13 DEADPOOL VARIANT
BY KHOI PHAM & MORRY HOLLOWELL

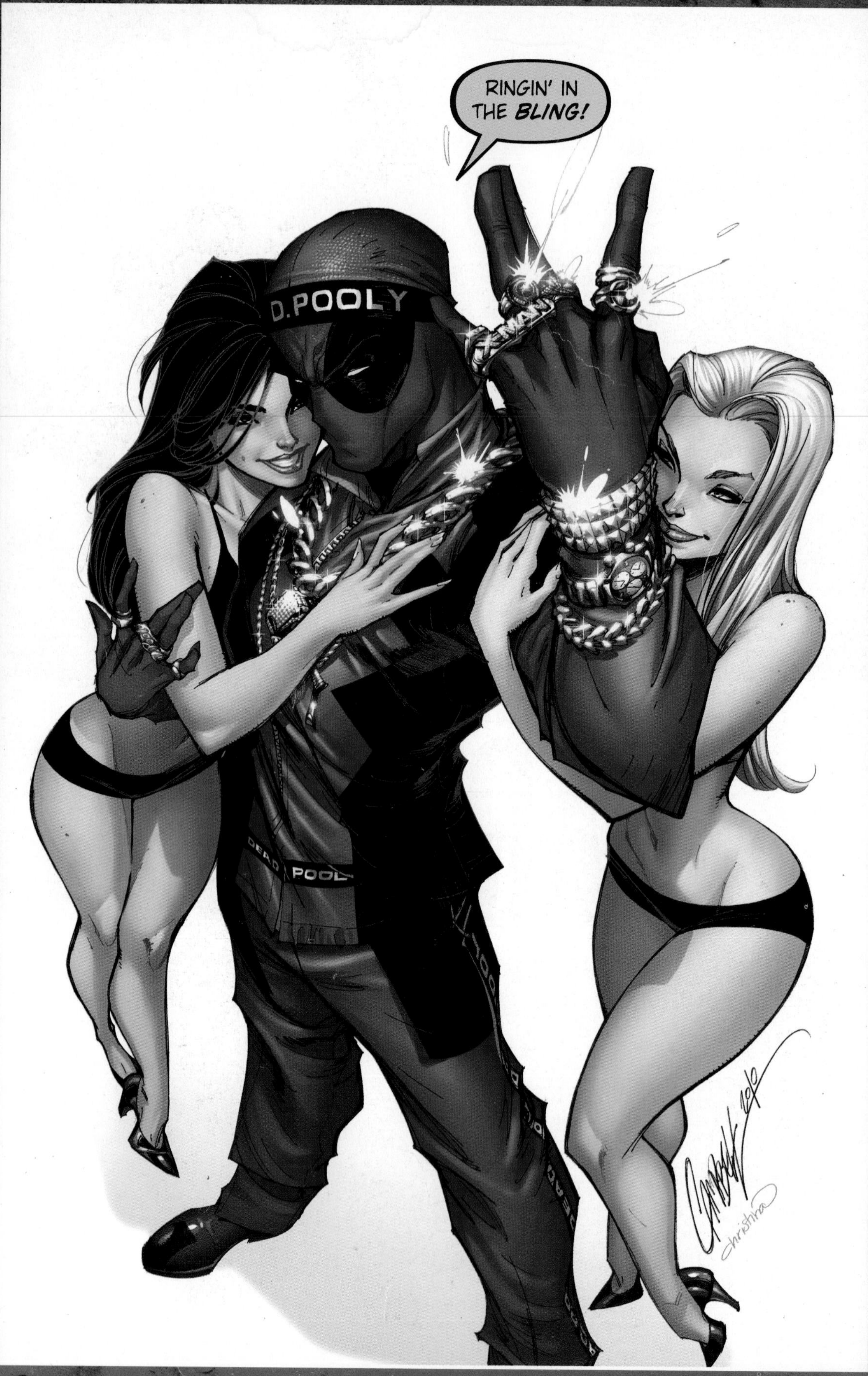
RINGIN' IN THE BLING!
D.POOLY
DEAD POOL

SIEGE #3 DEADPOOL VARIANT
BY J. SCOTT CAMPBELL & CHRISTINA STRAIN

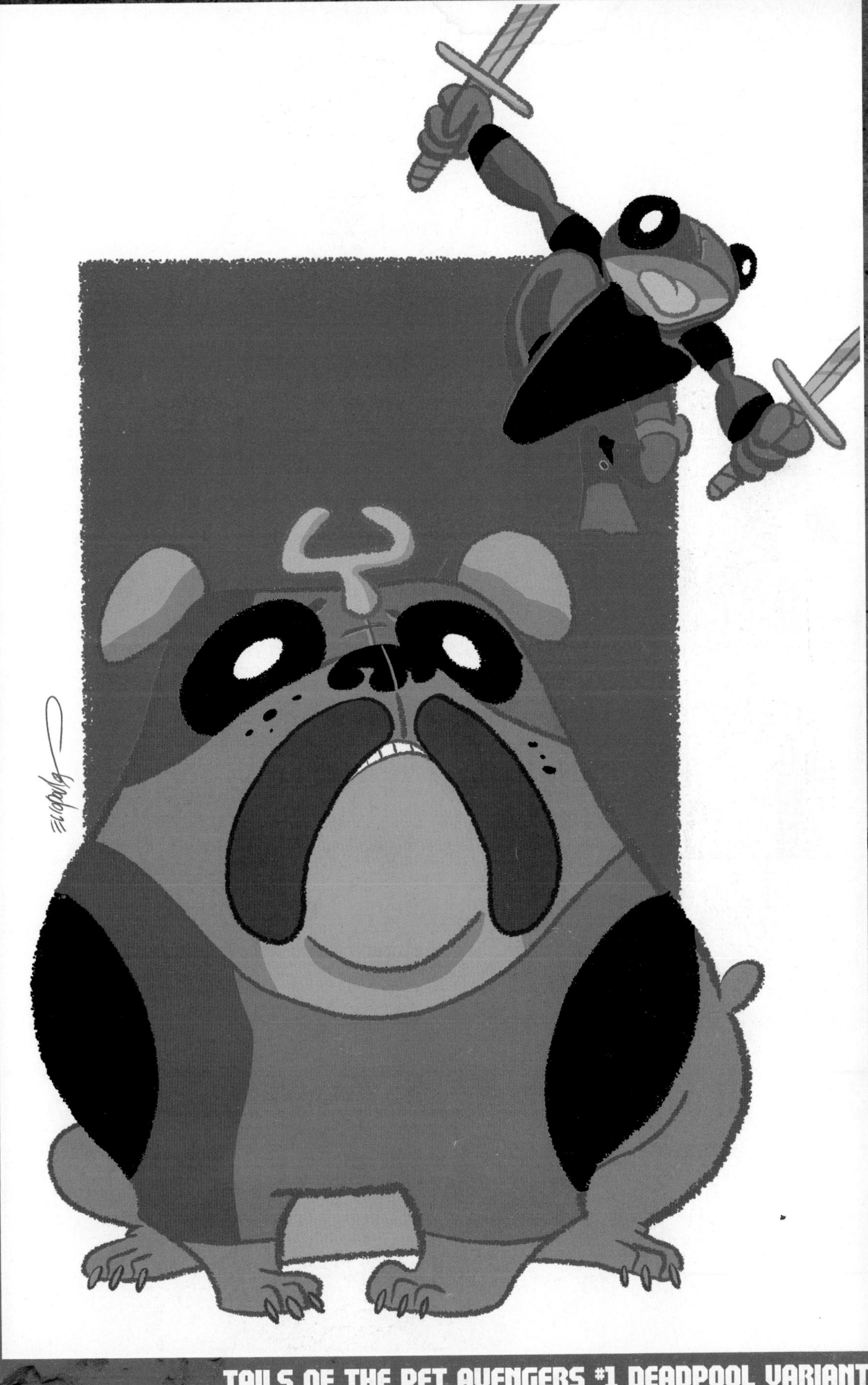

TAILS OF THE PET AVENGERS #1 DEADPOOL VARIANT
BY CHRIS ELIOPOULOS

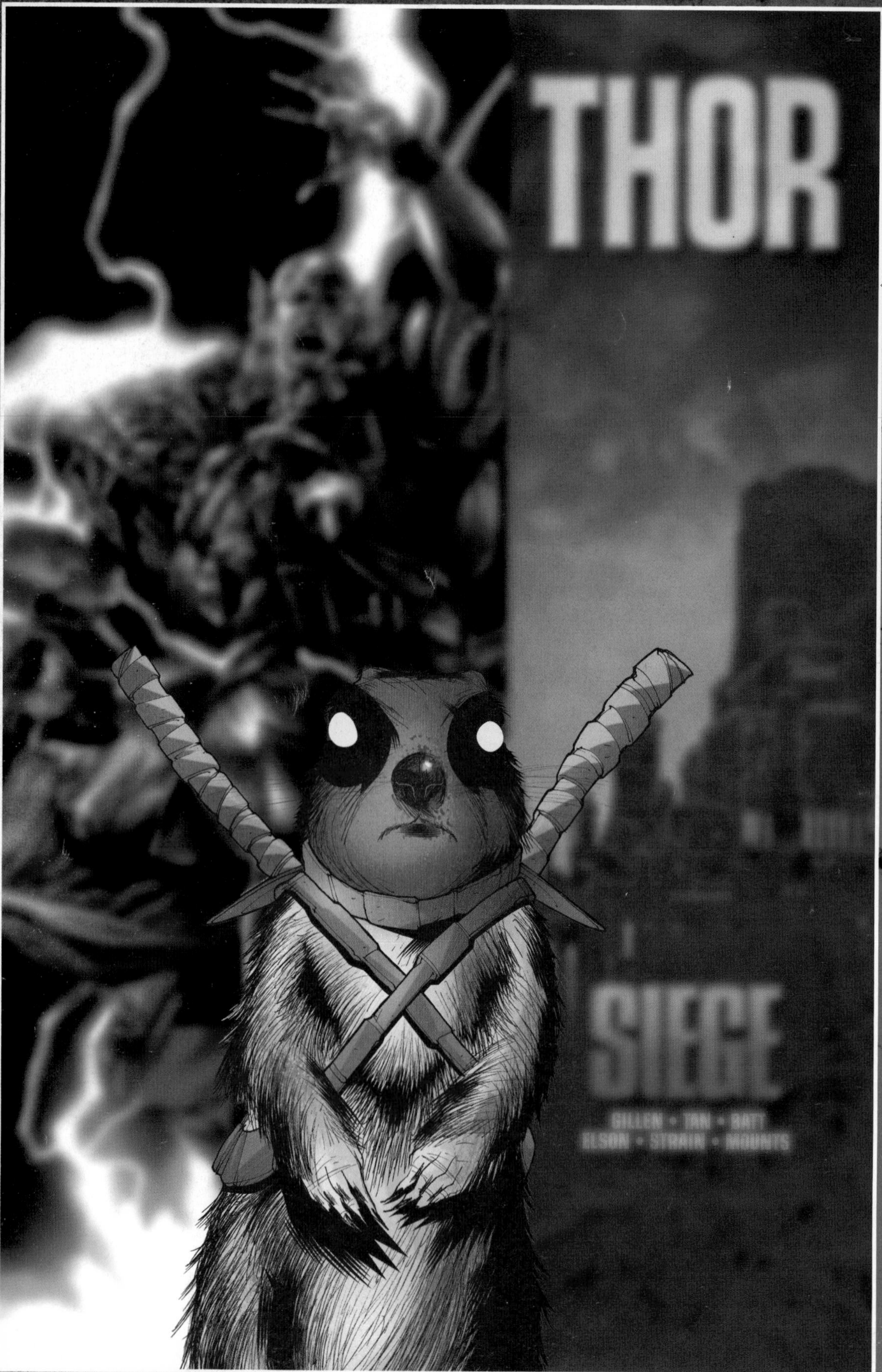
THOR
SIEGE

THOR #607 DEADPOOL VARIANT
BY JUAN DOE WITH MICO SUAYAN & LAURA MARTIN

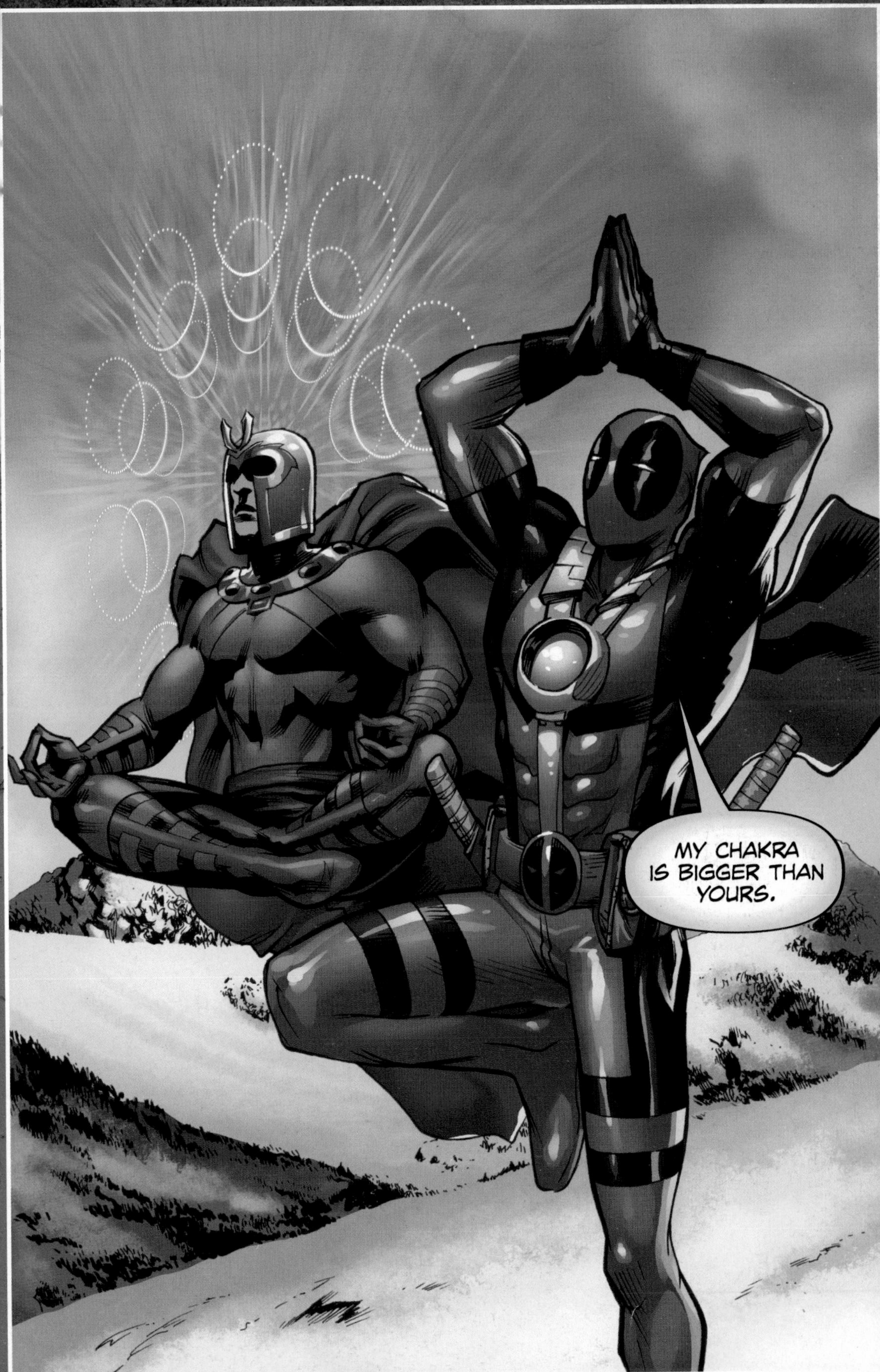
MY CHAKRA IS BIGGER THAN YOURS.

UNCANNY X-MEN #521 DEADPOOL VARIANT
BY KARL MOLINE, RICK MAGYAR & CHRISTINA STRAIN

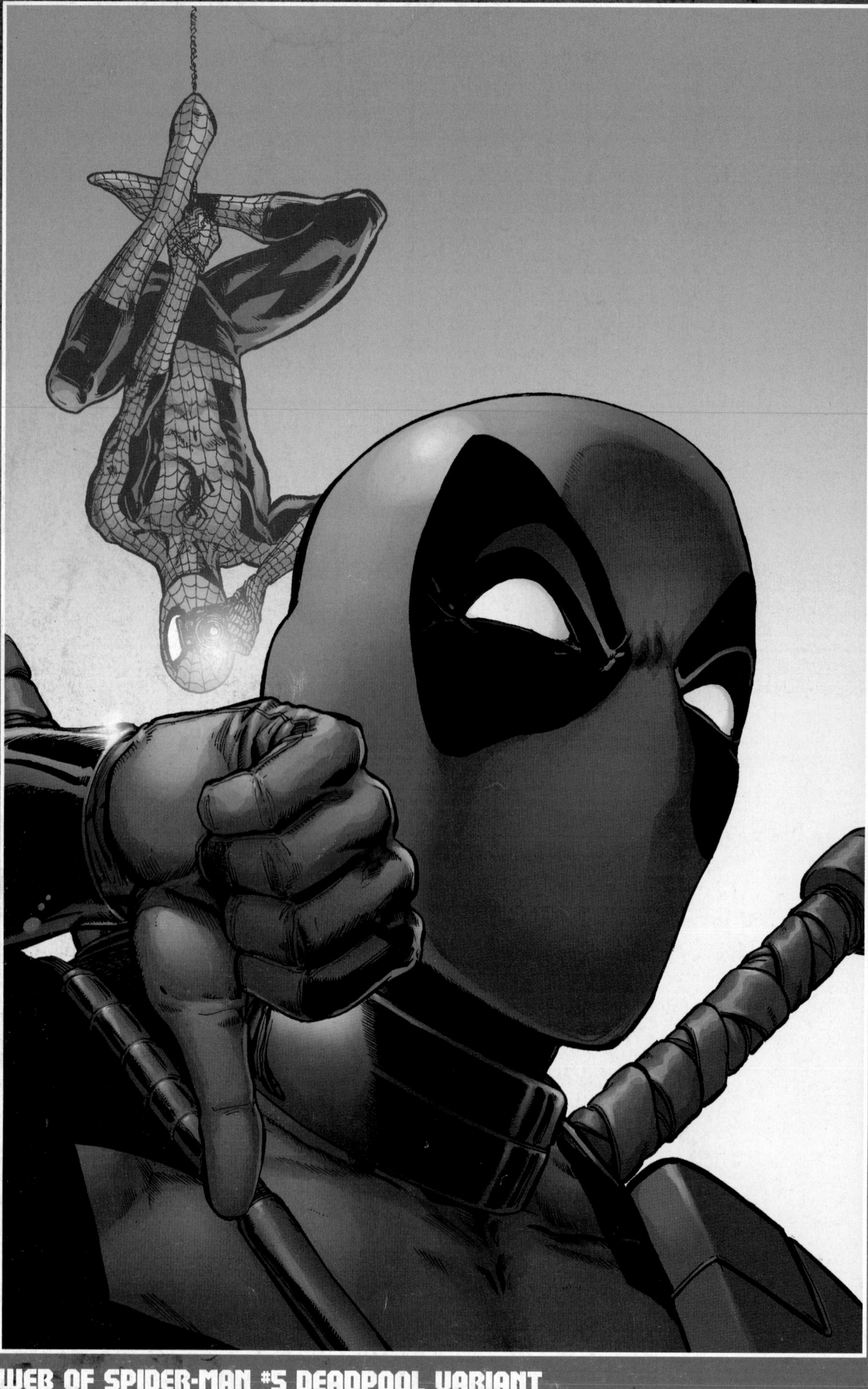

WEB OF SPIDER-MAN #5 DEADPOOL VARIANT
BY PHIL JIMENEZ & CHRIS CHUCKRY

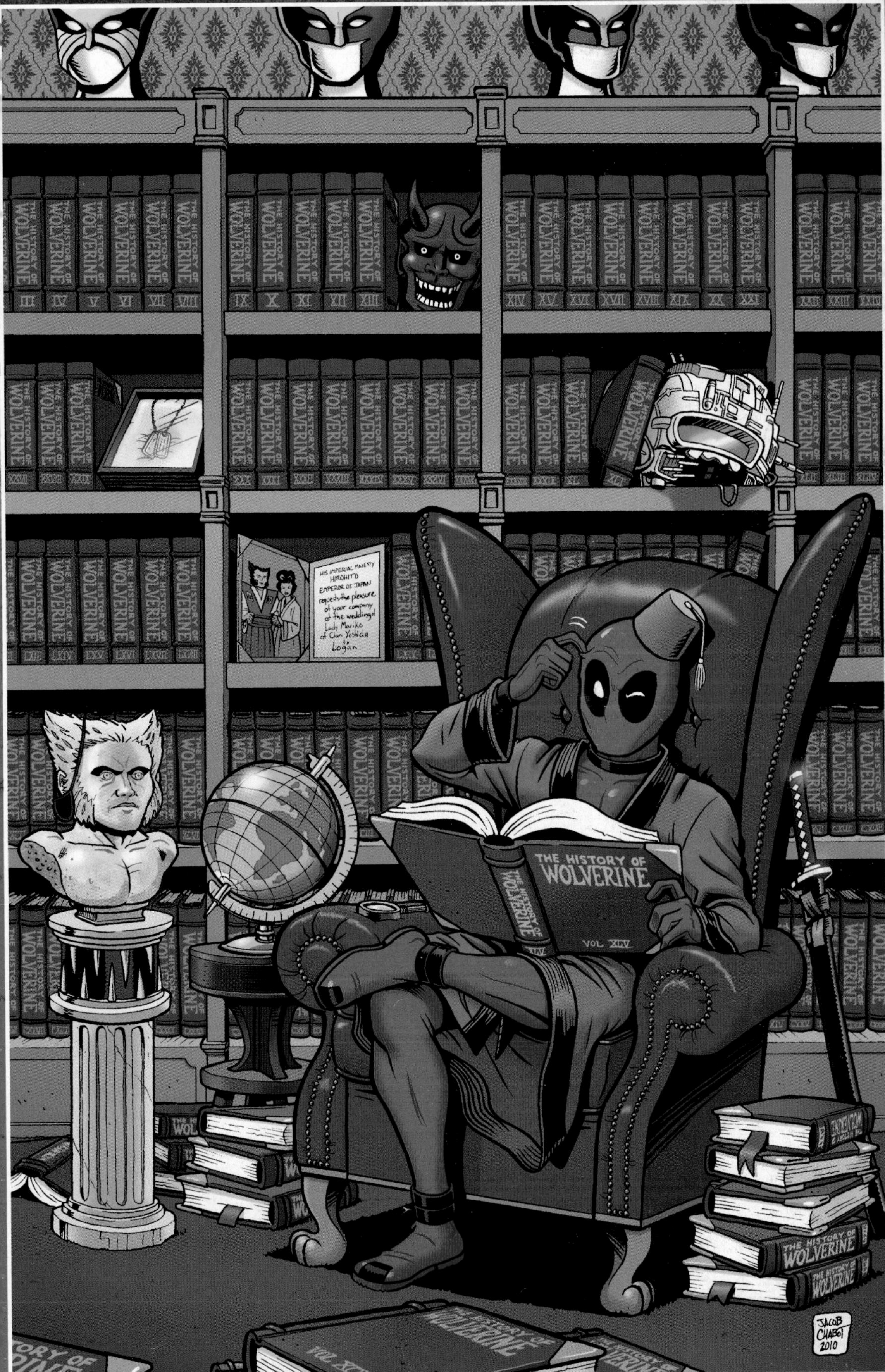
HIS IMPERIAL MAJESTY HIROHITO EMPEROR OF JAPAN requests the pleasure of your company at the wedding of Lady Mariko of Clan Yoshida to Logan
THE HISTORY OF WOLVERINE
VOL XLV
JACOB CHABOT 2010

WOLVERINE ORIGINS #45 DEADPOOL VARIANT
BY JACOB CHABOT

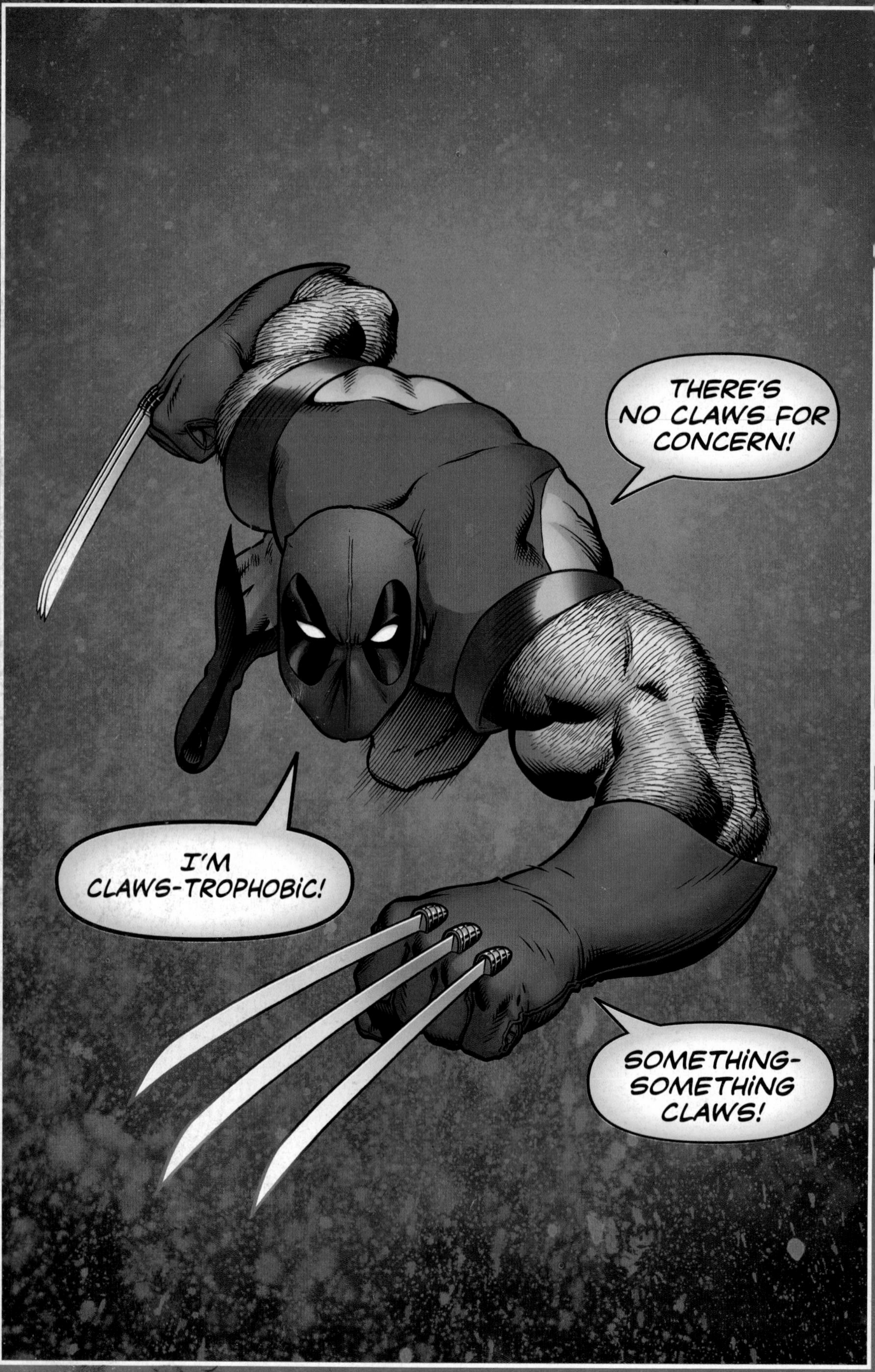
THERE'S NO CLAWS FOR CONCERN!
I'M CLAWS-TROPHOBIC!
SOMETHING-SOMETHING CLAWS!

WOLVERINE: SAVAGE #1 DEADPOOL VARIANT
BY CHRIS SOTOMAYOR WITH ED MCGUINNESS & MARK FARMER

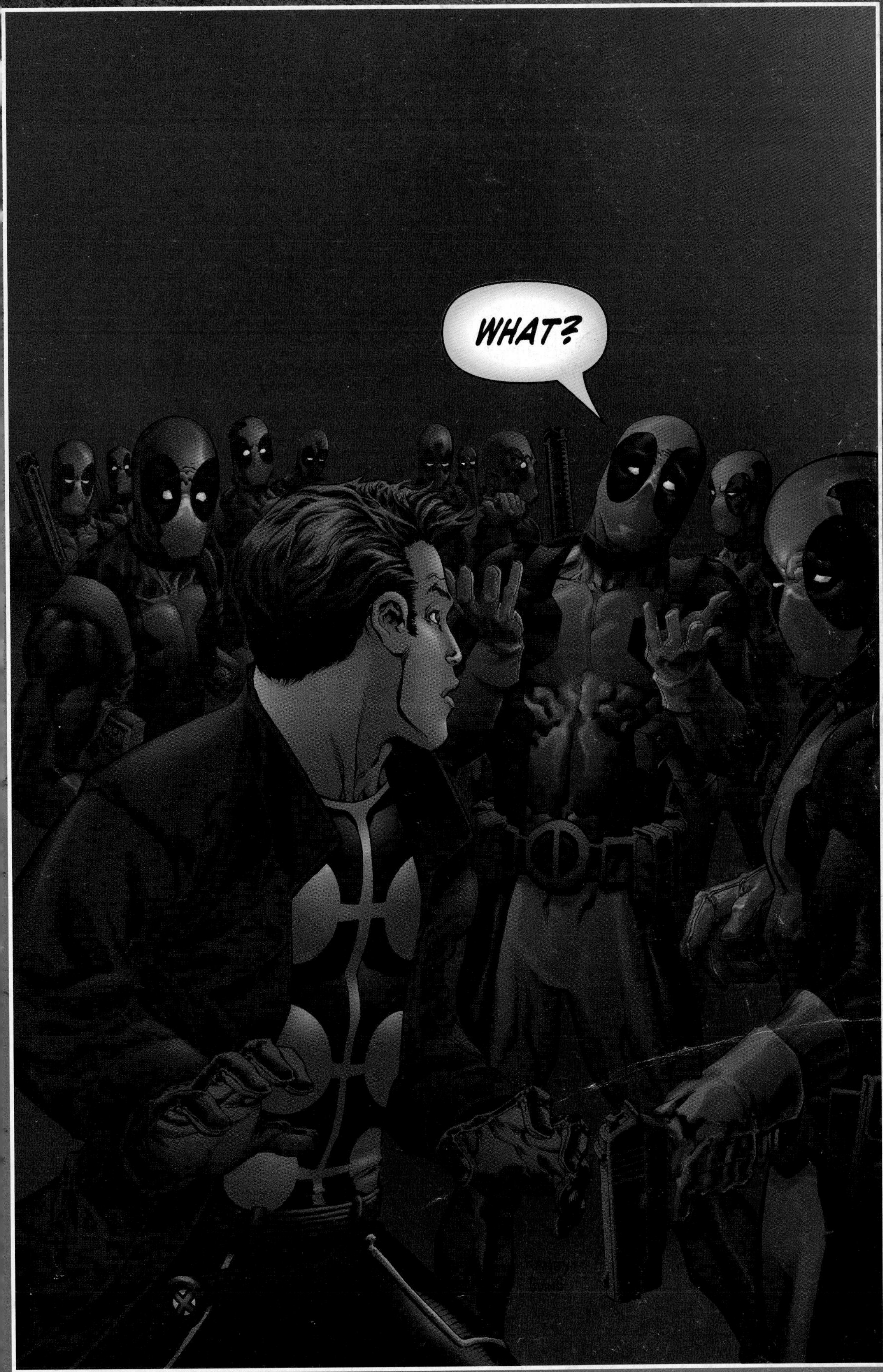
WHAT?

X-FACTOR #202 DEADPOOL VARIANT
BY TOM RANEY & GINA GOING

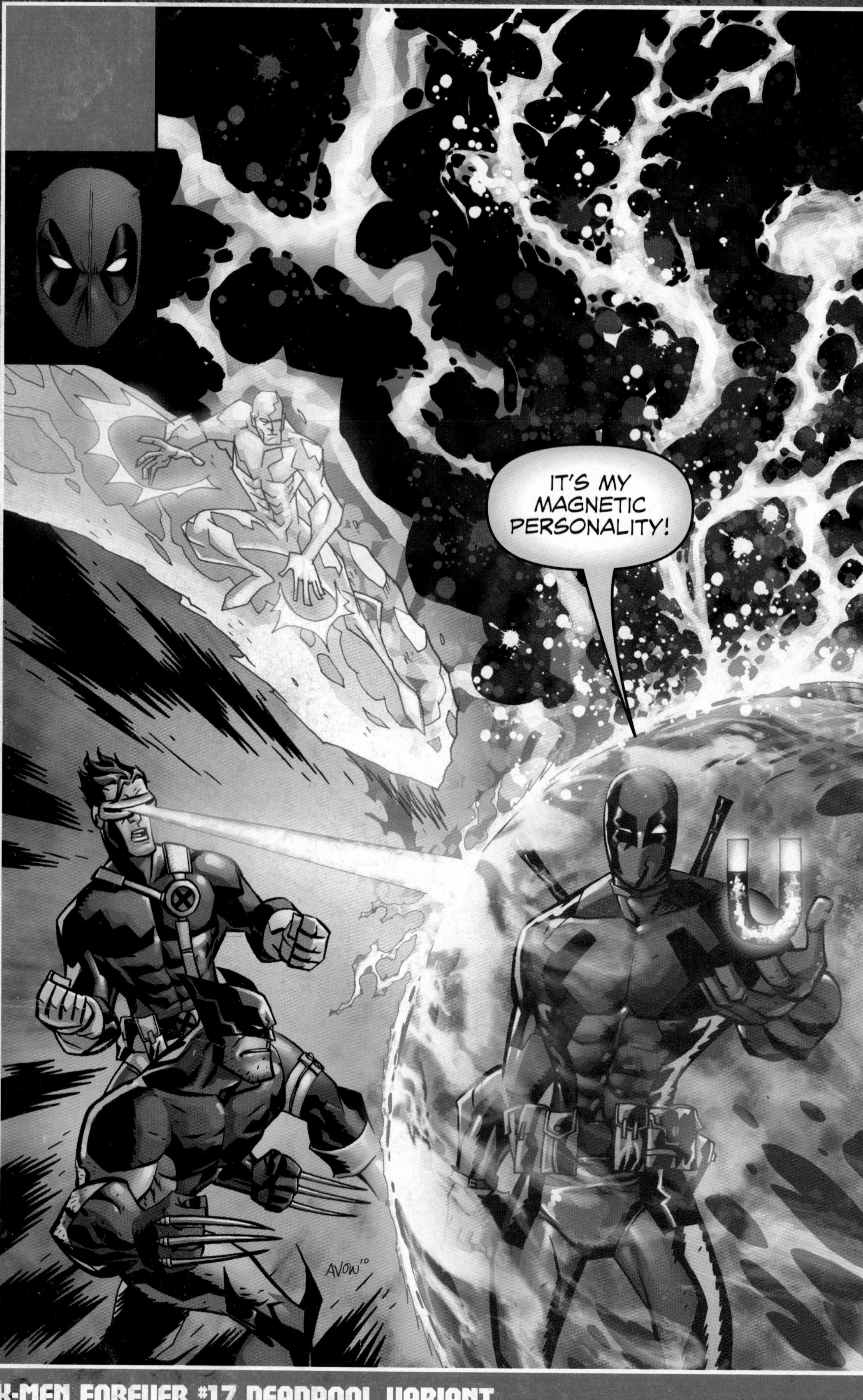
IT'S MY MAGNETIC PERSONALITY!
AVON '10

X-MEN FOREVER #17 DEADPOOL VARIANT
BY MICHAEL AVON OEMING & WIL QUINTANA

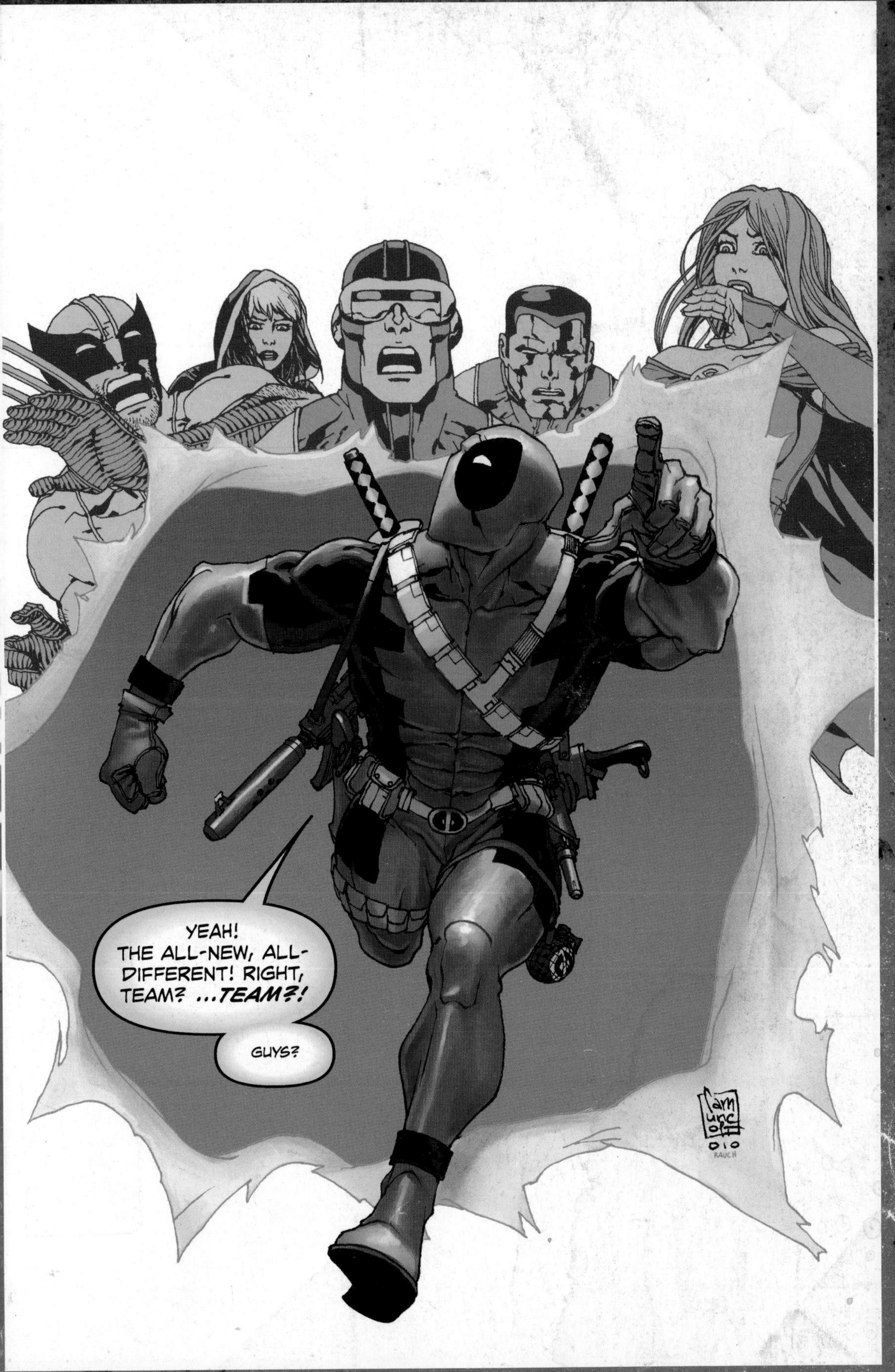
YEAH! THE ALL-NEW, ALL-DIFFERENT! RIGHT, TEAM? ...TEAM?!
GUYS?

X-MEN LEGACY #233 DEADPOOL VARIANT
BY GUISEPPE CAMUNCOLI & JOHN RAUCH

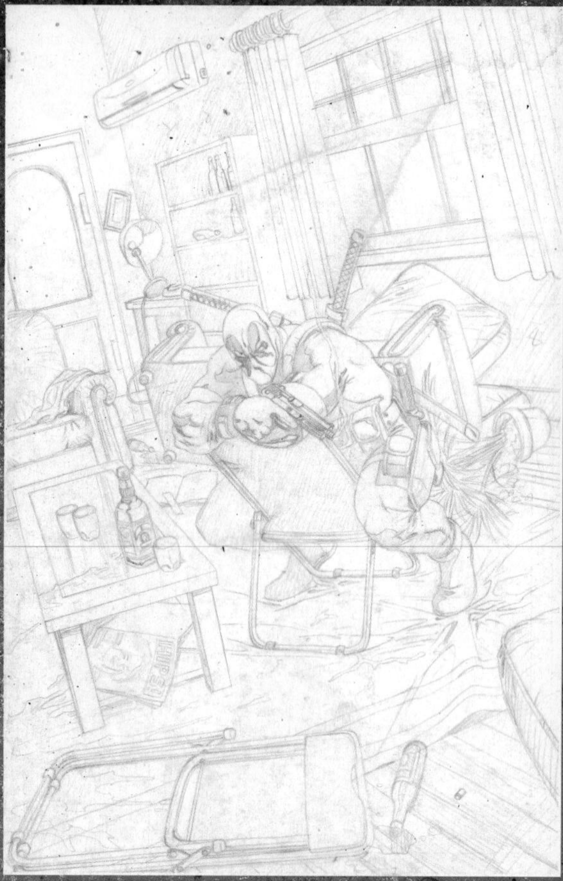

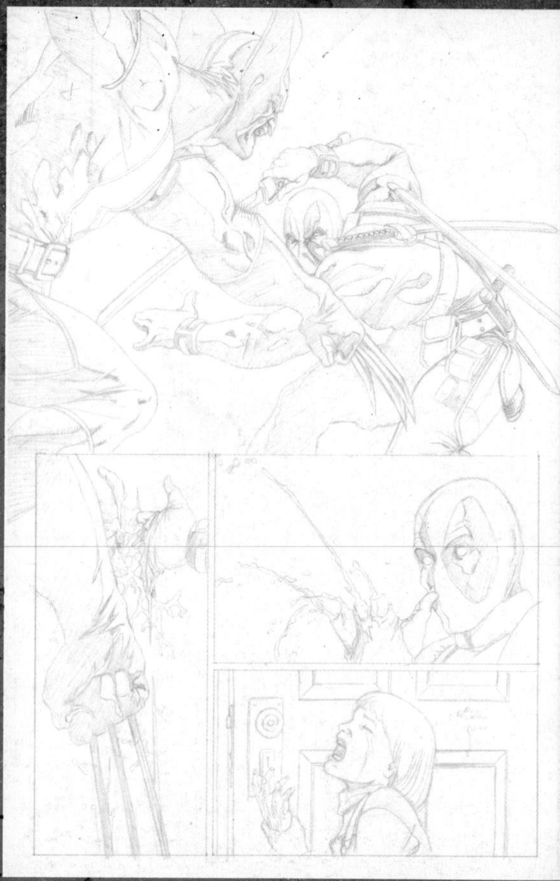

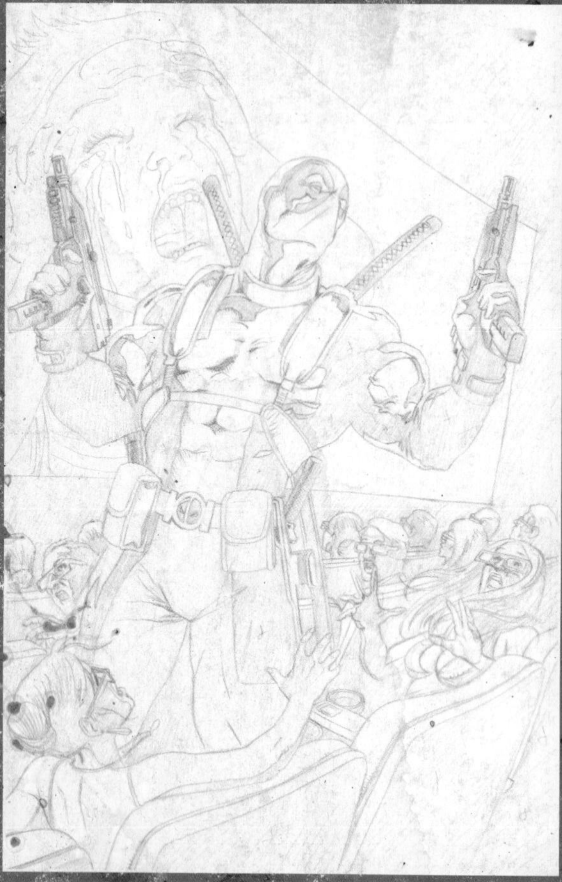

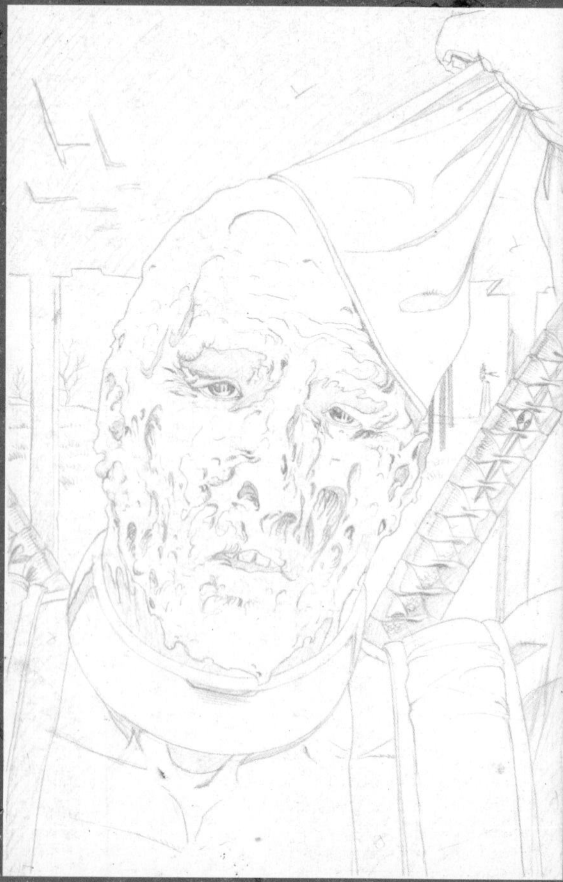

X-MEN ORIGINS: DEADPOOL
PENCILED PAGES 3, 22, 29 & 34 BY LEANDRO FERNANDEZ